Introduction to Comparative Politics

Contributors

Ervand Abrahamian
BARUCH COLLEGE

Joan Bardeleben
CARLETON UNIVERSITY

Louis DeSipio
UNIVERSITY OF CALIFORNIA, IRVINE

Merilee S. Grindle
HARVARD UNIVERSITY

William A. Joseph
WELLESLEY COLLEGE

Mark Kesselman
COLUMBIA UNIVERSITY

Darren Kew
UNIVERSITY OF MASSACHUSETTS,
BOSTON

Joel Krieger
WELLESLEY COLLEGE

Peter Lewis
AMERICAN UNIVERSITY

Introduction to Comparative Politics

AP Edition

Fourth Edition

General Editors

Mark Kesselman
Columbia University

Joel Krieger
Wellesley College

William A. Joseph
Wellesley College

Houghton Mifflin Company
Boston   New York

To our children, who are growing up in a complex and ever more challenging world;
MK—for Ishan and Javed
JK—for Nathan and Megan
WAJ—for Abigail, Hannah, and Rebecca

Sponsoring Editor: Katherine Meisenheimer
Development Editor: Leslie Kauffman
Project Editor: Andrea Dodge
Editorial Assistant: Kristen Truncellito
Production/Design Coordinator: Jill Haber
Marketing Manager: Nicola Poser
Cover Image: © Peter Adams/Digital Vision/Getty Images

Printed in the U.S.A.

Library of Congress Control Number: 2005937099

ISBN 13: 978-0-618-60449-4
ISBN 10: 0-618-60449-9

3 4 5 6 7 8 9-DOC-09 08 07

BRIEF CONTENTS

CONTENTS

PART ❸ Transitional Democracies   142

4 Russia   143
Joan DeBardeleben

6 Nigeria   253

Darren Kew and Peter Lewis

PART ❹ Authoritarian Regimes   310

7 Iran   311

Ervand Abrahamian

8 China   359

William A. Joseph

PREFACE

The preface to the third edition of *Introduction to Comparative Politics* (ICP) observed: "We hope that this thoroughly revamped edition of *Introduction to Comparative Politics* will help students analyze new (and old) political challenges and changing (and persistent) agendas." The same hope animates this thoroughly revised and updated edition of ICP.

The fact that the headings in the table of contents of the country chapters in this edition of *Introduction to Comparative Politics: Political Challenges and Changing Agendas* (ICP) are quite similar to those in the previous edition might appear to support Francis Fukuyama's prediction concerning the end of history.[i] Yet such an appearance is misleading: even a cursory review of the turbulent events of the few years since the publication of the previous edition of ICP in 2004 suggests both that it is difficult to discern a clear-cut trend to world history and that the profound changes since 2004 provide sufficient material to occupy historians—and students of comparative politics—for years to come.

Consider: since the third edition of this book was published, the "wave" of democratization that began to sweep much of the world beginning in the 1980s has reached Georgia, Ukraine, and Kyrgyzstan, former Soviet republics that many observers thought were locked into authoritarian regimes. In the Middle East, another part of the world often said to be inhospitable to democratic values, there have been important developments that suggest change may be coming to the region. There was a massive outpouring of "people power" in Lebanon in early 2005 that led to the withdrawal of Syrian troops from the country; in May 2005, the parliament in Kuwait voted to give women equal political rights with men; and Egypt's first multi-candidate presidential elections were held in September 2005.

However, any notion of an inexorable historical movement toward democracy and capitalism is belied by a host of other changes. In Russia, the state's manipulation of the courts and the media, as well as its suppression of political autonomy and dissent, suggest that the pendulum has swung away from democracy. More than two years after the United States-led coalition toppled the regime of Saddam Hussein in Iraq in 2003, the prospect of stable democracy continues to appear remote. The ability of authoritarian rulers in China, Iran, Togo, Uzbekistan, and Zimbabwe to retain or gain power challenges confident claims about the march of liberal democracy in the world. In a more theoretical vein, recent scholarship persuasively analyzes why one should not expect an orderly progression from democratic transitions to democratic consolidation.[ii] Also, *New York Times* commentator Thomas Friedman may celebrate globalization as the *deus ex machina* that is flattening the world in a way that promotes meritocracy on a global scale, but "altermondist" (other-world) activists

---

[i] Francis Fukuyama, "The End of History?" *The National Interest* 16 (Summer 1989); reprinted in Mark Kesselman and Joel Krieger, eds., *Readings in Comparative Politics: Political Challenges and Changing Agendas* (Boston: Houghton Mifflin, 2006). The outline of this anthology is parallel to that of *Introduction to Comparative Politics* and provides a range of readings that engage in comparative analysis of issues surveyed in ICP.

[ii] See, inter alia, Guillermo O'Donnell, "Illusions About Consolidation," *Journal of Democracy* 7, no. 2 (April 1996): 34–51; Thomas Carothers, "The End of the Transition Paradigm," *Journal of Democracy* 13, no. 1 (January 2002); and Steven Levitsky and Lucan A. Way, "The Rise of Competitive Authoritarianism," *Journal of Democracy* 13, no. 2 (April 2002): 51–65. These articles are reprinted in Kesselman and Krieger, *Readings in Comparative Politics*. From a different perspective, Fareed Zakaria, *The Future of Freedom: Illiberal Democracy at Home and Abroad* (New York: W. W. Norton, 2003) questions whether liberal democracy is the norm even in those countries considered to be its birthplace.

passionately proclaim, on the contrary, that globalization and U.S.-style neo-imperialism are accentuating the peaks and valleys of global inequality.[iii] As this text will amply demonstrate, neither history nor interpretive debates have ended.

The Advanced Placement Edition of *Introduction to Comparative Politics* reflects several significant developments, both in the world and the AP Comparative Politics Examination:

- We address the consequences of globalization on domestic politics in each country in a more focused and comprehensive manner than in the third edition.
- We analyze the consequences of the terrorist attacks on the United States on September 11, 2001, and the subsequent global war on terrorism for political institutions, processes, party competition, and potential regime change in each country case study.
- We consider the political repercussions of these developments—as well as the war in Iraq and its aftermath—for relations with the United States and for the changing contours of the world-of-states theme in its global dimensions.
- We underscore the significance of immigration for shaping—and for understanding the political challenges of—multi-ethnic and multi-religious societies.
- We analyze and reconceptualize the complex terrain of democratic transitions and uncertain consolidations and refine our typology of countries accordingly.
- We eliminate a number of chapters, including only those that cover countries tested on the new AP exam plus the United States for teachers wishing to add it to their classroom discussions.

Structure of the Book

Although we highlight certain key developments of the past few years, especially the reverberations of September 11 for countries throughout the world, the core elements of *Introduction to Comparative Politics* have not changed. In this edition, we have retained the basic framework and approach of past editions. We believe that the four constituent elements that comprise our analytical framework help students both to

highlight the particular features of the country case studies in ICP and to engage in rigorous cross-national comparisons.

We are pleased that teachers and students have generously praised the analytical framework, lively writing, and high level of scholarship in *Introduction to Comparative Politics*. Although we are committed to probing the complexity of developments when appropriate, we aim to make the book accessible to students with little or no background in political science. We value readable, direct prose that is free of jargon, and we have maximized symmetry in the topical outline of country chapters to facilitate cross-national comparison. We use vignettes to open the country chapters and elsewhere to engage students and highlight particular features of each country's political patterns, and provide an array of ancillary visual materials to complement the written text.

Introduction to Comparative Politics, Advanced Placement edition emphasizes patterns of state formation, political economy, domestic political institutions and processes, and the politics of collective identities within the context of globalization. A distinctive feature of the book is the use of four comparative themes to frame the presentation of each country's politics. We explain the themes in Chapter 1 and present an intriguing "puzzle" for each to stimulate student thinking. These themes—described in the first section of each country study and analyzed throughout the chapter—focus attention on the continuities and contrasts among the country studies:

- **A World of States** highlights the importance of state formation, the internal organization of the state, and the interstate system for political development. In this edition, we highlight how the events of September 11 have influenced political institutions and policies.
- **Governing the Economy** analyzes state strategies for promoting economic development and competitiveness and stresses the effects of economic globalization on domestic politics.

[iii] For spirited arguments on both sides, see Thomas L. Friedman, *The World is Flat: A Brief History of the Twenty-First Century* (New York: Farrar, Straus and Giroux, 2005); for opposing views, see John Cavanagh and Jerry Mander, eds., *Alternatives to Economic Globalization: A Better World is Possible,* 2nd ed. (San Francisco: Berrett-Koehler, 2004) and Leo Panitch and Colin Leys, eds., *The New Imperial Challenge: Socialist Register 2004* (New York: Monthly Review Press, 2003).

- **The Democratic Idea** explores the challenges posed by citizens' demands for greater control and participation in both democracies and authoritarian regimes.
- **The Politics of Collective Identities** considers the political consequences of race, ethnicity, gender, religion, and nationality and their complex interplay with class-based politics.

Through our four themes, the methods of comparative analysis come alive as students examine similarities and differences among countries and within and between political systems. The thematic approach facilitates disciplined analysis of political challenges and changing agendas within countries.

Introduction to Comparative Politics, Advanced Placement edition uses a country-by-country approach and strikes a balance between the richness of each country's national political development and cross-national comparative analysis. Chapter 1 explains the comparative method, analyzes the four key themes of the book, and describes core features of political institutions and processes. Each country chapter that follows consists of five sections. **Section 1** treats the historic formation of the modern state, its geographic setting, critical junctures in its political development, and the country's significance for the study of comparative politics. **Section 2** describes the political economy of past and current national development. **Section 3** outlines the major institutions of governance and policy-making. **Section 4** explains the widely varying processes of representation, participation, and contestation. Finally, **Section 5** reflects on the major issues that confront the country and are likely to shape its future.

Several special features assist in the teaching and learning process.

- At the beginning of each chapter, students will find a data box providing basic demographic, social, economic, and political information to aid in comparing countries. We have expanded the data presented for this edition and have redesigned their presentation.
- Throughout the chapters a wide array of maps, tables, charts, photographs, and political cartoons enliven the text and present key information in clear and graphic ways.
- Each country study includes several boxes that highlight interesting and provocative aspects of politics. These include **Leaders,** biographies of important political leaders; **Institutional Intricacies,** important features of a political system that warrant careful discussion; **Citizen**

Action, unconventional forms of participation; **Global Connection,** examples of connections between domestic and international politics; and **Current Challenges,** issues of today and the future that help shape important dimensions of national politics.

- Key terms are set in boldface when first introduced and are defined in the Glossary at the end of the book. Students will find that the Glossary defines many key concepts that are used broadly in comparative politics.
- Each chapter concludes with a list of suggested readings and links to websites that enable students to explore in greater depth issues relating to the country.

New to This Edition

Chapter 1 has been expanded to provide a more ample survey of the diversity of approaches to studying comparative politics as well as a richer analysis of democratic theory. At the same time that each country chapter has been slightly shortened to produce a leaner book, we provide a thoroughly updated description of current political developments to take account of major events and regime changes. We pay particular attention in the Advanced Placement edition of *Introduction to Comparative Politics* to the challenges posed by globalization and the aftermath of the events of September 11.

We retain the classification of countries used in the last edition, although we have changed the terminology: we now distinguish among *consolidated democracies*, *transitional democracies*, and *authoritarian regimes*. In the Introduction, we consider alternative ways to classify countries and warn against assuming that there is a linear movement from authoritarian regimes to transitional democracies to consolidated democracies. Democratization is often a protracted process with ambiguous results, rather than a clearly delineated path toward completion. As we noted above (and analyzed in the Introduction), we share the concerns of scholars who have identified the prevalence of "hybrid" regimes in which the trappings and some elements of democracy stably co-exist with authoritarian practices. We are especially concerned that students do not assume that the countries we classify as transitional democracies are on an historical escalator that mechanically leads to their becoming stable or consolidated democracies.

We have also pondered the classification of particular countries. For example, should Russia, a country placed in the intermediate category in the last edition of ICP, now be classified as authoritarian? (We decided to continue to place Russia in the category of transitional democracy, but the Russian chapter amply documents non-democratic tendencies under Vladimir Putin's leadership.) We emphasize that the boundaries dividing the three groups are not airtight. For one thing, politics is a moving target. For another, scholars disagree about the appropriate criteria for classifying regime types as well as about how to apply the criteria to particular cases. Indeed, teachers may find it fruitful and stimulating to organize discussion about how to best characterize the political system of a given country and about alternative conceptual schemes for classifying groups of countries.

This edition is streamlined to reflect the coverage of the AP examination. It provides chapters focusing on the six countries now on the test, as well as the United States for teachers who want to assign it. However, teachers who would prefer to cover more countries or a different selection of countries now have several choices. They can either adopt the complete college edition of the book or easily and inexpensively arrange for a **customized edition** of *Introduction to Comparative Politics* to be produced for their course. All the chapters of the regular college edition are posted in an **online database.** Also in the database are additional country choices, available only in a customized edition.

To learn more about the college edition or the database, or to create a custom edition, visit the Houghton Mifflin online catalog at *http://www. college.hmco.com* or contact your McDougal Littel representative by calling 1-800-323-5435.

Teaching and Learning Aids

For this edition of ICP, we have a much more robust website that offers a rich array of teaching and learning aids. For teachers, there is a website with interactive maps, an image library, interactive country profiles, interactive timelines, and a teacher's resource manual with useful teaching tips. Teachers also have access to the ClassPrep CD with HM Testing, an editable bank of test questions, and PowerPoint slides for classroom presentations. A correlation from the text to the Advanced Placement* course description ("acorn book") is available from your McDougal Littell representative.

For students, there is also a website that features a number of study aids including ACE self tests, flashcards for learning glossary terms, interactive maps, interactive country profiles, and interactive timelines.

Acknowledgments

We thank research assistants for their assistance in preparing some of the country chapters for this edition: Nicholas Toloudis and Matthew S. Winters for France; Anna Voronchikhina and Nadiya Ismaeva for Russia; Halbert Jones for Mexico; and Stephen Frenkel, Ifeoma Malo, and Victor Brobbey for Nigeria. We are also grateful to colleagues who have reviewed and critiqued the previous editions of this book: **Michael Bratton,** Michigan State University; **Rachel Califf,** PA Homeschoolers; **Liv Coleman,** University of Wisconsin-Madison; **William Crowther,** University of North Carolina; **Louise K. Davidson-Schmich,** University of Miami; **Chris Hamilton,** Washburn University; **Kenji Hayao,** Boston College; **Maria Perez Laubhan,** College of Lake County; **Richard Leich,** Gustavus Adolphus College; **Sherry L. Martin,** Cornell University; **Mahmood Monshipouri,** Quinnipiac University; **Vladimir Povov,** Carleton University; **Len Schoppa,** University of Virginia; **Peter M. Siavelis,** Wake Forest University; **Toshiyuki Yuasa,** University of Houston.

Finally, our thanks to the talented and professional staff who helped edit and publish ICP4: at Houghton Mifflin, Katherine Meisenheimer, sponsoring editor; Jeff Greene, senior development editor; Andrea Dodge, project editor; and Nicola Poser, executive marketing manager; at LEAP Publishing Services, Leslie Kauffman, senior development editor, Shay Carpenter, assistant project manager; and Jay Boggis, copyeditor.

M. K.
J. K.
W. A. J.

Introduction to
Comparative Politics

PART 1
Introduction

CHAPTER 1
Introducing Comparative Politics

CHAPTER 1

Introducing Comparative Politics

Mark Kesselman, Joel Krieger,
and William A. Joseph

When did our current era begin? Although a precise moment might be hard to identify, a frequently cited date is 1989, which marked the crumbling of the Berlin Wall. Until then, the wall separated communist-controlled East Berlin from West Berlin. More broadly, it separated the two Germanies: the German Democratic Republic, allied with the Soviet Union, and the Federal Republic of Germany, part of the **North Atlantic Treaty Organization (NATO)** alliance. At the most general level, the wall served as a powerful symbol of the division of the world into a communist bloc of countries, under the control of the Soviet Union, and the "Western" world, led by the United States. The collapse of the Berlin Wall swiftly ushered in a series of peaceful revolutions against the **communist party-states** of East Central Europe and the Soviet Union. The implosion of these **regimes,** and their replacement by governments proclaiming a commitment to democratic rule, marked the end of the grim and sometimes deadly **cold war** that had pitted the Soviet and American alliances against one another in many parts of the world.

At about the time when the Berlin Wall came tumbling down, an important and controversial analysis of world events was published with an audacious title, "The End of History?"[1] For its author, Francis Fukuyama, the failure of communism was of historic significance not only in itself, but also because it signified the end of any feasible alternative to Western-style regimes, that is, regimes that combine capitalist organization of the economy with a democratic political system. There was, he claimed, only one model of political and economic development for the world. He also claimed that history had ended, in the sense that never again would there be the kind of global struggle between competing ideologies that had marked previous eras and that, in the twentieth century alone, had led to two world wars and the cold war. He did recognize that the political and economic transitions to this new era would not be easy for many countries. He predicted that because of deeply entrenched nationalist and ethnic cleavages many parts of the world could not easily escape history and would "be a terrain of conflict for many years to come."

Was Fukuyama correct? Proving that "history" has ended is a long-term proposition. But in the short run, his analysis, despite its underlying ethnocentric triumphalism (*We won!*), does point to several crucial issues that present the contemporary world with both promise and peril in the uncertain international order following the cold war. Nearly every country (only a few isolated nations like North Korea and Burma are exceptions) faces the challenges of adjusting to a global economic system totally dominated by developed capitalist countries and international organizations committed to promoting free market capitalism. Many are also struggling, often under intense pressure, to build democratic governments in very difficult economic and social circumstances and after decades of **authoritarian** rule. And Fukuyama was certainly right—as the ethnic cleansing and genocide in Rwanda and the Sudan painfully remind us—that historically rooted antagonisms continue to exact a terrible toll in some countries and still fester just below the surface in many others.

By the year 2000, a new and distinctive lens for analyzing politics within and among countries seemed to be gaining great attention. This lens was **globalization.** The key new question that promised to dominate the political agenda of the early twenty-first century was whether the processes of globalization—the global diffusion of investment, trade, production, and electronic communication technologies—would promote a worldwide diffusion of opportunity and enhance human development or whether it would reinforce the comparative advantages of the more prosperous and powerful nations, transnational corporations, and peoples; undermine local cultures; and intensify regional conflicts.

These issues are very much with us today and frame the country studies in this book. Yet the terrorist attacks of September 11, 2001, on the United States and their aftermath have forced us to rethink, at least in part, the meaning of globalization. Before September 11, the economic aspects of globalization claimed major attention. Since 9/11, political and military concerns have been at the forefront, involving issues such as how U.S. power will recast global alliances and affect both national politics and people's lives throughout the world. We have also learned that international terror networks (another and especially sinister example of globalization) can strike anywhere—from the World Trade Center in New York and the Pentagon in Washington to a nightclub in Bali, Indonesia; and from a train station in Madrid, Spain, to an elementary school in Beslan, Russia, or in the subway and on a bus in London. Global politics has been transformed by 9/11. Security concerns have been placed at the top of nearly every government's agenda and transformed domestic politics. The war on terrorism has reshaped geopolitical alliances and redirected American foreign policy.

With wide international support and near-unanimity at home, the United States launched an attack in October 2001 on the Taliban regime in Afghanistan, which, President George W. Bush claimed, harbored the organization Al Qaeda and its leader, Osama Bin Laden, who had masterminded the September 11 attacks. International solidarity quickly dissolved, however, after the swift victory in Afghanistan of the coalition led by the United States. Despite the strong opposition of most governments and world public opinion, President Bush and prominent administration officials—as well as key allies such as Britain's prime minister Tony Blair—declared that there was irrefutable evidence that the Iraqi regime of Saddam Hussein possessed, and could rapidly deploy, weapons of mass destruction, including nuclear, biological, and chemical armaments, and that there were close links between Iraq and Al Qaeda. In 2003, the United States, Britain, and several other countries attacked Saddam's government, and "victory" quickly followed. However, establishing order and reconstructing Iraq proved far harder than toppling Saddam. Several years after President Bush declared in May 2003 that major combat operations were over, military hostilities in Iraq continued to claim the lives of Iraqi insurgents and citizens, as well as American, British, and other troops stationed there.

The events following September 11 have not replaced concerns about economic globalization. Instead, we are challenged to develop a more complex understanding of globalization and how it frames both politics and the study of comparative politics. More-over, the momentous events of the past few years have led many people to conclude that Fukuyama was premature and naive to predict that the history of global ideological conflict has ended.

Globalization and Comparative Politics

The terms *globalization* and *global era* are everywhere applied as general catch phrases to identify the growing depth, extent, and diversity of cross-border connections that are a key characteristic of the contemporary world. Discussion of globalization begins with accounts of economic activities, including the reorganization of production and the global redistribution of the work force (the "global factory"), as well as the increased extent and intensity of international trade, finance, and foreign direct investment. Globalization also involves the movement of peoples due to migration, employment, business, and educational opportunities.[2]

Globalization includes other profound changes that are less visible but equally significant. For example, new applications of information technology (such as the Internet and CNN) blur the traditional distinction between what is around the block and what is around the world—instantly transforming cultures and eroding the boundaries between the local and global. These technologies make instantaneous communication possible and link producers and contractors, headquarters, branch plants, and suppliers in real time anywhere in the world. Employees may be rooted in time and place, but employers can take advantage of the ebb and flow of a global labor market. A secure job today may be gone tomorrow. Globalization fosters insecurity in everyday life and presents extraordinary challenges to governments in all countries, large and small, rich and poor.

The dilemma that globalization represents for the post–cold war world can be illustrated by the theme "Global Inequalities" chosen by the American Political Science Association (the official organization of American political scientists) for its 2004 Annual Meeting. The program announcement for the Meeting declared, "While inequalities are hardly new, their relevance has become newly visible as the fading memory of the Cold War is replaced by the omnipresence of various North-South clashes. This invites systematic reflection. The enormous concentration of wealth and power in some parts of the world coexists with the marginalization of other countries and people."[3] The major source of international tensions has shifted from the East-West ideological conflict (between communist powers and capitalist democracies) to a North-South split between the "have" nations, often called the "North" because most developed countries are located in the northern hemisphere, against the "have not" nations, many of which are clustered in the southern half of the globe.

Globalization has forged new forms of international governance, from the **European Union (EU)** to the **World Trade Organization (WTO),** in an attempt to regulate and stabilize the myriad flows of globalization. An alphabet soup of other organizations and agreements—such as UNDP, IMF, IBRD, OECD, NAFTA, and APEC,[4] to name but a few—have also been enlisted in this attempt.

Globalization has also provoked challenges from grassroots movements in every region of the world that are concerned with its negative impact on, for example, poor people, the environment, and labor rights. The first such challenge occurred when the World Trade Organization sponsored a meeting of government ministers in Seattle in 1999 that was disrupted by fifty thousand protesters. Ever since then, conferences called to develop rules for global commerce have been the site of demonstrations by coalitions of environmental, labor-based, and community activists from around the world. Thus, to Seattle, one can add the names of cities on many continents—Washington, D.C., Prague, Genoa, Miami, and Cancun—where activists have assembled to protest the activity of international financial institutions. One can also identify sites, notably, Mumbai, India, and Porto Alegre, Brazil, where activists from around the world have assembled annually to exchange ideas and develop alternatives to the current form of economic globalization.[5]

All of these globalization processes complicate politics, just as they erode the ability of even the strongest countries to control their destinies. No state can secure the economic security and general well-being of its citizens in isolation from the rest of the world. None can preserve pristine national models of economic governance or distinctly national cultures, values, understandings of the world, or narratives that define a people and forge their unity. Many of the most important problems confronting governments are related to globalization, including pandemics like AIDS, global climate change, financial panics, and international terrorism. Although these problems may be global in scope, a government's popularity with its own people depends in considerable measure on how successfully it addresses these problems at home.

It is clear that countries face a host of challenges simultaneously from above and below. The capacities of states to control domestic outcomes and assert sovereignty are compromised by regional and global technological and market forces, as well as by growing security concerns. The very stability and viability of many countries are simultaneously assaulted by ethnic, nationalist, and religious divisions that often involve both internal and external components. The bright line separating domestic and international politics has been rubbed out by the complex set of cross-border economic, cultural, technological, governance, and security processes, institutions, and relations that constitute the contemporary global order.

Making Sense of Turbulent Times

The flash of newspaper headlines and television sound bites, the upheavals, rush of events, and sheer range and complexity of the cross-border phenomena of globalization tend to make politics look overwhelming and chaotic beyond comprehension. Although the study of comparative politics can help us understand current events in a rapidly changing world, it involves much more than snapshot analysis or Monday-morning quarterbacking. *Introduction to Comparative Politics* describes and analyzes in detail the government and politics of a range of countries and identifies common themes in their development that explain longer-term causes of both changes and continuities. The book provides cross-national comparisons and explanations based on four themes that we believe are central for understanding politics in today's world:

- The historical formation, internal organization, and interaction of states within the international order
- The role of the state in economic management
- The spread of democracy and the challenges of democratization

- The sources and political impact of diverse **collective identities**, including class, gender, ethnicity, and religion.

We also expect that these four themes will be useful for analyzing where the countries discussed in this book may be heading politically in the twenty-first century. Moreover, the themes illustrate how comparative politics can serve as a valuable tool for making political sense of even the most tumultuous times. The contemporary period presents an extraordinary challenge to those who study comparative politics, but the study of comparative politics also provides a unique opportunity for understanding this uncertain era.

In order to appreciate the complexity of politics and political transitions in countries around the world, we must look beyond any single national perspective. Today, business and trade, information technology, mass communications and culture, immigration and travel, as well as politics, forge deep connections—as well as deep divisions—among people worldwide. It is particularly urgent that we develop a truly global perspective as we explore the politics of different countries and their growing interdependence on one another.

There is an added benefit: by comparing political institutions, values, and processes in countries around the world, the student of comparative politics acquires analytical skills that can be used at home. After you study comparative politics, you begin to think comparatively. As comparison becomes more familiar, you will hopefully look at the politics of your own country differently, with a wider focus and new insights.

The contemporary world provides a fascinating laboratory for the study of comparative politics and gives unusual significance to the subject. We hope that you share our sense of excitement in the challenging effort to understand the complex and ever-shifting terrain of contemporary politics throughout the world. We begin by exploring what comparative politics actually compares and how comparative study enhances our understanding of politics generally.

Section ❷ What—and How—Comparative Politics Compares

To "compare and contrast" is one of the most common human mental exercises, whether in the classroom study of literature or politics or animal behavior—or in selecting dorm rooms or listing your favorite movies. In the observation of politics, the use of comparisons is very old, dating in the Western world to at least from Aristotle, the ancient Greek philosopher. Aristotle categorized Greek city-states in the fourth century B.C. according to their form of political rule: rule by a single individual, rule by a few, or rule by all citizens. He also added a normative dimension (a claim about how societies *should* be ruled) by distinguishing ("contrasting") good from corrupt versions of each type, according to whether those with power ruled in the interest of the common welfare of all citizens or only in their own interest. The modern study of comparative politics refines and systematizes the age-old practice of evaluating some feature of X by comparing it to the same feature of Y in order to learn more about it than isolated study would permit.

Comparative politics is a subfield within the academic discipline of political science as well as a method or approach to the study of politics.[6] The subject matter of comparative politics is the domestic politics of countries or peoples. Within the discipline of political science, comparative politics is one of four areas of specialization. In addition to comparative politics, most political science (or government) departments in U.S. colleges and universities include courses and academic specialists in three other fields: political theory, international relations, and American politics.

Because it is widely believed that students living in the United States should study American politics intensively and with special focus, it is usually treated as a separate subfield of political science. The pattern of distinguishing the study of politics at home from the study of politics abroad is also common elsewhere, so students in Canada may be expected to study Canadian politics as a distinct specialty, and Japanese students would be expected to master Japanese politics.

However, there is no logical reason that study of the United States should not be included within the field of comparative politics—and good reason to do so. In fact, many important studies in comparative politics (and an increasing number of courses) have integrated the study of American politics with the study of politics in other countries.[7] Comparative study can place U.S. politics into a much richer perspective and at the same time make it easier to recognize what is distinctive and most interesting about other countries.

Special mention should be made of the distinction between comparative politics and international relations. Comparative politics involves comparing domestic political institutions, processes, policies, conflicts, and attitudes in different countries; international relations involves the study of the foreign policy of and interactions among countries, the role of international organizations such as the United Nations, and the growing influence of a wide range of global actors from multinational corporations to terrorist networks. In a globalized world, the distinction sometimes becomes questionable, and there is a large gray zone where the two fields overlap. In 2005, the U.S. government announced that it would phase out subsidies for domestic cotton farmers in order to comply with a ruling by the World Trade Organization (WTO), an organization to which the United States belongs that is designed to facilitate cross-border trade and investment. Did this decision fall within the field of comparative politics or the field of international relations? The answer is both.[8]

However, it makes sense to maintain the distinction between comparative politics and international relations. Much of the world's political activity continues to occur within state borders, and comparisons of domestic politics, institutions, and processes enable us to understand critical features that distinguish one country's politics from another. Furthermore, we believe that, despite increased international economic integration (a key aspect of globalization), national states are the fundamental building blocks in structuring political activity. Therefore *Introduction to Comparative Politics* is built around in-depth case studies of a cross-section of important countries around the world.

The comparative approach principally analyzes similarities and differences among countries by focusing on selected institutions and processes. As students of comparative politics (we call ourselves **comparativists**), we believe that we cannot make reliable statements about most political situations by looking at only one case. We often hear statements such as: "The United States has the best health care system in the world." Comparativists immediately wonder what kinds of health care systems exist in other countries, what they cost and how they are financed, who is covered by health insurance, and so on. Besides, what does "best" mean when it comes to health care systems? Is it the one that provides the widest access? The one that is the most technologically advanced? The one that is the most cost-effective? The one that produces the healthiest population? None of us would announce the best movie or the best car without considering other alternatives or deciding what specific factors enter into our judgment.

Comparativists often analyze political institutions or processes by looking at two or more cases that are selected to isolate their common and contrasting features. The analysis involves comparing similar aspects of politics in more than one country. For example, a comparativist might analyze the similarities and differences in the executive branches of government in the United States, Britain, and Canada.[9] Some comparative political studies take a thematic approach and analyze broad issues, such as the causes and consequences of nationalist movements or revolutions in different countries.[10] Comparative studies may also involve comparisons of an institution, policy, or process through time, in one or several countries. For example, some studies have analyzed a shift in the orientation of economic policy that occurred in many advanced capitalist countries in the 1980s from Keynesianism, an approach that gives priority to government regulation of certain aspects of the economy, to neoliberalism, which emphasizes the importance of market-friendly policies.[11]

Level of Analysis

Comparisons can be useful for political analysis at several different levels. Political scientists often compare developments in different cities, regions, provinces, or states. Comparative analysis can also focus on specific institutions in different countries, such as the legislature, executive, political parties, social movements, or court systems, as well as specific processes and policies. The organization of *Introduction to Comparative Politics* reflects our belief that the best way to begin the study of comparative politics is with **countries.** Countries comprise distinct, politically defined territories that encompass political institutions, cultures, economies, and ethnic and other social identities. Although often highly divided by internal conflicts, countries have historically been the most important source of a people's collective political identity, and they are the major arena for organized political action in the modern world.

Within a given country, the **state** is almost always the most powerful cluster of institutions. But just what is the state? The way the term is used in comparative politics is probably unfamiliar to many students. In the United States, it usually refers to the states in the federal system—Texas, California, and so on. But in comparative politics, the state refers to the key political institutions responsible for making, implementing, enforcing, and adjudicating important policies in a country.[12] Thus, we use phrases such as the "German state" and the "Mexican state." In many ways, the state is synonymous with what is often called the "government."

The most important state institutions are the national **executive**—usually, the president and/or prime minister and the **cabinet**—but in some cases, the executive includes the Communist Party leader (such as in China), the head of a military government (as in Nigeria until 1999), or the supreme religious leader (as in the Islamic Republic of Iran). Other key state institutions include the military, police, administrative **bureaucracy,** the legislature, and courts.

States claim, usually with considerable success, the right to issue rules—notably, laws, administrative **regulations**, and court decisions—that are binding for people within the country. Even democratic states—in which top officials are chosen by procedures that authorize all citizens to participate—can survive only if they can preserve enforcement (or coercive) powers both internally and with regard to other states and external groups that may threaten them. A number of countries have highly repressive states whose political survival depends largely on military and police powers. But even in such states, long-term stability requires that the ruling regime have some measure of political **legitimacy;** that is, a significant segment of the citizenry (in particular, more influential citizens and groups) must believe that the state is entitled to command compliance from those who live under its rule. Political legitimacy is greatly affected by the state's ability to deliver the goods through satisfactory economic performance and an acceptable distribution of economic resources. Moreover, in the contemporary period, legitimacy seems to require that states represent themselves as democratic in some fashion, whether or not they are in fact. Thus, *Introduction to Comparative Politics* looks closely at both the state's role in governing the economy and the pressures exerted on states to develop and extend democratic participation.

The fact that states are the fundamental objects of analysis in comparative politics does not mean that all states are the same. Indeed, the organization of state institutions varies widely, and these differences have a powerful impact on political, economic, and social life. Hence, the country studies in this book devote considerable attention to variations in institutions of governance, participation, and representation—along with their political implications. Each country study begins with an analysis of how the institutional organization and political procedures of the state have evolved historically. The process of **state formation** fundamentally influences how and why states differ politically.

One critical difference among states that will be explored in our country studies involves the extent to which citizens in a country share a common sense of nationhood, that is, a belief that the state's geographic boundaries coincides with citizens' collective identity. When state boundaries and national identity coincide, the resulting formation is called a **nation-state**. A major source of political instability is that they often do not coincide. Countries in *Introduction to Comparative Politics* where there is a strong sense of national identity based on existing state boundaries include France, Japan, and the United States.

In many countries around the world, nationalist movements within a state's borders challenge existing boundaries and seek to secede to form their own state, sometimes in alliance with movements from neighboring countries with whom they claim to share a common heritage. Such is the case with the Kurds, who have large populations in Turkey, Syria, and Iraq, and have long sought and fought to establish an independent nation-state of Kurdistan. When a nationalist movement has distinctive ethnic, religious, and/or linguistic ties opposed to those of other groups in the country, conflicts are likely to be especially intense. Nationalist movements may pursue their separatist goal peacefully within established political institutions. Or, as we discuss in several of the country studies, they may act outside established institutions and engage in illegal activity, including violence against political authorities and civilians. One of the major sources of political instability throughout the world involves nationalist movements challenging established states. India and Nigeria have, for example, experienced particularly violent episodes of ethno-nationalist conflict.

Causal Theories

Because countries are the basic building blocks in politics and because states are the most significant political organizations and actors, these are the two critical units for comparative analysis. The comparativist seeks to measure and hopefully explain similarities and differences among countries or states. One influential approach in comparative politics involves developing causal theories—hypotheses that can be expressed formally in a causal mode: "If X happens, then Y will be the result." Such theories include factors (the independent variables, symbolized by X) that are believed to influence some outcome (the dependent variable, symbolized by Y) to be explained.

For example, it is commonly argued that if a country's economic pie shrinks, conflict among groups for resources will intensify. This hypothesis suggests what is called an inverse correlation between variables: as X varies in one direction, Y varies in the opposite direction. As the total national economic product (X) decreases, then political and social conflict over economic shares (Y) increases. This relationship might be tested by statistical analysis of a very large number of cases, a project facilitated in recent years by the creation of data banks that include extensive historical and contemporary data. Another way to study this issue would be to focus on one or several country cases and analyze how the relevant relationships have varied historically. Even when explanation does not involve the explicit testing of hypotheses (and often it does not), comparativists try to identify similarities and differences among countries and to discover significant patterns.

It is important to recognize the limits on just how "scientific" political science—and thus comparative politics—can be. Two important differences exist between the "hard" (or natural) sciences like physics and chemistry and the social sciences. First, social scientists study people who exercise free will. Because people have a margin for free choice, even if one assumes that they choose in a rational manner, their choices, attitudes, and behavior cannot be fully explained. This does not mean that people choose in a totally arbitrary fashion. We choose within the context of material constraint, institutional dictates, and cultural prescriptions. Comparative politics analyzes how such factors shape political preferences and choices in systematic ways; indeed, a recent study by three political scientists concluded that political beliefs are, to a certain degree, genetically determined.[13] But there will probably always be a wide gulf between the natural and social sciences because of their different objects of study.

A second difference between the natural and social sciences is that in the natural sciences, experimental techniques can be applied to isolate the contribution of distinct factors to a particular outcome. It is possible to change the value or magnitude of a factor—for example, the force applied to an object—and measure how the outcome has consequently changed. However, like other social scientists, political scientists and comparativists rarely have the opportunity to apply such experimental techniques.

Some political scientists have conducted experiments with volunteers in controlled settings. But laboratories provide crude approximations of natural settings since only one or several variables can be manipulated. The real world of politics, by contrast, consists of an endless number of variables, and they cannot easily be isolated or manipulated. Another attempt to deal with this problem is by statistical techniques that seek to identify the specific causal weight of different variables in explaining variations in political outcomes. But it is difficult to measure precisely how, for example, a person's ethnicity, gender, or income influences her or his choice when casting a ballot. Nor can we ever know for sure what exact mix of factors—conflicts among elites, popular ideological appeals, the weakness of the state, the organizational capacity of rebel leaders, or the discontent of the masses—precipitates a successful revolution. Indeed, different revolutions may result from different configurations of factors such that one cannot develop a single theory to explain the origins of all revolutions.

There is a lively debate about whether the social sciences should seek scientific explanations comparable to what prevails in the natural sciences, such as physics. Some scholars claim that political scientists should aim to develop what have been called covering laws to explain political outcomes: that is, political phenomena should be explained by universal laws in a similar way to how physicists develop universally applicable laws to explain specific features of the physical world. Critics of this view claim that the social world is essentially different from the natural world. Some contend that the social sciences should seek to identify particular patterns and structures that fulfill similar functions that operate in different settings—but they recognize that this is a more modest goal than fully explaining outcomes. Another group of scholars claims that social science should focus on identifying unique configurations of factors that coexist in a particular case. Proponents of this approach do not seek a definitive explanation or the development of covering laws.[14] And yet a fourth approach advocates what the anthropologist, Clifford Geertz, has designated "thick description," which seeks to convey the rich and subtle texture of any given historical situation, including the subjective and symbolic meaning of that situation for its participants.[15] Comparativists who favor this approach highlight the importance of understanding each country's distinctive **political culture**, which can be defined as the attitudes, beliefs, values, and symbols that influence political behavior.

An approach largely borrowed from economics, called **rational choice theory**, has been especially in-fluential—and highly controversial—in political science, as well as in comparative politics, in recent years.[16] Rational choice theory focuses on how individuals act strategically (that is, rationally) in an attempt to achieve certain goals or maximize their interests when it comes to things like voting for a particular candidate or rebelling against the government. Proponents of rational choice generally use highly quantitative methods to construct models and general theories of political behavior that they believe can be applied across all types of political systems and cultures. This approach has been criticized for claiming to explain large-scale and complex social phenomena by reference to individual choices. It has also been criticized for dismissing the importance of variations in historical experience, political culture, identities, institutions, and other factors that are key aspects of most explanations of the political world.

Issues involving the appropriate choice of theory, methodology, research approaches, and strategies are a vital aspect of comparative politics. However, students may be relieved to learn that we do not deal with such issues in depth in *Introduction to Comparative Politics*. We believe that students will be in a much better position to consider these questions after gaining a solid grasp of political continuities and contrasts in diverse countries around the world. It is this goal that we put front and center in this book.

Returning to our earlier discussion of the level of analysis, most comparativists probably agree on the value of steering a middle course that avoids both focusing exclusively on one country and combining all countries indiscriminately. If we study only individual countries without any comparative framework, comparative politics would become merely the study of a series of isolated cases. It would be impossible to recognize what is most significant in the collage of political characteristics that we find in the world's many countries. As a result, the understanding of patterns of similarity and difference among countries would be lost, along with an important tool for evaluating what is and what is not unique about a country's political life.

If we go to the other extreme and try to make universal claims, we would either have to stretch the truth or ignore significant national differences and patterns of variation. The political world is incredibly complex, shaped by an extraordinary array of factors and an almost endless interplay of variables. Indeed, after a brief period in the 1950s and 1960s when many comparativists tried—and failed—to develop a grand theory that would apply to all countries, most comparativists now agree on the value of **middle-level theory,** that is, theories focusing on specific features of the political world, such as institutions, policies, or classes of similar events, such as revolutions or elections.

For example, comparativists have analyzed the process in which many countries with authoritarian forms of government, such as military **dictatorships** and one-party states, have gone on to develop more participatory and democratic regimes. In studying this process, termed **democratic transitions,** comparativists do not treat each national case as unique or try to construct a universal pattern that ignores all differences. Applying middle-level theory, we identify the influence on the new regime's political stability of specific variables such as institutional legacies, political culture, levels of economic development, the nature of the regime before the transition, and the degree of ethnic conflict or homogeneity. Comparativists have been able to identify patterns in the emergence and consolidation of democratic regimes in southern Europe in the 1970s (Greece, Portugal, and Spain) and have compared them to developments in Latin America, Asia, and Africa since the 1980s and in Eastern and Central Europe since the revolutions of 1989.[17]

The study of comparative politics has many challenges, including the complexity of the subject matter, the fast pace of change in the contemporary world, and the impossibility of manipulating variables or replicating conditions. What can we expect when the whole political world is our laboratory? When we put the method of comparative politics to the test and develop a set of themes derived from middle-level theory, we discover that it is possible to discern patterns that make sense of a vast range of political events and link the experiences of states and citizens throughout the world. If we will doubtless not achieve definitive explanations, we will hopefully be able to better understand the daily headlines by reference to middle-range theoretical propositions.

Section ❸ Themes for Comparative Analysis

We began this introduction by emphasizing the extraordinary importance and fluid pace of the global changes currently taking place. Next, we explained the subject matter of comparative politics and described some of the tools of comparative analysis. This section describes the four themes we use in *Introduction to Comparative Politics* to organize the information on institutions and processes in the country chapters.

These themes help explain continuities and contrasts among countries and demonstrate what patterns apply to a group of countries and why, and what patterns are specific to a particular country. We also suggest a way that each theme highlights a particular puzzle in comparative politics.

Before we introduce the themes, a couple of warnings are necessary. First, our four themes cannot possibly capture the infinitely varied experience of politics throughout the world. Our framework in *Introduction to Comparative Politics,* built on these core themes, provides a guide to understanding many features of contemporary comparative politics. But we urge students (and rely on instructors!) to challenge and expand on our interpretations. Second, we want to note that a textbook builds from existing theory but does not construct or test new hypotheses. That task is the goal of original scholarly studies. The themes are intended to provide a framework to help organize some of the most significant developments in the field of contemporary comparative politics.

Theme 1: A World of States

The theme we call a world of states reflects the fact that for about 500 years, states have been the primary actors on the world stage. Although international organizations and private actors like transnational corporations—and ordinary citizens organized in political parties and social movements—may play a crucial role, for the most part it is the rulers of states who send armies to conquer other states and territories. It is the legal codes of states that make it possible for businesses to operate within their borders and beyond. States provide more or less well for the social protection of citizens through the provision—in one way or another—of health care, old age pensions, aid to dependent children, and assistance to the unemployed. It is states that regulate the movement of people across borders through immigration law. And the policies of even the most influential international organizations reflect to a considerable extent the balance of power among member states.

That said, and as we noted above when discussing globalization, there is increasing overlap between the study of international relations and the study of comparative politics. An important trend in political science is toward courses in international relations, which integrate a concern with how internal political processes affect states' behavior, and courses in comparative politics, which highlight the importance of transnational forces for understanding what goes on within a country's borders. Therefore, in *Introduction to Comparative Politics,* we emphasize the interactive effects of domestic politics and international forces.

We distinguish two important components of the world of states theme, one that focuses on a state's relationship to the international arena, the other focusing on its internal development. The external element highlights the impact on a state's domestic political institutions and processes of its relative success or failure in competing economically and politically with other states. What sphere of maneuver is left to states by imperious global economic and geopolitical forces? How do CNN, the Internet, McDonald's, television, and films (whether produced in Hollywood or in Bollywood, that is, Bombay, the city that has been renamed Mumbai and that is the site of India's thriving film industry) shape local cultures and values, influence citizen perceptions of government, and affect political outcomes?

A state's international geopolitical situation has a powerful impact on its domestic politics. When George Washington warned the United States, in his farewell address as president in 1796, not to "entangle our peace and prosperity" in alliances with other nations, he meant that the United States would be more successful if it could remain detached from the global power politics of the time (centered in Europe). That kind of disengagement might have been possible in the eighteenth century. But not in today's globalized world.

When President George W. Bush assumed office in 2001, he advocated a modest role for the United States in the world and opposed U.S. involvement in nation-building projects abroad. Months later, with the attacks of September 11, that policy orientation changed. Since then, the United States has toppled the Taliban regime in Afghanistan and sought to shape regimes in Iraq and elsewhere in the Middle East, as well as in other regions of the world, on the grounds that stable democratic regimes are in the interests of their own citizenry and, because terrorism is likely to flourish in such regimes, in the interests of the United States as well. Even a president who proclaimed the value of unilateralism—going it alone—has spent considerable time trying to assemble international coalitions to achieve his goals.

But no state, even the most powerful, such as the United States, can shape the world to suit its own designs. Nor is any state unaffected by influences originating outside its borders. A wide array of international organizations and treaties, including the United Nations, the European Union, the World Trade Organization, the **World Bank**, the **International Monetary Fund** (IMF), and the North American Free Trade Agreement (NAFTA), challenge the sovereign control of national governments. Transnational corporations, international banks, and currency traders in New York, London, Frankfurt, Hong Kong, and Tokyo affect countries and people throughout the world. A country's political borders do not protect its citizens from global warming, environmental pollution, or infectious diseases that come from abroad. More broadly, developments linked to technology transfer, the growth of an international information society, immigration, and cultural diffusion challenge state supremacy and have a varying but significant impact on the domestic politics of virtually all countries.[18]

Thanks to the global diffusion of radio, television, and the Internet, people nearly everywhere can become remarkably well informed about international developments. This knowledge may fuel popular local demands that governments intervene to stop atrocities in, for example, faraway Kosovo or Rwanda, or rush to aid the victims of natural disasters as happened after the great tsunami struck South and Southeast Asia in late 2004. And heightened global awareness may encourage citizens to hold their own government to internationally recognized standards of human rights and democracy. In the recent past, dictatorial rulers in Peru, Ukraine, and Kyrgyzstan have yielded power after popular movements took to the streets to challenge rigged election results. In mid-2005, hundreds of Iranian women demonstrated to protest sex discrimination in the Islamic Republic and to demand that candidates for the presidency discuss how they would address the issue.

States may collapse altogether when challenged by powerful rivals for power. And a similar outcome may occur when leaders of the state violate the rule of law and become predators, preying on the population. Political scientist Robert Rotberg suggested the term "failed states" to describe this extreme situation, and cited as examples Sierra Leone, Somalia, and Afghanistan before and under the Taliban.[19] The political situation in such countries has approached the anarchical state of nature described by the seventeenth-century English philosopher Thomas Hobbes. In a state of nature, he warned in the *Leviathan*, the absence of effective state authority produces a war of every man against every man, in which life involves "continual fear, and danger of violent death; and the life of man [is] solitary, poor, nasty, brutish, and short."

Although few states decline to the point of complete failure, all states in this new century are experiencing intense pressures from an expanding and increasingly complex mix of external influences. But international political and economic influences do not have the same impact in all countries, and a few privileged states have the capacity to shape the institutional structure and policy of international organizations in which they participate. It is likely that the more advantages a state possesses, as measured by its level of economic development, military power, and resource base, the more global influence it will have. Conversely, the policies of countries with fewer advantages are more extensively molded by other

states, international organizations, and broader international constraints.

The theme we identify as a world of states includes a second important component that recognizes the fact that individual states (countries) are still the basic building block in world politics. Our case studies emphasize the importance of understanding similarities and contrasts in state formation and design across countries. Here we study the ways that states have developed historically, diverse patterns of political institutions, the processes and limits of democratization, the ability of the state to control social groups and sustain power, and the state's economic management strategies and capacities. In our country chapters, we emphasize the importance of what we call critical junctures in state formation: that is, key events like colonial conquest, defeat in war, economic crises, or revolutions that had a durable impact on the character of the state.

The world-of-states theme is also intended to draw attention to the importance of regime variations among states, in other words, the overall mix of their political institutions that distinguishes, for example, democratic from authoritarian regimes. This theme is also intended to highlight the importance of variations in the configuration of institutions within a given regime type, such as the contrast between presidential and parliamentary forms in democratic states.

A puzzle: How do states in the modern world deal with the many challenges to their authority that they face from both internal and external forces? Increasingly, the politics and policies of states are shaped by diverse international factors often lumped together under the category of globalization. At the same time, many states face increasingly restive constituencies who challenge the power and legitimacy of central governments. In reading the country case studies in this book, try to assess what impact pressures from both above and below—outside and inside—have on the role of the state in carrying out its basic functions and in sustaining the political attachment of its citizens. To what extent can even the most powerful states (especially the United States) preserve their autonomy and impose their will on others? Or are all states losing their ability to control important aspects of policy-making and secure the political outcomes they desire? And in what ways are the poorer and less powerful countries particularly vulnerable to the pressures of globalization and disgruntled citizens?

Theme 2: Governing the Economy

The success of states in maintaining sovereign authority and control over their people is greatly affected by their ability to ensure that an adequate volume of goods and services is produced to satisfy the needs of their populations. Certainly, inadequate economic performance was an important reason for the rejection of communism and the disintegration of the Soviet Union. In contrast, the economic achievements of China's Communist Party are a major factor in explaining why communist rule has survived in that country.

Effective economic performance is near the top of every state's political agenda, and how a state "governs the economy"[20]—how it organizes production and the extent and character of its intervention in the economy—is a key element in its overall pattern of governance. It is important to analyze, for example, how countries differ in the balance between agricultural and industrial production in their economies, how successful they are in competing with other countries that offer similar products in international markets, and the relative importance of private market forces versus government direction of the economy.

The term **political economy** refers to how governments affect economic performance and how economic performance in turn affects a country's political processes. We accord great importance to political economy in *Introduction to Comparative Politics* because we believe that politics in all countries is deeply influenced by the relationship between government and the economy in both domestic and international dimensions. However, the term *economic performance* may convey the misleading impressions that there is one right way to promote successful economic performance and one single standard by which to measure performance. In fact, both issues are far more complex.

There are many wrong ways to manage an economy; there are multiple right ways as well. Economic historian Alexander Gerschenkron pointed out long ago that the major European powers were forced to develop distinctive ways to promote industrialism because of the different places they occupied in the sequence of industrializing powers.[21] Britain had the good fortune to be the first country in the world to industrialize. Britain enjoyed a head start in economic competition; hence, it was possible for the state to adopt a relatively hands-off posture and for a market system of production to develop slowly, an arrangement that came to be known by the French term **laissez-faire**, which literally means "let do," and more broadly refers to a free enterprise economy. All later developers, both those located in Europe in the nineteenth century and those located elsewhere in the world in the twentieth and twenty-first century, have had to catch up to an industrial leader. As a result, they did not have the luxury of adopting the British state's style of low-profile management but were forced to develop varieties of crash programs of economic development.

What formula of state management has made for success in this later period? On the one hand, both economic winners and losers display a pattern of extensive state intervention in the economy; thus, it is not the degree of state intervention that distinguishes the economic success stories from those that have fared less well. On the other hand, the winners do not share a single formula that enabled them to excel. For example, a study directed by Peter A. Hall and David Soskice of the world's affluent capitalist economies identifies two quite different patterns of political economy.[22] Studies seeking to explain the Asian "economic miracles"—Japan, South Korea, and more recently China—as well as the variable economic performance of other countries highlight the diversity of approaches that have been pursued.[23]

There is agreement on a list of practices that *hinder* economic development (although it borders on the commonsensical): such states tolerate dishonesty and corruption, set tax rates so high as to discourage productive economic activity, and fail to provide public goods like education and transportation facilities that promote a productive economy. However, there is less agreement on the economic policies that states *should* adopt.

The matter becomes even more complex when one considers the appropriate yardstick to measure economic success. Should economic performance be measured solely by how rapidly a country's economy grows? By how equitably it distributes the fruits of economic growth? By the quality of life of its citizenry, as measured by such criteria as life expectancy, level of education, and unemployment rate? What about the environmental impact of economic growth? There is now much greater attention than just a few decades ago given to this question, and more countries are emphasizing **sustainable development**, which promotes ecologically sound ways to modernize the economy and raise the standard of living. We invite you to consider these questions as you study the political economies of the countries analyzed in this book.

A puzzle: What is the relationship between democracy and successful national economic performance? This is a question that students of political economy have long pondered—and to which there are no fully satisfactory answers. Although all economies, even the most powerful, experience ups and downs, the United States, Canada, and the longer-standing countries of the European Union (in particular, the fifteen member-states prior to the 2004 enlargement to twenty-five members)—all durable democracies—have been notable economic success stories. On the other hand, several East Asian countries with authoritarian regimes also achieved remarkable records of development. The Republic of Korea (South Korea), Taiwan, and Singapore surged economically in the 1960s and 1970s, and Malaysia and Thailand followed suit in the 1980s and 1990s. (Korea, Taiwan, and Thailand subsequently adopted democratic institutions.) China, a repressive **communist party-state** that has enjoyed one of the highest growth rate in the world since the early 1990s, provides a vivid case of development without democracy.

In light of the contradictory evidence, Nobel Prize–winning economist and comparative public policy analyst Amartya Sen has argued, "There is no clear relation between economic growth and democracy in *either* direction."[24] As you read the country studies, try to identify why some states have been more successful than others in "governing the economy," that is, fostering successful economic performance. Are there any consistent patterns that apply across countries?

Theme 3: The Democratic Idea

One of the most important and astounding political developments in recent years has been the rapid spread of democracy throughout much of the world. There is overwhelming evidence of the strong appeal of the democratic idea, by which we mean the claim by citizens that they should, in some way, exercise substantial control over the decisions made by their states and governments.

According to Freedom House (a research organization based in the United States), in 1973 there were 43 countries that could be considered "free" (or democratic), 38 that were "partly free," and 69 that should be classified as "not free." By 2004, their count was 89 free, 54 partly free, and 49 not free. In terms of population, in 1973, 35 percent of the world's people lived in "free" countries, 18 percent in partly free, and 47 percent were citizens of countries ranked as "not free." In 2004, the percentages were 44 percent free, 21 percent partly free, and 35 percent not free.[25] And as authoritarian rulers have recently learned in Ukraine, Zimbabwe, Peru, and Kyrgyzstan, once persistent and widespread pressures for democratic participation develop, they are hard to resist (although not impossible, as China showed in its bloody 1989 crackdown on protestors). As Amartya Sen has put it, "While democracy is not yet uniformly practiced, nor indeed uniformly accepted, in the general climate of world opinion, democratic governance has now achieved the status of being taken to be generally right."[26]

What explains the recent trend toward democracy? Comparativists have devoted enormous energy to studying this question. One scholar notes, "For the past two decades, the main topic of research in comparative politics has been democratization."[27] Yet, for all the attention it has received, there is no scholarly consensus on how and why democratization occurs. Or, rather, what we have learned is that there is no one path to democracy. Some of the country studies in *Introduction to Comparative Politics* analyze the diverse causes and sources of support for democracy.

In certain historical settings, democracy may result from a standoff or compromise among political contenders for power, in which no one group can gain sufficient strength to control outcomes by itself.[28]

Democracy may appeal to citizens in authoritarian nations because democratic regimes often rank among the world's most stable, affluent, and cohesive countries. In some cases, a regional demonstration effect occurs, in which a democratic transition in one country provokes democratic change in neighboring countries. (This occurred in southern Europe in the 1970s, Latin America and parts of East Asia in the 1980s, and Eastern and Central Europe in the 1990s.) Another important pressure for democracy is born of the human desire for dignity and equality. Even when dictatorial regimes appear to benefit their countries—for example, by promoting economic development or nationalist goals—citizens are likely to demand democracy. Although authoritarian governments can suppress demands for democratic participation, the domestic and (in recent years) international costs of doing so are high. However, not all authoritarian regimes have crumbled. Indeed, China, the world's most populous country with most dynamic economy, remains resolutely undemocratic.

Is it possible to identify conditions that are necessary or sufficient for democracy to flourish? Comparativists have proposed, among the factors, secure national boundaries, a stable state, at least a minimum level of economic development, the widespread acceptance of democratic values, agreement on the rules of the democratic game among those who contend for power—one might extend the list, but the point should be clear! But democracy can and has flourished in unlikely settings—for example, in India, a country with a vast population whose per capita income is among the lowest in the world—and has failed where it might be expected to flourish—for example, in Germany in the 1930s. Democracies vary widely in terms of how they came into existence and in their concrete historical, institutional, and cultural dimensions.

Displacing authoritarian regimes and then holding elections does not mean that democracy will prevail or endure. A wide gulf exists between what comparativists have termed a *transition* to democracy and the *consolidation* of democracy. A transition involves toppling an authoritarian regime and adopting the rudiments of democracy; consolidation requires fuller adherence to democratic procedures and making democratic institutions more sturdy and durable. Below,

we further explore the important question of how to distinguish what we term *transitional democracies* from *consolidated democracies*. We consider the distinction of such great importance that it forms the basis for our classifying countries throughout the world.

We want to emphasize that the study of comparative politics does not support a philosophy of history or theory of political development that identifies a single (democratic) end point toward which all countries will eventually converge. One important work, published at the beginning of the most recent democratic wave, which began in Latin America in the 1970s, captured the tenuous process of democratization in its title: *Transitions from Authoritarian Rule: Tentative Conclusions About Uncertain Democracies.*[29] Scholars have suggested that it is far easier for a country to hold its first democratic election than its second or third. Historically, powerful groups have often opposed democratization because they fear that democracy will threaten their privileges. But disadvantaged groups may also oppose the democratic process because they see it as unresponsive to their deeply felt grievances. As a result, reversals of democratic regimes and restorations of authoritarian rule have occurred in the past and will doubtless occur in the future. In brief, the fact that the democratic idea is so powerful does not mean that all countries will adopt or preserve democratic institutions.

Finally, the theme of the democratic idea requires us to examine the incompleteness of democratic agendas, even in countries with the longest experiences of representative democracy. In recent years, many citizens in virtually every democracy have turned against the state when their living standards were threatened by high unemployment and economic stagnation.

At the same time, **social movements** have targeted the state because of its actions or inactions in such varied spheres as environmental regulation, reproductive rights, and race or ethnic relations. Comparative studies confirm that the democratic idea fuels political conflicts in even the most durable democracies because a large gap usually separates democratic ideals and the actual functioning of democratic political institutions. Moreover, social movements often organize because citizens perceive political parties—presumably an important established vehicle for representing *issues w/ democracy* ↗

citizen demands in democracies—as ossified and out of touch with the people. Even in countries with impressive histories of democratic institutions, citizens may invoke the democratic idea to demand that their government be more responsive and accountable.

A puzzle: Is there a relationship between democracy and political stability? Comparativists have debated whether democratic institutions contribute to political stability or, on the contrary, to political disorder. On the one hand, democracy by its very nature permits political opposition. One of its defining characteristics is competition among those who aspire to gain political office. Political life in democracies is turbulent and unpredictable. On the other hand, and perhaps paradoxically, the very fact that political opposition and competition are legitimate in democracies appears to deepen support for the state, even among opponents of a particular government. The democratic rules of the game may promote political stability by encouraging today's losers to remain in the game, rejecting the use of violence to press their claim to power, because they may win peacefully in future competition. Although there is a disturbing tendency for deep flaws to mar democratic governance in countries that have toppled authoritarian regimes, the odds are that, once a country adopts a democratic regime, that regime will endure.[30] As you learn about different countries, look for the stabilizing and destabilizing consequences of recent democratic transitions, the pressures (or lack of pressure) for democratization in authoritarian states, and the persistence of undemocratic elements even in established democracies.

Theme 4: The Politics of Collective Identity

How do individuals understand who they are in political terms? On what basis do groups of people form to advance common political aims? In other words, what are the sources of collective political identities? At one time, social scientists thought they knew. Observers argued that the age-old loyalties of ethnicity, religious affiliation, race, gender, and locality were being dissolved and displaced by economic, political, and cultural modernization. Comparativists thought that **social class**—solidarities based on the shared experience of work or, more broadly, economic position—had become the most important source of collective identity. They believed that most of the time, groups would pragmatically pursue their interests in ways that were not politically destabilizing. We now know that the formation of group attachments and the interplay of politically relevant collective identities are far more complex and uncertain.

In many long-established democracies, the importance of identities based on class membership has declined, although class and material sources of collective political identity remain significant in political competition and economic organization. Furthermore, contrary to earlier predictions, in many countries nonclass identities have assumed growing, not diminishing, significance. Such affiliations are based on a sense of belonging to particular groups sharing a common language, region, religion, ethnicity, race, nationality, or gender.

The politics of collective political identity involves struggles to form politically influential groups and to define which ones are influential participants in the political process and which are marginalized or even excluded. This struggle involves a constant tug of war among groups over relative power and influence, both symbolic and substantive. Issues of inclusion, political recognition, and priority remain pivotal in many countries, and they may never be fully settled.

In addition, questions of representation are hard to resolve. Who is included in a racial or ethnic minority community, for example? How is it determined who speaks for the community or negotiates with a governmental authority on its behalf? One reason that conflict around these questions can be so intense is that political leaders in the state and in opposition movements often seek to mobilize support by exploiting ethnic, religious, racial, or regional rivalries and by manipulating issues of identity and representation. Another reason is that considerable material and nonmaterial stakes derive from the outcome of these struggles.

Identity-based conflicts appear in every multiethnic society. And given the pace of migration and the tangled web of postcolonial histories that link colonizer to colonized, what country is not multiethnic? In Britain, France, and Germany, issues of nationality, citizenship, and immigration—often with ethnic or racial overtones—have been hot-button issues and have often spilled over into electoral politics. These conflicts have been particularly intense in postcolonial countries, such as Nigeria, where colonial powers forced ethnic groups together in order to carve out a country and where borders were drawn with little regard to preexisting collective identities. This process of state formation sowed seeds for future conflict in Nigeria and elsewhere and threatens the survival of democracy and perhaps the state itself in many postcolonial nations.

Even nations with a high degree of ethnic homogeneity, such as China and Japan, may experience political tensions based on ethnicity, although these tensions have certainly been much more extreme in China as reflected both in Tibet and in the Muslim regions of the country. Many states are also challenged (sometimes violently) by nationalist movements that seek to secede to form their own country. This was the root cause of the civil war in 1971 that led to the creation of Bangladesh, which was once part of Pakistan. The crisis in Northern Ireland, the separatist movement in Quebec, and the war in Chechnya show that developed countries like the United Kingdom, Canada, and Russia are not immune from high-stakes identity clashes.

Religion is another source of collective identity—as well as of severe political conflict, both within and among religious communities. Violent conflict among religious groups has recently occurred in many countries, including India, Sri Lanka, Nigeria, and the United Kingdom (again, in Northern Ireland). Such conflicts may spill over national boundaries and involve an especially ugly form of globalization. For example, Al Qaeda, the network responsible for the September 11 attacks in the United States, identified the presence of non-Muslim Western forces in what they regarded as the sacred territory of Saudi Arabia as a principal reason for its actions. At the same time, the political orientation of a particular religious community is not predetermined but is rather a product of what has been called "political entrepreneurship," that is, the efforts of leaders seeking power by mobilizing support within the community. The political posture associated with Christian, Jewish, Muslim, or Hindu beliefs cannot simply be read off the sacred texts, as is evidenced by the intense conflict *within* most religious communities today that pits more liberal, secular elements against those who defend what they claim is a more orthodox, traditional interpretation.

A puzzle: How does collective identity affect a country's **distributional politics**, that is, the process of deciding who gets what and how resources are distributed? Once identity demands are placed on the national agenda, can governments resolve them by distributing political, economic, and other resources in ways that redress the grievances of the minority or politically weaker identity groups? Collective identities operate at the level of symbols, attitudes, values, and beliefs as well as at the level of material resources. However, the contrast between material- and nonmaterial-based identities and demands should not be exaggerated. In practice, most groups are animated by both feelings of attachment and solidarity and by the desire to obtain material benefits and political influence for their members. Nonetheless, the analytical distinction between material and nonmaterial demands remains useful. Further, it is worth considering whether the nonmaterial aspects of collective identities make political disputes over ethnicity or religion or language or nationality especially divisive and difficult to resolve.

In a situation of extreme scarcity, it may prove nearly impossible to reach any compromise among groups with conflicting material demands. But if an adequate level of material resources is available, such conflicts may be easier to resolve through distributional politics because groups can negotiate at least a minimally satisfying share of resources.

However, the nonmaterial demands of ethnic, religious, and nationalist movements may be difficult to satisfy by a distributional style of politics. The distributional style may be quite ineffective when, for example, a religious group demands that the government require all citizens to conform to its social practices or when a dominant linguistic group insists that a single language be used in education and government throughout the country. In such cases, political conflict tends to move from the distributive realm to the cultural realm, where compromises cannot be achieved by simply dividing the pie of material resources. The country studies examine a wide range of conflicts involving collective identities. It is worth pondering whether, and under what conditions, they can be resolved by the normal give and take of political bargaining—and when, instead, they lead to the fury and blood of political violence.

These four themes provide our analytic scaffold. With an understanding of the method of comparative politics and the four themes in mind, we can now discuss how we have grouped the country studies that comprise *Introduction to Comparative Politics* and how the text is organized for comparative analysis.

Section ④ Classifying Political Systems

There are nearly 200 states in the world today, each with a political regime that is distinctive in some ways. How can we classify them in a manageable fashion? One possibility would be not to classify them at all, but simply to treat each state as different and unique. However, comparativists are rarely content with this solution—or nonsolution. It makes sense to highlight clusters of states that share important similarities, just as it is useful to identify what distinguishes one cluster of relatively similar states from other clusters. When comparativists classify a large number of cases into a smaller number of types or clusters, they call the result a **typology.** Typologies facilitate comparison both within the same type as well as between types of states. For example, what difference does it make that Britain has a parliamentary form of government and the United States a presidential one? Both are long-established democracies, but their different mix of democratic institutions provides an interesting laboratory case to study the impact of institutional variation.

We can also compare across clusters or types. In this type of comparison—comparativists call this **most different case analysis**—we analyze what produces the substantial differences we observe. Consider the fact that the world's two most populous countries, China and India, have such different political systems. How do their different political regimes affect such important issues as economic development, human rights, and the role of women?

How do we go about constructing typologies of states? Typologies exist as much in the eye of their beholder as in the nature of the beast. Typologies are artificial constructs, made rather than born. They are based on certain features that become the basis for classification and implicitly downplay the importance of others. It follows that what counts in evaluating a typology is not whether it is "true" or "false," but whether it is useful, and for what purpose. Typologies are helpful to the extent that they permit us to engage in useful comparisons.

What is the most useful typology for classifying political regimes or states? For almost half a century, from the end of World War II until the 1980s, there was a general consensus on the utility of one typology. Political scientists classified states as Western industrial democracies, dubbed the "First World"; communist states, the "Second World"; and the economically less developed countries in Asia, Africa, and Latin America, many of which had recently gained independence, the "**Third World.**" As with any typology, it was imperfect. For example, where should one assign Japan, a democratic country not in the West that rapidly developed in the 1960s and 1970s and became the world's second-leading economic power? Nevertheless, the typology was a generally adequate way to distinguish broad groups of countries because it corresponded to what appeared to be durable and important geopolitical and theoretical divisions in the world.

Today, the typology of First, Second, and Third Worlds is less useful. For one thing, in the past two decades, scores of countries have become democratic, or at least "partly free," that are neither highly industrialized nor located in the North Atlantic region, the geographic base of the "First World." From Argentina to Zambia, countries that were formerly colonies or undemocratic states have adopted democratic institutions, which we noted above is one of the most important and promising changes in the modern world.

Linked to the swelling of the ranks of democratic countries has been the near-disappearance of communist regimes, that is, the "Second World." Beginning in 1989, the implosion of communism in the former Soviet Union and Eastern and Central Europe set off a

Global Connection: *How Is Development Measured?*

This book makes frequent reference to three commonly used measures of the overall strength or power of a country's economy:

- **Gross Domestic Product** (GDP), which is a calculation of the total goods and services produced by the country during a given year.
- **Gross National Product** (GNP), which is GDP plus income earned abroad by the country's residents.
- **Gross National Income** (GNI), which is a new name for GNP that has been adopted by the World Bank.

The numbers generated by GDP or GNI/GNP are, of course, different, but not hugely so. As conventionally measured by GDP or GNI/GNP—which is the total output—the United States has, by far, the world's largest economy, followed by Japan, Germany, Britain, France, Italy, and China.

A better way to measure the level of development and the standard of living in different countries is to look at GDP/GNI per capita, in other words, total economic output divided by total population. From the perspective of GNP per capita, Luxembourg ranks first ($45,740), while the United States is fourth ($38,870), Japan is seventh ($34,180), and China is number 134 ($1,100) out of 208 countries measured.

But these figures use a calculation based on the American dollar and **official international currency exchange rates**, which would, for example, tell you how many Mexican pesos or Russian rubles you could get for US$1. Many economists believe this approach does not give a very accurate sense of the real standards of living in different countries because it does not tell what goods and services (such as housing, food, and transportation) people can actually buy with their local currencies.

An alternative and increasingly popular means of comparing levels of economic development across countries is called **purchasing power parity** (PPP). PPP takes into account the actual cost of living in a particular country by figuring what the purchasing price of the same "basket of goods" is in different countries. For example, how many dollars in the United States, pesos in Mexico, or rubles in Russia does it take to buy a certain amount of food or to pay for housing? Many analysts think that PPP provides a more reliable (and revealing) tool for comparing standards of living among countries.

The data boxes at the beginning of each country chapter in this text give both total and per capita GNI at official exchange rates and using PPP. As you will see, the differences between the two calculations can be quite dramatic, especially for developing countries. When PPP is used, China jumps from the seventh largest economy in the world to second place behind the United States. And, as noted above, China's exchange-rate GNP per capita is $1,100 (ranked 134th); using the PPP calculation it is $4,980, which places it at 119th out of 208 nations in 2003. Simply put, PPP takes into account that the cost of living in China is less than in the United States, so smaller incomes go farther when it comes to purchasing things.

The data boxes also give information about other ways to measure a country's development. The most important of these is the **Human Development Index** (HDI), which the United Nations introduced as a way to evaluate a country's level of development that considers more than just economic factors. The formula used to calculate a country's HDI takes into account *longevity* (life expectancy at birth), *knowledge* (literacy and average years of schooling), as well as *income* (according to PPP). Based on this formula, each country of the world, for which there are enough data, is assigned an HDI decimal number between 0 and 1; the closer a country is to 1, the better is its level of human development.

Out of 177 countries ranked according to HDI by the United Nations Development Programme on data collected in 2002, Norway (.956) was at the top and Sierra Leone (.273) was last. Countries such as the United States (8), Japan (9), Britain (12), France (16), Germany (19), the Republic of Korea (28), Poland (37), Cuba (52), and Mexico (53) were classified as having "high human development"; Russia (57), Brazil (72), China (94), Iran (101), South Africa (119), and India (127) were in the "medium human development" category; and Pakistan (142) and Nigeria (151) were scored as having "low human development."

revolutionary change in world politics. Only a handful of countries in the world—China, Cuba, Vietnam, Laos, and the Democratic People's Republic of (North) Korea—are now ruled by communist parties and declare an allegiance to communist ideology. Even some of these (particularly China and Vietnam) are adopting market-based economic policies and forging close ties with capitalist nations. It follows that the "Second World" has become a much less useful category to classify countries.

Finally, the "Third World" has also become less helpful in understanding the many countries formerly classified in this cluster. Countries that are often called Third World share few features, other than being less economically developed than industrialized nations (see "Global Connection: How Is Development Measured?"). Their colonial legacies have receded further and further into the past. In addition, some, such as Brazil and Mexico, have become more industrialized and economically powerful. Nevertheless, even in the period after the cold war, the term "Third World" may be a useful shorthand way to refer to the roughly 130 countries that the United Nations classifies as "developing" and that are still separated by a vast economic gulf from the 50 or so industrialized nations. However, when using this term, one should also take account of the fact that there are about four dozen countries—for example, Afghanistan, Ethiopia, and Haiti—that are classified by the UN as "least developed" and are so poor that the term "Fourth World" is sometimes used to describe them. This group of countries has become absolutely and relatively more poor in recent years due to the ravages of AIDS, civil war, and failed states.

If the "three worlds" method of classification is no longer as useful as it once was, what alternative is preferable? At present, there is no agreement among comparativists on this question. We suggest a typology based on one of the most important dimensions for understanding differences among countries in the contemporary world—the extent to which their governments are democratic. However, we preface the discussion by emphasizing that one might imagine an altogether different typology for classifying regimes. The categories we have established, the tools we use to measure, and the decisions we have made in classifying particular countries all lend themselves to discussion. We invite students to think critically about how to make sense of

the great variety of regimes in the world today and to devise alternative ways to classify countries.

Our typology classifies regimes into three groups: *consolidated democracies, transitional democracies,* and *authoritarian regimes.* The typology highlights the bedrock distinction between democratic and undemocratic regimes. Of course, the classification must carefully specify what is meant by democracy and authoritarianism.

What Is the Meaning—or Rather, Meanings—of Democracy?

As with many other important concepts, debate over the meaning of democracy is contentious. The wide popularity of the term conceals some important ambiguities. Should democracy be defined solely on the basis of the procedures used to select top governmental officeholders? That is, for a political system to qualify as democratic, is it sufficient that occupants of the highest offices of the state be selected on the basis of free and fair elections in which opposing parties are allowed to organize to present candidates and all citizens are entitled to cast a vote for a contending party? Or must there be respect for citizens' civil liberties (including rights of free expression, dissent, and privacy), regardless of what a democratically elected government might desire? What is the relationship between religious practice and the exercise of political power? To what extent must all citizens be guaranteed certain minimum economic and social rights and resources in a democratic regime, as distinct from political and civil rights (such as the right to vote and criticize the government)? Otherwise put, what is the relationship between democracy defined in purely procedural terms and democracy defined as a system that provides an adequate level of resources to its citizens and promotes substantive equalities?

Despite intense debates about the meaning(s) of democracy, a rough consensus has emerged among practitioners and scholars about the minimum political features required for a regime to qualify as democratic. It is generally agreed that the following conditions must be present:

- Selection to the highest public offices is on the basis of free and fair elections. For an election to qualify as fair, votes must be counted accurately, with the winning candidate(s) selected according

[margin note: continued 3rd/2nd/1st world]

to preexisting rules that determine the kind of plurality or majority required to gain electoral victory.

- Political parties are free to organize, present candidates for public office, and compete in elections. The opposition party or parties—those not in power—enjoy adequate rights of contestation, that is, the right to organize and to criticize the incumbent government.
- The elected government develops policy according to specified procedures that provide for due process, transparency in decision-making, and the accountability of elected executives (at the next election, through judicial action, and, in parliamentary systems, to the legislature).
- All citizens possess civil and political rights—the right to participate and vote in elections periodically held to select key state officeholders—and civil liberties—the rights of free assembly, conscience, privacy, and expression, including the right to criticize the government.
- The political system contains a judiciary with powers independent of the executive and legislature, charged with protecting citizens' political rights and civil liberties from violation by government and other citizens, as well as with ensuring that governmental officials respect constitutionally specified procedures.

Although these points make a useful checklist of the essential elements of a democracy, several qualifications should be added. First, this definition does not claim that electoral outcomes are always (or possibly even often) rational, equitable, or wise. Democracy specifies a set of procedures for making decisions, but it does not guarantee the wisdom of the outcomes. Indeed, as we discuss below, we believe that political outcomes in all democracies, both elections to office and the decisions of officeholders, are systematically and importantly influenced by economic inequalities that limit the ideal of "one person, one vote."

Second, no government has ever fully lived up to democratic standards. All democratic governments at various points in their histories have violated them to a greater or lesser extent. For example, Britain retained a system of plural votes for certain citizens until after World War II; French women did not gain the right to vote until 1945; and full suffrage did not

come to the United States until after the passage of the Civil Rights Act of 1964 and Voting Rights Act of 1965.

Third, how the constituent elements on the checklist of democracy are interpreted and implemented can be a contentious political issue. For example, in the 1990s, and again in 2004, there was intense controversy in France about whether Muslim girls should be permitted to wear a headscarf, signifying adherence to Islam, to public school. On the one hand, many public officials and citizens wanted to prohibit girls from wearing the scarf on the grounds that France is a secular state and that prominently displaying the scarf constitutes proselytizing in public schools and symbolizes girls' subordinate status. On the other hand, defenders of the practice argued that Muslim girls were entitled to exercise their fundamental right of self-expression.

Fourth, economic inequalities stack the political deck. Wealthy citizens, powerful interest groups, and business firms can use their substantial resources to increase their chances of winning an election or influencing public policy. This creates a tension in all democracies, to a greater or lesser degree, between the formal political procedures (such as voting), in which all are equal, and the actual situation, in which the affluent are, in novelist George Orwell's famous phrase from his satirical novel *Animal Farm,* "more equal than others" because of their greater political influence.

Finally, although all democracies share the five elements outlined above, they vary widely in the political institutions that implement these democratic principles. A common distinction among democracies involves differing relationships between the executive and the legislature. In presidential systems, such as in the United States, the chief executive (the president) is elected independently of the national legislature (the House and the Senate) and each branch has powers independent of the other, which means that there is a sharp separation of powers between the executive branch and the legislature. This system is actually an unusual form of democracy. Most of the world's democracies (including Britain, Germany, and Japan) have parliamentary governments in which executive and legislative powers are fused rather than separated: the chief executive

[margin handwritten notes: No Criticism of democracy · Solidated democracies]

(whether called prime minister, premier, or chancellor) and the cabinet are chosen from elected members of the legislature and generally are the leaders of the dominant party or party coalition in parliament. In fact, the chief executive in a parliamentary system remains a sitting member of the legislature even while serving as, for example, prime minister.

The formal and informal rules of the game for reaching and exercising power are very different in presidential and parliamentary systems. In presidential systems, members of the legislature jealously preserve their autonomy. Because the legislature is elected separately from the president, it is constitutionally authorized to set its own agenda, initiate policy proposals, defy presidential directives, and even impeach the president. Presidents have resources that they can deploy in an attempt to persuade the legislature to go along, but even when the same party controls both the presidency and the legislature, the key word is *persuade*. In most parliamentary systems, on the other hand, the legislature may serve as a forum for dramatic policy debate, but it rarely represents an independent source of policy initiatives or poses a decisive obstacle to prevent the government from legislating its own proposals.

The distinction between presidential and parliamentary systems does not exhaust the range of institutional variation within industrial democracies. For example, France's hybrid semi-presidential system is quite different from both. France has a dual executive, with both a directly elected president and a prime minister appointed by the president. These differences raise the kinds of questions that are at the heart of comparative politics: Which political institutions and procedures are more likely to represent citizens' demands? Which strike a better balance between participation and leadership? What consequences do these differences have for the effectiveness of government and the distribution of resources?

"So what?" you may ask in response to this discussion of political institutions. Good question![31] Ponder what difference the type of system makes to a country's politics as you study various types of parliamentary and presidential democracies in this book. And note how rare presidential systems are—a point that may surprise those who think that the U.S. presidential system is typical.

We believe that in understanding political similarities and differences among countries, it is fundamentally important to focus on whether a state is democratic. Our typology of political systems involves a further distinction between long-established, or *consolidated democracies*, and newly established, or *transitional democracies*. We claim that there is a difference in kind, and not just of degree, between the two groups. We use two criteria to distinguish these categories. The first criterion divides democratic regimes according to whether or not their democratic institutions and practices have been solidly and stably established for an ample period of time. (Precisely how much time is open to question: more than a few years, possibly at least a decade? In part, the answer depends on the degree to which the next requirement is met.)

The second criterion for distinguishing between consolidated and transitional democracies is the *extent* of their democratic practice. Consolidated democracies are regimes in which there is relatively consistent adherence to the five democratic principles that we specified above. We do not mean to claim that consolidated democracies never violate democratic norms—they do, and sometimes in shocking ways. For example, police abuse and unequal treatment of citizens who are poor or from a racial or ethnic minority are all too common in countries generally considered high in the democratic rankings, like Britain and the United States. More generally, a frequent source of conflicts in consolidated democracies involves demands for more and better-quality democracy. Examples of consolidated democracies are Britain, France, Germany, Japan, India, and the United States. All have been democracies for over fifty years and, again with flagrant exceptions, generally practice the democracy they preach.

The reason we highlight the quality of democracy becomes apparent when we turn to the second category of democracy. In many transitional democracies, a façade of democratic institutions conceals informal practices that violate the checklist of bedrock features of democracy.[32] As a general matter, there is greater legal protection of citizen rights and liberties in transitional democracies than in authoritarian regimes—but considerably less than in durable democracies. Transitional democracies are usually "hybrid regimes" in which democratic forms of governance coexist with a disturbing persistence of authoritarian elements.[33] In such systems, as compared to consolidated democracies, political authorities are much more likely to engage in corruption, control of the media, intimidation, and violence against opponents in order to limit criticism of the government, undermine opposition parties, and ensure that the ruling party is re-elected. Vote rigging and other abuses may be used if all else fails. Despite what the constitution may specify, the judiciary is often packed with ruling party faithful, and top military officers often exercise extraordinary political power. Among the countries that can be classified as transitional democracies are Russia, Brazil, Mexico, Nigeria, South Africa, and Indonesia.

How do we define authoritarian regimes? The simplest way to identify their principal features is to change the positive sign to negative in the checklist of democratic characteristics specified above. Thus, authoritarian regimes are those lacking effective procedures for selecting political leaders through competitive elections based on universal suffrage; there are no institutionalized procedures for holding those with political power accountable to the citizens of the country; oppositional politics and dissent are severely restricted; people of different genders, racial groups, religions, and ethnicities do not enjoy equal rights; and the judiciary is not an independent branch of government capable of checking the power of the state or protecting the rights of citizens.

Clearly, then, authoritarian states are nondemocracies. But it isn't good social science to define something only by what it is not. The term *authoritarianism* refers to political systems in which power (or authority) is highly concentrated in a single individual, a small group of people, a single political party, or institution. Furthermore, those with power claim an exclusive right to govern and use various means, including force, to impose their will and policies on all who live under their authority.

As with states that are classified as democracies, there is an enormous variety of authoritarian regime types: communist party-states (e.g., China and Cuba); theocracies in which sovereign power is held by religious leaders and law is defined in religious terms (e.g., present-day Iran), military governments (e.g., Pakistan and Burma); absolute monarchies (e.g.,

Saudi Arabia); and personalistic dictatorships (e.g., Iraq under Sadaam Hussein and Iran under the Shah). There are many ways in which these types of authoritarianism differ from one another, including fundamental beliefs (ideology) and the degree of repression used to quash opposition.

Authoritarian regimes frequently claim that they embody a form of democracy, particularly in the contemporary era when the democratic idea seems so persuasive and powerful. For example, according to the Chinese Communist Party, the political system of the People's Republic of China is based on "socialist democracy," which is superior to the "bourgeois democracy" of capitalist countries that, in the end, benefits wealthier citizens. But most political scientists would conclude that there is little substance to such claims and that in such states dictatorship far outweighs democracy.

Nevertheless, even in those countries that can be classified as authoritarian, we should not overlook certain features that reflect democratic values and practices. In Iran, which is a theocratic authoritarian regime, there are vigorously contested multiparty elections, although the extent of contestation is defined and limited by the Islamic clergy who ultimately exercise sovereign power. For the last decade or so, a form of grassroots democracy has been implemented in the more than 700,000 rural villages, where a majority of China's population lives. Even though the communist party still oversees the process to keep dissent from getting out of hand, China's rural dwellers now have a real choice when they elect their local leaders, and there have been many instances when exercising that choice has resulted in the ouster of corrupt and unpopular officials. Such democratic elements in Iranian and Chinese politics certainly make a difference in important ways to the citizens of those countries, but they do not alter the essential authoritarian character of the state in which they live.

One more important point about authoritarian states: like democracies, they, too, are not politically stagnant, but change and evolve over time in response to domestic and international influences. The Soviet Union under Joseph Stalin (1924–1952) and China under Mao Zedong (1949–1976) were extremely brutal dictatorships that closely approximated the model of **totalitarian** regimes that seek to control nearly every aspect of public and private life. Yet the successors to both Stalin and Mao began a process of reform that, to a significant degree, reduced the extent of repression and control while preserving the ultimate authoritarian power of the communist party. In the Soviet case, this eventually led to the collapse of communism, while in China the outcome actually strengthened communist rule. Why the difference? This is just the kind of interesting and important question that lies at the heart of comparative politics!

Although there are, we believe, fundamental differences between democracy and authoritarianism, we want to be clear that the categories we suggest for classifying political systems are not airtight; a gray zone exists such that some countries may straddle two categories. Which ones? Consider Brazil, which we designate as a transitional democracy. Ever since democracy was restored in 1974, following a period of brutal military rule, Brazil has compiled a solid record of democratic practice. For example, there have been several peaceful electoral alternations between dramatically different political coalitions. One might claim that Brazil should be classified as a durable democracy. We believe, however, that given some disquieting violations of democratic procedures, Brazil cannot at this point be classified as a durable democracy.

Another example of the difficulty of classifying states: we consider India a durable democracy because it has generally respected most of the democratic procedures on our checklist since it gained independence in 1947; there is intense political competition in India, elections are usually free and fair, and the Indian judiciary is quite independent. However, some might question our decision. For example, India has repeatedly experienced scenes of horrific communal violence, in which Muslim, Sikh, and Christian minorities have been brutally massacred, sometimes with the active complicity of state officials.

Furthermore, some of the countries that can be classified as transitional democracies are experiencing such political and economic turmoil that they could very well fall out of any category of democracy. Take Russia, for example. We consider Russia to be a transitional democracy because it has compiled a two-decade record of fairly free elections and partial adherence to the other elements on our checklist of democracy. However, under both Boris Yeltsin and Vladimir Putin's leadership, the Russian government has engaged in numerous undemocratic practices, including arbitrary detention and rigged trials of opponents, as well as repeated violations of its constitution. A strong case could be made that Russia should be classified as authoritarian. (In fact, Freedom House classifies Russia as "not free.") Such potential volatility illustrates our earlier point about the difference between a state that is going through a democratic transition and one where democracy has been consolidated with little chance of reversal.

Another comment on our typology: we do not mean to imply that there is an inevitable escalator of political development that transports a country from one category to the next "higher" one. History has demonstrated that one should beware of subscribing to a theory of inevitable progress—whether political, economic, or social. It is not inevitable that countries will remain anchored in one category or another. Regimes may become more democratic—or a democratic regime can be subverted and replaced by an authoritarian regime. When a new edition of this book appears, several countries classified here as transitional democracies may qualify, according to our criteria, as consolidated democracies—or, on the contrary, they may change in a way that tips the balance toward the authoritarian profile.

Section ❺ Organization of the Text

The core of this book consists of case studies selected for their significance in terms of our comparative themes and ability to provide a reasonable sample of types of political regimes and geographic regions. Although each of the country studies makes important comparative references, the studies are primarily intended to provide detailed descriptions and analyses of the politics of individual countries. At the same time, the country studies have common section and subsection headings to help you make comparisons and explore similar themes across the various cases. The following are brief summaries of the main issues and questions covered in the country studies.

1: The Making of the Modern State

Section 1 in each chapter provides an overview of the forces that have shaped the particular character of the state. We believe that understanding the contemporary politics of any country requires some familiarity with the historical process through which its current political system took shape. "Politics in Action" uses a specific event to illustrate an important political moment in the country's recent history and to highlight some of the critical political issues it faces. "Geographic Setting" locates the country in its regional context and discusses the political implications of this setting. "Critical Junctures" looks at some of the major stages and decisive turning points in the state's development. This discussion should give you an idea of how the country assumed its current political order and a sense of how relations between state and society have developed over time.

"Themes and Implications" shows how the past pattern of state development continues to shape the country's current political agenda. "Historical Junctures and Political Themes" applies the text's core themes to the making of the modern state. How has the country's political development been affected by its place in the world of states? What are the political implications of the state's approach to economic management? What has been the country's experience with the democratic idea? What are the important bases of collective identity in the country, and how do these relate to the people's image of themselves as citizens of the state? "Implications for Comparative Politics" discusses the broader significance of the country for the study of comparative politics.

2: Political Economy and Development

Section 2 in each chapter traces the country's recent and contemporary economic development. It explores the issues raised by the core theme of governing the economy and analyzes how economic development has affected political change. The placement of this section near the beginning of the country study reflects our belief that understanding a country's economic situation is essential for analyzing its politics. "State and Economy" discusses the basic organization of the country's economy, with emphasis on the role of the state in managing economic life and on the relationship between the government and other economic actors. How do the dynamics and historical timing of the country's insertion into the world economy—and its current position and competitiveness within the globalized economy—affect domestic political arrangements and shape contemporary challenges? This section also analyzes the state's social welfare policies, such as health care, housing, and pension programs. "Society and Economy" examines the social and political implications of the country's economic situation. It asks who benefits from economic change and looks at how economic development creates or reinforces class, ethnic, gender, regional, or ideological cleavages in society. "The Global Economy" considers the country's global role. How have patterns of trade and foreign investment changed over time? What is the country's relationship to regional and international organizations? To what degree has the country been able to influence multilateral policies? How have international economic issues affected the domestic political agenda?

3: Governance and Policy-Making

In Section 3, we describe the state's major policy-making institutions and procedures. "Organization of the State" lays out the fundamental principles—as reflected in the country's constitution, its official ideology, and its historical experience—on which the political system and the distribution of political power are based. It also sketches the basic structure of the state, including the relationship among different levels and branches of government. "The Executive" encompasses the key offices (for example, presidents, prime ministers, communist party leaders) that are at the top of the political system, focusing on those with the most power, how they are selected, and how they use their power to make policy. This section looks at the

What's in the Data Boxes?

At the beginning of each of the following chapters is a data box that presents important factual and statistical information about the country. We hope most of this information is self-explanatory, but a few points of clarification may be helpful.

- The social and economic data largely comes from the CIA *World Factbook*, the World Bank *World Development Indicators*, and the United Nations *Human Development Report*, all of which are issued annually.*
- The data presented is as up to date as possible. Unless otherwise indicated, it is from 2002–2005.
- Several important terms used in the data boxes are explained in the Glossary, including Gross Domestic Product (GDP), Gross National Product/Index (GNP/GNI), Purchasing Power Parity (PPP), and Gini Index.
- At the end of each data box are six broad categories that rate and rank countries on the basis of statistically derived measurements of various aspects of their political or economic development. We think these provide an interesting, if sometimes controversial approach to comparative analysis. The categories include the following:†
  - **The Human Development Index (HDI):** A summary composite index used by the United Nations "that measures a country's average achievements in three basic aspects of human development: longevity, knowledge, and a decent standard of living. Longevity is measured by life expectancy at birth; knowledge is measured by a combination of the adult literacy rate and the combined primary, secondary, and tertiary gross enrollment ratio; and standard of living by GDP per capita (PPP US$)." The higher the score, the better the HDI.
  - **The Gender-Related Development Index (GDI):** HDI "adjusted to account for inequalities between men and women" by comparing, for example, gender differentials in life expectancy, literacy, and income. The higher the score, the better the GDI.
  - **The Gender Empowerment Measure (GEM):** Also developed by the UN "to measure gender inequality in three basic dimensions of empowerment—economic participation and decision making, political participation and decision-making and power over economic resources." The higher the score, the better the GEM.
  - **The Corruption Perceptions Index (CPI):** A measure developed by Transparency International that "ranks countries in terms of the degree to which corruption is perceived to exist among public officials and politicians. It is a composite index, drawing on corruption-related data in expert surveys carried out by a variety of reputable institutions. It reflects the views of businesspeople and analysts from around the world, including experts who are locals in the countries evaluated." Range: 10 (highly clean) to 0 (highly corrupt).
  - **The Environmental Sustainability Index (ESI):** "A composite index developed at Yale and Columbia Universities tracking a diverse set of socioeconomic, environmental, and institutional indicators that characterize and influence environmental sustainability at the national scale." The current range is from 29.2 (worst) to 75.1 (best).
  - **Freedom in the World Rating:** An annual evaluation by Freedom House of the state of freedom in countries around the world measured according to political rights and civil liberties through "a multi-layered process of analysis and evaluation by a team of regional experts

(continued)

What's in the Data Boxes? (cont.)

and scholars." Countries are ranked in .5 gradations between 1.0 and 7.0, with 1.0–2.5 being "Free;" 3.0–5.0, "Partly Free;" and 5.5–7.0, "Not Free."

---

*These reports and other statistics can be found at www.cia.gov/cia/publications/factbook/index.html, www.worldbank.org/data/, and http://hdr.undp.org/.

†The explanatory quotations for the composite categories are taken from:

- The Human Development Index: http://hdr.undp.org/statistics/indices/about_hdi.cfm

- The Gender-Related Development Index: http://hdr.undp.org/statistics/data/indic/indic_282_1_1.html
- The Gender Empowerment Measure: http://hdr.undp.org/statistics/data/indic/indic_283_1_1.html
- The Corruption Perceptions Index: http://www.transparency.org/cpi/2004/cpi2004_faq.en.html
- The Environmental Sustainability Index: http://www.yale.edu/esi/
- Freedom in the World Rating: http://www.freedomhouse.org/research/freeworld/2004/methodology.htm.

---

national bureaucracy and its relationship to the chief executive and the governing party and its role in policy-making. "Other State Institutions" looks at the military, the judiciary and the legal system, semi-public agencies, and subnational government. "The Policy-Making Process" summarizes how public policy gets made and implemented. It describes the roles of formal institutions and procedures, as well as informal aspects of policy-making, such as patron-client relations and interest group activity.

4: Representation and Participation

The relationship between a country's state and society is the topic of Section 4. How do different groups in society organize to further their political interests, how do they participate and get represented in the political system, and how do they influence policy-making? Given the importance of the U.S. Congress in policy-making, American readers might expect to find the principal discussion of "The Legislature" in Section 3 ("Governance and Policy-Making") rather than Section 4. But the United States is quite exceptional in having a legislature that in much of the policy process is a coequal branch of government with the executive. In most other political systems, the executive dominates the policy process, even when it is ultimately responsible to the legislature, as in a parliamentary

system. In most countries other than the United States, the legislature functions primarily to represent and provide a forum for the political expression of various interests in government; it is only secondarily (and in some cases, such as China, only marginally) a policy-making body. Therefore, although this section does describe and assess the legislature's role in policy-making, its primary focus is on how the legislature represents or fails to represent different interests in society.

"Political Parties and the Party System" describes the overall organization of the party system and reviews the major parties. "Elections" discusses the election process and recent trends in electoral behavior. It also considers the significance of elections (or lack thereof) as a vehicle for citizen participation in politics and in bringing about changes in the government. "Political Culture, Citizenship, and Identity" examines how people perceive themselves as members of the political community: the nature and source of political values and attitudes, who is considered a citizen of the state, and how different groups in society understand their relationship to the state. The topics covered may include political aspects of the educational system, the media, religion, and ethnicity. How have globalization and events relating to September 11 shaped collective identities and collective action? "Interests, Social Movements, and Protests" discusses how various groups pursue their political interests outside the party system. When do they use formal organizations (such as unions) or launch movements (such as Green environmental, antiglobalization, or peace movements)? What is the relationship between the state and such organizations and movements? When and how do citizens engage in acts of protest? And how does the state respond to such protests?

5: Politics in Transition

In Section 5, each country study returns to the book's focus on the major challenges that are reshaping our world and the study of comparative politics. "Political Challenges and Changing Agendas" lays out the major unresolved issues facing the country and assesses which are most likely to dominate in the near future. Many of the country studies address issues that have generated intense conflicts around the world in the recent period—conflicts involving globalization, collective identities, human rights and civil liberties, the war in Iraq, and the consequences of America's exercise of global hegemony. "Politics in Comparative Perspective" returns to the book's four core themes and highlights the implications of the country case for the study of comparative politics. How does the history—and how will the fate—of the country influence developments in a regional and global context? What does this case study tell us about politics in other countries that have similar political systems or that face similar kinds of political challenges?

We realize that it is quite a challenge to set out on a journey with the goal of trying to understand contemporary politics around the globe. We hope that the timely information and thematic focus of *Introduction to Comparative Politics* will prepare and inspire you to explore further the often troubling, sometimes inspiring, but endlessly fascinating world of comparative politics.

Key Terms

North Atlantic Treaty Organization (NATO)
cold war
globalization
authoritarian
European Union (EU)
World Trade Organization (WTO)
collective identities
comparative politics
comparativists
country
state
executive
cabinet
bureaucracy
legitimacy
regulations
state formation
nation-state
political culture
rational choice theory
middle-level theory
democratic transitions
dictatorship
World Bank
International Monetary Fund (IMF)
political economy
laissez-faire
sustainable development
social movements
social class
distributional politics
typology
most different case analysis
gross domestic product (GDP)
gross national product (GNP)
gross national income (GNI)
official international exchange rates
purchasing power parity (PPP)
Human Development Index (HDI)
Gender-Related Development Index (GDI)
Gender Empowerment Measure (GEM)
Corruption Perceptions Index (CPI)
Environmental Sustainability Index (ESI)
Freedom in the World Rating
transitional democracies
consolidated democracies
totalitarian

Suggested Readings

Anderson, Benedict. *Imagined Communities: Reflections on the Origins and Spread of Nationalism.* Rev. ed. London: Verso, 1991.

Anderson, Lisa, ed. *Transitions to Democracy.* New York: Columbia University Press, 1999.

Berger, Suzanne, and Dore, Ronald, eds. *National Diversity and Global Capitalism.* Ithaca, N.Y.: Cornell University Press, 1996.

Brady, Henry E., and Collier, David, eds. *Rethinking Social Inquiry: Diverse Tools, Shared Standards.* Lanham, Md.: Rowman and Littlefield, 2004.

Calleo, David P. *Rethinking Europe's Future.* Princeton, N.J.: Princeton University Press: 2001.

Cammack, Paul. *Capitalism and Democracy in the Third World: The Doctrine for Political Development.* London: Leicester University Press, 1997.

Coates, David, ed. *Varieties of Capitalism, Varieties of Approaches.* Basingstoke, UK: Palgrave/Macmillan, 2005.

Diamond, Larry, and Plattner, Marc F., eds. *The Global Resurgence of Democracy.* 2d ed. Baltimore: Johns Hopkins University Press, 1996.

Diamond, Larry, Plattner, Marc F., Chu, Yun-han, and Tien, Hung-mao, eds. *Consolidating the Third Wave of Democracy.* 2 vols. Baltimore: Johns Hopkins University Press, 1997.

Evans, Peter. *Embedded Autonomy: States and Industrial Transformation.* Princeton, N.J.: Princeton University Press, 1995.

Evans, Peter B., Rueschemeyer, Dietrich, and Skocpol, Theda, eds. *Bringing the State Back In.* Cambridge: Cambridge University Press, 1985.

Friedman, Thomas L. *The World Is Flat: A Brief History of the Twenty-First Century.* New York: Farrar, Straus and Giroux, 2005.

Grindle, Merilee S. *Despite the Odds: The Contentious Politics of Education Reform.* Princeton, N.J.: Princeton University Press, 2004.

Hall, Peter A., and Soskice, David, eds. *Varieties of Capitalism: The Institutional Foundations of Comparative Advantage.* New York: Oxford University Press, 2001.

Katznelson, Ira, and Milner, Helen V., eds. *Political Science: The State of the Discipline.* New York: Norton, 2002.

King, Gary, Keohane, Robert O., and Verba, Sidney. *Designing Social Inquiry: Scientific Inference in Qualitative Research.* Princeton, N.J.: Princeton University Press, 1994.

Kohli, Atul. *State-Directed Development: Political Power and Industrialization in the Global Periphery.* Cambridge: Cambridge University Press, 2005.

Lahav, Gallya. *Immigration and Politics in the New Europe: Reinventing Borders.* Cambridge: Cambridge University Press, 2004.

Lichbach, Mark Irving, and Zuckerman, Alan S., eds. *Comparative Politics: Rationality, Culture, and Structure.* Cambridge: Cambridge University Press, 1997.

Linz, Juan J., and Stepan, Alfred. *Problems of Democratic Transition and Consolidation: Southern Europe, South America, and Post-Communist Europe.* Baltimore: Johns Hopkins University Press, 1996.

Mahoney, James, and Rueschemeyer, Dietrich, eds. *Comparative Historical Analysis in the Social Sciences.* Cambridge: Cambridge University Press, 2003.

Marx, Anthony. *Making Race and Nation: A Comparison of the United States, South Africa, and Brazil.* Cambridge: Cambridge University Press, 1998.

Norris, Pippa, and Inglehart, Ronald. *Sacred and Secular: Religion and Politics Worldwide.* New York: Cambridge University Press, 2004.

O'Donnell, Guillermo A., Schmitter, Philippe C., and Whitehead, Laurence, eds. *Transitions from Authoritarian Rule.* 4 vols. Baltimore: Johns Hopkins University Press, 1986.

Powell, G. Bingham. *Elections as Instruments of Democracy: Majoritarian and Proportional Visions.* New Haven: Yale University Press, 2000.

Przeworski, Adam. *Democracy and the Market: Political and Economic Reforms in Eastern Europe and Latin America.* Cambridge: Cambridge University Press, 1991.

————, et al. *Democracy and Development: Political Institutions and Well-Being in the World, 1950–1990.* Cambridge: Cambridge University Press, 2000.

Putnam, Robert, with Leonardi, Robert, and Nanetti, Raffaella Y. *Making Democracy Work: Civic Traditions in Modern Italy.* Princeton, N.J.: Princeton University Press, 1992.

Scott, James C. *Seeing Like a State: How Certain Schemes to Improve the Human Condition Have Failed.* New Haven, Conn.: Yale University Press, 1998.

Snyder, Jack. *From Voting to Violence: Democratization and Nationalist Conflict.* New York: W.W. Norton, 2000.

Stark, David, and Bruszt, Laszlo. *Postsocialist Pathways: Transforming Politics and Property in East Central Europe.* Cambridge: Cambridge University Press, 1998.

Stiglitz, Joseph E. *Globalization and Its Discontents.* New York: Norton, 2002.

Tarrow, Sidney. *Power in Movement: Social Movements and Contentious Politics.* 2nd ed. Cambridge: Cambridge University Press, 1998.

Tilly, Charles. *Coercion, Capital and European States, A.D. 990–1992.* Cambridge: Blackwell, 1990.

Toft, Monica Duffy, *The Geography of Ethnic Violence: Identity, Interests, and the Indivisibility of Territory.* Princeton, N.J.: Princeton University Press, 2003.

Wolf, Martin. *Why Globalization Works.* New Haven, Conn.: Yale University Press, 2004.

Woo-Cummings, Meredith, ed. *The Developmental State.* Ithaca, N.Y.: Cornell University Press, 1999.

Suggested Websites

Area Studies and Comparative Politics
www.psr.keele.ac.uk/area.htm
CIA World Factbook
www.cia.gov/cia/publications/factbook
Elections Around the World
www.electionworld.org
Foreign Government Resources on the Web
www.lib.umich.edu/govdocs/foreign.html

Freedom House
www.freedomhouse.org
NationMaster
www.nationmaster.com
Political Resources on the Net
www.politicalresources.net
World Audit
www.worldaudit.org

Endnotes

[1]Francis Fukuyama, "The End of History?" *The National Interest* 16 (Summer 1989), 3–18. The article is reprinted in Mark Kesselman and Joel Krieger, eds., *Readings in Comparative Politics: Political Challenges and Changing Agendas* (Boston: Houghton Mifflin, 2006).

[2]For collections of articles on globalization, see Mark Kesselman, ed., *Politics of Globalization* (Boston: Houghton Mifflin, 2006), and Joel Krieger, ed., *Globalization and State Power: A Reader* (New York: Pearson/Longman, 2006). For a lively account of changes involved in the current phase of globalization, see Thomas L. Friedman, *The World Is Flat: A Brief History of the Twenty-First Century* (New York: Farrar, Straus and Giroux, 2005).

[3]*PS: Political Science and Politics* 37, no. 6 (July 2004): 566. This issue also has the full program from the 2004 APSA annual meeting.

[4]United Nations Development Programme (UNDP), International Monetary Fund (IMF), International Bank for Reconstruction and Development (IBRD), Organization for Economic Cooperation and Development (OECD), North American Free Trade Agreement (NAFTA), and Asia Pacific Economic Cooperation (APEC) Forum.

[5]For descriptions by sympathetic participant-observers, see John Cavanagh and Jerry Mander, eds., *Alternatives to Economic Globalization: A Better World Is Possible,* 2nd ed. (San Francisco: Berrett-Koehler, 2004); and Robin Broad, ed., *Global Backlash: Citizen Initiatives for a Just World Economy* (Lanham, Md.: Rowman & Littlefield, 2002). For spirited defenses of globalization, see Jagdish Bhagwati, *In Defense of Globalization* (New York: Oxford University Press, 2004); and Martin Wolf, *Why Globalization Works* (New Haven, Conn.: Yale University Press, 2004).

[6]See Philippe Schmitter, "Comparative Politics," in Joel Krieger, ed., *The Oxford Companion to Politics of the World,* 2nd ed. (New York: Oxford University Press, 2001), 160–165. For a more extended discussion and different approach, see David D. Laitin, "Comparative Politics: The State of the Subdiscipline," in Ira Katznelson and Helen V. Milner, eds., *Political Science: The State of the Discipline* (New York: Norton, 2002), 630–659. For a collection of articles in the field of comparative politics, see Kesselman and Krieger, eds., *Readings in Comparative Politics.*

[7]See Anthony Marx, *Making Race and Nation: A Comparison of the United States, South Africa, and Brazil* (Cambridge: Cambridge University Press, 1998).

[8]For a landmark article that analyzed how political decisions often reflect pressures from both the domestic and international arena, see Robert Putnam, "Diplomacy and Domestic Politics: The Logic of Two-Level Games," *International Organization* 42 (Summer 1988): 427–460.

[9]See, for example, Colin Campbell, *Governments Under Stress: Political Executives and Key Bureaucrats in Washington, London, and Ottawa* (Toronto: University of Toronto Press, 1983).

[10]See, for example, Benedict Anderson, *Imagined Communities: Reflections on the Origins and Spread of Nationalism,* rev. ed. (London: Verso, 1991); and Theda Skocpol, *Social Revolutions in the Modern World* (Cambridge: Cambridge University Press, 1994).

[11]Peter A. Hall, *Governing the Economy: The Politics of State Intervention in Britain and France* (New York: Oxford University Press, 1986); and Mark Blyth, *Great Transformations: Economic Ideas and Institutional Change in the Twentieth Century* (Cambridge: Cambridge University Press, 2002).

[12]For reviews of recent literature on the state, see Margaret Levi, "The State of the Study of the State," Miles Kahler, "The State of the State in World Politics," and Atul Kohli, "State, Society, and Development," in Katznelson and Milner, eds., *Political Science: State of the Discipline.* 84–117.

[13]John R. Alford, Carolyn L. Funk, and John R. Hibbin, "Are Political Orientations Genetically Transmitted?", in *American Political Science Review,* vol. 99, no. 2, May 2005, 153–167.

[14]For diverse views, see Gary King, Robert O. Keohane, and Sidney Verba, *Designing Social Inquiry: Scientific Inference in Qualitative Research* (Princeton, N.J.: Princeton University Press, 1994); Mark Irving Lichbach and Alan S. Zuckerman, eds., *Comparative Politics: Rationality, Culture, and Structure* (Cambridge: Cambridge University Press, 1997); Katznelson and Milner, eds., *Political Science;* Henry E. Brady and David Collier, eds., *Rethinking Social Inquiry: Diverse Tools, Shared Standards* (Lanham, Md.: Rowman and Littlefield, 2004).

[15]Clifford Geertz, *The Interpretation of Cultures: Selected Essays* (New York, Basic Books, 1973).

[16]For discussion of rational choice theory in the popular press, see "Political Scientists Debate Theory of 'Rational Choice'," in the *New York Times,* February 26, 2000, p. B11; and Jonathan Cohn, "Irrational Exuberance: When Did Political Science Forget About Politics?," *New Republic,* October 25, 1999, 25–31. For an application of rational choice theory in comparative politics, see Robert H. Bates, Avner Greif, Margaret Levi, Jean-Laurent Rosenthal, and Barry R. Weingast, *Analytic Narratives* (Princeton, N.J.: Princeton University Press, 1998). For a lively exchange about the value of applying this approach to explaining large-scale historical

change, see a critical review of *Analytic Narratives* by Jon Elster, "Rational Choice History: A Case of Excessive Ambition," and a reply by the authors of the book: Elster, "Rational Choice History: A Case of Excessive Ambition," and Robert H. Bates et al., "The Analytic Narrative Project," *American Political Science Review* 94, no. 3 (September 2000): 685–702.

[17]For the most influential example, see Juan J. Linz and Alfred Stepan, *Problems of Democratic Transition and Consolidation: Southern Europe, South America, and Post-Communist Europe* (Baltimore: Johns Hopkins University Press, 1996). However, for a warning that generalizations of this kind may neglect important differences among countries, for example, between formerly authoritarian and communist countries, see Valerie Bunce, "Rethinking Democratization: Lessons from the Postcommunist Experience," *World Politics* 55, no. 2 (Jan. 2003): 170–189. Selections of both are included in Kesselman and Krieger, eds., *Readings in Comparative Politics*.

[18]One statement of the case that globalization has decisively weakened state supremacy is Martin van Creveld, "The Fate of the State," *Parameters* (Spring 1996): 4–17, reprinted in Kesselman and Krieger, *Readings in Comparative Politics*. Other articles in this collection develop the case that states retain a commanding position. See also Joel Krieger, *Globalization and State Power: Who Wins When America Rules?* (New York: Pearson/Longman, 2005).

[19]Robert I. Rotberg, "Failed States in a World of Terror," *Foreign Affairs* 81, no. 4 (July–August 2002). The article is reprinted in Kesselman and Krieger, *Readings in Comparative Politics*. Rotberg was referring in his article to Afghanistan when it was hijacked by the Taliban.

[20]This term is borrowed from Peter A. Hall, *Governing the Economy*.

[21]Alexander Gerschenkron, *Economic Backwardness in Historical Perspective* (Cambridge: Cambridge University Press, 1966).

[22]Peter A. Hall and David Soskice, eds. *Varieties of Capitalism: The Institutional Foundations of Comparative Advantage* (New York: Oxford University Press, 2001). Also see Herbert Kitschelt, Peter Lange, Gary Marks, and John Stephens, eds., *Continuity and Change in Advanced Capitalist Democracies* (New York: Cambridge University Press, 1998); and David Coates, ed., *Varieties of Capitalism, Varieties of Approaches* (Basingstoke, UK: Palgrave/Macmillan, 2005).

[23]For a sample of an enormous and diverse literature, see Chalmers Johnson, *MITI and the Japanese Miracle: The Growth of Industrial Policy* (Stanford: Stanford University Press, 1982); Stephan Haggard, *Pathways from the Periphery: The Politics of Growth in the Newly Industrializing Countries* (Ithaca, N.Y.: Cornell University Press, 1990); Mancur J. Olson, *The Rise and Decline of Nations: Economic Growth, Stagflation, and Social Rigidities* (New Haven, Conn.: Yale University Press, 1982); Peter Evans, *Embedded Autonomy:*

States and Industrial Transformation (Princeton, N.J.: Princeton University Press, 1995); Linda Weiss and John M. Hobson, *States and Economic Development: A Comparative Historical Analysis* (Cambridge: Polity Press, 1995); and Meredith Woo-Cummings, ed., *The Developmental State* (Ithaca, N.Y.: Cornell University Press, 1999). For a review article questioning many commonly offered explanations, see Robert Wade, "East Asia's Economic Success: Conflicting Perspectives, Partial Insights, Shaky Evidence," *World Politics*, 44, no. 2 (1992): 270–320. Recent important contributions are Atul Kohli, *State-Directed Development: Political Power and Industrialization in the Global Periphery* (Cambridge: Cambridge University Press, 2005), and Jeffrey D. Sachs, *The End of Poverty: Economic Possibilities for Our Time* (New York: The Penguin Press, 2005).

[24]Amartya Sen, "Democracy as a Universal Value," *Journal of Democracy* 10, no. 3 (July 1999): 3–17 (http://muse.jhu.edu/demo/jod/10.3sen.html). This article is included in Kesselman and Krieger, *Readings in Comparative Politics*. An influential study of this question, on which Sen draws, reaches a similar conclusion: Adam Przeworski et al., *Democracy and Development: Political Institutions and Well-Being in the World, 1950–1990* (Cambridge: Cambridge University Press, 2000). For a study that reaches a different conclusion—that there is a positive correlation between democracy and economic growth—see Yi Feng, *Democracy, Governance, and Economic Performance: Theory and Evidence* (Cambridge, Mass.: MIT Press, 2005).

[25]Assorted Comparative Charts and Graphs, Freedom in World Reports, 2003 (http://www.freedomhouse.org/research/freeworld/2003/tables.htm) and 2005 (http://www.freedomhouse.org/research/survey2005.htm).

[26]Sen, p. 3 (Internet text version).

[27]Andrew Roberts, "Review Article: The Quality of Democracy," *Comparative Politics* 37, no. 3 (April 2005), p. 357.

[28]This view was first developed by Dankwart Rustow. His original article and commentaries are the focus of Lisa Anderson, ed., *Transitions to Democracy* (New York: Columbia University Press, 1999). This approach has been further developed by Adam Przeworski, *Democracy and the Market: Political and Economic Reforms in Eastern Europe and Latin America* (Cambridge: Cambridge University Press, 1991).

[29]Guillermo O'Donnell and Philippe Schmitter, *Transitions from Authoritarian Rule: Tentative Conclusions About Uncertain Democracies* (Baltimore: Johns Hopkins University Press, 1986). The concept of waves of democratization is taken from Samuel Huntington, *The Third Wave: Democratization in the Late Twentieth Century.* (Norman, Ok.: University of Oklahoma Press, 1991).

[30]Przeworski et al., *Democracy and Development*.

[31]For attempts to answer this question, see Alfred Stepan and Cindy Skach, "Constitutional Frameworks and Democratic

Consolidation: Parliamentarism versus Presidentialism," *World Politics* 46, no. 1 (October 1993): 1–22, reprinted in Kesselman and Krieger, *Readings in Comparative Politics*; and Juan J. Linz and Arturo Valenzuela, eds., *The Failure of Presidential Democracy* (Baltimore: Johns Hopkins University Press, 1994).

[32]See, for example, Guillermo O'Donnell, "Illusions About Consolidation," *Journal of Democracy* 7, no. 2 (April 1996): 34–51; Thomas Carothers, "The End of the Transition Para-digm," *Journal of Democracy* 13, no. 1 (January 2002): 5–21; and Steven Levitsky and Lucan A. Way, "The Rise of Competi-tive Authoritarianism," *Journal of Democracy* 13, no. 2 (April 2002): 51–65. All are reprinted in Kesselman and Krieger, *Readings in Comparative Politics*.

[33]Larry Diamond, "Thinking about Hybrid Regimes," in *Journal of Democracy,* 13.2 (2002), 21–35.

PART 2

Consolidated Democracies

CHAPTER 2
Britain

CHAPTER 3
United States

CHAPTER 2

Britain

Joel Krieger

United Kingdom of Great Britain and Northern Ireland

Land and People

Capital	London
Total area (square miles)	94,251 (Slightly smaller than Oregon)
Population	60.4 million

Annual population growth rate (%)	1975–2000	0.2
	2000–2015 (projected)	0.3

Urban population (%)	89

Ethnic composition (%)	White	92.1
	Minority ethnic population	7.9
	Indian	1.8
	Pakistani	1.3
	Bangladeshi	0.5
	Other Asian	0.4
	Black Caribbean	1.0
	Black African	0.8
	Black Other	0.2
	Chinese	0.4
	Other ethnic groups	0.4
Major language(s)	English	
Religious affiliation (%)	All religions	76.8
	Christian	71.6
	Muslim	2.7
	Hindu	1.0
	Jewish	0.5
	Sikh	0.6
	Buddhist	0.3
	Other Religion	0.3
	No religion	15.5
	Not stated	7.3

Economy

Domestic currency	British pound (GBP) $US1 0.5462 GBP (2004)
Total GNI (US$)	1.68 trillion
GNI per capital (US$)	28,320
Total GNI at purchasing power parity (US$)	1.64 trillion

GDP annual growth rate (%)	1983–1993	2.5
	1993–2003	2.8
	2002	1.8
	2003	2.2
	2004	3.2
GDP per capita average annual growth rate (%)	1983–1993	2.2
	1993–2003	2.5

Inequality in income or consumption (1999) (%)	Share of poorest 10%	2
	Share of poorest 20%	6
	Share of richest 20%	44
	Share of richest 10%	28
	Gini Index (1999)	36.8
Structure of production (% of GDP)	Agriculture	1
	Industry	26.3
	Services	72.7
Labor force distribution (% of total)	Agriculture	1.5
	Industry	19.1
	Services	79.5
Exports as % of GDP	25.1	
Imports as % of GDP	28.1	

Society

Life expectancy at birth	77.6
Infant mortality per 1,000 live births	5.3
Adult illiteracy (% of population age 15+)	0*

The OECD estimates that Britain has a functional illiteracy rate of about 22%.

Access to information and communications (per 1,000 population)	Telephone lines	588
	Mobile phones	770
	Radios	1446
	Televisions	950
	Personal computers	366.2

Women in Government and the Economy

Women in the National Legislature	
Lower house or single house (%)	19.8
Upper house (%)	17.8
Female legislators, senior offices, and managers (% of total)	31
Women in Cabinet	30.4
Female professional and technical workers (% of total)	44
Female economic activity rate (age 15 and above) (%)	53.3

Estimated Earned Income (PPP US$)	Female	19,807
	Male	32,984

Composite Ratings and Rankings

Human Development Index (HDI) ranking (value) (out of 177 countries)	12 (.936)
Gender-Related Development Index (GDI) ranking (value) (out of 78 countries)	9 (.934)

Gender Empowerment Measure (GEM) ranking (value) (out of 78 countries)	18 (.698)
Corruption Perception Index (CPI) ranking (value) (out of 146 countries)	11 (8.6)
Environmental Sustainability (ESI) Index ranking (value) (out of 146 countries)	65 (50.2)
Freedom in World Rating	Free (1.0)

Political Organization

Political System   Parliamentary democracy, Constitutional monarchy.

Regime History   Long constitutional history, origins subject to interpretation, usually dated from the seventeenth century or earlier.

Administrative Structure   Unitary state with fusion of powers. UK parliament has supreme legislative, executive, and judicial authority. Reform in process to transfer limited powers to representative bodies for Scotland, Wales, and Northern Ireland.

Executive   Prime minister (PM), answerable to House of Commons, subject to collective responsibility of the cabinet;

member of Parliament who is leader of party that can control a majority in Commons.

Legislature   Bicameral. House of Commons elected by single-member plurality system with no fixed term but a five-year limit. Main legislative powers: to pass laws, provide for finance, scrutinize public administration and government policy. House of Lords, unelected upper house: limited powers to delay enactment of legislation and to recommend revisions; specified appeals court functions. Reform introduced to eliminate voting rights of hereditary peers and create new second chamber.

Judiciary   Independent but with no power to judge the constitutionality of legislation or governmental conduct. Judges appointed by Crown on recommendation of PM or lord chancellor.

Party System   Two-party dominant, with regional variation. Principal parties: Labour, and Conservative; a center party (Liberal Democrats); and national parties in Scotland, Wales, and Northern Ireland.

Section ❶ The Making of the Modern British State

Politics in Action

On Saturday, January 24, 2004, Prime Minister Tony Blair was facing the most dangerous week of his political life. He acknowledged that his job was on the line. On Tuesday, an extremely tough fight was anticipated over the Higher Education Bill to raise student fees in order to fund university education, a centerpiece of his legislative program. But Wednesday looked far more ominous, for that was the day when Blair would face the much-anticipated report of the Hutton inquiry on the suicide of David Kelly, the former UN weapons inspector and whistle-blower who had challenged a key tenet of the government's justification for the war in Iraq.

The report would bring to a climax the miserable saga that began in May 2003, when the BBC reported that the most compelling evidence for the claim that Saddam Hussein posed an imminent threat—that Iraq

could launch weapons of mass destruction on forty-five minutes' notice—was wrong. For an increasingly beleaguered Tony Blair, facing mounting criticism of the war in Iraq, the story could scarcely have been more damaging. Relying on an unnamed "senior official," the BBC asserted that Downing Street had ordered the government's claims against Saddam to be exaggerated or, as the BBC reporter unforgettably put it, "sexed up." After three weeks of merciless pounding in the media, Blair made a fateful decision: it was time to authorize a back-channel leak of the BBC's source, David Kelly. If Kelly were discredited, the BBC would be put in its place, and the prime minister might reclaim the offensive.

His name revealed, Kelly was promptly placed before the harsh glare of television cameras on July 15 and grilled by the House of Commons Foreign Affairs Committee. Then, just two days later, he left his home in a village near Oxford for his usual afternoon walk.

He chatted with a neighbor and never returned. His body was found the next day in a wooded area, close to his home in Oxfordshire, with a knife and a packet of pills nearby. There was little doubt that Kelly's death was suicide, but his tragedy put a human face on the misgivings many millions of Britons felt about the justifications for the Anglo-American invasion of Iraq. It unleashed a furious debate about the lengths Blair had gone to steamroll Parliament into backing his war aims and the pressure he was willing to exert to intimidate a well-meaning whistle-blower.

Blair was feeling the heat on all sides. Polls indicated that nearly 60 percent of the British people thought Blair should resign if Hutton found he had intentionally exaggerated the case for war. In addition, the prime minister made it clear that a defeat on the Education Bill on Tuesday would be taken as a vote of no confidence in his leadership and bring with it a likely resignation. London was buzzing with political intrigue, with many insiders speculating that by Wednesday, Blair's premiership might be crumbling.

So how bad a week did Blair have? On Tuesday, Blair's party deserted him in droves. His 161-seat majority all but evaporated, and his reputation was badly bruised, but the Education Bill squeaked through by five votes. A push from Hutton, and he could be on the way out. Then on Wednesday, the Hutton Report entirely vindicated his role in the Kelly affair, roundly blamed the BBC, and the Blair government was back in business.

The week's events signaled a short-term victory for Blair, but hardly a reversal in political fortunes. Blair's decision to support the U.S.-led war in Iraq was very unpopular in Britain, increasingly so as weapons of mass destruction—the key justification for war—never were found. Recurring questions about the war in Iraq hounded Blair right through the campaign leading to his third electoral victory in May 2005—a feat never before achieved by the leader of Britain's 105-year-old Labour Party.

Blair's victory, however, was bittersweet—and the slashing of his parliamentary majority by nearly 100 seats was not even the worst of it. British election night tradition has each candidate in a constituency standing side by side as the results are announced. Thus, television cameras captured a stony-faced

Blair's 2005 victory was both historic and humbling. In an image that promised to be replayed endlessly on television whenever the 2005 election was discussed, Blair visibly blanched as a defeated independent candidate, whose son died in Iraq, asked Blair to make amends to the families of those who lost loved ones in the war. *Source:* Jeff J. Mitchell/Reuters/Corbis

prime minister standing just behind Reg Keys, an independent antiwar candidate whose son had been killed in Iraq, as Keys solemnly intoned: "I hope in my heart that one day the prime minister will be able to say sorry . . . to the families of the bereaved." And before the final results were tabulated, the guessing game that threatened to engulf Blair's third term began, as pundits and Labour Party critics of the prime minister openly speculated about when Blair should resign in favor of Gordon Brown, his chancellor and much-anticipated successor as prime minister and leader of the Labour Party.

Geographic Setting

Britain is the largest of the British Isles, a group of islands off the northwest coast of Europe, and encompasses England, Scotland, and Wales. The second-largest island comprises Northern Ireland and the independent Republic of Ireland. The term *Great Britain* encompasses England, Wales, and Scotland, but not Northern Ireland. We use the term *Britain* as shorthand for the United Kingdom of Great Britain and Northern Ireland.

Covering an area of approximately 94,000 square miles, Britain is roughly two-thirds the size of Japan, or approximately half the size of France. In 2004, the population of the United Kingdom was 60.4 million people.

Although forever altered by the Channel Tunnel, Britain's location as an offshore island adjacent to Europe is significant. Historically, Britain's island destiny made it less subject to invasion and conquest than its continental counterparts, affording the country a sense of security. The geographic separation from mainland Europe has also created for many Britons a feeling that they are both apart from and a part of Europe, a factor that has complicated relations with Britain's EU partners to this day.

Critical Junctures

Our study begins with a look at the historical development of the modern British state. History shapes contemporary politics in very important ways. Once in place, institutions leave powerful legacies, and issues that were left unresolved in one period may present challenges for the future.

In many ways, Britain is the model of a united and stable country with an enviable record of continuity and resiliency. Nevertheless, the history of state formation reveals how complex and open-ended the process can be. Some issues that plague other countries, such as religious divisions, were settled long ago in Great Britain proper (although not in Northern Ireland). Yet others, such as multiple national identities, remain on the agenda.

British state formation involved the unification of kingdoms or crowns (hence the term United *Kingdom*). After Duke William of Normandy defeated the English in the Battle of Hastings in 1066, the Norman monarchy extended its authority throughout the British Isles. With the Acts of Union of 1536 and 1542, England and Wales were legally, politically, and administratively united. The unification of the Scottish and English crowns began in 1603, when James VI of Scotland ascended to the English throne as James I. Thereafter, England, Scotland, and Wales were known as Great Britain. Scotland and England remained divided politically, however, until the Act of Union of 1707. Henceforth, a common Parliament of Great Britain replaced the two separate parliaments of Scotland and of England and Wales.

At the same time, the making of the British state included a historic expression of constraints on monarchical rule. At first, the period of Norman rule after 1066 strengthened royal control, but the conduct of King John (1199–1216) fueled opposition from feudal barons. In 1215, they forced the king to consent to a series of concessions that protected feudal landowners from abuses of royal power. These restrictions on royal prerogatives were embodied in the Magna Carta, a historic statement of the rights of a political community against the monarchical state. Soon after, in 1236, the term *Parliament* was first used officially to refer to the gathering of feudal barons summoned by the king whenever he required their consent to special taxes. By the fifteenth century, Parliament had gained the right to make laws.

The Seventeenth-Century Settlement

The making of the British state in the sixteenth and seventeenth centuries involved a complex interplay of

Britain

0   100 Miles

0   100 Kilometers

Shetland Islands

Orkney Islands

Outer Hebrides

Inner Hebrides

SCOTLAND

North Sea

★Edinburgh

•Glasgow

NORTHERN IRELAND

Belfast★

Isle of Man

Irish Sea

REPUBLIC OF IRELAND

Dublin★

Isle of Anglesey

Manchester
•
•Liverpool

ENGLAND

WALES

•Birmingham

Thames

Cardiff★

•Bristol

London

Chunnel

Southampton•

Isle of Wight

ATLANTIC OCEAN

•Plymouth

English Channel

FRANCE

---

religious conflicts, national rivalries, and struggles between rulers and Parliament. These conflicts erupted in the civil wars of the 1640s and the forced abdication of James II in 1688. The bloodless political revolution of 1688, subsequently known as the Glorious Revolution, marked the "last successful political coup d'état or revolution in British history."[1]

By the end of the seventeenth century, the framework of a constitutional (or limited) monarchy, which would still exercise flashes of power into the nineteenth century, was established in Britain. For more than three hundred years, Britain's monarchs have been answerable to Parliament, which has held the sole authority for taxation and the maintenance of a standing army. The Glorious Revolution also resolved long-standing religious conflict. The replacement of the Roman Catholic James II by the Protestant William and Mary ensured the dominance of the Church of England (or Anglican Church). To this day, the Church of England remains the established (official) religion, and approximately two dozen of its bishops and archbishops sit as members of the House of Lords, the upper house of Parliament.

Thus, by the end of the seventeenth century, a basic form of parliamentary democracy had emerged. Except in Northern Ireland, the problem of religious divisions, which continue to plague many countries throughout the world, was largely settled (although Catholics and Jews could not vote until the 1820s). As a result of settling most of its religious differences early, Britain has taken a more secular turn than most other countries in Western Europe. The majority of Britons do not consider religion a significant source of identity, and active church membership in Britain, at 15 percent, is very low. These seventeenth-century developments became a defining moment for how the British perceive their history to this day. However divisive and disruptive the process of state building may have been originally, its telling and retelling have contributed significantly to a British political culture that celebrates democracy's continuity, gradualism, and tolerance.

The Industrial Revolution and the British Empire

Although the British state was consolidated by the seventeenth century, the timing of its industrial development and the way that process transformed Britain's role in the world radically shaped its form. The Industrial Revolution from the mid-eighteenth century onward involved rapid expansion of manufacturing production and technological innovation. It also led to monumental social and economic transformations and resulted in pressures for democratization. Externally, Britain used its competitive edge to transform and dominate the international order. Internally, the Industrial Revolution helped shape the development of the British state and changed forever the British people's way of life.

The Industrial Revolution.   The consequences of the Industrial Revolution for the generations of people who

Critical Junctures in Britain's Political Development	
1688	Glorious Revolution establishes power of Parliament
c. 1750	Industrial Revolution begins in Britain
1832	Reform Act expands voting rights
1837–1901	Reign of Queen Victoria; height of British Empire
1914–1918	World War I
1929–1939	Great Depression
1939–1945	World War II
1945–1979	Establishment of British welfare state; dismantling of British Empire
1973	Britain joins the European Community
1979–1990	Prime Minister Margaret Thatcher promotes "enterprise culture"
1997	Tony Blair elected prime minister
2001	Under Blair's leadership, Britain "stands shoulder to shoulder" with America in war against terror

experienced its upheavals can scarcely be exaggerated. The typical worker was turned "by degrees . . . from small peasant or craftsman into wage labourer," as historian Eric Hobsbawm observes. Cash and market-based transactions replaced older traditions of barter and production for local need.[2]

Despite a gradual improvement in the standard of living in the English population at large, the effects of industrialization were often profound for agricultural laborers and certain types of artisans. With the commercialization of agriculture, many field laborers lost their security of employment, and cottagers (small landholders) were squeezed off the land in large numbers. The mechanization of manufacturing, which spread furthest in the cotton industry, upset the traditional status of the preindustrial skilled craft workers and permanently marginalized them.

The British Empire.   Britain had assumed a significant role as a world power during the seventeenth century, building an overseas empire and engaging actively in international commerce. But it was the Industrial Revolution of the eighteenth century that established global production and exchange on a new and expanded scale, with particular consequences for the making of the British state. Cotton manufacture, the driving force behind Britain's growing industrial dominance, not only pioneered the new techniques and changed labor organization during the Industrial Revolution but also represented the perfect imperial industry. It relied on imported raw materials and, by the turn of the nineteenth century, already depended on overseas markets for the vast majority of its sales of finished goods. Growth depended on foreign markets rather than on domestic consumption. This export orientation fueled an expansion far more rapid than an exclusively domestic orientation would have allowed.

With its leading industrial sector dependent on overseas trade, Britain's leaders worked aggressively to secure markets and expand the empire. Toward these ends, Britain defeated European rivals in a series of military engagements, culminating in the Napoleonic Wars (1803–1815), which confirmed Britain's commercial, military, and geopolitical preeminence. The Napoleonic Wars also secured a balance of power on the European continent favorable for largely unrestricted international commerce (**free trade**). Propelled by the formidable and active presence of the British navy, international trade helped England to take full advantage of its position as the first industrial power. Many scholars suggest that in the middle of the nineteenth century, Britain had the highest per capita income in the world (it was certainly among the two or three highest), and in 1870, at the height of its glory, its trade represented nearly one-quarter of the world total, and its industrial mastery ensured highly competitive productivity in comparison with trading partners (see Table 1).

During the reign of Queen Victoria (1837–1901), the British Empire was immensely powerful and encompassed fully 25 percent of the world's population. Britain presided over a vast formal and informal empire, with extensive direct colonial rule over some four dozen countries, including India and Nigeria. At the same time, Britain enjoyed the advantages of an extensive informal empire—a worldwide network

Table 1

World Trade and Relative Labor Productivity

	Proprotion of World Trade (%)	Relative Labour Productivity[a] (%)
1870	24.0	1.63
1890	18.5	1.45
1913	14.1	1.15
1938	14.0	0.92

[a]As compared with the average rate of productivity in other members of the world economy.

Source: Robert O. Keohane, After Hegemony: Cooperation and Discord in the World Economy, p. 36. Copyright © 1984 by Princeton University Press. Reprinted by permission of Princeton University Press.

of independent states, including China, Iran, and Brazil—whose economic fates were linked to it. Britain ruled as a **hegemonic power,** the state that could control the pattern of alliances and terms of the international economic order, and that often could shape domestic political developments in countries throughout the world. Overall, the making of the British state observed a neat symmetry. Its global power helped underwrite industrial growth at home. At the same time, the reliance of domestic industry on world markets, beginning with cotton manufacture in the eighteenth century, prompted the government to project British interests overseas as forcefully as possible.

Industrial Change and the Struggle for Voting Rights. The Industrial Revolution shifted economic power from landowners to men of commerce and industry. As a result, the first critical juncture in the long process of democratization began in the late 1820s, when the "respectable opinion" of the propertied classes and increasing popular agitation pressed Parliament to expand the right to vote (franchise) beyond a thin band of men with substantial property, mainly landowners. With Parliament under considerable pressure, the Reform Act of 1832 extended the franchise to a section of the (male) middle class.

In a very limited way, the Reform Act confirmed the social and political transformations of the Industrial Revolution by granting new urban manufacturing centers, such as Manchester and Birmingham, more substantial representation. However, the massive urban working class created by the Industrial Revolution and populating the cities of Charles Dickens's England remained on the outside looking in. In fact, the reform was very narrow and defensive. Before 1832, less than 5 percent of the adult population was entitled to vote—and afterward, only about 7 percent. In extending the franchise so narrowly, the reform underscored the strict property basis for political participation and inflamed class-based tensions in Britain. Following the Reform Act, a massive popular movement erupted in the late 1830s to secure the program of the People's Charter, which included demands for universal male suffrage and other radical reforms intended to make Britain a much more participatory democracy. The Chartist movement, as it was called, held huge and often tumultuous rallies, and organized a vast campaign to petition Parliament, but it failed to achieve any of its aims.

Expansion of the franchise proceeded very slowly. The Representation of the People Act of 1867 increased the electorate to just over 16 percent but left cities significantly underrepresented. The Franchise Act of 1884 nearly doubled the size of the electorate, but it was not until the Representation of the People Act of 1918 that suffrage included nearly all adult men and women over age thirty. How slow a process was it? The franchise for men with substantial incomes dated from the fifteenth century, but women between the ages of twenty-one and thirty were not enfranchised until 1928. The voting age for both women and men was lowered to eighteen in 1969. Except for some episodes during the days of the Chartist movement, the struggle for extension of the franchise took place without violence, but its time horizon must be measured in centuries. This is British gradualism—at its best and its worst (see Figure 1).

World Wars, Industrial Strife, and the Depression (1914–1945)

With the matter of the franchise finally resolved, in one sense the making of the British state as a democracy

Figure 1

Expansion of Voting Rights

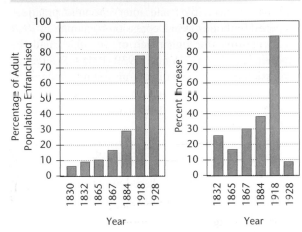

Expansion of the franchise in Britain was a gradual process. Despite reforms dating from the early nineteenth century, nearly universal adult suffrage was not achieved until 1928.

Source: Jorgen S. Rasmussen. *The British Political Process,* p. 151. Copyright © 1993 Wadsworth Publishing Company. Reprinted with permission of the publisher.

was settled. In another important sense, however, the development of the state was just beginning in the twentieth century with the expansion of the state's direct responsibility for management of the economy and the provision of social welfare for citizens. The making of what is sometimes called the *interventionist state* was spurred by the experiences of two world wars.

The state's involvement in the economy increased significantly during World War I (1914–1918). The state took control of a number of industries, including railways, mining, and shipping. It set prices and restricted the flow of capital abroad and channeled the country's resources into production geared to the war effort. After World War I, it remained active in the management of industry in a rather different way. Amid a set of tremendous industrial disputes, the state wielded its power to fragment the trade union movement and resist demands for workers' control over production and to promote more extensive state ownership of industries. This considerable government manipulation of the economy openly contradicted the policy of **laissez-faire** (minimal government interference in the operation of economic markets). The tensions between free-market principles and interventionist practices deepened with the Great Depression beginning in 1929 and continuing through much of the 1930s and the experiences of World War II (1939–1945). The fear of depression and the burst of pent-up yearnings for a better life after the war helped transform the role of the state and ushered in a period of unusual political harmony.

Collectivist Consensus (1945–1979)

In the postwar context of shared victory and common misery (almost everyone suffered hardships immediately after the war), reconstruction and dreams of new prosperity and security took priority over ideological conflict. In Britain today, a debate rages among political scientists over whether there was a postwar consensus. Critics of the concept contend that disagreements over specific policies concerning the economy, education, employment, and health, along with an electorate divided on partisan lines largely according to social class, indicated politics as usual.[3] It seems fair to say, however, that a broad culture of reconciliation and a determination to rebuild and improve the conditions of life for all Britons helped forge a postwar settlement based broadly on a collectivist consensus that endured until the mid-1970s.

Collectivism is the term coined to describe the consensus that drove politics in the harmonious postwar period when a significant majority of Britons and all major political parties agreed that the state should take expanded responsibility for economic governance and provide for the social welfare in the broadest terms. They accepted as a matter of faith that governments should work to narrow the gap between rich and poor through public education, national health care, and other policies of the **welfare state**, and they accepted state responsibility for economic growth and full employment. Collectivism brought class-based actors (representatives of labor and management) inside politics and forged a broad consensus about the expanded role of government. In time, however, economic downturn and political stagnation caused the consensus to unravel.

Margaret Thatcher and the Enterprise Culture (1979–1990)

In the 1970s, economic stagnation and the declining competitiveness of key British industries in international markets fueled industrial strife and kept class-based tensions near the surface of politics. No government appeared equal to the tasks of economic management. Each party failed in turn. The Conservative government of Edward Heath (1970–1974) could not resolve the economic problems or the political tensions that resulted from the previously unheard-of combination of increased inflation and reduced growth (stagflation). The Labour government of Harold Wilson and James Callaghan (1974–1979) fared no better. As unions became increasingly disgruntled, the country was beset by a rash of strikes throughout the winter of 1978–1979, the "winter of discontent." Labour's inability to discipline its trade union allies hurt the party in the election just a few months later, in May 1979. The traditional centrist Conservative and Labour alternatives within the collectivist mold seemed exhausted, and many Britons were ready for a new policy agenda.

Margaret Thatcher more than met the challenge. Winning the leadership of the Conservative Party in 1975, she wasted little time in launching a set of bold policy initiatives, which, with characteristic forthrightness, she began to implement after the Conservatives were returned to power in 1979. Reelected in 1983 and 1987, Thatcher served longer without interruption than any other British prime minister in the twentieth century and never lost a general election.

Thatcher was convinced that collectivism had contributed to Britain's decline by sapping British industry and permitting powerful and self-serving unions to hold the country for ransom. To reverse Britain's relative economic slide, Thatcher sought to jump-start the economy by cutting taxes, reducing social services where possible, and using government policy to stimulate competitiveness and efficiency in the private sector.

In many ways, the period of Margaret Thatcher's leadership as prime minister (1979–1990) marks a critical dividing line in postwar British politics. She set the tone and redefined the goals of British politics like few others before her. In November 1990, a leadership challenge within Thatcher's own

Conservative Party, largely over her anti-EU stance and high-handed leadership style, caused her sudden resignation and replacement by John Major. Major served as prime minister from 1990 to 1997, leading the Conservative Party to a victory in the 1992 general election before succumbing to Tony Blair's New Labour in 1997.

New Labour's Third Way

Some twenty electoral records were toppled as New Labour under the leadership of Tony Blair (see "Leaders: Tony Blair") won 419 of the 659 seats in Parliament, the largest majority it has ever held. Blair was propelled into office as prime minister with a 10 percent

Leaders: *Tony Blair*

Born in 1953 to a mother from Donegal, Ireland (who moved to Glasgow after her father's death), and a father from the Clydeside shipyards, Tony Blair lacks the typical pedigree of Labour Party leaders. It is very common in the highest ranks of the Labour Party to find someone whose father or grandfather was a union official or a Labour MP. The politics in the Blair family, by contrast, were closely linked to Conservatism (as chairman of his local Conservative Party club, his father Leo had a good chance to become a Conservative MP). Often, like Tony Blair's two predecessors—Neil Kinnock from Wales and John Smith from the West of Scotland—leaders of the Labour Party also have distinctive regional ties. In contrast, Blair moved to Durham in the north of England when he was five but spent much of his youth in boarding schools, moved south when he was old enough to set out on his own, studied law at Oxford, specialized in employment and industrial law in London—and returned to the north only to enter the House of Commons from Sedgefield in 1983. Thus, Blair has neither the traditional political or regional ties of a Labour Party leader.*

Coming of political age in opposition, Blair joined the shadow cabinet in 1988, serving in turn as shadow minister of energy, then of employment, and finally as shadow home secretary. An MP with no government experience, he easily won the contest for party leadership after his close friend and fellow modernizer John Smith died of a sudden heart attack in the summer of 1994. From the start, Blair boosted Labour Party morale and raised expectations that the party would soon regain power. As one observer put it, "The new Leader rapidly made a favorable impression on

the electorate: his looks and affability of manner appealed to voters whilst his self-confidence, lucidity and clarity of mind rendered him a highly effective communicator and lent him an air of authority."[†] As prime minister, Blair combined firm leadership, eclectic beliefs, and bold political initiatives as he transformed the Labour Party to "New Labour."

Even before the war in Iraq, his lack of familiar roots and ideological convictions made Blair, for many, an enigmatic figure. His very personal decision to support the U.S.-led invasion of Iraq deepened the impression that Blair would follow his own inner voice above the preferences of party. After the 2005 election, many both within and outside the party hoped that the prime minister's inner voice would tell him to live up to his end of a deal with Gordon Brown that has been long rumored: that in exchange for Brown backing Blair for party leadership in 1994, Blair would at some point in the future resign and hand the leadership of party and country to Brown. After he retires, Blair will doubtless be remembered as a towering figure in British politics. But two questions remained. In light of the war in Iraq, what would be Blair's legacy? And would he leave the scene gracefully, handing power to his rival, while the economy was still robust and Brown would still have the opportunity to make his mark as prime minister for a couple of years before having to face the electorate?

---

*See Andy McSmith, *Faces of Labour: The Inside Story* (London: Verso, 1997), pp. 7–96.

†Eric Shaw, *The Labour Party Since 1945* (Oxford: Blackwell, 1996), p. 195.

swing from Conservative to Labour, a postwar record. The Conservative Party, which had been in power since Margaret Thatcher's 1979 victory and was one of Europe's most successful parties in the twentieth century, was decimated.

New Labour aspired to recast British politics, offering what it referred to as a "third-way" alternative to Thatcherism and the collectivism of traditional Labour. Everything was at issue, from the way politics was organized to the country's underlying values, institutions, and policies. In electoral terms, New Labour rejected the notion of interest-based politics, in which unions and working people naturally look to Labour and businesspeople and the more prosperous look to the Conservatives. Labour won in 1997 by drawing support from across the socioeconomic spectrum. It rejected the historic ties between Labour governments and the trade union movement, choosing instead to emphasize the virtues of a partnership with business.

In institutional and policy terms, New Labour's innovations were intended to reverse the tendency of previous Labour governments in Britain to provide centralized statist solutions to all economic and social problems. Blair promised new approaches to economic, welfare, and social policy; British leadership in Europe; and far-reaching constitutional changes to revitalize democratic participation and devolve (transfer) specified powers from the central government to Scotland, Wales, and Northern Ireland.

In the early months of his premiership, Blair displayed effective leadership in his stewardship of the nation during the period after Lady Diana's death and in his aggressive efforts to achieve a potentially historic peace agreement for Northern Ireland, with far-reaching constitutional implications. By the summer of 2000, however, many began to say that New Labor was better at sounding innovative than at delivering the goods (better at spin than substance). In addition, a set of crises—from a set of fatal train crashes since 1997 to protests over the cost of petrol (gasoline) in September 2000 to an outbreak of mad cow disease in spring 2001—made Blair seem a little shopworn. Nevertheless, until the war in Iraq, Blair remained a formidable leader, and a few months before the cataclysmic events of September 11, 2001, New Labour won what it most sought: an electoral mandate in June 2001 for a second successive term.

After September 11. In the aftermath of the September 11, 2001, attacks on the World Trade Center and the Pentagon in the United States, Blair showed decisive leadership in assuming the role of a key ally to the United States in the war on terrorism. With Britain willing and able to lend moral, diplomatic, and military support, September 11 lent new credence to the **special relationship**—a bond of language, culture, and national interests, which creates an unusually close alliance—that has governed U.S.-UK relations for 50 years and catapulted Blair to high visibility in world affairs. Before long, however, especially when the central focus of the war on terrorism moved from Afghanistan to Iraq, many Britons became disenchanted. Blair's willingness to run interference with allies and add intellectual ballast to President George W. Bush's post-9/11 plans was a big help to the United States. But it locked Britain into a set of policies over which it had little or no control, vastly complicated its relationships with France and Germany (which opposed the war), and generated hostility toward the United Kingdom in much of the Arab and Muslim world. The devastating London bombings in July 2005, timed to correspond with the G-8 summit in Gleneagle, Scotland, appeared to confirm that Britain faced heightened security risks because of its participation in the war. The war in Iraq, which was very unpopular in the UK, eroded Blair's popularity. In addition, the conviction among many Britons that Blair led them into war under false premises seems to have permanently weakened his credibility and tarnished the legacy of New Labour.

Themes and Implications

The processes that came together in these historical junctures continue to influence developments today in powerful and complex ways. Our four core themes in this book, introduced in Part I, highlight some of the most important features of British politics.

Historical Junctures and Political Themes

The first theme suggests that a country's relative position in the world of states influences its ability to manage domestic and international challenges. A

One year after the start of the war in Iraq, Blair's credibility was hurt as key justifications for war such as WMDs and Al Queda links to Iraq remain unproven. During an anniversary demonstration, two protesters reached the clock face of Big Ben and unveiled banners reading "**Time for Truth.**" *Source:* © Graeme Robertson/Getty Images

weaker international standing makes it difficult for a country to control international events or insulate itself from external pressures. Britain's ability to control the terms of trade and master political alliances during the height of its imperial power in the nineteenth century confirms this maxim. In a quite different way, Blair's temptation to cling to the special relationship with the United States and Britain's reduced standing and influence today also confirm the theme of the world of states today.

As the gradual process of decolonization defined Britain's changing relationship to the world of states, Britain fell to second-tier status during the twentieth century. Its formal empire began to shrink in the interwar period (1919–1939) as the "white dominions" of Canada, Australia, and New Zealand gained independence. In Britain's Asian, Middle Eastern, and African colonies, the pressure for political reforms leading to independence deepened during World War II and in the immediate postwar period. Beginning with the formal independence of India and Pakistan in 1947, an enormous empire of dependent colonies more or less dissolved in less than twenty years. Finally, in 1997, Britain returned the commercially vibrant crown colony of Hong Kong to China. The process of decolonization ended any realistic claim Britain could make to be a dominant player in world politics.

Is Britain a world power or just a middle-of-the-pack country in Western Europe? It appears to be both. On the one hand, as a legacy of its role in World War II, Britain sits as a permanent member of the United Nations Security Council. On the other hand, Britain invariably plays second fiddle in its special relationship to the United States, a show of relative weakness that has exposed British foreign policy to extraordinary pressures since September 11.

In addition, British governments face persistent challenges in their dealings with the EU. As Margaret Thatcher learned too late to save her premiership, Europe is a highly divisive issue. Can Britain afford to remain aloof from the fast-paced changes of economic integration—symbolized by the headlong rush toward a common currency, the euro, which has already been embraced by every other leading member state—as well as several of the newest members from East-Central Europe, who only gained admission in May 2004? It is clear that Britain does not have the power to control EU policy outcomes, and the schism over the war in Iraq has, for a time at least, weakened the United Kingdom's influence as an honest broker between the United States and Europe.

A second theme examines the strategies employed in governing the economy. Since the dawn of Britain's Industrial Revolution, prosperity at home has relied on superior competitiveness abroad, and this is even truer in today's environment of intensified international competition and global production. When Tony Blair took office in 1997, he inherited a streak of prosperity in Britain dating from 1992—an enviable circumstance. The Blair government could thus work to modernize the economy and determine its budgetary priorities from economic strength. Will Britain's "less-is-more" laissez-faire approach to economic governance, invigorated by New Labour's business partnership, continue to compete effectively in a global context? Can Britain achieve a durable economic model with—or without—fuller integration into Europe? How can we assess the spending priorities and distributive implications of the third-way politics of the Blair government? Britain will never again assume the privileged position of hegemonic power, so a lot depends on how well it plays the cards it does have.

A third theme is the potent political influence of the democratic idea, the universal appeal of core values associated with parliamentary democracy as practiced first in the United Kingdom. Even in Britain, issues about democratic governance, citizen participation, and constitutional reform have been renewed with considerable force.

As the royal family has been rocked by scandal and improprieties, questions about the undemocratic underpinning of the British state are asked with greater urgency. Few reject the monarchy outright, but questions about the role of the monarchy helped place on the agenda broader issues about citizen control over government and constitutional reform. As a result, in November 1999, a bill was enacted to remove hereditary peers from Britain's upper unelected chamber of Parliament, the House of Lords, and although the final form of a reformed second chamber is not settled, the traditional House of Lords has been abolished.

Long-settled issues about the constitutional form and unity of the state have also reemerged with unexpected force. How can the interests of England, Wales, Scotland, and Northern Ireland be balanced within a single nation-state? Can the perpetual crisis in Northern Ireland be finally resolved? Tony Blair has placed squarely on the agenda a set of policies designed to reshape the institutions of government and reconfigure the fundamental constitutional

principles. Key policy initiatives have included the formation of a Scottish Parliament and a Welsh Senedd (the Welsh Assembly), and the negotiations of a peace agreement for Northern Ireland that contains a comprehensive set of new political institutions and power-sharing arrangements—some involving the Republic of Ireland—with far-reaching constitutional ramifications, should the stalemate be resolved. Clearly, democracy is not a fixed result, even in the United Kingdom, but a highly politicized and potentially disruptive process, as constitutional reform has taken a place front and center as perhaps the boldest item on Tony Blair's agenda.

Finally, we come to the fourth theme, collective identity, which considers how individuals define who they are politically in terms of group attachments, come together to pursue political goals, and face their status as political insiders or outsiders. In Britain, an important aspect of the politics of collective identity is connected to Britain's legacy of empire and its aftermath. Through the immigration of its former colonial subjects to the United Kingdom, decolonization helped create a multiracial society, to which Britain has adjusted poorly. As we shall see, issues of race, ethnicity, and cultural identity have challenged the long-standing British values of tolerance and consensus, and now present important challenges for policy and the prospects of cohesion in Britain today. With the exception of Iraq, there is no more hot-button issue in Britain than nationality and immigration, issues that in an important way drove the Conservative party election campaign in 2005. Indeed, the concept of "Britishness"—what the country stands for and who comprises the political community—has come under intense scrutiny. At the same time, gender politics remains a significant theme, from voting patterns to questions of equality in the workplace and positions of political leadership. Moreover, the specific needs of women for equal employment opportunities and to balance the demands of work and family have assumed an important place in debates about social and employment policies.

Implications for Comparative Politics

Britain's privileged position in comparative politics textbooks (it almost always comes first among country studies) seems to follow naturally from the important historical firsts it has enjoyed. Britain was the first nation to industrialize, and for much of the nineteenth century, the British Empire was the world's dominant economic, political, and military power, with a vast network of colonies throughout the world. Britain was also the first nation to develop an effective parliamentary democracy (a form of representative government in which the executive is drawn from and answerable to an elected national legislature). As a result of its vast empire, Britain had tremendous influence on the form of government introduced in countries around the globe. For these reasons, British politics is often studied as a model of representative government. Named after the section of London that is home to the British legislature, the **Westminster model** emphasizes that democracy rests on the supreme authority of a legislature—in Britain's case, the Parliament. Finally, Britain has served as a model of gradual and peaceful evolution of democratic government in a world where transitions to democracy are often turbulent, interrupted, and uncertain.

Today, more than a century after the height of its international power, Britain's significance in comparative terms must be measured in somewhat different ways. Even in tough times, as today, the advantages bestowed on prime ministers by the formidable levers of power they control, and the relative strength of the British economy provide a platform for success. Particularly in the aftermath of September 11, with signs of intolerance rampant, all economies facing new challenges, and European center-left politics in disarray, the stakes are high. Britain's ability to succeed (or not) in sustaining economic competitiveness, resolving the euro dilemma, and revitalizing the center-left will send important signals to governments throughout the world. Is significant innovation possible in established democracies? Can a politics beyond left and right develop coherent policies and sustain public support? Can constitutional reforms help bind together a multi-ethnic, multinational state? What geopolitical sphere of maneuver does any state have in a global order dominated by the United States (where it is not easy to tell whether the "special relationship" is a blessing, a curse, or a one-way street with little benefit for the United Kingdom)? In fact, contemporary Britain may help define what the prospects are for middle-rank established democracies in a global age.

Section ② Political Economy and Development

In the first decade of the new century, it appears that the trend in government management of the economy has gone in Britain's direction. The high unemployment and weak growth in the euro zone as well as the stagnation in the Japanese economy have breathed new life into the old economic doctrine of laissez-faire and raised doubts about the sustainability of more state-led models. In addition, the pressures of global competitiveness and the perceived advantages of a one size fits all style of minimalist government have encouraged the movement toward neoliberal approaches for economic management (free markets, free trade, welfare retrenchment, and an attractive investment climate as the end game of every state's politics). A legacy from Thatcher's Britain, **neoliberalism** is a touchstone premise of Tony Blair's New Labour. Government policies aim to promote free competition among firms, to interfere with the prerogatives of entrepreneurs and managers as little as possible, and to create a business-friendly environment to attract foreign investment and spur innovation.

This section analyzes and evaluates the range of strategies that Britain has applied in post–World War II Europe for managing the economy, culminating in New Labour's economic and social model. We then consider, in turn, the social consequences of economic developments, and the political repercussions of Britain's position in the international economic order.

State and Economy

Thirty years ago, there was not much to admire in the British economy. Growth was low, and unemployment was high, and in 1976 the country received a Third World–style bailout from the International Monetary Fund to help stabilize the economy. Britain was routinely called the "sick man of Europe." But times have changed for the better. Since the mid-1990s, Britain has avoided the high unemployment and recession that have plagued many of the member nations of the European Union (EU).

The pattern of growth reveals the two-track character of the UK economy, with growth in the service sector—the UK is especially competitive in financial services—offsetting a much weaker industrial sector performance. But in general the British economy exhibits overall strength, and stands up well in knowledge-intensive high-technology industrial sectors, which account for one-quarter of the country's total exports. International comparisons also reveal superior microeconomic competitiveness, with first- or second-place rankings in global comparisons of national business environment and company operations and strategy.

Although many are beginning to wonder how much longer the good times will continue to roll, with low unemployment, low interest rates, low inflation, and sustained growth, the UK performance profile through the middle of the century's first decade was one of the best in the OECD.

On the negative side, however, must be counted a productivity gap in manufacturing between the United Kingdom and key competitors, a persistent deficit in the UK balance of trade, as well as ongoing concern about low rates of domestic investment and spending on research and development. Housing prices have escalated rapidly beyond the reach of many middle-class Britons as home mortgage refinancing has fueled a huge boom in consumer spending for the "haves" and—augmented by a frenzy of credit card borrowing—pushed record numbers onto the edge of personal bankruptcy. Working-class families were largely excluded from this new affluence, spurred by a rapid rise in the equity generated by home ownership.[4] In addition, the British system of production tends to generate nonstandard and insecure jobs without the traditional social protections associated with the European social and economic model. Women and ethnic minorities are significantly overrepresented in this sector. As a result, within EU Europe (at least before the May 2004 enlargement eastward), Britain assumed a specialized profile as a producer of relatively low-technology, low-value-added products in the manufacturing sector, buttressed by a more competitive service economy.

Neoliberalism drives the economic policy orientation of Tony Blair's New Labour, and the economic performance of the UK economy today. Britain's sustained growth—which began during Major's government in 1993 and continued through eight years of New Labour governance—as well as its high inequality (discussed below in "Society and Economy"), reflects both the strengths and the weaknesses of the model. Government policies aim to promote free competition among firms, to interfere with the prerogatives of entrepreneurs and managers as little as possible, and to create a business-friendly environment to help attract foreign investment and spur innovation. At the same time, Britain's Labour government insists that its third way—as distinct from Conservative or conventional center-left projects—can blend the dynamism of market forces with the traditional center-left concern for social justice and commitment to the reduction of inequalities. How new is New Labour's approach to economic management? Are Britons across the board enjoying the fruits of the longest period of sustained economic growth, as Brown trumpeted, that Britain has enjoyed for over 200 years? How have the economic processes of globalization changed the equation? In this section, we analyze the politics of economic management in Britain and consider the implications of Britain's less-is-more, laissez-faire approach.

Two central dimensions, economic management and social policy, capture the new role of the state. Analysis of these policy areas also reveals how limited this new state role was in comparative terms.

Economic Management

Like all other states, whatever their commitment to free markets, the British state intervenes in economic life, sometimes with considerable force. However, the British have not developed institutions for state-sponsored economic planning or industrial policy. Instead, the British state has generally limited its role to broad policy instruments designed to influence the economy generally (**macroeconomic policy**) by adjusting state revenues and expenditures to achieve short-term goals. The Treasury and the Bank of England dominate economic policy, which has often seemed reactive and relatively ineffectual. Despite other differences, this generally reactive and minimalist orientation of economic management strategies in Britain bridges the first two eras of postwar politics in Britain: the consensus era (1945–1979) and the period of Thatcherite policy orientation (1979–1997). How has the orientation of economic policy developed and changed during the postwar period? How new is New Labour when it comes to economic policy?

The Consensus Era.   With control of crucial industries during World War I and the active management of industry by the state in the interwar years, the state assumed a more interventionist role that belied its laissez-faire traditions. After World War II, the sense of unity inspired by the shared suffering of war and the need to rebuild a war-ravaged country helped crystallize the collectivist consensus as the British state both broadened and deepened its responsibilities for the overall performance of the economy.

The state nationalized some key industries, assuming direct ownership of them. It also accepted the responsibility to secure low levels of unemployment (referred to as a policy of full employment), expand social services, maintain a steady rate of growth (increase the output or GDP), keep prices stable, and achieve desirable balance-of-payments and exchange rates. The approach is called Keynesian demand management, or **Keynesianism** (after the British economist John Maynard Keynes, 1883–1946). State budget deficits were used to expand demand in an effort to boost both consumption and investment when the economy was slowing. Cuts in government spending and a tightening of credit and finance were used to cool demand when high rates of growth brought fears of inflation or a deficit in balance of payments. Taken together, this new agenda of expanded economic management and welfare provision, sometimes referred to as the Keynesian welfare state, directed government policy throughout the era of the collectivist consensus.

Before Thatcher became leader of the Conservative Party in 1975, Conservative leaders in Britain generally accepted the terms of the collectivist consensus. By the 1970s, however, public officials no longer saw the world they understood and could master; it had become a world without economic growth and with growing political discontent. Edward Heath, the Conservative centrist who governed from 1970 to 1974, was the first prime minister to suffer the full burden of recession and the force of political opposition from both traditional business allies and resurgent trade union adversaries. Operating in an era marked by increased inflation and reduced growth (stagflation), Heath could never break out of the political constraints imposed on him by economic decline.

From 1974 to 1979, the Labour government of Harold Wilson and James Callaghan reinforced the impression that governments could no longer control the swirl of events. The beginning of the end came when trade unions became increasingly restive under the pinch of voluntary wage restraints pressed on them by the Labour government. Frustrated by wage increases well below inflation rates, the unions broke with the government in 1978. The number of unofficial work stoppages increased, and official strikes followed, all fueled by a seemingly endless series of leapfrogging pay demands that erupted throughout the winter of 1978–1979 (the "winter of discontent"). There is little doubt that the industrial unrest that dramatized Labour's inability to manage its allies, the trade unions, contributed a lot to Thatcher's electoral victory just a few months later in May 1979. The winter of discontent helped write the conclusion to Britain's collectivist consensus and discredit the Keynesian welfare state.

Thatcherite Policy Orientation.   In policy terms, the economic orientations that Thatcher pioneered and that Major substantially maintained reflected a growing disillusionment with Keynesianism. In its place, **monetarism** emerged as the new economic doctrine. Keynesian demand management assumed that the level of unemployment could be set and the economy stabilized through decisions of government (monetary and fiscal or budgetary policy). By contrast, monetarism assumed that there is a "natural rate of unemployment" determined by the labor market itself. Monetary and fiscal policy should be passive and intervention limited (so far as this was possible) to a few steps that would help foster appropriate rates of growth in the money supply and keep inflation low.

By implication, the government ruled out spending to run up budgetary deficits as a useful instrument for stimulating the economy. On the contrary, governments could contribute to overall economic efficiency and growth by reducing social expenditure and down-sizing the public sector, by reducing its work force or privatizing nationalized industries. Monetarism reflected a radical change from the postwar consensus regarding economic management. Not only was active government intervention considered unnecessary; it was seen as undesirable and destabilizing.

New Labour's Economic Policy Approach.   Can New Labour thinking on macroeconomic policy end the short-termism of economic policy and provide the cohesion previously lacking? In British commentaries on New Labour, much has been made of the influence of revitalized Keynesian ideas and reform proposals.[5] In some ways, government policy seems to pursue conventional market-reinforcing and probusiness policies (neoliberalism). In other ways, the New Labour program stands as an alternative to Thatcherite monetarism and traditional Keynesianism. Whether New Labour's approach to economic management constitutes a distinctive third way or a less coherent blend of disparate elements is the subject of endless political debate.

The first shot fired in the Blair revolution was the announcement within a week of the 1997 election by Gordon Brown, the chancellor of the exchequer (equivalent to the minister for finance or secretary of the treasury in other countries), that the Bank of England would be given "operational independence" in the setting of monetary policy, and charged with maintaining low inflation (which has been achieved). The decision transferred from the cabinet a critical, and highly political, prerogative of government. With Brown attuned to the pressures of international financial markets, and the control of inflation and stability the key goals of macroeconomic policy, the transfer of authority over monetary policy confirmed the neoliberal market orientation of economic policy.

Central to the concerns of Brown and his Treasury team from 1997 were issues of macroeconomic stability. Brown (the "iron chancellor") insisted on establishing a "platform of stability" through explicit acceptance of the preexisting (and Conservative specified) limits on public spending and gave a very high priority to policies designed to reduce the public debt. Only as he turned that debt into a surplus did the iron chancellor reinvent himself as a more conventionally Labour and social democratic chancellor.[6] Deciding to use economic growth to increase spending on key social policies (rather than cut taxes), spending on the National Health Service (NHS), which was 6 percent of GDP, jumped to 8 percent of GDP in 2005. Similarly, annual expenditure on education is scheduled to nearly double between 2002 and 2008.[7] Both Brown's success in achieving growth and economic stability and the credit he is given for a commitment to fund social policy position the chancellor well to make the most of his much-anticipated opportunity to assume leadership of the Labour Party.

Does the third way represent a genuine departure in economic policy? Although there is no ready agreement on how to best answer this question, the claim of a distinctive policy design is quite clear in the way Blair and Brown have articulated their priorities. Above all, New Labour's economic policy approach emphasizes pragmatism in the face of global economic competition. Since capital is international, mobile, and not subject to control, industrial policy and planning that focus on the domestic economy alone are futile. Rather, government can improve the quality of labor through education and training, maintain the labor market flexibility inherited from the Thatcher regime, and help to attract investment to Britain. Strict control of inflation and tough limits on public expenditure help promote both employment and investment opportunities. At the same time, economic policy is directed at enhancing the competitive strength of key sectors and developing a partnership with business through research and development, training, technology, and modernization policies. New Labour is very focused on designing and implementing policies to create new jobs and get people, particularly young people, into the work force.

Political Implications of Economic Policy.   Differences in economic doctrine are not what matter most in policy terms. In fact, British governments in the past have never consistently followed any economic theory, whether Keynesianism or monetarism. Today, the economic policy of New Labour is pragmatic and eclectic. The political consequences of economic orientations are more significant: each economic doctrine helps to justify a broad moral and cultural vision of society, to provide motives for state policy, and to advance alternative sets of values. Should the government intervene, work to reduce inequalities through the mildly redistributive provisions of the welfare state, and sustain the ethos of a caring society (collectivism/"Old Labour")? Should it back off and allow the market to function competitively and thereby promote entrepreneurship, competitiveness, and individual autonomy (Thatcherism)? Or should it help secure an inclusive "stakeholder" economy in which business has the flexibility, security, and mobility to compete and workers have the skills and training to participate effectively in the global labor market (New Labour)? As these questions make clear, economic management strategies are closely linked to social or welfare policy.

Social Policy

Observers have noted that the social and political role of the welfare state depends as much on policy goals and instruments as on spending levels. Does the state provide services itself or offer cash benefits that can be used to purchase services from private providers? Are benefits universal, or are they limited to those who fall below an income threshold (means-tested)? Are they designed to meet the temporary needs of individuals or to help reduce the gap between rich and poor?

The expanded role of government during World War II and the increased role of the Labour Party during the wartime coalition government led by Winston Churchill prepared the way for the development of the welfare state in Britain. The 1943 Beveridge Report provided a blueprint for an extensive but, in comparative European terms, fairly shallow set of provisions. The principal means-tested program is **social security**, a system of contributory and noncontributory benefits to provide financial assistance (not services directly) for the elderly, sick, disabled, unemployed, and others similarly in need of assistance.

In general, welfare state provisions interfere relatively little in the workings of the market, and policymakers do not see the reduction of group inequalities as the proper goal of the welfare state. The NHS provides comprehensive and universal medical care and has long been championed as the jewel in the crown of the welfare state in Britain, but it remains an exception to the rule. Compared with other Western European countries, the welfare state in Britain offers relatively few comprehensive services, and the policies

are not very generous. For the most part, Britons must rely on means-tested safety net programs that leave few of the recipients satisfied.

The Welfare State Under Thatcher and Major. The record on social expenditure by Conservative governments from 1979 to 1997 was mixed. Given Britons' strong support for public education, pensions, and health care, Conservative governments attempted more limited reform than many at first anticipated. The Thatcher and Major governments encouraged private, alongside public, provision in education, health care (insurance), and pensions. They worked to increase efficiency in social services, reduced the value of some benefits by changing the formulas or reducing cost-of-living adjustments, and contracted out some services (purchasing them from private contractors rather than providing them directly). In addition, in policy reforms reminiscent of U.S. "workfare" requirements, they tried to reduce dependency by denying benefits to youths who refused to participate in training programs. Despite these efforts, the commitment to reduced spending could not be sustained, partly because a recession triggered increases in income support and unemployment benefits.

To a degree, however, this general pattern masks specific and, in some cases, highly charged policy changes in both expenditures and the institutionalized pattern of provision. In housing, the changes in state policy and provision were the most extensive, with repercussions in electoral terms and in changing the way Britons think about the welfare state. By 1990, more than 1.25 million council houses (public housing maintained by local government) were sold, particularly the attractive single-family homes with gardens (quite unlike public housing in the United States). Two-thirds of the sales were to rental tenants. Thatcher's housing policy was extremely popular. By one calculation, between 1979 and 1983 there was a swing (change in the percentage of vote received by the two major parties) to the Conservative Party of 17 percent among those who had bought their council houses.[8]

Despite great Conservative success in the campaign to privatize housing, a strong majority of Britons remain stalwart supporters of the principle of collective provision for their basic needs. Thus, there were limits on the government's ability to reduce social spending or change institutional behavior. For example, in 1989, the Conservative government tried to introduce market practices into the NHS, with general practitioners managing funds and purchasing hospital care for their patients. Many voiced fears that the reforms would create a two-tier system of medical care for rich and poor.

More generally, a lack of confidence in the Conservatives on social protection hurt Major substantially in 1992, and it has continued to plague the party. Nothing propelled the Labour landslide in 1997 more than the concern for the "caring" issues. The traditional advantage Labour enjoys on these issues also helped secure victory for Blair in June 2001, and again when he needed a boost from traditional Labour supporters to offset their opposition to the prime minister on the war in Iraq.

New Labour Social Policy.   As with economic policy, social policy for New Labour presents an opportunity for government to balance pragmatism and innovation, while borrowing from traditional Labour as well as from Thatcherite options. Thus, the Blair government rejects both the attempted retrenchment of Conservative governments that seemed mean-spirited as well as the egalitarian traditions of Britain's collectivist era that emphasized entitlements. Instead, New Labour focuses its policy on training and broader social investment as a more positive third-way alternative. At the same time, New Labour draws political strength from the "Old Labour" legacy of commitment on the "caring" social policy issues.

For example, following Bill Clinton, Blair's New Democratic counterpart in the United States, the prime minister promised a modernized, leaner welfare state, in which people are actively encouraged to seek work. The reform of the welfare state emphasizes efficiencies and attempts to break welfare dependency. Efforts to spur entry into the labor market combine carrots and sticks. Positive inducements include training programs, especially targeted at youth, combined with incentives to private industry to hire new entrants to the labor market. The threats include eligibility restrictions and reductions in coverage. Referred to as the "New Deal" for the young unemployed, welfare reform in the United Kingdom has emphasized concerted efforts to create viable pathways out of

dependence. Although beginning with a focus on moving youth from welfare to work, New Deal reform efforts expanded in several directions.

The New Deal was quickly extended to single parents and the long-term unemployed. In 1999, the government launched a "Bridging the Gap" initiative to provide a more comprehensive approach for assisting sixteen- to eighteen-year-olds not in education, employment, or training to achieve clear goals by age nineteen through a variety of "pathways" (academic, vocational, or occupational). "Better Government for Older People" was launched in 1998 and was followed quickly by "All Our Futures," a government report issued in the summer of 2000 with twenty-eight recommendations to improve the quality of life and the delivery of public services for senior citizens. A new initiative, The IT New Deal, was launched in 2001 as a government-business partnership to address skill shortages in information technologies.

Although the jury is still out on the follow-through and effectiveness of New Labour social and welfare policy initiatives, the intent to create innovative policies and approach social policy in new and more comprehensive ways is clearly there. Late in 1997, the government inaugurated the Social Exclusion Unit, staffed by civil servants and external policy specialists. Initially located within the Cabinet Office and reporting directly to the prime minister, the Social Exclusion Unit moved to the Office of the Deputy Prime Minister in May 2002. It was charged broadly with addressing "what can happen when people or areas suffer from such problems as unemployment, poor skills, low incomes, poor housing, high crime environments, bad health, and family breakdown." The Social Exclusion Unit has been actively involved in developing the New Deal initiative as well as in writing reports and recommending policies to take on problems such as truancy and school exclusion, homelessness, neighborhood renewal, and teenage pregnancy. This effort to identify comprehensive solutions to society's ills and reduce the tendency for government to let marginalized individuals fall by the wayside captures the third-way orientation of the Blair project.

Nevertheless, New Labour, like all other governments in Britain and many other countries, will be accountable above all for the failure or success of more traditional social policies, especially health care and education. By 2004, there was mounting evidence that record growth in the NHS budget had netted results. Despite the report of a House of Commons select committee on the health dangers of obesity (particularly for children), there was widespread confidence that NHS quality and performance were improving, with waiting lists shorter and significant advances in the treatment of life-threatening diseases. After years of skepticism about New Labour's ability to deliver on promised improvements in the provision of key public services, by 2005 the tides of opinion—and massive budgetary increases—were beginning to have the desired effect. New Labour had gained considerable credibility on health care as well as education—and increasing success on core policies gave Labour a huge boost heading into the 2005 election.

Society and Economy

What were the *distributional effects*—the consequences for group patterns of wealth and poverty—of the economic and social policies of Thatcher and Major? To what extent have the policies of Tony Blair's Labour government continued—or reversed—these trends? How has government policy influenced the condition of minorities and women? It is impossible to ascertain when government policy creates a given distribution of resources and when poverty increases or decreases because of a general downturn or upswing in the economy. The evidence is clear, however, that economic inequality grew in Britain during the 1980s before it stabilized or narrowed slightly in the mid-1990s, and that ethnic minorities and women continue to experience significant disadvantages.

In general, policies initiated by the Conservative Party, particularly during the Thatcher years, tended to deepen inequalities. The economic upturn that began in 1992, combined with Major's moderating effects on the Thatcherite social policy agenda, served to narrow inequality by the mid-1990s. Since 1997, as one observer noted, Labour has "pursued redistribution by stealth, raising various indirect levies on the better-off to finance tax breaks for poorer workers."[9] As a result, Britain has witnessed a modest downward redistribution of income since 1997. Attention to social exclusion in its many forms, a 1999 pledge by the prime minister to eradicate child poverty (even though Britain at the time had one of the highest rates

of child poverty in EU Europe), and strong rates of growth augur well for a further narrowing of the gap between rich and poor in Britain. Data from 2004 indicates that in 2002–2003, 17 percent of the population lived in low-income households (down from a peak of 21 percent in the early 1990s). After rising to a peak of 27 percent in the early 1990s, the percentage of children living in low-income households has held steady at 21 percent for each of the three years from 1999–2000 to 2002–2003.[10]

Into Blair's third term, there were clear indications that the government was committed to an ambitious agenda to reduce childhood poverty through a new set of inclusive tax credits for children as well as other measures to transfer resources to poor families. In addition, since January 2005, the payment of vouchers to the parents of all British children born since 2002, with a promise to top up the funds periodically, represented an innovative effort to provide a sizeable nest egg of savings available for eighteen-year-olds. This "asset-based" welfare held the promise of reducing poverty and providing a new generation with new economic opportunities. Comparative analysis of poverty rates indicates that despite these efforts the United Kingdom has greater problems regarding income inequality than do many of its EU counterparts prior to the 2004 enlargement (see Figure 2).

Inequality and Ethnic Minorities

Poverty and diminished opportunity disproportionately characterize the situation of ethnic minorities (a term applied to peoples of non-European origin from the former British colonies in the Indian subcontinent, the Caribbean, and Africa). Official estimates place the ethnic minority population in Britain at 4.7 million in 2003 (the most recent data available) or 7.9 percent of the total population of the United Kingdom. Indians comprise the largest ethnic minority, at 21.7 percent; Pakistanis represent 16.7 percent, Bangladeshis, 6.1 percent, and Afro-Caribbeans and other blacks, 27.1 percent.[11] Because of past immigration and fertility patterns, the ethnic minority population in the United Kingdom is considerably younger than the white population. More than one-third of the ethnic minority population is younger than age sixteen, nearly half is under age twenty-five, and more than four-fifths is under age forty-five. Thus, despite the common and often

Figure 2

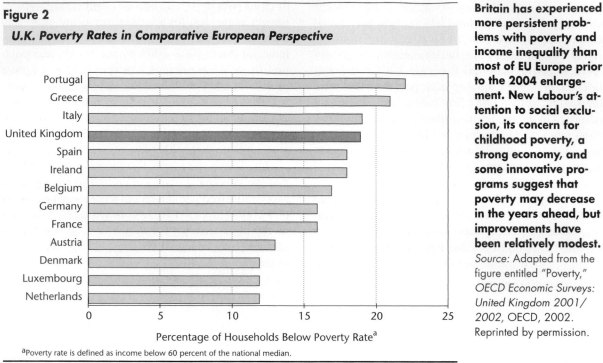

U.K. Poverty Rates in Comparative European Perspective

Percentage of Households Below Poverty Rate[a]

[a]Poverty rate is defined as income below 60 percent of the national median.

Britain has experienced more persistent problems with poverty and income inequality than most of EU Europe prior to the 2004 enlargement. New Labour's attention to social exclusion, its concern for childhood poverty, a strong economy, and some innovative programs suggest that poverty may decrease in the years ahead, but improvements have been relatively modest. *Source:* Adapted from the figure entitled "Poverty," *OECD Economic Surveys: United Kingdom 2001/2002,* OECD, 2002. Reprinted by permission.

disparaging reference to ethnic minority individuals as "immigrants," the experience of members of ethnic minority groups is increasingly that of a native-born population.[12]

Britain has adjusted slowly to the realities of a multicultural society. The postwar period has witnessed the gradual erosion of racial, religious, and ethnic tolerance in Britain and a chipping away at the right of settlement of postcolonial subjects in the United Kingdom. During the Thatcher era, discussion of immigration and citizenship rights was used for partisan political purposes and assumed a distinctly racial tone. Ethnic minority individuals, particularly young men, are subject to unequal treatment by the police and considerable physical harassment by citizens. They have experienced cultural isolation as well as marginalization in the educational system, job training, housing, and labor markets. There is considerable concern about the apparent rise in racially motivated crime in major metropolitan areas with significant ethnic diversity. Recognizing these problems, in 2000 the government brought to Parliament a bill to amend the Race Rela-

tions Act 1976 by outlawing direct and indirect discrimination in all public bodies and placing a "positive duty" on all public officials and authorities to promote racial equality. The Race Relations (Amendment) Act 2000 received final parliamentary approval in November 2000.

In general, poor rates of economic success reinforce the sense of isolation and distinct collective identities. Variations among ethnic minority communities are quite considerable, however, and there are some noteworthy success stories. For example, among men of African, Asian, Chinese, and Indian descent, the proportional representation in the managerial and professional ranks is actually higher than that for white men (although they are much less likely to be senior managers in large firms). Also, Britons of South Asian and, especially, Indian descent enjoy a high rate of entrepreneurship. Nevertheless, despite some variations, employment opportunities for women from all minority ethnic groups are limited.[13] In addition, a distinct gap remains between the job opportunities available to whites and those open to ethnic minorities in Britain. It is clear that people from ethnic minority communities are overrepresented among low-income households in the United Kingdom (see Figure 3). Almost 60 percent of Pakistani or Bangladeshi households are in low-income households (defined by income below 60 percent of the median). Just under half of black non-Caribbean households also live on low incomes after housing costs are deducted, as do nearly one-third of black Caribbeans. In contrast, only 16 percent of white people may be found in such low-income households before housing costs are deducted, and 21 percent after housing costs are deducted.[14]

Then there is the human side behind the statistics that reveals how difficult it remains in Britain for ethnic minorities to achieve top posts and how uneven the prospects of success are, despite some pockets of modest success. It seems that the police have been more effective in recent years in recruiting and retaining ethnic minority police officers, and moving them up

through the ranks, than have the further-education colleges (non-degree-giving institutions providing mainly vocational training for sixteen- to eighteen-year-olds not headed to university). "We don't have one black college principal in London in spite of having one of the most ethnically diverse student populations in the country," observed the mayor of London's senior policy director in 2004. There are many more young Afro-Caribbean men in prison than there are in university, and more black Met [London police] officers than there are teachers.[15] Ethnic minority police officers now make up 3 percent of the United Kingdom's 122,000-member police force, but only 2 percent of junior and middle managers in the more than four hundred colleges in Britain, only five of which have ethnic minority principals. It speaks volumes to the level of ethnic minority inequality that a 3 percent representation of ethnic minority police officers is considered evidence that "the police have in recent years

Figure 3

Distribution of Low-Income Households by Ethnicity

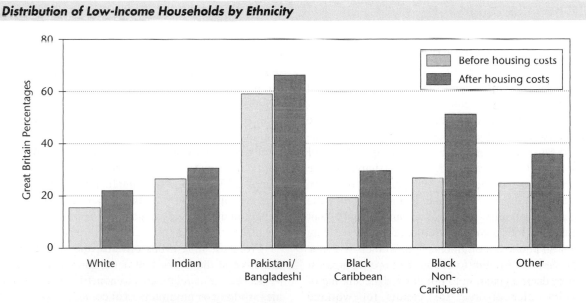

Households on low income: by ethnic group of head of household, 2001–02

People from Britain's ethnic minority communities are far more likely than white Britons to be in lower-income households, although there are important differences among ethnic minority groups. Nearly 60 percent of Pakistani or Bangladeshi households are low-income households, while about one-third of black Caribbean households live on low incomes.

Source: National Statistics Online: www.statistics.gov.uk/CCI/nugget.asp?ID=269&Pos=1&ColRank=2&Rank=384

been undertaking a much-needed overhaul of equal opportunities."[16]

Inequality and Women

Women's participation in the labor market when compared to that of men also indicates marked patterns of inequality. In fact, most women in Britain work part-time, often in jobs with fewer than sixteen hours of work per week and often with fewer than eight hours (in contrast, fewer than one in every fifteen men is employed part-time). More than three-quarters of women working part-time report that they did not want a full-time job, yet more women than men (in raw numbers, not simply as a percentage) take on second jobs. Although employment conditions for women in Britain trail those of many of their EU counterparts, the gap in the differential between weekly earnings of men and women in the United Kingdom has narrowed. In fact, in 2004 the **gender gap** in pay dropped to its lowest value since records have been kept: women's median hourly rate was 85.7 percent of men's.[17]

The Blair government remains committed to gender equality in the workplace and has affirmed its resolve to address women's concerns to balance work and family responsibilities. The government has implemented a set of "family-friendly" work-related policies, including parental leave and flexible working arrangements and working times. Most of these initiatives were at the minimum EU standard as required by treaty commitments (once the UK under Blair signed on to part of the Social Chapter of the 1991 Maastricht Treaty to which previous UK governments had opted out, and further took on the obligations under the 1997 Amsterdam Treaty). Other measures include a commitment in principle to filling half of all public appointments with women, a review of the pension system to ensure better coverage for women, draft legislation to provide for the sharing of pensions after divorce, tax credits for working families as well as for child care, and a National Childcare Strategy, to which the Blair government has committed extensive financial support and given high visibility. Nevertheless, the gap between child-care supply and demand is considerable, and the cost for many families remains prohibitive. Moreover,

despite its efforts to make it easier for women to balance work and family obligations, "Labour has focused its efforts on persuading employers as to the 'business case' for 'family friendly' working conditions."[18] This approach limits New Labour's agenda, as witnessed by the government's willingness to let employers opt out of a forty-eight-hour ceiling on the work week (a serious impediment to a healthy family-work balance, given that UK fathers work the longest hours in Europe).[19] Thus, New Labour's core commitment to management flexibility makes it likely that the general pattern of female labor market participation will change relatively little in the years ahead. A recent report commissioned by the Cabinet Office's Women's Unit confirms a significant pattern of inequality in lifetime earnings of men and women with an equal complement of skills, defined by both a gender gap and a "mother gap."

Britain in the Global Economy

Is Britain making the most of globalization? The answer to this critical question begins with the understanding that Britain plays a special role within the European and international economy, one that has been reinforced by international competitive pressures in this global age. For a start, **foreign direct investment** (FDI) favors national systems, like those of Britain (and the United States), that rely more on private contractual and market-driven arrangements and less on state capacity and political or institutional arrangements. Because of such factors as low costs, political climate, government-sponsored financial incentives, reduced trade union power, and a large pool of potential non-unionized recruits, the United Kingdom is a highly regarded location in Europe for FDI.

From the mid-1980s onward, the single-market initiative of the EU has attracted foreign investment by according insider status to non-EU-based companies, so long as minimum local content requirements are met. Throughout this period, all British governments have, for both pragmatic and ideological reasons, promoted the United Kingdom as a magnet for foreign investment. For the Thatcher and Major governments, FDI was a congenial market-driven alternative to state intervention as a means to improve sectoral competitiveness. It had the added benefit of exposing UK producers to lean production techniques and to management cultures and strategies that reinforced government designs to weaken unions and enforce flexibility. New Labour has continued this approach, which helps advance its key third-way strategy orientation to accept globalization as a given and to seek ways to improve competitiveness through business-friendly partnerships.

FDI is only one part of a bigger picture. In very important ways, New Labour accepted the legacy of eighteen years of Conservative assaults on trade union powers and privileges. It has chosen to modernize, but not reshape, the system of production in which non-standard and insecure jobs without traditional social protections proliferate—a growing sector in which women and ethnic minorities are significantly over-represented. As a result, within EU Europe, Britain has assumed a specialized profile as a producer of medium-technology, relatively low-value-added mass-market products through the use of a comparatively low-paid, segmented, weakly organized, and easily dismissible work force.

That said, the UK scores extremely well in international comparisons of growth competitiveness. It has also achieved significant competitive success in particular pockets of quality-competitive high technology industries. For example, the UK preserves an extremely strong position in its global market share in telecommunications equipment. It is second behind the United States in its exports, slightly ahead of

Japan, and 15 percent above Germany. B
strong in pharmaceuticals and aerospace.
ture of UK global competitiveness remains clou.
however, by weak industrial performance—illustrated by the 2005 closure of Rover, Britain's last mass-market automobile manufacturer.

Tony Blair's Britain preaches a globalization-friendly model of flexible labor markets throughout EU Europe, and its success in boosting Britain's economic performance in comparison with the rest of Europe has won some reluctant admirers, even converts. (For example, Chancellor Gerhard Schröder's economic reform package, Project 2010, had much in common with Blair's neoliberal approach to economic governance). Thus, Britain has been shaped by the international political economy in important ways and hopes to take full advantage of the economic prospects of globalization, even as it tries to reshape other European national models in its own image.

As our world-of-states theme suggests, a country's participation in today's global economic order diminishes autonomous national control, raising unsettling questions in even the most established democracies. Amid complicated pressures, both internal and external, can state institutions retain the capacity to administer policy effectively within distinctive national models? How much do the growth of powerful bureaucracies at home and complex dependencies on international organizations such as the EU limit the ability of citizens to control policy ends? We turn to these questions in Section 3.

Section ❸ Governance and Policy-Making

An understanding of British governance begins with consideration of Britain's constitution, which is notable for two significant features: its form and its antiquity. Britain lacks a formal written constitution in the usual sense; that is, there is no single unified and authoritative text that has special status above ordinary law and can be amended only by special procedures. Rather, the British constitution is a combination of statutory law (mainly acts of Parliament), common law, convention, and authoritative interpretations.

Although it is often said that Britain has an unwritten constitution, this is not accurate. Authoritative legal treatises are written, of course, as are the much more significant acts of Parliament that define crucial elements of the British political system. These acts define the powers of Parliament and its relationship with the Crown, the rights governing the relationship between state and citizen, the relationship of constituent nations to the United Kingdom, the relationship of the United Kingdom to the EU, and many other rights and legal arrangements. Thus, it is probably best to say that "what distinguishes the British constitution from others is not that it is unwritten, but rather that it is part written and uncodified."[21]

More than its form, however, the British constitution's antiquity raises questions. It is hard to know where conventions and acts of Parliament with constitutional implications began, but they can certainly be found dating back to the seventeenth century, notably with the Bill of Rights of 1689, which helped define the relationship between the monarchy and Parliament. "Britain's constitution presents a paradox," a British scholar of constitutional history has observed. "We live in a modern world but inhabit a pre-modern, indeed, ancient, constitution."[22] For example, several industrial democracies, including Spain, Belgium, and the Netherlands, are constitutional monarchies, in which policy-making is left to the elected government and the monarch fulfills largely ceremonial duties. In fact, Western Europe contains the largest concentration of constitutional monarchies in the world. However, Britain alone among Western democracies has permitted two unelected hereditary institutions, the Crown and the House of Lords, to participate in governing the country (in the case of the Lords, a process of reform was begun in 1999).

More generally, constitutional authorities have accepted the structure and principles of many areas of government for so long that appeal to convention has enormous cultural force. Thus, widely agreed-on rules of conduct, rather than law or U.S.-style checks and balances, set the limits of governmental power. This reality underscores an important aspect of British government: absolute principles of government are few. At the same time, those that exist are fundamental to the organization of the state and central to governance, policy-making, and patterns of representation. Yet, the government is permitted considerable latitude.

Organization of the State

The core constitutional principle of the British political system and cornerstone of the Westminster model is **parliamentary sovereignty:** Parliament can make or overturn any law; the executive, the judiciary, and the throne do not have any authority to restrict or rescind parliamentary action. In a classic **parliamentary**

democracy, the prime minister is answerable to the House of Commons (the elected element of Parliament) and may be dismissed by it. That said, by passing the European Communities Act in 1972 (Britain joined the European Economic Community in 1973), Parliament accepted significant limitations on its ability to act with power. It acknowledged that European law has force in the United Kingdom without requiring parliamentary assent and acquiesced to the authority of the European Court of Justice (ECJ) to resolve jurisdictional disputes. To complete the circle, the ECJ has confirmed its prerogative to suspend acts of Parliament.[23]

Second, Britain has long been a **unitary state.** By contrast to the United States, where powers not delegated to the national government are reserved for the states, no powers are reserved constitutionally for subcentral units of government in the United Kingdom. However, the Labour government of Tony Blair introduced a far-reaching program of constitutional reform that created, for the first time, a quasi-federal system in Britain. Specified powers have been delegated (the British prefer to say *devolved*) to legislative bodies in Scotland and Wales, and in Northern Ireland (although conflict there leaves the ultimate shape of the constitutional settlement still in doubt). In addition, some powers have been redistributed from the Westminster Parliament to an authority governing London with a directly elected mayor, and additional powers may be devolved to regional assemblies as well.

Third, Britain operates within a system of **fusion of powers** at the national level: Parliament is the supreme legislative, executive, and judicial authority and includes the monarch as well as the House of Commons and the House of Lords. The fusion of legislature and executive is also expressed in the function and personnel of the cabinet. Whereas U.S. presidents can direct or ignore their cabinets, which have no constitutionally mandated function, the British cabinet bears enormous constitutional responsibility. Through its collective decision making, the cabinet, and not an independent prime minister, shapes, directs, and takes responsibility for government. As we will see, this core principle, **cabinet government**, may at critical junctures be observed more in principle than in practice.

Finally, sovereignty rests with the Queen-in-Parliament (the formal term for Parliament). Britain is a **constitutional monarchy.** The position of head of state passes by hereditary succession, but the government or state officials must exercise nearly all powers of the Crown. Taken together, parliamentary sovereignty, parliamentary democracy, and cabinet government form the core elements of the British or Westminster model of government, which many consider a model democracy and the first effective parliamentary democracy.

It may seem curious that such a venerable constitutional framework is also vulnerable to uncertainty and criticism. Can a willful prime minister overstep the generally agreed-upon limits of the collective responsibility of the cabinet and achieve an undue concentration of power? How well has the British model of government stood the test of time and radically changed circumstances? These questions underscore the problems that even the most stable democracies face. They also help identify important comparative themes, because the principles of the Westminster model were, with some modifications, adopted widely by former colonies ranging from Canada, Australia, and New Zealand to India, Jamaica, and Zimbabwe. British success (or failure) in preserving citizens' control of their government has implications reaching well beyond the British Isles.

The Executive

The term *cabinet government* is useful in emphasizing the key functions that the cabinet exercises: responsibility for policy-making, supreme control of government, and coordination of all government departments. However, the term does not capture the full range of executive institutions or the scale and complexity of operations. The executive reaches well beyond the cabinet. It extends from ministries (departments) and ministers to the civil service in one direction, and to Parliament (as we shall see in Section 4) in the other direction.

Cabinet Government

After a general election, the Crown invites the leader of the party that emerges from the election with control of a majority of seats in the House of Commons to form a government and serve as prime minister. The prime minister usually selects approximately two dozen ministers to constitute the cabinet. Among the most significant assignments are the Foreign Office (equivalent to the U.S. department of state), the Home

Office (ministry of justice or attorney general), and the chancellor of the exchequer (a finance minister or a more powerful version of the U.S. treasury secretary).

The responsibilities of a cabinet minister are immense. "The Cabinet, as a collective body, is responsible for formulating the policy to be placed before Parliament and is also the supreme controlling and directing body of the entire executive branch," notes S. E. Finer. "Its decisions bind all Ministers and other officers in the conduct of their departmental business."[24] In contrast to the French Constitution, which prohibits a cabinet minister from serving in the legislature, British constitutional tradition *requires* overlapping membership between Parliament and cabinet. (In fact, this point was made in dramatic fashion after Blair's 2005 electoral victory when he appointed a former head of his policy unit to the House of Lords so that he could appoint him as a junior education minister.) Unlike the informal status of the U.S. cabinet, its British counterpart enjoys considerable constitutional privilege and is a powerful institution with enormous responsibility for the political and administrative success of the government.

The cabinet room at 10 Downing Street (the prime minister's official residence) is a place of intrigue as well as deliberation. From the perspective of the prime minister, the cabinet may appear as loyal followers or as ideological combatants, potential challengers for party leadership, and parochial advocates for pet programs that run counter to the overall objectives of the government. Against this potential for division, the convention of collective responsibility normally ensures the continuity of government by unifying the cabinet. In principle, the prime minister must gain the support of a majority of the cabinet for a range of significant decisions, notably the budget and the legislative program.

The only other constitutionally mandated mechanism for checking the prime minister is a defeat on a vote of no confidence in the House of Commons (discussed in Section 4). Since this action is rare and politically dangerous, the cabinet's role in constraining the chief executive remains the only routine check on his or her power. Collective responsibility is therefore a crucial aspect of the Westminster model of democracy. Does collective responsibility effectively constrain the power of prime ministers, or does it enable the prime minister to paint "presidential" decisions with the veneer of collectivity?

A politician with strong ideological convictions and a leadership style to match, Margaret Thatcher often attempted to galvanize loyalists in the cabinet and either marginalize or expel detractors. In the end, Thatcher's treatment of the cabinet helped inspire the movement to unseat her as party leader and stretched British constitutional conventions. John Major returned to a more consultative approach, in keeping with the classic model of cabinet government.

Tony Blair, like Thatcher, has narrowed the scope of collective responsibility. Cabinet meetings are often dull and perfunctory, and debate is rare. The prime minister, a few key cabinet members, and a handful of advisers take decisions in smaller gatherings. In a striking example of this process early in the Blair premiership, right after the election when the full cabinet had not yet met, the government announced the decision to free the Bank of England to set interest rates. Blair has accentuated the tendency for shorter cabinet meetings (they are usually less than an hour) that cannot seriously take up (much less resolve) policy differences.

More recently, the role of the cabinet in the decision to go to war in Iraq underscores its weakened capacity to exercise constitutional checks and balances. The subject was often discussed in cabinet—and endlessly in bilateral meetings with key ministers and unelected policy advisers—but was never subjected to the full-scale debate and formal cabinet approval that is associated with the model of cabinet government and collective responsibility. "We have not had cabinet government in the textbook sense for a very long time," affirmed Bernard Crick in *The Guardian*. "To gain assent for the Iraq war the prime minister had summoned cabinet ministers individually."[25] In addition, when the cabinet did take up the issue of the war in Iraq, the conversation was more desultory than the strict exercise of cabinet responsibility would imply.

The point is not that Blair lacked a majority in cabinet, but that cabinet meetings had become largely beside the point. In addition, with eyes turned toward bruising debates in Parliament, where, as Blair acknowledged, defeat would compel him to resign, the prime minister took no steps to discipline ministers who spoke out against the war plan. In fact, Blair

permitted both Robin Cook (former foreign secretary and the leader of the House of Commons) and Clare Short (secretary of state for international development) each to resign in a manner and at a time of their own choosing in protest of the decision to go to war. In March 2003, Blair won the formal support of Parliament he sought. In so doing, perhaps he set a precedent that the presumed prerogative power of the prime minister or Crown to declare war had been handed over to Parliament.[26] Alternatively, many contend that the real decision to go to war in Iraq had been taken by the prime minister and President Bush long before, probably at President Bush's ranch in April 2002. Either way, there is no denying that the cabinet played a minor, almost incidental role.[27]

As the decision to go to war in Iraq underscores, both Blair and his close aides seem skeptical about the effectiveness and centrality of the cabinet as well as cabinet committees. The prime minister prefers to coordinate strategically important policy areas through highly politicized special units in the Cabinet Office such as the Social Exclusion Unit, the Women's Unit, and the UK Anti-Drugs Co-ordination Unit. In June 2001, the Prime Minister's Delivery Unit was introduced to take strategic control of the delivery of public services, a central commitment of Blair's second term of office and one with great significance since it further eroded the principles of collective responsibility and the centrality of the cabinet.

On balance, cabinet government represents a durable and effective formula for governance, although the cabinet does not presently function in the role of supreme directing and controlling body it occupies in constitutional doctrine. It is important to remember that the cabinet operates within a broader cabinet system or core executive as it is sometimes called (see Figure 4) and that the prime minister holds or controls many of the levers of power in the core executive. Because the prime minister is the head of the cabinet, his or her office helps develop policy, coordinates operations, and functions as a liaison with the media, the party, interest groups, and Parliament. As Martin J. Smith puts it, "The culmination of a long-term process of centralization of power in the hands of the Prime Minister is seen in the declining role of the Cabinet and the increased development of resources inside Number 10."[28]

Figure 4

The Cabinet System

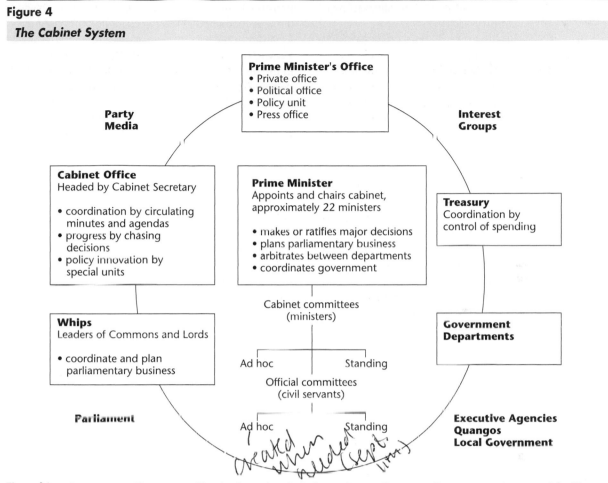

The cabinet is supported by a set of institutions that help formulate policy, coordinate operations, and facilitate the support for government policy. Acting within a context set by the fusion of legislature and executive, the prime minister enjoys a great opportunity for decisive leadership that is lacking in a system of checks and balances and separation of powers among the branches of government.

Source: Her Majesty's Treasury Budget Bulletin as found in *British Politics: Continuities and Change,* Third Edition, by Dennis Kavanagh, p. 251, Oxford University Press, 1996.

Both cabinet committees (comprising ministers) and official committees (made up of civil servants) supplement the work of the cabinet. In addition, the Treasury plays an important coordinating role through its budgetary control, while the Cabinet Office supports day-to-day operations. Leaders in both the Commons and the Lords, the *whips,* help smooth the passage of legislation sponsored by the government, which is more or less guaranteed by a working majority.

The cabinet system, and the complex interplay of resources, interdependencies, and power within the core executive that tend to concentrate power at the top, ensure that there is no Washington-style gridlock (the inability of legislature and executive to agree on policy) in London. On the contrary, if there is a problem at the pinnacle of power in the United Kingdom, it is the potential for excessive concentration of power by a prime minister who is prepared to manipulate the cabinet and flout the conventions of collective responsibility.

Bureaucracy and Civil Service

Policy-making at 10 Downing Street may appear to be increasingly concentrated in the prime minister's hands. At the same time, when viewed from Whitehall, the executive may appear to be dominated by its vast administrative agencies. The range and complexity of state policy-making mean that in practice, the cabinet's authority must be shared with a vast set of unelected officials.

How is the interaction between the civil service and the cabinet ministers (and their political assistants) coordinated? A very senior career civil servant, called a permanent secretary, has chief administrative responsibility for running a department. Other senior civil servants, including deputy secretaries and undersecretaries, in turn assist the permanent secretaries. In addition, the minister reaches into his or her department to appoint a principal private secretary, an up-and-coming civil servant who assists the minister as gatekeeper and liaison with senior civil servants.

Successful policy requires the effective translation of policy goals into policy instruments. Since nearly all legislation is introduced on behalf of the government and presented as the policy directive of a ministry, civil servants in Britain do much of the work of conceptualizing and refining legislation that is done by committee staffers in the U.S. Congress. Civil servants, more than ministers, assume operational duties, and, despite a certain natural level of mutual mistrust and incomprehension, the two must work closely together. In the eyes of the impartial, permanent, and anonymous civil servants, ministers are too political, unpredictable, and temporary—*they* are tireless self-promoters who may neglect or misunderstand the needs of the ministry. To a conscientious minister, the permanent secretary may be protecting *his* or *her* department too strenuously from constitutionally proper oversight and direction. Whatever they may think, no sharp line separates the responsibilities of ministers and civil servants, and they have no choice but to execute policy in tandem. Many of the activities traditionally undertaken by civil servants are now carried out in executive agencies established since a 1988 report on more effective government management. In addition, quite a range of administrative func-

tions previously performed in house are now provided through contracting out services to the private sector.

Like ministers, civil servants are servants of the Crown, but they are not part of the government (taken in the more political sense, like the term *the administration* in common American usage). The ministers, not the civil servants, have constitutional responsibility for policy and are answerable to Parliament and the electorate for the conduct of their departments. Since the early 1980s, the pace of change at Whitehall has been very fast, with governments looking to cut the size of the civil service, streamline its operations, replace permanent with casual (temporary) staff, and enhance its accountability to citizens. As a result of the ongoing modernization of Whitehall (known as new public management, NPM), the civil service inherited by New Labour is very different from the civil service of thirty years ago. It has been downsized and given a new corporate structure (divided into over 120 separate executive agencies). Few at the top of these agencies (agency chief executives) are traditional career civil servants. More generally, the old tradition of a career service is fading, a service in which nearly all the most powerful posts were filled by those who entered the bureaucratic ranks in their twenties. Many top appointments nowadays are advertised widely and filled by outsiders. The Blair government has continued the NPM trends toward accountability, efficiency, and greater transparency in the operations of the executive bureaucracy.

In recent years, many observers have expressed concern, however, that New Labour has done—and will continue to do—whatever it can to subject the Whitehall machine to effective political and ministerial direction and control.[29] A related concern, that the centrality and impartiality of civil servants is being eroded by the growing importance of special advisers (who are both political policy advisers and civil servants), came to a head as Blair made the case for war in Iraq. Key special advisers played critical roles in making the case in the famous "dodgy dossier" of September 2002 that the threat of weapons of mass destruction justified regime change in Iraq. In recent years, many observers have noted that the political neutrality of the civil service is a core element in British governance and policymaking. Some have expressed concern that the boundaries between ministers and civil servants as well as between special advisers and civil servants are not as clearly drawn as they should be.

Public and Semipublic Institutions

Like other countries, Britain has institutionalized a set of administrative functions that expand the role of the state well beyond the traditional core executive functions and agencies. We turn now to a brief discussion of semipublic agencies—entities sanctioned by the state but without direct democratic oversight.

Nationalized Industries   The nationalization of basic industries—such as coal, iron and steel, gas and electricity supply—was a central objective of the Labour government's program during the postwar collectivist era. By the end of the Thatcher era, the idea of public ownership had clearly run out of steam. For New Labour, a return to the program of public ownership of industry is unthinkable. Instead, when thinking of expanding state functions, we can look to a growing set of semipublic administrative organizations.

Nondepartmental Public Bodies.   Since the 1970s, an increasing number of administrative functions have been transferred to bodies that are typically part of the government in terms of funding, function, and appointment of staff, but operate at arm's length from ministers. They are officially called nondepartmental public bodies (NDPBs) but are better known as quasi-nongovernmental organizations or **quangos.** Quangos have increasing policy influence and enjoy considerable administrative and political advantages. They take responsibility for specific functions and can combine governmental and private sector expertise. At the same time, ministers can distance themselves from controversial areas of policy.

Despite Thatcher's attempts to reduce their number and scale back their operations, by the late 1990s, there were some six thousand quangos, 90 percent operating at the local level. They were responsible for one-third of all public spending and staffed by approximately fifty thousand people. Key areas of public policy previously under the authority of local governments are now controlled by quangos, which are nonelected bodies. Increasingly, the debate about NDPBs is less about the size of the public, semipublic, or private sector, and more about the effective delivery of services. For example, in 2004, the health secretary announced detailed plans for a quango purge: the number of quangos sponsored by the department would be cut by one-half in order to reduce 20 percent of their spending (nearly one billion dollars) and streamline the staff by 25 percent.[30]

The elected authority in London, as well as the Welsh Assembly and Scottish Parliament, acquired extensive powers to review and reform many of the quangos under their responsibility. We will return later to consider local government in Britain, but we move now to a discussion of a set of formal institutions within and outside the executive.

Other State Institutions

In this section, we examine the military and the police, the judiciary, and subnational government.

The Military and the Police

From the local bobby (a term for a local police officer derived from Sir Robert Peel, who set up London's metropolitan police force in 1829) to the most senior military officer, those involved in security and law enforcement have enjoyed a rare measure of popular support in Britain. Constitutional tradition and professionalism distance the British police and military officers from politics. Nevertheless, both institutions have been placed in more politically controversial and exposed positions in recent decades.

In the case of the military, British policy in the post–cold war period remains focused on a gradually redefined set of North Atlantic Treaty Organization (NATO) commitments. Still ranked among the top five military powers in the world, Britain retains a global presence, and the Thatcher and Major governments deployed forces in ways that strengthened their political positions and maximized Britain's global influence. In 1982, Britain soundly defeated Argentina in a war over the disputed Falkland/Malvinas Islands in the South Atlantic. In the Gulf War of 1991, Britain deployed a full armored division in the UN-sanctioned force arrayed against Iraq's Saddam Hussein. Under Blair's leadership, Britain was the sole participant alongside the United States in the aerial bombardment of Iraq in December 1998. In 1999, the United Kingdom strongly backed NATO's Kosovo campaign and pressed for ground troops. Indeed, the Kosovo campaign and Blair's "doctrine of international community," which the prime minister rolled out in a major speech in Chicago on the eve of NATO's fiftieth anniversary in 1999, assumed an important role in

Blair's justification for the war in Iraq.[31] According to Blair, global interdependence rendered isolationism obsolete and inspired a commitment to a new ethical dimension in foreign policy. Throughout the war in Iraq and its bloody aftermath, Blair has persistently sought to characterize Iraq as an extension of Kosovo, an effort to liberate Muslims from brutal dictatorships, whether Serbia's Milosevic or Iraq's Saddam Hussein.

Until Blair's decision to support the American plan to shift the venue of the war on terror from Afghanistan to Iraq, the use of the military in international conflicts generated little opposition. Indeed, even in the case of the 2003 war in Iraq, the role of the military (as distinct from the decision to go to war) has generated relatively little controversy. Allegations of mistreatment raised far fewer questions than those directed at the United States for its abuse of prisoners at Abu Ghraib. In addition, UK forces are widely credited with operations in and around Basra that have been as culturally sensitive and effective as could be expected under very difficult circumstances.

As for the police, which traditionally operate as independent local forces throughout the country, the period since the 1980s has witnessed growth in government control, centralization, and level of political use. During the coal miners' strike of 1984–1985, the police operated to an unprecedented, and perhaps unlawful, degree as a national force coordinated through Scotland Yard (London police headquarters). Police menaced strikers and hindered miners from participating in strike support activities. This partisan use of the police in an industrial dispute flew in the face of constitutional traditions and offended some police officers and officials. During the 1990s, concerns about police conduct focused on police-community relations, including race relations, corruption, and the interrogation and treatment of people held in custody. In particular, widespread criticism of the police for mishandling their investigation into the brutal 1993 racist killing of Stephen Lawrence in South London resulted in a scathing report by a commission of inquiry in 1999.

The Judiciary

In Britain, the principle of parliamentary sovereignty has limited the role of the judiciary. Courts have no power to judge the constitutionality of legislative acts (judicial review). They can only determine whether policy directives or administrative acts violate common law or an act of Parliament. Hence, the British judiciary is generally less politicized and influential than its U.S. counterpart.

Jurists, however, have participated in the wider political debate outside court, as when they have headed royal commissions on the conduct of industrial relations, the struggle in Northern Ireland, and riots in Britain's inner cities. Some observers of British politics are concerned that governments have used judges in these ways to secure partisan ends, deflect criticism, and weaken the tradition of parliamentary scrutiny of government policy. Nevertheless, Sir Richard Scott's harsh report on his investigation into Britain's sales of military equipment to Iraq in the 1980s, for example, indicates that inquiries led by judges with a streak of independence can prove highly embarrassing to the government and raise important issues for public debate. The intensely watched inquiry conducted by Lord Hutton, a senior jurist, into the death of David Kelly confirmed this important public role of judges in the United Kingdom, although the question of Hutton's independence became very controversial in light of a "verdict" that exonerated the prime minister.

Beyond the politicization of jurists through their role on commissions and public inquiries, potentially dramatic institutional changes in law and the administration of justice are under consideration. In June 2003, Blair announced the government's intention to abolish the office of Lord Chancellor and move the law lords (who hold the ultimate authority of appeal in British law) from the House of Lords to a new "supreme court." The constitutional reform bill, introduced in 2004, faced strong opposition in the Lords (where Labour does not hold a majority), and the prospects for ultimate passage remain clouded.

The European dimension has also significantly influenced law and the administration of justice. As a member of the EU, Britain is bound to abide by the European Court of Justice (ECJ), as it applies and develops law as an independent institution within the EU. For example, two decisions by the ECJ led to the enactment of the Sex Discrimination Act of 1986, since previous legislation did not provide the full guarantees of women's rights in employment mandated to all members by the EU's Equal Treatment Directive. Moreover, with the passage of the Human

Rights Act in 1998, Britain is required to comply with the European Convention on Human Rights (ECHR) as well as with the rulings of the European Court of Justice on Human Rights (ECJHR). This has far-reaching potential for advancing a "pluralistic human rights culture" in Britain and providing new ground rules in law for protecting privacy, freedom of religion, and a wider respect for human rights.[32] Perhaps an indication of its broad influence to come, the adoption of the ECHR forced Britain to curtail discrimination against gays in the military. The Human Rights Act has also provided the judiciary with a legal framework (which Parliament cannot rescind) for addressing specific concerns such as asylum.[33] In addition, the UK Parliament's Joint Committee on Human Rights now reviews all bills for their compatibility with the Human Rights Act, thus imposing an important filter on controversial legislation as well as reporting on positive steps to secure human rights—for example, through a bill prohibiting the physical punishment of children.[34]

Subnational Government

Since the United Kingdom is a state comprised of distinct nations (England, Scotland, Wales, and Northern Ireland), the distribution of powers involves two levels below the central government: national government and local (municipal) government. Because the British political framework has traditionally been unitary, not federal, no formal powers devolved to either the nation within the United Kingdom or to subnational (really subcentral or sub-UK) units as in the United States or Germany.

Although no powers have been constitutionally reserved to local governments, they historically had considerable autonomy in financial terms and discretion in implementing a host of social service and related policies. In the context of increased fiscal pressures that followed the 1973 oil crisis, the Labour government introduced the first check on the fiscal autonomy of local councils (elected local authorities). The Thatcher government tightened the fiscal constraints on local government. Finally, in 1986, the Thatcher government abolished the multicultural-oriented city government (the Greater London Council, GLC) under the leadership of Ken Livingstone, as well as several other metropolitan

councils. In 1989, the Thatcher government introduced a poll tax, an equal per capita levy for local finance, to replace the age-old system of local property taxes. This radical break with tradition, which shifted the burden of local taxes from property owners and businesses to individuals, and taxed rich and poor alike, was monumentally unpopular. The poll tax proved a tremendous political liability, made local politics a hot-button national issue, and helped lead to Thatcher's departure.

Although much of New Labour's agenda concerning subcentral government is focused primarily on the political role of nations within Britain, devolution within England is also part of the reform process. Regional Development Agencies (RDAs) were introduced throughout England in April 1999 as part of a decentralizing agenda, but perhaps even more to facilitate economic development at the regional level. Despite the fairly low-key profile of RDAs and their limited scope (they are unelected bodies with no statutory authority), they opened the door to popular mobilization in the long term for elected regional assemblies. Since 2002, the government's chief economic advisor has argued for a "new localism" to link local initiative and public policy coordinated through the No. 10 Delivery Unit.[35]

In addition, the Blair government placed changes in the governance of London on the fast track. The introduction of a directly elected mayor of London in May 2000 proved embarrassing to Blair, since the government's efforts to keep Livingstone out of the contest backfired and he won handily. Livingstone has introduced an expansive agenda to spur long-term sustainable growth and advance a policy agenda that emphasizes ethnic diversity and the enhanced representation and leadership of women in London public life. In addition, London's determined effort to reduce traffic congestion by levying per day per vehicle charges within a central London zone have won widespread admiration for one of England's most controversial political leaders.

The Policy-Making Process

Parliamentary sovereignty is the core constitutional principle of the British political system. However, when it comes to policy-making and policy implementation, the focus is not on Westminster (the legislative arena) but rather on Whitehall (the administrative center of UK government). In many countries, such as Japan, India, and Nigeria, personal connections and informal networks play a large role in policy-making and implementation. How different is the British system?

Unlike the U.S. system, in which policy-making is concentrated in congressional committees and subcommittees, Parliament has little direct participation in policy-making. Policy-making emerges primarily from within the executive. There, decision making is strongly influenced by policy communities—informal networks with extensive knowledge, access, and personal connections to those responsible for policy. In this private hothouse environment, civil servants, ministers, and members of the policy communities work through informal ties. A cooperative style develops as the ministry becomes an advocate for key players in its policy community and as civil servants come perhaps to overidentify the public good with the advancement of policy within their area of responsibility.

This cozy insider-only policy process has been challenged by the delegation of more and more authority to the EU. As one observer neatly summarized this development, "The result is a new kind of multilevel political system in which political power is shared between the EU, national and subnational levels, and decisions taken at one level shape outcomes at others."[36]

When it comes to policy-making, the consequences of the European dimension are profound. Both ministers and senior civil servants spend a great deal of time in EU policy deliberations and are constrained both directly and indirectly by the EU agenda and directives. Although still effectively in charge of many areas of domestic policy, more than 80 percent of the rules governing economic life in Britain are determined by the EU. Even when the United Kingdom has opted out, as in the case of the common currency, European influences are significant. Decisions by the Council of Finance Ministers and the European Central Bank shape British macroeconomic, monetary, and fiscal policies in significant ways. Nor are foreign and security policy, the classic exercises of national sovereignty, immune from EU influences, since multilevel governance has been extended to these spheres by the EU's Common Foreign and Security Policy. Little is certain about the processes of European integration. But if the history of UK-EU relations is a prologue to future developments, the increasing Europeanization of policy-making will be one of the most interesting and potentially transformative developments in British politics in the next decade.

Section ❹ Representation and Participation

As discussed in Section 3, parliamentary sovereignty is the core constitutional principle defining the role of the legislature and, in a sense, the whole system of British government. The executive or judiciary can set no act of Parliament aside, nor is any Parliament bound by the actions of any previous Parliament. Nevertheless, in practice, the control exerted by the House of Commons (or the Commons) is not unlimited. In this section we investigate the powers and role of Parliament, both Commons and Lords, as well as the party system, elections, and contemporary currents in British political culture, citizenship, and identity. We close by offering an analysis of surprising new directions in political participation and social protest.

The Legislature

Is Parliament still as sovereign in practice as it remains in constitutional tradition? Clearly, it is not as powerful as it once was. From roughly the 1830s to the 1880s, it collaborated in the formulation of policy, and members amended or rejected legislation on the floor of the House of Commons. Today, the Commons does not so much legislate as assent to government legislation, since (with rare exceptions) the governing party has a majority of the seats and requires no cross-party voting to pass bills. In addition, the balance of effective oversight of policy has shifted from the legislature to executive agencies. In this section we discuss, in turn, the legislative process, the House of

Commons, the House of Lords, and reforms and pressures for change.

The House of Commons

In constitutional terms, the House of Commons, the lower house of Parliament (with 646 seats at the time of the 2005 election), exercises the main legislative power in Britain. Along with the two unelected elements of Parliament, the Crown and the House of Lords, the Commons has three main functions: (1) to pass laws, (2) to provide finances for the state by authorizing taxation, and (3) to review and scrutinize public administration and government policy. (The elaborate path followed by prospective legislation is described in "Institutional Intricacies: The Legislative Process.")

In practical terms, the Commons has a limited legislative function; nevertheless, it serves a very important democratic function. It provides a highly visible arena for policy debate and the partisan collision of political worldviews. The high stakes and the flash of rhetorical skills bring drama to the historic chambers, but one crucial element of drama is nearly always missing: the outcome is seldom in doubt. The likelihood that the Commons will invoke its ultimate authority, to defeat a government, is very small. MPs from the governing party who consider rebelling against their leader (the prime minister) are understandably reluctant in a close and critical vote to force a general election, which would place their jobs in jeopardy. Only once since the defeat of Ramsay MacDonald's government in 1924 has a government been brought down by a defeat in the Commons (in 1979). Today, the balance of institutional power has shifted from Parliament to the governing party and the executive.

Institutional Intricacies: **The Legislative Process**

To become law, bills must be introduced in the House of Commons and the House of Lords, although approval by the latter is not required. The procedure for developing and adopting a public bill is quite complex. The ideas for prospective legislation may come from political parties, pressure groups, think tanks, the prime minister's policy unit, or government departments. Prospective legislation is then normally drafted by civil servants, circulated within Whitehall, approved by the cabinet, and then refined by one of some thirty lawyers in the office of Parliamentary Counsel.*

According to tradition, in the House of Commons the bill usually comes to floor three times (referred to as *readings*). The bill is formally read upon introduction (the *first reading*), printed, distributed, debated in general terms, and after an interval (from a single day to several weeks), given a *second reading*, followed by a vote. The bill is then usually sent for detailed review to a standing committee of between sixteen and fifty members chosen to reflect the overall party balance in the House. It is then subject to a report stage during which new amendments may be introduced. The *third reading* follows; normally, the bill is considered in final form (and voted on) without debate.

After the third reading, a bill passed in the House of Commons follows a parallel path in the House of Lords. There the bill is either accepted without change, amended, or rejected. According to custom, the House of Lords passes bills concerning taxation or budgetary matters without alteration, and can add technical and editorial amendments to other bills (which must be approved by the House of Commons) to add clarity in wording and precision in administration. After a bill has passed through all these stages, it is sent to the Crown for royal assent (approval by the queen or king, which is only a formality), after which it becomes law and is referred to as an Act of Parliament.

*See Dennis Kavanagh, *British Politics: Continuities and Change*, 3d ed. (Oxford: Oxford University Press, 1996), 282–288.

The House of Lords

The upper chamber of Parliament, the House of Lords (or Lords), is an unelected body that is comprised of hereditary peers (nobility of the rank of duke, marquis, earl, viscount, or baron), life peers (appointed by the Crown on the recommendation of the prime minister), and law lords (life peers appointed to assist the Lords in its judicial duties). The Lords also include the archbishops of Canterbury and York and two dozen senior bishops of the Church of England. There are roughly 1,200 members of the House of Lords, but there is no fixed number, and membership changes with the appointment of peers. Not surprisingly, the Conservatives have a considerable edge in the upper house, with just over one-half of peers; Labour runs a distant second at roughly one-sixth. About one-third are crossbenchers, or independents.

Traditionally, the House of Lords has also served as the final court of appeal for civil cases throughout Britain and for criminal cases in England, Wales, and Northern Ireland. This judicial role, performed by the law lords, drew international attention in 1998 and 1999 when a Spanish court attempted to extradite General Augusto Pinochet of Chile on charges of genocide, torture, and terrorism. As discussed in Section 5, if made into law, the constitutional reform bill, which was introduced in 2004, would transfer that function from the Lords to a new "supreme court."

In modern times, however, the Lords, which has the power to amend and delay legislation, has served mainly as a chamber of revision, providing expertise in redrafting legislation. Recently, for example, the House of Lords, which considered the Nationality, Immigration and Asylum Bill too harsh, battled the government for weeks and forced revisions before approving the legislation.

In 1999, the Blair government appointed a Royal Commission on the Reform of the House of Lords (the Wakeham commission) and in the same year introduced legislation to remove the right of hereditary lords to speak and vote. With the passage of House of Lords Act 1999, the number of hereditary peers was reduced to 92. In January 2000, the commission recommended a partly elected second chamber, enumerating alternative models. In February 2003, the Commons rejected seven options, ranging from a fully appointed chamber (Blair's preference) to an entirely elected one. The failure of a joint committee of MPs and peers to achieve consensus left reform plans in tatters. The government remains committed to the removal of hereditary peers and to an upper house that would be largely elected, but multiple divisions cloud the fate of reform legislation.

Reforms in Behavior and Structure

How significant are contemporary changes in the House? How far will they go to stem the tide in Parliament's much-heralded decline?

Behavioral Changes: Backbench Dissent. Since the 1970s, backbenchers (MPs of the governing party who have no governmental office and rank-and-file opposition members) have been markedly less deferential than in the past. A backbench rebellion against the Major government's EU policy took a toll on the prestige of the prime minister and weakened him considerably. Until the war in Iraq was on the horizon, Blair seemed less likely to face significant rebellion from Labour MPs, although divisions did occur—relatively early in his premiership, for example, over social welfare policy and the treatment of trade unions. The opening vignette in Section 1 described the rebellion Blair faced in January 2004 over the Education Bill. The defection of some one-third of Labour MPs on key votes in February and March 2003 authorizing the use of force in Iraq represents a far more historic rebellion. Looking ahead, it is likely that any vote to adopt the euro would inspire significant backbench dissent once more.

Structural Changes: Parliamentary Committees. In addition to the standing committees that routinely review bills during legislative proceedings, in 1979 the Commons revived and extended the number and "remit" (that is, responsibilities) of select committees. Select committees help Parliament exert control over the executive by examining specific policies or aspects of administration.

The most controversial select committees are watchdog committees that monitor the conduct of major departments and ministries. Select committees hold hearings, take written and oral testimony, and question senior civil servants and ministers. They then issue reports that often include strong policy recommendations at odds with government policy. As one side effect of the reform, the role of the civil service has been complicated. For the first time, civil servants have been required to testify in a manner that might damage their ministers, revealing culpability or flawed judgments. As discussed in Section 4, the powerful norms of civil service secrecy have been compromised and the relationship with ministers disturbed. On balance, the committees have been extremely energetic, but not very powerful.

Political Parties and the Party System

Like the term *parliamentary sovereignty,* which conceals the reduced role of Parliament in legislation and the unmaking of governments, the term *two-party system,* which is commonly used to describe the British party system, is somewhat deceiving. It is true that since 1945, only leaders of the Labour or Conservative parties have served as prime ministers. Also, from 1945 through 2001, the Conservative and Labour parties have each won eight general elections, with 2005 tipping the lead to Labour. It is also true that throughout the postwar period, these two parties have routinely divided at least 85 percent of the seats in the House of Commons. But since the 1980s center parties have assumed a high profile in British electoral politics, with the Liberal Democrats (Lib Dems) emerging as an important alternative to Conservative and Labour—or perhaps a coalition partner with Labour in the not too distant future. In addition, Britain has several national parties, such as the Scottish National Party (SNP) in Scotland or the Plaid Cymru in Wales as well as a roster of parties competing in Northern Ireland. (These parties are described below under "Trends in Electoral Behavior.")

The Labour Party

As one of the few European parties with origins outside electoral politics, the Labour Party was launched by trade union representatives and socialist societies in the last decade of the nineteenth century and formally took its name in 1906. But it would be decades before the Labour Party became a contender for government leadership. Its landslide 1945 victory promoted the party to major player status. At the same time, Labour began moderating its ideological appeal and broadening its electoral base by adopting the collectivist consensus

described in Section 1. In the 1950s and early 1960s, those not engaged in manual labor voted Conservative three times more commonly than they did Labour; more than two out of three manual workers, by contrast, voted Labour. During this period, Britain conformed to one classic pattern of a Western European party system: a two-class/two-party system.

The period since the mid-1970s has been marked by significant changes in the party system and a growing disaffection with even the moderate social democracy associated with the Keynesian welfare state and Labourism. The party suffered from divisions between its trade unionist and parliamentary elements, constitutional wrangling over the power of trade unions to determine party policy at annual conferences, and disputes over how the leader would be selected. Divisions spilled over into foreign policy issues as well. On defense issues, there was a strong pacifist and an even stronger antinuclear sentiment within the party. Support for unilateral nuclear disarmament (the reduction and elimination of nuclear weapons systems with or without comparable developments on the Soviet side) was a decisive break with the national consensus on security policy and contributed to the party's losses in 1983 and 1987. Unilateralism was then scrapped.

The 1980s and 1990s witnessed a period of relative harmony within the party, with moderate trade union and parliamentary leadership agreeing on major policy issues. Labour has become a moderate left-of-center party in which ideology takes a backseat to performance and electoral mobilization, although divisions over the war in Iraq have inspired some soul searching about what values the party represents.

The Conservative Party

The pragmatism, flexibility, and organizational capabilities of the Conservative Party, a party that dates back to the eighteenth century, have made it one of the most successful and, at times, innovative center-right parties in Europe. Although it has fallen on hard times in recent years, it would be unwise to underestimate its potential as both an opposition and a governing party.

Although the association of the Conservative Party with the economic and social elite is unmistakable, it is also true that it was the Conservative government of Prime Minister Benjamin Disraeli (1874–1880) that served as midwife to the birth of the modern welfare state in Britain. The creation of a "long-lasting alliance between an upper-class leadership and a lower-class following" made the Conservative Party a formidable player in British politics.[37] Throughout the postwar period, it has also routinely (with some exceptions) provided the Tories, as Conservatives are colloquially called, with electoral support from about one-third or more of the manual working class.

Contemporary analysis of the Conservative Party must emphasize the cost to the party of its internal divisions over Britain's role in the EU. Wrangling among the Conservatives over Europe lead to Thatcher's demise as leader and weakened Major throughout his years as prime minister. The bitter leadership contest that followed Major's resignation after the 1997 defeat only reinforced the impression of a party in turmoil; subsequent rapid departures of party leaders after electoral defeat in 2001 as well as the forced resignation of the leader in 2003 lent an aura of failure and self-doubt to the Conservatives.

Once the combative, experienced, and highly regarded Michael Howard—who had served in the cabinets of both Margaret Thatcher and John Major—assumed the party leadership in 2003, the Conservatives seemed revitalized. But it was not easy for Howard to translate his assured performances from the front bench in Parliament into popular support. Although Howard pounded Blair on the failures of intelligence in the run-up to the war in Iraq and his handling of the David Kelly affair, Conservatives gave the prime minister far less trouble on Iraq than did members of the Labour Party itself. Nor could he make much headway against New Labour on central social and economic policy concerns—and thus despite an energetic campaign, one which will likely be remembered for its xenophobic edge, Howard succumbed to the same fate as his recent predecessors: electoral defeat followed by a quick resignation as party leader.

Liberal Democrats

Since the 1980s, a changing roster of centrist parties has posed a potentially significant threat to the two-party dominance of Conservative and Labour. Through the 1970s, the Liberal Party, a governing party in the pre–World War I period and thereafter the traditional centrist third party in Britain, was the only centrist challenger to the Labour and Conservative parties. In 1981, the Social Democratic Party (SDP) formed out of a split within the Labour Party. In the 1983 election, the Alliance (an electoral arrangement of the Liberals and the SDP) gained a quarter of the vote. The strength of centrist parties in the mid-1980s led to expectations of a possible Alliance-led government (which did not occur). After the Conservative victory in 1987, the Liberal Party and most of the SDP merged to form the Social and Liberal Democratic Party (now called the Liberal Democrats or Lib Dems). Especially against the backdrop of an ineffectual Tory opposition to New Labour, the Lib Dems have become a major political player.

Their success in the 2001 general election—the party increased its vote tally by nearly one-fifth and won fifty-two seats, the most since 1929—positioned the party as a potentially powerful center-left critic of New Labour. That said, Labour has not made it easy for them. As the Blair government began to spend massively to improve education and health care, it narrowed the range of policy issues on which the Liberal Democrats could take on New Labour. Although Charles Kennedy, party leader since 1999 and a highly regarded figure in British politics, won the political gamble in spring 2003 by opposing the war in Iraq, challenging the weapons of mass destruction (WMD) claim, and even attending the huge antiwar rally in February, it has not been easy for him—or the party—to take electoral advantage of Blair's political weakness.

Elections

British elections are exclusively for legislative posts. The prime minister is not elected as prime minister but as an MP from a single constituency (electoral district), averaging about 65,000 registered voters. Parliament has a maximum life of five years, with no fixed term. General elections are held after the Crown, at the request of the prime minister, has dissolved Parliament. Although Blair has in effect set a precedent of elections with four-year intervals, the ability to control the timing of elections is a tremendous political asset for the prime minister. This contrasts sharply with a presidential system, characteristic of the

United States, with direct election of the chief executive and a fixed term of office.

The Electoral System

Election for representatives in the Commons (who are called members of Parliament, or MPs) is by a "first-past-the-post" (or winner-take-all) principle in each constituency. In this single member plurality system, the candidate who receives the most votes is

elected. There is no requirement of a majority and no element of proportional representation (a system in which each party is given a percentage of seats in a representative assembly roughly comparable to its percentage of the popular vote). Table 2 shows the results of the general elections from 1945 to 2005.

This winner-take-all electoral system tends to exaggerate the size of the victory of the largest party and to reduce the influence of regionally dispersed lesser parties. Thus, in 2005, with 35.2 percent of the

Table 2

British General Elections, 1945–2005

		Percentage of Popular Vote						Seats in House of Commons					
	Turnout	Conser-vative	Labour	Liberal[a]	National Parties[b]	Other	Swing[c]	Conser-vative	Labour	Liberal[a]	National Parties[b]	Other	Government Majority
1945	72.7	39.8	48.3	9.1	0.2	2.5	−12.2	213	393	12	0	22	146
1950	84.0	43.5	46.1	9.1	0.1	1.2	+3.0	299	315	9	0	2	0.5
1951	82.5	48.0	48.8	2.5	0.1	0.6	+0.9	321	295	6	0	3	17
1955	76.7	49.7	46.4	2.7	0.2	0.9	+2.1	345	277	6	0	?	60
1959	78.8	49.4	43.8	5.9	0.4	0.6	+1.2	365	258	6	0	1	100
1964	77.1	43.4	44.1	11.2	0.5	0.8	−3.2	304	317	9	0	0	4
1970	72.0	46.4	43.0	7.5	1.3	1.8	+4.7	330	288	6	1	5	30
Feb. 1974	78.7	37.8	37.1	19.3	2.6	3.2	−1.4	297	301	14	9	14	−34[d]
Oct. 1974	72.8	35.8	39.2	18.3	3.5	3.2	−2.1	277	319	13	14	12	3
1979	76.0	43.9	37.0	13.8	2.0	3.3	+5.2	339	269	11	4	12	43
1983	72.7	42.4	27.6	25.4	1.5	3.1	+4.0	397	209	23	4	17	144
1987	75.3	42.3	30.8	22.6	1.7	2.6	−1.7	376	229	22	6	17	102
1992	77.7	41.9	34.4	17.8	2.3	3.5	−2.0	336	271	20	7	17	21
1997	71.4	30.7	43.2	16.8	2.6	6.7	−10.0	165	419	46	10	19	179
2001	59.4	31.7	40.7	18.3	2.5	6.8	+1.8	166	413	52	9	19	167
2005	61.5	32.3	35.2	22.1	2.1	8.4	+3.0	197	355	62	9	22	65[e]

[a]Liberal Party, 1945–1979; Liberal/Social Democrat Alliance, 1983–1987; Liberal Democratic Party, 1992–2005.

[b]Combined vote of Scottish National Party (SNP) and Welsh National Party (Plaid Cymru).

[c]"Swing" compares the results of each election with the results of the previous election. It is calculated as the average of the winning major party's percentage point increase in its share of the vote and the losing major party's decrease in its percentage point share of the vote. In the table, a positive sign denotes a swing to the Conservatives, a negative sign a swing to Labour.

[d]Following the February 1974 election, the Labour Party was thirty-four seats short of having an overall majority. It formed a minority government until it obtained a majority in the October 1974 election.

[e]Due to the death of a candidate in one constituency, only 645 parliamentary seats were contested in the May 2005 general election, with one additional seat to be filled through a by-election.

Source: Anthony King, ed., *New Labour Triumphs: Britain at the Polls* (Chatham, N.J.: Chatham House, 1998), p. 249. Copyright © 1998 by Chatham House. Reprinted by permission. For 2001 results, http://news.bbc.co.uk/hi/english/static/vote2001/results_constituencies/uk_breakdown/uk_full.stm. For 2005 results, http://news.bbc.co.uk/1/hi/uk_politics/vote_2005/constituencies/default.stm.

popular vote, Labour won 355 seats. With 22.1 percent of the vote, the Liberal Democrats won only 62 seats. Thus, the Liberal Democrats achieved a share of the vote that was approximately two-thirds of that achieved by Labour, but won less than one-fifth of the seats won by Labour. Such are the benefits of the electoral system to the victor (as well as the second major party).

With a fairly stable two-and-a-half party system (Conservative, Labour, and Liberal Democrat), the British electoral system tends toward a stable single-party government. However, the electoral system raises questions about representation and fairness. The system reduces the competitiveness of smaller parties with diffuse pockets of support. In addition, the party and electoral systems have contributed to the creation of a Parliament that has been a bastion of white men. The 1997 election represented a breakthrough for women: the number of women MPs nearly doubled to 120 (18.2 percent). The 2001 election saw the number of women MPs decline to 118 (17.9 percent). But a record 128 women were elected in 2005 (19.8 percent). As a result of using women-only shortlists for the selection of candidates in many winnable seats, Labour sent far more women (94) to Parliament than any other party.

In 1992, 6 ethnic minority candidates were elected, up from 4 in 1987, the first time since before World War II that Parliament included minority members. The number of ethnic minority (black and Asian) MPs rose in 1997 to 9 (1.4 percent), to 12 in 2001 (1.8 percent), and to 15 in 2005 (2.3 percent). Despite the general trend of increased representation of women and minorities, they remain substantially underrepresented in Parliament.

Trends in Electoral Behavior

Recent general elections have deepened geographic and regional fragmentation on the political map. British political scientist Ivor Crewe has referred to the emergence of two two-party systems: (1) competition between the Conservative and Labour parties dominates contests in English urban and northern seats, and (2) Conservative-center party competition dominates England's rural and southern seats.[38] In addition, a third two-party competition may be observed in Scotland, where competition between Labour and the Scottish National Party dominates.

The national parties have challenged two-party dominance since the 1970s. The Scottish National Party (SNP) was founded in 1934 and its Welsh counterpart, the Plaid Cymru, in 1925. Coming in a distant second to Labour in Scotland in 1997, the SNP won 21.6 percent of the vote and six seats. In 2001, support for the SNP declined by 2 percent, and the party lost one of its seats. The 2005 election showed some interesting results in Scotland. Labour lost five seats and the SNP gained 2 seats (for a total of 6). But the Lib Dems overtook the SNP's share of the vote. Both electoral and polling data indicate that Scottish voters are more inclined to support the SNP for elections to the Scottish parliament than to Westminster and that devolution may have stemmed the rising tide of nationalism.[39] In both 1997 and 2001, the Plaid Cymru won four seats where Welsh is still spoken widely. In 2005, after an absence of eight years, three Conservative MPs were elected in Wales, as the Plaid Cymru lost one seat.

How can we come to terms with the May 2005 election? All three major parties could claim some kind of victory, but also had to come to terms with elements of failure. Blair secured an historic third term with a cautious campaign, riding a strong economy and improvements in education and health care—and recurrent images of Gordon Brown by his side—to victory. But the election nevertheless left Blair humbled, his majority slashed, his support often grudging. New Labour won by putting off tough decisions—on pension reform, public spending, climate change, Europe, and a timetable for the withdrawal of British troops from Iraq. They won, too, by locking in the middle of the electoral sentiment. They are perfectly positioned: slightly center-right on security and immigration; slightly center-left on the economy and social policy.

Hence, the other parties couldn't lay a glove on Blair on the core issues that drive domestic politics. With little to say about the government's solid economic record or about the war in Iraq (which they supported, whatever criticisms they might muster about Blair's credibility), the Conservatives played the race card. As *The Economist* put it, their campaign was an "unseemly scramble for the anti-immigrant vote." The Tories could take solace in the fact that they had a net gain of 31 seats, but Michael Howard's hasty departure made it obvious that the campaign was a failure.

One of the most significant features of the 2005 election, an element of continuity with 2001, was the growing importance of the Liberal Democrats. They enjoyed a net gain of 10 seats and, perhaps more importantly, their share of the popular vote rose to an impressive 22 percent. On the down side, like Howard, Kennedy could not chip away at Labour's dominant position on the core economic and social policies. But he benefited from a consistent and articulate opposition to the war in Iraq, which paid dividends especially in constituencies with a strong presence of students or Muslims. With a Labour majority down to 67, a lot of backbench opposition to the prime minister within Labour ranks, and the Conservatives left with little to offer, Kennedy could look forward to the role of de facto leader of the opposition. And he could dream of a scenario full of delight for the Lib Dems—a diminished Labour party needing a coalition partner when the next election rolled around.

Political Culture, Citizenship, and Identity

In their classic study of the ideals and values that shape political behavior, political scientists Gabriel Almond and Sidney Verba wrote that the civic (or political) culture in Britain was characterized by trust, deference to authority and competence, pragmatism, and the balance between acceptance of the rules of the game and disagreement over specific issues.[40] Viewed retrospectively, the 1970s appear as a crucial turning point in British political culture and group identities.

During the 1970s, the long years of economic decline culminated in economic reversals in the standard of living for many Britons. Also for many, the historic bonds of occupational and social class grew weaker. Union membership declined with the continued transfer of jobs away from the traditional manufacturing sectors. More damaging, unions lost popular support as they appeared to bully society, act undemocratically, and neglect the needs of an increasingly female and minority work force. At the same time, a growing number of conservative think tanks and the powerful voice of mass-circulation newspapers, which are overwhelmingly conservative, worked hard to erode the fundamental beliefs of the Keynesian welfare state. New social movements (NSMs), such as feminism, antinuclear activism, and environmentalism, challenged basic tenets of British political culture. Identities based on race and ethnicity, gender, and sexual orientation gained significance. Thus, a combination of economic strains, ideological

assaults, and social dislocations helped foster political fragmentation and, at the same time, inspired a shift to the right in values and policy agendas.

Thatcher's ascent reflected these changes in political culture, identities, and values. It also put the full resources of the state and a bold and determined prime minister behind a sweeping agenda for change. As a leading British scholar put it, "Thatcher's objective was nothing less than a cultural revolution."[41] Although most observers agree that Thatcher fell considerably short of that aim, Thatcherism cut deep. It touched the cultural recesses of British society, recast political values, and redefined national identity.

To the extent that the Thatcherite worldview took hold (and the record is mixed), its new language and ethos helped transform the common sense of politics and redefined the political community. Monetarism (however modified) and the appeal to an enterprise culture of competitive market logic and entrepreneurial values fostered individualism and competition—winners and losers. It rejected collectivism, the redistribution of resources from rich to poor, and state responsibility for full employment. Thatcherism considered individual property rights more important than the social rights claimed by all citizens in the welfare state. Thus Thatcherism set the stage in cultural terms for the New Labour consolidation of neoliberalism and the core political-cultural orientation in Britain.

Social Class

One of the key changes in political culture in Britain in the last quarter-century has been the weakening of bonds grounded in the experience of labor. During the Thatcher era, the traditional values of "an honest day's work for an honest day's pay" and solidarity among coworkers in industrial disputes were characterized as "rigidities" that reduced productivity and competitiveness. New Labour has persisted in the negative characterization of social class as an impediment to competitiveness.

As many have noted, being "tough on the unions" is a core premise of New Labour, and this has contributed to a fundamental erosion of the ability of working people in the United Kingdom to improve their lot through collective bargaining or to exert influence over public policy through the political muscle of the trade union movement. Class still matters in the United Kingdom, but not in the dominating way that it did in the nineteenth century or in the collectivist era. Importantly, it no longer explains more than about 2 percent of voting behavior.

The sources and relative strength of diverse group attachments have shifted in Britain in recent decades under the combined pressures of decolonization, which created a multiethnic Britain, and a fragmentation of the experiences of work, which challenges a simple unitary model of class interest. National identity has become especially complicated in the United Kingdom. At the same time, gender politics has emerged as a hot-button issue.

Citizenship and National Identity

Questions about fragmented sovereignty within the context of the EU, the commingled histories of four nations (England, Scotland, Wales, and Ireland/Northern Ireland), and the interplay of race and nationality in postcolonial Britain have created doubts about British identity that run deep. As ethnicity, intra-UK territorial attachments, and the processes of Europeanization and globalization complicate national identity, it becomes increasingly difficult for UK residents automatically to imagine themselves Britons, constituting a resonant national community.

Thus, the British political community fragmented into smaller communities of class, nation, region, and ethnicity that existed side by side but not necessarily in amiable proximity. Can New Labour recreate a more cohesive political culture and foster a more inclusive sense of British identity? Unlike Thatcher, Blair is a conciliator, and he has worked hard to revitalize a sense of community in Britain and to extend his agenda to the socially excluded. But the results are mixed, with every effort to eradicate an emerging underclass, it seems, offset by the divisive aftereffects of 9/11 and fingers pointed at ethnic minorities, immigrants, and asylum seekers.

Ethnicity

Britain is a country of tremendous ethnic diversity. Beyond the numbers—nearly 8 percent of the people who live in Britain are of African, African-Caribbean, or Asian descent—there is the growing reality of life in a multiethnic society. The authors of a recent commission report on multiethnic Britain explained: "Many communities overlap; all affect and are affected by others. More and more people have multiple identities—they are Welsh Europeans, Pakistani Yorkshirewomen, Glaswegian Muslims, English Jews and black British. Many enjoy this complexity but also experience conflicting loyalties."[42]

While there are many success stories, ethnic minority communities have experienced police insensitivity, problems in access to the best public housing, hate crimes, and accusations that they are not truly British if they do not root for Britain's cricket team. In addition, harsh criticism directed at immigrants and asylum seekers, coming as it does in the wake of intense scrutiny of the Muslim community since September 11, contributes to the alienation of the ethnic minority community, particularly sections of the Muslim citizenry. And yet, in the aftermath of the attack on the World Trade Center and the Pentagon, public debate included a range of articulate, young, and confident Muslims from a variety of perspectives, and Faz Hakim, chief race relations adviser to the prime minister, played a visible public insider role. It is true that ordinary law-abiding Muslims—or people perceived to be Muslims—have experienced intensified mistrust and intimidation since the terror attacks by British Muslims in London in July 2005. But it is equally true that Muslim university graduates are assuming leading roles in the professions, while there are more than 160 Muslim elected city councilors, and British society has become increasingly sensitive to Muslim concerns.[43]

Gender

Historically, the issues women care about most—child care, the treatment of part-time workers, domestic violence, equal pay, and support for family caregivers—have not topped the list of policy agendas of any political party in Britain. Has New Labour significantly changed the equation?

It is probably fair to say, on balance, that Labour does well among women voters less because of any specific policies and more because it has made the effort to listen to concerns that women voice. Labour stalwarts would insist that they have addressed key concerns that women (and men) share concerning health care, crime, and education. They would point with pride to the policy directions spurred by the Social Exclusion and Women's units; to the implementation of a national child-care strategy; to policies intended to help women to balance work and family commitments; and to the creation of women-only shortlists in 2005 for candidates to compete in safe Labour constituencies.

As a result, New Labour has obliterated the old gender gap in which women favored the Conservatives and has begun to establish a new pro-Labour women's vote, which may be particularly significant, for its ability to mobilize young women (and more than a few young men, too). These developments are discussed in detail in "Current Challenges: Gender and Generation Gaps and Trends."

Interests, Social Movements, and Protest

In recent years, partly in response to globalization, political protest has been on the rise in Britain. As protesters demand more accountability and transparency in the operations of powerful international trade and development agencies, London became the site of protests timed to correspond with the Seattle meeting of the World Trade Organization (WTO), which generated some 100,000 protesters in November 1999.

In addition, since the mid-1990s, the level and intensity of environmental activism really took off with the growing attention to genetically modified (GM) crops in the late 1990s. A newly radicalized movement, worried that long-term consumption of GM food might be harmful and that once let loose, GM crops—referred to as "Frankenstein food"— might cross-pollinate with "normal" plants, captured the popular imagination. Opinion polls indicated that nearly 75 percent of the population did not want GM crops in the United Kingdom, and in November 1999, the government announced a ban on commercially grown GM crops in Britain.

In a movement that galvanized the country and raised critical questions about Blair's leadership,

massive demonstrations that cut across constituencies and enjoyed huge popular support erupted in September 2000 to protest high fuel prices. A very successful and well-coordinated week-long protest stalled fuel delivery throughout the country, forced 90 percent of the petrol stations to run out of unleaded gasoline, and required the Queen, on the advice of the prime minister, to declare a state of emergency. By the time the blockades came down, opinion polls for the first time in eight years showed the Conservatives for the moment surging past Labour. In fact, polling data indicates that Blair's popularity has never recovered from the bump it took over fuel prices.[44]

A quite different kind of activism spread to the countryside among a population not usually known for political protest. Farmers who had been badly hurt by the BSE (bovine spongiform encephalopathy, more popularly known as "mad cow disease") crisis and other rural populations concerned about the perceived urban bias of the Labour government launched massive protests.[45] As the banning and licensing of fox hunting roiled Parliament, the Countryside Alliance, which represents country dwellers who see restrictions on fox hunting as emblematic of domineering urban interests, held mass demonstrations in an effort to block restrictive legislation. Even after a law banning the hunt went into effect in 2005, they kept up the heat with legal challenges.

On the far more significant matter of war in Iraq, a series of antiwar rallies were held in London. In September 2002, a huge protest rally was organized in London, led by the Stop the War Coalition and the Muslim Association of Britain. It was one of Europe's biggest antiwar rallies. Another antiwar rally in mid-February 2003 challenged Blair's stand on Iraq with at least 750,000 demonstrators.

Both within the United Kingdom and among observers of British politics and society, many still endorse the view that British culture is characterized by pragmatism, trust, and deference to authority. This may be true, but the persistence and mobilizing potential of a wide range of social movements suggest that quite powerful political subcurrents persist in Britain, posing significant challenges for British government.

Current Challenges: *Gender and Generation Gaps and Trends*

The issue of a gender gap in voting behavior has long been a mainstay of British electoral studies. From 1945 to 1992, women were more likely than men to vote Conservative. In addition, since 1964 a gender-generation gap has become well established and was very clear in the 1992 election. Among younger voters (under thirty years old), women preferred Labour, while men voted strongly for the Conservatives, producing a fourteen-point gender gap favoring Labour; among older voters (over sixty-five years old), women were far more inclined to vote Conservative than were their male counterparts, creating a gender gap of eighteen points favoring the Conservatives.

The modest all-generation gender gap that favored the Tories in 1992 (6 percent) was closed in 1997 as a greater percentage of women shifted away from the Conservatives (11 percent) than did men (8 percent). As a result, women and men recorded an identical 44 percent tally for Labour. The gender-generation gap continued, however, with younger women more pro-Labour than younger men and the pattern reversing in the older generation. Moreover, one of the most striking features of the 1997 election was the generational dimension: the largest swing to Labour was among those in the age group eighteen to twenty-nine years (more than 18 percent), and among first-time voters; there was no swing to Labour among those over age sixty-five.*

After the 2001 election, analysis pointed to a generation gap in turnout. BBC exit polls revealed that young voters had the lowest turnout, most often saying the election "didn't matter." The home secretary worried aloud that youth had "switched off politics." Polling data tend to confirm the impression that there is a gender gap in the connection between citizens and mainstream politics, and that younger Britons are more divorced from politics than older ones. Three-quarters of young people aged fifteen to twenty-four have never met their local councilor, compared with just over half of those aged fifty-five or older. Also, older

citizens are more than twice as likely to say that they know the name of their local councilor (46 percent compared with 20 percent of fifteen- to twenty-four-year-olds).†

That said, the unprecedented participation of British youth in the massive antiwar protests in February and March 2003 tells a different story—one of young people with strong political views and an unexpected taste for political engagement. A BBC poll of schoolchildren in February 2003 reported that 80 percent opposed the war, while Britain as a whole was more evenly divided. As part of a coordinated day of antiwar protests, thousands of teenagers across the country walked out of school and congregated in city centers, while some five hundred protested at the Houses of Parliament. "What's shocking isn't their opposition but the fact they're doing something about it," noted one electronic journalist on a youth-oriented website. "Considering that most 18–25 year olds couldn't even be bothered to put a cross in a box at the last general election this is a pretty big thing."‡ It was a big enough thing that New Labour strategists were left to ponder the consequences, knowing that the mobilization of support among young people, which was already a cause for concern, was likely to become more difficult in the aftermath of the war in Iraq.

What are the gender and generational storylines in Blair's historic third electoral victory in May 2005? The most talked about theme regarding youth was their continued disaffection from electoral politics. According MORI, Britain's highly regarded political polling organization, only 37 percent of the possible 18–24-year-old voters turned out to vote in 2005 (down from 39 percent in 2001). But this is only one side of the generational story. The other side is that the "grey vote" rose. Voters 55 and older made up 35 percent of the electorate in 2005 (up 2 percent from 2001) and since 75 percent voted, they represented 42 percent of those casting ballots. As for women— they delivered a very big chunk of Blair's majority. While men split evenly between Conservatives

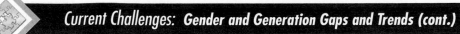

Current Challenges: *Gender and Generation Gaps and Trends (cont.)*

and Labour an identical 34 percent (and 23 percent for the Lib Dems), women swung decisively to Labour, giving them a 10 percent advantage over the Conservatives (32 percent to 22 percent).[§]

---

*Pippa Norris, *Electoral Change in Britain Since 1945* (Oxford: Blackwell, 1997), pp. 133–135; Pippa Norris, "A Gender-Generation Gap?" in Pippa Norris and Geoffrey Norris, eds., *Critical Elections: British Parties and Voters in Long-Term Perspective* (London: Sage, 1999).

[†]Market & Opinion Research International, "Many Councillors 'Divorced' from the Electorate," April 30, 2002, www.mori.com/polls/2002/greenissues.shtml.

[‡]David Floyd, "British Youth Oppose 'Bomber Blair,'" *Wiretap*, March 28, 2003; www.wiretapmag.org/story.html?StoryID=15505.

[§]Robert Worcester, "Women's Support Give Blair the Edge," *Guardian Unlimited*, May 8, 2005, http://politics.guardian.co.uk/election/story/0,15803,1479238,00.html#article_continue.

Section ⑤ British Politics in Transition

In the fall of 1994, cease-fire declarations made by the Irish Republican Army (IRA) and the Protestant paramilitary organizations renewed hope for a peace settlement in Northern Ireland. Then, in a dramatic new development in early spring 1995, British prime minister John Major and Irish prime minister John Bruton jointly issued a framework agreement, inspiring mounting optimism about a political settlement. Although Major did what he could to secure public and parliamentary support, he lacked the necessary political capital to bring the historic initiative to fruition.

With his 1997 landslide victory, Tony Blair had political capital to spend, and he chose to invest a chunk of it on peace in Northern Ireland. Blair arranged to meet Gerry Adams, president of Sinn Fein, the party in Northern Ireland with close ties to the IRA—and shook his hand. He was the first prime minister to meet with a head of Sinn Fein since 1921. Blair later spoke of the "hand of history" on his shoulder.

Under deadline pressure imposed by Blair and the new Irish prime minister, Bertie Ahern, and thirty-three hours of around-the-clock talks, an agreement was reached on Good Friday 1998. It specified elections for a Northern Ireland assembly, in which Protestants and Catholics would share power, and the creation of a North-South Council to facilitate "all-Ireland" cooperation on matters such as economic development,

agriculture, transportation, and the environment. Both parts of Ireland voted yes in May 1998 in a referendum to approve the peace agreement. It appeared that a new era was dawning in Northern Ireland.

Handshake or not, devastating bombs have exploded from time to time in Northern Ireland since the agreement, and violent turf battles within and between each camp have created fear and repeated crises in the peace process. Insisting that Sinn Fein cabinet ministers be barred from discussion until the IRA disarmed, hardliners in the Protestant camp created a rash of challenges to David Trimble, the Ulster Unionist leader who remained committed to the success of the process. Sinn Fein, in turn, accused Trimble of sabotage and warned that the IRA would not be able to control its own dissidents if the power-sharing arrangements were unilaterally dismantled.

In October 2001, the IRA began disarming under the sponsorship of third-party diplomats, and yet violence rose despite cease-fires by paramilitary groups. In October 2002, home rule government was suspended, and British direct rule was reimposed. Since then, on numerous occasions, Tony Blair and his Irish Republic counterpart, Bertie Ahern, have pledged to redouble efforts to get Northern Ireland's faltering peace process back on track, but progress has not been easy.

In January 2005, hope for a settlement was dashed by the blockbuster announcement that linked the IRA to a $40 million bank robbery. In February, the brutal murder of Robert McCartney, a Sinn Fein supporter, by IRA members in a Belfast bar—who had accused him of looking inappropriately at one of their female companions—may have permanently shattered support for the IRA. McCartney's murder, the wall of silence the IRA imposed on some 70 witnesses, and the IRA's offer to kill the men responsible, have had significant political repercussions. Despite the May 2005 election, which ousted Unionist moderate David Trimble and strengthened the hands of the more radical parties (Sinn Fein and Democratic Unionist Party), the increasingly vocal popular demands for an end to sectarian violence may finally break the deadlock. By mid-2005, the IRA had exhausted its leverage, Gerry Adams seemed ready to press for their dissolution, and—despite denials—insiders spoke of a pending settlement or even a secret deal that is all but agreed upon.

The decades-long crisis in Northern Ireland confirms the important proposition that unresolved tensions in state formation shape political agendas for generations. Northern Ireland, however, is but one of a host of challenges facing Britain and New Labour as Tony Blair begins his third term under relentless pressure to yield power to Gordon Brown.

Political Challenges and Changing Agendas

As our democratic idea theme suggests, no democracy, however secure it may be, is a finished project. Even in Britain, with its centuries-old constitutional settlement and secure institutional framework, issues about democratic governance and citizens' participation remain unresolved.

Constitutional Reform

Questions about the role of the monarchy and the House of Lords have long been simmering on Britain's political agenda. "Why is the House of Commons not sovereign?" wondered one observer somewhat caustically. "Why does it have to share sovereignty with other, unelected institutions?"[46] In addition, the balance of power among constitutionally

critical institutions raises important questions about a democratic deficit at the heart of the Westminster model. Britain's executive, whose strength in relation to that of the legislature may be greater than in any other Western democracy, easily overpowers Parliament. Add to these concerns the prime minister's tendency to bypass the cabinet on crucial decisions and the bias in the electoral system that privileges the two dominant parties, and it seems appropriate to raise questions about the accountability of the British government to its citizens.

In fact, in the heady days after Blair's 1997 election victory, amidst talk of an expanding array of constitutional reforms, it was commonplace to suggest that constitutional reform might become New Labour's most enduring legacy. But the reform agenda has been sidetracked or subjected to powerful political crosscurrents—or administrative complexities—that have slowed or stalled agreement on key elements. For example, the Freedom of Information Act was passed in 2002, but a second stage of implementation began only in January 2005. It was also weakened by the extensive range of information it permitted ministers to withhold and by its limited provision for independent review of such ministerial decisions.[47] The Blair government has begun to implement far-reaching reforms of Parliament, including the removal of the right of hereditary peers to speak and vote in the House of Lords, and the redesign of the historic upper chamber, but as discussed in Section 4, the form of the new upper chamber has yet to take shape. In addition, the European Convention on Human Rights has been incorporated into UK law, and, more controversially, plans have been announced for the creation of a "supreme court," but strenuous opposition in both chambers has clouded the prospects for passage. New systems of proportional representation have been introduced for Welsh and Scottish elections, as well as for the European Parliament. But the potential use of proportional representation in UK general elections will come only from a Labour government in dire straights: if it is unable to control a majority in the next election without the support of the Lib Dems and the Lib Dems are able to wrest a commitment to proportional representation from Labour as a condition for backing Labour or forming a Labour–Lib Dem government. Such is political life in a country without an entrenched constitution!

Finally, the power-sharing initiatives in Northern Ireland (if the political deadlocks are ever broken) and arrangements among Westminster, the Welsh Assembly, and, most importantly, the Scottish Parliament represent basic modifications of UK constitutional principles. Devolution implies both an element of federalism and some compromise in the historic parliamentary sovereignty at the heart of the Westminster model. But the potentially unsettling consequences feared by some have not come to pass.

New Labour's constitutional reform agenda represents a breathtaking illustration of a core premise of our democratic idea theme: that even long-standing democracies face pressures to narrow the gap between government and citizens. At the same time, the relatively limited results and slowed pace of reforms are an important reminder that democratic changes are not easy to implement.

Identities in Flux

Although the relatively small scale of the ethnic minority community limits the political impact of the most divisive issues concerning collective identities, it is probably in this area that rigidities in the British political system challenge tenets of democracy and tolerance most severely. Given Britain's single-member, simple-plurality electoral system and no proportional representation, minority representation in Parliament is very low, and there are deep-seated social attitudes that no government can easily transform.

The issues of immigration, refugees, and asylum still inspire a fear of multiculturalism among white Britons and conjure up very negative and probably prejudiced reactions. In fall 2000, the report of the Commission on the Future of Multi-Ethnic Britain raised profound questions about tolerance, justice, and inclusion in contemporary UK society. In a powerful and controversial analysis, the report concluded that "the word 'British' will never do on its own. . . . Britishness as much as Englishness, has systematic, largely unspoken, racial connotations."[48]

Against the backdrop of intensified finger pointing directed at the Muslim community, the post–September 11 period has witnessed a hardening of government policy on asylum, refuge, and immigration. This controversial process culminated in the formal announcement in November 2003 that the Asylum Bill would force a heart-wrenching choice on failed asylum seekers: they must either "voluntarily" accept a paid-for return flight to the country from which they fled or see their children taken into government care.[49] By spring 2004, race, immigration, and asylum issues were even stealing headlines from the war in Iraq. Charges that there had been widespread fraud in the treatment of East European applications for immigration as well as efforts by the minister in charge of immigration and asylum, Beverly Hughes, to mislead Parliament led to her resignation. Official government data revealed record levels of hate crimes in England and Wales. After an episode in which British-born Muslims set fire to the Union Jack in London, debate raged about the validity of "separateness" among ethnic communities, and the chairman of the Commission for Racial Equality, Trevor Phillips, called for a return to "core British values" and the abandonment of the government's commitment to building a multicultural society. As Britain experienced increased ethnic tension, polls indicated widespread unease with ethnic diversity. By the start of the election campaign in April 2005, nearly one-quarter (23 percent) of the British people ranked immigration and asylum as the single most important issue facing the nation—nearly double the percentage who thought health care (13 percent) was the biggest issue. A strong majority thought that laws on immigration should be tougher (nine out of ten supporters of the Conservatives, but also six out of ten Labour supporters).[50]

How about other dimensions of collective identity? The situation is fluid. In political terms, the gender gap has tilted quite strongly toward Labour, as it has responded to concerns about women's employment, the disparate impact of social policy, the problems of balancing family and work responsibilities, and parliamentary representation. The electoral force of class identity has declined almost to the vanishing point in Britain. By Labour's second term, however, the country faced an upsurge in industrial action. Public sector workers such as local government staff and firefighters have led the unrest. A new generation of militant leaders in two railway unions, the postal workers' union, and the government and health workers' union has created new challenges for the government. Any downturn in the economy will likely intensify union militancy during Labour's third term.

The Challenges of Europe and the World

Tony Blair came to office determined to rescue Europe for Britain—to redress the problems caused by Thatcher's anti-Europe stance and to reposition the United Kingdom both as a major player in Europe and as a powerful interlocutor (respected in both camps) to build bridges, when necessary, between the United States and EU Europe. To advance this agenda, Blair enthusiastically supported initiatives for a common foreign and security policy and helped bring Europe into the war in Kosovo in accordance with Blair's doctrine of international community, which insisted on military interventions when necessary to prevent or contain humanitarian catastrophes, such as ethnic cleansing. As one lesson of Kosovo, Europe tried to come to terms with its reliance on America's military muscle and unrivaled wartime technological capacities. Hence, Blair worked with France and Germany to develop a more robust European military capability.

Yet the ambivalence of Britain toward Europe remains very strong. Britain remains on the outside looking in when it comes to the euro (it is one of but three of the fifteen members of the EU before enlargement on May 1, 2004, to remain outside the euro zone). On another European front, in April 2004, under merciless sniping from the Conservatives, and worried that his own declining political fortunes made parliamentary passage of a bill on the EU Constitution increasingly contentious, Blair suddenly—and with virtually no consultation—announced that the EU Constitution would also be put to a referendum.

As the French and Dutch votes approached, nearly everyone thought that Blair was hoping that another country might reject the constitution before any referendum in the UK, to minimize the wrath of EU stalwarts that would otherwise be directed at Britain, where defeat of the Constitution—should it ever come

to a vote—was a foregone conclusion. (Assent by each of the twenty-five member states was required.)

In the end, however, even the French and Dutch no votes on the Constitution in May–June 2005 did not make life easier for Blair. Both German Chancellor Gerhard Schröder and French President Jacques Chirac pinned as much blame as possible on Blair, if not directly for the defeat of the Constitution, then for Britain's insistence that agricultural subsidies and the UK's longstanding budgetary rebate be considered in tandem as part of a reform package to resolve the increasingly acrimonious budget wrangling.

Especially against the backdrop of Britain's break with Germany and France over the war in Iraq—and with the limited time remaining for him as prime minister—Blair is unlikely to realize his expectations that Britain could, under his leadership, assume a leading role in Europe, heal old wounds, and bridge the gap between Europe and the United States. That said, during the first year of his final premiership, Blair will have an unusual opportunity for EU and global leadership, as the UK assumes the rotating presidency of both the EU and the G8.

Together with Brown, Blair has an extremely ambitious agenda for far-reaching global commitments: to eliminate poverty and disease in Africa, to increase financial aid and narrow the development gap, and to make significant progress on climate change. They are also issues—as are his commitment to make progress toward peace in the Middle East and insistence on diplomacy, not force, in the showdown with Iran over nuclear weapons—that burnish his progressive credentials, reconnect Britain with key European allies, and are likely to place the United States and the UK in opposing camps. These are all legacy issues for Blair, with solid mainstream support in Britain, that present him with the opportunity—perhaps the last opportunity—to leave his mark on European and global affairs.

British Politics, Terrorism, and Britain's Relationship with the United States

In the immediate aftermath of the terror attacks on the United States, Blair's decisive support for President Bush struck a resonant cord in both countries and (despite some grumbling) boosted Britain's influence in Europe. But by the spring and summer of 2002,

Blair's stalwart alliance with Bush was looking more and more like a liability.

As Britons' instinctive post–September 11 support for America faded, many wondered whether Tony Blair had boxed himself into a corner by aligning himself too closely with George W. Bush—without knowing where the president's foreign policy initiatives might lead in the Middle East and Asia—and in a host of policy areas from trade policy to the conduct of the continuing campaign in Afghanistan, to global warming, to the International Criminal Court. Yet, throughout the diplomatic disputes in the run-up to war in early 2003, Blair persevered in his staunch support for Bush's decision to go to war—this despite Blair's strong preference for explicit Security Council authorization for the use of force and his strong preference that significant progress in resolving the Israeli-Palestinian dispute be made before any military intervention to topple the Saddam Hussein regime.

Nonetheless, despite his inability to achieve either of these preferences, Blair refused all advice (including advice from members of his cabinet as well as his chief of defense staff) to make support of the war conditional on achievement of these ends. Blair was convinced that the threats of weapons of mass destruction

(WMDs), Al Qaeda terrorism, and rogue states justified the invasion of Iraq and that Britain should and must support the United States in its leadership of a global war against terrorism. Despite initial denials by the prime minister, most Britons instinctively drew a connection between the war in Iraq and the bombs that exploded in London in July 2005. Britons who displayed enormous resolve in the face of terrorism were shaken by a set of troubling revelations—first, that the July 7th bombers were all British and, second, after a botched bombing attempt two weeks later, that London police had shot and killed an innocent man on a subway. Thus, the repercussions of Iraq continued.

As we know from the 2005 election, Blair's unconditional commitment to support America's war in Iraq has cost Blair and New Labour dearly in political terms, especially as the initial justifications for war lost credibility. In the years ahead, the experience of the war in Iraq may contribute to a constructive reconsideration of the "special relationship" between the United States and the United Kingdom. It will certainly loom large in any assessment of Blair's contribution to British politics and the legacy of New Labour.

Throughout the 2005 election campaign, it appeared as if the prime minister was running on the chancellor's coattails, relying on Brown's credibility, the strong economy, and improvements in health care and education to bring reluctant Labour and Lib Dem voters into the fold. With the election over, one question was on everyone's lips: "When do we get Brown?" *Source:* Steve Bell, Guardian Unlimited. http:// www. guardian.co.uk/cartoons/archive/stevebell/ 0,7371,33776400.html

British Politics in Comparative Perspective

Until the Asian financial crisis that began in 1997, it was an axiom of comparative politics that economic success required a style of economic governance that Britain lacks. Many argued that innovation and competitiveness in the new global economy required the strategic coordination of the economy by an interventionist state. Interestingly, however, the United Kingdom escaped the recession that plagued the rest of Europe for much of the 1990s. Britain is outperforming most major world economies and exhibits a good overall performance with low unemployment and inflation and with steady growth. Britain is not an economic paradise, but there is cause for continued optimism, notwithstanding persistent poverty, weak investment, problems with productivity, and trade imbalances. In many countries throughout the world, politicians are looking for an economic model that can sustain economic competitiveness while improving the plight of the socially excluded. Tony Blair's third way—a political orientation that hopes to transcend left and right in favor of practical and effective policies—will be carefully watched. If the third way can be sustained, and make the expected transition from Blair to Brown, it will be widely emulated.

Beyond the impressive size of Blair's victory, nothing about the May 1997 election was clearer than the unprecedented volatility of the electorate. In previous elections, commitment to party (partisan identification) and interests linked to occupation (class location) had largely determined the results. In 1997, attachments to party and class had far less influence.

Beginning with the historically low turnout, the 2001 election underscored, as one journalist put it, that "instinctive party support" based on class and partisan traditions has been replaced by "pick and choose" politics. The tendency of voters to behave as electoral shoppers lends a perpetual air of uncertainty to elections. It seems that Blair's success in transforming Labour into New Labour blunted the social basis of party identification. At the same time, the modernization agenda of New Labour resolutely emphasized fiscal responsibility over distributive politics. The 2005 election continued this trend. It saw a slight upswing in participation, with a turnout of 61.5 percent (up 2.1 percent from 2001)—but substantially below the postwar average of just over 76 percent.

Without the traditional constraints of partisan and class identities, citizens (whether as voters or as political activists) can shift allegiances with lightning speed. "What have you done for me lately?" becomes the litmus test for leaders and politicians. As the dictates of a post-9/11 war against terror, European integration, and globalization blur the distinction between governing the economy and the world of states, the scope of the "What have you done for me lately?" test may be expanding, and the ways to fail in the eyes of the electorate may be growing. It is clear that lately Blair has lost the trust of many Britons over his rationale for going to war in Iraq. Blair has also, as David Sanders argues, become a victim of his own (or was it Gordon Brown's?) success. The better the economy has performed, the less voters worried about the economy, and the less salient it became in the voters' decisions about which party to support.[51]

Clearly these are tough times for national governments to maintain popular support and achieve desirable goals. They are sufficiently demanding that on the day after Blair's third victory in a row—the first time this has ever been achieved by a Labour prime minister—he was routinely referred to as "humbled" or "chastised" and felt called upon to acknowledge that he'd gotten the message. Victory brought immediate calls for his resignation in favor of Brown—and a relentless guessing game about when he would depart and under what circumstances. In fact, Labour supporters, anticipating a decline in Britain's economic performance—due to credit bubbles, deficits, underinvestment, and the vulnerabilities of the global economy—were heard to mutter that this would have been a good election to lose! The world will be watching to see whether Blair stumbles and falls during his last years in office. Or can he depart on his terms, after a settlement in Northern Ireland, perhaps, or success in his global development initiatives? If not, many will conclude that these tough times just got tougher.

Key Terms

free trade

hegemonic power

laissez-faire

welfare state

special relationship

Westminster model

neoliberalism

macroeconomic policy

Keynesianism

monetarism

social security

gender gap

foreign direct investment

parliamentary sovereignty

parliamentary democracy

unitary state

fusion of powers

cabinet government

constitutional monarchy

quangos

Suggested Readings

Beer, Samuel H. *Britain Against Itself: The Political Contradictions of Collectivism*. New York: Norton, 1982.

Coates, David. *Prolonged Labour*. London: Palgrave/Macmillan, 2005.

Coates, David, and Krieger, Joel. *Blair's War*. Cambridge, UK, and Malden Mass.,: Polity Press, 2004.

Coates, David, and Lawler, Peter, eds. *New Labour in Power*. Manchester: Manchester University Press, 2000.

Cook, Robin. *The Point of Departure*. London: Simon & Schuster, 2003.

Cronin, James E. *New Labour's Pasts*. Harrow, UK: Pearson/Longman, 2004.

Dunleavy, Patrick, et al. *Developments in British Politics* 7. New York: Palgrave/Macmillan, 2003.

Gamble, Andrew. *Between Europe and America: The Future of British Politics*. London: Palgrave/Macmillan, 2003.

George, Bruce. *The British Labour Party and Defense*. New York: Praeger, 1991.

Giddens, Anthony. *The Third Way: The Renewal of Social Democracy*. Cambridge: Polity Press, 1998.

Gilroy, Paul. *"There Ain't No Black in the Union Jack": The Cultural Politics of Race and Nation*. Chicago: University of Chicago Press, 1991.

Hall, Stuart, and Jacques, Martin, eds. *The Politics of Thatcherism*. London: Lawrence and Wishart, 1983.

Hobsbawm, E. J. *Industry and Empire*. Harmondsworth, UK: Penguin/Pelican, 1983.

Howell, Chris. *Trade Unions and the State: The Construction of Industrial Relations Institutions in Britain, 1890–2000*. Princeton: Princeton University Press, 2005.

Kampfner, John. *Blair's Wars*. London: Free Press, 2003.

Kavenagh, Dennis, and Seldon, Anthony. *The Powers Behind the Prime Minister: The Hidden Influence of Number Ten*. London: Harper-Collins, 1999.

King, Anthony, ed. *Britain at the Polls, 2001*. New York and London: Chatham House, 2002.

Krieger, Joel. *Globalization and State Power*. New York: Pearson Longman, 2005.

Krieger, Joel. *British Politics in the Global Age. Can Social Democracy Survive?* New York: Oxford University Press, 1999.

Landes, David S. *The Unbound Prometheus: Technological Change and Industrial Development in Western Europe from 1750 to the Present*. Cambridge: Cambridge University Press, 1969.

Lewis, Philip. *Islamic Britain: Religion, Politics and Identity among British Muslims*. London and New York: I. B. Taurus, 2002.

Marsh, David, et al. *Postwar British Politics in Perspective*. Cambridge: Polity Press, 1999.

Marshall, Geoffrey. *Ministerial Responsibility*. Oxford: Oxford University Press, 1989.

Middlemas, Keith. *Politics in Industrial Society: The Experience of the British System Since 1911*. London: André Deutsch, 1979.

Modood, Tariq. *Multicultural Politics: Racism, Ethnicity, and Muslims in Britain*. Minneapolis: University of Minnesota Press, 2005.

Norris, Pippa. *Electoral Change in Britain Since 1945*. Oxford: Blackwell Publishers, 1997.

Parekh, Bhiku, et al., *The Future of Multi-Ethnic Britain: The Parekh Report*. London: Profile Books, 2000.

Riddell, Peter, *The Thatcher Decade*. Oxford: Basil Blackwell, 1989.

Särlvik, Bo, and Crewe, Ivor. *Decade of Dealignment: The Conservative Victory of 1979 and Electoral Trends in the 1970s*. Cambridge: Cambridge University Press, 1983.

Shaw, Eric. *The Labour Party Since 1945*. Oxford: Blackwell Publishers, 1996.

Thompson, E. P. *The Making of the English Working Class*. New York: Vintage, 1966.

Wright, Tony, ed. *The British Political Process*. London: Routledge, 2000.

Suggested Websites

Directgov – Portal to public service information from the UK government

www.direct.gov.uk

National Statistics Online—Home of official UK statistics

www.statistics.gov.uk

The UK Parliament
www.parliament.uk
The cabinet office
www.cabinet-office.gov.uk
The Scottish Parliament
www.scottish.parliament.uk
British Broadcasting Corporation (BBC)
www.bbc.co.uk
Market & Opinion Research International (MORI), Britain's leading political polling organization
www.mori.com

Endnotes

[1]Jeremy Black, *The Politics of Britain, 1688–1800* (Manchester: Manchester University Press, 1993), p. 6.

[2]E. J. Hobsbawm, *Industry and Empire* (Harmmondsworth, UK: Penguin/Pelican, 1983), pp. 29–31.

[3]See Duncan Fraser, "The Postwar Consensus: A Debate Not Long Enough?" *Parliamentary Affairs* 53, no. 2 (April 2000): 347–362.

[4]David Coates, *Prolonged Labour* (London: Palgrave, 2005), p. 172.

[5]Will Hutton, *The State We're In* (London: Jonathan Cape, 1995).

[6]This discussion of the tenets of the third way and the evaluation of its economic policy draws heavily on collaborative work with David Coates. See Joel Krieger and David Coates, "New Labour's Model for UK Competitiveness: Adrift in the Global Economy?"

[7]Andrew Gamble, "The British Economic Miracle: New Labour and the Economy," paper presented at the Conference on *Cool Britannia: Britain After Eight Years of Labour Government*, Montreal, Cerium, May 4–6, 2005.

[8]Ivor Crewe, "Labor Force Changes, Working Class Decline, and the Labour Vote: Social and Electoral Trends in Postwar Britain," in Frances Fox Piven, ed., *Labor Parties in Postindustrial Societies* (New York: Oxford University Press, 1992), p. 34. See also David Marsh and R. A. W. Rhodes, "Implementing Thatcherism: Policy Change in the 1980s," *Parliamentary Affairs* 45, no. 1 (January 1992): 34–37.

[9]Steven Fielding, "A New Politics?" in Patrick Dunleavy et al., eds., *Developments in British Politics* 6 (New York: St. Martin's Press, 2000), p. 2.

[10]National Statistics Online, "Low Income: Fewer Children in Poverty in Recent Years," March 31, 2004; www.statistics.gov.uk/cci/nugget_print.asp?ID=333. See also Adrian Sinfield, "UK Shows the Way on Child Poverty," *New Zealand Herald,* May 26, 2004; www.nzherald.co.nz/storydisplay.cfm?storyID=3568524&thesection=news&thesubsection=dialogue.

[11]National Statistics Online, "Population Size: 7.9% from a Minority Ethnic Group," February 13, 2003; www.statistics.gov.uk/cci/nugget.asp?id=273.

[12]Office of National Statistics Social Survey, *Living in Britain: Results from the 1995 General Household Survey* (London: The Stationery Office, 1997).

[13]Gail Lewis, "Black Women's Employment and the British Economy," in Winston James and Clive Harris, eds., *Inside Babylon: The Caribbean Diaspora in Britain* (London: Verso, 1993), pp. 73–96.

[14]National Statistics Online, "Low Income for 60% of Pakistanis/Bangladeshis," December 12, 2002; www.statistics.gov.uk/CCI/nugget.asp?ID=269&Pos=1&ColRank=2&Rank=384.

[15]"All White at the Top," *Guardian,* May 25, 2004; http://education.guardian.co.uk/egweekly/story/0,5500,1223478,00.html.

[16]Ibid.

[17]National Statistics Online, "Gender Pay Gap: Narrows slightly to record low,"; www.statistics.gov.uk/cci/nugget.asp?id=167.

[18]Jane Lewis, "The Pursuit of Welfare Ends and Market Means and the Case of Work/Family Reconciliation Policies," p. 10, paper presented at the Conference on *Cool Britannia: Britain After Eight Years of Labour Government*, Montreal, Cerium, May 4–6, 2005.

[19]Lewis, ibid.

[20]See Joel Krieger, *Globalization and State Power* (New York: Pearson Longman, 2005), p. 67.

[21]See Philip Norton, *The British Polity,* 3rd ed. (New York: Longman, 1994), p. 59, for a useful discussion of the sources of the British constitution.

[22]Stephen Haseler, "Britain's Ancien Régime," *Parliamentary Affairs* 40, no. 4 (October 1990): 415.

[23]See Philip Norton, "Parliament in Transition," in Robert Pyper and Lynton Robins, eds., *United Kingdom Governance* (New York: St. Martin's Press, 2000), pp. 82–106.

[24]S. E. Finer, *Five Constitutions* (Atlantic Highlands, N.J.: Humanities Press, 1979), p. 52.

[25]Bernard Crick, "Blair Should Beware the Boiling Up of Little Irritations," September 29, 2003; www.guardian.co.uk/comment/story/0,3604,1051720,00.html.

[26]Iain Byrne and Stuart Weir, "Democratic Audit: Executive Democracy in War and Peace," *Parliamentary Affairs* 57, no. 2 (April 2004): 455.

[27]See Kampfner, *Blair's Wars* (London: The Free Press, 2005), p. 294.

[28]Martin J. Smith, "The Core Executive and the Modernization of Central Government," in Patrick Dunleavy et al., eds., *Developments in British Politics* 7 (New York: Palgrave/Macmillan, 2003), p. 60.

[29]See Kevin Theakston, "Ministers and Civil Servants," in Pyper and Robins, eds., *United Kingdom Governance,* pp. 39–60.

[30]Nicholas Timmins, "Health Ministers Back Purge of Quangos," *Financial Times,* May 21, 2004.

[31]Tony Blair, "Doctrine of the International Community," speech to the Economic Club of Chicago, Hilton Hotel, Chicago, April 22, 1999. For a detailed discussion of the speech and its implications for the war in Iraq, see David Coates and Joel Krieger, *Blair's War* (Malden, Mass.: Polity Press, 2004), chap. 6.

[32]See Bhiku Parekh et al., *The Future of Multi-Ethnic Britain: The Parekh Report* (London: Profile Books, 2000), pp. 90–102.

[33]See Andrew Gamble, "Remaking the Constitution," in Patrick Dunleavy et al., eds., *Developments in British Politics 7* (New York: Palgrave/Macmillan, 2003), pp. 34–36.

[34]Sue Prince, "The Law and Politics: Upsetting the Judicial Apple-Cart," *Parliamentary Affairs* 57, no. 2 (2004): 288.

[35]Andrew Gray and Bill Jenkins, "Government and Administration: Too Much Checking, Not Enough Doing?" *Parliamentary Affairs* 57, no. 2 (2004): 274.

[36]Ibid., p. 48.

[37]Samuel H. Beer, *The British Political System* (New York: Random House, 1973), p. 157.

[38]Ivor Crewe, "Great Britain," in I. Crewe and D. Denver, eds., *Electoral Change in Western Democracies* (London: Croom Helm, 1985), p. 107.

[39]John Bartle, "Why Labour Won—Again," in Anthony King et al., eds., *Britain at the Polls, 2001* (New York: Chatham House, 2002), p. 171.

[40]See Gabriel A. Almond and Sidney Verba, *The Civic Culture: Political Attitudes and Democracy in Five Nations* (Princeton, N.J.: Princeton University Press, 1963); Almond and Verba, eds., *The Civic Culture Revisited* (Boston: Little, Brown, 1980); and Samuel H. Beer, *Britain Against Itself: The Political Contradictions of Collectivism* (New York: Norton, 1982), pp. 110–114.

[41]Ivor Crewe, "The Thatcher Legacy," in King et al., eds., *Britain at the Polls 1992,* p. 18.

[42]Bhiku Parekh et al., *The Future of Multi-Ethnic Britain: The Parekh Report* (London: Profile Books, 2000), p. 10.

[43]For an excellent treatment of the complex experiences of British Muslims, see Philip Lewis, *Islamic Britain* (London and New York: I. B. Tauris, 2002).

[44]David Sanders, "The Political Economy of Labour Support, 1997–2005," paper presented at the Conference on *Cool Britannia: Britain After Eight Years of Labour Government*, Montreal, Cerium, May 4–6, 2005.

[45]See: Helen Margetts, "Political Participation and Protest," in Patrick Dunleavy et al., eds., *Developments in British Politics* 6 (New York: St. Martin's Press, 2000), pp. 185–202.

[46]Stephen Haseler, "Britain's Ancien Régime," *Parliamentary Affairs* 40, no. 4 (October 1990): 418.

[47]Iain Byrne and Stuart Weir, "Democratic Audit: Executive Democracy in War and Peace," *Parliamentary Affairs* 57, no. 2 (2004): 453–468.

[48]Bhiku Parekh et al., *The Future of Multi-Ethnic Britain: The Parekh Report* (London: Profile Books, 2000), p. 38.

[49]See Liza Schuster and John Solomos (and respondents), "Debate: Race, Immigration and Asylum," *Ethnicities* 4, no. 2 (June 2004): 267–300.

[50]MORI, "State of the Nation," April 10, 2005; http://www.mori.com/pubinfo/rmw/state-of-the-nation.shtml.

[51]Sanders, "The Political Economy of Labour Support, 1997–2005," paper presented at the Conference on *Cool Britannia: Britain After Eight Years of Labour Government*, Montreal, Cerium, May 4–6, 2005.

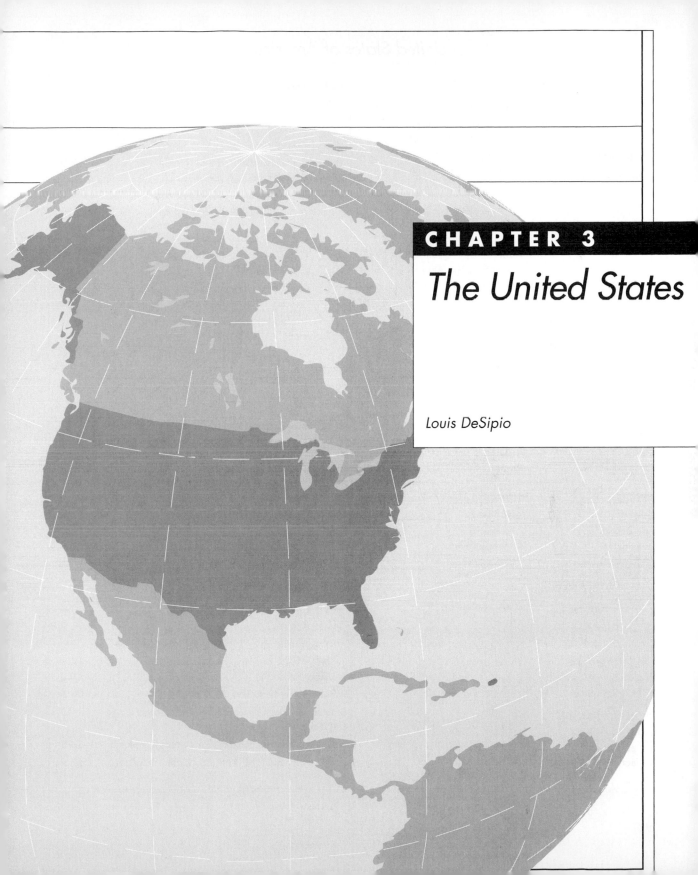

CHAPTER 3
The United States

Louis DeSipio

United States of America

Land and People

Capital	Washington, D.C.
Total area (square miles)	3,794,083 (about one half the size of Russia)
Population	295,976,000

Annual population growth rate (%)	1975–2000	1.0
	2002–2015 (projected)	1.0

Urban population (%)		79.8

Ethnic composition (%)	White	76.2
	Black	12.1
	Asian	4.2
	Amerindian and Alaska native	0.8
	Native Hawaiian and other Pacific Islander	0.1
	Other races	4.8
	Two or more races	1.9

Note: Hispanics make up about 14% of the U.S. population. The Census considers Hispanic to be an ethnic rather than a racial category and includes Hispanics in the racial categories above.

Major language(s)	English; Spanish *(about 30 million U.S. residents over the age of 5 speak Spanish at home)*
	Asian languages *(approximately 8 million U.S. residents over the age of 5 speak Asian languages at home)*

Religious affiliation (adults) (2001) (%)	Protestant	55.2
	Roman Catholic	25.9
	Jewish	1.4
	Muslim/Islamic	0.6
	Other	1.9
	None	15.0

Economy

Domestic currency	U.S. Dollar USD
Total GNI (US$)	11.01 trillion
GNI per capita (US$)	37,870
Total GNI at purchasing power parity (US$)	10.98 trillion
GNI per capita at purchasing power parity (US$)	37,750

GDP annual growth rate (%)	1983–1993	3.0
	1993–2003	3.4
	2002	2.4
	2003	2.9
	2004	4.4

GDP per capita average annual growth rate (%)	1983–1993	2.0
	1993–2003	2.1

Inequality in income or consumption (2000) (%)	Share of poorest 10%	1.9
	Share of poorest 20%	5.4
	Share of richest 20%	45.8
	Share of richest 10%	29.9
	Gini Index	.462

Structure of production (% of GDP)	Agriculture	0.9
	Industry	19.7
	Services	79.4

Labor force distribution (% of total)	Agriculture	0.7
	Industry	22.7
	Services	76.7

Exports as % of GDP (2004)	9.3
Imports as % of GDP (2004)	14.2

Society

Life expectancy at birth	77.2
Infant mortality per 1,000 live births	6.63
Adult illiteracy (% of population age 15+)	3*

*The OECD estimates that the U.S. has a functional illiteracy rate of about 21%.

Access to information and communications (2001) (per 1,000 population)	Telephone lines	6,667
	Mobile phones	451
	Radios	2,117
	Televisions	835
	Personal computers	625

Women in Government and the Economy

Women in the national legislature (2005)	
Lower House or Single House (%)	14.9
Upper House (%)	14.0
Women at ministerial level (2005) (%)	26.7
Female legislators, senior officials, and managers (% of total)	46
Female professional and technical workers (% of total)	55
Female economic activity rate (age 15 and above) (%)	60.9

Female labor force (% of total)		47
Estimated earned income	Female	27,338
(PPP US$)	Male	43,797

Composite Indices and Rankings

Human Development Index (HDI) ranking (value) out of 177 countries	8 (.939)
Gender-related Development Index (GDI) ranking (value) out of 144 countries	8 (.936)
Gender Empowerment Measure (GEM) ranking (value) out of 78 countries	14 (.769)
Corruption Perception Index (CPI) ranking (value) out of 145 countries	17 (7.5)
Environmental Sustainability Index (ESI) ranking (value) out of 146 countries	45 (52.9)
Freedom House Freedom in the World Rating	Free (1.0)

Political Organization

Political System   Presidential system.

Regime History   Representative democracy, usually dated from the signing of the Declaration of Independence (1776) or the Constitution (1787).

Administrative Structure   Federalism, with powers shared between the national government and the fifty state governments; separation of powers at the level of the national government among legislative, executive, and judicial branches.

Executive   President, "directly" elected (with Electoral College that officially elects president and vice president) for four-year term; cabinet is advisory group of heads of major federal agencies and other senior officials selected by president to aid in decision-making but with no formal authority.

Legislature   Bicameral. Congress composed of a lower house (House of Representatives) of 435 members serving two-year terms and an upper house (Senate) of 100 members (two from each state) serving six-year terms; elected in single-member districts (or, in the case of the Senate, states) by simple plurality (some states require a majority of voters).

Judiciary   Supreme Court with nine justices nominated by president and confirmed by Senate, with life tenure; has specified original and appellate jurisdiction and exercises the power of judicial review (can declare acts of the legislature and executive unconstitutional and therefore null and void).

Party System   Essentially two-party system (Republican and Democrat), with relatively weak and fractionalized parties; more than in most representative democracies, the personal following of candidates remains very important.

Section ❶ The Making of the Modern American State

Politics in Action

In a news conference two days after his reelection (and the day after his opponent, Massachusetts Senator John Kerry, conceded defeat), President Bush answered a reporter's question about how he would be able achieve the many objectives he has set for his second term. He said, "I earned capital in the campaign, political capital, and now I intend to spend it." Bush's victory in the 2004 election was by a surprisingly large margin. He won the popular vote by approximately 3.5 million votes (out of 121 million cast) and was the first presidential candidate to win an outright majority of the popular vote since his father's 1988 victory. President Bush's party, the Republicans, also increased their representation in the U.S. Senate and House of Representatives. The Republicans raised their majority from 51 senators of the 100 members to 55 in the 2004 elections and from 229 of the 435 members to 231 in the House of Representatives. Even with President Bush's sizeable victory and the Republican's stronger position in the Congress, however, the President will have difficulty spending what he believes to be his political capital. The design of the U.S. government, particularly the divisions between the branches of the federal government and between the federal and state governments, ensures that he will face many roadblocks and that his stock of political capital will decline before he succeeds in achieving more than a few of his objectives.

President Bush's goals for his second term are quite ambitious. He seeks to partially privatize **Social**

President Bush's assertion that he earned political capital with his 2004 victory may prove overly optimistic considering the many institutional barriers to changing popular programs, such as Social Security.
Source: Dick Wright

Security (a federal pension program for elderly and disabled workers and their survivors), make permanent tax cuts that were passed during his first term (at a significant cost to the federal budget), reform immigration and establish a guest worker program, pass a constitutional amendment prohibiting gay marriage, and continue the U.S. commitment to an international war on terror that involves a significant U.S. troop presence in Afghanistan and Iraq, along with sizeable expenditures to rebuild those nations. President Bush has also had the opportunity to appoint one member of the Supreme Court—John Roberts, Jr.—to replace Sandra Day O'Connor and will likely have the opportunity to appoint other members of the Court, including the Chief Justice. President Bush must also face increasingly vocal challenges to U.S. policies in Iraq coming from the families of service members killed in Iraq and from Democrats and Republicans in Congress.

To achieve his goals in each of these areas and the confirmation of his judicial nominees, President Bush requires more than simply his own commitment and a clear articulation of his goals (see "Leaders: George Walker Bush"). Congress must also agree; and, on each of these issues, dissent from President Bush's positions is considerable. President Bush must also demonstrate to international financial markets that the United States can afford to cut taxes, spend money on international security and its military presence abroad, and pay the short-term costs of introducing private accounts to the Social Security system within the constraints of its current tax

system and borrowing ability. Ultimately, President Bush must be able to sell his program to the American people. With their support, Congress will be more likely to pass the Bush agenda. But should the American public become dissatisfied with President Bush's ability to deliver in any of these areas, he could find that he has quite suddenly lost not just the political capital that he believes that he earned in the 2004 election, but also the support (that of approximately half of the American electorate) that he had on election day.

The constitutional design of the U.S. government limits the power of the presidency, even when the president and the majority of both houses of Congress are of the same party. Efforts to concentrate policy design in the presidency often generate opposition among members of Congress who share many of the president's goals, but don't want the presidency and the executive branch to become too powerful. In addition, any second-term president faces limits on his ability to pressure Congress, and recent two-term presidents have faced scandals that have further undermined their leadership abilities. Unlike members of Congress, President Bush will not again face re-election and will quickly come to be perceived as a lame duck (an officeholder who can no longer exact retribution if he is crossed). The controversies over whether presidential advisor Karl Rove leaked the name of a CIA agent to the press that consumed the media and political debates in the summer of 2005 are an example of the increasing weakness of a second-term president to shape the political agenda. So, while

Leaders: *George Walker Bush*

Georg Bush is the forty-third president of the United States. He was elected in a disputed election in 2000, but saw a dramatic rise in his popularity in the period after the September 11, 2001, terrorist attacks on the World Trade Center and the Pentagon. In 2004, Bush won a majority of the popular vote (the first president to do so since 1988) that included a 3.5 million-vote victory over Senator John Kerry. In 2000, Bush was elected on a platform of educational reform, tax cuts, the introduction of private sector managerial approaches to government, and ethics in government. By 2004, his focus shifted to national security, defense, the war in Iraq, and protection of traditional values.

President Bush was born in 1946 and grew up in Texas, where his father had moved after World War II to make his fortune in the oil industry. President Bush grew up in a political family. His father served as the forty-first president of the United States (1989–1993) and his grandfather served as senator from Connecticut (1952–1963). His brother Jeb was elected governor of Florida in 1998 and reelected in 2002.

Previous U.S. presidents have seen similar multigenerational success in election to the nation's highest offices. John Adams, for example, served as the second president of the United States, and his son John Quincy Adams was the sixth. The large number of Bushes in politics has begun a conversation about whether they are a dynasty. In the past, political success has dwindled after the second or third generation in most political families.

President Bush surprised many by his quick rise in politics, including perhaps many in his own family, who expected Jeb to follow his father in the White House. Prior to President Bush's election to the Texas governorship in 1994, he had a rather undistinguished academic and professional career. He had followed his father into the oil business and had seen his investments fail. Nevertheless, he was able to turn a small investment in the Texas Rangers baseball club into a sizeable profit. He used his innate political skills, as well as perhaps some of his father's political connections, to negotiate a very favorable plan for building a new stadium for the team at public expense. He moved from this position to the Texas governorship. Although the Texas governorship is relatively weak, he used what political capital he had to promote educational reform and business development. He was re-elected by an overwhelming margin in 1998, and most Texans expected that he would run for president in 2000.

In that election, he easily defeated his Republican opponents and was able to unify the moral conservative and economic conservative wings of the Republican Party (which had not been able to cooperate in the 1990s) to win a come-from-behind victory. Bush benefited, in an odd way, from the low expectations that many held for him. In the presidential debates in particular, he did much better than people expected, a pattern that was repeated in 2004. He also benefited from his ability to identify skilled staff people to direct his campaign. Most notable among these is Karl Rove, who had guided President Bush's political career from its start. Rove now serves as senior adviser to the president in the White House.

President Bush's presidency was changed in profound ways by the events of September 11, 2001. The domestic agenda that had shaped his campaign shifted to an all-encompassing war on terror that began with an invasion of Afghanistan to destroy Osama bin Laden, the leadership of Al Qaeda, and the Taliban leadership of Afghanistan and quickly transitioned to invasion of Iraq and the removal of Saddam Hussein. President Bush began this war on terror with much international support, but as the focus shifted to Iraq, support from U.S. allies diminished considerably. Support among the U.S. population also declined such that President Bush won reelection with an approval rating that hovered around 50 percent, low for a successful reelection capaign.

Second terms have generally not been as successful as first terms for presidents who have been

(continued)

Leaders: *George Walker Bush* (cont.)

reelected. President Clinton's second term was defined by his dalliance with Monica Lewinsky, his impeachment by the House of Representatives, and his tentative efforts to rebuild his reputation. His influence declined in the two years after the Senate's decision not to convict him (and remove him from office). President Reagan's second term saw scandal, with charges that administration officials secretly sold armaments to Iran and sent the proceeds to rebels fighting to overthrow the government of Nicaragua; both actions violated acts of Congress. Neither president was able to achieve as much in his second term as his first. Although it is too early to assess the relative success of Bush's second term, he has proposed a broad and controversial agenda that includes the continuation—and possible expansion—of the U.S. military role in Iraq and Afghanistan, the partial privatization of Social Security, the introduction of a guest worker immigration program, and the extension of tax cuts enacted in his first term. Soon after the election, President Bush responded at a press conference that the election had conferred "political capital" on him that he intended to spend. To achieve his ambitious goals and to avoid the pattern of scandal and reduced effectiveness of presidential second terms, President Bush will have to manage his political capital carefully.

President Bush may have earned political capital, its value in his second term may decline as quickly as the U.S. dollar.

Geographic Setting

The 3.79 million square miles of the United States occupy approximately half of the North American continent and represent an area about half of the size of the Russian Federation and slightly larger than China. Its population, approximately 295 million people, is dwarfed by the populations of China and India.

The United States has only two neighbors, Mexico and Canada, which do not present a military threat and are linked in a comprehensive trade agreement: the **North American Free Trade Agreement (NAFTA).** U.S. territory is rich in natural resources (such as coal, oil, and metals), arable land, navigable rivers, and protected ports. The abundance of land and natural resources has engendered a national ethos that there will always be enough resources to meet national needs. This abundance explains in part the low support for environmental protection laws in the United States. Finally, the nature of the land leads to a final characteristic of U.S. society: the territory has always had low population densities and has served as a magnet for international migration. In 2005, for example, the United States had approximately 80 people per square mile. This compares to 578 people per square mile in Germany, 835 in India, and 17,685 in Singapore.[1]

Although the time period is regularly debated, the settlement of the territory that is now the United States appears to have begun at least 12,000 years ago, with the arrival of migrants from Asia into what is now Alaska. European settlers and involuntary African migrants came much later, but in the end, they came in larger numbers.

European colonization led to the eventual unification of the territory that became the United States under one government and the expansion of that territory from the Atlantic to the Pacific Ocean. This process began in the early 1500s and reached its peak in the nineteenth century, when rapid population expansion was reinforced by an imperialist national ideology **(manifest destiny)** to push the westward boundary of the nation from the Appalachians to the Pacific. The indigenous residents of the western territories were pushed aside in the process of expansion. The United States experimented with colonialism at the turn of the twentieth century, leading to the annexation of Hawaii, Guam, the Northern Marianas Islands, and Puerto Rico. Hawaii became a state in 1959.

The United States faces little challenge to its territorial boundaries today. Although some in Puerto Rico seek independence, most want either a continuation of Commonwealth or statehood. Commonwealth status for Puerto Rico reflects something of a semantic compromise; Puerto Rico is a colony of the United States that has been granted autonomy in local governance, but has limited autonomy in trade and foreign policy. Puerto Ricans are U.S. citizens by birth and can travel freely to the United States. Guam is an "unincorporated territory" (a U.S. territory that is not on the road to statehood and does not have all of the protections of the U.S. Constitution). The Northern Marianas petitioned for and received Commonwealth status in 1975. Neither Guam nor the Northern Marianas has active independence movements.

Critical Junctures

The first four critical junctures in U.S. political history appeared at points when mass discontent became sufficiently organized to alter governing institutions or relationships. Each of these junctures challenged dominant paradigms of who should have a voice in democratic government and what the relationship between government and citizen should be. Although these demands for democratic voice and changed citizen-state relations are ongoing in U.S. political history, four periods of focused popular demand are explored here: the period from the beginning of the American Revolution through the ratification of the U.S. Constitution, the Civil War and Reconstruction, the New Deal, and a contemporary period of routinely

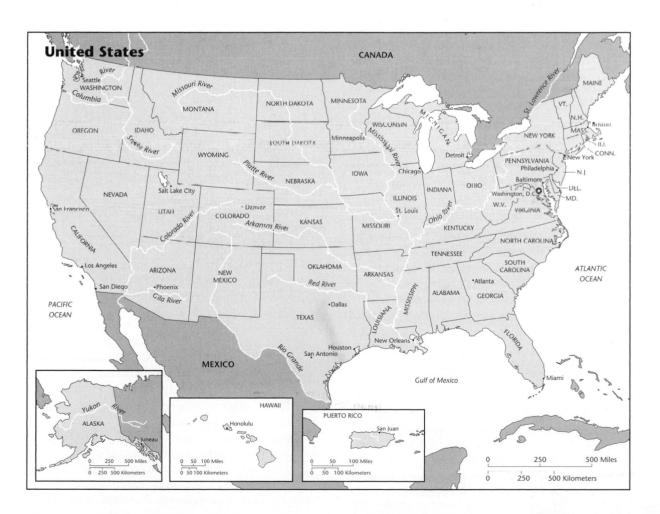

divided national government that began with the 1968 national elections. This last period, which is ongoing, is somewhat less focused than the other three because we cannot know its ultimate outcome. It was into this ongoing period of divided national government that the United States experienced the attacks of September 11, 2001, the final critical juncture analyzed here.

Critical Junctures in U.S. Political Development

1776	Independence from Great Britain declared
1788	U.S. Constitution replaces Articles of Confederation
1803	Supreme Court establishes judicial review in *Marbury* v. *Madison*
1803	Louisiana Purchase
1830s	Mass political parties emerge, and electorate expands to include a majority of white men
1861–1865	U.S. Civil War
1865–1876	Reconstruction era: the United States establishes but fails to guarantee voting rights for freed slaves
1896	Voter turnout in elections begins century-long decline
1933–1940	The New Deal responds to the economic distress of the Great Depression
1941–1945	U.S. participates in World War II
1964	Tonkin Gulf Resolution authorizes military actions in Vietnam
1974	Richard Nixon resigns the presidency in the face of certain impeachment
1978	California passes Proposition 13
1996	Federal government ends the guarantee of social welfare programs to the poor established during the New Deal
1998–1999	U.S. House of Representatives impeaches and the U.S. Senate acquits President Clinton
2000	George W. Bush (R) defeats Al Gore (D) in a disputed election resolved by a ruling from the U.S. Supreme Court
2001	The World Trade Center and the Pentagon are targets of terrorist attacks using hijacked civilian airliners

The Revolutionary Era (1773–1789)

The American Revolution was sparked by mass and elite discontent with British colonial rule that resulted in the signing of the **Declaration of Independence** on July 4, 1776. The Revolution itself was only the beginning of a process of creating a new form of government. Mass interests sought to keep government close to home, in each colony, and wanted each colony to have substantial autonomy from the others. Elite interests advocated a national government with control over foreign policy, national assumption of state Revolutionary War debts, and the ability to establish national rules for commerce.

Mass interests won this battle initially. From 1777 to 1788, the **Articles of Confederation** governed the nation. The Articles' weaknesses, specifically the inability of the national government to implement foreign or domestic policy, to tax, or to regulate trade between the states without the acquiescence of the individual governments of each of the states, allowed elite interests to gain support for their replacement with the Constitution. The limited powers of the national government under the Articles rested in a legislature, but the states had to ratify most key decisions. In this period, states established their own foreign policies, which were often divergent with each other. They also established their own fiscal policies and financed state budgets through extensive borrowing.

The Constitution maintained most power with the states but granted the federal (or national) government authority over commerce and foreign and military policy. It also provided the federal government with a source of financing independent of the states. And, most important, it created an executive officer, the president, who had powers independent of the legislature. Initially, the U.S. presidency was quite weak, but its power grew in the twentieth century. The Constitution delegated specific, but limited, powers to the national government. These included establishing post offices and roads, coining money, promoting the progress of science, raising and supporting an army and a navy, and establishing a uniform rule of naturalization. These powers can be found in Article I, Section 8 of the Constitution and tend to vest the federal government with the power to create a national economy. Finally, the Constitution sought to limit the citizenry's voice in government. Presidents were elected indirectly, through the Electoral College. Members of the Senate were elected by state legislatures. Only the members of the House of Representatives were elected by the people, but regulation of who could vote for members of the House was left to the states.

(See "Institutional Intricacies: The Electoral College.") In the nation's early years, only property-holding men held the vote in most states. By the 1840s, most white adult men were enfranchised. Women did not receive voting rights nationally until 1920.

Institutional Intricacies: *The Electoral College*

Until votes started to be counted in the 2000 election, most Americans did not realize that voters do not directly elect the president or the vice president. Instead, they learned, the president and vice president are elected by the Electoral College, which in turn is elected by the voters on Election Day.

The framers of the Constitution designed the Electoral College to act as a check on the passions of the citizenry. Like the indirect election of senators by state legislatures that survived until 1913, the Electoral College was a device to place community leaders between voters and the selection of leaders. Senators are now elected directly, but the Electoral College remains. On Election Day, voters actually vote for a slate of electors who are pledged to vote for a particular candidate. The number of electors in a state is equal to the state's number of representatives plus its two senators. With the ratification of the Twenty-Third Amendment to the Constitution in 1961, the District of Columbia also has three electors, although it has no voting representation in Congress. To win, a candidate must earn half the total number plus one, or 270, of the Electoral College votes.

The electors, who are not named on the ballot, are selected by the state parties and, in some cases, by the candidates. They are usually state party leaders who are named as an honor for past service. As a result, they are very likely to support the candidate to whom they are pledged when the electors meet in each state capital early in December. Most states also require (by law) that an elector vote for the candidate to whom he or she is pledged. But there are examples, as recently as the 2004 election, where electors did not vote for their pledged candidate.

Such "faithless" electors have not affected the outcome of any election so far. What would happen in a close election if a handful of electors did not vote for the candidate to whom they were pledged? Congress, under the Constitution, would have to count their votes as reported. Thus, in this hypothetical close election, a few stray electors could deny the winner a majority by voting for a third candidate. This would throw the election into the House of Representatives. More unlikely, the electors could vote for the losing candidate and give him or her the ultimate victory in the Electoral College.

As the 2000 election demonstrated, the Electoral College system can make a winner out of the person who places second in the popular vote. Al Gore won the popular vote by more than 500,000 votes, but he lost the Electoral College by a vote of 271 to 266 (one faithless elector from the District of Columbia did not vote for Al Gore, who had won a majority of the District of Columbia's popular vote). All but two states award electoral votes on a winner-take-all basis. This practice maximizes the influence of their voters and increases the likelihood that candidates will campaign in that state; no large state is likely to sacrifice this practice unless all do. Thus, the candidate who receives the most votes in these winner-take-all states wins all of the state's Electoral College votes. In races with three or more serious candidates, these votes can be awarded to candidates who received far less than a majority of the state's votes.

In the 2004 election, President Bush won small victories in key states. These victories, even by small margins, ensured him all of these states' electoral votes. John Kerry won some of the largest states by large margins. Thus, Bush won a higher share of the electoral vote than the popular vote.

As popular support for ratification of the Constitution began to rise, many who had supported the Articles of Confederation made a new demand: that the newly drafted U.S. Constitution include enumerated protections for individuals from governmental power. Meeting this demand for a **Bill of Rights,** a specific set of prohibitions on the new national government was necessary to ensure the ratification of the Constitution. Although the specific rights guaranteed in the Bill of Rights had little substantive meaning for Americans in the 1790s, over time they came to offer fundamental guarantees against the excesses of national and state government. Interpretation of the meaning of these rights ensured that the federal courts would play an increasingly significant role in U.S. national government, particularly in the twentieth century.

The Civil War and Reconstruction (1861–1876)

The second critical juncture in U.S. political history was the Civil War. While the morality of slavery convulsed the nation prior to the war, the war itself began over the question of whether the states or the national government should be dominant. Despite the seeming resolution of this question during the Revolutionary era, many states still believed they could reject specific federal laws. Any time Congress threatened to pass legislation that would restrict slavery in the South, the legislation would be met by a threat by one or more southern state legislatures to nullify the law. From the perspective of most in the North and some in the South, the potential for any state to nullify federal laws put the union at risk (and would return the nation to the system of governance under the Articles of Confederation). The Civil War resolved this issue in favor of the indivisibility of the union. A second long-term consequence was to establish an enforceable national citizenship to supplement the state citizenship that had predated the ratification of the Constitution.[2] This establishment of a national citizenship began a slow process that culminated in the New Deal, as the nation's citizens looked to the federal government to meet their basic needs in times of national crisis.

As part of the process of establishing full citizenship for the freed slaves after the war, Congress revisited the question of individual liberties and citizenship for the first time since the debate over the Bill of Rights at the end of the Revolutionary era. These post–Civil War debates on the relationship of citizens to the national government established several important principles in the Fourteenth Amendment to the Constitution (1868) that shape citizenship today. First, it extended the protections of the Bill of Rights to cover actions by states as well as by the federal government (the courts slowed the implementation of this provision). Second, it extended citizenship to all persons born in the United States. This made U.S. citizens of freed slaves (a legal necessity because an 1857 Supreme Court ruling, *Dred Scott* v. *Sanford,* had held that all blacks, slave or free, were not and could never be U.S. citizens) but also guaranteed that children of the tens of millions of immigrants who migrated after 1868 would become U.S. citizens at birth. Without this constitutional protection, the children of immigrants could have formed a legal underclass—denied citizenship but with no real tie to a foreign land. (This kind of excluded status characterized the children of many immigrants to Germany until 2000.) Third, Congress sought to establish some federal regulation of voting and to grant the vote to African Americans (these provisions were strengthened in the Fifteenth Amendment, ratified in 1870). Failure of the federal government to continue to enforce black voting rights meant that African Americans, particularly in the South, could not routinely exercise the vote until the passage of the Voting Rights Act in 1965. These fundamental guarantees that ensure electoral opportunities today limit prerogatives recognized as the states' responsibilities in the Constitution. The Voting Rights Act and subsequent nationalization of voting rights and voting procedures would have likely been found to be unconstitutional without these Civil War–era amendments.

The New Deal Era (1933–1940)

The third critical juncture in U.S. political development was the New Deal, the Roosevelt administration's response to the economic crisis of the Great Depression. The federal government tapped its constitutional powers to regulate interstate commerce to vastly expand federal regulation of business (which had begun tentatively around the turn of the century with antitrust legislation). It also established assistance programs for targeted groups, such as Social Security to provide monthly payments to the elderly who had worked, housing programs to provide housing for the working poor, and food subsidies for children in poor households. Finally, the federal government began to directly subsidize the agricultural sector and to offer farmers protections against the cyclical nature of demand. These programs, which had traditionally been understood as being within the purview of the states to the extent that they existed at all, expanded dramatically in the fifty years after the New Deal. The legislative and judicial battles to establish such policies are direct outcomes of the New Deal and represent a fundamental expansion of the role of the federal government in the lives of individual Americans.

This juncture also saw the federal government assert dominance over the states in delivering services to the people that gave substantive meaning to the national citizenship that was established during the critical juncture of the Civil War and Reconstruction. Equally important, the critical juncture of the New Deal saw the presidency assert dominance over the Congress in terms of policymaking. The U.S. president during the New Deal, Franklin D. Roosevelt, found powers that no previous president had exercised and permanently changed the office of the presidency. Despite many changes in U.S. politics since 1933 and a significant reduction in the scope of federal assistance programs to the poor, all post–New Deal presidents remain much more powerful than any of their predecessors, except perhaps for Abraham Lincoln, who served during the Civil War. Beginning in the 1960s, however, Congress began to regularly challenge growth in executive power, a challenge that President Bush continues to face today.

The expanded role of the federal government in this era should be seen in the context of demands for even more dramatic changes. Unemployment rates as high as 40 percent, a worldwide decline in demand for U.S. manufactures, and climatological changes that made much agricultural land unproductive spurred widespread demand for wealth redistribution and centralization of power in the federal government that had not been seen either before or after in American politics. Although the New Deal programs represented a significant change from the policies that preceded the Great Depression, they also reflected underlying American political values (see Section 4) relative to other visions for the U.S. government that were

discussed in the era. Even in the New Deal era, class-based politics was kept to a minimum.

As the depression came to a close, the United States geared up for its involvement in World War II. Although the United States had previously been involved in an international conflict beyond its borders (World War I), the experience of World War II was different at the inception of U.S. involvement and at the conclusion. The United States entered the war after U.S. territory was attacked (the Japanese bombing of Pearl Harbor). Throughout the war, U.S. leaders made a commitment not to follow the U.S. pattern of isolation after World War I. Although the lessons of World War I and its aftermath may have driven this response, the expansive multilateral approach to the post–World War II era must also be seen as a response to popular support for the newly interventionist U.S. government that emerged during the New Deal.

Divided Government and Political Contestation of the Scope of Government (1968 to the Present)

The fourth critical juncture, which began with the 1968 presidential election, is ongoing today. This critical juncture has two dimensions. First, the national government has been routinely divided between the two political parties. Division such as this cannot exist in parliamentary systems. This division exacerbates the inefficiency that was designed into the American constitutional order and increases popular distrust of government (see Section 3).

The second ongoing dimension of the contemporary critical juncture began a few years later but emerges from the apparent inefficiency caused by divided government. Many in the United States began to question the steady increase in the scope of governmental services that was ongoing throughout the twentieth century, and particularly since the New Deal. The electoral roots of this popular discontent can be found in the passage of Proposition 13 by California voters in 1978. Proposition 13 limited governments' abilities to increase **property taxes.** The dissatisfaction expressed by Californians with the cost and scope of government, and efforts to limit them soon spread to other states. The passage of Proposition 13 began an era that continues today, in which many citizens reject the expansion of government and its role in citizens' lives that began with the New Deal. President Bush's proposals to partially privatize Social Security benefits can be understood as part of a program to reduce the scope of government protections for individual citizens.

The 1968 election saw the election of Richard Nixon (a California Republican) to the presidency. Through Nixon's term and that of his Republican successor, Gerald Ford, the Democrats maintained control of both houses of Congress. In the period since 1968, one of the parties has controlled the presidency, the U.S. Senate, *and* the U.S. House of Representatives only four times. The Democrats controlled all three from 1977 to 1981 and from 1993 to 1995. The Republicans controlled all three from late January to early June 2001 and again beginning in January 2003.

This division of the federal government between the parties and the emergence by the end of the 1990s of a near equal division between the parties in Congress (and of the electorate in the 2000 and 2004 elections) make it more difficult for government to respond to national needs. The division also reflected a growing division in the populace about the size and scope of government. Although the roots of this debate can be traced to the nation's earliest days, the origin of its current manifestation can be traced to California's passage of Proposition 13 in 1978. California, like a handful of other states, allows citizens to propose ballot initiatives—legislation that appears on the state ballot. If passed by the voters, it cannot be reversed by the legislature. This is one of the few forms of direct democracy in the U.S. system.

Popular discontent in the contemporary era is not limited to taxes; it also focuses on the scope of government. This same period saw popular mobilization to reshape government's involvement in "values" issues. This era saw the emergence of pro- and antiabortion organizations, fundamentalist religious movements, advocates of "traditional" values, and movements of people (such as feminists, gay men, and lesbians) who oppose their exclusion from such agendas. Each group seeks to use the government to protect its interests, while condemning government for allegedly promoting the interests of groups with alternative positions on the same issues. The U.S. government offers individuals and groups with differing positions the opportunity to influence policy in different (governmental) arenas.

As a result, U.S. governing institutions cannot directly resolve conflicts over values issues.

Popular concerns about the scope of government reached their apogee with the passage by Congress in 1996 of the Personal Responsibility and Work Opportunity Reconciliation Act, better known as the welfare reform bill. This legislation was quickly signed into law by President Clinton in response to election-year pressures. The consequences of this bill were twofold. First, it ended a commitment that the federal government had made to poor people during the Great Depression and established time limits for eligibility for needs-based federal social welfare programs. The entitlement, based largely on low incomes and having minor children in the household, was replaced with a lifetime period of eligibility and the requirement that the parent receiving the benefit train for employment during this period of limited eligibility. Second, the legislation eliminated permanent residents (immigrants who have entered the country legally but have not been naturalized as U.S. citizens) from eligibility for most social welfare benefits, at least during their initial years of U.S. residence. That this bill received support in Congress from many Democrats and was signed with moderate enthusiasm by a Democratic president indicates how far the national debate about the size and scope of government had come since California passed Proposition 13 in 1978.

While divided government had become the norm in 1968, the division became even more razor thin in the late 1990s. Each election raises the possibility of a switch in partisan control of the House and the intense focus of both parties and **interest groups** on winning the handful of seats that could switch from one party to the other. This nearly even legislative division makes judicial nominations more contentious as well. This nearly equal division between the parties also exists at the state legislative level. After the 2004 elections, the Republicans held a one-person advantage in state legislatures nationwide: 3,657 Republican legislators to 3,656 Democrats. In state legislatures, Republicans had held a 64-person advantage prior to the 2004 elections.

September 11, 2001, and Its Aftermath

It is in this environment—one of routinely divided government and national and local debates about the size and scope of government—that the United States responded to the September 11, 2001, terrorist attacks. Initially, Congress and the nation rallied behind the president to significantly increase the scope of federal law enforcement powers and to provide financial assistance for New York City, the families of the victims of the attack, and the airlines. Quickly, however, partisan divisions and concerns about the powers the president was seeking for the federal government (a concern related to the size and scope of government) began to appear. With Congress so closely divided and neither side actively seeking compromise, the nation soon saw the consequences of the structure and scope of

government in the period of the fourth critical juncture. These divisions were exacerbated by the preparations that the Bush administration made in 2002 and early 2003 to invade Iraq and by its willingness to pursue domestic tax cuts and dramatically increase the size of the federal budget deficit.

In the weeks after September 11, 2001, the United States experienced a rare period of national consensus and international support. Domestically, President Bush's popularity surged to 90 percent. Largely without debate (or significant dissent), Congress passed a dramatic expansion of government's ability to conduct surveillance, to enforce laws, to limit civil liberties,

A jet crashes into the World Trade Center on September 11, 2001.
Source: © Moshe Bursurker/AP/Wide World Photos.

and to fight terrorism—the United and Strengthening America by Providing Appropriate Tools to Intercept and Obstruct Terrorism Act (or **USA PATRIOT Act**) of 2001. Just 65 of the 435 members of the U.S. House of Representatives and 1 of the 100 members of the U.S. Senate voted against this bill. Congress also rallied to provide financial support for communities affected by the terrorist attacks and for segments of the economy adversely affected by the attacks, such as the airlines. The Federal Reserve lowered interest rates to ensure that investors would continue to have confidence in the economy (in the short term) and that individuals and businesses would be able to borrow.

Popular support for President Bush and his administration's initial efforts to respond to the challenges of September 11 continued as the administration moved toward an invasion of Afghanistan. Bush justified this military action with evidence that the September 11 hijackers were trained in Afghanistan and that the Al Qaeda network received protection from the Taliban regime that ruled Afghanistan. At the beginning of the war, nearly nine in ten Americans supported military action in Afghanistan.

The United States also experienced a period of international support immediately following the September 11, 2001, attacks. In addition to immediate offers of humanitarian assistance, initial U.S. military responses to the attacks won widespread backing around the world. U.S. allies joined the United States in what President Bush characterized as a "war against international terrorism." When the United States invaded Afghanistan in October 2001, the coalition included forty nations including all NATO member states. What was perhaps more significant, popular support in other countries was high for an international coalition to remove the Taliban government in Afghanistan. Support for participation of their own governments exceeded 65 percent among Danes, the French, Indians, Italians, the Dutch, and the British. Nearly two-thirds of Germans supported U.S. military action in Afghanistan.

The initial domestic cohesion and international support for the United States in the months after September 11, 2001, dissipated quickly in 2002 and 2003. Although the causes were numerous and differed considerably domestically and internationally, U.S. efforts to extend the war on terrorism to Iraq

became the focus of many of the objections to growing U.S. power and unilateralism in international affairs.

Domestically, Bush faced several challenges but has been able to hold onto support from a bare majority of the population. Only in the spring of 2005 did his popularity dip below 50 percent, in some polls. For the first time since September 11, 2001, more Americans disapproved of the way he was handling the presidency than approved.

Why had his support slipped so dramatically? Domestic and international issues each played a role. A sizeable minority of the U.S. population opposed the U.S. invasion of Iraq without the support of the United Nations or other international bodies. This opposition grew in the period after the military phase of the war ended when it became evident that the peace would be harder fought than the war. U.S. and coalition force casualties, for example, numbered 173 in March and April 2003, the period of combat. Over the next year, the period prior to turning sovereignty over to Iraq on June 28, 2004, U.S. and coalition casualties numbered 803. In the period between June 28, 2004, and the Iraqi elections in January 2005, U.S. and coalition force casualties numbered 632. Bush's support also declined when he continued to advocate strongly partisan positions on contentious domestic issues such as tax cuts that benefited high-income earners, support for moral conservative positions, and, after the 2004 elections, proposals to partially privatize Social Security. While these positions did not differ from those taken prior to September 11, 2001, some expected that Bush would govern more consensually during a period of national crisis. Instead, the Bush positions returned the country to the near-even partisan division that had characterized the country in the 1990s. In the 2004 elections, President Bush beat Senator John Kerry of Massachusetts by approximately 3.5 million votes out of the 121 million cast. While a somewhat greater margin than the 2000 race, the switch of one state in the Electoral College (Ohio—which President Bush won by 119,000 votes) would have given the presidency to John Kerry.

The United States also faced significant opposition from its allies. Germany and France, in particular, opposed U.S. intervention in Iraq and prevented both United Nations and NATO support for U.S. military activities. Although initially part of the U.S.-led coalition, Spain, Poland, Italy, and the Philippines, among other countries, reduced or eliminated their military support as opposition increased at home. The growing opposition to U.S. unilateralism in international affairs resulted in a dramatic decline in positive feelings for the United States among residents of other countries. In the summer of 2002, 75 percent of UK residents and 61 to 63 percent of French, Germans, and Russians had a favorable view of the United States. Just two years later, the share reporting favorable views of the United States declined to 58 percent in the United Kingdom, 37 percent in France, 38 percent in Germany, and 47 percent in Russia. Surveys conducted in March 2003—at the beginning of the Iraq war—saw even lower evaluations of the United States.[3]

In the years after the September 11, 2001, attacks on the United States, the United States has won and squandered international support, and the Bush administration has lost some of the domestic support that it enjoyed in the months after the attack. In retrospect, neither of these outcomes is surprising. Allies of the United States have increasingly sought multilateral solutions to international affairs and are suspicious of U.S. unilateralism. Domestically, the electorate was largely divided prior to 2001, and these divisions reappeared as the shock of the 2001 attacks diminished and other, largely domestic issues returned to their traditional spot at the top of most citizens' policy agendas. In the era of divided government and political contestation of the scope of government, national unity will be the exception rather than the rule.

Themes and Implications

Historical Junctures and Political Themes

The conflict between the president and Congress, the centralization of federal power in the twentieth century, and the growing opposition to the cost and scope of government represent ongoing themes in U.S. politics. These are not quickly or easily resolved in the United States because the Constitution slowed resolution of such conflicts by creating a system of federalism and separation of powers (see Section 3). As will be evident, the period of consensus after the September 11, 2001, attacks was an exceptional moment in American politics. When the Constitution

was drafted in 1787, its framers were wary of allowing the federal government to intervene too readily in matters of individual liberties or states' prerogatives, so they created a governing system with multiple powers. These limits remain today even as the United States has achieved sole superpower status in the world, and other nations, as well as U.S. citizens, expect the nation to lead.

In the modern world, the United States may be at a disadvantage with such a system relative to other governing systems that can react more quickly and decisively to societal needs and shifts in public opinion. Leadership in parliamentary systems changes when leaders lose support from the legislature. In parliamentary systems, even when they are burdened by the compromises necessary to maintain coalition governments, a prime minister can exercise power in a way that a U.S. president or Congress can never expect to do. When a prime minister loses the support of his or her party on key issues, elections are called. In the United States, elections are held on a regular cycle, and the presidency and Congress have come to be routinely controlled by the two major opposing parties. In addition to the differences between the parliamentary and the presidential systems, **federalism** (a division of governing responsibilities between the national government and the states) further slows government action.

The tensions inherent in a system designed to impede governmental action are seen in each of the cross-national themes explored in this book: the world of states, governing the economy, the democratic idea, and the politics of collective identities.

Until the New Deal era and World War II, the United States pursued a contradictory policy toward the rest of the world of states: it sought isolation from international politics but unfettered access to international markets. World War II changed the first of these stances, at least at elite levels (see Section 2): the United States sought to shape international relations through multilateral organizations and military force. It designed the multilateral organizations so that it could have a disproportionate voice (for example, in the United Nations Security Council). The United States used military force to contain communism around the world. With the decline of communism and the end of the cold war, this postwar internationalism has declined somewhat, and some now call for a reduced role of the U.S. government in the world of states or, at a minimum, a greater willingness to use a unilateral response to international military crises. This willingness to move unilaterally manifested itself in the shallow coalition that supported the United States in the Iraq War. This decline in interest in the U.S. role in the world among some in U.S. society reflects the fact that foreign policy has never been central to the evolution of U.S. politics and governance.

The federal government and the states have sought to manage the economy by building domestic manufacturing and exploiting the nation's natural resources while interfering little in the conduct of business (see Section 2). Thus, the United States has governed the economy only selectively. To build industry and exploit resources, the government built roads and other infrastructure, educated citizens, and opened its borders to guarantee a work force. It also sought access to international markets. Only in exceptional circumstances has it limited the operations of business through antitrust regulation. Yet its ability to continue to promote the nation's commerce is today limited by the challenge to the size and scope of government.

The democratic idea inspired the American Revolution and all subsequent efforts to secure and increase freedom and liberty. The democratic idea in the U.S. context was one of an indirect, representative democracy with checks on democratically elected leaders. The emergence of a strong national government after the New Deal era meant that national coalitions could often focus their demands on a single government. The decline in mediating institutions that can channel these demands reduces the ability of individual citizens to influence the national government (see Section 4).

A continuing challenge in U.S. governance is the politics of collective identities. As a nation of immigrants, the United States must unite immigrants and descendants of immigrants from Europe, Africa, Latin America, and Asia with the established U.S. population. Previous waves of immigrants experienced only one to two generations of political and societal exclusion based on their differences from the larger society. Whether today's immigrants experience the same

relatively rapid acculturation remains an open question. Preliminary evidence indicates that the process may be even quicker for immigrants who possess skills and education but slower for those who do not. National economic decline or the rise of a virulent anti-immigrant sentiment could slow or even stop the acculturation process. Despite the acculturation of previous waves of immigrants and their children, the United States has never fully remedied its longest-lasting difference in collective identities with full economic and political incorporation of African Americans.

Implications for Comparative Politics

Scholars of U.S. politics have always had to come to terms with the idea of American exceptionalism—the idea that the United States is unique and cannot easily be compared to other nations. In several respects, the United States *could* be considered exceptional. As indicated, its geography and natural resources offer it advantages that few other nations can match. Its experience with mass representative democracy is longer than that of other nations. It has been able to expand the citizenry beyond the descendants of the original members. And, finally, U.S. society has been much less divided by class than have the societies of other states.[4]

The United States has influenced other nations both because of its success and because it sometimes imposes its experiences on others. The U.S. Constitution, for all of its limitations, has served as the model for the constitutions of many newly independent nations. Some form of **separation of powers** (see Section 3) has become the norm in democratic states. Similarly, district-based and single-member-plurality electoral systems (see Section 4) have been widely adapted to reduce conflict in multiethnic states, of which the United States was the first large-scale example. Through its active role in multilateral institutions such as the United Nations (UN) and international financial institutions such as the International Monetary Fund (IMF), the United States also attempts to impose its will on other nations. Thus, for all of its strengths and weaknesses, it is necessary to know about the U.S. experience to understand more fully the shape of modern democracies throughout the world.

Section ② Political Economy and Development

State and Economy

When national leaders present the accomplishments of the United States, they often hold its economy up as an example of what the nation offers to the world and what it offers to its citizens. By governing the economy less, the United States allows the private economy to thrive. In this simplified version of this story, the private sector is the engine of national growth, and this private sector is most successful when left alone by government. Economic success, then, is tied to the **free market**—the absence of government regulation and the opportunity for entrepreneurs to build the nation's economy.

Relative to other advanced democracies, the U.S. economy is much less regulated. The U.S. government has traditionally taken a **laissez-faire** attitude toward economic actors. This absence of regulation allowed for the creation and expansion of many new types of production that subsequently spread throughout the world, such as the assembly line early in the twentieth century, industrialized agriculture at mid-century, and Internet commerce at its end.

The Constitution reserves for the federal government authority to regulate interstate commerce and commerce with foreign nations. As a result, state and local governments—those most knowledgeable about business or consumer interests in their areas—are limited in their ability to shape the economy. When states have tried to regulate commerce, their efforts have been ruled unconstitutional by the Supreme Court. Over time, however, states have established the ability to regulate workplace conditions as part of their **police powers** or of jurisdiction over public health and safety.

With the exception of agriculture, higher education, and some defense-related industries, the size of various sectors of the economy is almost entirely the result of the free market. The federal government does try to incubate some new industrial sectors, but it primarily uses grants to private agencies—often universities—to accomplish this end. This stimulation of new economic activity makes up a very small share of the nation's gross national product. The United States

also occasionally supports ailing industries, as it did with grants and subsidies to the airline industry in the days after the September 11 attacks, for example. While these account for more in terms of federal expenditures than does stimulation for new industries, political support for propping up ailing industries usually dies quickly. With limited government intervention, the shape of the economy is determined almost entirely by market forces.

Agriculture is something of an exception to this pattern. Since the New Deal, the federal government has guaranteed minimum prices for most agricultural commodities and has sought to protect agriculture by paying farmers to leave some land fallow. It has also considerably reduced the costs of production and risks associated with agriculture by providing subsidized crop insurance, subsidies for canals and aqueducts to transport water, and flood control projects. It has subsidized the sale of U.S. agricultural products abroad. In the 1990s, the federal government began to move away from the guarantees of minimum prices for crops, although it continued to provide funds to sell U.S. crops abroad. Although a less explicit, and perhaps less intentional, form of subsidy, weak regulation of U.S. immigration laws has ensured that agriculture has always had a reliable and inexpensive labor source.

The federal government has also limited its own ability to regulate the economy. With the formation of the **Federal Reserve Board** in 1913, for example, it removed control of the money supply from democratically elected officeholders. Today, unelected leaders on the Federal Reserve Board, many with ties to the banking industry, control the volume of money in the economy and the key interest rates that determine rates at which private lenders lend. Furthermore, the United States has not regulated the flow of capital, which has allowed many large U.S.-based firms to evolve over time into multinational corporations and hence remove themselves from much U.S. government regulation and taxation.

While the United States has taken a more laissez-faire approach to its economy than have other advanced democracies, it is important to recognize that from the nation's earliest days, the federal government has promoted agriculture and industry, spurred exports, and (more recently) sought to stabilize the domestic and international economy. These promotional efforts included tariffs, which sought to disadvantage products that competed with U.S. manufactures; roads and canals, so that U.S.-produced goods could be brought to market cheaply and quickly; the distribution of federally owned lands in the West to individuals and to railroads, so that the land could contribute to national economic activity; and large-scale immigration, so that capital would have people to produce and consume goods (see Section 3).

These efforts to promote U.S. industry often came at the expense of individual citizens, who are less able to organize and make demands of government. Tariffs, for example, kept prices high for domestic consumers, and the enhanced road system and consequent cheap transportation forced native producers to compete in a world economy where their locally produced goods might be more expensive than the same goods produced elsewhere in the United States or abroad.

Through much of the nation's history, the United States used its diplomatic and military resources to establish and maintain markets for U.S.-produced commodities and manufactures abroad. During the nineteenth century, as industry and agriculture geared up to produce for mass markets at home and abroad, the United States entered into bilateral trading agreements to sell its natural resources, agricultural produce, and manufactured products abroad. The U.S. military protected this commerce. Today, the United States uses its position in the world economy and on multilateral lending institutions to open markets, provide loans for nations facing economic distress, and protect some U.S.-produced goods from foreign competition. In sum, despite national rhetoric to the contrary, the United States has consistently promoted economic development, though not by regulating production or spurring specific industries.

The U.S. economy has increasingly come to rely on two unintentional forms of international subsidy. First, it has built up a steadily increasing international trade deficit. In other words, the United States has bought much more abroad than it has sold. In 2004, for example, the United States imported $617.1 billion

more in goods and services than it exported. This represented a substantial increase from the $496.5 billion trade deficit in 2003. Although some aspects of these trade deficits could well reflect a strength in the U.S. economy (for example, being able to purchase goods produced inexpensively abroad), continuing deficits of this level will act as a downward pressure on the U.S. dollar in the long run (see Figure 1). Slowing this downward pressure for the time being is the second form of international subsidy: the U.S. dollar has become the international reserve currency. This means that many nations and individual investors keep their reserves (their savings) in dollars, or more specifically in dollar-denominated bonds issued by the U.S. government. By doing this, they keep demand for the dollar up, and this reduces the downward pressure that comes from repeated annual trade deficits. To the extent that they are buying U.S. government bonds, they are lending the United States money.

As the European common currency, the euro, increasingly comes to be used as a reserve currency, the United States may see less demand for dollar-denominated investments. This could lead to a decline in the value of the dollar relative to the euro (and other currencies) and an increasing cost for goods produced abroad. Over time, such a scenario will damage the U.S. economy.

The long-term stability of the U.S. economy and the value of the dollar as a reserve currency will be challenged by an increasing national debt (discussed later) and market concerns about unfounded liabilities in federal and state pension, health care, and insurance programs. Although the dollar value of these unfounded liabilities is debated, most agree that reforms—both tax increases and benefit cuts—made now can considerably reduce the long-term costs of these programs to the economy. In an environment of divided government and political contestation of the scope of government, however, there is little likelihood of the compromises necessary to enact these reforms.

The government, both federal and state, regulates aspects of the economy and employer-labor relations. Beginning in 1890, the United States enacted antitrust legislation that gave it the ability to break up large businesses that could, by the nature of their size, control an entire market. These antitrust powers have been used sparingly. Antitrust legislation gives the

Figure 1

U.S. Trade Deficit, 1994–2004

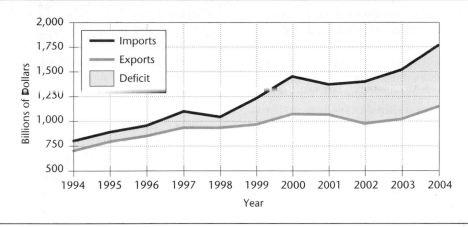

Source: U.S. Bureau of the Census, U.S. Trade in Goods and Services—Balance of Payments (BOP) Basis. http://www.census.gov/foreign-trade/statistics/historical/gands.pdf [viewed April 15, 2005].

government a power that is very much at odds with a laissez-faire ideology, but its unwillingness to use this authority except in the most egregious cases (and the courts' occasional rejection of government antitrust initiatives) reflects the underlying hands-off ideology.

In the twentieth century, the U.S. government took on new responsibilities to protect citizens and to tax businesses, in part, to provide government-mandated services for workers. The government also expanded regulation of workplace safety, pension systems, and other worker-management relations issues that limit the ability of industry to operate in a free market relative to its workforce (see Section 3). Despite this expansion of the government role in providing protections to workers, the United States offers fewer guarantees to its workers than do other advanced democracies.

The public sector has traditionally been smaller in the United States than in other advanced democracies. Nevertheless, the U.S. government and the states conduct activities that many believe could be better conducted by the private sector. The federal government operates hospitals for veterans (through the Veterans Administration), provides water and electrical power to Appalachian states (through the Tennessee Valley Authority), manages lands in the West and Alaska

(through the Department of Interior), runs the civilian air traffic control system (through the Federal Aviation Administration), and, after September 11, manages passenger and luggage screening at commercial airports. Roads have traditionally been built and maintained by the state and federal governments, and waterways have been kept navigable (and open to recreational use) by the federal government.

The U.S. government privatized some activities in recent years. The postal service, for example, became a semi-independent corporation in 1970. The federal government is now trying to end subsidies for the semi-independent passenger rail corporation (Amtrak) that it inherited when the company's private sector owners went bankrupt.

Often left out of the story of the development of the U.S. economy is the role of its natural resources and the environment. The nation's territory is unique. Although it is not the largest country in the world, it is the most diverse in terms of natural resources and environments, stretching from tropical to arctic. The territory includes arable land that can produce more than enough year round for the domestic market as well as for extensive exports. These lands have not been subject to invasion for much of the nation's history. Land has become increasingly concentrated in a few hands, but in the past, it was held in small plots tilled at least in part by the owners. This tradition of equitable land distribution (encouraged by government policies in the nineteenth century that distributed small plots to resident landholders) dampened the class tensions that appeared in societies with entrenched landholding elites. Not all Americans were eligible for this land giveaway, however. The recently freed slaves could not obtain free lands in the West, and some share of the gap in wealth between whites and blacks today can be attributed to the access that whites had to western lands in the last century.[5] In today's economy, public benefits and public employment are increasingly limited to U.S. citizens. Over time, these policies could enhance differences between the non-Hispanic white and black populations, on the one hand, and ethnic groups with large shares of immigrants, such as Latinos and Asian Americans, on the other.

The United States has also been advantaged in terms of trade. It has protected ports and navigable rivers and few enemies that can challenge U.S. control over these transportation resources. For over a century, it was able to expand trade while not investing in a large standing military to defend its trade routes. This long history of safety in U.S. territory made the events of September 11 all the more unnerving for Americans. The symbolic importance of the name of one of the September 11 targets, New York's World Trade Center, raised for many Americans questions about whether the buildings were targeted in part because they represented the increasing presence of American commerce abroad.

One area in which the United States has taken a limited role in regulating the activities of private actors in the American economy is environmental regulation. When the environment first became an issue in international politics, the United States took aggressive action to clean the air and the nation's oceans and navigable waterways. In each of these regulatory areas, federal legislation had dramatic impacts. Emissions standards have made the air much healthier, even in the nation's most car-focused cities. Waterways that were dangerous to the touch are now open to swimming.

These 1970s-era environmental **regulations** have not been followed by a continuing national commitment to environmentalism. President Ronald Reagan opened federal lands to further commercial exploitation. President George W. Bush has proposed opening the Arctic National Wildlife Refuge (ANWR) to oil exploration, and in 2005 both houses of Congress appeared ready to approve this request by narrow majorities. Presidents of both parties have reduced auto fuel efficiency standards. In some sense, the successes of the early environmental regulations, which had a tangible and visible impact in areas where most Americans live, has reduced the salience of environmental issues, particularly those that would have impact in areas where few people live. As the environment has diminished as a popular concern, traditional laissez-faire attitudes toward governmental regulation have allowed presidents and Congress to trade economic gains for environmental losses.

Society and Economy

The United States adheres more strictly to its laissez-faire ideology in terms of the outcomes of the economic system. The distribution of income and wealth is much more unequal in the United States than in other advanced democracies. In 2003, for example, the richest fifth of families earned approximately 50 percent of the nation's income. The poorest fifth, on the other hand, earned just 3 percent of the nation's income (see Figure 2). The top 5 percent alone earned more than 21 percent of the total amount earned in the United States in 2003. Wide differences exist between women and men and between racial groups. Women, on average, earned $12,000 annually less than men in 2003. Non-Hispanic whites and Asian Americans earned an average of $32,000 annually. Blacks and Hispanics, on the other hand, have average incomes of slightly more than $21,000.

The nation has always tolerated these conditions and sees them as an incentive for people at the lower end of the economic spectrum. Wealth and income have become more skewed since 1980 (when the top 20 percent of households earned approximately 44 percent of what was earned), a phenomenon that has not been an issue of national political concern. In fact, the mere mention in an election of the class implications of a policy, particularly tax policy, will usually lead to the charge of fomenting class warfare.

Figure 2

Share of Aggregate Income Received by Households, Quintiles, 1980–2003

Source: U.S. Bureau of the Census, Historical Income Data, Table H-2 "Historical Income Tables—Households." http://www.census.gov/hhes/income/histinc/h02ar.html [accessed April 17, 2005].

Federal income taxation of individuals is progressive, with higher income people paying a higher share of their income in taxes. Rates range from 0 percent for individuals with incomes less than $8,200 to 35 percent for individuals with incomes exceeding approximately $320,000. These rates are scheduled to decline between now and 2010. The highest rate will drop to 33 percent. The progressive nature of federal taxes is reduced considerably by two factors. Upper-income taxpayers receive a much higher share of their income from investments, which are taxed at lower rates. Second, all taxpayers with salary income are subject to regressive tax for Social Security and disability benefits. The tax for Social Security and Medicare is currently 7.65 percent paid by the worker and 7.65 percent paid by the employer. The Social Security share of this tax is imposed only on the first $90,000 of income and not at all on higher incomes. This is a regressive tax: higher income taxpayers pay a lower share of their income for Social Security than do lower income taxpayers.

State and local taxes tend to be much less progressive. Most states levy a sales tax. This is a flat tax, ranging between 2.9 and 8.25 percent depending on the state, on most consumption; some states exempt food and other items from sales taxation. For lower-income people, sales taxes act as a flat tax on most or all of their income. Upper-income people pay a smaller share of their income because they do not have to dedicate all of their income to consumption. Not all states have income taxes. Among those that do, no state has an income tax that is as progressive as the federal income tax. The final major form of individual taxation is property taxes. All people pay these in one way or another. Property owners pay them directly and can deduct the tax payment from their federal and, in some cases, state income taxes. Renters pay them as part of their rent payment but do not directly get any tax benefits.

Thus, the vast gap between rich and poor in the United States is not remedied by progressive taxation. This gap might well have led to the emergence of class-based political movements, but immigration policy, which also promoted economic development, focused workers' attention away from class and toward cultural differences that reduced the salience of class divisions in U.S. society. Unions, which could also have promoted a class-based politics and focused workers' attentions on income inequalities, have traditionally been weak in the United States. This weakness reflects individual-level antipathy toward unions, but also state and federal laws that limit the abilities of unions to organize and collectively bargain. Today, approximately 12.5 percent of American workers are unionized; this rate steadily declined in the twentieth century.

Agriculture and industry could not have grown in the United States without the importation of this immigrant labor. With only a few exceptions, the nation has sought to remedy labor shortages with policies that encouraged migration. Today, the United States is one of just four countries that allow large-scale migration of those who do not already have a cultural tie to the receiving nation. (The others—Canada, Australia, and New Zealand—share a colonial history with the United States.) Contemporary immigration to the United States numbers approximately 900,000 people annually, who immigrate under the provisions of the law to a permanent status that allows for eventual eligibility for U.S. citizenship.[6] Another 450,000 migrate without

Figure 3

Immigration to the United States, 1821–2000

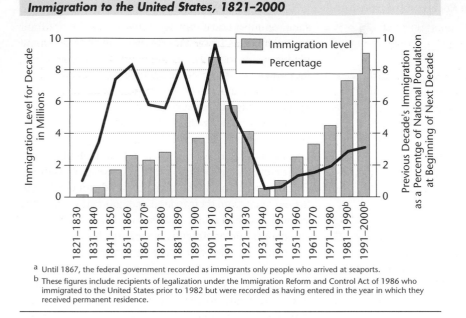

a Until 1867, the federal government recorded as immigrants only people who arrived at seaports.

b These figures include recipients of legalization under the Immigration Reform and Control Act of 1986 who immigrated to the United States prior to 1982 but were recorded as having entered in the year in which they received permanent residence.

Source: Adapted from DeSipio, Louis, and Rodolfo O. de la Garza, 1998. *Making Americans/Remaking America: Immigration and Immigrant Policy* (Boulder, Colo.: Westview Press), Table 2.1.

legal status each year and stay (many more who migrate as undocumented immigrants come and go during any year). Migration at this level adds about 4 percent to the U.S. population each decade (see Figure 3).

Although the United States tolerates the unequal distribution of income and wealth, in the twentieth century it intervened directly in the free market to establish protections for workers and, to a lesser degree, to guarantee the welfare of the most disadvantaged in the society. The programs for workers, which are primarily distributive policies, receive much more public support than do programs to assist the poor, which are primarily redistributive policies. **Distributive policies** allocate resources into an area that policymakers perceive needs to be promoted without a significant impact on income or wealth distribution. **Redistributive policies** take resources from one person or group in society and allocate them to a more disadvantaged group in the society. It should be noted that most worker benefits, such as health insurance, childcare, and pensions, are provided by private employers, if they are provided at all, but are regulated by the government.

In 2003, approximately 45 million people, or about one in six Americans, did not have health insurance. Nearly 21 million of the uninsured are full-time workers. Many poor families are eligible for a needs-based health insurance program, Medicaid, provided by the federal government. In the early 1990s, Congress and President Bill Clinton sought to craft a policy solution to insure the uninsured, but their efforts collapsed around questions of cost and control.

Employers and the health care industry are again looking to government for assistance in providing insurance, and the uninsured (and the potentially uninsured) will demand government action. It seems even less likely today than it did in the early 1990s that the federal government will assume a responsibility for providing health insurance to the American populace. The cost, estimated to be at least $135 billion annually, is too high, and there is no consensus in Congress as to who should manage such a program: the public or private sectors. Finally, President Bush learned a lesson from the Clinton administration's experience with trying to reform health care: that there is little to be gained because the financial cost of successful health care reform is very high and any reform would require new taxes that would generate much opposition in the electorate. Future presidents may very well learn the same lesson.

Best known among the federal programs aimed toward workers is Social Security, which taxes workers and their employers to pay for benefits for retired and disabled workers (and nonworker spouses). In the past, retirees almost always received more than they had paid into the system (a form of intergenerational redistribution), but it will take some reform to guarantee that this outcome continues when today's workers reach retirement age. In 2005, President Bush proposed changes to Social Security that would allow workers to invest a share of their Social Security taxes in stock and bond market funds in exchange for reductions in the size of their guaranteed payments from the government upon retirement. While this plan was initially popular at the mass and congressional level because of the sense that individuals would have control of their retirement savings rather than the government, much support disappeared when it became clear how sizeable the reductions in guaranteed payments would be for all younger workers. At this writing, significant changes in the program along the lines proposed by President Bush seem unlikely.

The government also established a minimum wage and a bureaucratic mechanism to enforce this wage. Some states and localities have established higher minimum wages than the federal minimum wage. Citizen groups in several cities nationwide over the past decade have promoted a further expansion of the idea of a minimum wage to a "living wage," a wage sufficient to live in high-cost cities and is often double the federal minimum wage. These living wage campaigns seek to force cities and municipal contractors to pay such wages.

In addition to Social Security retirement benefits and the minimum wage, the federal government provides a health insurance program for elderly retirees and their nonworking spouses (Medicare), paid for by workers and their employers; programs to provide financial and health care assistance for disabled workers (through Social Security); and insurance for private pension plans (paid for by employers). With

health care costs on the rise and the number of elderly Americans increasing, Medicare faces a deficit. Sometime early in the 2010s, the government will face the dilemma of having to lower benefits or to pay for health care for the elderly out of general revenues. Changing the tax basis of Medicare now (or lowering benefits now) would delay this point of reckoning, but there is little incentive for Congress to act in this area and suffer the political consequences.

The states also regulate worker-employer relations through unemployment insurance and insurance against workplace injuries. Benefits and eligibility requirements vary dramatically by state, although the federal government mandates that all workers be eligible for twenty-six weeks of benefits (assuming the worker has been employed for more than six months).

Beginning in the 1930s, the United States also established social welfare programs to assist the economically disadvantaged. As one would expect in a system organized around the free market, these programs have never been as broad-based or as socially accepted as in other economies. These programs, which expanded in the 1960s and 1970s and were restructured in 1996, provided food, health care, housing assistance, some job training, and some cash assistance to the poor. The states administered these programs with a combination of federal and state funds, established benefit levels, and were responsible for moving recipients off the programs. Eligibility and benefit levels varied dramatically from state to state. Prior to 1996, there was a federal guarantee of some food and cash assistance for everyone who met eligibility thresholds. This guarantee disappeared in 1996 when recipients were limited in the duration of their eligibility and states were entrusted with developing programs to train recipients for work and to get them jobs. Although enacted separately from the 1996 welfare reform, the federal government also reduced the availability of federally managed housing for the poor and expanded subsidies for the poor to secure housing in the private market.

The federal and state governments have one final recurring impact on the national economy that is more indirect but will likely be of increasing importance in the coming years: both the federal and state governments are entering a period of high deficit spending. Current estimates suggest that the federal government spent $412 billion more than it raised in 2004. Thirty states had 2005 budget deficits totaling approximately $40 billion. Most states will be required to close this deficit very quickly by raising taxes or cutting services. The federal government, on the other hand, can continue to run a large annual deficit (as it did from the early 1980s until 1997).

Current projections show that the federal government will continue to have deficits in the $200 to $400 billion range throughout the rest of the decade. These deficits will add to the approximately $7.7 trillion national debt (which reflects the cumulative deficits of the past 218 years). Deficits can have a salutary effect on the national economy during weak economic times because the federal government can more easily borrow and then spend this money to stimulate the economy and support individuals who are out of work. In the long run, however, this federal debt absorbs money that could be invested in private sector activities and will slow national economic growth. In 2004, the federal government paid approximately $322 billion in interest on its debt.

The United States in the Global Economy

Since colonial times, the United States has been linked to world trade. By the late twentieth century, the United States had vastly expanded its role in international finance and was an importer of goods produced abroad (often in low-wage countries that could produce goods less expensively than U.S. factories) as well as an exporter of agricultural products.

After World War II, the United States reversed its traditional isolationism in international politics to take a leading role in the regulation of the international economy. The increasing interdependence of global economies was the result, in part, of conscious efforts by world leaders at the end of World War II, through the Bretton Woods Agreement, to establish and fund multinational lending institutions. These were to provide loans and grants to developing economies in exchange for their agreement to reduce government regulation of their economies and open their domestic markets to internationally produced goods. Chief among these institutions were the World Bank and the International Monetary Fund. Since their establishment in the 1940s, they have been supplemented by a network of international lending and regulatory

agencies and regional trading agreements. The Group of Eight (G-8), for example, conducts annual meetings of the leaders of the eight largest industrial democracies (the United States, Japan, Germany, Britain, France, Italy, Canada, and Russia).

The United States is also part of regional trading networks, such as NAFTA with Canada and Mexico. NAFTA did not initially have extensive support in Congress, but President Clinton used all the powers of the presidency to win the support of members of his own party, and the treaty narrowly passed. Despite the initial opposition of many in Congress to NAFTA, it has come to be seen as a boon to the American economy. After its passage, the United States entered into an agreement with neighboring countries in the Caribbean to reduce tariffs on many goods.

NAFTA and the Caribbean Basin Initiative are likely the precursors of other regional trading agreements in the Americas. In 2002, Congress passed, and the president signed into law, authority for the president to negotiate an expansion of regional trading alliances along the lines of NAFTA. This legislation allows the president to circumvent constitutional limits on the powers of the office. By passing this legislation, Congress agreed that it would review any trade agreement negotiated by the president with a simple yes or no vote. In other words, Congress will not have power to amend trade legislation in any way. Advocates of expanded trade agreements argue that this presidential authority is necessary so that other nations entering into the agreement with the United States can be assured that what they negotiate will become the law. Critics note that such trade authority circumvents constitutional mandates that the Congress have a role in shaping policy and limits the ability of labor and environmental interests (or other groups who might oppose freer trade) to shape trade relations. Now that the president holds this trade authority, the United States is more likely to enter into a free trade area of the Americas that could potentially include as many as thirty-four nations in the Americas and would serve as a counterweight to the European Community (and currency zone).

The U.S. government plays a central role in the international political economy. It achieves this through its domination of international lending agencies and regional defense and trade organizations. Although these international organizations reflect a desire by policymakers to address some international financial issues multilaterally (at least with the other advanced democracies), these efforts are ultimately limited by domestic politics. Some in Congress and a significant minority of the citizenry oppose U.S. involvement in multilateral organizations. Thus, while presidents may promote an international agenda, Congress often limits the funding for international organizations. The United States then appears to many outside the country as a hesitant and sometimes resentful economic leader.

In recent years, another multilateral institution has emerged that can potentially challenge U.S. economic dominance. The European Union (EU) is much more than a trading alliance. It is an organization of twenty-five European nations with growing international influence. Twelve EU members share a common currency, the euro. As the euro comes into widespread use, the dollar will face its first challenge in many years as the world's dominant trading currency. Increasingly, the euro has joined the dollar as a reserve currency for nations and wealthy individuals, and is also being used as a pricing currency for international trade. Each of these trends has the potential to reduce the dominance of the dollar in the world financial markets. Preliminary evidence may show that this trend has already begun. In spring 2005, financial analysts concluded that Asian central banks were reducing their dollar holdings and replacing them with euros, which contributed to a steep decline in the value of the dollar.

In addition to contributing to multilateral institutions, the United States funds binational international lending through such agencies as the Export-Import Bank and the Overseas Private Investment Corporation. These agencies make loans to countries and private businesses to purchase goods and services from U.S.-owned businesses. The United States also provides grants and loans to allies to further U.S. strategic and foreign policy objectives or for humanitarian reasons.

The new role of the United States in multilateral economic and defense organizations, and the growth in bilateral aid reflect a change in the nation's approach to its role in the world economy. The United States has slowly, and grudgingly, adapted to a world where it can no longer rest on its exceptionalism or simply assert its central role. Its economy and the larger society feel the effects of economic changes abroad. Thus, the U.S. government and, more slowly, the American people have seen their problems and needs from a global perspective. This incorporation into the larger world is certainly not complete. The separation of powers between the executive and legislative branches, and the local constituencies of members of Congress, ensures continuing resistance to this new international role.

The role of the United States in the international economy may be tested in coming years in a way that it has not been since the formation of the multilateral organizations after World War II. The strength of these international organizations is inherently limited by the increasing presence of multinational corporations that are able to transfer capital and production across national boundaries with little control by governments. While this change in the political economy is a political problem that all countries will face in the twenty-first century, the United States is and will be central to this problem. As the domestic U.S. economy is increasingly shaped by these international forces, U.S. citizens will demand economic stability from their government. The U.S. government was designed to be weak (see Section 3), so it will not easily be able to respond. The seeming lack of response will lead to strengthened calls by some in U.S. society to isolate the United States from the regulation of the international economy that it has helped shape. If these voices become dominant, the United States may find itself at odds with the international organizations that it helped create and that promote U.S. trade internationally.

Section ❸ Governance and Policy-Making

Organization of the State

The governing document of the United States is the Constitution. It was drafted in 1787 and ratified by the necessary nine states the following year (all thirteen colonies had ratified it by 1790). The Constitution was not the first governing document of the United States. It was preceded by the Articles of Confederation, which concentrated most power in the states. The revision of the Articles established a central government that was independent of the states but left the states most of their pre-existing powers (particularly police powers and public safety, the most common area of interaction between citizens and government). Although it had limited powers, the new U.S. government exercised powers over commerce and foreign policy that were denied to the states.

The Constitution has been amended twenty-seven times since 1787. The first ten of these amendments make up the Bill of Rights, the set of protections of individual rights that were a necessary compromise to ensure that the Constitution was ratified. These first ten amendments were ratified in 1791. The remaining seventeen amendments have extended democratic election practices and changed procedural deficiencies in the original Constitution that came to be perceived as inconsistent with democratic practice. Examples of amendments to extend democratic election practices would be the extension of the vote to women and to citizens between the ages of eighteen and twenty (the Nineteenth and Twenty-Sixth Amendments, respectively) or the prohibition of poll taxes, a tax that had to be paid before an individual could vote (the Twenty-Fourth Amendment). Changes to procedural deficiencies in the Constitution included the linking of presidential and vice-presidential candidates on a single ticket, replacing a system where the candidate with the most votes in the Electoral College won the presidency and the second-place candidate won the vice presidency (the Twelfth Amendment), and establishing procedures to replace a president who becomes incapacitated (the Twenty-Fifth Amendment).

Each amendment requires three-quarters of the states to agree to the change. Although the Constitution allows states to initiate amendments, all twenty-seven have resulted from amendments passed by Congress. When Congress initiates an amendment to the Constitution, two-thirds of senators must vote in favor of the amendment before it is sent to the states. States set their own procedures for ratifying constitutional amendments. In some, a simple majority in the legislature is sufficient, while others require support from a higher share of the legislature (such as two-thirds of those voting). Some require that a special convention be called to review the amendment.

Understanding two principles is necessary to understand American constitutional government: federalism and separation of powers. Federalism is the division of authority between multiple levels of government. In the case of the United States, the division is between the federal and state governments. Separation of powers is an effort to set government against itself by vesting separate branches with independent powers so that any one branch cannot permanently dominate the others.

These two characteristics of American government—federalism and separation of powers—were necessary compromises to guarantee the ratification of the Constitution. They should not, however, be viewed simply as compromises. On the contrary, they reflect a conscious desire by the constitutional framers to limit the federal government's ability to control citizens' lives. To limit what they perceived of as an inevitable tyranny of majorities over numerical minorities, the framers designed a system that set each part of government against all the other parts. Each branch of the federal government could limit the independent action of the other two branches, and the federal government and the states could limit each other. Although the potential for tyranny remained, the framers hoped that the individual ambitions of the members of each branch of government would cause each branch to fight efforts by other branches to undermine individual liberties.[7]

Federalism and separation of powers have a consequence that could not be fully anticipated by the framers of the Constitution: U.S. government is designed to be inefficient. Because each part of government is set against all others, policymaking is difficult. Inefficiencies can be partly overcome through extragovernmental mediating institutions such as political parties, but no single leader or branch of government can unequivocally dominate policymaking as the prime minister can in a parliamentary system. Although a consensus across branches of government can sometimes appear in times of national challenge, such as in the period immediately after the September 11 attacks, this commonality of purpose quickly dissolves as each branch of government seeks to protect its prerogatives and position in the policymaking process. As an example the USA PATRIOT Act passed Congress with few dissenting voices, but there was much more dissent four years later to renew provisions of the bill set to expire or to pass new legislation expanding the powers granted to the executive branch.

Federalism is the existence of multiple sovereigns. A citizen of the United States is simultaneously a citizen of the nation and of one of the states. Each citizen has responsibilities to each of these sovereigns and can be held accountable to the laws of each. Over the nation's 200-year history, the balance of power between the two principal sovereigns has shifted, with the federal government gaining power relative to the states, but to this day, states remain responsible for many parts of citizens' lives and act in these areas independently of the federal government.

Over time, many powers traditionally reserved to the states have shifted to the federal government. The period of the most rapid of these shifts was the New Deal, when the federal government tapped its commerce regulation powers to create a wide range of programs to address the economic and social needs of the people.

The second organizing principle of American government is separation of powers. While each of the states has adopted some form of separation of powers, its purest form exists at the federal level. Each of the three branches of the federal government—the executive, the legislature (see Section 4), and the judiciary—shares in the responsibilities of governing and has some oversight over the other two branches. In order to enact a law, for example, Congress (the legislative branch) must pass the law, and the president (the executive branch) must sign it. The president can block the action of Congress by vetoing the law. Congress can override the president's veto through a two-thirds vote in both houses of Congress. The courts (the judiciary) can review the constitutionality of laws passed by Congress and signed by the president. Congress and the states acting in unison, however, can reverse a Supreme Court ruling on the constitutionality of a law by passing a constitutional amendment by a two-thirds vote that is subsequently ratified by three-quarters of the states. The Senate (the legislative branch) must ratify senior appointments to the executive branch, including members of the cabinet, as well as federal judges. The president nominates these judges, and Congress sets their salaries and much of their jurisdiction (except in constitutional matters). In sum, the separation of powers allows each branch to limit the others and prevents any one branch from carrying out its responsibilities without the others' cooperation. It also allows a phenomenon unanticipated by the framers of the Constitution: the divided government in which different political parties control the executive and legislative branches of government, which has been the norm for the federal government since 1968 (the Republicans have controlled all branches of government since Congress convened in 2003).

Federalism and separation of powers create a complexity in U.S. government that cannot be found in other advanced democracies. This complexity encourages an ongoing competition for political power. The states traditionally played a greater role in these battles but are relatively less important now than they were before the 1930s.

The Executive

The Presidency

The American presidency has grown dramatically in power since the nation's first days. The president, who is indirectly elected, serves a fixed four-year term and is limited to two terms by a constitutional amendment ratified in 1951. The president is both head of state and head of government. The roots of presidential power are found in these roles more than in the powers delegated to the presidency in the Constitution.

Through much of the political history of the United States, the president was not at the center of the federal government. Quite the contrary. The Constitution established Congress as the central branch of government and relegated the president to a much more poorly defined role whose primary responsibilities are administering programs designed and funded by Congress. Although twentieth-century presidents found new powers and exercised powers unimaginable to earlier presidents, the structural weaknesses of the presidency remain. The president must receive ongoing support from Congress to ensure the implementation of his agenda. But the president cannot control Congress except to the degree that public opinion (and, to a much lesser degree, party loyalty) encourages members of Congress to support the president. As a result, U.S. presidents are far weaker than prime ministers in parliamentary systems; they can, however, stay in office long after they have lost popular support.

The president is the commander in chief of the military and may grant pardons, make treaties (which are ratified with the approval of two-thirds of the Senate), and make senior appointments to the executive branch and to judicial posts (again with congressional concurrence). The president is required to provide an annual state of the union report to Congress and may call Congress into session. Finally, the president manages the bureaucracy, which at the time of the Constitution's ratification was small but has subsequently grown in size and responsibility. Thus, in terms of formal powers, the president is far weaker than Congress is.

With one exception, presidents until the turn of the twentieth century did not add considerably to the delegated powers. Instead, nineteenth-century presidents largely served as clerks to the will of Congress. The exception among nineteenth-century presidents was Abraham Lincoln, who dominated Congress during the Civil War. His example was one that twentieth-century presidents followed. He became a national leader and was able to establish his own power base directly in the citizenry. Lincoln realized that each member of Congress depended on a local constituency (a district or state) and was able to label their activities as being local or sectional. Lincoln created a national power base for the presidency by presenting himself as the only national political leader, an important position during the Civil War. He had an advantage in being commander in chief during wartime; however, the foundation of his power was not the military but his connection to the people.

In the twentieth century, presidents discovered that they had a previously untapped resource. Beginning with Theodore Roosevelt, twentieth-century presidents used the office of the president as a bully pulpit to speak to the nation and propose public policies that met national needs. No member of Congress or the Senate could claim a similar national constituency (although several have tried in the last sixty years). Roosevelt began a trend that has been tapped by each of his successors. He used the mass media (in his case, newspapers) to present a national agenda to the American people. The most successful of his successors used newly available media to reach over the heads of Congress to the people. Most successful among these twentieth-century presidents using new media technologies was Franklin Roosevelt, whose radio broadcast Fireside Chats unified much of the nation in support of elements of the New Deal.

Later in the twentieth century, presidents found a new power. As the role of the federal government expanded, they managed a much larger federal bureaucracy that provided goods and services used by nearly all citizens. Thus, a program like Social Security connects almost all citizens to the executive branch. Although Congress appropriates the funds for Social Security and played a significant role in its design, the executive branch sends the checks each month. Beginning with the New Deal, presidents proposed programs that expanded the federal bureaucracy and, consequently, the connection between the people and the president. In 2003, for example, President Bush proposed and Congress passed an expansion to the Medicare program providing prescription drug insurance for Medicare recipients. Estimates indicate that this program will cost the government $1.2 trillion over its first decade, a considerable increase from the $500 to $600 billion estimated when Congress passed the legislation.

Finally, twentieth-century presidents learned an important lesson from the experience of Abraham Lincoln. The president has an authority over the military that places the office at the center of policymaking in military and international affairs. This centrality is particularly evident in times of war when immediate decisions may have to be made. Thus, in the period from World War II to the collapse of the Soviet Union, the presidency gained strength from the widely perceived need for a single decision maker. After September 11, the president assumed direction of the U.S. response, although Congress quickly sought to reestablish its prerogatives.

Even as Congress balked at some presidential initiatives in the post-9/11 period, the public looked to the executive branch, and more specifically to President Bush, to lead. President Bush used these popular expectations strategically in the 2002 elections to support Republican candidates in close races. Republicans won control of the Senate and gained several seats in the House of Representatives and added to these margins in 2004. Gains by the incumbent party in an off-year election and at the beginning of a second presidential term are unusual in politics today.

Although the presidency gained powers in the twentieth century, the office remains structurally weak relative to Congress. Despite popular expectations for presidential leadership in the period after 9/11, presidential dominance in policymaking has declined relative to the period between World War II and the end of the cold war. Presidential power is particularly undercut by the norm of divided government: presidents have little power over Congresses controlled by the other party. The bureaucracy is a weak link on which to build institutional power. Congress has significant powers to shape it. Congress has become increasingly restive about ceding power in international affairs to the president. Since Congress retains the power to appropriate funds, the president must ultimately yield to its will on the design and implementation of policy.

To date, all presidents have been men, all have been white, and all but one (John F. Kennedy) have been Protestant. While being a former general was once a stepping-stone to the presidency, in today's politics having served as a governor works to a candidate's advantage. Presidents from 1976 to 2003 included four former governors (Georgia's Jimmy Carter, California's Ronald Reagan, Arkansas's Bill Clinton, and Texas's George W. Bush). Only President George H.W. Bush had extensive service in the federal government (including serving as President Reagan's vice president) prior to winning the presidency. Despite a common assumption, only four vice presidents have been elected to the presidency immediately at the end of their terms. It is more common for vice presidents to move to the presidency on the death (or, in one case, the resignation) of the president. As the media have become more central to the electoral process, presidents (as well as presidential candidates) have on average been getting younger. Bill Clinton was forty-six when he was elected president in 1992. George W. Bush was fifty-four in 2000.

The Cabinet and the Bureaucracy

To manage the U.S. government, the president appoints (and the Senate confirms) senior administrators to key executive branch departments. The chief officers at each of the core departments make up the president's cabinet. These senior officers include heads of prominent departments such as the secretary of state, the attorney general, and the secretary of defense, as well as lesser-known officials such as the secretary of veterans affairs. Contrary to the case in parliamentary systems, the U.S. cabinet has no legal standing, and presidents frequently use it only at a symbolic level. The president is also free to extend membership to other senior appointed officials (such as the U.S. ambassador to the United Nations), so the number of cabinet members fluctuates from administration to administration.

The senior officers of the executive branch agencies manage a work force of approximately 1.9 million civilian civil servants (the bureaucracy). Although formally part of the executive branch, the bureaucracy must also be responsive to Congress. Under certain circumstances, it operates independent of both elective branches and, rarely, under the direction of the courts. The presidential appointees establish broad policy objectives and propose budgets that can expand or contract the responsibilities of executive branch offices. Congress must approve these budgets, and it uses this financial oversight to encourage bureaucrats to behave as their congressional monitors wish. Although the size of the federal bureaucracy had been in steady decline since the early 1980s, the new federal military and security responsibilities established after the September 11 attacks have reversed this trend. The federalization of airport baggage screening alone added approximately 45,000 workers to the federal bureaucracy.

September 11 also spurred a challenge to the protections traditionally guaranteed to the federal bureaucracy that would not have been politically possible prior to the attacks. When the Department of Homeland Security was formed to unite many federal agencies responsible for domestic security, Congress exempted the approximately 170,000 federal workers in the twenty-two agencies from civil service protections. President Bush argued that this change would ensure the agency would be more responsive to public security threats. Opponents expressed concern that the Bush administration, or a subsequent administration, could use the new Department of Homeland Security to reward political supporters with patronage appointments and impede its mission of homeland security.

Arguably, the inability of either Congress or the president to control the bureaucracy fully should give it some independence. Although this may be true in the case of policy areas that are of little interest to the elected branches, the bureaucracy as a rule does not have the resources to collect information and shape the laws that guide their operations. Interest groups have steadily filled this informational role, but the information comes at a cost. Bureaucracies often develop symbiotic relations with the interests that they should be regulating. The interest groups have more access to Congress and can shape the operations of the regulatory agencies. These **iron triangle relationships** (among a private interest group, a congressional committee or subcommittee overseeing the policy in questions, and a federal agency implementing the policy) often exclude new players who represent alternative views on how policies should be implemented. Thus, without an independent source of authority, the bureaucracy is dependent not just on the elected branches but also on interest groups.

Other State Institutions

Besides the presidency and the Congress (see Section 4), several other institutions are central to the operation of U.S. government: the military, national security agencies, the judiciary, and state and local governments.

The Military

The U.S. Army, Navy, Marine Corps, Coast Guard, and Air Force are made up of approximately 1.3 million active duty personnel plus an additional 1.3 million reserve and national guard troops (who are increasingly asked to serve overseas for extended periods of deployment). The president is commander in chief of the U.S. military, but on a day-to-day basis, U.S. forces serve under the command of a nonpolitical officers corps made up of graduates of the nation's military academies and officer candidate training programs at civilian universities and from the ranks of the military services.

Because of the unique geographic advantages of the United States, the military has had to dedicate few of its resources to defending U.S. territory. In the nineteenth century, its primary responsibilities were to defend U.S. shipping on the high seas and to colonize the West. In the twentieth century, U.S. troops have seen more service abroad. Beginning with the new U.S. geopolitical role after World War II, the military was given new responsibilities to support U.S. multilateral and regional defense agreements. In the 1990s, the U.S. military was committed to multilateral military operations and United Nations peacekeeping efforts. In Kosovo, for example, the North Atlantic Treaty Organization (NATO) sought to remove President Milosevic from power in response to his government's attacks on ethnic Albanians. The United States committed 31,600 troops to the NATO force of approximately 114,000. U.S. involvement in multilateral military operations and U.N. peacekeeping efforts is highly controversial among the American public and some members of Congress. The U.S., for example, slowed efforts to put peacekeepers in Somalia and impeded U.N. efforts to respond to the Rwandan genocide. The U.S. commitment to multilateral military operations is happening with sufficient frequency, however, to suggest that it will be an ongoing responsibility.

The United States increasingly looks to its allies to support U.S. military objectives abroad. In preparation for war with Iraq, U.S. military leaders designed an invasion force of 130,000, with 100,000 ground troops and the remainder in support positions abroad. These 100,000 U.S. military ground troops were supported by at least 15,000 British ground troops. By the end of 2004, this force had grown to 148,000 U.S. troops and 22,000 allied troops (approximately 45 percent from the UK).

As was the pattern in the civilian bureaucracy in the 1990s, the military saw its size reduced. Many of the traditional responsibilities of the military, such as support of troops and specialized technical activities, have been transferred to reserve units. Reserve troops are now called to active duty more frequently and for longer periods.

With the increased expectations for the military came increased reliance on defense technologies. U.S. nuclear weapons, intelligence technologies, and space-based defense technologies, as well as the maintenance of conventional weaponry and troop support, have significantly raised the cost of maintaining the military. This has led to ongoing national debates about the cost of the military and whether defense resources should be expended for technology or for troops. Industries have emerged to provide goods and services to the military. Proposals to cut defense spending often face opposition from these industries.

In response to the September 11 attacks, the president quickly proposed, and Congress appropriated, a record increase in defense spending of more than 10 percent, from approximately $330 billion to $380 billion. By 2005, this budget increased to $401 billion. These new funds included pay raises for the U.S. troops and resources to expand the size of the military. A considerable share, however—as much as a third of the increase—was made up of grants to state and local governments for homeland security. These appropriations provided operating funds to local police and fire and rescue departments. Although U.S. policymakers have long used the military budget to support the domestic economy (military base placement, for example), this $15 billion in new commitments represented an unprecedented new use of the defense budget to support state and local activities.

National Security Agencies

The September 11, 2001, attacks focused the attention of policy-makers on domestic security to an unprecedented degree. Agencies with responsibility in this area that had been dispersed throughout the federal government were united in the Department of Homeland Security under a single cabinet secretary. Responsibility for airport screening was federalized, and funding for border enforcement increased dramatically. Although it took somewhat longer, intelligence-gathering agencies were placed under the administrative control of a director of national intelligence (see Section 4). Funding for domestic security and international intelligence gathering increased by approximately one-third. Despite these dramatic administrative reorganizations and added appropriations, however, there is little evidence that intragovernmental communication has improved or that the citizenry has a greater sense of security.

Legislation passed in the months after September 11, 2001, also subjected U.S. citizens and permanent residents to greater levels of government scrutiny and

to potential violations of civil rights. Government and banks subjected financial transactions to new levels of review. Immigrants, in particular, faced limits on services available from government. The Bush administration asserted (and the courts rejected) a position that suspected terrorists could be seized and held indefinitely, without charges. Reserve troops have been required to serve multiple long-term commitments in Iraq and Afghanistan and have been prohibited from leaving the reserves at the end of their commitments. The military has had difficulty reaching its recruitment goals, and this has raised the specter of a draft.

The Judiciary

Of the three branches of federal government, the courts are the most poorly defined in the Constitution. Initially, it was unclear what check the courts had on other branches of government. Equally important, the courts were quite dependent on the president, who appointed judges, and on Congress, which approved the nomination of judges and set the jurisdictional authority for the courts. The early days of the federal courts confirmed this weakness. In the Judiciary Act of 1789, Congress created a Supreme Court and a network of lower federal courts—thirteen district courts and three circuit courts. Judges, who often had to travel from city to city to hear cases, saw a higher turnover in the early years than in any subsequent period of American history.

In 1803, the Supreme Court established the foundation for a more substantial role in federal policy-making. It ruled in *Marbury* **v.** *Madison* that the courts inherently had the right to review the constitutionality of the laws. This ruling, though used rarely in the nineteenth century, gave the judiciary a central place in the system of **checks and balances.** The Court that ruled in *Marbury* v. *Madison* recognized the weakness of the federal courts in this era. While asserting their power to review the constitutionality of a piece of federal legislation, the substantive effect of the ruling was to give a political victory to the sitting president, Thomas Jefferson, against the partisan and ideological interests of a majority of the members of the Court. The majority of the Court at the time had been nominated to the judiciary by political opponents of Jefferson. Had the same justices ruled against President Jefferson, he would likely have disregarded this ruling and demonstrated the fundamental weakness of the federal courts.

Even with the power of judicial review, the judicial branch remained weaker than the other branches. In addition to Congress's ability to establish court jurisdiction in nonconstitutional cases and the president's ability to fill the courts with people of his choosing, the courts have other weaknesses. They must rely on the executive branch to enforce their decisions. Enforcement proves particularly difficult when a court's rulings are not in line with public opinion, such as when the courts ruled that organized prayer did not belong in the public schools or that busing should be used as a tool to accomplish racial integration in the schools. The courts' own rules have also limited their powers. Traditionally, the courts limit standing—the ability to bring suits—to individuals who saw their rights directly challenged by a law, policy, or action of government.

Beginning in the second half of the twentieth century, the federal courts gained power relative to the other branches of government. In part, this was accomplished by expanding the rules of standing so that groups as well as individuals could challenge laws, policies, or government actions and by maintaining longer jurisdiction over cases as a tool to establish limited enforcement abilities. The courts also gained relative power because of the expansion of federal regulatory policy. Unclear laws and regulations, often requiring technical expertise to implement, placed the courts at the center of many policy debates. The courts have also gained power because they became a venue for individuals and groups in society whose interests were neglected by the democratically elected institutions but who could make claims based on constitutional guarantees of civil rights or civil liberties. African Americans, for example, received favorable rulings from federal courts before Congress and the president responded to their demands. Since the September 11 attacks, the executive branch and majorities in Congress manifested a willingness to limit individual rights in a search for collective security. Courts—including the Supreme Court—have been more cautious. In 2004, the Supreme Court rejected administration assertions that it could seize and hold suspected terrorists indefinitely. Instead, the court ruled that U.S. citizens and foreign nationals detained as terrorists can challenge their status in the federal courts.

The steady increase in judicial power in the twentieth century should not obscure the fundamental weaknesses of the courts relative to the elected branches. Although courts in some cases have been able to establish connections with the citizenry around specific issues, the courts are more dependent on the elected branches than the elected branches are on them.

Subnational Government

State governments serve as an important part of government in the United States. Their responsibilities include providing services to people more directly than does the federal government. Most important among these is education, which has always been a state and local responsibility in the United States. Until the New Deal era, state and local governments served as the primary point of interaction between the citizenry and the government.

States and localities continue to serve a critical function in contemporary U.S. governance. They are able to experiment with new policies. If a policy fails in a single state, the cost is much lower than if the entire nation had undertaken a new policy that eventually failed. Successes in one state can be copied in others or nationally. For example, Wisconsin experimented with welfare reform in the early 1990s before the federal government changed national welfare laws in 1996. Policy-makers outside Wisconsin saw these reforms as a success and implemented similar (although more draconian) reforms nationally. Had these reforms not been perceived to be successful in Wisconsin, they would not have become the model for federal welfare reform, and the cost of experimentation would have been confined to Wisconsin. Even after the implementation of this reform, Wisconsin spends far more than many other states on social welfare programs.

In addition to state governments, citizens pay taxes to, and receive services from, an array of local governments that include such entities as counties, cities, districts for special services such as water and fire protection, and townships. These local entities have a different relationship to the states, however, than do states to the federal government. The local entities are statutory creations of the state and can be altered or eliminated by the state (and are not a form of federalism).

Local governments are nevertheless very important in the system of American governance. They provide many of the direct services that the citizenry receives from the government. Because states and localities have different resources (often based on local property taxes) and different visions of the responsibilities of government, people in the United States may receive vastly different versions of the same government service, depending simply on where they live. Education provides an example. Property tax–poor areas may spend only a few thousand dollars per year educating students, while property tax–rich areas may spend $15,000 to $20,000 per student. Some states try to equalize education spending within the state, while others see disparities this great within the state, but there is no national effort, or constitutional authority, to equalize spending across states.

The Policy-Making Process

Separation of powers and constitutional limits on each branch of government create a federal policy-making process with no clear starting or ending point. Instead, citizens and organized interests have multiple points of entry and can contest outcomes through multiple venues. There is little centralization of policy-making except in a few areas where there is consensus among national leaders. Without centralization, policies often conflict with each other (for example, the United States currently subsidizes tobacco cultivation but seeks to hamper tobacco companies from selling cigarettes through high taxes, health warnings, and limits on advertising). Federalism further complicates policy-making. Each of the states sets policy in many areas, and states often have contradictory policies. State policy-making institutions are often used strategically to shape the debate around an issue or to influence other states or the federal government. In sum, policy advocates have many venues in which to propose new policies or change existing policies: congressional committees, individual members of Congress, executive branch regulatory agencies, state governments, and, in some states, direct ballot initiatives.

With so many entrance points, there are equally many points at which policies can be blocked. Once

Congress passes a law, executive branch agencies must issue regulations to explain specifically how the law will be implemented. Subtle changes can be inserted as part of this process. On controversial issues, senior political appointees set policy for the writing of regulations. Laws that must be implemented by several agencies raise a possible role for the cabinet to craft government-wide solutions to policy needs, but recent presidents have not used the cabinet as a whole to structure policy-making in this way.

Furthermore, people or interest groups that feel disadvantaged by the regulations can contest regulations in the courts. They also can contest the law itself, if the assertion can be made that the law is unconstitutional or conflicts with another law or with state government responsibilities. Once a policy is in place, it can be opposed or undermined by creating a competing policy in another agency or at the state level.

The Constitution gives no guidance about the origins and outcomes of policy initiatives. The president is directed to present an annual report to Congress on the state of the nation. Over time, this has evolved into an organized set of policy proposals. In the absence of presidential leadership in policymaking, Congress partially filled the void. Enumerated powers in the Constitution direct Congress to take action in specific policy areas, such as setting tax policy, establishing a post office, and building public roads. Once Congress established committees to increase its efficiency (see Section 4), these committees offered forums for discussion of narrow policy areas of importance to society. These committees, however, are not mandated in the Constitution and are changed to reflect the policy needs of each era. Thus, while presidents can propose policies (and implement them), only Congress has the ability to deliberate about policy and pass it into law.

The courts have long provided a forum for debating the outcome of policy decisions, but have rarely initiated policies on their own. Beginning in the 1970s, however, some federal courts experimented with initiating policy as a way of maintaining jurisdiction in cases brought before them. These efforts, such as court-mandated busing of public school students to achieve racial integration and control of state prison or mental health care systems, spurred much national controversy and caused the judiciary to decline in public opinion.

Today, the courts are much more likely to block or reshape policies than to initiate them.

Because there is no clear starting point for initiating policies, individual citizens have great difficulty when they seek to advocate a new policy. Into this void have come extragovernmental institutions, some with narrow interests and some promoting collective interests. Prominent or wealthy individuals or groups can get Congress's or the president's attention through campaign contributions and other types of influence in support for their candidacies and the causes they support.

Mediating institutions have also emerged to represent mass interests. Political parties, organized on a mass basis in the 1830s, organize citizen demands and channel them to political leaders. The parties balance the needs of various interests in society and come as close as any other group in society to presenting comprehensive policy proposals (often summarized in the parties' platforms). Group-based interests also organize to make narrow demands. Veterans are an early example of a group in society that made a group-specific demand on federal policymaking. In the twentieth century, as both federal and state governments began to implement more widespread distributive and redistributive policies, more organized interest groups appeared. These interest groups have become the dominant form of mediating institution in U.S. politics (see Section 4). Unlike political parties, however, interest groups represent only a single issue or group of narrowly related issues. Thus, the complexity of policymaking in the United States has created an equally complex structure of making demands.

Section ❹ Representation and Participation

The Legislature

Of the three branches in the federal government, the founders envisioned that Congress would be at the center and would be the most powerful. They concentrated the most important powers in it and were most explicit about its responsibilities. For most of the nation's history, their expectations for the powers of Congress have been met.

One of the most important compromises of the Constitutional Convention involved the structure of Congress. States with large populations wanted seats in the national legislature to be allocated based on population. Small states feared they would be at a disadvantage under this system and wanted each state to have equal representation. The compromise was a **bicameral** system with two houses, one allocated by population—the House of Representatives—and the other with equal representation for each state—the Senate. This compromise has remained largely uncontested for the past two hundred years despite the growing gap in population between large and small states. Today, for example, the 507,000 residents of Wyoming elect two senators, the same number elected by the more than 36 million residents of California. The senatorial vote of each resident of Wyoming has seventy-one times the impact of each Californian. In this pattern, the U.S. Senate is unique among legislatures in the world's democracies.

These two legislative bodies are structured differently. The House has 435 members (a number that has been fixed since 1910) and is designed to be more responsive to the popular will. Terms are short (two years), and the districts are smaller than Senate seats except in the smallest states. After 2000, the average House seat had 646,952 constituents and will continue to grow. The Senate has only 100 members and is designed to be more deliberative, with six-year, staggered terms. Although unlikely, it is possible every two years to vote out an entire House of Representatives; the Senate could see only one-third of its members unseated during any election year.

Membership in the U.S. Congress is slightly more diverse than the people who have held the presidency, although most members of Congress are white male Protestants. In the 1990s, approximately 12 percent of officeholders were women, 9 percent were African American, 4 percent were Latino, and 0.5 percent were Asian American. Most members of Congress, regardless of gender, race, or ethnicity, are highly educated professionals. Law is the most common profession. The Senate is less racially diverse but has a slightly higher share of women: two Latinos, two Asian Americans, one African American, and fourteen women serve in the Senate in 2005.

The two central powers of Congress are legislation and oversight. For a bill to become law, it must be passed in the same form by both the House and the Senate and signed by the president. Equally important, Congress has the ability to monitor the implementation of laws that it passes. Since it continues to control the appropriation of funds for programs each year (all government spending must begin with an appropriations bill in the House of Representatives), Congress can oversee programs being administered by the executive branch and shape their implementation through allocations of money or by rewriting the law.

Congress has organized itself to increase its efficiency. Discussion and debate take place primarily in committees and subcommittees. The committee system permits each member to specialize in specific areas of public policy. Committees are organized topically, and members often seek to serve on committees that are of particular interest to their constituencies— for instance, a member of Congress from a rural area may seek to serve on the Agriculture Committee. All members seek to serve on committees that have broad oversight of a wide range of government activities, such as the Appropriations Committee through which all spending bills must pass. Specialization allows each member to have some influence while not requiring that she or he know the substance of all facets of government.

For a bill to become law, it must be reviewed by the committee and subcommittee that have responsibility for the substantive area that it covers. When a member proposes a bill, it is referred to committee based on the subject matter of the legislation and usually never gets any further. In each session, relatively few bills are given hearings before a subcommittee or committee. The House and Senate leadership (the speaker of the House, the Senate majority leader, and committee chairs) are central to deciding which bills receive hearings. If the bill receives support from the committee, it must then be debated by the body as a whole. In the House, this may never occur because that institution has another roadblock: the Rules Committee, which determines what can be debated on the floor and under what terms. Only in the Senate can debate

be unlimited (although it can be limited by cloture, a vote of sixty senators to limit debate). These hierarchical structures strengthen the powers granted to the House and the Senate in the Constitution because they allow Congress to act efficiently and to use its powers to investigate federal programs, even though it does not administer them. As a result, Congress places itself at the center of the policymaking process. When Woodrow Wilson, in his years as a political scientist before he ran for president, studied U.S. government, he saw Congress as the central branch of government and the committee system as its central organizational tool.[8] Although congressional power waned somewhat in the late twentieth century, it remains the foremost branch of American government. This specialization and hierarchy ensure that congressional leaders are more central to the design and oversight of policy than are members of European parliaments.

This tension between the constitutional powers of Congress and the national focus on the president as the national leader became evident in the federal government's response to the September 11 attacks. Initially, President Bush shaped the public policy response, including a large emergency appropriation that included financial assistance for New York City, grants and loans to the airlines, an increase in defense and intelligence spending, and military action against Afghanistan. Congress quickly followed the presidential lead and appropriated funds, federalized airport security screening, and supported military action in Afghanistan that targeted the Al Qaeda movement that took responsibility for the September 11 attacks and the Taliban government that provided a safe haven for Al Qaeda.

As Bush administration policies evolved and the response came to focus on structural changes in the federal government, however, Congress began to reassert its constitutional prerogatives. Congressional concern about the growth in executive power after September 11 was probably most evident in its reaction to Bush administration reorganization of more than fifty federal agencies into the cabinet-level Department of Homeland Security. In addition to centralizing many (but not all) federal agencies with responsibilities for domestic intelligence collection and public safety, the Bush administration limited the protections federal workers in this new agency would have. The selection of federal agencies with responsibilities for security to exclude from the new department (most notably the Federal Bureau of Investigation) reflected White House sensitivities to agencies with strong support in Congress that would, though logically placed in the new agency, make the Department of Homeland Security less likely to receive congressional approval. Democrats, and perhaps some Republicans, in Congress feared that granting the new Department of Homeland Security an exemption from worker civil service protections would make the new agency more subject to political pressures. When combined with its responsibilities for intelligence gathering and law enforcement, this gave many in Congress concerns about the growth of executive power and for the potential of new restrictions on civil liberties.

Congress also asserted itself to ensure that the National Commission on Terrorist Attacks on the United States, unofficially known as the 9/11 Commission, would be formed, funded, and given sufficient time to conduct its investigation and write its report. Initially, the Bush administration opposed the formation of such an investigative commission and, once it relented in the face of strong congressional opposition to its position, sought to limit the scope, funding, and longevity of the commission. The commission documented executive branch intelligence-gathering failures and provided the political pressure necessary to force the Bush administration to create a new federal official—the Director of National Intelligence—who would oversee most U.S. intelligence-gathering agencies.

As the Bush administration moved toward war with Iraq, Congress also forced the president to seek and obtain congressional approval for any U.S. military action against Iraq and for the costs of conducting the war. In October 2002, the House voted 296 to 133 and the Senate voted 77 to 23 to authorize President Bush to attack Iraq if Saddam Hussein refused to give up weapons of mass destruction as required by the United Nations. The president has also had to seek congressional approval for war-related expenditures. Much of the cost of the wars in Afghanistan and Iraq as well as the reconstruction of the two countries has been paid for through supplemental appropriations, not the Defense Department's annual appropriation. The debates over these supplemental appropriations, totaling more than $240 billion by 2005, have allowed

Congress to investigate the conduct of the wars and reconstructions and hold administration officials accountable for their previous assurances to Congress. To date, these appropriations have not faced serious opposition. As public concern about the Iraqi reconstruction grows, Congress has increasingly been willing to use the supplemental appropriation bill debates as venues for criticism of the administration and to amend the appropriations bills to shape unrelated federal programs, such as immigration, that the Bush administration would rather not have debated.

As congressional responses to presidential leadership in the U.S. response to September 11 and the wars in Afghanistan and Iraq should indicate, Congress did not yield as the president gained power. It passed legislation to undermine presidential power and, equally important, applied its traditional authority to investigate federal programs to weaken the presidency. Beginning with Watergate (the Nixon administration scandals in which Nixon and his aides used the institutions of the federal government to investigate and intimidate Nixon's political opponents), Congress directly investigated presidents. These investigations of presidents and their senior appointees weaken the connection between the presidency and the people (regardless of the specific charges being investigated or the outcome of the investigation). Investigations of modern presidents weaken not just the presidents as individuals but also the presidency as an office.

Political Parties and the Party System

Electoral politics in the United States is organized around two political parties. The roots of two-party politics can be found both in the nation's political culture and in the legal structures that govern elections. Today, the two major parties are the Democrats and the Republicans. The Democrats can trace their origins to the 1800 election, while the Republicans first appeared in 1856. Despite the fact that today's parties have consistently competed against each other in each of the past thirty-eight presidential elections, the coalitions that support them (and which they, in turn, serve) have changed continually.

Today, the Republicans depend on a coalition of upper-income voters, moral and religious conservatives, small-business owners, residents of rural areas, and evangelical Christians. They receive more support from men than from women and are strongest in the South and the Mountain West. In 2004, voters identifying "moral values" as the most important issue facing the nation were particularly important to President Bush's victory in several states, including Ohio. Bush won nearly four out of five votes of voters who identified moral values as the most important issue facing the nation.

The Republicans have tried to make inroads in minority communities but have been largely unsuccessful, with the exception of Cuban Americans and some Asian American groups (see Table 1). President Bush has sought to bring a higher share of the Latino vote into the Republican fold. Some exit polls indicate that he was modestly successful in 2004, but these results are disputed by scholars who study Latino voting patterns. For Republicans to win Latino (or African American) votes on a wider scale, the party would have to be willing to alienate some core Republican constituencies.[9]

The contemporary Democratic coalition includes urban populations, the elderly, racial and ethnic minorities, workers in export-oriented businesses, unionized labor, and, increasingly, working women. Suburban voters have increasingly joined the Democratic coalition. Today's Democrats are in the Northeast and on the West Coast. The Democrats have built a steady advantage among women voters. This is a double advantage for the Democrats: women have higher turnout rates than do men, and men split their votes more evenly.

Each party sees support from approximately 34 percent of registered voters. Approximately 31 percent of registered voters are independents, with a slightly larger share of these independents leaning toward the Democrats than the Republicans. Generally, Democrats, who are more likely to be poor, less educated, and younger than Republican voters, are less likely to turn out on Election Day. As a result, the Republicans have been the dominant party at the presidential level since 1968 and have had a slight advantage in governorships and state legislatures. After the 2004 election, the Republicans controlled governorships in twenty-eight states, and the Democrats controlled twenty-two. The majority of members of the House of Representatives have been Republican since

Table 1

Candidate Vote in Presidential Elections, by Race and Ethnicity, 1976–2004 (in percentages)

	Whites	Blacks	Hispanics	Asian Americans
1976				
Carter (D)	47	83	76	n.a.
Ford (R)	52	16	24	n.a.
1980				
Reagan (R)	56	11	33	n.a.
Carter (D)	36	85	59	n.a.
Anderson (I)	7	3	6	n.a.
1984				
Reagan (R)	64	9	37	n.a.
Mondale (D)	35	90	62	n.a.
1988				
Bush (R)	59	12	30	n.a.
Dukakis (D)	40	86	69	n.a.
1992				
Clinton (D)	39	83	61	31
Bush (R)	40	10	25	55
Perot (I)	20	7	14	15
1996				
Clinton (D)	43	84	72	43
Dole (R)	46	12	21	48
Perot (I)	9	4	6	8
2000				
Bush (R)	54	8	31	41
Gore (D)	42	90	67	54
Nader (I)	3	1	2	4
2004				
Bush (R)	58	11	43	44
Kerry (D)	41	88	56	58

Note: Data not collected on Asian Americans until 1992. Data do not always add up to 100 because of votes for other candidates.

Source: New York Times, "How Americans Voted: A Political Portrait." *The New York Times National Edition*, November 7, 2004.

1994. In 2005, the Republicans have a 232-to-202 majority (with one independent voting with the Democrats on organizational matters). The Republicans hold an eleven-vote majority in the Senate.

The relative Republican advantage in holding federal offices in the last two decades of the twentieth century may be changing at this writing. Internal conflicts in the Democratic Party in the 1970s and 1980s limited its ability to present a cohesive message and reach out to new constituencies. As a result, it was not able to recruit new followers at rates comparable to the Republicans. These conflicts—particularly disputes over the size and scope of government, affirmative action (programs designed to redress past discrimination against racial and ethnic minorities and women) and other race-sensitive programs, and taxation and the deficit—subsided during the Clinton presidency and have remained quiet since he completed his term. Beginning in the 1990s, internal conflicts grew in the Republican Party that President Bush was able to sooth. Moral conservatives and fiscal conservatives each wanted the party to focus on their interests and jettison the others' issues as a way of expanding the party's base of support. The future of each party's coalition is unclear at this writing, although it is worth noting that Democrats are more successful in the parts of the country seeing population growth (particularly suburbs of major cities) than are Republicans. The Republicans have begun to see growth in support in the so-called exurbs, or areas in transition from rural to suburban on the fringes of metropolitan areas.

These party divisions lead to speculation that new parties might emerge. The political culture of the United States limits the likelihood that a faction of one of the parties (such as the religious right from the Republicans) will break off and form a party that competes in election after election. Instead, two coalitional parties are the norm, an unusual pattern among advanced democracies.

Electoral law reinforces this situation. Most U.S. elections are conducted under a **single-member plurality (SMP) election system** in district-based elections, again an unusual pattern among advanced democracies, where proportional representation systems and multi-member districts are much more common. In the United States, the candidate who wins the most votes wins the election, and only one person is elected from each district. Single-member district-based elections reward coalitional parties and diminish opportunities for single-issue parties or narrowly focused parties, such as the Green Party in today's politics. Broad coalitional parties can contest a seat election after election, while smaller parties are likely to dissolve after a number of defeats. Finally, since the existing parties have written the electoral laws in each of the states (the laws vary dramatically from state to state), they have made it difficult for new parties to get on the ballot.

Geography reinforces the difficulty faced by small and single-issue parties in an SMP system. There are more than 600,000 elected offices in the United States. To compete regularly in even a small percentage of these, a party must have a national presence and a national infrastructure. Most third parties fail long before they are able to compete in more than a few hundred of these 600,000 races. The Green Party, for example, fielded only 433 candidates in 2004, or just 7 of every 10,000 elective offices.

Thus, it is unlikely that a new major party will emerge in the United States. Much more than in countries with proportional representation, the electoral law in the United States limits the ability of new parties to emerge and, if they do, to survive. Both the political culture and the geography of the United States, however, make this unlikely. The heterogeneity of the U.S. population and the range of regional needs and interests advantage a system that forces coalitions prior to elections, as does a system with just two political parties. The Constitution-driven inefficiency of U.S. government would become all the more dramatic if multiple parties (rather than two that must, by their nature, be coalitions) were competing in legislatures to shape outcomes.

Elections

The United States takes pride in its long practice of democracy. As an example of its commitment to democratic norms, it points to the frequency of elections and the range of offices filled through elections. As is not the case in parliamentary systems, these elections are conducted on a regular schedule: presidential elections every four years, Senate elections every six years, House of Representatives elections every two years. States and localities set the terms of state and local offices, but almost all have fixed terms. (Local judicial offices in some states are the rare exception.) General elections for federal offices are held the first Tuesday after the first Monday in November. States and localities establish dates for primary elections and for general elections for nonfederal offices. Thus, while elections are regularly scheduled, there are frequently multiple elections in the same year.

Fundamental to understanding U.S. elections is federalism. States set the rules for conducting elections and for who can participate and how votes are counted. When the nation was founded, this authority was almost complete, since the Constitution said little about elections. At the nation's founding, most states limited electoral participation to white male landholders. By the 1830s, many states had reduced or eliminated the property-holding requirement, in part in response to the emergence of competitive political parties that sought to build their memberships.

Further expansion of the U.S. electorate required the intervention of the federal government and amendment of the Constitution. The first of the efforts to nationalize electoral rules was initially a failure. This was the effort to extend the franchise to African Americans after the Civil War through the Fourteenth and Fifteenth Amendments. More successful was the Nineteenth Amendment, ratified in 1920, which extended the vote to women.[10] The Civil War amendments finally had an impact with the passage of the Voting Rights Act (VRA) in 1965, which secured African Americans access to the ballot box. In 1975, Congress extended the VRA to other ethnic and racial groups who had previously seen their right to vote abridged because of their origin or ancestry—groups including Hispanics, Asian Americans, Native Americans, and Alaskan Natives. The Twenty-Sixth Amendment gave the vote to all citizens between the ages of eighteen and twenty in 1971.

States continue to be able to regulate individual participation in elections through their control of the registration process. In most advanced democracies, the state is responsible for voter registration rather than the individual. Individual registration prescreens potential voters to ensure they meet the state's requirements for voting: residence in the jurisdiction for a set amount of time and the absence of felony convictions. While this may appear minimal and necessary to prevent voter fraud such as an individual's voting multiple times in the same election, the requirement to register in advance of the election prevents many from being able to vote.[11] In 1993, Congress sought to expand opportunities for registration by requiring the distribution of voter registration materials at certain state agencies such as motor vehicle offices (hence, the designation "motor voter" legislation). While not as sweeping in impact as the VRA, motor voter was a continuing effort to nationalize the rules for voting.

There is a second consequence of federalism on U.S. elections: the responsibility for holding elections, deciding which nonfederal offices are filled through elections, and determining how long nonfederal officeholders will serve before again having to be elected is the responsibility of the states and, if the states delegate the power, to localities. Thus, a local office that is elected in one state could be an appointed office in another. Terms for state and local offices, such as governors, vary. Elections are held at different points throughout the year. In states that have primary elections to determine each party's candidates, the primary can be just a month before the general election or as many as ten months before.

Finally, federalism shapes elections by delegating to the states responsibilities for determining how votes are collected and how they are counted, even in elections to national office. This became evident to the nation as a result of the controversy after the 2000 elections. Florida allowed local jurisdictions to design ballots, select voting machines, and establish rules for counting the ballots. One of the most controversial design decisions was Palm Beach County's "butterfly ballot," which led many voters who thought they were casting their vote for Al Gore actually to vote for Pat Buchanan. The several legal challenges filed by the Gore and Bush campaigns in state and federal courts after the elections focused on questions of the legality and constitutionality of ballot designs, counting rules, and deadlines established by Florida counties and the state.

What are the consequences of this federalist system of elections? At a minimum, it leads to confusion and burnout among potential voters. Many voters are unaware of elections that are not held on the same schedule as national elections. Others who are aware become overloaded with electoral responsibilities in jurisdictions that have frequent elections and so choose not to vote in local races.

One result of this decentralized system with a legacy of group-based exclusion is that increasing numbers of citizens do not vote. In the late 1800s, for example, turnout in national elections exceeded 80 percent of those eligible to vote, and the poor participated at rates comparable to the rich. By 1996, turnout in the

The confusing design of Palm Beach, Florida's, presidential ballot appears to have caused more than 3,000 Gore supporters to vote for Pat Buchanan. Had Gore won these votes, he would have won the presidency. *Source:* © Gary Rothstein/ Getty Images.

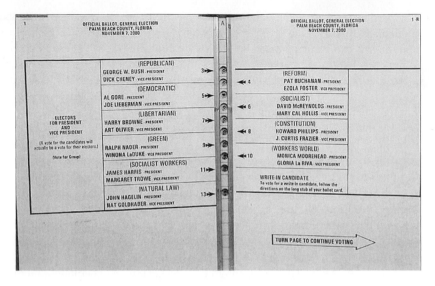

presidential election dropped below 50 percent. Although turnout increased to 55 percent in 2004, this election may not represent the norm for the future; the division of the electorate after the disputed 2000 race and popular mobilization over issues ranging from the war in Iraq to state-level propositions to ban gay marriage mobilized the electorate. It is not clear that these mobilizing forces will be repeated in U.S. presidential politics. In state and local races, turnouts in the range of 10 to 20 percent are the norm. Perhaps more important, turnout varies dramatically among different groups in society. The poor are less likely to vote than the rich, the young less likely than the old, and the less-educated less likely than the more educated.[12] Because blacks and Hispanics are more likely to be young, poor, and have lower levels of formal education, they are less likely to vote than are whites. Hence, political institutions are less likely to hear their demands and respond to their needs.

These class- and age-driven differences in participation are not entirely the result of federalism and variation in the rules for individual participation and the conduct of elections. Declining party competitiveness at the state level also plays a role. Nevertheless, it is important to observe that the steady elimination of formal group-based exclusion has been replaced by the informal exclusion of the majority of some groups, such as

African Americans and Hispanics. Thus, despite the expansion of the electorate to almost all adults, the nation has yet to live up to its democratic ideals.

This declining participation should not obscure the dramatic changes in leadership and issues addressed that result from elections. The 1994 elections saw an unprecedented increase in Republican members of the House of Representatives that allowed Republicans to take control of the House for the first time in forty years (see Figure 4). Republicans also took control of the Senate in that year and were able to pass legislation that dramatically changed the nation's welfare system and slowed the growth of the federal government. In 1998, Democrats unexpectedly gained seats in the sixth year of a presidential term by a member of their party for the first time since 1822. This victory ensured the Senate's acquittal of President Clinton in his impeachment trial. In 2002, Republicans bucked a historical trend and gained seats at the midpoint of the presidential term of a member of their party (the first time since 1934 that the party controlling the presidency won seats in the House of Representatives in the off-year election following its election to the presidency). In 2004, Republicans gained in the House due to a mid-decade redistricting in Texas that forced Democratic incumbents to compete against other Democratic incumbents or to retire.

Despite a steady liberalization of rules on who can vote, voting rates in the United States have declined for the past 100 years.
Source: By permission of Gary Varvel and Creators Syndicate, Inc.

Political Culture, Citizenship, and Identity

The United States is a large nation with distinct regional cultures, ongoing immigration leading to distinct languages and cultures, class divisions, and a history of denying many Americans their civil rights. Despite these cleavages, the United States has maintained almost from its first days a set of core political values that have served to unify the majority of the citizenry. These values are liberty, equality, and democracy.

Liberty, as it is used in discussions of U.S. political culture, refers to liberty from restrictions imposed by government. A tangible form of this notion of liberty appears in the Bill of Rights—the first ten amendments to the U.S. Constitution, which provide for the rights of free speech, free assembly, free practice of religion, and the absence of cruel and unusual punishment. Support for liberty takes a second form: support for economic liberty and free enterprise. Property rights and contract rights, for example, are protected at several places in the Constitution. Furthermore, Congress is empowered to regulate commerce.

Clearly, these liberties are not mutually exclusive. Protections of the Bill of Rights often conflict with

Figure 4

Party Control of the U.S. House of Representatives, 1930–2005

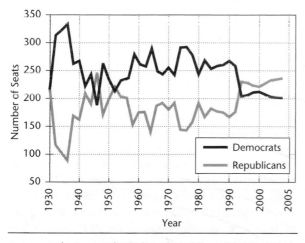

Source: Author's compilation based on Office of the Clerk, U.S. House of Representatives. http://clerk.house.gov/histHigh/Congressional_History/partyDiv.html (accessed April 17, 2005).

each other: economic liberties reward some in the society at the cost of economic opportunities for others. Nevertheless, the idea that citizens should be free to pursue their beliefs and their economic objectives with only limited government interference has been a unifying element in U.S. political culture.

Equality is the second unifying American political value. In the Declaration of Independence, it is "self-evident" that "all men are created equal." Nevertheless, at various times in the nation's history, women, Native Americans, African Americans, Mexican Americans, Chinese Americans, Japanese Americans, and immigrants have been excluded from membership in the polity and, consequently, from access to this equality. But each of the excluded groups, such as African Americans during the civil rights movement, has used the widespread belief in equality to organize and demand that the nation live up to its ideals.

It is important to observe what this belief in equality is not. The equality that has long been sought is equality of opportunity, not equality of result, such as that sought in the communist states. There is support for the notion that people should have an equal opportunity to compete for economic rewards, not that they should end up at the same point.

The final unifying value is representative democracy. Throughout the nation's history, there has been a belief that government is legitimate only to the degree that it reflects the popular will. As with the notion of equality, the pool of citizens whose voices should be heard has changed over time, from white male property holders at the time of the founding to most citizen adults today (convicted felons are excluded from the franchise in many states). Nevertheless, excluded populations have continually sought to influence the polity.

The United States have never had a national religion and, at times in the nation's history, conflicts between Protestants and Catholics have been divisive. In contemporary society, division over religion is more between those for whom religion provides routine guidance in politics and social interactions and those for whom religion is a more private matter that does not shape political activities. Divisions along these lines appeared dramatically in the 2004 elections with evangelical churches taking on new roles in voter mobilization and claiming credit for President Bush's victory and the passage of gay marriage prohibitions in nine states.

Approximately 56 percent of Americans are Protestants and 28 percent are Roman Catholics. Jews make up 4 percent of the population. Because of high levels of immigration from Latin America, the Catholic share of the population is increasing slightly. Despite the fact that there is no national religion in the United States, religion plays a more central role in U.S. politics than it does in the politics of European democracies. Church attendance is higher in the United States and church membership is growing. Moral issues—such as abortion and gay rights—guide the votes of a sizeable minority of the population. Many elected leaders are overt in their religiosity to a degree that would not be acceptable in European politics (and would not have been in U.S. politics as recently as twenty-five years ago).

Values are very much at the heart of contemporary political debates. Leaders have marshaled these values throughout the nation's history to reduce potential cleavages in U.S. society. Since the United States cannot look to a common ethnicity of its people (as, for example, Germany can), to a sovereign with a historical tie to the citizenry (as in a monarchy like the United Kingdom), or to a purported common religion or ideology among its citizens (as does Iran or Cuba), the belief in these values has been used to unify the diverse peoples of the United States.[13] Voluntary membership based on belief in this creed serves to unify the disparate peoples of the United States.

Interests, Social Movements, and Protest

In the United States, political participation has long included activities other than elections and party politics. In the nation's story about its origins, protest proves central; the Revolution was spurred by acts of civil disobedience such as the Boston Tea Party. Similarly, protest and social movements repeatedly forced the nation to live up to its democratic ideals. From the woman's suffrage movement of the nineteenth century to the civil rights movement of the 1950s and 1960s, people defined as being outside the democratic community organized to demand that they be included. The success of these movements was enhanced by their ability to tap the political values discussed in the previous section.

These protest movements have also been able to tap the willingness of Americans to become involved in collective action. First chronicled by a visitor from France in the 1830s, Alexis de Tocqueville, this voluntarism and civic involvement have long been identified as stronger in the U.S. democracy than in other advanced democracies.

In recent years, however, observers of U.S. politics have noted a decline in this pattern of rich civic involvement, a decline that has also appeared in the other advanced democracies. Although social movements remain, they have become much more driven by elites than their predecessors were. At the same time, voluntarism and civic involvement have declined, and the likelihood of participation has followed the patterns of voting, with the more educated, wealthier, and older generally more likely to volunteer and be civically engaged.[14] This decline in civic involvement in U.S. politics has serious long-term implications for society. As civic involvement declines, Americans talk about politics less with their peers and have a lessened sense that they can shape political outcomes. Political scientist Robert Putnam has identified this as the "bowling alone" phenomenon.[15] Americans traditionally had many social venues, such as bowling leagues, where they had an outlet to talk about politics and, potentially, to organize when they were frustrated with political outcomes. There are fewer of these today (people are busier, have more job responsibilities, and spend more time watching television), and the decline in civic engagement has led to reduced political efficacy and greater frustration with the course of politics.

Protest, of course, remains an option for people who feel neglected by the political order. The decline in social movements and other ways to organize the politically marginalized (such as labor unions), however, has shifted the focus of protest from organized collective actions to more isolated and, often, violent protests (such as the 1995 bombing of the federal building in Oklahoma City or the antiglobalization protests in Seattle in 1999) that fail to build more support for the demands of the people organizing the protest. Militia movements—organizations of individuals willing to take up arms to defend their own notion of U.S. political values and the Constitution, for example—represent the concerns of some in today's society, but few support their activities.

The twentieth century saw the rise of a new form of organized political activity: interest groups (see Citizen Action: MoveOn). Like political parties and candidates for office, these organizations try to influence the outcome of public policy by influencing policymakers. They differ, however, in that they are usually organized to influence a single issue or a tightly related group of issues. Also unlike social movements, they rely on money and professional staff rather than on committed volunteers. Interest groups increased in prominence as the federal and state governments increasingly implemented distributive and redistributive policies. Beginning in the 1970s, a specialized form of interest group, the **political action committee (PAC),** appeared to evade restrictions on corporations and organized labor to make financial contributions to political candidates and political parties.

Interest groups are so numerous in contemporary U.S. politics that it is not possible to even venture a guess as to their number. To show their diversity, however, it is important to realize that they include national organizations, such as the National Rifle Association, as well as local groups, such as associations of library patrons who seek to influence city council appropriations. They include mass organizations, such as the American Association of Retired Persons, which claims to represent the interests of more than 35 million people over the age of fifty, and very narrow interests, such as oil producers seeking to defend tax protections for their industry.

Although interest groups and PACs are now much more common than social movements in U.S. politics, they do not replace one key function traditionally fulfilled by the social movements, which seek to establish accountability between citizens and government. Interest groups by definition are organized to protect the needs of a cohesive group in the society and to make demands that government allocate resources in a way that benefits the interests of that group. Thus, they tend to include as members people who already receive rewards from government or are seeking new benefits. Their membership, then, tends to include more socially, financially, and educationally advantaged members of U.S. society. There is no place in the network of interest groups for individuals who are outside the democratic community or whose voices are ignored by the polity. The key role that social movements and protest

Citizen Action: *MoveOn*

The twentieth century has seen a steady decline in popular involvement in politics and civic life. Voting has declined, as has membership in civic organizations and participation in community-based activities. Robert Putnam has described this phenomenon as "bowling alone," reflecting the decline of bowling leagues (and other voluntary membership organizations) and the regular opportunity that they offered to talk about issues and to develop collective solutions to shared societal problems. MoveOn seeks to bring mass participation back into politics. It believes that by increasing mass participation in politics, elected representatives will be more accountable to the popular will and will be less beholden to corporate interests and rich individuals who can fund electoral campaigns in an age when running for office requires huge sums of money (largely to buy media advertising). MoveOn seeks to link citizens on the left side of the political spectrum, but reflects efforts across the ideological spectrum to re-engage mass publics in politics. Evangelical churches and the Christian Coalition are seeking a comparable mobilization, though more often from the right.

MoveOn, which began in 1998 in the wake of the Clinton impeachment, builds electronic advocacy groups around issues. Claiming a membership of more than two million individuals. MoveOn uses the power of the Internet to create an electronic community that connects individual citizens with shared interests. MoveOn members determine the top issues for each election (campaign finance reform and the environment in 2000 and Iraq and media reform in 2004, as examples) and have the opportunity through the organization's ActionForum software to converse and plan with others who share similar interests. Members plan local as well as national political action, converse about candidates and policy issues before legislative bodies and Congress, and provide a forum for candidates seeking their support.

In 2004, Democratic presidential candidate Howard Dean, a little-known ex-Vermont governor before the race, tapped into the MoveOn network and used the support of many MoveOn members and their activism to rise to the top of the Democratic field in the months before the 2004 primaries and caucuses. MoveOn provided for Dean what money traditionally provides: name recognition and buzz. Although the Dean campaign fizzled, MoveOn continued to play a role in Democratic politics and the Kerry campaign throughout the 2004 race. It challenged some traditional Democratic leaders and traditional Democratic issues, but also engaged a new generation of citizens in politics by ensuring that Kerry could not neglect the strong antiwar sentiment among Democratic voters.

As much as MoveOn seeks to engage individual citizens in a more community-focused collective politics of issues, it also seeks to develop resources for political influence that follow the contemporary modes of politics. MoveOn has formed a political action committee (PAC) that funnels contributions from MoveOn members to congressional campaigns. In 2000, the MoveOn PAC raised $2 million, primarily through small contributions, and donated these funds to a handful of congressional candidates in close races who committed to support positions identified by MoveOn. This amount increased to $3.5 million in the 2002 race and $4.6 million in 2004. The MoveOn PAC distributed these 2004 funds to 25 candidates. Most lost their races, but the candidates who won were underdogs in their races and, consequently, had difficulty raising funds from the traditional sources of campaign funds, who tend to back incumbents and likely winners, with the hope of having influence after the election. Among these unexpected winners was Colorado House congressional candidate John Salazar, who won in a Republican-leaning district, and Illinois congressional candidate Melissa Bean, who beat a Republican incumbent who had been in office for over thirty years. Also included on the MoveOn PAC list of candidates funded in 2004 was Colorado Senate candidate Ken Salazar (John's brother) who, though he had a better chance at victory overall, faced Peter Coors, heir to the brewery fortune, who contributed $2 million to his own campaign. Salazar was one of two Latinos elected to the Senate in 2004, a body in which no Latino had served for 30 years.

have played in U.S. politics is being replaced by a more elite and more government-focused form of political organization. This is not to say that social movements and collective protest will not reappear in the future, but such a reappearance would require that the insider-focused strategy employed by interest groups could no longer ensure the outcomes that their members seek from government.

Section ❺ United States Politics in Transition

Political Challenges and Changing Agendas

The United States today faces some familiar and some new challenges that result from the nation's new place in the world of states. Primary among the continuing challenges is the need to live up to its own definition of the democratic idea and to balance this goal of representative government elected through mass participation with the divergent economic outcomes that result from its laissez-faire approach to governing the economy. As it has throughout its history, the United States must address these challenges with a system of government that was designed to impede the actions of government and a citizenry that expects much of government but frequently does not trust it to serve popular needs.

Although challenges to achieve the democratic idea are not new to U.S. political life, the circumstances in which they are debated are new for several reasons. Most important, the United States has assumed a relatively new role and set of responsibilities in the world of states, at least new as far as the past sixty years; U.S. governing institutions must now respond not just to their own people but more broadly to an international political order that is increasingly interconnected and seeks rapid responses to international security, political, and economic crises. The institutional arrangements of U.S. government reduce the potential for quick responses and increase the likelihood of parochial responses that the rest of the world can hear as isolationism or unilateralism. These institutional arrangements are reinforced by a citizenry that for the most part cares little about foreign policy (except when war threatens), expects quick and often painless solutions to international crises, and has little respect, and sometimes open animosity, for multinational political and economic institutions such as the U.N. and the I.M.F. Despite the citizenry's continued focus on domestic concerns, U.S. jobs and national economic well-being are increasingly connected to international markets and to the willingness of governments and individuals to buy U.S. bonds. Over time, many in the United States may come to resent this economic integration.

Economics is not the only role that the United States plays in the world of states, as has been brought home in the period since the September 11 attacks. Its military and its bilateral and multilateral defense arrangements guarantee that the U.S. military will have a global presence. Again, this represents a substantial change from the nation's historical role prior to World War II. Although the citizenry has demonstrated a willingness to pay the financial cost of a global military, it has been much less willing to sacrifice the lives of members of the military. As a result, U.S. leaders must continually balance their military objectives and responsibilities to allies and international organizations with an inability to commit U.S. forces to conflicts that might lead to substantial casualties.

This tension between U.S. reliance on a global economic order among developed nations and a willingness to pursue a unilateral military and defense policy appeared repeatedly after the September 11 attacks. The initial approach of national leaders as well as the citizenry was to pursue military actions against Afghanistan and Iraq alone if necessary. Although alliances formed for each military engagement, this threat of unilateral action made the building of long-term multilateral alliances all the more difficult.

In addition to its economic and military roles in the world of states, the United States exports its culture and language throughout the world. Certainly, this process contributes to economic development in the United States; equally important, it places the United States at the center of an increasingly homogenizing international culture. The process also can generate hostile reactions in defense of national and local cultures.

The substantial changes in the U.S. connections to the world of states have not been matched by equally dramatic changes in the U.S. role in governing the economy. The laissez-faire governance that has characterized the nation from its earliest days continues. The United States tolerates income and wealth disparities greater than those of other advanced democracies. Equally important, business is less regulated and less taxed in the United States than in other democracies. Few in the polity contest this system of economic regulation.

Since the Great Depression, the United States has seen an expansion of redistributive programs to assist the poor. Beginning with Proposition 13 and coming to fruition with the 1996 welfare reform legislation, however, the nation has reduced its commitment to assisting the poor and has established time limits for any individual to collect benefits. While some programs will undoubtedly survive, the current pattern indicates that the United States will not develop targeted programs to assist citizens in need that come anywhere close to those of other advanced democracies.

Distributive programs targeted to the middle class, such as Social Security, Medicare, and college student loans, have also been implemented in the twentieth century. These have much more support among voters and will be harder to undermine or significantly change, even if they challenge traditional laissez-faire approaches to the U.S. role in governing the economy. The costs of these programs, however, are putting an increasing long-term burden on the federal budget and, because of deficit spending, on the national economy. As is evident in the public and congressional responses to President Clinton's health care reform proposals and President Bush's partial privatization of Social Security, the political will to deal with these long-term costs is absent. Particularly in the case of Social Security, relatively mild changes in the program in the first decade of the 2000s could extend the life of the program will into the 2070s (from the current 2040s).

Regardless of whether the focus is domestic or international policy, the U.S. government faces a challenge to its sense of its own democratic idea that is more dramatic than that faced by other advanced democracies. Fewer Americans participate in the electoral politics of the nation. The 55 percent of the electorate who turned out in 2004 was high by recent standards, but it's not clear that this pattern will continue (even turnout at this level is well below turnout in the 1950s and before). Turnout in non-presidential-year elections is even lower: approximately 39 percent of registered voters in 2002. As has been indicated, participation is not spread evenly across the population. Older, more affluent, and more educated citizens are much more likely to vote than are the young, the less-educated, and the poor. As a result, non-Hispanic whites vote at considerably higher rates than blacks, Latinos, and Asian Americans. Thus, elected representatives are simultaneously receiving less guidance from a narrower subset of the people. Contributing to this process is the increasing cost of campaigns in the United States and the burdensome need to raise ever-increasing sums of money.

The breadth of nonelectoral politics is also narrowing. Previous study of the United States found rich networks of community-based organizations, voluntary organizations, and other forms of nonelectoral political activity. Community politics in the United States, however, began to decline in the 1950s (roughly when electoral turnout began to decline) and appears to be at record lows today. This is the "bowling alone" phenomenon discussed above.

This decline in electoral and nonelectoral politics magnifies a final dilemma that the United States faces as it looks to the future. The politics of collective identities has always been central to U.S. politics because the nation has been a recipient of large numbers of immigrants through much of its history. Each wave of immigrants has differed from its predecessors in terms of culture and religion. These differences forced the nation to redefine itself in order to live up to its democratic idea. The "old" group of each era also perceived the "new" group as a threat to the political values of the nation. Today, Asian and Hispanic immigrants are perceived as a challenge by the descendants of European immigrants who populated the nation before large-scale immigration of the newer groups began in 1965.[16] These political fears lead to periodic spasms of anti-immigrant rhetoric that disappear rapidly when it becomes evident that the new wave of immigrants has adopted the political values of the nation (in the long run, cultural differences are more tolerated).

The United States has experienced a long period of sustained high levels of immigration since 1965.

The current period of high immigration (roughly from 1965 to the present) has seen higher levels of overall immigration than the previous period of sustained high immigration (beginning after the Civil War and extending to the 1920s). In this previous period, however, the final fifteen years were characterized by increasingly vitriolic national debates about limiting the volume of immigration and limiting immigration from parts of Europe (southern and eastern) that had only recently begun to send large numbers of immigrants to the United States. Some in Congress are proposing to further deter undocumented migration, but there have been no serious proposals to reduce the opportunities for immigration to permanent residents. President Bush has proposed an expansion of immigration: a guest worker program that would allow some undocumented immigrants to regularize their status and would open new immigration opportunities to others. While these migrants would officially be in a temporary status, evidence from previous guest worker programs in the United States and Europe demonstrate that the temporary status will lead either to subsequent legal immigration or unauthorized migration at even higher levels in the future. Finally, Democrats in Congress are proposing legalization programs to allow some of the approximately 10 million unauthorized migrants in the United States to become permanent residents. In sum, it seems likely that sustained high levels of immigration, quite diverse in terms of its origins, will continue well into the future. (See "Current Challenges: Incorporating Immigrants.")

Current Challenges: *Incorporating Immigrants*

That the United States is a nation of immigrants is a truism. What is often overlooked, however, is that the flow of immigrants to the United States is not evenly spread across its history. Instead, some periods, such as the current one, see high levels of immigration, and others see much more moderate levels. As each of these periods of high immigration reaches maturity, the nation has to relearn how to ensure that the new immigrants achieve the same levels of success as the children of previous periods of immigration.

In 2003, approximately 33 million residents of the United States were born abroad. These foreign-born residents make up nearly 12 percent of the U.S. population. Although the number of foreign-born residents in the United States is at a historic high, they make up a lower share of the national population than in previous periods of high immigration because the national population is so much larger. Today's immigrants overwhelmingly trace their origins to Latin America and to Asia, two regions that sent few immigrants to the United States prior to the current immigrant wave (which began when U.S. immigration law was reformed in 1965).

Immigrants are generally more educated and better skilled than the average person from their countries of origin, but they have less education and fewer professional skills than the U.S. work force. While some immigrants are at the top of the U.S. work force and many can be found in positions in the technology industry, the average immigrant works in service, administrative, agriculture, or manufacturing. Immigrants are much more urban than the population as a whole. Immigrant households include more members than households headed by a U.S.-born resident and are more likely to have more than two generations in the household.

The experience of previous waves of immigrants offers a partial lesson for immigrant incorporation today. Immigrants bring with them a drive that facilitates economic advance. Immigrants, on average, work more hours and have more jobs than do the U.S.-born. Immigrant households have more workers than do households headed by the U.S.-born. This economic drive allows immigrant households in part to overcome the low salaries associated with the sectors of the

(continued)

Current Challenges: *Incorporating Immigrants* (cont.)

economy in which they work. Even with this drive, however, immigrant households tend to earn less than those headed by the U.S.-born. This gap is particularly large for recent immigrants and those without legal status in the United States.

The U.S. economy is much changed from a century ago. Manufacturing and agriculture have declining labor needs, and the number of low-skill jobs that have absorbed immigrants over the past three decades is not growing. There are few job-training resources to prepare low-skill immigrants for the needs of the U.S. economy. Thus, economic gains seen in immigrant populations over the past several decades may not continue in the future.

Immigrants are demonstrating a steady development of political ties to the United States, although they are slower to make these connections formal through naturalization. Survey data demonstrate that immigrants quickly develop ties to the political values of the United States (liberty, equality, and democracy), sometimes at levels greater than those of the U.S.-born. Immigrants show only moderate interest in the politics of their native lands. When disputes arise between the United States and the nation of origin, immigrants most often agree with the U.S. government's position on the issue. Immigrants, however, are somewhat slow to naturalize. Slightly more than one-third of immigrants have naturalized. While this may reflect a failure among immigrants to choose to become citizens, a more likely explanation is

that some immigrants are ineligible (those who are undocumented and those who immigrated legally within the past five years) and others are interested but find the application requirements too onerous or too expensive. With time, most eligible immigrants naturalize, although most do only a few years after they become eligible (after five years of legal residence).

A final measure supplements economic and political incorporation to assess whether immigrants are becoming full members of U.S. society, and, in this area, there is much less evidence. For the current wave of immigration to be successful, their children—the second generation—must have opportunities comparable to those of other Americans. These children start with a structural disadvantage: they overwhelmingly reside in urban and suburban areas with poor tax bases and, hence, poor schools. It was schooling that allowed previous generations of immigrant children to improve their position in U.S. society. If equal educational opportunities are denied to today's children of immigrants, these past successes will likely not be repeated. Perhaps the greatest domestic challenge that the nation faces in the coming years is ensuring that its commitment to large-scale immigration is matched by a commitment to ensuring that those immigrants and the second generation become equal participants in the opportunities and political responsibilities of membership in the American polity.

The absence of strong political parties, mediating institutions, and nonelectoral community politics may dampen the political integration of these immigrants and their children. The preliminary evidence is that naturalization rates are increasing, but that naturalized citizens vote and participate in other forms of politics at lower levels than comparably situated U.S.-born citizens. If these patterns continue, the nation faces a risk that has not come to pass in its long history of high levels of immigration: contemporary immigrants and their children may not be represented in the polit-

ical order, even when these immigrants achieve formal political equality by naturalizing as U.S. citizens.

In the past, the weaknesses of the U.S. constitutional system could be overcome in part through institutional arrangements and mediating institutions. In terms of institutions, Congress dominated the executive until the New Deal era, after which the president dominated Congress until Watergate. This institutional dominance reflected the Framers' intent through the Great Depression and after, at least in terms of the dominance of one branch. It is unclear that the Framers envisioned a system where two, and occasionally all three, branches of government would compete for dominance and where the Congress and the presidency would be routinely controlled by different political parties.

Mediating institutions also played a role in the past that they are incapable of addressing today. Once they formed as mass institutions in the 1830s, the parties served a necessary role in unifying popular opinion and forcing elite compromise. Today, parties are in decline and have been replaced by a distinct type of mediating institution that does not seek compromise across issues and instead promotes narrow interests. Interest groups connect the citizenry to political institutions, as did parties, but the purpose of this connection is to advance a narrow agenda.

Thus, the United States faces the challenges that it has confronted throughout its history and continues to be limited by a governing system that seeks to inhibit government activity. In the past, it has been able to overcome these challenges through active citizen participation, often channeled through mediating institutions and the mobilization of new groups to active political participation. With citizen participation in decline (or becoming more selective) and mediating institutions less broadly based, the nation is more poorly situated to face challenges. As the United States is now centrally positioned in the international economic and political order, its ability to overcome challenges has implications not just for the people of the United States but also for people throughout the world.

United States Politics in Comparative Perspective

From the perspective of the study of comparative politics, the United States may well remain an enigma. Its size, wealth, unique experiences with immigration, history of political isolation from the world, and reliance on separation of powers and federalism do not have clear parallels among the other advanced democracies. This distinctness comes through perhaps most clearly in the way the nation engages its international political responsibilities. While the president has traditionally directed the scope of U.S. foreign policy, Congress, as it reasserts power relative to the president, will likely play an increasing role. Members of Congress, who represent narrow geographic districts and are more directly connected to mass interests, are less likely to

take an internationalist perspective than is the president. When Congress speaks on international issues, it is often with multiple voices, including some that oppose U.S. involvement in multilateral organizations. This conflict over control and direction of foreign policy has become more evident since the end of the cold war. An example would be tensions over U.S. payments to support the United Nations. The objections of one, admittedly well-placed, senator, Jesse Helms, chair of the Senate Foreign Relations Committee, and his perceptions of excessive bureaucracy at the United Nations caused the United States to slow its support payments to the organization and risk its voice in the activities of U.N. agencies. Because Helms controlled the actions of the Foreign Relations Committee, which had to authorize the U.S. payments, he was able to alter U.S. policy and ultimately force the United Nations to change its policies. Most nations, let alone, individual legislators, do not have this sort of power. Only in the United States can a senator have more power than a president.

The impact of the constitutionally mandated structural and institutional weaknesses of U.S. government is not limited to the American people. The United States plays a dominant role in the world economy, as well as a central political role in international organizations. Thus, the inefficiencies and multiple entry points into U.S. policymaking shape the ability of the United States to respond to crises and develop coherent long-term policies in conjunction with its allies. In 1998, for example, as the world economy declined, the president, with the support of the chair of the Federal Reserve, proposed that the United States increase its contribution to the IMF by $18 billion so that the IMF could expand its ability to provide short-term loans to Asian and Latin American countries. Congress initially balked at this request for several reasons, none of which were apparent to the U.S. allies. Some opposed the new appropriations because of concerns about international organizations in general, reflecting the tradition of isolationism. Others sought to block presidential initiatives in general, because of the president's political weaknesses. Still others, likely the majority of those who opposed the initiative, thought that they could bargain with the president to earn his support for initiatives that they sought to pass. While the power of intransigence and horse trading makes a great deal of sense to analysts of U.S. politics, analysts abroad cannot so easily understand the seeming failure of the United States to act in a time of crisis. Eventually Congress passed the added IMF appropriation.

In sum, despite its central role in the international economic system and in multilateral organizations, the United States often remains reluctant to embrace fully the international system that it helped shape. This hesitancy appears despite the active role of U.S. economic interests abroad and the importance of international trade to the U.S. economy. The United States does not hesitate to impose its will abroad when it perceives its security threatened, as was evident in the period leading up to the Iraq war, or when it perceives that the rules made by the international organizations undermine its economic or political interests. Thus, despite its central role in the world of states, the United States is sometimes a hesitant leader. While this has been the case since the emergence of the United States as a global political leader in the post–World War II era, the new challenges of the post-9/11 world potentially make this a much more difficult position to sustain. The challenge of the contemporary era is not states—as it was in the Cold War era—but instead international non-state-based networks. These cannot so easily be controlled through economic dominance and multilateral political alliances. As the United States faces the new challenges of a post-9/11 world, it must again reexamine the degree to which it is willing to act unilaterally and to pay the price for global concern about its occasional unilateralism.

Key Terms

Social Security

North American Free Trade Agreement (NAFTA)

manifest destiny

Declaration of Independence

Articles of Confederation

Bill of Rights

property taxes

interest group

USA PATRIOT Act

federalism

separation of powers

free market

laissez-faire

police powers

Federal Reserve Board

regulations

distributive policies

redistributive policies

iron triangle relationships

Marbury v. *Madison*

checks and balances

bicameral

single-member plurality (SMP) electoral system

political action committee (PAC)

Suggested Readings

Amar, Akhil Reed. *The Bill of Rights: Creation and Reconstruction.* New Haven, Conn.: Yale University Press, 1998.

Burns, Nancy, Schlozman, Kay Lehman, and Verba, Sidney. *The Private Roots of Public Action: Gender, Equality, and Political Participation.* Cambridge, Mass.: Harvard University Press, 2001.

Dawson, Michael C. *Black Visions: The Roots of Contemporary African-American Political Ideologies.* Chicago: University of Chicago Press, 2002.

Deering, Christopher J., and Smith, Steven S. *Committees in Congress.* 3d ed. Washington, D.C.: Congressional Quarterly Books, 1997.

DeSipio, Louis. *Counting on the Latino Vote: Latinos as a New Electorate.* Charlottesville: University Press of Virginia, 1996.

Elkins, Stanley, and McKitrick, Eric. *The Age of Federalism.* New York: Oxford University Press, 1993.

The Federalist Papers. Edited by Clinton Rossiter. New York, Mentor, 1961.

Fenno, Jr., Richard F. *Home Style: House Members in Their Districts.* Glenview, Ill.: Scott, Foresman, 1978.

Hartz, Louis. *The Liberal Tradition in America.* New York: Harvest/HBJ, 1955.

Judis, John B., and Teixeira, Ruy. *The Emerging Democratic Majority.* New York: Scribner, 2002.

Kupchan, Charles. *The End of the American Era: U.S. Foreign Policy and the Geopolitics of the Twenty-First Century.* New York: Knopf, 2002.

Levinson, Sanford. *Constitutional Faith.* Princeton, N.J.: Princeton University Press, 1988.

Lowi, Theodore J. *The End of Liberalism: The Second Republic of the United States.* 2d ed. New York: Norton, 1979.

Nye, Joseph, Jr. *The Paradox of American Power: Why the World's Only Superpower Can't Go It Alone.* New York: Oxford University Press, 2002.

Sniderman, Paul, and Piazza, Thomas. *The Scar of Race.* Cambridge: Harvard University Press, 1993.

Tulis, Jeffrey A. *The Rhetorical Presidency.* Princeton, N.J.: Princeton University Press, 1988.

Verba, Sidney, Schlozman, Kay Lehman, and Brady, Henry. *Voice and Equality: Civic Voluntarism in American Politics.* Cambridge, Mass.: Harvard University Press, 1995.

Wilson, Woodrow. *Congressional Government: A Study in American Politics.* Baltimore: Johns Hopkins University Press, 1885.

Wolfinger, Raymond, and Rosenstone, Steven. *Who Votes?* New Haven, Conn.: Yale University Press, 1980.

Zaller, John. *The Nature and Origins of Mass Opinion.* New York: Cambridge University Press, 1992.

Suggested Websites

The 9/11 Commission Report
http://www.gpoaccess.gov/911/
FindLaw—Cases and Codes: U.S. Constitution
findlaw.com/casecode/constitution/
The New York Times
www.nytimes.com
Thomas—Legislative Information from the Library of Congress
thomas.loc.gov
U.S. Census Bureau
www.census.gov
White House
www.whitehouse.gov

Endnotes

[1] U.S. Bureau of the Census, *Statistical Abstract of the United States 2001* (Washington, D.C.: U.S. Bureau of the Census, 2001), Table 1374.

[2] Rogers Smith, *Civic Ideals: Conflicting Visions of Citizenship in U.S. History* (New Haven, Conn.: Yale University Press, 1997).

[3] The Pew Research Center for the People & the Press, *A Year After the Iraq War: Mistrust of America and Europe Ever Higher, Muslim Anger Persists* (Washington, D.C.: The Pew Research Center for the People & the Press, 2004).

[4] Louis Hartz, *The Liberal Tradition in America* (New York: Harvest/HBJ, 1955).

[5] Randall Robinson, *The Debt: What America Owes to Blacks* (New York: Plume, 2001).

[6] U.S. Immigration and Naturalization Service, *2000 Statistical Yearbook of the Immigration and Naturalization Services* (Springfield, Va.: National Technical Information Service, 2002).

[7] See *The Federalist Papers,* ed. Clinton Rossiter (New York: Mentor, 1961), particularly *Federalist* Nos. 10 and 51.

[8] Woodrow Wilson, *Congressional Government: A Study in American Politics* (Baltimore: Johns Hopkins University Press, 1885).

[9] Louis DeSipio, *Counting on the Latino Vote: Latinos as a New Electorate* (Charlottesville: University Press of Virginia, 1996).

[10] Kristi Anderson, *After Suffrage: Women in Partisan and Electoral Politics Before the New Deal* (Chicago: University of Chicago Press, 1996).

[11] Ruy A. Teixeira, *The Disappearing American Voter* (Washington, D.C.: Brookings Institution, 1992).

[12] Raymond Wolfinger and Steven Rosenstone, *Who Votes?* (New Haven, Conn.: Yale University Press).

[13] Sanford Levinson, *Constitutional Faith* (Princeton, N.J.: Princeton University Press, 1988).

[14] Sidney Verba, Kay Lehman Schlozman, and Henry Brady, *Voice and Equality: Civic Voluntarism in American Politics* (Cambridge: Harvard University Press, 1995).

[15] Robert D. Putnam, *Bowling Alone: The Collapse and Revival of American Community* (New York: Simon and Schuster, 2000).

[16] Louis DeSipio and Rodolfo O. de la Garza, *Making Americans/Remaking America: Immigration and Immigrant Policy* (Boulder, Colo.: Westview Press, 1998).

PART 3

Transitional Democracies

CHAPTER 4

Russia

Joan DeBardeleben

Russian Federation

Land and People

Capital	Moscow
Total area (square miles)	6,520,800 (about 1.8 times larger than the U.S.)
Population	143.5 million

Annual population growth rate (%)	1975–2000	0.0
	2002–2015 (projected)	−.6

Urban population (%)	73

Ethnic composition (%)	Russian	81.5
	Tatar	3.8
	Ukrainian	3.0
	Chuvash	1.2
	Bashkir	0.9
	Belorussian	0.8
	Moldavian	0.7
	Other	8.1

Major language(s)	Russian

Religious affiliation (%)	Russian Orthodox	16.3
	Muslim	10.0
	Protestant	0.9
	Jewish	0.4
	Roman Catholic	0.3
	Other (mostly nonreligious)	72.1

Economy

Domestic currency	Ruble (RUR)
	US$1 = 28.5 RUR
Total GNI (US$)	374.8 billion
GNI per capita (US$)	$2,610
Total GNI, purchasing power parity (US$)	1.283 trillion
GNI per capita, purchasing power parity (US$)	$8,950

GDP annual growth rate (%)	1993–2003	1.4
	2002	4.7
	2003	7.3
	2004	7.1

GDP per capita average annual growth rate (%)	1993–2003	1.8

Inequality in income or consumption (2002)	GINI Index (2001)	39.9

Structure of production (% of GDP)	Agriculture	4.9
	Industry	33.9
	Services	61.2

Labor force distribution (% of total)	Agriculture	12.3
	Industry	22.7
	Services	65

Exports as % of GDP	31.7
Imports as % of GDP	20.8

Society

Life expectancy at birth	65.7
Infant mortality per 1,000 live births	16
Adult illiteracy (% of population age 15+)	0

Access to information & communications (per 1,000 population)	Telephone lines	243
	Mobile phones	38
	Radios	418
	Televisions	538
	Personal computers	49.7

Women in Government and the Economy

Women in the national legislature	
Lower house or single house (%)	9.8
Upper house (%)	3.4
Female professional and technical workers (% of total)	59.1
Female economic activity rate (age 15 and above) (%)	64

Estimated earned income (PPP US$)	Female	6,508
	Male	10,189

Composite Ratings & Rankings

Human development index (HDI) ranking (value) out of 177 countries	57 (.795)
Gender-related development index (GDI) ranking (value) out of 78 countries	49 (.794)
Gender empowerment measure (GEM) ranking (value) out of 78 countries	55 (.467)
Corruption perception index (CPI) ranking (value) out of 146 countries	90 (2.8)
Environmental sustainability index (ESI) ranking (value) out of 146 countries	33 (56.1)
Freedom in world rating	Not free (5.5)

Political Organization

Political System Constitutionally a federal state, presidential system.

Regime History Re-formed as an independent state with the collapse of communist rule in December 1991; current constitution since December 1993.

Administrative Structure Federal system, originally with eighty-nine subnational governments including twenty-one republics, fifty-five provinces (*oblast', krai*), eleven autonomous districts or regions (*okrugs or autonomous oblast*), and two cities of federal status. As of December 2005 the number of subnational governments was reduced to eighty-eight, through a merger of two regions; further mergers are expected.

Executive Dual executive (president and prime minister). Direct election of president; prime minister appointed by the president with the approval of the lower house of the parliament (State *Duma*).

Legislature Bicameral. Upper house (Federation Council) appointed by heads of regional executive and representative organs. Lower house (State *Duma*) chosen by direct election until 2003, with half of the 450 deputies chosen through a proportional representation system and half from single-member constituencies, but the next elections (scheduled for 2007) will be based on a proportional representation system for all 450 deputies. Powers include proposal and approval of legislation, approval of presidential appointees.

Judiciary Independent constitutional court with nineteen justices, nominated by the president and approved by the Federation Council, holding twelve-year terms with possible renewal.

Party System Multiparty system with a dominant party (United Russia).

Section ❶ The Making of the Modern Russian State

Politics in Action

For children of Middle School No. 1 in the town of Beslan in southern Russia (population about 34,000), the first day of the 2004–2005 school year was marked by tragedy. As parents accompanied children to school, for what is traditionally a festive opening day, terrorist forces with explosives strapped to their bodies herded the children and families into the school gymnasium, for what was to become a 52-hour siege. Not permitting the victims food or water, the hostage takers made demands that were unacceptable to the Russian government: the removal of Russian troops from the neighboring secessionist region, the Republic of Chechnya, and the release of Chechen rebels held by the government. On Friday, September 3, Russian special forces heard an explosion inside. Fearing the worst, they stormed the building in an effort to release the victims. Over 300 of the 1,000 hostages, the majority children, were dead.

The Beslan massacre followed numerous other terrorist attacks in Russia since 1999. Just the previous month, two Russian passenger planes crashed simultaneously, killing at least eighty-nine passengers. In May 2004, a hidden bomb killed the president of Chechnya, Akhmad Kadyrov, at a gathering in a stadium in Grozny, the Chechen capital; Kadyrov had been installed by elections that some contested as unfairly controlled by Moscow. Two years earlier, over 700 hostages were held by bomb-laden terrorists in a Moscow theater; in this case, at least 120 died, including the hostage takers. Other attacks targeted theaters, apartment buildings, and public transport.

Although experts consider that Chechen terrorists do have links to international networks, including Al Qaeda, the origins and context of the Russian problem is decidedly local. Terrorist acts are a response to an extended war in the Russian republic of Chechnya that has resulted from the Russian government's unsuccessful efforts to control rebel secessionist forces. An increasingly prominent role for Chechen women among the suicide bombers (the so-called black widows) suggests the depth of the social alienation that underlies the terrorist wave.

Following the Beslan tragedy, the Russian president, Vladimir Putin, announced reforms to bring increased central control over selection of regional governors, and a counterterrorism law was proposed that would make it easier to restrict press freedom and civil liberties in the face of alleged terrorist threats. Allegations that bribes to local figures may have facilitated terrorists' access to the besieged Beslan school helped to justify such measures. Even as economic growth in Russia had taken a positive turn since 1999, worries about personal and collective security have instilled renewed concern about the capacity of the Russian state to ensure the well-being of its citizens. Many Russians appear to think that democracy is of less importance than ensuring stability and security. While Western experts debate whether Putin's most recent reforms to strengthen state power will undermine democratization, many Russians just hope they will give the government the authority it needs to ensure a decent way of life.

Geographic Setting

In December 1991, the Soviet Union ceased to exist. Each of the fifteen newly independent states that emerged in early 1992 began the process of forming a new political entity. In this section, we focus on the Russian Federation, the most important of these fifteen successor states. With a population of 143.5 million, Russia is the largest European country in population and in size. In territory, it is the largest country in the world, spanning ten time zones.

Russia underwent a period of rapid industrialization and urbanization in the Soviet period; only 18 percent of the population lived in urban areas in 1917; 73 percent do now. Despite its vast expanses, less than 8 percent of Russia's land is arable, while 45 percent is forested. Russia is rich in natural resources, which are generally concentrated in the vast regions of western Siberia and the Russian north, far from Moscow, the Russian capital. Russia's wealth includes deposits of oil, natural gas, mineral resources (including gold and diamonds), and extensive forestland. Oil and natural gas exports are now the main sources of Russia's economic wealth and trade potential.

Before the Communists took power in 1917, the Russian empire extended east to the Pacific, south to the Caucasus mountains and the Muslim areas of Central Asia, north to the Arctic Circle, and west into present-day Ukraine, eastern Poland, and the Baltic states. Unlike the empires of Western Europe, with their far-flung colonial possessions, Russia's empire bordered its historic core. With its unprotected location spanning Europe and Asia, Russia had been repeatedly invaded and challenged for centuries. This exposure to outside intrusion encouraged an expansionist mentality among the leadership; some historians argue that

this factor, combined with Russia's harsh climate, encouraged Russia's rulers to craft a centralizing and autocratic state.[1]

With the formation of the Soviet Union after World War I, the Russian Republic continued to form the core of the new multiethnic state. Russia's ethnic diversity and geographic scope have always made it a hard country to govern, evidenced by the current Chechen crisis. Russia has also, on and off, faced pockets of instability and regional warfare on several of its borders, most notably in the Central Asian countries of Tajikistan and Afghanistan and in the countries of Georgia and Azerbaijan on Russia's southern border. On the west, Russia's neighbors include Ukraine, Belarus, and several EU member states (Finland and those that joined in May 2004—Estonia, Latvia, Lithuania, and Poland). Some have described Russia as Eurasian, reflecting the impact of both Asian and European cultural influences. Indeed, Russia is located at a critical juncture between Europe, the Islamic world, and Asia. While this position creates opportunities, it means that Russia's position of influence is not undisputed in its former sphere of influence.

Critical Junctures

The Decline of the Russian Tsarist State

Until the revolution of 1917, Russia was ruled through an autocratic system headed by the tsar, the Russian monarch and emperor. The historian Richard Pipes explains that before 1917, Russia had a **patrimonial state,** that is, a state that not only ruled the country but also owned the land as well.[2] The economic and agricultural system tied the majority of the population (peasants) to the nobles (through serfdom), the state, or the church, whose land they worked. The serfs were emancipated by the tsar in 1861 as a part of his effort to modernize Russia, to make it militarily competitive with the West, and thus to retain its status as a world power. Emancipation freed the peasants from bondage to the nobility but did not destroy the traditional communal peasant organization in the countryside, the *mir.* Individual peasant farming did not develop in Russia on a significant scale.

A Russian bourgeoisie, or entrepreneurial class, also failed to emerge in Russia as it had in Western

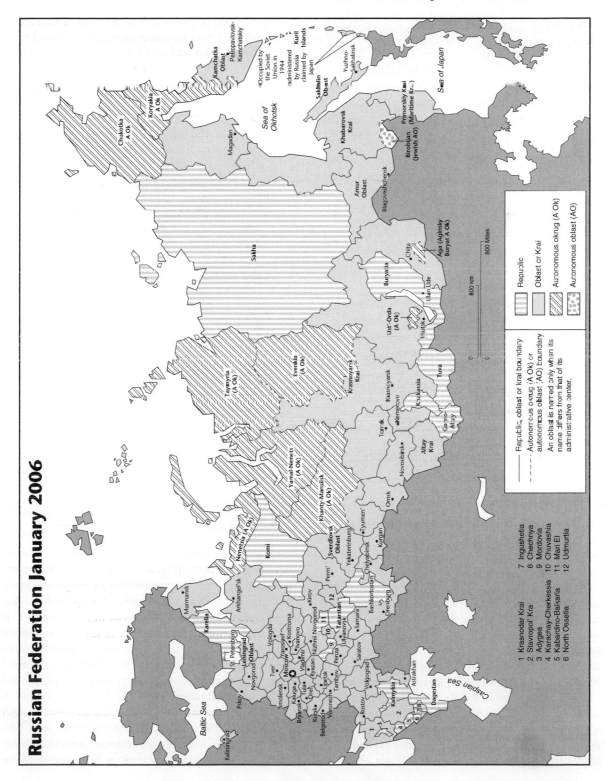

Russian Federation January 2006

Occupied by the Soviet Union in 1944 administered by Russia claimed by Japan

Kuril Islands

Sea of Japan

Sea of Okhotsk

Kamchatka Oblast
Petropavlovsk-Kamchatskiy

Koryakia A Ok

Chukotka A Ok

Magadan

Yuzhno-Sakhalinsk

Sakhalin Oblast

Primorskiy Krai (Maritime Kr.)

Khabarovsk Krai

Birobijan (Jewish AO)

Amur Oblast

Blagoveshchensk

Sakha

Chita

Aga (Aginsky Buryat A Ok)

Buryatia

Ulan Ude

Ust-Orda (A Ok)

Irkutsk

Tuva

Evenkia (A Ok)

Krasnoyarsk Krai

Krasnoyarsk

Khakassia

Gorno-Altay

Taymyria (A Ok)

Kemerovo

Tomsk

Altay Krai

Yamal-Nenets (A Ok)

Khanty-Mansiisk (A Ok)

Novosibirsk

Omsk

Nenetsia (A Ok)

Komi

Sverdlovsk Oblast

Yekaterinburg

Tyumen

Kurgan

Chelyabinsk

Perm

Kirov

Bashkortostan

Orenburg

Murmansk

Arkhangel'sk

Karela

St. Petersburg

Leningrad Oblast

Vologda

Yaroslavl

Kostroma

Ivanovo

Nizhnii Novgorod

Tatarstan

Samara

Saratov

Novgorod Oblast

Tver

Smolensk

Moscow

Vladimir

Ryazan

Ulyanovsk

Penza

Pskov

Kaluga

Tula

Orel

Lipetsk

Tambov

Bryansk

Kursk

Belgorod

Voronezh

Volgograd

Rostov

Astrakhan

Kalmykia

Dagestan

Baltic Sea

Kaliningrad

Caspian Sea

800 Miles

800 km

Legend

Republic

Oblast or Krai

Autonomous okrug (A Ok)

Autonomous oblast (AO)

Republic, oblast or krai boundary

Autonomous okrug (A Ok) or autonomous oblast (AO) boundary

An oblast is named only when its name differs from that of its administrative center.

1 Krasnodar Krai
2 Stavropol' Kra
3 Adygea
4 Karachay-Cherkessia
5 Kabardino-Balkaria
6 North Ossetia
7 Ingushetia
8 Chechnya
9 Mordovia
10 Chuvashia
11 Mari El
12 Udmurtia

Europe. The key impetus for industrialization came from the Russian state and from injections of foreign capital (especially French, English, German, and Belgian), in the form of joint-stock companies and foreign debt incurred by the tsarist government. The dominant role of state and foreign capital was accompanied by the emergence of large factories alongside small, private workshops. Trade unions were illegal until 1906, and even then their activities were carefully controlled. Worker discontent grew, alongside that of liberal intellectuals, students, and, later, peasants, in the wake of the defeats in the Russo-Japanese war and continued tsarist repression. This culminated in the revolution of 1905, which involved widespread strikes in the cities and rural uprisings. The tsarist regime was able to maintain control through repression and a measure of economic reforms, until its collapse in 1917.

The Bolshevik Revolution and the Establishment of Soviet Power (1917–1929)

In 1917, at the height of World War I, two revolutions occurred in Russia. The March revolution threw out the tsar (Nicholas II) and installed a moderate provisional government. In November, the Bolsheviks, led by Vladimir Lenin, overthrew that government. This second revolution marked a major turning point in the history of Russia. Instead of trying to imitate Western European patterns, the Bolsheviks applied a dramatically different blueprint for economic, social, and political development.

The Bolsheviks were Marxists who believed their revolution reflected the political interests of a particular social class, the proletariat (working class). Most of the revolutionary leaders, however, were not themselves workers but were from a more educated and privileged stratum, commonly referred to as the intelligentsia. But in 1917, the Bolsheviks' slogan, "Land, Peace, and Bread," appealed to both the working class and the discontented peasantry, which made up over 80 percent of Russia's population.

The Bolsheviks formed a tightly organized political party based on their own understanding of democracy. Their strategy was founded on the notions of democratic centralism and vanguardism, concepts that differed significantly from the liberal democratic notions of Western countries. **Democratic centralism** mandated a hierarchical party structure in which leaders were elected from below, with freedom of discussion until a decision was taken, but strict discipline was required in implementing party policy. Over time, the centralizing elements of democratic centralism took precedence over the democratic elements, as the party tried to insulate itself first from informers of the tsarist forces and later from both real and imagined threats to the new regime. The concept of a **vanguard party** governed the Bolsheviks' (and later the Communist Party's) relations with broader social forces: party leaders claimed that they understood the interests of the working people better than the people did themselves. Over time, this philosophy was used to rationalize virtually all actions of the Communist Party and the state it dominated. Neither democratic centralism nor vanguardism emphasized democratic procedures or accountability of the leaders to the public. Rather, these concepts focused on achieving a "correct" political outcome that would reflect the "true" interests of the working class, as defined by the leaders of the Communist Party.

Once in power, the Bolsheviks formed a new government, which in 1922 brought the formation of the first Communist Party state, the Union of Soviet Socialist Republics (USSR), henceforth referred to as the Soviet Union. In the early years, the Bolsheviks felt compelled to take extraordinary measures to ensure the survival of the regime. The initial challenge was an extended civil war (1918–1921) for control of the countryside and outlying regions. The Bolsheviks introduced war communism to ensure the supply of materials necessary for the war effort. The state took control of key economic sectors and forcibly requisitioned grain from the peasants. Political controls also increased: the *Cheka,* the security arm of the regime,

was strengthened, and restrictions were placed on other political groups, including other socialist parties. By 1921, the leadership recognized the political costs of war communism: the peasants resented the forced requisitioning of grain, and the policy blocked economic initiative. In an effort to accommodate the peasantry, the New Economic Policy (NEP) was introduced in 1921 and lasted until 1928. State control over the economy was loosened so that private enterprise and trade were revived. The state, however, retained control of large-scale industry and experimented with state control of the arts and culture.

Gradually, throughout the 1920s, the authoritarian strains of Bolshevik thinking eclipsed the democratic elements. Lacking a democratic tradition and bolstered by the vanguard ideology of the party, the Bolshevik leaders engaged in internecine struggles following Lenin's death in 1924. These conflicts culminated in the rise of Joseph Stalin and the demotion or exile of prominent party figures such as Leon Trotsky and Nikolai Bukharin. By 1929, all open opposition, even within the party itself, had been silenced. Sacrifices of democratic procedure were justified in the name of protecting class interests.

The Bolshevik revolution also initiated a period of international isolation for the new state. To fulfill their promise of peace, the new rulers had to cede important chunks of territory to Germany under the Brest-Litovsk Treaty (1918). Only the defeat of Germany by Russia's former allies (the United States, Britain, and France) reversed some of these concessions. However, these countries were hardly pleased with internal developments in Russia. Not only did the Bolshevik revolution bring expropriation of foreign holdings and Russia's withdrawal from the Allied powers' war effort, it also represented the first successful challenge to the capitalist order. As a result, the former allies sent material aid and troops to oppose the new Bolshevik government during the civil war.

Lenin had hoped that successful working-class revolutions in Germany and other Western countries would bolster the fledgling Soviet regime and bring it tangible aid. When this did not occur, the Soviet leaders had to rely on their country's own resources to build a viable economic structure. In 1924, Stalin developed the idea of building "socialism in one country." This policy defined Soviet state interests as synonymous with the promotion of socialism, suggesting that socialism could be built in Russia even without successful revolutions in other countries. It simultaneously set the Soviet Union on a course of economic isolation from the larger world of states. To survive in such isolation, the new Soviet state pursued a policy of rapid industrialization and increased political control.

The Stalin Revolution (1929–1953)

From 1929 until Stalin's death in 1953, the Soviet Union faced another critical juncture. During this time, Stalin consolidated his power as Soviet leader by establishing the basic characteristics of the Soviet regime that substantially endured until the collapse of the Communist system in 1991.

The Stalin revolution brought changes to virtually every aspect of Soviet life. The result was an interconnected system of economic, political, and ideological power. The state became the engine for rapid economic development, with state ownership and control of virtually all economic assets (land, factories, housing, and stores). By 1935, over 90 percent of agricultural land had been taken from the peasants and made into state or collective farms. This **collectivization** campaign was justified as a means of preventing the emergence of a new capitalist class in the countryside, but it actually targeted the peasantry as a whole, leading to widespread famine and the death of millions. Survivors who resisted were arrested or exiled to Siberia. In the industrial sector, a program of rapid industrialization favored heavy industries (steel mills, hydroelectric dams, machine building); production of consumer goods was neglected. Economic control was exercised through a complex but inefficient system of central economic planning, in which the state planning committee (Gosplan) set production targets for every enterprise in the country. The industrialization campaign was accompanied by social upheaval. People were uprooted from their traditional lives in the countryside and catapulted into the rhythm of urban industrial life. Media censorship and state control of the arts strangled creativity as well as political opposition. The party/state became the authoritative source of truth; anyone deviating from the authorized interpretation could be charged with treason.

In the early 1920s, the Communist Party was the only political party permitted to function, and by the early 1930s, open opposition or dissent within the party itself had been eliminated. Gradually, the party became subject to the personal whims of Stalin and his secret police. Party bodies ceased to meet on a regular basis, and they no longer made important political decisions. Party ranks were periodically cleansed of potential opponents, and previous party leaders as well as citizens from many other walks of life were violently purged (arrested, sentenced to labor camps, sometimes executed). Overall, an estimated 5 percent of the Soviet population was arrested at one point or another under the Stalinist system, usually for no apparent cause. The arbitrary and unpredictable terror of the 1930s left a legacy of fear. Only among trusted friends and family members did people dare to express their true views. Forms of resistance, when they occurred, were evasive rather than active: peasants killed their livestock to avoid giving it over to collective farms; laborers worked inefficiently, and absenteeism was high.

Isolation of the Soviet citizen from interaction with the outside world was a key tool of Stalinist control. Foreign news broadcasts were jammed; travel abroad was highly restricted; and contacts with foreigners brought citizens under suspicion. The economy was isolated from interaction with the international economic system. Although this policy shielded Soviet society from the effects of the Great Depression of the 1930s, which shook the capitalist world, it also allowed an inefficient system of production to survive in the USSR. Protected from foreign competition, the economy failed to keep up with the rapid pace of economic and technological transformation in the West.

In 1941, Nazi Germany invaded the Soviet Union, and Stalin had little choice but to join the Allied powers. Wartime casualties were high, about 27 million people, including 19 million civilians. Therefore, it is no wonder that even today wartime sacrifices and losses are frequently recalled, since World War II had such a profound impact on the outlook of an entire generation of Soviet citizens. Soviet propaganda dubbed it the Great Patriotic War, evoking images of Russian nationalism rather than of socialist internationalism; the sacrifices and heroism of the war period remained a powerful symbol of Soviet pride and unity until the collapse of Communist power. The war period was marked by support for traditional family values and a greater tolerance for religious institutions, whose support Stalin sought for the war effort. Among the social corollaries of the war effort were a declining birthrate and a long-lasting gender imbalance as a result of high wartime casualties among men. The war also affected certain minority ethnic groups that were accused of collaborating with the enemy during the war effort and were deported to areas farther east in the USSR. These included Germans, Crimean Tatars, and peoples of the northern Caucasus regions such as the Chechens, Ingush, and Karachai-Balkar. Their later rehabilitation and resettlement caused renewed disruption and conflict, contributing to the ethnic conflicts of the post-Soviet period.

The Soviet Union was a major force in the defeat of the Axis powers in Europe. After the war, the other Allied powers allowed the Soviet Union to absorb new territories into the USSR itself (these became the Soviet republics of Latvia, Lithuania, Estonia, Moldavia, and portions of western Ukraine), and they implicitly granted the USSR free rein to shape the postwar governments and economies in eastern Germany, Poland, Hungary, Czechoslovakia, Yugoslavia, Bulgaria, and Romania. Western offers to include parts of the region in the Marshall Plan were rejected under pressure from the USSR. With Soviet support, local Communist parties gained control of all of these countries; only in Yugoslavia were indigenous Communist forces sufficiently strong to gain power largely on their own and thus later to assert their independence from Moscow.

Following World War II, the features of Soviet communism were largely replicated in those areas newly integrated into the USSR and in the countries of Eastern Europe. The Soviet Union tried to isolate its satellites in Eastern Europe from the West and to tighten their economic and political integration with the USSR. The Council for Mutual Economic Assistance (CMEA) and the Warsaw Treaty Organization (a military alliance) were formed for this purpose. With its developed industrial economy, its military stature bolstered in World War II, and its growing sphere of regional control, the USSR emerged as a global superpower. But the enlarged Soviet bloc still remained insulated from the larger world of states. Some countries within the Soviet bloc, however, had strong historic links to Western Europe (especially Czechoslovakia, Poland, and Hungary), and in these areas, domestic resistance to Soviet dominance forced some alterations or deviations from the Soviet model. Over time, these countries served not only as geographic buffers to direct Western influence on the USSR but also as

conduits for such influence. In the more Westernized Baltic republics of the USSR itself, the population firmly resisted assimilation to Soviet rule and eventually spearheaded the disintegration of the Soviet Union in the late 1980s.

Attempts at De-Stalinization (1953–1985)

Stalin's death in 1953 triggered another critical juncture in Soviet politics. Even the Soviet elite realized that Stalin's system of terror could be sustained only at great cost to the development of the country. The terror destroyed initiative and participation, and the unpredictability of Stalinist rule inhibited the rational formulation of policy. The period from Stalin's death until the mid-1980s saw a regularization and stabilization of Soviet politics. Terror abated, but political controls remained in place, and efforts to isolate Soviet citizens from foreign influences continued.

Nikita Khrushchev, who succeeded Stalin as the party leader from 1955 until his removal in 1964, embarked on a bold policy of de-Stalinization. Although his specific policies were only minimally successful, he initiated a thaw in political and cultural life, an approach that planted the seeds that ultimately undermined the Stalinist system. Khrushchev rejected terror as an instrument of political control and revived the Communist Party as a vital political institution able to exercise political, economic, and cultural authority. The secret police (KGB) was subordinated to party authority, and party meetings were resumed on a regular basis. However, internal party structures remained highly centralized, and elections were uncontested. In the cultural sphere, Khrushchev allowed sporadic liberalization, with the publication in the official media of some literature critical of the Stalinist system.

Leonid Brezhnev, Khrushchev's successor, who headed the party from October 1964 until his death in 1982, partially reversed the de-Stalinization efforts of the 1950s and early 1960s. Controls tightened again in the cultural sphere. Individuals who expressed dissenting views (members of the so-called dissident movement) through underground publishing or publication abroad were harassed, arrested, or exiled. However, unlike in the Stalinist period, the political repression was predictable: people knew when they were transgressing permitted limits of criticism. The Brezhnev regime could be described as primarily bureaucratic and conservative, seeking to maintain existing power structures rather than to introduce new ones.

During the Brezhnev era, a **tacit social contract** with the population governed state-society relations.[3] In exchange for political compliance, the population enjoyed job security; a lax work environment; low prices for basic goods, housing, and transport; free social services (medical care, recreational services); and minimal interference in personal life. Wages of the worst-off citizens were increased relative to those of the more educated and better-off portions of the population. The intelligentsia (historically Russia's social conscience and critic) was allowed more freedom to discuss publicly issues that were not of crucial importance to the regime.

Nonetheless, from the late 1970s onward, an aging political leadership was increasingly ineffective at addressing the mounting problems facing Soviet society. Economic growth rates declined, and improvements in the standard of living were minimal. Many consumer goods were still in short supply, and quality was often mediocre. As the economy stagnated, opportunities for upward career mobility declined. To maintain the Soviet Union's superpower status and competitive position in the arms race, resources were diverted to the military sector, gutting the capacity of the consumer and agricultural spheres to satisfy popular expectations. Russia's rich natural wealth was squandered, and the costs of exploiting new resource deposits (mostly in Siberia) soared. High pollution levels lowered the quality of life and health in terms of morbidity and declining life expectancy. At the same time, liberalization in some Eastern European states and the telecommunications revolution made it increasingly difficult to shield the population from exposure to Western lifestyles and ideas. Among a certain critical portion of the population, aspirations were rising just as the capacity of the system to fulfill them was declining. It was in this context that the next critical transition occurred.

Perestroika *and* Glasnost *(1985–1991)*

Mikhail Gorbachev took office as a Communist Party leader in March 1985 at the relatively young age of fifty-three. He hoped to reform the system in order to spur economic growth and political renewal, but without undermining Communist Party rule or its basic ideological precepts. Four important concepts formed the basis of Gorbachev's reform program: *perestroika, glasnost, demokratizatsiia,* and "New Thinking." *Perestroika* (restructuring) involved decentralization and rationalization of economic structures to enable individual enterprises to increase efficiency and take initiative. The central planning system was to be reformed, but not disbanded. To counteract the resistance of entrenched central bureaucracies, Gorbachev enlisted the support of the intelligentsia, who benefited from his policy of *glasnost*. *Glasnost* (openness) involved relaxing controls on public debate, the airing of diverse viewpoints, and the publication of previously prohibited literature. *Demokratizatsiia* (Gorbachev's conception of democratization) was an effort to increase the responsiveness of political organs to public sentiment, both within and outside the party, introducing some elements of competitive elections, a **law-based state,** and freer political expression. Finally, "New Thinking" in foreign policy involved a rethinking of international power in nonmilitary terms. Gorbachev advocated integration of the USSR into the world of states and the global economy, emphasizing the common challenges facing East and West, such as the cost and hazards of the arms race and environmental degradation.[4]

Gorbachev's policies triggered a fundamental change in the relationship between state and society in the USSR. Citizens pursued their interests and beliefs through a variety of newly created organizations at the national and local levels. These included ethnonationalist movements, environmental groups, groups for the rehabilitation of Stalinist victims, charitable groups, new or reformed professional organizations, political clubs, and many others. The existence of these groups implicitly challenged the Communist Party's monopoly of power. By March 1990, pressures from within and outside the party forced the Supreme Soviet (the Soviet parliament) to rescind Article 6 of the Soviet constitution, which provided the basis for single-party rule. Embryonic political parties challenged the Communist Party's monopoly of political control. In the spring of 1989, the first contested elections since the 1920s were held for positions in the Soviet parliament. These were followed by elections at the republic and local levels in 1990, which, in some cases, put leaders in power who pushed for increased republic and regional autonomy.

The most divisive issues facing Gorbachev were economic policy and demands for republic autonomy. Only 50.8 percent of the Soviet population was ethnically Russian in 1989. In several of the fourteen non-Russian republics that made up the USSR, popular front organizations formed. First in the three Baltic republics (Latvia, Lithuania, and Estonia) and then in other union republics (particularly Ukraine, Georgia, Armenia, Moldova [formerly Moldavia], and Russia itself), demands for national autonomy and, in some cases, for secession from the USSR were put forth. Gorbachev's efforts to bring consensus on a new federal system for the fifteen union republics failed, as popular support and elite self-interest took on an irreversible momentum, resulting in a separatism mania.

Gorbachev's economic policies failed as well. They involved half-measures that sent contradictory messages to enterprise directors, producing a drop in output and undermining established patterns that had kept the Soviet economy functioning, albeit inefficiently. The economic decline reinforced demands by union republics for economic autonomy. To protect themselves, regions and union republics began to restrict exports to other regions, despite planning mandates. Separatism mania was accompanied by "the war of laws," as regional officials openly defied central directives. In response, Gorbachev issued numerous decrees; their number increased as their efficacy declined.

Gorbachev achieved his greatest success in foreign policy. Just as his domestic support was plummeting in late 1990 and early 1991, he was awarded the Nobel Peace Prize, reflecting his esteemed international stature. Under the guidance of his New Thinking, the military buildup in the USSR was halted, important arms control agreements were ratified, and many controls on international contacts were lifted. In 1989, Gorbachev refused to prop up unpopular communist governments in the East European countries. First in Hungary and Poland, then in the German Democratic Republic (East Germany) and Czechoslovakia, pressure from below pushed the communist parties out of power, and a process of democratization and market reform ensued. Politicians in both East and West declared the cold war over. However, to Gorbachev's dismay, the liberation of Eastern Europe fed the process of disintegration in the Soviet Union itself.

Collapse of the USSR and the Emergence of the Russian Federation (1991 to the Present)

On August 19, 1991, a coalition of conservative figures attempted a coup d'état, temporarily removing Gorbachev from the leadership post to stop the reform initiative and prevent the collapse of the USSR. The failed coup proved to be the death knell of the Soviet system. While Gorbachev was held captive at his summer house (*dacha*), Boris Yeltsin, the popularly elected president of the Russian Republic, climbed atop a tank loyal to the reform leadership and rallied opposition to the attempted coup. Yeltsin declared himself the true champion of democratic values and Russian national interest. The Soviet Union collapsed at the end of 1991 when Yeltsin joined the leaders of Ukraine and Belorussia (later renamed Belarus) to declare the formation of a loosely structured entity, called the Commonwealth of Independent States, to replace the Soviet Union. In December 1991, the Russian Federation stepped out as an independent country in the world of states. Its independent status (along with that of the other fourteen former union republics of the USSR) was quickly recognized by the major world powers.

Yeltsin quickly proclaimed his commitment to Western-style democracy and market economic reform, marking a radical turn from the Soviet past. However, that program was controversial and proved hard to implement. The market reform produced severe and unpopular economic repercussions because traditional economic patterns were disrupted. The Russian parliament, elected in 1990, mirrored popular skepticism in its hesitancy to embrace the radical reform project. The executive and legislative branches of the government failed to reach consensus on the nature of a new Russian constitution; the result was a bloody showdown in October 1993, after Yeltsin disbanded what he considered to be an obstructive parliament and laid siege to its premises, the Russian White House. The president mandated new elections and a constitutional referendum in December 1993. The constitution, adopted by a narrow margin of voters, put in place a set of institutions marked by a powerful president and a relatively weak parliament.

The White House, seat of the Russian parliament, burns while under assault from troops loyal to President Yeltsin during the confrontation in October 1993. *Source:* AP/Wide World Photos.

Leaders: *Boris Nikolaevich Yeltsin*

On February 1, 1931, Boris Yeltsin was born to a working-class family in a village in the Russian province of Sverdlovsk located in the Ural Mountains. Like so many men of his generation who later rose to top Communist Party posts, his education was technical, in the field of construction. His early jobs were as foreman, engineer, supervisor, and finally director of a large construction combine. Yeltsin joined the Communist Party of the Soviet Union (CPSU) in 1961, and in 1968 he took on full-time work in the regional party organization. Over the next ten years, he rose to higher positions in Sverdlovsk *oblast*, first as party secretary for industry and finally as head of the regional party in 1976. In 1981, Yeltsin became a member of the Central Committee of the CPSU and moved onto the national stage.

Because of Yeltsin's reputation as an energetic figure not tainted by corruption, Mikhail Gorbachev drafted Yeltsin into his leadership team in 1985. Yeltsin's first important post in Moscow was as head of the Moscow party organization. Gorbachev also selected Yeltsin to be a nonvoting member of the USSR's top party organ, the Politburo.

Yeltsin soon gained a reputation as an outspoken critic of party privilege. He became a popular figure in Moscow as he mingled with average Russians on city streets and public transport. In 1987, party conservatives launched an attack on Yeltsin for his outspoken positions; Gorbachev did not come to his defense. Yeltsin was removed from the Politburo and from his post as Moscow party leader in 1988; he was demoted to a position in the construction sector of the Soviet government. At the party conference in June 1988, Yeltsin defended his position in proceedings that were televised across the USSR. Yeltsin's popular support soared as the public saw him single-handedly taking on the party establishment.

Rivalry between Gorbachev and Yeltsin formed a backdrop for the dramatic events that led to the collapse of the Soviet Union in December 1991.

(continued)

Leaders: *Boris Nikolaevich Yeltsin (cont.)*

Yeltsin represented a radical reform path, while Gorbachev supported gradualism. Yeltsin established his political base within the Russian Republic; thus Russia's self-assertion within the USSR was also a way for Yeltsin to secure his own position. Under his guidance on June 8, 1990, the Russian Republic declared sovereignty (not a declaration of independence, but an assertion of the right of the Russian Republic to set its own policy). One month later, Yeltsin resigned his party membership. On June 12, 1991, Yeltsin was elected president of the Russian Republic by direct popular vote, establishing his legitimacy as a spokesman for democratization and Russian independence.

During the attempted coup d'état by party conservatives in August 1991, Yeltsin reinforced his popularity and democratic credentials by taking a firm stand against the plotters while Gorbachev remained captive at his dacha in the Crimea. Yeltsin's defiance gave him a decisive advantage in the competition with Gorbachev and laid the groundwork for the December 1991 dissolution of the USSR engineered by Yeltsin (representing Russia) and the leaders of Ukraine and Belorussia. In an unusual turn of events, the rivalry between Yeltsin and Gorbachev, as well as between their differing approaches to reform, was decided through the disbanding of the country Gorbachev headed.

In 1992, Yeltsin embarked on the difficult task of implementing his radical reform policy in the newly independent Russian Federation. Economic crisis, rising corruption and crime, and a decline of state authority ensued. Yeltsin's popularity plummeted. His reputation as a democratic reformer was marred by his use of force against the Russian parliament in 1993 and in the Chechnya war in 1994–1996. Although Yeltsin's campaign team managed to orchestrate an electoral victory in 1996, Yeltsin's day was past. Plagued by poor health and failed policies, Yeltsin could hope only to serve out his presidential term and groom a successor. He succeeded in the latter, designating Vladimir Putin as acting president upon Yeltsin's own resignation in December 1999. Since that time, he has not been a visible figure on the Russian political scene except in 2004, when, in reaction to Putin's move to end the election of governors, Yeltsin remarked, "The stifling of freedoms and the rolling back of democratic rights will mean, among other things, that the terrorists will have won."[1]

---

[1]"Yeltsin fears for Russia freedoms," *BBC News*, September 17, 2004, http://news.bbc.co.uk/2/hi/europe/3669700.stm (accessed May 12, 2005).

Yeltsin's economic reform program, while fundamentally altering economic relations, failed to produce an effective market economy; a major financial crisis in August and September 1998 was the culmination of this failed reform process. The financial crisis triggered a political one. In 1999, Yeltsin nominated a surprise candidate to the post of prime minister of Russia. Vladimir Putin, a little-known figure from St. Petersburg, was a former KGB operative in East Germany. His political advance was swift, and the rise in his popularity was equally meteoric. In December 1999, Yeltsin, apparently ill and unable to command the reins of power, resigned from his position as president of the Russian Federation. Elections were announced for March 2000; the result was a resounding victory for Putin, with an even stronger show of support in elections that followed for the *Duma* in December 2003 and for the presidency in March 2004. Putin's tenure as president benefited from auspicious conditions, as high international gas and oil prices fed tax dollars into the state's coffers. In 1999, the economy experienced its first real growth in over a decade, a trend that has continued into the new millennium.

After September 11, 2001

Following the terrorist attacks on the World Trade Center and the Pentagon on September 11, 2001,

President Putin expressed solidarity with the American people in their struggle against terrorism. Terrorist attacks in Russia reinforced a sense of common purpose between the two world leaders, but Russia withheld its support for the American incursion into Iraq. In recognition of Russia's terrorist challenges, Western criticism of Russian human rights abuses in Chechnya were muted, and in response to Russia's desire for recognition as an important international and regional actor Russia was granted an enhanced status in relationship to organizations such as NATO and the Group of 7 (G-7, a group of leading industrial nations, which became the G-8 with Russia's addition). Still an outsider as more and more neighboring states joined NATO and the European Union (EU), Russia faced the issue of how to balance its global, European, and Eurasian roles. In his 2005 address to the Federal Assembly, Putin affirmed his conviction that "above all else Russia, was, is, and will, of course, be a major European power" and

defined as a task to "continue its civilizing mission on the Eurasian continent."[5]

Themes and Implications

Historical Junctures and Political Themes

Following the collapse of the USSR in 1991, international support for the new reform-oriented government in Russia surged, with the proliferation of aid programs and international financial credits. The honeymoon is now, however, over. When it comes to the world of states, Russia is no longer a world power, and the expansion of Western organizations (NATO, EU) to Russia's western border has undermined its sphere of influence in Central and Eastern Europe. The events of September 11, however, provided a new impetus for Russia's claim to be a key link in the antiterrorist chain, alongside the United States. Ironically, however, the war on terrorism also brought the expansion of American influence into Russia's traditional sphere of influence as U.S. bases

The relationship between President George W. Bush and Russian President Vladimir Putin reflects moments of tension in the light of Russian objections to the U.S.-led invasion of Iraq and U.S. criticism of Russian political developments. *Source:* AP/Wide Photos

September brought Russia closer 2 us

were established in post-Soviet Central Asia (neighboring Afghanistan). Russia's defense of a disputed presidential election outcome during Ukraine's Orange Revolution in November 2004 suggested the primacy of Russian national interest over democratic values. With its "near abroad," Russia has not found an effective manner to establish itself as a respected regional leader. Its eastern neighbors, except Belarus, look more to Europe than to Russia as a guidepost for the future.

For nearly a decade following the collapse of the Soviet system, the Russian Federation seemed mired in a downward spiral of economic collapse and political paralysis. By the late 1990s, the Russian public was disillusioned and distrustful of its leaders, and resentment remained over the dismal results of the Western-inspired reform program. In the new millennium, growth rates have, however, seen a process of recovery, budget surpluses have become routine, and the population has shown a marked increase in economic confidence. Questions, however, remain about the depth of the apparent economic recovery. Some experts attribute the economic turnaround to high oil prices rather than to effective government policy; global economic trends could, however, also push Russia back into a renewed slump. At the same time, wide disparities in wealth and income, as well as important regional inequalities, continue to plague the system. Although many important policy problems have been addressed, others remain unresolved, including inadequate levels of foreign investment, capital flight, continuing high levels of poverty, the decline in the agricultural sector, and corruption. Furthermore, in 2005 reforms of the welfare system elicited broad public protest, as vulnerable groups feared a collapse of the social safety net they rely on for basic subsistence. The public remains skeptical of many of the features of a market economic system, feeding suspicions that public optimism could easily turn sour in the face of a new economic jolt, such as occurred in 1998.

Concerns about the fate of Russian democracy are even more widespread. On the positive side, the constitution adopted in 1993 seems to have gained a surprising level of public acceptance. However, observers continue to express concern about the democratic credentials of the Russian president, since key reforms introduced after 2000 seem to undermine prospects for real political competition, and were accompanied by increased controls on the electronic media (especially TV). These changes are justified by the regime as necessary to ensure state capacity to govern and to secure continuing economic growth, but critics wonder whether the Russian desire for order could lead to an authoritarian outcome.

Finally, Russians continue to seek new forms of collective identity. The loss of superpower status, the dominance of Western economic and political models, and the absence of a widely accepted ideology have all contributed to uncertainty about what it means to be Russian and where Russia fits into the world as a whole. Meanwhile, Russia itself suffers from internal divisions. Although overt separatism has been limited to the Republic of Chechnya, differing visions of collective identity have emerged in some of Russia's ethnic republics, particularly in Muslim areas. Other aspects of identity are also being reconsidered. Social class, a linchpin of Soviet ideology, may take on increasing importance in defining group solidarity, as working people seek new organizational forms to assert their rights. Changing gender roles have challenged both men and women to reconsider not only their relationships to one another, but also the impact of these changes on children and community values.

Implications for Comparative Politics

Many countries in the world today are attempting a transition from authoritarian rule to democratic governance. In Russia's case, one of the most important factors affecting this process is the tradition of strong state control, stretching from tsarist times, through the Soviet period, and now influencing present developments. In addition, the intertwined character of politics, economics, and ideology in the Soviet Union has made democratization and economic reform difficult to realize at the same time. In effect, four transition processes were initiated simultaneously in the early 1990s: democratization, market reform, a redefinition of national identity, and integration into the world economy. Whereas other democratizing countries may have undergone one or two of these transitions, Russia has tackled all four at once, and this has complicated each aspect of the process. The difficulties of extricating political from economic power are particularly stark. Because the former Communist elites had no private wealth to fall back on, corrupt or illegal methods were sometimes used to maintain former privileges—methods taken over by Russia's new capitalist class. Citizens, confronted with economic decline and an ideological vacuum, have been susceptible to appeals for strong state control, as well as nationalist appeals. No doubt economic uncertainty has made the Russian public willing to accept strong leadership and limits on political expression that would be resisted in many Western countries. Examining these linkages between political and economic forces in Russia may provide insights for understanding other political settings. The Russian case also offers an opportunity to explore how differing cultural characteristics and diverse economic settings may affect how people understand the meaning of democracy.

Section ❷ Political Economy and Development

The collapse of the Soviet system in late 1991 ushered in a sea change, radically reducing the state's traditionally strong role in economic development and opening the Russian economy to foreign influence. The process of market reform that the Russian government pursued after 1991 brought with it a dramatic decline in economic performance as well as fundamental changes in social relationships. To respond, the Russian government struggled to create tools to regulate the new market forces and to manage impacts of global economic forces. Since 1999, after experiencing an unprecedented period of economic depression from 1991 to 1998, Russia has experienced renewed economic growth (see Table 1). Many experts believe, however, that this sustained upturn has less to do with government policies under Putin and more to do with the 1998 ruble devaluation and high energy prices. If dependent on such volatile factors, Russia's economic revival may fade as quickly as it appeared.

State and Economy

The Soviet Economic System

Under the Soviet command economy, land, factories, and all other important economic assets belonged to the state. Short- and long-term economic plans defined production goals, but these were frequently too ambitious to be fulfilled. Productivity and efficiency were low in Soviet enterprises, and innovation was not rewarded. Prices were controlled by the state; only in the peasant markets and the illegal black market did prices fluctuate in response to conditions of shortage or surplus. Because enterprises were weakly motivated by the need to turn a profit, they had neither the incentive nor the resources to increase production of goods in short supply or to respond to consumer demands. Retail stores piled up stocks of unwanted goods, while goods in high demand were often unavailable. Shortages forced citizens to wait in line for basic items.

Environmental quality deteriorated under Soviet rule because ecological goals were subordinate to production quotas. Large nature-transforming projects (hydroelectric dams, huge factory complexes) were glorified as symbols of Soviet power. Energy intensity was among the highest in the world, and many priority industries (metallurgy, machine building, chemicals, energy production) were highly polluting, resulting in a visibly higher incidence of respiratory and other ailments. Inadequate technological safeguards and an insufficient regulatory structure led to the disastrous nuclear accident at Chernobyl (in Ukraine) in 1986, which contaminated immense areas of agricultural land in Ukraine and Belorussia (now Belarus), as well as some areas of Russia.

Although Russia is rich in natural resources, by the 1970s the most easily accessible deposits in the western part of the country approached depletion. To deal with this, Soviet leaders gave priority to the development of northern Siberia to permit exploitation of oil, natural gas, and precious metals located there. However, Siberian development proved to be complicated and expensive, due to permafrost conditions, transport distances, and the necessity of paying higher wages to attract workers.

Firms and individuals were not permitted to develop direct links to foreign partners; these were all

Table 1

Economic Indicators for the Russian Federation (percent change from the previous year unless otherwise indicated)

	1991	1992	1993	1994	1995	1996	1997	1998	1999	2000	2001	2002	2003	2004
Economic growth	–5.0	–14.5	0.7	12.6	1.0	3.5	0.9	–5.3	6.4	10.0	5.1	4.7	7.3	7.1
Industrial production	–8.0	–18.8	–16.2	–22.6	4.7	–6.5	0.3	–5.2	11.0	11.9	4.9	3.7	7.0	7.3
Consumer price inflation	93	1526	875	307	197	48	15	28	86	21	22	16	14	12
Unemployment rate	n.a.	4.8	5.5	7.5	8.8	9.3	10.7	12.3	12.6	9.8	8.9	8.6	8.4	8.0
Rubles per one USD[a]	169	415	1247	3550	4640	5560	5960	20.7	26.8	28.2	30.1	31.8	29.5	28.5
Population (in millions, Jan. 1)[b]	148.3	148.9	148.7	148.4	148.3	148.0	147.1	146.5	146.0	145.2	144.5	144.0	145.0	144.2

[a]At year end; figures for 1998 and after are in new redenominated rubles, where one new ruble = 1,000 old rubles. The redenomination occurred in January 1998.

[b]January 21, 2005—143.5.

Sources: Data from 1991–2001 are reprinted from *Introduction to Comparative Politics* (Houghton Mifflin, 2004), 361; updates for 2002–2004 and some adjustments to previous data are from *EBRD Transition Report* 2004, and World Bank, *Russian Economic Report* (April 2005) (www.worldbank.org.ru); population figures are from State Statistical Agency of the Russian Federation, http://194.04.30.65/mdb/upload/RERIO.eng.pdf

channeled through the central economic bureaucracy. This international isolation shielded the economy from economic recessions and depressions that plagued Western economies, but lacking foreign competition, the quality of many Russian consumer goods was low by international standards. Both producers and consumers were denied access to many advances available in Western industrial society.

Despite these weaknesses, the Soviet economic model registered some remarkable achievements: rapid industrialization, provision of social welfare and mass education, relatively low levels of inequality, and advances in key economic sectors such as the military and space industries. Nonetheless, over time, the top-heavy nature of Soviet planning and the isolation of the Soviet economy could no longer deliver increased prosperity at home and competitive products for export. These inadequacies spurred Mikhail Gorbachev to initiate his program of restructuring (*perestroika*). However, Gorbachev's efforts to reform the economic system were halting and contradictory. The results were declining economic performance,

increasing regionalism, and an uncertain economic environment. Only after the collapse of the USSR in 1991 did a concerted effort at fundamental economic change take place.

State and Economy in the Russian Federation

In 1992, Boris Yeltsin immediately endorsed radical **market reform,** sometimes referred to as **shock therapy** because of the radical rupture it implied for the economy. The changes were to be rapid and thorough, jolting the Russian economy into a new mode of operation. Although shock therapy would inevitably throw large parts of the economy into a downward spin, reformers hoped that the recovery would be relatively quick and that citizens would accept short-term economic sacrifices, including rising unemployment and higher prices, in order to achieve longer-term economic benefits.

Four main pillars of reform were the lifting of price controls, encouragement of small private businesses, the privatization of most state-owned enterprises, and opening the economy to international influences. Economic decision making would be turned over to new private owners, who would be forced to respond to consumer demands and to increase efficiency and quality by exposure to a competitive economic environment governed by market prices. The more open economic environment would attract foreign investment capital, eliminating the need for state subsidies. These measures would propel the economy to become internationally competitive and responsive to consumer demands—assuring long-term prosperity and stability.

Yeltsin's team quickly took first steps to implement the economic reform program. In January 1992, price controls on most goods were loosened or removed entirely. The result was a period of high inflation; the consumer price index increased by about 2,500 percent between December 1991 and December 1992. Inflation was fueled by a soft monetary policy pursued by the Central Bank of Russia; money was printed with nothing tangible to back it up. Real wages (after controlling for the effects of inflation), on average, declined by an estimated 50 percent between late 1991 and January 1993. International lenders, most notably the International Monetary Fund (IMF), placed strict conditions on Russian loans in order to try to control inflationary tendencies, but the restrictions on the money supply that these policies implied produced their own problems.[6]

Some private business activity was allowed even in the late Soviet period, but private entrepreneurs were more actively encouraged by the new Russian leadership. However, these new ventures faced a number of obstacles, which included confusing regulations, high taxes, lack of capital, and a poor infrastructure (transport, banking, communications) for doing business. With the breakdown of the Soviet distribution system, trade became the most lucrative arena for upstart businesses. These included thousands of small kiosks on city streets; over time, the most successful moved into permanent quarters, alongside a wide range of restaurants, cafes, and entertainment establishments. Although the number of small businesses increased quickly in the early 1990s, they have provided only about 10–15 percent of employment and GNP, compared to over 50 percent in most European countries.[7]

Another important component of the government's program was rapid privatization of the state sector. In 1992, a privatization law was passed, and by early 1994, an estimated 80 percent of medium-sized and large state enterprises in designated sectors of the economy had been transformed into **joint-stock companies.** The most widely adopted method for privatizing state enterprises gave managers and workers of the enterprise (jointly) the right to acquire a controlling packet (51 percent) of enterprise shares at virtually symbolic prices. Each citizen of Russia was issued a **privatization voucher** with a nominal value of 10,000 rubles (about ten U.S. dollars). This privatization method allowed workers to use these vouchers to acquire shares in the enterprises where they worked. Many experts consider that this approach, called **insider privatization,** placed substantial obstacles to reform of business operations because it made managers reluctant to increase efficiency by firing excess labor, which kept work discipline lax. Some managers extracted personal profit from enterprise operations rather than investing available funds to improve production. In addition, many managers did not have the necessary skills to restructure enterprise operations effectively, and some resisted badly needed outside investment that might threaten insider ownership. This path also did not bring real workers' control; protection of shareholder rights was weak, so that savvy managers found ways, over time, to buy out worker shares or prevent workers from having a real impact on decision making. In August 2001, legislation strengthening shareholder rights was signed by the president.

In 1995, the second stage of privatization was launched. At that point, firms could sell remaining shares for cash or investment guarantees. However, this phase of privatization proceeded much more slowly than expected. Many enterprises were unattractive to potential Russian and foreign investors because they were white elephants with backward technology that would require massive infusions of capital for restructuring. Some of the more attractive enterprises (in sectors such as oil and gas production, telecommunications, mass communications, and minerals) fell into the hands of developing financial-industrial conglomerates that had acquired their wealth through positions of power or connections in the government. The loans-for-shares program of 1996 was a particularly controversial approach and is credited by some observers with helping to secure the position of Russia's wealthy and powerful business elite. Under this program, favored businessmen were granted control of lucrative enterprises (through control of state shares) in exchange for loans to the cash-strapped Russian government. When the government could not repay the loans, the favored businesses gained ownership of the shares. In other cases, securities auctions gave advantages to large business interests that became an increasingly powerful force on the Russian political scene in the late 1990s as politicians tried to win their favor, particularly before elections, to secure sources of campaign financing.

Despite all of its problems, on balance the pace and scope of privatization in Russia were rapid and thorough compared to other postcommunist countries. However, the new joint-stock companies did not meet expectations. Productivity and efficiency did not increase significantly; unprofitable firms continued to operate; investment was weak; and the benefits of ownership were not widely or fairly distributed. The government continued to subsidize ineffective operations through various means, making most Russian firms uncompetitive and unattractive to potential investors. Renationalization of some enterprises came under discussion and was, for the most part, rejected, but some believed it would undermine investor confidence and the economic power of important elements of the Russian elite. However, some consider the controversial purchase of the large oil company Yukos to be de facto nationalization.

Reform of agriculture produced even less satisfactory results than industrial privatization. Large joint-stock companies and associations of individual households were created on the basis of former state and collective farms. These privatized companies operated inefficiently, and agricultural output declined throughout the 1990s. Foreign food imports (including meat and a whole range of processed goods) also undercut domestic producers, contributing to a downward spiral in agricultural investment and production. In 2003, a new Land Code took effect, allowing the sale of agricultural land for agricultural purposes, with some restrictions, including the exclusion of foreigner buyers.[8]

By the late 1990s, it appeared that the government's reform program had not achieved most of its underlying goals (see Figure 1a). Russia was in the grip of a severe depression, more sustained than the

Figure 1a

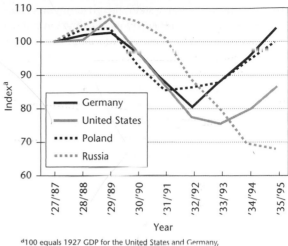

Downturn of the Russian Economy

[a]100 equals 1927 GDP for the United States and Germany, and 1987 GDP for Poland and Russia.

Source: Copyright © 2002 by the National Bureau of Asian Research. Reprinted from Millar, James, R. "Normalization of the Russian Economy: Obstacles and Opportunities for Reform and Sustainable Growth," *NBR Analysis 13,* no. 2, April 2002, by permission of the National Bureau of Asian Research.

Great Depression of the 1930s in the United States and Western Europe. Industrial production was less than half the 1990 level. Basic industrial sectors such as machine building, light industry, construction materials, and wood products were the worst off. The depression fed on itself, as declining capacity in one sector deprived other sectors of buyers or suppliers. Consumer purchasing power dropped with the decline in real wages. Firms were unable to pay their suppliers, were in arrears to their employees, and owed taxes to the government. Even the state was behind in its wage, social benefit, and pension payments. Under these conditions, barter arrangements, often involving intertwined linkages of several enterprises or organizations, became common.

A key obstacle to the success of the market reform agenda has been the very weakness of state institutions. This may seem ironic, since one of the main ideas underlying market economic reform is to reduce state control of the economy. However, even in established market economies a well-functioning state apparatus is essential to carry out needed regulatory and law-enforcement functions. Two examples illustrate the point: tax collection and law enforcement. Without an effective tax collection system, the government cannot acquire revenues needed to pay its own bills on time, to provide essential services to the population, and to ensure a well-functioning economic infrastructure (such as transportation, energy, public utilities). The state would also not be able to fulfill key regulatory functions, for example, those regarding the banking sector, health and safety regulations, and assurance of labor standards. If government cannot provide these services efficiently, businesses may take matters into their own hands, for example, by hiring private security services, turning to the mafia for protection, or by paying bribes. Weak government capacity feeds corruption and criminality, producing risks both to business and to the population at large. This is the situation Russia faced in the 1990s and still does to a considerable extent today.

Other centers of power undermined the central government's reform efforts. The central state had difficulty exerting its authority in relation to the regions of the Russian Federation, of which there were eighty-nine until December 2005, when the first merger of regions occurred (see Section 3). A second problem was the increasing power of the business **oligarchs,**

wealthy individuals who had benefited from the privatization process and who often held significant political influence as well.[9] These new Russian capitalists were able to gain control of important economic assets but often did not reinvest their profits to spur business development; rather, wealth was siphoned off through capital flight, in which money was removed from the country and deposited in foreign accounts or assets. Diverse methods of laundering money to avoid taxes became widespread. Corruption involving government officials, the police, and operators abroad fed a rising crime rate, which spilled over into many Western countries. Rich foreigners, Russian bankers, and outspoken journalists became targets of the Russian **mafia.** Rather than controlling these abuses, policies of the Russian government itself had contributed to the creation of this new group of financial and business oligarchs.

A financial crisis in August 1998 brought the situation to a head. Underlying the crisis was the Russian government's inability to pay its many creditors. The government successively took on new loans at progressively higher rates of interest in order to pay off existing debts, creating a structure of **pyramid debt.** Because the revenues the government acquired through these short-term loans were used, in large

"Welcome to the Russian Market." The market economy is not always a friendly place for the small firm.
Source: Elkin, *Izvestiia,* August 29, 2002.

Figure 1b

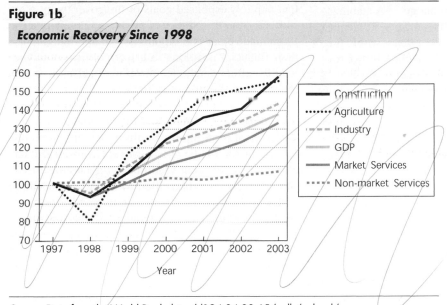

Economic Recovery Since 1998

Legend:
— Construction
······ Agriculture
– – – Industry
GDP
Market Services
······ Non-market Services

Source: Data from the World Bank; http://194.84.38.65/mdb/upload/
PAR_020805_eng pdf

part, to pay interest on debt, they did not generate any usable income for the government. Following a sharp upturn in 1996–1997, in August 1998 the Russian stock market lost over 90 percent of its value, and the government defaulted on its bonds. Many Russian banks, holders of the Russian government's short-term bonds, were facing imminent bankruptcy. The government began to print more of the increasingly valueless rubles, threatening to undermine the ruble's value further and thus intensify the underlying financial crisis.

The government was finally forced to allow a radical devaluation of the overvalued ruble. Within a two-week period, the ruble lost two-thirds of its value against the U.S. dollar, banks closed or allowed only limited withdrawals, supplies of imported goods decreased, and business accounts were frozen—forcing some firms to lay off employees and others to close their doors. In retrospect, despite its immediate disastrous effects, the 1998 financial crisis ushered in positive changes. First, the devalued ruble led to a sharp reduction in imports of Western commodities, making

Russian producers competitive. Firms were able to improve their products, put underused labor back to work, and thus increase productivity. The state budget benefited from improved tax revenues; barter declined, as did payment arrears.[10] Economic growth registered 5.4 percent in 1999 and has remained in positive territory ever since, with 7 percent growth in GDP in 2003 and 2004, representing the first years of sustained economic recovery since the Soviet collapse.[11] See Figure 1b.

A second effect was less tangible. Relying on international credits and aid, Russian policymakers had been subject to Western conditions that often involved unpopular choices with debatable economic benefits. This system undermined the motivation to seek indigenous solutions. Following the 1998 crisis, under Putin's leadership, Russian policymakers were more determined to fashion Russian solutions to Russian problems. A third positive influence emerged in the late 1990s: international oil and gas prices rose sharply, generating new sources of revenue, which also spilled into government tax coffers, making up as much as 20 to 30 percent of the budget.[12] A stabilization fund, created in 2004, hold a portion of revenues generated by export duties and other taxes, would presumably cushion the effects of a decline in tax revenue associated with a fall in world energy prices.

Experts have continued to debate the contribution of government policy to Russia's economic recovery. While Yeltsin's economic policies were associated with economic decline, President Putin tried to chart a new course. After a sluggish first year, an active legislative program emerged in 2001 and 2002. A new Ministry for Economic Development and Trade was charged with developing the underlying concept. One of the first steps was a simplification of the tax system, intended to increase tax compliance and facilitate enforcement. A 13 percent flat income tax was one very visible aspect of the package, and adjustments were also made to corporate taxes as well. Other government initiatives included amendments to the corporate governance law to protect shareholders' rights; legislation to control money laundering; provision for the sale of land to both domestic and foreign buyers (in the first instance, commercial and urban land only); a new labor code that tightened conditions for trade union organization; a new system governing the distribution of authority and of tax revenues among the center, the regions, and local organs; a new customs code; pension reform; amendments to the bankruptcy law; and initiatives to reduce subsidization of housing and communal services. Other developments fueled optimism about Russia's economic future. A budget surplus replaced a deficit, and the foreign debt load declined from 90 percent of GDP in 1998 to 28 percent in 2004.[13] Prospects for Russia's membership in the World Trade Organization also fueled optimism about Russia's trade growth. However, by early 2005, criticism was again emerging that the government was sluggish in pushing forward further reforms, that the economic bubble could be burst by falling energy prices, and that the exchange rate for the ruble was again reaching levels that could undermine the competitiveness of domestic production.

Another important feature of Putin's policy has involved efforts to rein in the power of the economic oligarchs. In the Yeltsin period, bartering of economic concessions in exchange for political support meant that publicly espoused goals of the government often succumbed to the politics of private economic interest. Putin made clear that oligarchs who attempted to use their financial positions to affect political outcomes would suffer sanctions. Several attacks on media moguls were the first stage in this process, as business magnates Vladimir Gusinsky and Boris Berezovksy were targeted. Gusinsky's NTV was the nearly sole TV critic of the Kremlin's military action against the secessionist Republic of Chechnya; Gusinsky also had close ties to President Vladimir Putin's political rival, Moscow mayor Luzhkov. Berezovksy was also a thorn in the Kremlin's side, threatening to broadcast charges on TV-6 linking the government to 1999 apartment bombings that had been attributed to terrorists. Charges of tax evasion and fraud were brought against both men, defended as part of the government's campaign to assure proper business practices by business oligarchs. Berezovsky fled to self-imposed exile in Europe, while Gusinsky fled to Spain.

A controversial new chapter in Putin's battle with the oligarchs was opened in October 2003 when Mikhail Khodorkovsky, the chief executive officer and major shareholder of the giant Russian oil company Yukos, was placed under arrest for fraud and tax evasion. Cited by Forbes as Russia's richest man, his company was forced to dispose of its major asset, Yuganskneftegas, to pay tax bills presented by the Russian government. Following a high-profile trial, in May 2005, Khodorkovsky was sentenced by a Russian court to nine years in prison on charges of fraud, tax evasion, and embezzlement. Critics of the government charged that the process was both motivated and influenced by political considerations, and that it marked a step back from democratic reform and due process. Many critics felt the attacks on Khodorkovsky, Gusinsky, and Berezovsky were cases of selective enforcement to rid the president of economically powerful critics. Khodorkovsky had publicly opposed key government initiatives, provided support to opposition political parties (particularly the liberal Union of Rights Forces and Yabloko), and proposed radical changes in political structures that would weaken the power of the Russian presidency. The attack on Yukos has undermined investor confidence (including foreign investors) among shareholders who fear government pretexts for economic takeovers.

These events spurred debates about the status of press freedom, democracy, and privatization in Russia. Shortly after his arrest, Khodorkovsky presented himself as a defender of Russian democracy. "The biggest threat is that we do not have a civil society, and so there are people, groups of people, who want to have the power in their hands, basically bypassing democratic procedures, by keeping the shell, but taking out the meaning."[14] However, with Russian citizens deeply concerned about crime and corruption in high places, Putin's commitment to restoring legal order and a strong state apparatus strikes a chord with the Russian public. Putin's personal background in the Soviet secret service has, however, evoked suspicions about his intentions. Attacks on independent power sources, whether they be critical media outlets or powerful financial figures, could give the Russian president decisive control over the formation of public opinion, influencing electoral outcomes and creating an atmosphere of fear and intimidation. While the oligarchs Putin has targeted may not have clean hands, Putin's attacks seem strangely focused on political opponents.

Society and Economy

Soviet Social Policy

The Soviet system allowed the leadership to establish priorities with little input from society. One such priority was military production, but realization of social goals was also a policy focus, producing some of the most marked achievements of the Soviet system. Benefits to the population included free health care, low-cost access to essential goods and services, maternity leave (partially paid), child benefits, and disability pensions. Mass education was another social priority of the Soviet regime, taking the form of universal access to primary and secondary schooling—leading to nearly universal literacy in a short period of time. Postsecondary education was free of charge, with state stipends provided to university students.

Guaranteed employment and job security were other core elements of the tacit social contract; only in

exceptional cases could an enterprise fire an employee. Participation in the labor market was high: almost all able-bodied adults, men and women, worked outside the home. Citizens received many of these benefits through their place of employment, thus making the Soviet workplace a social as well as an economic institution. The full-employment policy made unemployment compensation unnecessary. The retirement age was fifty-five for women and sixty for men, although in the early 1980s about one-third of those beyond retirement age continued to work. Modest pensions were guaranteed by the state, ensuring a stable but minimal standard of living for retirement.

Although basic social needs were met in the Soviet Union, the system was plagued by shortages and low-quality service. For example, the availability of advanced medical equipment was limited, and sometimes under-the-table payments were required to prompt better-quality service. Many goods and services, although economically in the reach of every citizen, were in short supply, so queues were a pervasive part of everyday life. Housing shortages restricted mobility and forced young couples and their children to share small apartments with parents. An irony of the system was that labor in many sectors was in constant short supply, reflecting the inefficient use of the work force. Labor productivity was low by international standards and work discipline weak: drunkenness and absenteeism were common. A Soviet saying of the time captured this element of the tacit social contract: "We pretend to work, they pretend to pay us." Whereas the lax work atmosphere reduced the likelihood and frequency of labor conflicts, it also kept production inefficient. Alcoholism was also a significant source of low labor productivity.

Another feature of the system was the relatively low level of inequality. As a matter of state policy, wage differentials between the best- and worst-paid were lower than in Western countries. This approach seemed in harmony with overriding cultural values, but it also reduced the incentive for outstanding achievements and innovation. Because land and factories were state owned, individuals could not accumulate wealth in the form of real estate, stocks, or ownership of factories. Any privileges that did exist were modest by Western standards. Political elites did have access to scarce goods, higher-quality health care, travel, and vacation homes, but these privileges were hidden from public view. An underlying assumption of this approach seemed to be that a dismal equality was superior to the tensions and discontent that visible inequality might evoke.

Economic Reform and Russian Society

The Soviet experience led Russians to expect a broad range of social welfare support from the state, expectations hard to realize in a market economy and in the face of declining economic performance. In the 1990s, budget constraints necessitated cutbacks in state welfare programs at a time when there was a growing need for them. Pensions had less and less buying power, and state services proved inadequate to deal with increasing problems of homelessness and poverty. In line with the new market ideology, tuition fees for postsecondary education were introduced in many cases, and although a system of universal health care remained, higher-quality health care was made more obviously dependent on ability to pay. The cost of medicine rose beyond the reach of many citizens. Benefits provided through the workplace were cut back, as even viable businesses faced pressures to reduce costs and increase productivity.

Some groups have benefited from the reform process, while others have suffered sharp declines. Wage rates are highest for highly skilled employees in the natural resource sectors (such as oil and gas), in banking and finance, and for individuals with marketable skills such as knowledge of English or German. At the extreme end, the wealthiest enjoy a standard of living luxurious even by Western standards. These people, many of them multimillionaires with Western bank accounts, were able to take advantage of the privatization process to gain positions in lucrative sectors like banking, finance, oil, and gas.

Poverty is highest among rural residents, the unemployed, the less educated, pensioners, and the disabled. The number of homeless and beggars has skyrocketed, especially in large cities like Moscow, a magnet for displaced persons and refugees from war zones on Russia's perimeter. Nonetheless, as a result of low wage levels, the majority of those in poverty are the working poor. Dramatic declines in income have affected those without easily marketable skills, including unskilled laborers in low-priority sectors of the economy and people working in areas of public service such as education. Consumer price inflation gradually declined over the 1990s but still had an important impact on incomes; in 1999 the rate of inflation was 86 percent, falling to an acceptable 11.7 percent in 2004.[15] Unemployment has been lower than might be expected because many enterprises kept underemployed staff on the rolls. Official estimates are about 9.8 percent in 2000 and between 8 and 9 percent in 2003 and 2004.[16] But these figures hide short-term layoffs, workers still employed but only sporadically paid, or people who have shifted to partial employment. On the other hand, employment in the shadow economy goes unreported. Levels of unemployment are particularly high in some regions, including republics and regions with high ethnic minority populations. Aboriginal groups in Russia's far north have suffered especially adverse effects as a result of the economic decline. Northern regions depend on the maintenance of a fragile transport and communications system for deliveries of basic necessities such as fuel and food.

Although income differentials overall have declined only minimally since 1999 when growth was restored, the World Bank estimates that by 2002 poverty had been cut in half—to 19.6 percent of the Russian population.[17] Social impacts of economic stress include higher rates of crime, suicide, and mortality; alcoholism continues to be a significant problem, particularly for males. All of these factors increase the likelihood of dysfunctional family structures, producing a particularly marked impact on children. Only in the last two years have these social indicators of economic stress begun to decline. Since 2000, levels of personal consumption have grown following years of decline, but many individuals (particularly men) have two to three jobs just to make ends meet. Public opinion surveys indicate that in 2004, most Russians expected little change in the economic situation of their families in the near future, and they continued to worry most about economic issues such as low income, poor social protection, unemployment, and crime.[18]

Russians line up at the money exchange kiosk. The longer line wants to receive social benefits rather than money, whereas the shorter line is happy to give up social benefits in exchange for money. *Source:* Rossii skie vesti, p. 3, August 18, 2004.

A particularly contentious issue, which led to massive street demonstrations in several Russian cities in early 2005, involves changes to social welfare policy. Referred to as the "monetarization of social benefits," the reforms include rescinding the provision of certain services (such as public transport, medicine) free of charge to a wide range of disadvantaged groups (pensioners, veterans, the disabled), and their replacement by a modest monetary payment, lower than the cost people would have to pay for the services. Subsidies for public utilities and housing were also reduced. Viewed as part of the liberal market reform process, these reforms were intended to increase the role of the market and reduce the direct financial burden on local governments. Many Russians viewed the change, however, as a direct reduction in social welfare for the neediest in society, including people who had served the country through years of hardship. Following large-scale demonstrations throughout the country, the government agreed to accompany the reforms by a modest increase in pensions and to

restore subsidized transport to ensure that actual costs did not rise. It was generally acknowledged that the reform was poorly implemented, with inadequate preparation. Although Putin's popularity suffered a temporary decline during this episode, it rebounded quickly. Nonetheless, the issue galvanized popular discontent, providing the political opposition with the opportunity to mobilize population protests against the government.

Women still endure many of the same hardships from which they suffered in the Soviet period. They continue to carry the bulk of domestic responsibilities, including shopping, cooking, housework, and childcare. In addition, most women feel compelled to work outside the home to help make ends meet. Many women take advantage of the permitted three-year maternity leave, which is only partially paid. Fathers play a relatively small role in child raising; many women rely on grandparents to help out. Employers are sometimes reluctant to hire women of childbearing age, since exercise of maternity leave is often viewed as disruptive in the workplace. Some data suggest, however, that while women are more likely to register with unemployment offices and take longer to find new jobs, levels of actual unemployment are about equal for men and women.[19]

The birth rate in Russia fell from 16.6 births per 1,000 people in 1985 to a rate of 10.5 in 2004, while the death rate was 16.0.[20] These figures underlie a progressive decline in the population of the country. Life expectancy for Soviet men fell from 66 years in 1966–1967 to under 59 in 2003 (from 74 to 72 for women).[21] The decline in population has been tempered only by the immigration of ethnic Russians from other former Soviet republics (see Figure 2). Although declining birth rates are a common corollary of economic modernization, in the 1990s many couples in Russia were especially reluctant to have children because of daily hardships, future uncertainty, a declining standard of living, and continuing housing shortages—a line of thinking that reflects a dangerous demoralization of public life and an indicator of the social costs of economic transformation. Today, contraceptive devices and sanitary products are more widely available than in the past, but the former are expensive if they are of reliable quality.

Russian Political Culture and Economic Change

Alongside more objective factors, culture affects processes of economic change. Several aspects of Russian culture may have inhibited adaptation to a market economy. These include a weak tradition of individual entrepreneurship, a widespread commitment to egalitarian values, and a reliance on relations of personal trust rather than written contracts. Profit, as a measure of success, is less important to many Russians than is support for friends and coworkers; thus, firing redundant workers may be an unpalatable approach. Selection of business partners or recruitment of personnel may be strongly influenced by personal contacts and relationships rather than by merit. Incentive structures of the Soviet period also have been internalized by older population groups, including features that encourage risk avoidance, low productivity, poor punctuality, absenteeism, lack of personal responsibility and initiative, and a

Figure 2

Immigration Into Russia, 1995–2004

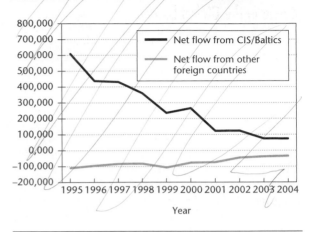

Year

Source: Russian Annual Statisical Report 2003; Current Statistical Survey, no. 1 (48) 2004; and website of the Federal Statistical Agency of the Russian Federation, www.gks.ru.

preference for security over achievement.[22] However, young people in Russia are being socialized in a new cultural environment and when offered appropriate incentives, Russian employees tend to operate at high levels of efficiency and, after a period of time, adopt work habits rewarded by the employing organization.

Younger Russians are also better equipped to adapt to the new economic conditions. Not only are they more flexible due to their age, but they also have different expectations from their elders. Consequently, they are more supportive of the market transition and are more oriented toward maximizing self-interest and demonstrating initiative. Thus, generational change is an important factor in understanding Russia's economic development. Nevertheless, a significant portion of Russians of all age groups still question values underlying the market reform process, preferring an economy that is less profit driven and more oriented to equality and the collective good. Survey data suggest that although Russians support the idea of democracy and appreciate the freedom they have gained since the collapse of communism, they are much less enamored with the basic notions underlying the capitalist economic system.[23]

Russia in the Global Economy

Right up to the end of the Soviet period, the economy remained relatively isolated from outside influences. Most of the USSR's trade (53 percent of imports, 51 percent of exports, in 1984) was carried out with the countries of Eastern Europe.[24] The ruble was nonconvertible, meaning that its exchange rate was set by the state and did not fluctuate freely in response to economic forces. All foreign trade was channeled through central state organs, so individual enterprises had neither the possibility nor the incentive to seek external markets. Accounts in Western currencies (so-called hard currency) were under state control. Russia's rich natural resource base, particularly oil and gas, provided an important source of hard currency income.

Gorbachev sought to integrate the USSR into the global economy by permitting some foreign investment through joint ventures and by reducing barriers to foreign contacts. The new Russia has pursued this policy even more aggressively. Over time, restrictions on foreign investment have been lifted, the value of the ruble has been allowed to respond to market conditions, and firms are allowed to conclude agreements directly with foreign partners. In response, Western governments (with Germany at the top of the list) have made fairly generous commitments of technical and humanitarian assistance. Assistance programs have included training programs to help government officials, individual entrepreneurs, and social organizations adapt to the new challenges of market reform. The World Bank, the IMF, and the EU have also contributed substantial amounts of economic assistance, often in the form of repayable credits. In the past, release of IMF credit, issued to stabilize the ruble, was made contingent on Russia's pursuing a strict policy of fiscal and monetary control and lifting remaining price controls. The Russian government had difficulties in meeting these conditions, and thus the funds were released intermittently. After the August 1998 crisis, the Russian government defaulted first on the ruble-denominated short-term debt and then on the former Soviet debt. Since then, debt repayments have been made on time. In 2001, the Russian government decided to forgo additional IMF credits. By 2004, it had paid off its IMF debt and, bit by bit, has cut its remaining debt obligation.[25]

Russia has had problems attracting foreign investment, even in its improved economic circumstances since 1999, and levels still remain low compared to other East European countries: less than 4 percent of the per capita level in the Czech Republic and Slovakia, and about a quarter of the Polish level in 2002. An upward trajectory was interrupted by the 1998 financial crisis. Major sources of foreign direct investment in 2003 were Cyprus (19.3 percent but this is mainly recycled Russian capital, exported earlier for tax reasons), the United States (16.4 percent), and Great Britain and the Netherlands (just under 11 percent each).[26] Continued uncertainty and instability regarding government policy, reinforced by the Khodorkovsky case, and a few highly visible murders of prominent business figures have prevented a stabilization of investor confidence. On the other hand, the focus of Russia's foreign trade activity has shifted significantly since the Soviet period. Whereas in 1994, Ukraine was Russia's most important trading partner, now Germany holds first place, receiving 7.7 percent of Russian exports, followed by the United States, with 6.9 percent in 2004. Germany provided 10.7 percent of imports in 2004, followed by Belarus (6.5, down from 11.1 percent in 2000), China (5.5 percent), and Ukraine (5.0 percent). In 2004, Russia's foreign trade with countries of the expanded EU (more than 50 percent of the total) far exceeded combined exports to countries of the Commonwealth of Independent States (CIS).[27] In 2004, the EU confirmed its support for Russian membership in the World Trade Organization (WTO), as observers speculated a quid pro quo had been reached in exchange for Russian agreement to raise domestic oil prices (since their low level allegedly gives Russian producers an unfair competitive advantage) and to ratify the Kyoto Accord on Climate Change, an important priority of the European Union.

Russia's position in the international political economy remains undetermined. With a highly skilled work force and an advanced technological base in certain sectors (especially military sectors), Russia has many of the ingredients necessary to become a competitive and powerful force in the global economy. However, if the country's industrial capacity is not restored, reliance on natural resource exports will leave Russia vulnerable to global economic fluctuations in supply and demand. At the same time, its wealth in natural resources has given Russia advantages compared to its neighbors, since these expensive materials do not need to be imported. In 2003, over 50 percent of exports were fuels or energy, whereas only about 10 percent were machinery and equipment, with other resources such as metals and timber making up a large part of the balance.[28] Ultimately, Russia's position in the global economy will depend on the ability of the country's leadership to fashion a viable approach to domestic economic challenges and to facilitate differentiation of the country's export base.

Section ❸ Governance and Policy-Making

When Russia became an independent country in December 1991, dramatic changes in state structure and governing processes followed. The new Russian leadership endorsed liberal democratic principles as the basis of its new political institutions, and in April 2005 Putin declared, "[T]he development of Russia as a free and democratic state [is] the main political and ideological goal."[29] Critics, however, were less certain about the fate of democracy in Russia, as measures introduced by Putin to strengthen presidential power seemed to undermine some of the Russian Federation's founding democratic principles. Disagreement over the status of Russian democracy and its future form the backdrop for our examination of Russian state structures and policy-making that we explore in this chapter.

Organization of the State

As we noted in Section 1, ratification of the new Russian constitution in 1993 was a contested political process that followed a violent confrontation between the president and the parliament. The process culminated in a narrowly successful popular referendum on a document reflecting Yeltsin's own preferences. Nonetheless, by 2005 public opinion polls suggest that the new constitution has acquired broad-based popular legitimacy, even if its interpretation is sometimes hotly contested. The document affirms many established principles of liberal democratic governance—competitive elections within a multi-party context, separation of powers, an independent judiciary, federalism, and protection of individual civil liberties. However, another key feature is the strength of the president's executive power. This feature is both a response to the demands for leadership required in a period of radical change and a reflection of Russia's political tradition, which has been characterized by strong central political authority. Despite the constitutional basis for strong executive power, in practice throughout the 1990s the state demonstrated only a weak capacity to govern. Associated declines in economic performance elicited a countertendency after Putin's election in 2000 in the form of a recentralization of political power.

The constitution laid the groundwork for institutional conflict between governing structures, which has not always taken a constructive form. The Russian Federation inherited a complex structure of regional subunits from the Soviet period. Between 1991 and 1993, negotiations between the central government and the various regions led to the establishment of a complicated federal structure with eighty-nine federal units. Some of these subnational governments demanded increased autonomy, even sovereignty (and one, Chechnya, demanded independence; see "Current Challenges: The Chechnya Crisis"), generating a process of negotiation and political conflict between the center and the regions that sometimes led to contradictions between regional and federal laws. The relationship between organs of the federal government itself has also been conflictual. The constitution makes the executive dominant but still dependent on the agreement of the legislative branch to realize its programs. Tension between the two branches of government, which are selected in separate electoral processes, was a persistent obstacle to effective governance in the Yeltsin years. The executive itself has two heads (the president and the prime minister), introducing another venue for intrastate tension. Relations between the executive and judicial branches were strained in the Yeltsin years, and the establishment of real judicial independence

remains a significant political challenge. Finally, poor salaries and lack of professionalism in the civil service opened the door to corruption and political influence. Putin's centralizing measures have sought to address all of these areas of contention, but, some would argue, in so doing may be undermining the very checks and balances that are supposed to offer protection against reestablishment of authoritarian control.

Current Challenges: The Chechnya Crisis

Despite its small size and population (estimated at 600,000 in 1994), the breakaway republic of Chechnya holds an important position on Russia's southern border. The republic is widely perceived as a safe haven for criminal elements that operate in Russia. In the early 1990s, the Russian leadership feared that Chechnya's attempted secession from the Russian Federation might embolden other republics to pursue a similar course. These concerns motivated Russia to send troops into Chechnya on December 11, 1994, fueling a regional civil war.

The desire for independence has deep roots in Chechnya. Prior to its incorporation into the Russian Empire in 1859 and again after the Bolshevik revolution in 1917, local forces fought to maintain Chechnya's independence. In 1924, Chechnya was made part of the USSR, and in 1934 it was joined with an adjacent region, Ingushetia, to form a single autonomous republic within the Soviet Union. During World War II, following an anti-Soviet uprising, Stalin deported hundreds of Chechens to Soviet Central Asia.

Taking advantage of the ongoing political upheaval in the USSR, in October 1991 the newly elected president of the republic, Dzhokar Dudaev, declared Chechnya's independence from Russia. In 1992, Checheno-Ingushetia was officially recognized by the Russian government as two separate republics. Following the split,

Chechen leaders continued to pursue independence, a claim rejected by the Russian government. Intervention by Russian military forces in December 1994 evoked criticism within the Russian Federation and its leadership circles. Some opposed the intervention completely, favoring a political solution; others were primarily critical of the ineffective manner in which the war effort was carried out. The campaign was poorly organized and internal dissension within the army and security forces demoralized the troops. Civilians in Chechnya and the surrounding regions suffered at the hands of both sides. In 1995 and 1996, hostage takings by Chechen rebels in the adjacent regions, Stavropol krai and the republic of Dagestan, took the conflict beyond Chechnya's borders.

The unpopular war became an important issue in the 1996 presidential campaign and threatened to undermine Yeltsin's already fragile support. In late May 1996, a cease-fire agreement was signed, and in June, Yeltsin decreed the beginning of troop withdrawals. In September 1996, an agreement with the rebels was again signed. The joint declaration put off a decision on Chechnya's status for five years, leaving the issue unresolved.

On January 27, 1997, an election was held for the president of the Republic of Chechnya. Observers generally considered the vote to be fair, with 79 percent of the eligible population

(continued)

Current Challenges: The Chechnya Crisis (cont.)

participating. In a race involving thirteen candidates, Aslan Maskhadov received 59 percent of the vote. Relative to other leading candidates, Maskhadov was considered to be a moderate. However, he publicly supported Chechnya's independence, and later, removed from power by Moscow, he became a rebel leader, killed by Russian forces in March 2005.

In 1999, terrorist bombings, attributed to Chechen rebels, occurred in apartment buildings in Moscow and two other Russian cities, causing about 300 deaths. The second war against Chechnya was launched as Yeltsin sent nearly 100,000 Russian troops to regain control of the breakaway republic. The troops occupied the Chechen capital Grozny; refugees spilled into surrounding areas and beyond Chechnya's borders. Allegations of human rights violations were made both against Russian troops and Chechen rebels; Western governments and international organizations such as Human Rights Watch demanded that the Russian government comply with international human rights standards. Russian authorities continue to resist external involvement in the situation, maintaining that the Chechnya crisis is a domestic political issue. At the same time, President Putin has repeatedly emphasized the existence of links between Chechen rebels and international

terrorist networks, including Al Qaeda, in an effort to gain Western acceptance for Russia's military actions.

Since 1999, Russian authorities have periodically claimed imminent victory in the military struggle. However, Russian forces have proven unable to rout rebels from the mountainous regions of the republic. A string of terrorist attacks by Chechen rebels since 1999, intensifying in 2004 with the Beslan tragedy, placed the problem clearly in the public mind. In March 2003, Russian authorities tried to set Chechnya on a track of normalization by holding a referendum on a new constitution in the republic that would confirm Chechnya's status within the Russian Federation. This symbolic act has not stopped the conflict. In October 2003, Akhmad Kadyrov was elected president of Chechnya with Russian support in a controversial process, only to be killed by Chechen rebels the next year. In March 2005, former Chechen president Aslan Maskhadov was killed by Russian forces, but the more radical insurgent leader Shamil Basayev, who claimed responsibility for the Beslan hostage taking, was still at large.

Source: Adapted from *Introduction to Comparative Politics*, 3rd ed. Copyright 2004 by Houghton Mifflin Company. Reprinted with permission.

Many of the difficulties facing the new Russian state are, at least in part, legacies of the Soviet period. Following the collapse of the USSR, the new political leadership tried to wipe the slate clean and start anew. However, some political scientists emphasize the importance of "path dependence," that is, the manner in which past experience shapes the choices and options available for change.[30] Some observers see in Putin's reforms a reversion to practices and patterns reminiscent of the Soviet period, namely, centralization of power and obstacles to effective political competition. Other analysts interpret these

measures as necessary to solidify rule of law and the state's capacity to govern; both are prerequisites of democratic development. To assess this debate, first let's review the nature of Soviet political institutions themselves.

The Soviet State

Before Gorbachev's reforms, top organs of the Communist Party of the Soviet Union (CPSU) dominated the state. The CPSU was a hierarchical structure in which lower party bodies elected delegates to higher party organs, but these elections were uncontested, and top organs determined candidates for lower party posts. The Politburo, the top party organ, was the real decision-making center. A larger body, the Central Committee, represented the broader political elite, including regional party leaders and representatives of various economic sectors. Alongside the CPSU were Soviet state structures that formally resembled Western parliamentary systems but had little decision-making authority. The state bureaucracy had day-to-day responsibility in both the economic and political spheres but operated in subordination to the party's directives. People holding high state positions were appointed through the *nomenklatura* system, a mechanism that allowed the CPSU to fill key posts with politically reliable individuals. The Supreme Soviet, the parliament, was a rubber-stamp body; its members were directly elected by the population, but the single candidate who ran in each district was chosen by higher CPSU organs (but was not necessarily a party member).

In theory, the Soviet state was governed by a constitution, the last one adopted in 1977. In practice, however, the constitution was of symbolic rather than operational importance since many of its principles were ignored. The constitution provided for legislative, executive, and judicial organs, but separation of powers was considered inapplicable to Soviet society because the CPSU claimed to represent the interests of society as a whole. With the power of appointment firmly under party control, it made little sense to speak of legislative or judicial independence. When the constitution was violated (as it frequently was), the courts had no independent authority to protect its provisions.

The Soviet Union was also designated a federal system; that is, according to the constitution, certain powers were granted to the fifteen union republics (which have since become independent states). However, this was phony federalism since all aspects of life were overseen by a highly centralized Communist Party. Nonetheless, the various subunits that existed within the Russian Republic (***autonomous republics, krais, oblasts,*** and ***okrugs***) were carried over into the Russian Federation in an altered form, an example of path dependence.

Gorbachev began a process of radical institutional change through the introduction of competitive elections, increased political pluralism, reduced Communist Party dominance, a revitalized legislative branch of government, and renegotiation of the terms of Soviet federalism. He also tried to bring the constitution into harmony with political reality, and many constitutional amendments were adopted that altered existing political institutions. Together, these changes moved the political system haltingly and unevenly in a direction resembling the liberal democratic systems of the West.

The New Russian State

Even before the collapse of the USSR, political institutions began to change in the Russian Republic, a constituent unit of the Soviet Union. A new post of president was created, and on June 12, 1991, Boris Yeltsin was elected by direct popular vote as its first incumbent, giving him a base of popular legitimacy. Once the Russian Federation became an independent state, a crucial turning point was the adoption by referendum of a new Russian constitution in December 1993; this constitution provides the legal foundation for current state institutions (see Figure 3). However, as in any other country, political practice goes far beyond constitutional provisions and sometimes alters their interpretation. In some ways, the evolution of governance and policymaking in the Russian Federation since 1991 can be seen as a laboratory for engineering democratic governance, somewhat analogous to the experience of Germany and Japan after World War II.

The Executive

The constitution establishes a semipresidential system, formally resembling the French system but with stronger executive power. The president, who holds primary power, is the head of state, and the prime minister, appointed by the president but approved by the lower house of the parliament (the State *Duma*), is the head of government. This dual executive can introduce tensions within the executive branch, as well as between the president and the *Duma*. As a

Figure 3

Political Institutions of the Russian Federation (R.F.), 2005

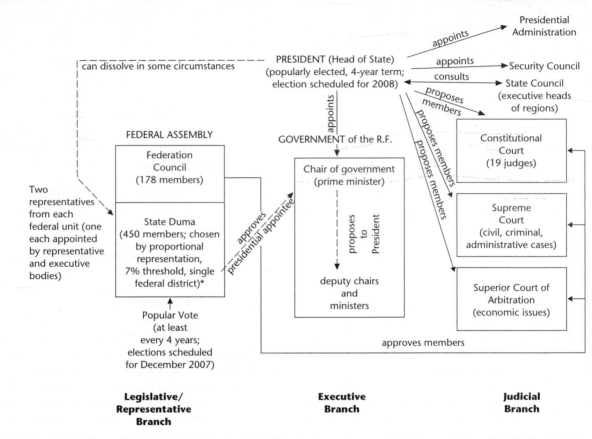

* Effective for the 2007 Duma elections; 2003 elections involved 225 seats chosen by proportional representation with a 5% threshold.

rule of thumb, the president has overseen foreign policy, relations with the regions, and the organs of state security, while the prime minister has focused his attention on the economy and related issues. However, with Yeltsin's continuing health problems in 1998 and 1999, operative power shifted in the direction of the prime minister. Ever since the election of Vladimir Putin in March 2000, however, the primary locus of power has returned to the presidency, with economic powers gradually shifting back into the hands of the prime minister.

The president is elected directly by the population every four years, with a limit of two consecutive terms. In 1996, the first presidential elections returned Yeltsin to power, despite his waning popularity. In December 1999, Yeltsin resigned from office, making the prime minister, Vladimir Putin, acting president until the March 2000 elections, which he won handily. Putin's 2004 electoral victory was even more stunning (winning 71 percent of the vote, with his closest competitor getting under 14 percent), but some international observers alleged that media bias raised questions about its genuine democratic character. The constitution excludes a third consecutive term, so speculation is rife about whom Putin is grooming as a successor; Putin has pointed out that he could run again after stepping out for one term.

One of the president's most important powers is the authority to issue decrees, which Yeltsin used frequently to address contentious issues such as privatization, salaries of state workers, the running of the economy, and anticrime measures. Presidential decrees have the force of law until formal legislation is passed, but because they can be annulled as quickly as they are approved, they do not command the same respect as actual laws. Although presidential decrees may not violate the constitution or specific legislation passed by the bicameral legislature (the Federal Assembly), policymaking by decree can allow the president to ignore an uncooperative or divided parliament. Yeltsin's decision in 1994, and again in 1999, to launch the offensive in Chechnya was not approved by either house of parliament, despite strong objections from a broad range of political groups. President Putin has used his power of decree less extensively than Yeltsin did, in part because Putin has managed to forge a more cooperative relationship with the parliament and has been able to resolve many policy debates through the legislative process.

The president has other powers, including the right to call a state of emergency, impose martial law, grant pardons, call referenda, and temporarily suspend actions of other state organs if he deems them to contradict the constitution or federal laws. Some of these actions must be confirmed by other state organs (such as the upper house of the parliament, the Federation Council). The president is commander in chief of the armed forces and conducts affairs of state with other nations. Impeachment of the president is a complicated process involving the *Duma,* the Federation Council, the Supreme Court, and the Constitutional Court. If the president dies in office or becomes incapacitated, the prime minister fills the post until new presidential elections can be held.

The Russian government is headed by the prime minister, flanked by varying numbers of deputy prime ministers. The president's choice of prime minister must be approved by the *Duma.* During Yeltsin's presidency, six prime ministers held office, the longest being Viktor Chernomyrdin, from December 1992 until March 1998, and the final one being Vladimir Putin, appointed in August 1999. The current prime minister, Mikhail Fradkov, was appointed in March 2004. A technocrat who rose through the Foreign Trade Ministry and Federal Tax Service, Fradkov also served as Russia's permanent representative to the European Union beginning in May 2003. He is generally considered to be a Putin loyalist with no political ambitions of his own.

The prime minister can be removed by the *Duma* through two repeat votes of no confidence passed within a three-month period; although the process has been attempted several times in the past decade, usually spearheaded by the Communist Party faction, it has never succeeded. A recent no-confidence attempt occurred in February 2005, spurred by objections from the Communist and Rodina factions to government changes to the provision of social benefits (see Section 2). The attempt received only 112 of the needed 226 votes. The president has also, on occasion, had difficulty gaining approval of his nominee for prime minister, most notably following the 1998 financial crisis when three prime ministers were in office over a seventeen-month period. Here, too, the *Duma* has ultimately been reluctant to defy the president because rejection of the candidate three times can lead to dissolution of the *Duma* itself. The prime minister has never been a member of the dominant party or coalition in the *Duma*; thus, principles of party accountability that apply in most Western parliamentary systems are not operative in Russia. Without disciplined parties and with no formal links between parties and the executive branch, the process of gaining *Duma* acceptance of government proposals depends on the authority of the president and on the particular configuration of power at the moment.

The National Bureaucracy

The new Russian state inherited a large bureaucratic apparatus. Despite proclaimed intentions, efforts to downsize the executive bureaucratic apparatus have been only partially successful. Alongside the state bureaucracy is the presidential administration, which serves the president directly. With some 2,000 employees, the presidential administration can duplicate or compete with the formal agencies of the state, while some government ministries (such as the Foreign Affairs Ministry, the Federal Security Service, and the Defense Ministry) report directly to the president.[31] The State Legal Office reviews all legislation before the president signs it. The president has created various advisory bodies that solicit input from important political and economic actors and also co-opt them into support for government policies. These organs have no constitutional status and thus could be abolished at will. The most important are the Security Council and the State Council. Formed in 1992, the Security Council advises the president in areas related to foreign policy and security (broadly conceived) and includes heads of appropriate government bodies (the so-called power ministries such as Defense and the Federal Security Service), the prime minister, and the heads of seven newly created federal districts. The State Council was formed in September 2000 as part of Putin's attempt to redefine the role of regional leaders in federal decision making (see below). The State Council, which includes all of the regional heads, has a consultative role, but without giving the regional executives any real power. A smaller presidium, made up of seven of the regional heads selected by the president, meets monthly. While Putin appointed business leader, Aleksandr Abramov, as first secretary of the council, the president himself chairs the body and seems to keep a tight rein on its discussion agenda.

The bureaucratic agencies that make up the executive branch itself include ministries, state committees, and other agencies. Ministers other than the prime minister do not require parliamentary approval. The prime minister makes recommendations to the president, who appoints these officials. In mid-2005, there were sixteen ministries alongside numerous other executive bodies, such as state committees, commissions, and federal services, such as the Federal Security Service and the Tax Inspectorate. Ministers and other agency heads are generally career bureaucrats who have risen through an appropriate ministry, although sometimes more clearly political appointments are made. Many agencies have been reorganized, often more than once. Reorganization of the state's bureaucracy results not only from restructuring of the economy and of state functions; top leaders also use restructuring to induce political loyalty and place their clients and allies in key positions in the new agencies. **Patron-client networks,** which were important in the Soviet period, continue to play a key role in both the presidential administration and other state organs. These linkages are similar to old-boy networks in the West (and they most often involve men in the Russian case); they underscore the importance of personal career ties between individuals as they rise in bureaucratic or political structures. For example, Putin has drawn heavily on colleagues with whom he worked earlier in St. Petersburg or in the security establishment, referred to as *siloviki,* in staffing a variety of posts in his administration. With the collapse of the *nomenklatura* system, politicians and government officials looked to people they knew and trusted to staff their organizations.[32] In an effort to increase the role of merit and the professional character of the civil service, the president himself initiated a process of civil service reform in August 2002; legislation to begin the reform passed in 2004.

In Putin's restructuring of government agencies, a new Ministry for Economic Development and Trade, headed by German Gref, took over functions of several previously existing ministries, as did a new Ministry of Industry, Science, and Technology. Observers question whether such reorganizations produce substantive benefits, and some are particularly controversial. For example, the State Committee for Environmental Protection was abolished by a May 2000 decree, with its responsibilities transferred to the Ministry of Natural Resources. The mixing of responsibility for overseeing both use and protection of natural resources in this single agency may be an indicator of the low priority of environmental protection (as compared to resource use). Functions of the State Committee on Northern Affairs were transferred to the Ministry for Economic Development and Trade, viewed by some as a downgrading of northern concerns on the government's agenda.

Other State Institutions

The Military and Security Organs

Because of Vladimir Putin's career background in the Soviet security agency (the KGB), he has drawn many of his staff from this arena. Thus, while the formal rank of the Federal Security Service has not changed, the actual impact of the security establishment has taken on increasing importance in the Putin era. This development preceded the events of September 11, 2001, and the important role placed on security concerns reflects the orientation of the current Russian state under Putin's leadership. Because many Russians are alarmed by the crime rate and terrorist bombings in the country, restrictions on civil liberties have not elicited the popular concern typical of many Western countries. At the same time, there is widespread public cynicism about the honesty of the ordinary police (*militsiia*); many believe that payoffs by the mafia and even by ordinary citizens can buy police cooperation in overlooking crimes or ordinary legal infractions such as traffic tickets. Such suspicions are likely often correct.[33]

The Russian government attributes repeated bombings since 1999 to Chechen terrorists and has claimed that the terrorists have international links to the Al Qaeda network. The year 2004 was particularly traumatic with the downing of two airliners and a suicide-bomb attack in Moscow in August, followed by the Beslan incident in September. The visibility of female suicide bombers in the incidents suggests the deep penetration of resistance within Chechen society. Attacks on civilians by Russian forces in Chechnya have elicited Western human rights protests. Since the September 11 attacks, cooperation between Russian and Western security agencies has increased, as Russia has shared security information and accepted an American presence in neighboring Georgia and Tajikistan. In turn, Western governments have muted their public criticism of Russian actions in Chechnya.

The Soviet military once ranked as one of the largest and most powerful forces in the world, second only to that of the United States and justifying the country's designation as a superpower. Since the military was represented in the political structures (almost always having at least one representative on the Politburo), political loyalty to the civilian authorities represented a good bargain for the military establishment. The Communist Party controlled military appointments, and, although the military did lobby for particular policies and sometimes played a role in

Kremlin intrigues, it never usurped political power. During the August 1991 coup attempt, troops remained loyal to Yeltsin and Gorbachev, even though the Minister of Defense was among the coup plotters; there were no orders to fire on Soviet citizens who took to the streets in defense of the government. In October 1993, despite some apparent hesitancy in military circles, military units defended the government's position, this time firing on civilian protesters and shocking the country. It is noteworthy that in not a single postcommunist country has the military intervened to take power, which suggests that communist rule helped to cement the principle of civilian political control, earlier exercised through the Communist Party and now through elected political figures.

In the postcommunist period, the political power and prestige of the military have declined radically. Both Gorbachev and Yeltsin oversaw a reduction in military expenditures, which undermined the privileged position of military interests, bringing a decline in facilities for military personnel and a reduction in conventional and nuclear forces. Plans to downsize the military have been a source of tension between the political leadership and the military establishment, and the Putin government has also proclaimed its commitment to continue the process. The military's failure to implement a successful strategy in the Chechnya war has led the government to increase the role of the Federal Security Service there instead of relying on the army alone.[34] Reports of deteriorating conditions in some Russian nuclear arsenals have raised international concerns about nuclear security. In addition, the situation of military personnel, from the highest officers to rank-and-file soldiers, has deteriorated dramatically, producing a potential source of political unrest.

As of 2005, the Russian Federation still maintains a system of universal male conscription, but noncompliance and draftees rejected for health reasons have been persistent problems; a law to permit alternative military service for conscientious objectors took effect in 2004. Although critics of the military service law welcome the concept, they are critical of the restrictive conditions that the law imposes on alternative service. Government proposals to supplement the conscript army by a smaller professional military corps are on the agenda, but in April 2005 there were no plans to abolish the military draft.[35]

The Judiciary

Concepts such as judicial independence and the rule of law were poorly understood in both pre–Revolutionary Russia and the Soviet era. Gorbachev, however, emphasized the importance of constructing a law-based state, judicial independence, and due process. These concepts have been embedded in the new Russian constitution and are accepted both by the public and political elites. However, their implementation has been difficult and not wholly successful.

In Russia, a Constitutional Court was formed in 1991. Its decisions were binding, and in several cases even the president had to bow to its authority. After several controversial decisions that challenged the president's authority, Yeltsin suspended the operations of the court in late 1993. However, the new Russian constitution again provided for a Constitutional Court with the power to adjudicate disputes on the constitutionality of federal and regional laws, as well as jurisdictional disputes between various political institutions. Justices are nominated by the president and approved by the Federation Council, a procedure that produced a stalemate after the new constitution was adopted, so that the court became functional only in 1995. Among the justices are political figures, lawyers, legal scholars, and judges. Since 1995, the court has established itself as a vehicle for resolving conflicts relating to the protection of individual rights and conformity of regional laws with constitutional requirements. The court has been cautious in confronting the executive branch, on which it depends to enforce its decisions.

Alongside the Constitutional Court is an extensive system of lower and appellate courts, with the Supreme Court at the pinnacle. These courts hear ordinary civil and criminal cases. In 1995, a system of commercial courts was also formed to hear cases dealing with issues related to privatization, taxes, and other commercial activities. The Federation Council must approve nominees for Supreme Court judgeships, and the constitution also grants the president power to appoint judges at other levels. Measures to shield judges from political pressures include criminal prosecution for attempting to influence a judge, protections from arbitrary dismissal, and improved salaries for judges. The Russian judicial system operates on a civil code system, similar to most of continental Europe. One innovation in the legal system has included introduction of jury trials for some types of criminal offenses.

Subnational Government

The collapse of the Soviet Union was precipitated by the demands of some union republics for more autonomy and, then, independence. After the Russian Federation became an independent state, the problem of constructing a viable federal structure resurfaced. The Russian Federation inherited a complex structure of regional subunits from the Soviet period. Between 1991 and 1993, negotiations between the central government and the various regions led to the establishment of a federal structure that includes eighty-nine units, which have different historical origins and designations (twenty-one republics, forty-nine *oblasts,* six *krais,* ten autonomous *okrugs,* one autonomous *oblast,* and two cities with federal status, namely, St. Petersburg and Moscow). Discussion of possible mergers of proximate federal units to reduce their number has been ongoing; such changes are subject to approval by popular referendum. The first instance is the merger of Perm Region and the Komi-Permyak Autonomous District, which occurred in December 2005, with others under active consideration. For example, through a referendum on April 17, 2005, voters in three Siberian regions approved the merger of the two smaller autonomous okrugs into the larger Krasnoyarsk krai, setting that consolidation process on track.

One of the first issues to arise in the development of Russia's federal system was whether all of the eighty-nine units should have equal status. The republics have viewed themselves as a special category because of their different status in the Soviet period and the presence of significant minority groups within their borders. They have also been the most assertive in putting forth claims for autonomy or even sovereignty. The most extreme example is Chechnya, whose demand for independence has led to a protracted civil war. The Russian government's determination to oppose Chechen secession is reflective of its fear that separatist sentiment could spread. This has not happened, although other republics have declared sovereignty, an ambiguous claim rejected by the Constitutional Court. The ethnic dimension complicates political relations with some of the republics. For example, in Tatarstan, one of the most populous and most assertive of the republics, the titular nationality (the Tatars) forms about half of the population. In the Republic of Sakha (formerly Yakutia), which has valuable diamond reserves, Yakuts formed one-third of the population. The republics tend to be in peripheral areas of the Russian Federation, except for Tatarstan and Bashkortostan, which lie in the center of the country. The titular nationalities (Tatars and Bashkirs) in these two republics, as well as in some of the republics of the Caucasus region, are of Islamic cultural background, but Islamic fundamentalism has not been a significant problem in Russia since decades of Soviet socialization seems to have acculturated most parts of the Muslim population to secular, scientific values.

Despite the fact that the constitution grants equal status to all units of the federation, republics have been given some special rights, such as declaring a second state language (in addition to Russian) and adopting their own constitutions. From 1994 to 1998, forty-six individual treaties were signed, first between the federal government and several of Russia's republics and then with other units of the federation. These documents may not contradict the federal constitution, but some provisions in fact do so. These treaties outlined the jurisdiction of each level of government and granted special privileges, including special rights in relation to natural resource revenues and division of tax revenue—often to the benefit of the ethnic republics. This ad hoc approach produced a system of **asymmetrical federalism,** giving different regions varying privileges. The result was an escalation of regional demands and a drop in the perceived fairness of central policy.

Figure 4

Level of Trust in Various Institutions in Russia

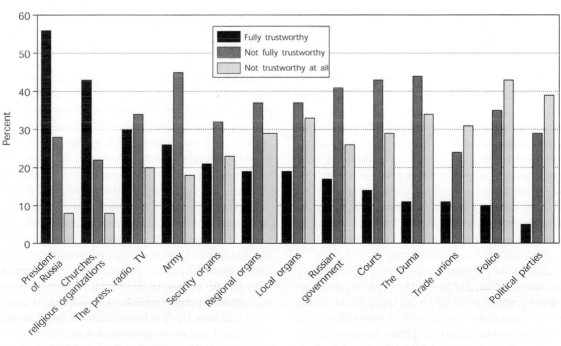

Source: Levada Center, http://www.levada.ru/press/2004092702.html (accessed April 28, 2005).

It is no wonder that following the March 2000 election Putin identified the establishment of a uniform system of federal-regional relations, governed by uniform legal principles, as an important priority. He immediately took several steps to realize this objective, first by harmonizing regional laws and republic constitutions with federal legislation and constitutional provisions. More contentious was the 2002 deadline for rescinding the special bilateral treaties that Yeltsin had concluded. Although several regions resisted giving up privileges that the treaties afforded, all but a handful have been annulled. Among remaining treaties is the one with Tatarstan; negotiations about its amendment to satisfy federal and republic concerns continued in 2005. Another new measure gave the president the power, pending approval by a court, to remove a governor and disband a regional legislature if they engage in anticonstitutional activity. In 2002, the Constitutional Court upheld the measure, but with many restrictions on its use.[36]

Other reforms to the federal system introduced by Putin in 2000 were even stronger measures to strengthen what Putin has called the **"power vertical."** This concept involves the strengthening of an integrated structure of executive power from the top (presidential) level down through to the local level. Critics have questioned whether the idea is actually consistent with federal principles. A first step in this direction was the creation of seven federal districts on top of the existing federal units. Although not designed to replace regional governments, the districts were intended to oversee the work of federal offices operating in these regions and to ensure compliance with federal laws and the constitution. Putin's appointees to head these new federal districts included several individuals (all male) with backgrounds in the security services, reinforcing concerns that the federal districts could become a powerful instrument of central control. In practice, the federal districts have been less intrusive in the affairs of the regions than many feared.

A second set of changes to create the power vertical has involved the position of the governors (and republic presidents) themselves. In the Yeltsin period, there was extensive political conflict over the method of selecting governors: initially, they were appointed by the president, but Yeltsin finally agreed to their

popular election, which has given them greater legitimacy and independence from Moscow. Beginning in 1996, the governors, along with the heads of each regional legislative body, also sat as members of the upper house of the Russian parliament, the Federation Council. This arrangement gave the regional executives a direct voice in national legislative discussions and a presence in Moscow, but it divided their attention between their executive responsibilities in their home regions and their duties in Moscow. In 2001, Putin gained approval for a revision to the composition of the Federation Council; regional executives were, as of January 2002, no longer members of the Federation Council. Rather, one regional representative is appointed by the regional executive and the other by the regional legislature. Some governors resisted this change, seeing it as an assault on their power (they also lost the legal immunity that goes along with being a member of parliament). Putin made concessions to make the change more palatable, for example, giving governors the right to recall their representatives. The State Council was formed to try to assure the regional executives that they would retain some role in the federal policymaking arena, although losing their seats in the Federation Council.

Following the 2000 election, implementation of these changes was accompanied by the exercise of "soft" power mechanisms, namely, the strengthening of patron-client relations between central authorities and the governors and presidents of republics. A striking feature of this reform process has been the minimal protest that has issued from governors themselves, even as their power and independence have been progressively undermined. No doubt, some governors were hesitant to take an opposing stance that might alienate the powerful president in the belief that cooperation would yield more benefits. Thus, in addition to formal changes, some observers have noted the capacity of federal authorities, particularly the president, to use administrative pressure to gain acquiescence, if not compliance, in pursuing a particular reform design. This use of administrative pressure reinforces a personalistic and clientelistic system of political power.

Following the Beslan massacre, Putin identified corruption and ineffective leadership at the regional level as culprits in allowing terrorists to carry out the devastating school hostage taking. Accordingly, he proposed an additional reform that created a decisive element of central control over regional politics. Approved by the State *Duma* in December 2004, the change eliminated popular election of governors. From now on, as current gubernatorial terms run out, the president nominates regional heads for approval by the regional legislature. Similar to the system for approval of the prime minister, if the regional legislature refuses the nomination three times, the president may disband the body and call for new elections. With governors and republic presidents dependent on the goodwill of the president for appointment and reappointment, a self-perpetuating political process has taken on a formal character, leading some observers to declare the death of Russian federalism. Shortly after these changes occurred, demonstrators in Bashkortostan demanded the removal of the republic's president, an action Putin was apparently reluctant to take because it could have a domino effect, triggering more widespread public activism; as Russian specialist Nikolai Petrov noted: "We are facing a new wave of social activism, and it is dangerous because there is a lack of democratic institutions through which this energy can be channeled."[37] As of mid-2005 several regional executives had been reappointed and a much smaller number had been replaced.

Fiscal federalism (the process of distribution of tax revenues among the various levels of government) has been another problematic area in center-regional relations. Although the Soviet state pursued a considerable degree of regional equalization, regional differences have increased in the Russian Federation. The Putin government has accepted the principle of regional equalization and has tried to create a more regularized system for determining the distribution of revenues, taking account of both the regional tax base and differences in the needs of various regions (for instance, northern regions have higher expenses to maintain basic services). An additional area requiring attention is the role and powers of local governments. A new law on local self-government, adopted in 2003, elicited praise for more clearly defining the jurisdictions of the various levels of government, and criticism for increasing the dependence of local officials on regional authorities.

The Policy-Making Process

Policy-making occurs through both formal and informal mechanisms. The Russian constitution laid the ground rules for the adoption of legislation, one formal mechanism of policy-making. Although the federal government proposes most legislation, regional legislatures, the president and his administration, individual deputies, and some judicial bodies may also do so. Various organizations may be involved in the drafting of legislation, including the presidential administration, the parliamentary staff, and a special office within the federal government responsible for drafting economic legislation. Often, expert consultants or a special commission are also involved in the process, as well as bodies such as the Security Council. In August 2000, the president formed the Entrepreneurship Council to solicit input from the business elite; meetings were also held with the Russian Union of Industrialists and Entrepreneurs regarding issues relating to economic and social policy affecting the business sector.[38] Whereas in the Yeltsin years only 35 to 40 percent of legislation was based on initiatives issuing from the executive branch, the proportion rose to 60 percent in the first half of 2001.[39]

Sometimes, the government, deputies, or parliamentary factions offer competing drafts of laws, leading to protracted and complicated bargaining. In order for a bill to become law, it must be approved by both houses of the parliament in three readings and signed by the president. If the president vetoes the bill, it must be passed again in the same wording by a two-thirds majority of both houses of parliament in order to override the veto. Budgetary proposals can be put forth only by the government, and they usually elicit sharp controversy in the parliament since proposed budget reductions affect key interests and groups, such as regional and local governments, other state agencies, the military, trade unions, enterprise directors, state employees, and pensioners. Many policy proclamations are made through presidential or governmental decrees, without formal consultation with the legislative branch. This decision-making process is much less visible and may involve closed-door bargaining rather than an open process of debate and consultation.

Informal groupings also have an important indirect impact on policymaking, very evident in the Yeltsin years. A prominent example is the industrialist lobby, which represents the managerial interests of some of Russia's large privatized industries. Business magnates were able to exert behind-the-scenes influence to gain benefits in the privatization of lucrative firms in sectors such as oil, media, and transport. Putin has attempted to reduce the direct political influence of these powerful economic figures and to formalize business input through bodies such as the Entrepreneurship Council. Some observers see this development as an example of corporatism, a system in which the government identifies (or sometimes helps create) organizations that are consulted to represent designated societal interests (in this case, business interests) in the policymaking process. The emerging Russian corporatism seems to be a state corporatist variant, a top-down variety in which the government itself plays an active role in defining these vehicles of societal input.[40] One problem with this approach is that some interests, particularly those that are less powerful or well organized, may be excluded from the process. Another less formal linkage between the government and business is through continued government ownership of enterprise shares, which gives the government the ability to influence leadership positions in key firms such as Gasprom, the main exporter of natural gas. Through such personal links, the president can maintain some leverage in the economic sphere, even without a clear policy or legislative basis. In almost all cases, participation in policymaking does not extend to representatives of more broadly based citizens' groups.

A continuing problem is the inefficacy of policy implementation. Under Communist rule, the party's control over political appointments enforced at least some degree of conformity to central mandates. Under Yeltsin, fragmented and decentralized political power gave the executive branch few resources to ensure compliance. The government faced massive tax evasion, avoidance of military conscription, circumvention of a wide variety of regulations in spheres ranging from environmental protection to export of foreign currency, and regional policies violating federal laws. Pervasive corruption, including bribery and selective enforcement, hindered enforcement of policy decisions. Although Putin has stated his commitment to restrict these types of irregularities, they no doubt continue. However, his commitment to reestablishing order and a rule of law has been an important foundation of his public support and his justification for the centralization of power we have discussed in this chapter.

Section ❹ Representation and Participation

Gorbachev's policies in the 1980s brought a dramatic change in the relationship between state and society, as *glasnost* sparked new public and private initiatives. Most restrictions on the formation of social organizations were lifted, and a large number of independent groups appeared. Hopes rose that these trends might indicate the emergence of **civil society,** an autonomous sphere of social life that could act on the state without being dependent on it. However, just a few years later, only a small stratum of Russian society was actively engaged; the demands of everyday life as well as cynicism about politicians and state institutions led many people to withdraw into the private domain and to endorse strong political leadership that would ensure stability and continued economic growth. With minor fluctuations, Putin's approval rating stabilized at 65 to 70 percent after his election in 2000, while trust in public institutions remained low and the public's ability to affect policy seemed questionable. Some analysts suspect that Russia may be on the verge of a new set of social upheavals, as public discontent finds few legitimate outlets and public activism in neighboring countries (Georgia, Ukraine, Kyrgyzstan) has spurred change. On the other hand, other observers see the strengthening of the presidency as offering an opportunity to marshal resources in order to address fundamental social ills.

The Legislature

The Russian legislature, the Federal Assembly, came into being after the parliamentary elections of December 12, 1993, when the referendum ratifying the new Russian constitution was also approved. The upper house, the Federation Council, represents Russia's constituent federal units. The lower house, the *Duma,* has 450 members and involves direct popular election of candidates and parties. This body was named after the short-lived assembly formed by the tsar following the revolution of 1905 and thus emphasizes continuity with the Russian (rather than the Soviet) tradition. The first Federal Assembly served only a two-year term. Subsequent elections to the *Duma* have occurred every four years, in 1995, 1999, and 2003. As noted in Section 3, in some special circumstances, earlier elections can be called.

Within the *Duma,* factions unite deputies from the same or allied parties. The *Duma* also has a number of standing committees. Up until 2001, committee chairships were distributed among the most important factions of the *Duma;* however, in 2005 all 29 heads came from the dominant United Russia faction, with just four committees having first deputy chairs from other party factions.[41] The *Duma* elects its own speaker (or chair); since July 2003 this has been Boris Gryzlov, head of the United Russia Party, who, in Putin's circles, enjoys the highest level of support besides the president.[42] After the 1995 and 1999 elections, the speaker of the *Duma* came from the Communist Party, which had the highest electoral showing in those votes.

Compared to the Communist period, deputies reflect less fully the demographic characteristics of the population at large. For example, in 1984, 33 percent of the members of the Supreme Soviet were women;[43] in 2005 they constitute less than 10 percent. Women head four committees, two in the traditionally "female" areas of health, and women/family/children. (The other two areas are nationalities and the North/Far East.[44]) In 2000, manual workers made up less than 1 percent of *Duma* deputies, in contrast to 35 percent in the 1985 Supreme Soviet.[45] It is important, however, to remember that the implicit demographic quotas that the CPSU enforced in the Soviet period were primarily symbolic since the Supreme Soviet was largely powerless. On the other hand, the underrepresentation of women and workers in the present *Duma* indicates the extent to which Russian politics is primarily the domain of male elites.

The upper house of the Federal Assembly, the Federation Council, has two members from each of Russia's federal regions and republics, but the method of selection has varied over time. A new procedure, phased in between 2000 and 2002, involves appointment of one representative by the regional executive and the other by the regional legislature, whereas from 1995 until that time, the elected governor/president of each region and the regional legislative head were themselves members. Since 2000, the Federation Council has gradually become quite a compliant organ, although formally it plays a role in approval of federal laws.[46] Many prominent businessmen are among the appointees, and in some cases the posts may be granted in exchange for political loyalty, raising doubts about the likelihood that the body adequately represents interests of the regions. Party factions do not play a significant role in the Federation Council. Deputies to the Federation Council, as well as to the *Duma,* are granted immunity from criminal prosecution.

The constitution grants parliament powers in the legislative and budgetary areas, but if there is conflict with the president or government, these powers can be exercised effectively only if parliament operates with a high degree of unity. In practice, the president can often override the parliament through mechanisms such as the veto of legislation. To override the veto, two-thirds of the members of the Federal Assembly must support the original wording of the bill. Each house of parliament has the authority to confirm certain presidential appointees, in addition to the prime minister. For example, the *Duma* confirms the chair of the Central Bank of Russia, and the Federation Council confirms judges of higher courts. The Federation Council must also approve presidential decrees relating to martial law and state emergency, as well as deploying troops abroad.[47] In some cases, failure to approve the president's nominees has produced stalemate or prevented certain offices from functioning for a period of time.

Conflict between the president and the legislative branch was frequent in the 1990s. Following electoral rebuffs in the 1993 and 1995 parliamentary elections, Yeltsin confronted a parliament that obstructed many of his proposed policies, but the parliament did not have the power or unity to offer a constructive alternative. Following the 1999 elections, the situation was somewhat less conflictual, and since the 2003 election the *Duma* has cooperated with the president, since about two-thirds of the deputies are tied to the United Russia faction, closest to the president.[48] However, with conflict over the monetarization of social benefits (discussed in Section 2), cracks have marred the unity of the United Russia faction.

Society's ability to affect particular policy decisions through the legislative process is minimal. First, the blocs and parties in the parliament are isolated from the public at large and suffer low levels of popular respect. Many of the mechanisms that link parties and parliaments to citizens in Western democracies do not exist in Russia: interest associations to lobby the parliament are weak, and the internal decision-making structures of parties are generally elite-dominated. Public hearings on controversial issues are rare. Proposed changes in methods of selection of deputies for the *Duma* (discussed below) may make elections less competitive than previously, possibly undermining further the degree to which the body represents a diverse Russian public.

Political Parties and the Party System

One of the most important political changes following the collapse of communism was the shift from a single-party to a multiparty system. In the USSR, the CPSU not only dominated state organs but also oversaw all social institutions, such as the mass media, trade unions, youth groups, educational institutions, and professional associations. It defined the official ideology for the country, set the parameters for state censorship, and, through the *nomenklatura* system, ensured that loyal supporters occupied all important offices. Approximately 10 percent of adults in the Soviet Union were party members, but there were no effective mechanisms to ensure accountability of the party leadership to its members. Because the CPSU did not have to compete for political office, it was a party of a special kind, whose authority could not be openly questioned.

National competitive elections were held for the first time in the USSR in 1989, but new political parties were not formal participants in Russia until 1993. Since then, a confusing array of political organizations have run candidates in elections (see Table 2). Until 2003, these included not only political parties but also political and socioeconomic movements. A new law on political parties went into effect in July 2001; the law tightened the conditions for party formation and registration. It required that parties have at least 10,000 members, with branches of at least 100 members in at least half of the regions of Russia. In December 2004, revisions to the law raised the membership bar to 50,000 and 500, respectively, to be implemented by January 2006. In early 2005, only a small minority of the 41 registered parties[49] would be able to meet the target, but all four parties represented in the *Duma* claimed memberships above the 50,000 mark. Only organizations registered as political parties are now permitted to run candidates, and legislation under consideration in 2005 would put further restrictions disallowing party coalitions to compete. Although critics have portrayed these changes as artificially reducing voter choice, defenders argue that they will help to bring order to a chaotic and fragmented party system.

Russian political parties have some peculiarities when compared to their Western counterparts. In the 1990s, many parties formed around a prominent individual. The Yabloko party, for example, was named from the first letters of its founders' names, forming the Russian word for "apple." Most of the liberal (pro-market) parties and the nationalist Liberal Democratic Party also were leader-centered. The *Duma* ballots list not only the names of the blocs and parties but also their leaders.[50] Most Russian parties do not have a firm social base or stable constituency. Many Russians are hesitant to join a political party, perhaps due to unhappy experiences with the CPSU, and others simply distrust politics and politicians. Furthermore, other than the Communist Party of the Russian Federation (CPRF), Russian parties are young, so deeply rooted political identifications have not had time to develop. Finally, many citizens do not have a clear conception of their own interests or of how parties might represent them. In this context, image making is as important as programmatic positions, so parties appeal to transient

Table 2

Top Parties in the 2003 State Duma Elections[a]

Party or Bloc	Percent of 1995 Party List Vote[b]	Percent of 1999 Party List Vote[b]	Comments	Leader at Time of Most Recent Election	Percent of 2003 Party List Vote[b]	Duma Seats from 2003 Party List Vote	Duma Seats from Single-Member Districts	Total Duma Seats 2003[c]	% of Duma Seats
Centrist									
United Russia All-Russia	—	23.3	Formed as Unity Party in 1999, then merged with Fatherland,	Boris Gryzlov	37.6	120	102	222	49.3
Fatherland, All-Russia	—	13.3	Merged into United Russia (2001)	Yuri Luzhkov, Evgenii Primakov (1999)	—	—	—	—	—
Our Home is Russia	10.1	1.2	Chernomyrdin was prime minister from 1992–1998	Viktor Chernomyrdin (1995, 1999)	—	—	—	—	—
Liberal/Reform									
Union of Rightist Forces	3.9	8.5	Russia's Democratic Choice/United Russia (1995)	Sergey Kirienko	4.0	0	3	3	0.7
Yabloko	6.9	5.9	Opposition liberal/reform party	Grigoriy Yavlinsky	4.3	0	4	4	0.9
Communist/Socialist									
Communist Party of the Russian Federation	22.3	24.3		Gennady Zyuganov	12.6	40	12	52	11.6
Nationalist/Patriotic									
Liberal Democratic Party of Russia	11.2	6.0	Participated in 1999 elections as Bloc Zhirinovsky	Vladimir Zhirinovsky	11.5	36	0	36	8.0
Rodina (Motherland Bloc)	—	—	Left/center nationalist party	Dmitiy Rogozin, Sergei Glaziev	9.0	29	8	37	8.2

[a] Figures may not add to 100 percent or to the total number of deputies in the State *Duma* because smaller parties and independents are excluded. Table includes only parties winning at least 4.0 percent of the national party list vote in one of the three elections (but not all such parties).

[b] Percentage of the total popular vote the party or bloc received on the proportional representation portion of the ballot in the year indicated. A dash indicates that the party or bloc was not included on that ballot or did not win a significant portion of the vote. Numbers in parentheses are votes for predecessor parties, similar to the one running in 2003.

[c] The sum of seats won in the proportional representation (party list) vote and the single-member district vote. Number of deputies in the faction changed over time following the elections.

Source: Revised from DeBardeleben, Joan, "Russia" in *Introduction to Comparative Politics.* Copyright 2004 by Houghton Mifflin Company. Reprinted with permission. For the 2003 figures, *The Economist. Country Briefings: Russia.* http://www.economist.com, April 25, 2005.

voter sentiments. Nonetheless, party membership has grown in recent years, but observers wonder whether monetary incentives are sometimes the reason. As the situation in the country stabilizes, the interests of particular groups (for example, blue-collar workers, business entrepreneurs, or groups based on age, gender, or region) may take a more central role in the formation of parties.

Despite the personalistic nature of party politics, some key cleavages help explain the political spectrum. A major cleavage relates to economic policy. Nearly all parties mouth support for the market transition, but those on the communist/socialist end of the spectrum are markedly muted in their enthusiasm. They support renationalization of some firms, continued state subsidies, more extensive social welfare policies, and limits on foreign economic investment. At the other end of the spectrum are liberal/reform groupings, which support rapid market reform, including privatization, free prices, and limited government spending. The now dominant United Russia Party charts a middle ground, permitting it to appeal to voters from a wide ideological spectrum, supporting market reform but in a less radical form than the more strongly liberal reformist groups would prefer.

Parties and blocs are also divided on noneconomic issues, particularly those involving national identity and Westernization. The nationalist/patriotic parties emphasize the defense of Russian interests over Westernization. They strongly criticize the expansion of NATO to include former Soviet bloc countries such as Poland, Hungary, and the Baltic states. They also favor a strong military establishment, protection from foreign economic influence, and reconstitution of some former Soviet republics into a larger federation. Liberal/reform parties, on the other hand, advocate integration of Russia into the global market and the adoption of Western economic and political principles—positions that go along with their general support for radical market reform. Again, the United Russia Party has articulated an intriguing combination of these viewpoints, identifying Europe as the primary identity point for Russia, but at the same time insisting on Russia's role as a regional power, pursuing its own unique path to democratization and market reform.

It is striking that despite Russia's ethnic diversity, ethnic and regional parties have not had a significant impact on the national scene and only a minimal one in particular regions. Amendments to the party law make it even more difficult than previously for regional parties to emerge. Similarly, religion has not been an important political cleavage, probably because religious sentiments, although reviving among certain sectors of the population, have not developed a firm enough organizational or identity base, given their suppression in the communist period. Religion appears to have personal meaning rather than being a source of group identity, at least for ethnic Russians, who primarily adhere to the Russian Orthodox strain of Christianity. Ethnic and religious distinctions do overlap, particularly for the Islamic population, but even these groupings have not taken on a significant political character in the form of political parties.

Russian political parties do not fit neatly on a left-right spectrum. Nationalist sentiments crosscut economic ideologies, producing the following party tendencies:

- The traditional left, critical of market reform and often mildly nationalistic
- Liberal/reform forces, supporting assertive Western-type market reform and political norms
- Centrist "parties of power," representing the political elite
- Nationalist/patriotic forces, primarily concerned with identity issues and national self-assertion

The most important parties in all four groupings, when not in power, have acted throughout as a loyal opposition; that is, they have not challenged the structure of the political system but have chosen to work within it. The unique feature of the now-dominant United Russia Party is that it draws on elements of the other tendencies, forming what in the West might be called a catchall party.

The Russian Left: The Communist Party of the Russian Federation

Consistently represented in the *Duma* since 1993, the CPRF was by far the strongest parliamentary party after the 1995 elections, winning over one-third of the seats in the *Duma*. While maintaining strong electoral performance, the CPRF's relative position was weakened after the 1999 election because the Unity Party gained almost an equal number of votes and seats. In the 2003 elections, the party's support dropped by about one-half, to 12.6 percent of the party list vote compared to 24.3 percent in 1999 and 22.3 percent in 1995. In May 2005, only 10.4 percent of deputies were in the CPRF faction, compared to about 25 percent after the 1999 election and close to 35 percent after the 1995 election.[51] The CRRF, the clearest successor of the old CPSU, appears to be a party in decline.

In addition to its socialist economic approach, Russian nationalism is also evident in the party program. The party defines its goals as being democracy, justice, equality, patriotism and internationalism, a combination of civic rights and duties, and socialist renewal. The CPRF opposes the private sale of agricultural land but accepts substantial elements of the market reform package, favoring a combination of state and private ownership. Primary among the party's concerns are the social costs of the reform process. Thus, it has supported state subsidies for industry to ensure timely payment of wages and to prevent enterprise bankruptcies. The party's detractors see its leaders as opportunistic rather than as true democrats, but others point out that communist governors in some of Russia's regions have acted pragmatically rather than ideologically. The party has operated within the constitutional framework in pursuing its political goals. Support for the party is especially strong among older Russians, the economically disadvantaged, and rural residents. The party is no longer credible as a vanguard organization representing the working class. Instead, it appears to represent those who have adapted less successfully to the radical and uncertain changes that have occurred since the collapse of the Communist state, as well as some individuals who remain committed to socialist ideals. Despite a readymade base of voters sympathetic to a left-leaning or social democratic perspective, the party has not capitalized on this potential. Its principle failures have been an inability to adapt its public position to attract significant numbers of new adherents, particularly among the young, as well as the absence of a charismatic and attractive political leader.

Centrist Parties: United Russia

In 2001, the party originally formed as the Unity Party joined with a potential establishment rival, Fatherland/ All-Russia, taking the name United Russia in 2004. Even though Putin is not formally head of the party, Putin and the Unity Party rose to prominence together in the elections of 1999 and 2000, and are closely associated with one another. A remarkable feature of the Unity Party was its ability, within a few months after its formation, to finish a close second runner to the CPRF in the 1999 *Duma* elections. In this first electoral foray, the party won 23.3 percent of the party-list vote and seventy-three seats in the *Duma*; this increased to 37.6 percent of the party list in 2003. In 2005, through the merger of Unity with other parties and attraction of other deputies, 67 percent of deputies joined the United Russia faction.

Previous centrist formations, despite their close association with the government and regional political elites, had failed to develop a base of popular support. What explains United Russia's success? An important factor is the association with Putin, but the party has also built an effective political machine that could generate persuasive incentives for regional elites. Even some governors not in the party agreed to appear on the party's *Duma* electoral list. A bandwagon effect and desire to be on the winning side have bolstered the party's fortunes. The party has a rather poorly defined program, which emphasizes the uniqueness of the Russian approach (as distinct from Western models), an appeal to values of order and law, and a continued commitment to moderate reform. Its official website[52] indicates that the party is more focused on prominent people than on ideas, justifying its designation as a cadre party, in contrast to the CPRF, for example, which is clearly of the programmatic party type. At the same time, United Russia's voters represent a broad spectrum of the population and have drawn support from every other part of the political spectrum, making the party a catchall electoral organization.

As noted, other centrist parties have been markedly less successful than United Russia. Fatherland, which joined with Unity to form United Russia, was also a party of established political elites. Founded in 1998, the prominence of the party's leader, Yuri Luzhkov, mayor of Moscow, was more important than its platform. Although associated with Moscow, a capital city whose privileges are both envied and resented in the regions, Luzhkov's success in modernizing the city gave him the image of an effective leader. The party joined with another centrist grouping, All-Russia, headed by the relatively popular former foreign minister and short-time prime minister, Evgenii Primakov, in 1999. Fatherland/All-Russia won a respectable 13.3 percent of the vote in the 1999 *Duma* party-list vote, bringing the total centrist vote (with Unity) up to 36.6 percent. It was widely expected that Primakov would run for president in March 2000, but presumably due to Putin's overwhelming popularity, he too climbed on the Unity bandwagon.

Another unsuccessful centrist party was Women of Russia. With a surprisingly good showing in the 1993 elections (8 percent of the party-list vote), this party was an alliance of women's groups, most prominently the Union of Women of Russia, a renamed version of an official organization of women formed by the Soviet regime. Its program emphasized social welfare issues. The party's success in the 1993 vote put twenty-three women in the *Duma,* otherwise dominated by men. But in the 1995 election the party-list vote dropped to 4.6 percent of the party-list vote, and then to just over 2 percent in 1999. Possible explanations for the decline include limited campaign funds, minimal media coverage of the party during the electoral campaign, and the failure of the party to make its positions adequately clear to the voters.[53]

Liberal/Reform Parties

More than any other part of the political spectrum, the liberal/reform parties have found it hard to build a stable and unified electoral base. Many Russians held aspects of the liberal program, such as privatization and shock therapy, responsible for Russia's economic decline. Leaders from this grouping, such as Yegor Gaidar, who was Yeltsin's first prime minister, and Anatoly Chubais, who oversaw Yeltsin's privatization plan, even now have low ratings with the population. Another liberal reformer, the economist Grigoriy, who has consistently taken a critical stance toward the government's policies, enjoys a more loyal following, particularly among intellectuals. Until 1999 Yavlinsky, Yabloko enjoyed the most success among these parties.[54] Four parties or blocs running on a promarket reform plank won seats in the *Duma,* his party, in the

1993 elections, and several liberal/reform parties split the vote in 1995, reducing their representation in the *Duma.* On November 21, 1998, the brutal murder by contract killers of the liberal/reform politician and *Duma* member Galina Starovoitova (one of Russia's most prominent female politicians) resulted in renewed efforts to form a united political bloc in the form of the Union of Rightist Forces (URF).[55] In 1999, the URF received only 8.5 percent of the party-list vote, while Yabloko, with its more critical stance toward the government, ran separately, pulling just 5.9 percent. In 2003, for the first time, neither Yabloko nor the URF reached the 5 percent cutoff; thus, this tendency is currently not represented in the *Duma* at all.

These groups espouse a commitment to traditional liberal values, such as a limited economic role for the state, support for free-market principles, and the protection of individual rights and liberties. Although this philosophy provided the impetus for Yeltsin's original reform agenda, his refusal to associate himself with any political party deprived these groups of a strong organizational resource. The unpopularity of Yeltsin's reform approach also undermined support for its ideological soulmates. While liberal/reform figures are often referred to as the "democrats" because of their Westernizing approach, many Russians associate them with Russia's economic and national decline. Support for liberal/reform parties generally is stronger among the young, the more highly educated, urban dwellers, and the well-off. Thus, ironically, those with the best prospects for succeeding in the new market economy have been among the least successful in constructing an effective political party.

Nationalist/Patriotic Parties

To the surprise of many observers, the Liberal Democratic Party of Russia (LDPR), headed by Vladimir Zhirinovsky, got the strongest support on the party ballot in 1993, winning almost 23 percent of the vote; this declined to 11 percent in 1995 and 6 percent in 1999, but rebounded to 11.5 percent in 2003, placing a close third behind the Communist Party. Neither liberal nor particularly democratic in its platform, the party might more properly be characterized as nationalist and populist. Its populism is based on Zhirinovsky's personal charismatic appeal. Some Russians say, "He speaks our language"; while others radically oppose his provocative style and nationalist rhetoric. In his speeches, Zhirinovsky openly appeals to the anti-Western sentiments that grew in the wake of Russia's decline from superpower status and the government's perceived groveling for Western economic aid. The party has supported revival of an expanded Russian state to include Ukraine, Belarus, and possibly other neighboring areas. Concern with the breakdown of law and order seems to rank high among its priorities. However, despite Zhirinovsky's radical demeanor, he has often supported the government on key issues, most notably the war in Chechnya. Zhirinovsky's support has been especially strong among working-class men and military personnel. Other parties and leaders have taken up a softer version of the patriotic theme, including Putin, so the resurgence of support for the LDPR in 2003 suggests that nationalist sentiment in Russia is increasing, not declining.

A new political party, Rodina (Motherland), was registered in 2002 on the basis of the Party of Russian Regions, formed in 1998. While we include it in the nationalist category, it might legitimately also be dubbed a left-leaning formation. Led by Dmitrii Rogozin and Sergei Glaz'ev, this relative newcomer received 9 percent of the party-list vote in 2003 and has about 9 percent of the deputies in its *Duma* faction. In informed Russian circles, the party's creation is considered to have been fostered by the Kremlin, in an effort to divert support from the more threatening CPRF. The party defines the "central political problem for our country [as] the formation and development of a strong, effective Russian government, capable of assuring the necessary conditions for a proper life for the Russian citizen."[56] Generally loyal to the Kremlin, in January 2005 some Rodina *Duma* deputies embarked on a visible hunger strike to protest the effects of the government's monetarization of social benefits. Some media critics, however, called the strike a stunt rather than a real expression of political opposition. Reported tension between the two party leaders, however, has also drawn media attention in Russia since both seem to have political ambitions of their own.

Elections

In the postcommunist period, elections seemed to be a constant phenomenon in Russia, partly because presidential, legislative, and regional/local elections are generally held on separate occasions. The initial euphoria with the competitive electoral structure has been replaced by voter fatigue, although turnout in federal elections remains respectable, generally between 60 and 70 percent, but down to 56 percent in the 2003 *Duma* election. In regional and local contests, participation rates have at times fallen below the required minimum of 25 or 50 percent of eligible voters, necessitating repeat balloting. National elections receive extensive media coverage, and campaign activities begin as long as a year in advance. Candidates and parties make extensive use of polling firms and public relations experts, so that elections are now big business. Up until 2003, national elections were generally considered to be reasonably fair and free, but international observers expressed serious concerns about the conduct of the 2003 vote and the campaign that preceded it.[57]

Up through 2003, the electoral system for selecting the *Duma* resembled the German system, combining **proportional representation** with winner-take-all districts. Half of the 450 deputies have been selected on the basis of nationwide party lists, with any party gaining 5 percent of the national vote entitled to a proportional share of these 225 seats. In 1995, a large percentage of voters chose small parties that did not cross the 5 percent threshold, and voters are also given the explicit option of voting against all candidates or parties. In the 2003 *Duma* election, 4.7 percent of voters chose this option. The remaining 225 deputies in the current *Duma* were elected in **single-member plurality districts;** these races usually have involved local notables. Most winning candidates have been associated with particular parties. Some independent candidates joined party factions once they were in the *Duma*; in 2005, the *Duma* had 21 independent deputies. The final balance of forces in the parliament after the 2003 election was determined by the combined result of the party-list vote and the single-member district votes. Until 1999, despite the electoral rebuffs in 1993 and 1995, Yeltsin did not install a prime minister reflecting party strength in the *Duma*. In 1999 and 2003, parliamentary elections offered qualified support for the government.

In 2005, changes to the electoral law were approved, to take effect before the next Duma elections in 2007. These involve abolition of the single-member districts, subsuming selection of all 450 deputies on the party-list ballot into one national proportional representation district, with a minimum threshold for representation raised to 7 percent. Parties are required to include regional representatives on their lists from across the country. For those parties above the 7 percent threshold, choice of deputies from the list would reflect strength of the vote in the various regions. Although this aspect of the legislation seeks to prevent dominance by Moscow-based or other regional cliques, nonetheless the reform has a strongly centralizing character. The number of successful parties is likely to decline, and these parties will probably be more dependent on national party machines. Higher hurdles for competing parties to gain representation may mean reduced opportunities for public input. These changes, plus allegations of interference with nomination and party registration processes, may reduce the effectiveness of elections as vehicles of popular control.

Since 1999, opposition parties have experienced a sharp decline in electoral success, with the rapid ascent of the United Russia Party. One reason is genuine popular support for Putin, as well as the failure of the opposition parties to develop appealing programs or field attractive candidates. However, other factors also play a role. Media coverage has favored the "party of power" and the president. Administrative control measures and selective enforcement have delimited the scope of acceptable political opposition, particularly when this has involved potential elite support for challengers, the Khodorkovsky instance being a case in point. In addition, the carrot-and-stick method has wooed regional elites, producing a bandwagon effect, reinforced by the abolition of gubernatorial elections. Dependent on the president's nomination for reappointment, regional leaders have a further incentive to join the Putin team. Finally, potential opposition forces have been co-opted through party mergers and through formation of fellow-traveler parties (such as the Rodina Party before the 2003 election).

Results of presidential elections have not mirrored parliamentary election outcomes, and Russia has yet to experience a real transfer of power from one political grouping to another, which some scholars consider a first step in consolidating democratic governance. While the CPRF topped the list in the 1995 *Duma* elections, the party leader, Zyuganov, was not able to defeat Yeltsin in the presidential election of 1996. Zyuganov did even more poorly against Putin in the 2000 vote; even in areas of traditional support (the so-called Red Belt in central European Russia), Putin generally outscored him. In 2003, Zyuganov did not run. Under the Russian constitution, presidential elections are held every four years. If no candidate receives a majority of the votes in the first round, a runoff election is held between the two top contenders. Although the 1995 election went to a second round (Yeltsin won 35 percent in the first and 54 percent in the second round against Zyuganov), in 2000 Putin won handily, with nearly 53 percent of the vote against ten other candidates in the first round, and in 2004, he got an even stronger 71 percent in the first round. Attention is already focused on the 2008 race because, given current constitutional provisions, Putin may not run again for a third term, so speculation is rife about who may be groomed as a successor and whether Putin may run again after sitting out one term.

Political Culture, Citizenship, and Identity

Political culture can be a source of great continuity in the face of radical upheavals in the social and political spheres. Attitudes toward government that prevailed in the tsarist period seem to have endured with remarkable tenacity. These include acceptance of a tradition of personalistic authority, highly centralized leadership, and a desire for an authoritative source of truth. The Soviet regime embodied these and other traditional Russian values, such as egalitarianism and collectivism; at the same time, the Soviet development model glorified science, technology, industrialization, and urbanization—values superimposed on the traditional way of life of the largely rural population. When communism collapsed, Soviet ideology was discredited, and the government embraced political and economic values from the West. Many citizens and intellectuals are skeptical of this "imported" culture, partly because it conflicts with other traditional civic values such as egalitarianism, collectivism, and a broad scope for state activity. A crisis of identity resulted for both elites and average citizens, and the current government priorities collide with some traditional values while appealing to others. Can Russian political culture generate its own variant of democracy and economic prosperity, distinct from both the Soviet and the Western models?

One way to study political culture is to examine evidence from public opinion surveys. Such surveys suggest that there is considerable support for liberal democratic values such as an independent judiciary, a free press, basic civil liberties, and competitive elections. Colton and McFaul conclude from survey results that "a significant portion of the Russian population acquiesces in the abstract idea of democracy without necessarily looking to the West for guidance."[58] The authors find that Russians are divided on the proper balance between defense of individual rights and the maintenance of order; other experts conclude that Russians' desire for a strong state and strong leaders does not imply support for authoritarian government.[59] On the other hand, democratic values may not be deeply enough entrenched to provide a safeguard against authoritarian rule.

Another dimension of the search for identity relates to what it means to be Russian. In the USSR, just over 50 percent of the population was ethnically Russian. Since most of the major ethnic minorities now reside in independent states, the Russian Federation is considerably more ethnically homogeneous than was the USSR, with Russians making up over 80 percent of the population. The largest minority group is the Tatars, a traditionally Muslim group residing primarily in Tatarstan, a republic of Russia. Other significant minorities are the neighboring Bashkirs, various indigenous peoples of the Russian north, the many Muslim groups in the northern Caucasus region, and ethnic groups (such as Ukrainians and Armenians) of other former Soviet republics. At the same time, some 25 million ethnic Russians reside outside the Russian Federation in other former Soviet republics.

Given this situation, it is significant whether one considers Russianness to be defined by ethnicity or by citizenship. Indeed, the Russian language itself has two distinct words for "Russian": *russkii,* which refers to an ethnicity, and *Rossiiskii,* a broader concept referring to people of various ethnic backgrounds included in Russia as a political entity. Although the civic definition forms the basis of citizenship, both anti-Semitic and anti-Muslim sentiments do surface in everyday life. Muslim groups from Russia's southern regions have been the target of ethnic stereotyping. In addition, refugee flows from some of the war-torn regions of the Tran Caucasus (Georgia, Azerbaijan, and neighboring regions of southern Russia such as Chechnya and Ingushetia) have heightened national tensions. Individuals from these regions play an important role in Russia's trade sector and are viewed by many Russians as speculators and crooks. Recent terrorist attacks have heightened these prejudices. Religion has long played a role in shaping Russian identity. Today, the Russian Orthodox Church appeals to many citizens who are looking for a replacement for the discredited values of the Communist system. A controversial law passed in 1997 made it harder for new religious groups to organize themselves; the law was directed primarily at Western proselytizers. Human rights advocates and foreign observers protested strongly, again raising questions about the depth of Russia's commitment to liberal democratic values.

In the Soviet period, the mass media, the educational system, and a variety of other social institutions played a key role in propagating the party's political values. Now, students are presented with a wider range of views, and the print media represent a broad spectrum of political opinion, but the electronic media increasingly reflects the government position. As noted in Section 1, the government itself has exerted pressure on the media to present issues favorably. The electronic media are particularly susceptible to political pressure, given the costs and limited availability of the technology needed to run television stations. Unequal media access, in favor of the pro-presidential forces, was criticized by international observers in relation to the 2003 and 2004 federal elections. Financial interests and mafia attacks on investigative journalists have an inhibiting effect on press freedom. The print media is considerably more diverse than TV, but on occasion political and economic pressure is used by national and regional governments to limit the publication of highly critical viewpoints. The continued political interference in media affairs is but one example of the difficult process involved in transforming political culture.

Interests, Social Movements, and Protest

Dozens and usually hundreds of political and social organizations exist in every region of Russia, alongside a large number of nationwide organizations representing the interests of children, veterans, women, environmental advocates, pensioners, the disabled, and cultural interests. Other groups are professional unions, sports clubs, trade unions, and organizations concerned with various aspects of social welfare. Most locally based interest associations have small staffs and rely for support on local government, contracts for work carried out, commercial activities, and grants from international organizations or Western governments. Dependence on Western aid can divert nongovernmental organizations' (NGOs') agendas from concerns of their constituents to priorities of their foreign sponsors. Organizations generally must register with local authorities, and some develop such close relationships with the local administration as to possibly undermine their independence. The most successful interest associations have been those formed by better-off elements of society (such as new business entrepreneurs), officials, or groups receiving funding from international or foreign agencies.

Many groups are successors to Soviet-era associations, such as the trade union organizations and nature protection societies, but now they can mobilize openly to influence state policy and spawn new independent offshoots or competitors. The official trade unions established under Soviet rule have survived under the title of Federation of Independent Trade Unions (FITU). However, FITU has lost the confidence of large parts of the work force. In some sectors, such as the coal industry, new independent trade unions have formed, mainly at the local level. Labor actions have become an important form of social protest through spontaneous strikes, transport blockages, and even hunger strikes. In the mid- to late 1990s, the main grievance was late payment of wages, and strikes were most prevalent among coal miners, in the transportation sector, and in the public service. Other important social groups include the Committee of Soldiers' Mothers of Russia, the

Socio-Ecological Union, the "Chernobyl" Union, and the Society of Veterans.

The government has attempted to channel public activism through official forums, such as the Civic Forum, an unprecedented all-Russian congress of nongovernmental organization activists held in November 2001 in Moscow. Organized with government support, the event elicited both enthusiasm and skepticism in NGO circles. While pleased with the official recognition given to civil society organizations, some activists viewed the event as mainly a public relations effort to indicate the government's openness to social input. A new initiative is the Public Chamber, created in 2005 by legislation proposed by the president. Based on voluntary participation by presidential appointees and representatives recommended by national and regional societal organizations, the organization is presented as a mechanism for public consultation and input, as well as a vehicle for creating public support for government policy. It appears to reflect a corporatist approach that might serve to co-opt public activists from more disruptive forms of self-expression. In 2001, at the Civic Forum, then–prime minister Mikhail Kasyanov referred to an age-old Russian malady—the "lack of connectedness and communication between the authorities and society."[60] The question remains whether these government-sponsored organizations and events really will address this problem or whether they are a reflection of the Kremlin's efforts to co-opt potential opposition and maintain firm control.

The year 2005 commenced with an outburst of public protests, mainly associated with cutbacks in social benefits, as noted in Section 2. Also, in 2005, demonstrators demanded the removal of regional executives in some regions, notably Bashkortostan; with the abolition of elections for this office in late 2004, citizens appealed directly to the president, who seemed reluctant to bow to this pressure. In 2005, following the Orange Revolution in Ukraine in the previous year, Russian authorities seemed concerned about a potential contagion effect in the face of these new sources of popular discontent (see "Citizen Action: Will Russia Have Its Own Color or Flower Revolution?") At the time of this writing, one cannot say that civil society has really formed in Russia. Whatever forms of collective identity have emerged, social forces do not easily find avenues to exert constructive and organized influence on state activity. As Russian citizens awaken to political awareness, they seem to sway between activism and apathy, and the political system wavers along a path between fledgling democratic innovations and renewed authoritarianism. Only the future will tell.

Citizen Action: Will Russia Have Its Own Color or Flower Revolution?

With popular activism on the rise in neighboring countries, speculation is rife as to whether it will have a contagion effect in Russia. Between November 2003 and March 2005, three post-Soviet countries experienced largely nonviolent upheavals, which threw out establishment figures. In each case, a color or flower was adopted as a symbol for the opposition, and the events came to be associated with that symbol. The popular protests followed fraudulent elections; elections were effective in bringing change, but not in the expected way, through the ballot box, but rather by exposing corruption in the system. In two cases (Ukraine and Georgia), repeat elections were held following a court ruling, reversing the original outcome. Foreign support for the protest groups was a point of hot discussion. In fact, in commenting on the Ukrainian protests, the Russia press depicted this as a case of external intervention in the domestic affairs of Ukraine because of foreign financial support for the protestors camped out in Kiev.

November 2003: Georgia

Georgia's Rose Revolution saw public protests against rigged parliamentary elections; the court declared them invalid. New presidential and parliamentary elections in early 2004 replaced Eduard Shevardnadze, the long-time incumbent, with opposition figure Mikheil Saakashvilli. Support from the Open Society Foundation, funded by George Soros, was alleged by critics to have played a pivotal role in activating opposition forces.

November 2004: Ukraine

Ukraine's Orange Revolution followed the fraudulent presidential runoff election of November 21, 2004, when Viktor Yanukovich was declared to have defeated Viktor Yushchenko. Following a court ruling, repeat elections made Yushchenko the winner. An east/west regional split was an important factor in the contest, with Yushchenko favoring more assertive efforts for integration with the EU, while Viktor Yanukovich followers were more inclined to close relations with Russia. Russia provided aid to Yanukovich and objected to the repeat vote, while Western organizations assisted Yushchenko supporters. (Orange was the color of Yushchenko's party.)

March 2005: Kyrgyzstan

Kyrgyzstan's Tulip Revolution occurred after parliamentary elections in February 2005. This resulted in the ouster of incumbent president Askar Akayev one month later, who fled the country to Kazakhstan and Moscow in the face of the protests, which included minor violence. Akayev finally resigned in early April with new elections scheduled for July.

Could Russia experience its own color or flower revolution? Analysts disagree, and they also argue over what color or symbol it would take if it did occur. Many observers emphasize that "Russia isn't Ukraine." Reasons for reaching that conclusion vary. Defenders of the system emphasize the broad popular support for Vladimir Putin. Critics point to the more subtle methods of achieving popular compliance in Russia, so that a fraudulent election of the Ukrainian variety would be unnecessary to keep incumbents in power; others cite the absence of checks and balances to permit a redressing of undemocratic

(continued)

Citizen Action: Will Russia Have Its Own Color or Flower Revolution? (cont.)

outcomes.[1] Yegor Gaidar argues that in countries like Ukraine, democracy, nationalism, and European values are associated with one another, while Russia suffers from a "postimperial syndrome" that makes it hard for westernizing democrats to link to nationalist sentiments.[2]

What color might a Russian revolution be? Gaidar implies it would be red, but not communist red, rather bloody red: the problem is that, unlike in Ukraine, "it is impossible to unite nationalists and democrats in street politics without the possibility of a dangerous, violent development occurring." Another idea is that any popular "revolution" in Russia might soon turn gray, since it would be controlled by the gray suits in Moscow.

---

[1]Masha Lipman, "How Russia is Not Ukraine: The Closing of Russian Civil Society," Policy Outlook Carnegie Endowment for International Peace, January 2005.

[2]"The Economic and Political Situation in Eurasia: Why Russia Is Not Ukraine," Policy Outlook Carnegie Endowment for International Peace, April 21, 2005, http://www.carnegieendowment.org/events/index.cfm?fa=eventDetail&id=770. Summary on website prepared by Alina Tourkova, Junior Fellow with the Russian and Eurasian Program at the Carnegie Endowment for International Peace.

Section ⑤   Russian Politics in Transition

In April 2005, in his annual political address to the Federal Assembly, Putin made a dramatic admission: "Above all, we should acknowledge that the collapse of the Soviet Union was a major geopolitical disaster of the century. As for the Russian nation, it became a genuine drama."[61] About the same time, in several cities throughout Russia, local officials decided to erect new monuments to Joseph Stalin to commemorate the sixtieth anniversary of the end of World War II in Europe, a move that Putin neither approved nor obstructed. President George Bush, in visiting Latvia before arrival in Moscow to celebrate the events, also evoked images of the past, referring to the Soviet Union's unlawful annexation and occupation of the Baltic states.[62] A Kremlin spokesperson vehemently denied this depiction of the postwar events. The verbal sparring was followed by two apparently congenial leaders in Moscow, honoring the veterans who brought the defeat of Naziism. These events show how the Soviet past continues to haunt and obscure not only Russia's path forward, but also relations with neighbors and potential allies.

Political Challenges and Changing Agendas

When the first edition of this book was published in 1996, five possible scenarios for Russia's future were presented:

- A stable progression toward marketization and democratization
- The gradual introduction of "soft authoritarianism"
- A return to a more extreme authoritarianism of a quasi-fascist or communist variety
- The disintegration of Russia into regional fiefdoms or de facto individual states
- Economic decline, civil war, and military expansionism[63]

Just before Putin's appearance as a major political figure, it appeared that the more pessimistic scenarios were the more likely. Optimism grew at the beginning of the new millennium that a strong leader like Putin might move Russia towards its own self-defined version of democracy. At the time of this writing, the "soft authoritarian" scenario seems to be most likely.

Russia in the World of States

In the international sphere, Russia's flirtation with Westernization in the early 1990s produced ambiguous results, leading to a severe transitional recession and placing Russia in the position of a supplicant state requesting international credits and assistance. Russia's protests against unpalatable international developments, such as NATO expansion, the Desert Fox operation against Iraq in December 1998, and NATO's bombing of Yugoslavia in 1999, revealed Moscow's underlying resentment against Western dominance, as well as the country's relative powerlessness in affecting global developments. With a weakened military structure and economy, Russia could do little more than issue verbal protests. The West's recognition that Russia's involvement was crucial to finding a diplomatic solution to the Kosovo crisis in 1999 marked the beginning of a turning point, heralding a new period of increased cooperation between Russia and the Western world. The events of September 11 reinforced these cooperative ventures, as Russia expressed solidarity with American losses and a commitment to join the battle against international terrorism. Evidence of warmer relations included the formation of a NATO-Russia Council in May 2002, marking an era of closer cooperation in areas such as control of international terrorism, arms control, nonproliferation, and crisis management.[64] The next month, at the 2002 G-8 summit meeting in Kanaskis, Canada, it was announced that Russia would assume the presidency of the organization in 2006 and host the annual summit meeting.[65] The G-8 statement affirmed that "Russia has demonstrated its potential to play a full and meaningful role in addressing the global problems that we all face" and referred to "the remarkable economic and democratic transformation that has occurred in Russia in recent years and in particular under the leadership of President Putin."[66] As a further sign of the positive trend in United States–Russia relations, in May 2002 Presidents Bush and Putin agreed to a treaty involving further reductions in the nuclear arsenals of the two countries.

Against this positive background, new tensions emerged in the face of American withdrawal from the Anti-Ballistic Missile Treaty and Russian objections to the American incursion into Iraq in March 2003. Although criticism of Russia's Chechnya policies by Western governments was tempered after the events of September 11, organizations such as Human Rights Watch have continued to charge Russia with acts of violence against the Chechen civilian population, as well as instances of arbitrary arrests and sexual attacks on women.[67] In 2004 and 2005, American officials openly criticized Putin's centralizing moves as antidemocratic, and figures in American business circles viewed the attack on Khodorkovsky as interference in business operations, producing inhibitions to investments in the crucial energy sector.

A critical element of Russia's relations with both the United States and its West European neighbors rests with Russia's rich endowment of oil and natural gas. The source of about 10 percent of the world's oil production and the country most richly endowed with natural gas (about a third of the world's total reserves), Russia has been dubbed by one expert as a "new energy superpower." (See Figure 5) The United States began an "energy dialogue" with Russia in 2002, as the United States hoped to increase energy imports from Russia to diversify its international energy dependence. At the Bush-Putin meeting in Bratislava in February 2005, this was again reaffirmed as a bilateral priority, along with efforts to counter terrorism, facilitate space

Figure 5

Exports from Russia, 2003

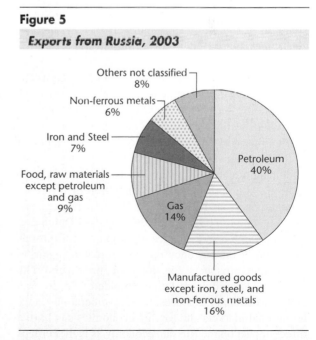

Others not classified
8%

Non-ferrous metals
6%

Iron and Steel
7%

Food, raw materials
except petroleum
and gas
9%

Petroleum
40%

Gas
14%

Manufactured goods
except iron, steel, and
non-ferrous metals
16%

Source: OECD Economic Survey of the Russian Federation 2004: The Sources of Economic Growth, p. 15, 2004.

cooperation, and assure Russia's WTO accession.[68] An energy dialogue had been initiated between the EU and Russia even earlier, in 2000, with a goal of increased integration of EU-Russian energy markets and assurances of energy security for the EU.[69] Russian imports support almost 20 percent of EU gas consumption and 16 percent of oil consumption. In 2004, the EU agreed to support Russia's bid to join the WTO in an implicit quid pro quo involving Russian ratification of the Kyoto climate change protocol, but also Russian agreement to bring a gradual adjustment of its domestic gas prices to bring them closer to world market levels. Will Russia be able to lever energy and other resources to reestablish itself as a regional and potentially a global power? This may depend on whether the leadership can build a stable economic and political structure within the country.

Governing the Economy

The upturn in the Russian economy that began in 1999 may have been a watershed in the struggle to overcome the transitional recession that plagued Russia from the late 1980s onward. At the same time, severe disparities in income and wealth remain, meaning that a restoration of economic growth may not bring an improved standard of living for large numbers of Russian citizens, particularly the elderly, children, the disabled, and those living in poorer northern regions. Questions also remain about whether income from oil and gas exports will feed the investment needs of other sectors of the economy, or whether they will be appropriated by a privileged elite. Making the economy attractive to foreign investors will require a continued development of the banking sector, legal institutions to ensure enforcement of contracts, and controls on crime and corruption. Although the 1998 devaluation of the ruble brought decreased reliance on Western imports (as they become too expensive), the so-called Dutch disease, in which heavy reliance on export income pushes the value of the currency up, now threatens again to undermine prospects for domestic producers. The Russian economy is no longer shielded from foreign and international influences; thus, reverberations in international markets and foreign economies can have a direct impact on the Russian economy as well. Perhaps the greatest economic challenge facing the Putin

administration is establishing policies to ensure a greater diversity of Russia's economic base, which will require reaching a new social accommodation that will bring a stable environment for investment and confidence among Russia's own economic elite as well as among foreign investors. At the same time, the Russian leadership still struggles to find appropriate vehicles for limiting the influence of powerful economic forces on policymaking without undermining political pluralism.

The Democratic Idea

Russia's attempted democratization has been formally successful, but it is marred by corruption, the power of big money, and the limited accountability of its leaders. The political structures put in place by the 1993 constitution have not produced the strong and effective government most Russians desire, nor have these measures permitted ordinary people to feel that their interests are being considered. Opinion surveys indicate that Russians consider government performance less than satisfactory across a wide range of policy areas such as crime control, dealing with unemployment, social security, and health care.[70] The continuing disjuncture between high personal support for the president and a continuing lack of confidence in the ability of political central institutions to address the country's problems effectively suggests that the legitimacy of the system is still on thin ice. The more positive working relationship between the executive and legislative branches that has emerged under Putin's leadership, as well as efforts to regularize relations between the center and regions, provides prospects for improved institutional performance, but the reduction of vehicles for popular input already shows signs of producing poor policy choices that may elicit public protests and reinforce public cynicism about the motives of politicians and the trustworthiness of institutions.

It is difficult to conceive that the freedoms that have been exercised since 1986 could be easily withdrawn. Russians value the personal freedom they have gained since the collapse of communism. Expanding contacts with the West have made increasingly broad circles aware of the benefits of civic participation, even if the Russian system does not yet realize these potentials. Yet a reversion to a more centralized and predictable set of political practices may, on a conscious or unconscious level, seem familiar and therefore comfortable for many Russians. If the security and stability can be combined with rising prosperity, then many Russians may be willing to accept a reduction in democratic rights in exchange for economic improvement and political stability.

The Politics of Collective Identities

Despite changes in social consciousness, the formation of new political identities remains unfinished business. In the Soviet period, the state-imposed homogeneity of interests and political repression hindered the formation of diverse interest associations. Now, other obstacles prevail. Most people are still preoccupied by the struggle to make ends meet or to increase personal welfare; they have little time or energy to forge new forms of collective action to address underlying problems. Under such circumstances, the appeal to nationalism and other basic sentiments can be powerful. Indications of this are already evident in the fact that political parties with nationalist messages seem to be doing better than liberal forces. However, if President Putin is able to channel these sentiments into support for the current constitutional order, then the danger of extreme populist appeals may be minimized. The weakness of Russian intermediary organizations (interest groups, political parties, or associations) means that politicians can more easily appeal directly to emotions because people are not members of groups that help them evaluate the politicians' claims. These conditions are fertile ground for authoritarian outcomes, which the government itself might use to keep the public compliant. Still, the high level of education and increasing exposure to international media may work in the opposite direction. Also, many Russians identify their country as part of Europe and its culture, an attitude echoed by the government. (See Table 3.) Exposure to alternative political systems and cultures may make people more critical of their own political system and seek opportunities to change it. A significant portion of the intelligentsia and some political elites provide potential leaders for this democratic subculture.

Russia remains in what seems to be an extended period of transition. Radical upheavals have been frequent over the past century—a source of some solace

Table 3

Attitudes Toward Foreign Countries

In general what is your attitude toward the following foreign countries:

	USA	The European Union	Ukraine
Very positive	6%	6%	7%
Basically positive	57	67	60
Basically negative	22	12	19
Very negative	7	3	4
Hard to say	8	12	10

Note: Based on a survey carried out April 15–18, 2005, among 1,600 residents of Russia (128 sampling points in 46 regions).
Source: Levada Center, http://www.levada.ru/press/2005050401.html.

to Russians, as they see their current conditions in continuity rather than in contrast to the past. History has been hard on Russians, but the country has always muddled through. In the early 1990s, Russians frequently hoped for "normal conditions," that is, an escape from the shortages, insecurity, and political controls of the past. As the new situation becomes familiar, *normality* has been redefined in less glowing terms than those conceived in the late 1980s. Russians seem to have a capability to adapt to change and uncertainty that North Americans find at once alluring, puzzling, and disturbing.

Russian Politics in Comparative Perspective

The way in which politics, economics, and ideology were intertwined in the Soviet period has profoundly affected the nature of political change in all of the former Soviet republics and generally has made the democratization process more difficult. Unlike developing countries currently experiencing democratization and economic transformation, Russia is a highly industrialized country with a skilled and educated work force. Although this offers advantages, the high level of development is associated with a host of problems: a heavily damaged natural environment, obsolescent industries, entrenched bureaucratic structures, a nuclear arsenal that must be monitored and controlled, and a public that expects the state to provide a stable system of social welfare. Unlike modernizing elites in the developing world, Russian leaders must first deconstruct existing modern structures before constructing new ones. For example, inefficient or highly polluting factories need to be closed or radically renovated, the military-industrial complex has to be cut back or converted to other uses, and the state must accustom the public to more modest expectations about the ability of the state to provide the array of social benefits that the Soviet system offered. These problems make it more difficult for the state to manage the domestic and international challenges it confronts.

How is Russia faring compared to some of the other postcommunist systems that faced many of these same challenges? The nations of Eastern Europe and the former Soviet Union were all subjected to a similar system of economic, political, and ideological power during the period of communist rule. Some were under communist rule for a shorter period of time, but most parts of the Soviet Union shared with Russia more than seven decades of the Communist Party state. Despite the efforts of the Soviet leadership to establish conformity throughout the region, national differences did emerge. The countries of Eastern Europe had a history of closer ties and greater cultural exposure to Western Europe; ideas of liberalism, private property, and individualism were less foreign to citizens in countries such as Czechoslovakia, East Germany, and Hungary than in regions farther east, including Russia. The Roman Catholic Church in Poland provided a focal point for national identity, and Poland's historical antipathy to Russia produced a stronger resistance to the imposition of the Soviet model than in other Slavic countries of the region. Such cultural, geopolitical, and historical differences affected the shape that communist rule took in the various countries.

Within the Soviet Union, too, there was considerable variation among the union republics. The Baltic republics of Latvia, Lithuania, and Estonia took a more experimental approach in many spheres of activity and had a more Western European atmosphere; at the other extreme, the Central Asian republics retained aspects of traditional Muslim culture, preserved the extended family structure, and maintained within the structure of the Communist Party a greater prominence for links rooted in the clan system indigenous to the region. Only in Russia and Yugoslavia (as well as in China and Cuba) was communism largely an indigenous phenomenon rather than a pattern imposed by an outside force. In many ways, Russia's culture helped to define the character of the communist system that it imposed throughout its sphere of influence.

All fifteen countries that gained independence after the collapse of the Soviet Union, as well as several countries of Central and Eastern Europe, have experienced the collapse of the communist system of power since 1989. Given the diversity of nations that were subject to the system, it is not surprising that paths of extrication from communist rule should also vary widely. A rule of thumb, simple as it seems, is that the further east one goes in the postcommunist world, the more difficult and prolonged the transition period has been. This is partly because the more westerly countries of Central Europe that were outside the USSR (Poland, Hungary, Czech Republic, Slovakia), as well as the Baltic states, faced the realistic prospect of EU accession and thus had a strong motivation to embark on fundamental reform to meet the EU's conditions. Also, these countries were under communist rule for a shorter period of time. Although political and economic liberalization generally follows this West-East axis, an exception is Belarus, which has liberalized less than Russia.

In terms of economic performance, postcommunist countries that liberalized the least, such as Uzbekistan and Belarus, suffered lesser recessions in the 1990s because state institutions remained more fully intact. However, these less-reformed economies may face painful adjustments in the future. Because Russia possesses rich deposits of natural resources (including energy resources), it has been able to cope with the ruptured economic ties resulting from the collapse of the Soviet Union better than some of the less-well-endowed states. In addition, Ukraine and particularly Belarus are still suffering from the severe economic and health effects of the accident at the Chernobyl nuclear power plant, and the Central Asian states confront the disastrous effects of Soviet-imposed emphasis on cotton production and associated environmental degradation (the Aral Sea crisis). Russia (along with Ukraine) has been the focal point of international economic assistance because of its large nuclear arsenal, its size, and its geopolitical importance (see "Global

Global Connection: Joining the West or Aid Recipient?

With the collapse of the Iron Curtain, the Russian Federation opened up to global influences, in contrast to the isolation imposed by the Soviet government. As part of this opening, the Russian government has sought equal membership in some international organizations from which it was previously excluded, and it has forged partnerships with others. Western governments and international agencies were welcomed by Russian authorities as they provided aid to Russia's developing market economy and fledgling democratic political structures.

An important aspect of these processes has been the notion of **conditionality,** namely, the requirement that Russia meet certain conditions to be eligible to receive international assistance or to join certain international clubs. Conditionality is a controversial foreign policy tool because it grants foreign governments and agencies a certain leverage over domestic political and economic policy. It has been a particularly powerful tool used by the European Union in relation to candidate countries since strict conditions are set for membership. These requirements helped to speed transition processes in Central Europe (Czech Republic, Slovakia, Poland, Hungary, Slovenia) and the Baltic States before they were admitted as members in May 2004. Russia, viewing itself as a regional power that should have an equal partnership role, has been more resistant to some elements of conditionality, and this may be one reason that Russia has not adopted the goal of EU accession.

Following are some of the most important international agencies that Russia has become involved with in one way or another over the past fifteen years.

The International Monetary Fund (IMF). The IMF was founded in 1944, and during most of the 1990s it was the most influential international agency in Russia. Its general mandate is to oversee the international monetary system and help maintain stability in exchanges between its 184 member countries, which can draw on the fund's resources. The Soviet Union applied for membership in 1991

but was dissolved before acceptance; Russia was admitted to the IMF in 1992, and funds were issued to Russia as short- and medium-term credits to help stabilize the ruble and Russia's internal and external monetary balance. The dispersal of these funds was made contingent on the fulfillment of certain conditions by the Russian government, particularly the maintenance of noninflationary fiscal and monetary policies. These policies, in turn, necessitated cutbacks in social services and subsidies to troubled economic sectors. Through conditions on its loans, the IMF was able to influence the direction of the Russian reform program. In 1999, a final loan was granted, and since then Russia has forgone further credits, choosing to manage its own macroeconomic fiscal policy. By 2004, Russia had paid off its IMF debt (www.imf.org).

The World Bank. Also founded in 1944, the World Bank has as its purpose to promote and finance economic development in the world's poorer countries. After World War II, this involved assistance in financing reconstruction in war-torn Europe. The agency is an investment bank with 184 member countries. As with the IMF, the Russian Federation was admitted in 1992. Through its International Bank for Reconstruction and Development (IBRD), the World Bank has provided loans to support development programs in Russia in sectors such as agriculture, the environment, energy, and social welfare. From 1991 to 2002, Russia borrowed US$12.5 billion from the IBRD, and in January 2005 its outstanding debt stood at $5.7 billion[1] (www.worldbank.org).

The European Bank for Reconstruction and Development (EBRD). The EBRD, formed in 1991, promotes the development of market economies in postcommunist countries. Specific current priorities include measures to "advance technological modernization and efficiency improvements in key sectors of the economy"[2] and helping economic diversification as well as supporting small business development. The EBRD provides loans and guarantees, and supports equity investments (www.ebrd.com).

(continued)

Global Connection: Joining the West or Aid Recipient? (cont.)

The European Union (EU). The EU initiated the Tacis program in 1991 as a vehicle for providing grants to finance the transfer of knowledge to Russia and other countries in the former Soviet Union. Now the largest source of aid to Russia, annual contributions ran at about 90 million Euros in 2002 and 2003. In addition to such assistance efforts, the EU's Partnership and Cooperation Agreement with Russia sets out a strategy for development of four "Common Spaces": Common Economic Space (to create an integrated market), Common Space for Freedom, Security, and Justice (relating to media, travel, human contact); Common Space for External Security (multilateralism, crisis management, antiterrorism); and Common Space for Research, Education, and Culture (http://europa.eu.int/comm/external_relations/russia/summit_05_05/index.htm).

North Atlantic Treaty Organization (NATO). NATO was formed in 1949 by ten European countries, the United States, and Canada to safeguard the security of its members in response to the perceived Soviet threat. Following the collapse of the communist system in Eastern Europe, NATO has had to reconceptualize its mandate and the nature of potential threats. Among its duties are crisis management, peacekeeping, opposing international terrorism, and prevention of nuclear proliferation. In 2004, Bulgaria, Estonia, Latvia, Lithuania, Romania, Slovakia, and Slovenia became NATO members, following Hungary, the Czech Republic, and Poland in 1999. Albania, Croatia, and Macedonia (FYROM) are preparing for possible future membership. After raising strong objections to NATO expansion into its former sphere of influence, Russia has, over time, developed a stronger working relationship with the organization. The Partnership for Peace program was the first important step in the process in 1994, and in 1997, the NATO-Russia Founding Act on Mutual Relations, Cooperation and Security was concluded. A further step was taken in 2002 with the establishment of the NATO-Russia Council, in which Russia holds an equal seat with the twenty-six NATO member states. Working groups

deal with issues such as peacekeeping actions, international terrorism, and nuclear proliferation (http://www.nato.int/issues/nrc/index.html).

The G-8 and Russia. In 1998, Russia was accepted as a full member into the G-8 (Group of Eight), an expanded G-7. The G-8 is an informal international body consisting of the leading industrial nations; G-8 countries hold regular summits dealing with such issues as the international economy, trade relations, and foreign exchange markets. Although Russia is still too weak to exert much influence on G-8 issues, its membership in the organization is widely perceived to be valuable, allowing Russia to maintain a presence on the world stage. Russia is currently looking forward to hosting the G-8 for the 2006 summit.

The World Trade Organization (WTO). The WTO is a powerful international organization, responsible for regulating international trade, settling trade disputes, and designing trade policy through meetings of its 148 member countries. Because of the increasingly global nature of trade, membership in the WTO is seen as an essential prerequisite for increasing economic prosperity and for avoiding international economic isolation. Russia's membership is supported by powerful actors such as the European Union, but Russia still must conclude bilateral agreements with some member countries before accession can proceed. The World Bank estimates that membership will bring Russian annual benefits of $19 billion through increased exports, opening the country to multilateral services and increased foreign direct investment[3] (www.wto.org).

---

[1]Central Bank of the Russian Federation website, at http://www.cbr.ru/statistics/credit_statistics/print.asp?file=debt.htm (accessed May 10, 2005).

[2]European Bank for Reconstruction and Development website, at http://www.ebrd.com/about/strategy/country/russia/main.htm (accessed May 10, 2005).

[3]"Russian Economic Report #10: April 2005," *The World Bank Group,* http://194.84.38.65/mdb/upload/RER10_eng.pdf (accessed May 10, 2005).

Connection: Joining the West or Aid Recipient?"). Although this aid has been insufficient to make the government's overall reform program successful, other parts of the former Soviet Union (with the likely exception of the Baltic states) have received even less international assistance, despite their weaker economic position.

Progression along the various dimensions of the quadruple transition are uneven across postcommunist countries, and Russia seems now to be progressing economically, while regressing politically, with nationalism on the rise and aspirations to status of a regional superpower resurfacing. In the political sphere, virtually all of the postcommunist states claim to be pursuing some form of democratization, but in some cases, this is more in name than in practice, particularly in Central Asia and parts of the Tran Caucasian area. Belarus has a distinctively authoritarian government. In all of the postcommunist states, the attempt to construct democratic political institutions has been characterized by repeated political crises, weak representation of popular interests, executive-legislative conflict, faltering efforts at constitutional revision, and corruption. These features are more marked in the countries farther east.

In Russia, there is considerable skepticism about adopting the Western model of political development, and the political elites who mouth Western values have, to some degree, not understood or internalized them. The question might be asked whether the patrimonial, collectivist, and egalitarian thrust of Russian culture, as well as some features of the cultures of Central Asia, Ukraine, and Belarus, are really compatible with Western economic and political ideas. Although the concept of democracy has a distinct appeal in the region (partly because it has been associated with Western affluence), to much of the population in these countries it means, above all, personal freedom rather than support for notions of political accountability, rule of law, or the civic role of the citizen.

Although Russian politics has been highly contentious and the government has operated at very low levels of efficacy and legitimacy for most of the past decade, with the exception of the Chechnya conflict, Russia has escaped major domestic violence and civil war, unlike Yugoslavia, Armenia, Azerbaijan,

Georgia, Moldova, and the Central Asian state of Tajikistan. For all their problems, Russian politicians have conducted themselves in a relatively civil manner, and neither Yeltsin nor Putin has appealed to exclusivist definitions of Russian identity. Citizenship rights for all ethnic groups have been maintained, and state-sponsored racism is largely absent. Some opposition figures have not been so restrained in their political rhetoric, but the Russian government can be credited with avoiding marginalization of any major social groups.

Russia will undoubtedly continue to be a key regional force in Europe and Asia. Its vast geographic expanse, rich resource base, large and highly skilled population, and the legacy of Soviet rule will ensure this. Yet its former allies in Central Europe, as well as the Baltic states, are gradually drifting into the orbit of Western Europe economically and politically. Following the 2004 EU enlargement, Russia's most important Western neighbor, Ukraine, aspires to EU membership, a goal the Russian leadership has not articulated. Although Ukraine is divided internally over its future course, the European dream is an increasingly important reference point. Russian leaders seem to appreciate the isolation this could imply, but seem unwilling to adopt certain crucial aspects of Western political practice. Thus, over the past few years, while Russia has resisted a monopolar world order dominated by the United States and its leaders have shown a desire and willingness to identify as a European country, Russia has an ambivalent relationship to accepting crucial norms that would underlie an effective and enduring partnership.

Will Russia be able to find a place for itself in the world of states that meets the expectations of its educated and sophisticated population? Five years into the new millennium, prospects are still unclear. One thing is certain: Russia will continue to be an important factor by virtue of its size, its energy resources, its historic role, and its nuclear arsenal. If Russia's experiment produces a stable outcome that benefits the majority of the population, then it may offer a path of quasi-democratic development that could serve as a model for countries further east. If instability and popular discontent rise, then incipient democracies elsewhere in the region may also take a further backward step.

Key Terms

patrimonial state

mir

democratic centralism

vanguard party

collectivization

tacit social contract

perestroika

glasnost

demokratizatsiia

law-based state

market reform

shock therapy

joint-stock companies

privatization voucher

insider privatization

oligarchs

mafia

pyramid debt

autonomous republics

krai

oblast

okrug

patron-client networks

siloviki

asymmetrical federalism

"power vertical"

civil society

proportional represen-
    tation

single-member plurality
    district

conditionality

Suggested Readings

Aslund, Anders. *Building Capitalism: The Transformation of the Former Soviet Bloc.* Cambridge, UK, and New York: Cambridge University Press, 2002.

Black, J. L. *Vladimir Putin and the New World Order: Looking East, Looking West?* Lanham MD: Rowman and Littlefield, 2004.

Blasi, R. Joseph, Kroumova, Maya, and Kruse, Douglas. *Kremlin Capitalism: The Privatization of the Russian Economy.* Ithaca, N.Y.: Cornell University Press, 1997.

Colton, Timothy J. *Transitional Citizens: Voters and What Influences Them in the New Russia.* Cambridge: Harvard University Press, 2000.

DeBardeleben, Joan, ed. *Soft or Hard Borders: Managing the Divide in an Enlarged Europe.* Aldershot, UK: Ashgate, 2005.

Eckstein, Harry, Fleron, Frederic J., Jr., Hoffman, Erik P., and Reisinger, William M. *Can Democracy Take Root in Russia? Explorations in State-Society Relations.* Lanham, Md.: Rowman & Littlefield, 1998.

Freeland, Chrystia. *Sale of the Century: Russia's Wild Ride from Communism to Capitalism.* New York: Doubleday, 2000.

Getty, J. Arch. *Origins of the Great Purges: The Soviet Communist Party Reconsidered.* Cambridge: Cambridge University Press, 1985.

Hoffman, David E. *The Oligarchs: Wealth and Power in the New Russia.* New York: Public Affairs Press, 2002.

Hough, Jerry, and Fainsod, Merle. *How the Soviet Union Is Governed.* Cambridge: Harvard University Press, 1979.

Humphrey, Caroline. *The Unmaking of Soviet Life: Everyday Economies after Socialism.* Ithaca, N.Y.; London: Cornell University Press, 2002.

Lewin, Moshe. *The Gorbachev Phenomenon: A Historical Interpretation.* Berkeley: University of California Press, 1991.

Motyl, Alexander J., Ruble, Blair A., and Shevtsova, Lilia, eds. *Russia's Engagement with the West: Transformation and Integration in the Twenty-First Century.* Armonk, New York: M. E. Sharpe, 2005.

Pål, Kolsto, and Blakkisrud, Helge, eds. *Nation-Building and Common Values in Russia.* Lanham Md.: Rowman and Littlefield Publishers, 2004.

Pipes, Richard. *Russia Under the Old Regime.* New York: Scribner, 1974.

Reddaway, Robert, and Orttung, Robert, eds. *The Dynamics of Russian Politics: Putin's Reform of Federal-Regional Relations.* 2 vols. Rowman & Littlefield, 2004 (volume 1); forthcoming, 2005 (volume 2).

Remington, Thomas F. *Politics in Russia.* 3rd ed. Boston: Pearson Education, 2004.

Robinson, Neil, ed. *Institutions and Political Change in Russia.* Houndsmill, Basingstoke, UK; Macmillan; New York: St. Martin's Press, 2000.

Sakwa, Richard. *Putin: Russia's Choice.* London and New York: Routledge, 2004.

Shevstsova, Lilia, *Putin's Russia.* rev. ed. Moscow: Carnegie Institute, 2004.

Solomon, Peter H., Jr., and Fogelson, Todd S. *Courts and Transition in Russia: The Challenge of Judicial Reform.* Boulder, Colo.: Westview Press, 2000.

Tolz, Vera. *Russia.* London: Arnold; New York: Oxford University Press, 2001.

Weigle, Marcia A. *Russia's Liberal Project: State-Society Relations in the Transition From Communism.* University Park: Pennsylvania State University Press, 2000.

Suggested Websites

The Carnegie Moscow Center
www.carnegie.ru/en/
Center for Russian and East European Studies, University of Pittsburgh
www.ucis.pitt.edu/reesweb
Itar-TASS News Agency
www.itar-tass.com/eng/
Johnson's Russia List
www.cdi.org/russia/johnson/default.cfm
Radio Free Europe/Radio Liberty
www.rferl.org/newsline/
Moscownews.com
www.mosnews.com

Endnotes

[1]Richard Pipes, *Russia Under the Old Regime* (London: Widenfelt & Nicolson, 1974).

[2]Ibid., pp. 22–24.

[3]Peter Hauslohner, "Politics Before Gorbachev: De-Stalinization and the Roots of Reform," in Alexander Dallin and Gail W. Lapidus (eds.), *The Soviet System in Crisis. A Reader of Western and Soviet Views* (Boulder, Colo.: Westview Press, 1991), 37–63.

[4]Mikhail Gorbachev, *Perestroika: New Thinking for Our Country and the World* (New York: Harper, 1987).

[5]Vladimir Putin, Address to the Federal Assembly, April 25, 2005, http://www.kremlin.ru/eng/speeches/2005/04/25/2031_type70029_87086.shtml (accessed April 25, 2005).

[6]See, for example, Joseph Stiglitz, *Globalization and Its Discontents* (New York: W. W. Norton & Co., 2002).

[7]Interview with Irina Khakamada, "Razvitie malogo biznesa v Rossii" (Development of Small Business in Russia), March 3, 2003, website of the Foundation for Assistance to Small Innovative Enterprises (FASIE) http://fasie.tradition.ru/index.php?nid=17 (accessed May 2, 2005).

[8]Gregory Feifer, "Putin Tries Incrementation Rather than Radical Reform in the Countryside," *RFE/RL Russian Political Weekly* 3, No. 8 (February 21, 2003), http://www.rferl.org/reports/rpw/2003/02/8-210203.asp (accessed September 16, 2005).

[9]Sergei Peregudov, "The Oligarchic Model of Russian Corporatism," in Archie Brown (ed.), *Contemporary Russian Politics: A Reader* (New York: Oxford University Press, 2001), 259.

[10]Jacques Sapir, "Russia's Economic Rebound: Lessons and Future Directions," *Post-Soviet Affairs* 18, no. 1 (January–March 2002): 6.

[11]Economist Intelligence Unit (EIU), *Country Report: Russia* (London: EIU, March 8, 2005).

[12]E. T Gurvich, "Makroekonomicheskaia otsenka roli rossiiskogo neftegazovogo sektora," (Macroeconomic Evaluation of the Role of the Russian Oil-Gas Sector), *Voprosy ekonomiki*, no. 10 (2004); also under "Publications" (p. 15) at http://www.eeg.ru/DOWNLOADS/PUBLICATIONS/SCIENTIFIC/2004_009.pdf (accessed May 2, 2005).

[13]Central Intelligence Agency, CIA Factbook, 2004, Russia http://www.cia.gov/cia/publications/factbook/geos/rs.html.

[14]Public Broadcasting Service, "Interview with Mikhail Khodorkovsky: Money, Power Politics," conducted by Sabrine Travernise, *Frontline:* World, October 31, 2003.

[15]EIU, Country Report: Russia (March 2005).

[16]EIU, *Country Report: Russia* (March 2002), 13; *Rossiiskii statisticheskii ezhegodnik* (Russian Statistical Yearbook), Moscow: Goskomstat, 2004.

[17]World Bank, *Russian Federation: Reducing Poverty through Growth and Social Policy Reform,* Report No. 28923-RU, February 24, 2005, pp. iv, viii.

[18]Levada Centre, *Vestnik obshchestvennogo mnenia* (November–December 2004), p. 104; and Levada Center data, online, http://www.levada.ru/press/2005041202.html (accessed April 27, 2005).

[19]Sarah Ashwin and Elaine Bowers, "Do Russian Women Want to Work?" in Mary Buckley (ed.), *Post-Soviet Women: From the Baltics to Central Asia* (Cambridge: Cambridge University Press, 1997), 23. Also *Rossiiskii statisticheskii ezhegodnik* (2004)

[20]Goskomstat (Russian Statistical Agency), http://www.gks.ru/bgd/free/b05_00/IswPrx.dll/Stg/d010/i010180r.htm (accessed May 2, 2005).

[21]*Rossiiskii statisticheskii ezhegodnik* (Russia Statistics Annual). Moscow: Federal Service of State Statistics, 2004.

[22]Victor Zaslavsky, "From Redistribution to Marketization: Social and Attitudinal Change in Post-Soviet Russia," in Gail W. Lapidus (ed.), *The New Russia: Troubled Transformation* (Boulder, Colo.: Westview Press, 1994), 125.

[23]Joan DeBardeleben, "Attitudes Toward Privatization in Russia," *Europe-Asia Studies* 51, no. 3 (1999): 447–465, as well as subsequent data from surveys organized in Russia by the author.

[24]Figures adapted from Economist Intelligence Unit, *EIU Quarterly Economic Review of the USSR,* Annual Supplement (London: EIU, 1985), 20.

[25]*"Putin Urges Early Repayment of Russia's Whole External Debt,"* Moscow News Online, Feb. 11, 2005, http://www.mosnews.com/money/2005/02/11/putindebt.shtml (accessed April 14, 2005).

[26]OECD, "Obzory investitsionnoi politiki: Rossiiskaia Federaltisiia" (OECD Investment Policy Review: Russian Federation) (2004) http://www.oecd.org/dataoecd/3/27/34464365.pdf, pp. 20, 24 (accessed April 27, 2005).

[27]Economist Intelligence Unit, Russia: Country Profile 2004, pp. 53, 63.

[28]Ibid, p. 51.

[29]Vladimir Putin, Address to the Federal Assembly, April 25, 2005, http://www.kremlin.ru/eng/speeches/2005/04/25/2031_type70029_87086.shtml (accessed April 25, 2005).

[30]For an example of path-dependent analysis, see David Stark and Laszlo Bruszt, *Postsocialist Pathways: Transforming Politics and Property in East Central Europe* (Cambridge and New York: Cambridge University Press, 1998).

[31]Thomas Remington, *Politics in Russia,* 2nd ed. (New York: Longman, 2001), 53–54.

[32]The beginning of a regularized competitive system for civil service appointments was provided in a July 1995 law, but its provisions have not been widely implemented. See Natalia Joukovskaia, "The Development State in Russia" (master's research essay, Carleton University, September 2002), 59–61.

[33]Thomas Remington, *Politics in Russia,* 2nd ed. (New York: Longman, 2001), 53–54.

[34]Fred Weir, "Putin's Endgame for Chechen Beartrap," *Christian Science Monitor,* January 25, 2001.

[35]"Society is Afraid of Our Army," interview with Defense Minister Sergei Ivanov, April 13, 2005, http://mosnews.com/interview/2005/04/13/ivanov.shtml (accessed April 20, 2005). Interview conducted by Natalia Kalashnikova, summarized and translated from Itogi.ru, April 20, 2005, http://www.itogi.ru/Paper2005.nsf/Article/Itogi_2005_04_11_13_3960.

[36]Svetlana Mikhailova, "Constitutional Court Confirms Federal Authorities' Ability to Fire Governors, Disband Legislatures," *Russian Regional Report,* April 10, 2002, http://www.iews.org/rrabout.nsf/ (accessed Sept. 6, 2002).

[37]Quoted by Steven Lee Meyers, in "Protest in Urals Seeking Ouster of Putin Ally," *New York Times,* April 26, 2005, p. A6.

[38]I am grateful to Natalia Joukovskaia for her assistance relating to these issues. See Aleksei Zudin, "Biznes i gosudarstvo pri Putina: stanovlenie novoi sistemy vzaimootnoshenii" (Business and the state under Putin: The creation of a new system of interrelations), *Russian Journal,* December 18, 2000, http://old.russ.ru/politics/grammar/20001.2118_zudin.html (accessed April 18, 2003).

[39]EIU, *Country Report: Russia* (September 2001), 13.

[40]On corporatism, see Philippe C. Schmitter and Gerhard Lehmbruch, *Trends Towards Corporatist Intermediation* (Thousand Oaks, Calif.: Sage, 1979).

[41]Compiled by the author from the website of the State Duma, http://www.duma.gov.ru/ (accessed May 2, 2005).

[42]Levada Center, public opinion poll, March 18, 2005, http://www.levada.ru/press/2005041801.html (accessed May 2, 2005).

[43]David Lane, *State and Politics in the USSR* (Oxford: Blackwell, 1985), 184–185.

[44]Compiled by the author from the website of the State Duma, http://www.duma.gov.ru/ (accessed May 2, 2005).

[45]Thomas Remington, *Politics in Russia* (New York: Longman, 2001), 102.

[46]See the Constitution of the Russian Federation, Articles 105 and 106, http://www.constitution.ru/en/10003000-06.htm (accessed May 5, 2005).

[47]Ibid., Article 102.

[48]http://www.duma.gov.ru (May 2, 2005).

[49]For a listing of registered parties, see the website of the Russian Electoral Commission, http://www.cikrf.ru/m_menu_i.htm (accessed May 5, 2005).

[50]For a copy of the 1999 ballot, see Remington, *Politics in Russia,* 182–183.

[51]These numbers also include seats won in single-member districts, as discussed below.

[52]http://www.edinros.ru/index.html (accessed May 5, 2005)

[53]Mary Buckley, "Adaptation of the Soviet Women's Committee: Deputies' Voices from 'Women of Russia,' " in Mary Buckley (ed.), *Post-Soviet Women: From the Baltics to Central Asia* (Cambridge: Cambridge University Press, 1997), 158, 163, 180.

[54]See the Yabloko website at http://www.eng.yabloko.ru/ (accessed May 5, 2005).

[55]See the official website at http://www.sps.ru/ (accessed May 5, 2005).

[56]Rodina official website, http://www.rodina.ru/programma/show/?id=37 (accessed May 5, 2005).

[57]Office for Democratic Institutions and Human Rights, "Russian Federation: Election to the State Duma 7 December 2003, OSCE/ODHIR Election Observation Mission Report" (Warsaw, January 27, 2004), http://unpan1.un.org/intradoc/groups/public/documents/UNTC/UNPAN016105.pdf (accessed May 2, 2005).

[58]Timothy J. Colton and Michael McFaul, "Are Russians Undemocratic," *Post-Soviet Affairs* 18 (April–June 2002): 102.

[59]William M. Reisinger, Arthur H. Miller, Vicki L. Hesli, and Kristen Hill Maher, "Political Values in Russia, Ukraine, and Lithuania: Sources and Implications," *British Journal of Political Scien*ce 24 (1994): 183–223.

[60]Paraphrased by Oksana Alekseyev, "Premier Performance," *Kommersant,* Nov. 23, 2001, excerpted and translated in *The Current Digest of the Post-Soviet Press,* Dec. 19, 2001.

[61]http://kremlin.ru/eng/speeches/2005/04/25/2031_type70029_87086.shtml (accessed May 9, 2005).

[62]Elisabeth Bumille, "Bush, Arriving in Baltics, Steps Into Argument With Russia," *New York Times,* May 7, 2005.

[63]Joan DeBardeleben, "Russia," in Mark Kesselman, Joel Kreiger, and William A. Joseph (eds.), *Comparative Politics at the Crossroads* (Lexington, Mass.: Heath, 1996): 355–357.

[64]For the official statement, see the NATO website, "NATO-Russia Relations: A New Quality" Declaration by Heads of State and Government of NATO Member States and the Russian Federation, http://www.nato.int/docu/basictxt/b020528e.htm (accessed Sept. 12, 2002).

[65]For background on the G-8, see the Canadian government site, "About the G8," http://www.g8.gc.ca/menu-en.asp. (accessed May 8, 2005).

[66]Fiona Hill, "Russia: The 21st Century's Superpower?" *Brookings Review,* Spring 2002, Vol. 20, no. 2, pp. 28–31.

[67]Human Rights Watch webpage, http://hrw.org/english/docs/2005/05/07/russia10586.htm (accessed May 7, 2005).

[68]White House Press Release, http://www.whitehouse.gov/news/releases/2005/02/20050224-7.html, February 24, 2005 (accessed May 7, 2005).

[69]EU-Russia Energy Dialogue, Fifth Progress Report, November 2004, Moscow-Brussels http://europa.eu.int/comm/energy/russia/joint_progress/doc/progress5_en.pdf (accessed May 7, 2005).

[70]Based on a survey carried out by the author in conjunction with Russian partners headed by Viktor Khitrov and the Institute of Sociology of the Russian Academy of Sciences. The research was conducted by regional partners in Stavropol *krai,* Nizhnegorodskaia *oblast,* and Orlov *oblast* in 1998 and 2000, and in the same locations in 2004.

CHAPTER 5

Mexico

Merilee S. Grindle

United Mexican States

Land and People

Capital	Mexico City	
Total area (square miles)	756,066 (about 3 times the size of Texas)	
Population	104.96 million	
Annual population growth rate (%)	1975–2002	2.0
	2002–2015 (projected)	1.2
Urban population (%)	75.2%	
Major language(s) (%)	Spanish	94.1
	Mayan, Nahuatl, and other indigenous languages	5.9
Religious affiliation (%)	Roman Catholic	89
	Protestant	6
	Other	5

Economy

Domestic currency	Peso (MXN)	
	US$1: 11.29 MXN (2005)	
Total GNI (US$)	637.2 billion	
GNI per capita (US$)	6,230	
Total GNI at purchasing power parity (US$)	918.5 billion	
GNI per capita at purchasing power parity (US$)	8,980	
GDP annual growth rate (%)	1983–1993	2.4
	1993–2003	3.2
	2002	0.7
	2003	1.3
	2004	4.1
GDP per capita average annual growth rate (%)	1983–1993	0.4
	1993–2003	1.7
Inequality in income or consumption (2000) (%)	Share of poorest 10%	1.0
	Share of poorest 20%	3.1
	Share of richest 20%	59.1
	Share of richest 10%	43.1
	Gini Index (2000)	54.6
Structure of production (% of GDP)	Agriculture	4
	Industry	27.2
	Services	68.9
Labor force distribution (% of total)	Agriculture	18
	Industry	24
	Services	58
Exports as % of GDP	28.4	
Imports as % of GDP	30.1	

Society

Life expectancy at birth	74.94	
Infant mortality per 1,000 live births	21.69	
Adult literacy (%)	Male	94
	Female	90.5
Access to information and communications (per 1,000 population)	Telephone lines	147
	Mobile phones	255
	Radios	330
	Televisions	283
	Personal computers	82.0

Women in Government and the Economy

Women in the national legislature		
Lower house or single house (%)		22.6
Upper house (%)		15.6
Women at ministerial level (%)		11.1
Female economic activity rate (age 15 and above) (%)		40.2
Female labor force (% of total)		32
Estimated earned income (PPP US$)	Female	4,915
	Male	12,967

Composite Rankings and Ratings

2004 Human Development Index ranking (value) out of 177 countries	53
Gender-related Development Index (GDI) ranking (value) out of 144 countries	53 (.802)
Gender Empowerment Measure (GEM) ranking (value) out of 78 countries	34 (.563)
Corruption Perception Index (CPI) ranking (value) out of 146 countries	64 (3.6)
Environmental Sustainability Index (ESI) ranking (value) out of 146 countries	95 (46.2)
Freedom in World rating	Free (2.0)

Political Organizations

Political System   Federal republic.

Regime History   Current form of government since 1917.

Administrative Structure   Federal with 31 states and a federal district.

Executive   President, elected by direct election with a six-year term of office; reelection not permitted.

Legislature   Bicameral Congress. Senate (upper house) and Chamber of Deputies (lower house); elections held every three years. There are 128 senators, 3 from each of the 31 states, 3 from the federal (capital) district, and 32 elected nationally by proportional representation for six-year terms. The 500 members of the Chamber of Deputies are elected for three-year terms from 300 electoral districts, 300 by simple majority vote and 200 by proportional representation.

Judiciary Independent federal and state court system headed by a Supreme Court with 11 justices appointed by the president and approved by the Senate.

Party System Multiparty system. One-party dominant (Institutional Revolutionary Party) system from 1929 until 2000. Major parties: National Action Party, Institutional Revolutionary Party, and the Democratic Revolutionary Party.

Section ❶ The Making of the Modern Mexican State

Politics in Action

On December 1, 2000, Vicente Fox Quesada became president of Mexico. Although most of the inauguration ceremony followed long-established tradition, the event was historic. For the first time in seventy-one years, the president of Mexico did not represent the Institutional Revolutionary Party (PRI, pronounced "pree"), which had governed the country without interruption since 1929. Fox assumed the presidency under the banner of the National Action Party (PAN, pronounced "pahn"), a center-right party that had long opposed the PRI. He won the election largely because the old civil-authoritarian system could no longer ensure political stability, economic progress, and responsiveness to the demands of a society that was increasingly characterized by inequality.

The inauguration of Fox signaled a new stage in Mexico's quest for democracy. Under the PRI, political conflict had been largely limited to internal struggles within the party, and those who questioned its monopoly of power were usually co-opted into quiescence with promises and benefits, or they were quietly but effectively repressed. The regime was sometimes called "the perfect dictatorship." For several decades, this system produced political stability and economic growth. Yet, increasingly during the 1980s and 1990s, Mexicans began to press for fairer elections and more responsive public officials. They demanded the right of opposition parties to compete for power on an equal basis with the PRI. They argued that the president had too much power and that the PRI was riddled with corruption. By 2000, a significant number of

the country's 100 million citizens wanted political change.

Just six years before, in 1994, despite widespread disillusionment with the political system, PRI candidate Ernesto Zedillo had easily won the presidency. At that time, many voters feared that political change might bring violence and instability more than they feared politics as usual under the continuation of a PRI government. And having spent all their lives under the PRI, some citizens remembered the party's triumphs of decades past and continued to support it. By 2000, however, a majority of the voters had had enough. Yet it was natural that they should be concerned about what government under the PAN would bring. Along with trepidation about change, many were expecting a great deal from the new government—more open political debate, more open government, more capacity to influence public policies, more economic growth, improved public services. President Fox had his job cut out for him.

Today, Mexicans are proud that their country has demonstrated its ability to move toward more democratic politics. Yet political and economic dissatisfaction continues to characterize the country. Regime change did not bring much evidence of improved capacity to respond to the needs of many. For elites, the opportunities of globalization have provided unprecedented wealth and cosmopolitan lifestyles. Yet indicators of increased poverty are everywhere. At least a quarter of the population lives on less than two dollars a day. The public education and health systems struggle to meet demand. In the countryside, the peasant population faces destitution. In urban areas, the poor are forced to find meager sources of income however they can.

Thus, the advent of the Fox administration drew attention to ongoing and interrelated challenges of Mexico's development:

- Would a country with a long tradition of authoritarian government be able to sustain a democratic political system in the face of increasing demands and high expectations?
- Would a country that had long sought economic development through government activism and the domestic market be able to compete effectively in a competitive, market-driven global economy?
- Would a country long noted for severe inequalities between the rich and the poor be capable of providing better living standards for its growing population?

Geographic Setting

Mexico is one of the most geographically diverse countries in the world, encompassing snow-capped volcanoes, coastal plains, high plateaus, fertile valleys, rain forests, and deserts within an area slightly less than three times the size of Texas. To the north, it shares a 2,000-mile-long border with the United States, to the south, a 600-mile-long border with Guatemala and a 160-mile-long border with Belize. Two imposing mountain ranges run the length of Mexico: the Sierra Madre Occidental to the west and the Sierra Madre Oriental to the east. As a result, the country is noted for peaks, plateaus, and valleys that produce an astonishing number of microclimates and a rich diversity of plants and animals. Mexico's varied geography has historically made communication and transportation between regions difficult and infrastructure expensive. The mountainous terrain tends to limit large-scale commercial agriculture to irrigated fields in the northern part of the country, while the central and southern regions produce a wide variety of crops on small farms. Soil erosion and desertification are major problems because of the steep terrain and unpredictable rainfall in many areas. The country is rich in oil, silver, and other natural resources, but it has long struggled to manage those resources wisely.

The human landscape is equally dramatic. With some 100 million inhabitants, Mexico is the world's eleventh most populous country—the second-largest nation in Latin America after Portuguese-speaking Brazil and the largest Spanish-speaking nation in the world. Sixty percent of the population is *mestizo,* or people of mixed **Amerindian** and Spanish descent. About 30 percent of the population claims indigenous (Amerindian) descent, although only about 6 percent of the population speaks an indigenous language rather than Spanish. The rest of the population is made up of Caucasians and people with other backgrounds. The largest **indigenous groups** are the Maya in the south and the Náhuatl in the central regions, with well over 1 million members each. There are also dozens and perhaps hundreds of smaller linguistic and social groups throughout the country. Although Mexicans pride themselves on their Amerindian heritage, problems of racism and classism run deep.

Mexico was transformed from a largely rural to a largely urban country in the second half of the twentieth century, with over 75 percent of the population now living in urban areas. Mexico City has become one of the world's largest cities, with about 20 million inhabitants.[1] Annual population growth has slowed to about 1.4 percent, but society continues to adjust to the baby boom of the 1970s and early 1980s as these twenty- to thirty-year-olds seek jobs and form families. Migration both within and beyond Mexico's borders has become a major issue. Greater economic opportunities in the industrial cities of the north lead many men and women to seek work there in the *maquiladoras,* or assembly industries. As a result, border cities like Tijuana and Ciudad Juárez have experienced tremendous growth in the past twenty years. Many job seekers continue on to the United States, lured by a larger job market and higher wages. The problem repeats itself in reverse on Mexico's southern border, with many thousands of Central Americans looking for better prospects in Mexico and beyond.

Critical Junctures

Mexicans are deeply affected by the legacies of their collective past, including centuries of colonialism and decades of political instability after the end of Spanish rule. The legacies of the distant past are still felt, but the most formative event in the country's modern history was the Revolution of 1910. Mexico

Mexico

0   300 Miles

0   300 Kilometers

experienced the first great social revolution of the twentieth century, a conflict that lasted for more than a decade and claimed the lives of as many as 1 million people. The revolution was fought by a variety of forces for a variety of reasons, which made the consolidation of power that followed as significant as the revolution itself. The institutions and symbols of the current political regime emerged from these complex conflicts.

Independence and Instability (1810–1876)

Spain ruled Mexico for three centuries, administering a vast economic, political, and religious empire in the interests of the imperial country, its kings, and its representatives in North America (see "Global Connection: Conquest or Encounter?"). Colonial policy was designed to extract wealth from the territory then known as New Spain and to limit the

possibilities for Spaniards in the New World to benefit from agriculture, commerce, or industry without at the same time benefiting the mother country. It was also designed to ensure commitment to the Roman Catholic religion and the subordination of the Amerindian population.

In 1810, a parish priest in central Mexico named Miguel Hidalgo called for an end to Spanish misrule. At the head of a motley band of insurgents, he began the first of a series of wars for independence that pitted rebels against the Spanish Crown for eleven years. Although independence was gained in 1821, Mexico struggled to create a stable and legitimate government for decades after. Liberals and conservatives, federalists and centralists, those who sought to expand the power of the church and those who sought to curtail it, and those who wanted a republic and those who wanted a monarchy were all engaged in the battle for Mexico's soul during the nineteenth century. Between

Critical Junctures in Mexico's Political Development

1521	Spaniards led by Hernán Cortés capture the Aztec capital, initiating three centuries of colonial rule.
1810–1821	War of independence from Spain
1876–1911	Dictatorship of Porfirio Díaz
1910–1920	Mexican Revolution
1917	Mexican Constitution
1929	Plutarco Elías Calles founds PRI.
1934–1940	Presidency of Lázaro Cárdenas; entrenchment of corporatist state
1968	Massacre of Tlaltelolco; hundreds of protesting students killed
1978–1982	State-led development reaches peak with petroleum boom and bust.
1982	Market reformers come to power in PRI.
1988	Carlos Salinas is elected amid charges of fraud.
1989	First governorship is won by an opposition party.
1994	NAFTA goes into effect; uprising in Chiapas; Colosio assassinated.
1996	Political parties agree on electoral reform.
1997	Opposition parties advance nationwide; PRI loses absolute majority in congress for first time in its history.
2000	PRI loses presidency; Vicente Fox of PAN becomes president, but without majority support in congress.

1833 and 1855, thirty-six presidential administrations came to power.

Adding insult to injury during this disorganized period, Mexico lost half its territory to the United States. Its northern territory of Texas proclaimed and then won independence in a war ending in 1836. Then the Lone Star Republic, as Texas was then called, was annexed by the United States in 1845, and claims on Mexican territory north of the Rio Grande were increasingly heard from Washington. On the basis of a dubious claim that Mexico had invaded U.S. territory, the United States declared war on its southern neighbor in 1841. The war was first fought along what was later to become the border between the two countries, and then, in 1847, the U.S. army invaded the port city of Veracruz. With considerable loss of civilian lives, U.S. forces marched toward Mexico City, where they engaged in the final battle of the war at Chapultepec Castle. An 1848 treaty gave the United States title to what later became the states of Texas, New Mexico, Utah, Nevada, Arizona, California, and part of Colorado for about $18 million, leaving a legacy of deep resentment toward the United States, which many Mexicans still consider to be the "Colossus of the North."

The loss in this war did not make it any easier to govern Mexico. Liberals and conservatives continued their struggle over issues of political and economic order and, in particular, the power of the Catholic Church. The Constitution of 1857 incorporated many of the goals of the liberals, such as a somewhat democratic government, a bill of rights, and limitations on the power of the church. The constitution did not guarantee stability, however. In 1861, Spain, Great Britain, and France occupied Veracruz to collect debts owed by Mexico. The French army then continued on to Mexico City, where it subdued the weak government, and established the rule of Emperor Maximilian (1864–1867). Conservatives welcomed this respite from the liberal rule. Benito Juárez returned to the presidency in 1867 after defeating and executing Maximilian. Juárez, a Zapotec Indian from Oaxaca who came to be a liberal hero, is still hailed in Mexico today as an early proponent of more democratic government.

The Porfiriato (1876–1911)

Over the next few years, a popular retired general named Porfirio Díaz became increasingly dissatisfied with what he thought was a "lot of politics" and "little action" in Mexico's government. After several failed attempts to win and then take the presidency, he finally succeeded in 1876. His dictatorship lasted thirty-four years and was at first welcomed by many because it brought sustained stability to the country.

Díaz imposed a highly centralized authoritarian system to create political order and economic progress. Over time, he came to rely increasingly on a small clique of advisers, known as *científicos* (scientists), who wanted to adopt European technologies and values to modernize the country. Deeply disdainful of the

Global Connection: **Conquest or Encounter?**

The year 1519, when the Spanish conqueror Hernán Cortés arrived on the shores of the Yucatán Peninsula, is often considered the starting point of Mexican political history. But the Spanish explorers did not come to an uninhabited land waiting to be excavated for gold and silver. Instead, the land that was to become New Spain and then Mexico was home to extensive and complex indigenous civilizations that were advanced in agriculture, architecture, and political and economic organization—civilizations that were already over a thousand years old. The Mayans of the Yucatán and the Toltecs of the central highlands had reached high levels of development long before the arrival of the Europeans. By 1519, diverse groups had fallen under the power of the militaristic Aztec Empire, which extended throughout what is today central and southern Mexico.

The encounter between the Europeans and these indigenous civilizations was marked by bloodshed and violence. The great Aztec city of Tenochtitlán—the site of Mexico City today—was captured and largely destroyed by the Spanish conquerors in 1521. Cortés and the colonial masters who came after him subjected indigenous groups to forced labor; robbed them of gold, silver, and land; and introduced flora and fauna from Europe that destroyed long-existing aqueducts and irrigation systems. They also brought alien forms of property rights and authority relationships, a religion that viewed indigenous practices as the devil's work, and an economy based on mining and cattle—all of which soon overwhelmed existing structures of social and economic organization.

Within a century, wars, savage exploitation at the hands of the Spaniards, and the introduction of European diseases reduced the indigenous population from an estimated 25 million to 1 million or fewer. The Indian population took three hundred years just to stop decreasing after the disaster of the conquest.

Even so, the Spanish never constituted more than a small percentage of the total population, and massive racial mixing among the Indians, Europeans, and to a lesser extent Africans produced a new *raza*, or *mestizo* race. This unique process remains at once a source of pride and conflict for Mexicans today. What does it mean to be Mexican? Is one the conquered or the conqueror? While celebrating Amerindian achievements in food, culture, the arts, and ancient civilization, middle-class Mexico has the contradictory sense that to be "Indian" nowadays is to be backward. Many Amerindians are stigmatized by mainstream society if they speak a native dialect. But perhaps the situation is changing, with the upsurge of indigenous movements from both the grass roots and the international level striving to promote ethnic pride, defend rights, and foster the teaching of Indian languages.

The collision of two worlds resonates in current national philosophical and political debates. Is Mexico a Western society? Is it colonial or modern? Third or First World? South or North? Is the United States an ally or a conqueror? Perhaps most important, many Mexicans at once welcome and fear full integration into the global economy, asking themselves: Is globalization the new conquest?

---

vast majority of the country's population, Díaz and the *científicos* encouraged foreign investment and amassed huge fortunes. During this period, known as the *Porfiriato*, this small elite group monopolized political power and reserved lucrative economic investments for itself. Economic and political opportunities were closed off for new generations of middle- and upper-class Mexicans, who became increasingly resentful of the greed of the Porfirians and their own lack of opportunities.

The Revolution of 1910 and the Sonoran Dynasty (1910–1934)

In 1910, conflict broke out as reformers sought to end the dictatorship. Díaz had pledged himself to an open election for president, and in 1910, Francisco I. Madero, a landowner from the northern state of Coahuila, presented himself as a candidate. The slogan "Effective Suffrage, No Reelection" summed up the reformers' goals in creating opportunities for a new class of politically ambitious citizens to move into positions of power. When this opposition swelled, Díaz jailed Madero and tried to repress growing dissent. But it was too late. The clamor for change forced Díaz into exile. Madero was elected in 1911, but he was soon using the military to put down revolts from reformers and reactionaries alike. When Madero was assassinated during a **coup d'état** in 1913, political order in the country virtually collapsed.

At the same time that middle-class reformers struggled to displace Díaz, a peasant revolt that focused on land claims erupted in the central and southern states of the country. This revolt had roots in legislation that made it easy for wealthy landowners and ranchers to claim the lands of peasant villagers. Encouraged by the weakening of the old regime and driven to desperation by increasing landlessness, villagers armed themselves and joined forces under a variety of local leaders. The most famous of these was Emiliano Zapata, who amassed a peasant army from Morelos, a state in southern Mexico. Zapata's manifesto, the Plan de Ayala, became the cornerstone of the radical agrarian reform that would be incorporated into the Constitution of 1917.

In the northern part of the country, Francisco (Pancho) Villa rallied his own army of workers, small farmers, and ranch hands. He presented a major challenge to the national army, now under the leadership of Venustiano Carranza, who inherited Madero's middle-class reformist movement and eventually became president. Villa's forces recognized no law but that of their chief and combined military maneuvers with banditry, looting, and warlordism in the territories under their control. In 1916, troops from the United States entered Mexico to punish Villa for an attack on U.S. territory. Although this badly planned, poorly executed military operation failed to locate Villa, the presence of U.S. troops on Mexican soil resulted in increased public hostility toward the United States, against which feelings were already running high because of a 1914 invasion of Veracruz.

The Mexican Constitution of 1917 was forged out of the diverse and often conflicting set of interests represented by the various revolutionary factions. The document established a formal set of political institutions and guaranteed citizens a range of progressive social and economic rights: agrarian reform, social security, the right to organize in unions, a minimum wage, an eight-hour workday, profit sharing for workers, universal secular education, and adult male suffrage. Despite these socially advanced provisions, the constitution did not provide suffrage for women, who had to wait until 1953 to vote in local elections and 1958 to vote in national elections. In an effort to limit the power of foreign investors, the constitution declared that only Mexican citizens or the government could own land or rights to water and other natural resources. It also contained numerous articles that severely limited the power of the Roman Catholic Church, long a target of liberals who wanted Mexico to be a secular state. The signing of the document signaled the formal end of the revolution and the intent of the contending parties to form a new political regime. Despite such noble sentiments, violence continued as competing leaders sought to assert power and displace their rivals. By 1920, a modicum of stability had emerged, but not before many of the revolutionary leaders—including Zapata and President Carranza—had been assassinated in struggles over power and policy. There were, however, occasional outbreaks of violence among local warlords during the twenties.

Despite this violence, power was gradually consolidated in the hands of a group of revolutionary leaders from the north of the country. Known as the Sonoran Dynasty, after their home state of Sonora, these leaders were committed to a capitalist model of economic development. Eventually, one of the Sonorans, Plutarco Elías Calles, emerged as the *jefe máximo*, or supreme leader. After his presidential term (1924–1928), Calles managed to select and dominate his successors from 1929 to 1934. The consolidation of power under his control was accompanied by extreme **anticlericalism**, which eventually resulted in warfare between the government and the conservative leaders of the Catholic Church and their followers.

In 1929, Calles brought together many of the most powerful contenders for leadership, including

In 1914, Pancho Villa (right) met with Emiliano Zapata in Mexico City to discuss the revolution and their separate goals for its outcome.   *Source:* Robert Freck/Odyssey/Chicago.

many regional warlords, to create a political party. The bargain he offered was simple: contenders for power would accommodate each other's interests in the expectation that without political violence, the country would prosper and they would be able to reap the benefits of even greater power and economic spoils. They formed a political party, whose name was changed in 1938 and again in 1946, to consolidate their power; and for the next seven decades, Calles's bargain was effective in ensuring nonviolent conflict resolution among elites and the uninterrupted rule of the Institutional Revolutionary Party (PRI) in national politics.

Although the revolution was complex and the interests contending for power in its aftermath were numerous, there were five clear results of this protracted conflict. First, the power of traditional rural landowners was undercut. But in the years after the revolution, wealthy elites would again emerge in rural areas, even though they would never again be so powerful in national politics nor would their power be so unchecked in local areas. Second, the influence of the Catholic Church was strongly curtailed. Although the church remained important in many parts of the country, it no longer participated openly in national political debates. Third, the power of foreign investors was severely limited; prior to the

revolution, foreign investors had owned much of the country's land as well as many of its railroads, mines, and factories. Henceforth, Mexican nationalism would shape economic policymaking. Fourth, a new political elite consolidated power and agreed to resolve conflicts through accommodation and bargaining rather than through violence. And fifth, the new constitution and the new party laid the basis for a strong central government that could assert its power over the agricultural, industrial, and social development of the country.

Lázaro Cárdenas, Agrarian Reform, and the Workers (1934–1940)

In 1934, Plutarco Elías Calles handpicked Lázaro Cárdenas, a revolutionary general and former state governor, as the official candidate for the presidency. The *jefe máximo* fully anticipated that Cárdenas would go along with his behind-the-scenes management of the country and that the new president would continue the economic policies of the postrevolutionary coalition. To his great surprise, Cárdenas executed a virtual coup that established his own supremacy and sent Calles packing to the United States for an "extended vacation."[2] Even more unexpectedly, Cárdenas mobilized peasants and workers in pursuit of the more radical goals of the 1910 revolution. He encouraged peasant associations to petition for land and claim rights promised in the Constitution of 1917. During his administration, more than 49 million acres of land were distributed, nearly twice as much as had been parceled out by all the previous postrevolutionary governments combined.[3] Most of these lands were distributed in the form of *ejidos* (collective land grants) to peasant groups. *Ejidatarios* (those who acquired *ejido* lands) became one of the most enduring bases of support for the government. Cárdenas also encouraged workers to form unions and demand higher wages and better working conditions. He established his nationalist credentials in 1938 when he wrested the petroleum industry from foreign investors and placed it under government control.

During the Cárdenas years (1934–1940), the bulk of the Mexican population was incorporated into the political system. Organizations of peasants and workers, middle-class groups, and the military were added to the official party, and the voices of the poor majority were heard within the councils of government, reducing the risk that they would become radicalized outside them. In addition, the Cárdenas years witnessed a great expansion of the role of the state as the government encouraged investment in industrialization, provided credit to agriculture, and created infrastructure.

Lázaro Cárdenas continues to be a national hero to Mexicans, who look back on his presidency as a period when government was clearly committed to improving the welfare of the country's poor. His other legacy was to institutionalize patterns of political succession and presidential behavior that continue to set standards for Mexico's leaders. He campaigned extensively, and his travels took him to remote villages and regions, where he listened to the demands and complaints of humble people. Cárdenas served a single six-year term, called a *sexenio,* and then relinquished full power to his successor—a pattern of presidential succession that still holds in Mexican politics. Cárdenas's conduct in office created hallowed traditions of presidential style and succession that all subsequent national leaders have observed.

The Politics of Rapid Development (1940–1982)

Although Cárdenas had directed a radical reshuffling of political power in the country, his successors were able to use the institutions he created to counteract his reforms. Ambitious local and regional party leaders and leaders of peasants' and workers' groups began to use their organizations as pawns in exchange for political favors. Gradually, the PRI developed a huge patronage machine, providing union and *ejido* leaders with jobs, opportunities for corruption, land, and other benefits in return for delivering their followers' political support. Extensive chains of personal relationships based on the exchange of favors allowed the party to amass far-reaching political control and limit opportunities for organizing independent of the PRI. These exchange relationships, known as **clientelism,** became the cement that built loyalty to the PRI and the political system.

This kind of political control enabled post-Cárdenas presidents to reorient the country's development away from the egalitarian social goals of the 1930s toward a development strategy in which the state actively encouraged industrialization and the accumulation of wealth. Initially, industrialization created jobs and made available a wide range of basic consumer goods to Mexico's burgeoning population. Economic growth rates were high during the 1940s, 1950s, and 1960s, and Mexicans flocked to the cities to take advantage of the jobs created in the manufacturing and construction industries. By the 1970s, however, industrial development policies were no longer generating rapid growth and could not keep pace with the rapidly rising demand for jobs.

The country's economy was in deep crisis by the mid-1970s. Just as policymakers began to take actions to correct the problems, vast new amounts of oil were discovered in the Gulf of Mexico. Soon, rapid economic growth in virtually every sector of the economy was refueled by extensive public investment programs paid for with oil revenues. Based on the promise of petroleum wealth, the government and private businesses borrowed huge amounts of capital from foreign lenders, who were eager to do business with a country that had so much oil. Unfortunately for Mexico, international petroleum prices plunged sharply in the early 1980s. Almost overnight, there was no more credit to be had and much less money from petroleum to pay for economic expansion or the interest on the debts incurred in preceding years. Mexico plunged into a deep economic crisis that affected many other countries around the world.

Crisis and Reform (1982–2001)

This economic crisis led two presidents, Miguel de la Madrid (1982–1988) and Carlos Salinas (1988–1994), to introduce the first major reversal of the country's development strategy since the 1940s. New policies were put in place to limit the government's role in the economy and to make it easier for Mexican producers to export their goods. This period clearly marked the beginning of a new effort to integrate Mexico more fully into the global economy. In 1993, by signing the **North American Free Trade Agreement (NAFTA),** which committed Mexico, the United States, and Canada to the elimination of trade barriers among them, Mexico's policymakers signaled the extent to which they envisioned that the future prosperity of

Mexican presidential candidates are expected to campaign hard, traveling to remote locations, making rousing campaign speeches, and meeting with citizens of humble origins. Here, presidential candidate Vicente Fox Quesada is on the campaign trail. *Source:* R. Kwiotek/Zeitenspiegel/Corbis/Sygma.

their country would be linked to that of its two neighbors to the north.

The economic reforms of the 1980s and 1990s were a turning point for Mexico and meant that the country's future development would be closely tied to international economic conditions. A major economic crisis at the end of 1994, in which billions of dollars of foreign investment fled the country, was indicative of this new international vulnerability. The peso lost half of its value against the dollar within a few days, and the government lacked the funds to pay its debt obligations. Suddenly, Mexico's status among nations seemed dubious once more, and the country felt betrayed by outgoing President Salinas, convinced that he had patched together a shaky house of cards only long enough to get himself out of office. The Mexican economy shrank by 6.2 percent in 1995, inflation soared, taxes rose while wages were frozen, and the bank system collapsed. The United States orchestrated a $50 billion bailout, $20 billion of which came directly from the U.S. Treasury. Faced with limited options, the administration of Ernesto Zedillo (1994–2000) implemented a severe and unpopular economic austerity program, which restored financial stability over the next two years.

Economic crisis was exacerbated by political concerns. On January 1, 1994, a guerrilla movement, the Zapatista Army of National Liberation (EZLN),

seized four towns in the southern state of Chiapas. The group demanded land, democracy, indigenous rights, and an immediate repeal of NAFTA. Many citizens throughout the country openly supported the aims of the rebels, pointing out that the movement brought to light the reality of two different Mexicos: one in which the privileged enjoyed the fruits of wealth and influence and another in which citizens were getting left behind because of poverty and repression. The government and the military were also criticized for inaction and human rights abuses in the state.

Following close on the heels of rebellion came the assassination of the PRI's presidential candidate, Luis Donaldo Colosio, on March 23, 1994, in the northern border city of Tijuana. The assassination shocked all citizens and shook the political elite deeply. The murder opened wide rifts within the PRI and unleashed a flood of speculation and distrust among the citizenry. Many Mexicans were convinced that the assassination was part of a conspiracy of party "dinosaurs," political hardliners who opposed any kind of democratic transformation.[4] Although that has never been proved, speculation about who was behind the assassination has continued to this day. Fear of violence helped provide the PRI with strong support in the August 1994 elections.

The PRI was able to remain in power, but these shocks provoked widespread disillusionment and frustration with the political system. Many citizens, especially in urban areas, decided that there was no longer any reason to support the PRI. Buoyed by a 1996 electoral reform, the opposition made important gains in the legislative elections the following year. For the first time in modern Mexican history, the PRI lost its absolute majority in the Chamber of Deputies, the lower house of the national legislature. Since then, the congress has shown increasing dynamism as a counterbalance to the presidency, blocking executive decisions, demanding unrestricted information, and initiating new legislation. In addition, opposition parties have won important governorships and mayorships. The 2000 election of Vicente Fox as the first non-PRI president in seven decades was the culmination of this electoral revolution.

The Fox Presidency and Post–September 11 Mexico (2001 to the Present)

When Vicente Fox entered Los Pinos, the official residence of the Mexican president, in December 2000, hopes were high that his administration would transform the country, consolidating the progress towards democracy that had been made, while also improving public services and reducing poverty. However, Fox found it difficult to bring about the changes that he had promised to the Mexican people. The difficulties faced by the new president as he attempted to implement his ambitious agenda arose in part because he and his team lacked experience in addressing the challenges of governance on a national scale. However, a bigger problem for Fox was that new structural factors placed significant limits on the president's ability to secure approval for his policies. Because he lacked the compliant congressional majority and the close relationship with his party that his PRI predecessors had enjoyed, Fox was unable to overcome opposition to many of his initiatives. Proposals for a reform of the tax code and for the restructuring of the government-controlled electricity corporation went down to defeat, and the president was subjected to catcalls and heckling when he made his annual reports to the congress.

With his legislative agenda stalled, Fox hoped that achievements in international policy would enhance his prestige at home. He was particularly hopeful that a close personal connection with the new U.S.

president, George W. Bush, would facilitate an agreement under which a greater number of Mexicans would be able to migrate to the United States and work there. During his first months in office, Fox had good reasons to be optimistic that he might be successful in building a more constructive relationship with Mexico's powerful neighbor. Bush had indicated that building a partnership with Mexico would be an important component of his foreign policy program, and the two governments initiated talks on a possible migration accord in 2001.

The events of September 11, 2001, dramatically changed the outlook, however. After the terrorist attacks on the World Trade Center and the Pentagon, top U.S. officials immediately turned their attention away from Mexico and Latin America and toward Afghanistan and the Middle East, diminishing the prospects for significant breakthroughs in U.S.-Mexican relations. It did not help that some in Washington felt that Mexico had been slow to express its solidarity with the United States in the wake of the attacks. The possibility of an agreement on migration disappeared as Washington moved to assert control over its borders and to restrict access to the United States. In the months that followed, Mexican officials cooperated with their U.S. counterparts in efforts designed to improve security at border crossings between the two nations, but many in Mexico City were frustrated that no progress was being made on issues like migration that were important to their country.

In 2002, Mexico began a two-year term as a member of the United Nations Security Council. The Fox administration intended the country's return to the council after a twenty-year absence to signal the desire of a democratic Mexico to play a larger role in international affairs. Serving on the Security Council presented the Mexican government with a new set of dilemmas, however. Deliberations at the UN headquarters in New York focused increasingly on U.S. proposals for the use of force against Iraq. The Bush administration, aware of Mexico's close economic ties with the United States and of Fox's personal friendship with the U.S. president, believed that Mexico could be convinced to support its position on the issue. Public opinion in Mexico was so deeply opposed to an invasion of Iraq, however, that Fox's government decided to reject U.S.-sponsored resolutions on the subject. The U.S. officials who had counted on Mexican support were bitterly disappointed, but what they had failed to realize was that memories of past U.S. invasions and occupations still made questions involving national sovereignty very sensitive in Mexico and that any Mexican government that effectively sponsored a U.S. attack on a smaller, weaker country would have to confront a tremendous backlash. This episode, and the Fox administration's post-9/11 foreign policy more generally, show that nationalism and ambivalence about Mexico's proximity to the United States remained important factors in the country's politics at the beginning of the twenty-first century.

Themes and Implications

Historical Junctures and Political Themes

The modern Mexican state emerged out of a popular revolution that proclaimed goals of democratic government, social justice, and national control of the country's resources. In the chaotic years after the revolution, the state created conditions for political and social peace. By incorporating peasants and workers into party and government institutions, and by providing benefits to low-income groups during the 1930s, it became widely accepted as legitimate. In encouraging considerable economic growth in the years after 1940, it also created a belief in its ability to provide material improvements in the quality of life for large portions of the population. These factors worked together to create a strong state capable of guiding economic and political life in the country. Only in the 1980s did this system begin to crumble.

In its external relations, Mexico has always prided itself on ideological independence from the world's great powers. For many decades, its large population, cultural richness, political stability, and front-line position regarding the United States prompted Mexico to consider itself a natural leader of Latin America and the developing world in general. After the early 1980s, however, the government rejected this position in favor of rapid integration into a global economy. The country aspired to the status enjoyed by the newly industrialized countries of the world, such as South Korea, Malaysia, and Taiwan. While the reforms of the 1980s and 1990s, and especially NAFTA, have advanced this

goal, many citizens are concerned that the government has accepted a position of political, cultural, and economic subordination to the United States.

Mexico enjoyed considerable economic advancement after the 1940s, but economic and political crises after 1980 shook confidence in its ability to achieve its economic goals and highlighted the conflict between a market-oriented development strategy and the country's philosophical tradition of a strong and protective state. The larger questions of whether a new development strategy can generate growth, whether Mexican products can find profitable markets overseas, whether investors can create extensive job opportunities for millions of unemployed and part-time workers, and whether the country can maintain the confidence of those investors over the longer term continue to challenge the country.

Politically, after the Revolution of 1910, the country opted not for true democracy but for representation through government-mediated organizations within a **corporatist state,** in which interest groups became an institutionalized part of state structure rather than an independent source of advocacy. This increased state power in relation to **civil society.** The state took the lead in defining goals for the country's development and, through the school system, the party, and the media, inculcated in the population a broad sense of its legitimate right to set such goals. In addition, the state had extensive resources at its disposal to control or co-opt dissent and purchase political loyalty. The PRI was an essential channel through which material goods, jobs, the distribution of land, and the allocation of development projects flowed to increase popular support for the system or to buy off opposition to it.

This does not mean that Mexican society was unorganized or passive. Indeed, many Mexicans were actively involved in local community organizations, religious activities, unions, and public interest groups. But traditionally, the scope for challenging the government was very limited. At the same time, Mexico's strong state did not become openly repressive except when directly challenged. On the contrary, officials in the government and the party generally worked hard to find ways to resolve conflicts peacefully and to use behind-the-scenes accommodation to bring conflicting interests into accord.

By the 1980s, cracks began to appear in the traditional ways in which Mexican citizens interacted with the government. As the PRI began to lose its capacity to control political activities and as civic groups increasingly insisted on their right to remain independent from the PRI and the government, the terms of the state-society relationship were clearly in need of redefinition. The administration of President Zedillo signaled its willingness to cede political power to successful opposition parties in fair elections, and electoral reform in 1996 and competitive elections in 1997 were significant steps that led to the defeat of the PRI in 2000. Mexico's future stability depends on how well a more democratic government can accommodate conflicting interests while at the same time providing economic opportunities to a largely poor population.

Implications for Comparative Politics

The Mexican political system is unique among developing countries in the extent to which it managed to institutionalize and maintain civilian political authority for a very long time. In a world of developing nations wracked by political turmoil, military coups, and regime changes, the PRI regime established enduring institutions of governance and conditions for political stability. Other developing countries have sought to emulate the Mexican model of stability based on an alliance between a dominant party and a strong development-oriented state, but no other government has been able to create a system that has had widespread legitimacy for so long. Among developed nations, perhaps Japan comes closest to this model. The PRI's revolutionary heritage, as well as its ability to maintain a sense of national identity, were important factors in accounting for its political continuity.

Currently, Mexico is a nation undergoing significant political change without widespread violence, transforming itself from a corporatist state to a democratic one for the first time in its long history. At the same time, it struggles to resolve the conflicts of development through integration with its North American neighbors. Mexico has been categorized as an upper middle-income developing country, and its per capita income is comparable to countries such as Latvia, Malaysia, South Africa, and Chile.[5] It has made significant strides in industrialization, which accounts for about 27.2 percent of the country's gross domestic product (GDP). Agriculture contributes about 4.0 percent to GDP, and services contribute some 68.9 percent.[6] This structure is very similar to the economic profiles of Argentina, Brazil, Poland, and Hungary. But unlike those countries, Mexico is oil rich. The government-owned petroleum industry is a ready source of revenue and foreign exchange, but this commodity also makes the economy extremely vulnerable to changes in international oil prices.

Mexico's industrial and petroleum-based economy gives the country a per capita income higher than those of most other developing nations. If income were spread evenly among all Mexicans, each would receive $6,230 annually—far more than the per capita incomes of Nigeria ($320), India ($530), and China ($1,100), but considerably less than those of France ($24,770), Germany ($25,250), Britain ($28,350), and Mexico's wealthy neighbor, the United States ($37,500).[7] Of course, income is not spread evenly. Mexico suffers from great inequalities in how wealth is distributed, and poverty continues to be a grim reality for millions of Mexicans. The way the country promoted economic growth and industrialization is important in explaining why widespread poverty has persisted and why political power is not more equitably distributed.

Section ❷ Political Economy and Development

State and Economy

During the years of the Porfiriato (1876–1911), Mexico began to produce some textiles, footwear, glassware, paper, beer, tiles, furniture, and other simple products. At that time, however, policymakers were convinced that Mexico could grow rich by exporting its raw materials to more economically advanced countries. Their efforts to attract domestic and international investment encouraged a major boom in the production and export of products such as henequin (for making rope), coffee, cacao (cocoa beans), cattle, silver, and gold. Soon, the country had become so attractive to foreign investors that large amounts of land, the country's petroleum, its railroad network, and its mining wealth were largely controlled by foreigners. Nationalist reaction against the power of these foreign interests played a significant role in the tensions that produced the Revolution of 1910.

In the postrevolutionary Mexican state, this nationalism combined with a sense of social justice inspired by popular revolutionary leaders such as Zapata. Mexicans widely shared the idea that the state had the responsibility to generate wealth for all its citizens. As a result, the country adopted a strategy in which the government guided the process of industrial and agricultural development. Often referred to as **state capitalism,** this development strategy relied heavily on government actions to encourage private investment and reduce risks for private entrepreneurs. In the twenty years following the revolution, many of those concerned about the country's development became convinced that economic growth would not occur unless Mexico could industrialize more fully. They argued that reliance on exports of agricultural products, minerals, and petroleum—called the agro-export model of development—forced the country to import manufactured goods, which, over the long term, would always cost more than what was earned from exports. Mexico, they believed, should begin to manufacture the goods that it was currently importing.

Import Substitution and Its Consequences

Between 1940 and 1982, Mexico pursued a form of state capitalism and a model of industrialization known as import substitution, or **import substituting industrialization (ISI).** Like Brazil and other Latin American countries during the same period, the government promoted the development of industries to supply the domestic market by encouraging domestic and international investment; providing credit and tax incentives to industrialists; maintaining low rates of inflation; and keeping wage demands low through subsidized food, transportation, housing, and health care for workers. It also fostered industrialization by establishing state-owned steel mills, electric power generators, ports, and petroleum production and by using tariffs and import licenses to protect Mexican

industries from foreign competition. These policies had considerable success. Initially, the country produced mainly simple products like shoes, clothing, and processed foods. But by the 1960s and 1970s, it was also producing consumer durables (refrigerators, automobiles, trucks), intermediate goods (steel, petrochemicals, and other products used in the manufacturing process), and capital goods (heavy machinery to produce manufactured items).

Mexican agriculture was also affected by this drive to industrialize. With the massive agrarian reform of the 1930s (see Section 1), the *ejido* had become an important structure in the rural economy, accounting for half the cultivated area of the country and 51 percent of the value of agricultural production by 1940. After Cárdenas left office, however, government policymakers moved away from the economic development of the *ejidos*. They became committed instead to developing a strong, entrepreneurial private sector in agriculture. For them, "the development of private agriculture would be the 'foundation of industrial greatness.'"[8] They wanted this sector to provide foodstuffs for the growing cities, raw materials for industry, and foreign exchange from exports. To encourage these goals, the government invested in transportation networks, irrigation projects, and agricultural storage facilities. It provided extension services and invested in research. It encouraged imports of technology to improve output and mechanize production. Since policymakers believed that modern commercial farmers would respond better to these investments and services than would peasants on small plots of land, the government provided most of its assistance to large landowners.

The government's encouragement of industry and agriculture set the country on a three-decade path of sustained growth. Between 1940 and 1950, GDP grew at an annual average of 6.7 percent, while manufacturing increased at an average of 8.1 percent. In the following two decades, GDP growth rates remained impressive, and manufacturing growth continued to outpace overall growth in the economy. In the 1950s, manufacturing achieved an average of 7.3 percent growth annually and in the 1960s, 10.1 percent annually. Agricultural production grew rapidly as new areas were brought under cultivation and green revolution technology (scientifically improved seeds, fertilizers, and pesticides) was extensively adopted on large farms. These were years of great optimism as foreign investment increased, the middle class grew larger, and indicators for health and welfare steadily improved. Even the poorest Mexicans believed that their lives were improving. Table 1 presents data that summarize a number of advancements during this period. So impressive was Mexico's economic performance that it was referred to internationally as the Mexican Miracle.

While the government took the lead in encouraging industrialization, it was not long before a group of domestic entrepreneurs developed a special relationship with the state. Government policies protected their products through high tariffs or special licensing requirements, limiting imports of competing goods. Business elites in Mexico received subsidized credit to invest in equipment and plants; they benefited from cheap, subsidized energy; and they rarely had to pay

taxes. These protected businesses emerged as powerful players in national politics. In the 1940s and 1950s, they led a set of industry-related interest groups that worked to promote and sustain favorable policies. With this organizational foundation, groups like the chambers of industry, commerce, and banking began to play increasingly important roles in government policymaking. They were able to veto efforts by the government to cut back on their benefits, and they lobbied for even more advantages. The government remained the source of most policy initiatives, but generally it was not able to move far in the face of opposition from those who benefited most from its policies.

Workers also became more important players in national politics. As mentioned in Section 1, widespread unionization occurred under Cárdenas, and workers won many rights that had been promised in the Constitution of 1917. Cárdenas organized the

Table 1

Mexican Development, 1940–2003

	1940	1950	1960	1970	1980	1990	2003
Population (thousands)	19,815	26,282	38,020	52,771	70,416	88,598	102,300
Life expectancy (years)[b]	–	51.6	58.6	62.6	67.4	68.9	73.6
Infant mortality (per 1,000 live births)	–	–	86.3	70.9	49.9	42.6	23.0
Illiteracy (% of population age 15 and over)	–	42.5	34.5	25.0	16.0	12.7	9.0
Urban population (% of total)	–	–	50.7	59.0	66.4	72.6	75.0
Economically active population in agriculture (% of total)	–	58.3	55.1	44.0	36.6	22.0	18.0[a]

	1940–1950	1950–1960	1960–1970	1970–1980	1980–1990	1990–2003
GDP growth rate (average annual percent)	6.7	5.8	7.6	6.7	1.6	1.3
Per capita GDP growth rate	–	–	3.7	3.7	–0.7	–0.2

[a]2001

[b]Five-year average.

Sources: Statistical Abstract for Latin America (New York: United Nations, Economic Commission for Latin America, various years); Roger Hansen, *The Politics of Mexican Development* (Baltimore, Md.: Johns Hopkins University Press, 1971); *Statistical Bulletin of the OAS.* World Bank Country Data for Mexico, http://www.worldbank.org/data/countrydata/countrydata.html; World Bank, World Development Indicators.

unions into the Confederation of Mexican Workers (CTM), which became the most powerful voice of organized labor within the PRI. The policy changes initiated in the 1940s, however, made the unions more dependent on the government for benefits and protection; the government also limited the right to strike. Despite the fact that unions were closely controlled organized workers continued to be an elite within the country's working classes. Union membership meant job security and important benefits such as housing subsidies and health care. These factors helped compensate for the lack of democracy within the labor movement. Moreover, labor leaders had privileged access to the country's political leadership and benefited personally from their control over jobs, contracts, and working conditions. In return, they guaranteed labor peace.[9]

In agriculture, those who benefited from government policies and services were primarily farmers who had enough land and economic resources to irrigate and mechanize, as well as the capacity to make technological improvements in their farming methods and crops. By the 1950s, a group of large, commercially oriented farmers had emerged to dominate the agricultural economy.[10] Like their urban counterparts in business, they became rich and powerful. These rural landowners also became firm supporters of the continuation of government policies that provided them with special advantages.

There were significant costs to this pattern of economic and political development. Most important, government policies eventually limited the potential for further growth.[11] Industrialists who received extensive subsidies and benefits from government had few incentives to produce efficiently. High tariffs kept out foreign competition, further reducing reasons for efficiency or quality in production. Importing technology to support industrialization eventually became a drain on the country's foreign exchange. In addition, the costs of providing benefits to workers increased beyond the capacity of the government to generate revenue, especially because tax rates were kept low as a further incentive to investors. Mexico's tax rates, in fact, were among the lowest in the world, and opportunities to avoid payment were extensive. Eventually, the ISI strategy became less effective in generating new jobs, as industrialists moved from investing in labor-intensive industries such as processed foods and textiles to capital-intensive industries such as automobiles, refrigerators, and heavy equipment.

Moreover, as the economy grew, and with it the power of industrial, agricultural, and urban interests, many were left behind. The ranks of the urban poor grew steadily, particularly from the 1960s on. Mexico developed a sizable **informal sector**—workers who produced and sold goods and services at the margin of the economic system and faced extreme insecurity. By 1970, a large proportion of Mexico City's population was living in inner-city tenements or squatter settlements surrounding the city.[12]

Also left behind in the country's development after 1940 were peasant farmers. Their lands were often the least fertile, plot sizes were minuscule, and access to markets was impeded by poor transportation and exploitive middlemen who trucked products to markets for exorbitant fees. Farming in the *ejido* communities, where land was held communally, was particularly difficult. Because *ejido* land could not be sold or (until the early 1980s) rented, *ejidatarios* could not borrow money from private banks because they had nothing to pledge as collateral if they defaulted on their payments. Government banks provided credit, but usually only to those who had political connections. The government invested little in small infrastructure projects throughout the 1960s, and agricultural research and extension focused on the large-farm sector. Not surprisingly, the *ejido* sector consistently reported low productivity.

Increasing disparities in rural and urban incomes, coupled with high population growth rates, contributed to the emergence of rural guerrilla movements and student protests in the mid- and late 1960s. The government was particularly alarmed in 1968, when a student movement openly challenged the government on the eve of the Mexico City Olympic Games. Moreover, by the early 1970s, it was becoming evident that the size of the population, growing at a rate of some 3.5 percent a year, and the structure of income distribution were impeding further industrial development. The domestic market was limited by poverty; many Mexicans could not afford the sophisticated manufactured products the country would need to produce in order to keep growing under the import substitution model.

The Mexican government had hoped that industrialization would free the economy from excessive dependence on the industrialized world, and particularly on the United States, making the country less subject to abrupt swings in prices for primary commodities. Industrialization, however, highlighted new vulnerabilities. Advanced manufacturing processes required ever more foreign investment and imported technology. Concern grew about powerful multinational companies, which had invested heavily in the country in the 1960s, and about purchasing foreign technology with scarce foreign exchange. By the late 1960s, the country was no longer able to meet domestic demand for basic foodstuffs and was forced to import increasingly large quantities of food, costing the government foreign exchange that it could have used for better purposes. By the 1970s, some policymakers had become convinced that industrialization had actually increased the country's dependence on advanced industrial countries and particularly on the United States.

Sowing the Oil and Reaping a Crisis

In the early 1970s, Mexico faced the threat of social crisis brought on by rural poverty, chaotic urbanization, high population growth, and the questioning of political legitimacy. The government responded by increasing investment in infrastructure and public industries, regulating the flow of foreign capital, and increasing social spending. It was spending much more than it generated, causing the public internal debt to grow rapidly and requiring heavy borrowing abroad. Between 1971 and 1976, inflation rose from an annual average of 5.3 percent to almost 16 percent, and the foreign debt more than tripled. In response to mounting evidence that its policies could not be sustained, the government devalued the peso in 1976 to encourage exports and discourage imports. It also signed a stabilization agreement with the International Monetary Fund (IMF) to reduce government spending, increase tax collection, and control inflation. Little progress was made in changing existing policies, however, because just as the seriousness of the economic situation was being recognized, vast new finds of oil came to the rescue.

Between 1978 and 1982, Mexico was transformed into a major oil exporter. As international oil prices

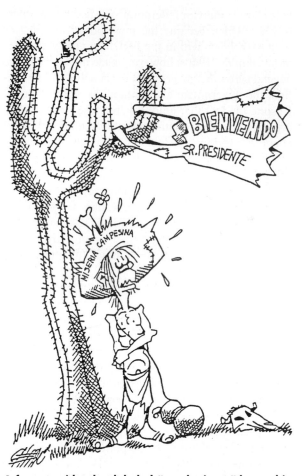

A farmer with a hat labeled "rural misery" hangs his shirt on a cactus: "Welcome, Mr. President." Among those who have benefited least from the government's development policies are the rural poor.
Source: Ausencias y Presencias Gente de Ayer y Hoy en su Tinta: Problematica Politica, Social, Vista por un Cartoonista Potosino by Luis Chessal, Unversidad Autonoma de San Luis Potosi, Mexico, 1984.

rose rapidly, from $13.30 per barrel in 1978 to $33.20 per barrel in 1981, so too did the country's fortunes, along with those of other oil-rich countries such as Nigeria, Iran, Indonesia, and Venezuela. The administration of President José López Portillo (1976–1982) embarked on a policy to "sow the oil" in the economy and "administer the abundance" with vast investment projects in virtually all sectors and major new initiatives to reduce poverty and deal with declining agricultural productivity. Oil revenues paid for much of this expansion, but the foreign debt also mounted as both public and private sectors borrowed heavily to finance investments and lavish consumer spending.

By 1982, Mexico's foreign debt was $86 billion, and the peso was seriously overvalued, making Mexican products more expensive on the world market. Oil accounted for 77.2 percent of the country's exports, causing the economy to be extremely vulnerable to changes in oil prices. And change they did. Global overproduction brought the international price for Mexican petroleum down to $26.30 a barrel in 1982 and to even lower levels in the years that followed. Revenues from exports declined dramatically. At the same time, the United States tightened its monetary policy by raising interest rates, and access to foreign credit dried up. Wealthy Mexicans responded by sending vast amounts of capital out of the country just as the country's international creditors were demanding repayment on their loans. In August 1982, the government announced that the country could not pay the interest on its foreign debt, triggering a crisis that reverberated around the world. The impact of these conditions on the Mexican economy was devastating. GDP growth in 1982 was –0.6 percent and fell to –4.2 percent the following year.

The economic crisis had several important implications for structures of power and privilege in Mexico. First, faith in the import substitution policy was destroyed. The crisis convinced even the most diehard believers that import substitution created inefficiencies in production, failed to generate sufficient employment, cost the government far too much in subsidies, and increased dependency on industrialized countries. In addition, the power of interest groups and their ability to influence government policy declined. Bankruptcy and recession exacted their toll on the fortunes of even large entrepreneurs. As economic hardship affected their members, traditional business organizations lost their ability to put strong pressure on the government.

Similarly, the country's relatively privileged unions lost much of their bargaining power with government over issues of wages and protection. Union leaders loyal to the PRI emphasized the need for peace and order to help the nation get through tough times, while inflation and job loss focused many of the country's workers on putting food on the table. A shift in employment from the formal to the informal economy further fragmented what had once been the most powerful sector of the party. Cuts in government subsidies for public transportation, food, electricity, and gasoline created new hardships for workers. The combination of these factors weakened the capacity of labor to resist policy changes that affected the benefits they received.

In addition, new voices emerged to demand that the government respond to the crisis. During the recession years of the 1980s, wages lost between 40 and 50 percent of their value, increasingly large numbers of people became unemployed, inflation cut deeply into middle-class incomes, and budgets for health and education services were severely cut back. A wide variety of interests began to organize outside the PRI to demand that government do something about the situation. Massive earthquakes in Mexico City in September 1985 proved to be a watershed for Mexican society. Severely disappointed by the government's failure to respond to the problems created by death, destruction, and homelessness, hundreds of communities organized rescue efforts, soup kitchens, shelters, and rehabilitation initiatives. A surging sense of political empowerment developed, as groups long accustomed to dependence on government learned that they could solve their problems better without government than with it.[13]

Moreover, the PRI was challenged by the increased popularity of opposition political parties, one of them headed by Cuauhtémoc Cárdenas, the son of the country's most revered president, Lázaro Cárdenas. The elections of 1988 became a focus for protest against the economic dislocation caused by the crisis and the political powerlessness that most citizens felt. Carlos Salinas, the PRI candidate, received a bare majority of 50.7 percent, and opposition parties claimed widespread electoral fraud.

New Strategies: Structural Reforms and NAFTA

Demands on the Salinas administration to deal with the economic and political crisis were extensive. At the same time, the weakening of the old centers of political power provided the government with a major opportunity to reorient the country's strategy for economic development. Between 1988 and 1994, the mutually dependent relationship between industry and government was weakened as new free-market policies were put in place. Deregulation gave the private sector more freedom to pursue economic activities and less reason to seek special favors from government. A number of large government industries were reorganized and sold to private investors. A constitutional revision made it possible for *ejidatarios* to become owners of individual plots of land; this made them less dependent on government but more vulnerable to losing their land. In addition, financial sector reforms that changed laws about banking and established a stock exchange encouraged the emergence of new banks, brokerage firms, and insurance companies.

Salinas pursued, and Zedillo continued, an overhaul of the federal system and the way government agencies worked together. Called the New Federalism, it was an attempt to give greater power and budgetary responsibilities to state and local governments, which had been historically very weak in Mexico. Beginning with education and health, the presidents hoped decentralization would make government more efficient and effective. Additionally, the central bank, the institution responsible for making national monetary policy, became independent from the government in 1994, although exchange rates are still determined by the finance ministry.

Among the most far-reaching initiatives was NAFTA. This agreement with Canada and the United States created the basis for gradual introduction of free trade among the three countries. These changes were a major reversal of import substitution and economic intervention that had marked government policies in the past. However, the liberalization of the Mexican economy and opening of its markets to foreign competition increased the vulnerability of the country to changes in international economic conditions. These factors, as well as mismanaged economic policies, led to a major economic crisis for the country at the end of 1994 and profound recession in 1995. NAFTA has meant that the fate of the Mexican economy is increasingly linked to the health of the American economy. For example, the economic strength of Mexico's northern neighbor sheltered the country from the contagion of the 1997–1998 Asian financial crisis, while the economic cooldown in the United States slowed growth in Mexico in the early 2000s.

Society and Economy

Mexico's economic development has had a significant impact on social conditions in the country. Overall, the standard of living rose markedly after the 1940s. Rates of infant mortality, literacy, and life expectancy have steadily improved. Provision of health and education services expanded until government cutbacks on social expenditures in the early 1980s. Among the most important consequences of economic growth was the development of a large middle class, most of whom live in Mexico's numerous large cities. By the 1980s, a third or more of Mexican households could claim a middle-class lifestyle: a steady income, secure food and shelter, access to decent education and health services, a car, some disposable income and savings, and some security that their children would be able to experience happy and healthy lives.

These achievements reflect well on the ability of the economy to increase social well-being in the country. However, the impressive economic growth through the early 1970s and between 1978 and 1982 could have produced greater social progress. In terms of standard indicators of social development—infant mortality, literacy, and life expectancy—Mexico fell behind a number of Latin American countries that grew less rapidly but provided more effectively for their populations. Costa Rica, Colombia, Argentina, Chile, and Uruguay had lower overall growth but greater social development in the period after 1940. These countries paid more attention to the distribution of the benefits of growth than did Mexico. Moreover, rapid industrialization has made Mexico City one of the most polluted cities in the world, and in some rural areas, oil exploitation left devastating environmental damage.

Mexico's economic development also resulted in a widening gap between the wealthy and the poor and among different regions in the country. Although the poor are better off than they were in the early days of the country's drive toward industrialization, they are worse off when compared to middle- and upper-income groups. In 1950, the bottom 40 percent of the country's households accounted for about 14 percent of total personal income, while the top 30 percent had 60 percent of total income.[14] In 2000, it is estimated, the bottom 40 percent accounted for about 10.3 percent of income, while the top 40 percent shared 78.1 percent.[15] As the rich grew richer, the gap between the rich and the poor increased.

Among the poorest are those in rural areas who have little or no access to productive land. Harsh conditions in the countryside have fueled a half-century of migration to the cities. Nevertheless, some 25 million Mexicans continue to live in rural areas, many of them in deep poverty. Many work for substandard wages and migrate seasonally to search for jobs in order to sustain their families. Among rural inhabitants with access to land, almost half have five hectares or less. This land is usually not irrigated and depends on erratic rainfall. It is often leached of nutrients as a result of centuries of cultivation, population pressure, and erosion. The incidence of disease, malnutrition, and illiteracy is much higher in Mexico's rural areas than in urban areas. When the rebels in Chiapas called for jobs, land, education, and health facilities, they were clearly reflecting the realities of life in much of the country.

Poverty has a regional dimension in Mexico. The northern areas of the country are significantly better off than the southern and central areas. In the north, large commercial farms using modern technologies grow fruits, vegetables, and grains for export. The U.S. border, the principal destination of agricultural products, is close at hand, and transportation networks are extensive and generally in good condition. Moreover, industrial cities such as Monterrey and Tijuana provide steady jobs for skilled and unskilled labor. Along the border, a band of manufacturing and assembly plants, called *maquiladoras,* provides many jobs, particularly for young women who are seeking some escape from the burdens of rural life or the constraints of traditional family life.

In the southern and central regions of the country, the population is denser, the land poorer, and the number of *ejidatarios* eking out subsistence greater. Transportation is often difficult, and during parts of the year, some areas may be inaccessible because of heavy rains and flooding. Most of Mexico's remaining indigenous groups live in the southern regions, often in remote areas where they have been forgotten

by government programs and exploited by regional bosses for generations. The conditions that spurred the Chiapas rebellion are found throughout the southern states.

The economic crisis of the 1980s had an impact on social conditions in the country as well. Wages declined by about half, and unemployment soared as businesses collapsed and the government laid off workers in public offices and privatized industries. The informal sector expanded rapidly. Here, people eked out a living by hawking chewing gum, umbrellas, sponges, candy, shoelaces, mirrors, and a variety of other items in the street; jumping in front of cars at stoplights to wash windshields and sell newspapers; producing and repairing cheap consumer goods such as shoes and clothing; and selling services on a daily or hourly basis. While the informal sector provides important goods and services, conditions of work are often dangerous, and uncertainty as to where the next peso will come from is endemic.

The economic crisis of the 1980s also reduced the quality and availability of social services. Expenditures on education and health declined after 1982 as the government imposed austerity measures. Salaries of primary school teachers declined by 34 percent between 1983 and 1988, and many teachers worked second and even third jobs in order to make ends meet. Per capita health expenditures declined from a high of about $19 in 1980 to about $11 in 1990. Although indicators of mortality did not rise during this troubled decade, the incidence of diseases associated with poverty—malnutrition, cholera, anemia, and dysentery—increased. The crisis began to ease in the early 1990s, however, and many came to believe that conditions would improve for the poor. The government began investing in social services. When a new economic crisis occurred, however, unemployment surged, and austerity measures severely limited investments. Despite considerable recovery in the late 1990s, wages remain low for the majority of workers while taxes and the cost of living have increased.

Mexico in the Global Economy

The crisis that began in 1982 altered Mexico's international policies. In response to that crisis, the government relaxed restrictions on the ability of foreigners to own property, reduced and eliminated tariffs, and did away with most import licenses. Foreign investment was courted in the hope of increasing the manufacture of goods for export. The government also introduced a series of incentives to encourage the private sector to produce goods for export. In 1986, Mexico joined the General Agreement on Tariffs and Trade (GATT), a multilateral agreement that seeks to promote freer trade among countries that later became the basis for the World Trade Organization (WTO), and in the 1990s and early 2000s Mexico signed trade pacts with many countries in Latin America, Europe, and elsewhere.

The government's effort to pursue a more outward-oriented development strategy culminated in the ratification of NAFTA in 1993, with gradual implementation beginning on January 1, 1994. This agreement is important to Mexico. In 2000, 89 percent of the country's exports were sent to the United States, and 74 percent of its imports came from that country.[16] Access to the U.S. market is essential to Mexico and to domestic and foreign investors. NAFTA signaled a new period in U.S.-Mexican relations by making closer integration of the two economies a certainty.

NAFTA also entails risks for Mexico. Domestic producers worry about competition from U.S. firms. Farmers worry that Mexican crops cannot compete effectively with those grown in the United States; for example, peasant producers of corn and beans have been hard hit by the availability of lower-priced U.S.-grown grains. In addition, many believe that embracing free trade with Canada and the United States indicates a loss of sovereignty. Certainly, Mexico's economic situation is now more vulnerable to the ebb and flow of economic conditions in the U.S. economy. Some are also concerned with increasing evidence of "cultural imperialism" as U.S. movies, music, fashions, and lifestyles increasingly influence consumers. Indeed, for Mexico, which has traditionally feared the power of the United States in its domestic affairs, internationalization of political and economic relationships poses particularly difficult problems of adjustment.

On the other hand, the United States, newly aware of the importance of the Mexican economy to its own economic growth and concerned about instability on its southern border, hammered together a $50 billion economic assistance program composed of U.S., European, and IMF commitments to support its neighbor when crisis struck in 1994. The Mexican government imposed a new stabilization package that contained austerity measures, higher interest rates, and limits on wages. Remarkably, by 1998, Mexico had paid off all of its obligations to the United States.

Globalization is also stripping Mexico of some of the secrecy that traditionally surrounded government decision making, electoral processes, and efforts to deal with political dissent. International attention increasingly focuses on the country, and investors want clear and up-to-date information on what is occurring in the economy. The Internet and email, along with lower international telephone rates, are increasing information flows across borders. The government can no longer respond to events such as the peasant rebellion in Chiapas, alleged electoral fraud, or the management of exchange rates without considering how such actions will be perceived in Tokyo, Frankfurt, Ottawa, London, or Washington.

Section ❸ Governance and Policy-Making

Mexico is a federal republic, although until the 1990s, state and local governments had few resources and a limited sphere of action when compared with the national level. Under the PRI, the executive branch held almost all power, while the legislative and judiciary branches followed the executive's lead and were considered rubber-stamp bodies. During the years of PRI hegemony, the government was civilian, authoritarian, and corporatist. Currently, Mexico has multiparty competitive elections, and power is less concentrated in the executive branch and the national government. Since the mid-1980s, great efforts have been made to reinvigorate the nation's laws and institutions and to make the country more democratic.

Organization of the State

According to the supreme law of the land, the Constitution of 1917, Mexico's political institutions resemble those of the United States. There are three branches of government, and a set of checks and balances limits the power of each. The congress is composed of the Senate and the Chamber of Deputies. One hundred twenty-eight senators are elected, three from each of the country's thirty-one states; three from the Federal District, which contains the capital, Mexico City; and another thirty-two elected nationally by **proportional representation.** The 500 members of the Chamber of Deputies are elected from 300 electoral districts— 300 by simple majority vote and 200 by proportional representation. State and local governments are also elected. The president, governors, and senators are elected for six years, and deputies (representatives in the lower house) and municipal officials are elected for three.

In practice, the Mexican system is very different from that of the United States. The constitution is a very long document that is easily amended, especially when compared to that of the United States. It lays out the structure of government and guarantees a wide range of human rights, including familiar ones such as freedom of speech and protection of the law, but also economic and social rights such as the right to a job and the right to health care. Economic and social rights are acknowledged but in practice do not reach all of the population. Although there has been some decentralization of power, the political system is still much more centralized than that of the United States. Congress is now more active as a decision-making arena and as a check on presidential power, but the executive remains central to initiating policy and managing political conflict.

The Executive

The President and the Cabinet

The presidency is the central institution of governance and policymaking in Mexico. Until the 1990s, the incumbent president always selected who would run as the PRI's next presidential candidate, appointed officials to all positions of power in the government and

the party, and often named the candidates who almost automatically won elections as governors, senators, deputies, and local officials. Even with a non-PRI incumbent, the president continues to set the broad outlines of policy for the administration and has numerous resources to ensure that those policy preferences are adopted. Until the mid 1970s, Mexican presidents were considered above criticism in national politics and revered as symbols of national progress and well-being. While economic and political events of the 1980s and 1990s diminished presidential prestige and politicians are showing an increasing willingness to stand up to the chief executive in today's multiparty system, the extent of presidential power remains a legacy of the long period of PRI ascendance.

Mexican presidents have a set of formal powers that allows them to initiate legislation, lead in foreign policy, create government agencies, make policy by decree or through administrative regulations and procedures, and appoint a wide range of public officials. More important, informal powers provide them with the capacity to exert considerable control. The president manages a vast patronage machine for filling positions in government and initiates legislation and policies that were, until recently, routinely approved by the congress. When Vicente Fox became president in 2000, he promised many fewer personnel changes in government than under previous incumbents. He promised more open government and greater diversity among his cabinet and other appointees. His powers have been curtailed to some degree by a more forceful congress and his administration's lack of experience in governing.

Under the PRI, presidents were always male and almost always members of the outgoing president's cabinet. Four of the five presidents who served between 1946 and 1976 had previously been ministers of the interior, with responsibility for the maintenance of law and order in the country. With the expansion of the government's role in economic development, candidates in the 1970s and 1980s were selected from the ministries that managed the economy. José López Portillo (1976–1982) had been minister of finance, and Miguel de la Madrid (1982–1988) and Carlos Salinas (1988–1994) had served as ministers of planning and budgeting. The selection of Luis Donaldo Colosio, who had been minister of social development and welfare, was thought by political observers to signal renewed concern with social problems. When Colosio was assassinated in 1994, the selection of Ernesto Zedillo, who had first been minister of planning and budgeting and then minister of education, was interpreted as reflecting an ongoing concern with social issues and as an effort to maintain the policies of economic liberalization that Salinas had introduced. With the victory of the PAN in 2000, this long tradition came to an end. Prior to running for president, Vicente Fox had been in business and had served as the governor of the state of Guanajuato.

Mexican presidential candidates since the mid-1970s have had impressive educational credentials and have tended to be trained in economics and management rather than in the traditional field of law. Presidents since López Portillo have had postgraduate training at elite institutions in the United States. By the 1980s, a topic of great debate in political circles was the extent to which a divide between *políticos* (politicians) and *técnicos* (**technocrats**) had emerged within the national political elite. Among the old guard of the PRI, there was open skepticism about the ability of young technocrats like Carlos Salinas and Ernesto Zedillo to manage political conditions in the country. During the presidential campaign of 1994, considerable efforts were made to stress the more humble origins of Colosio and Zedillo and the fact that they had had to work hard to get an education. Under Fox, the ties of the president to business elites raised similar fears that the government would not respond to the concerns of everyday citizens.

Once elected, the president moves quickly to name a cabinet. Under the PRI, he usually selected those with whom he had worked over the years as he rose to political prominence. He also used cabinet posts to ensure a broad coalition of support; he might, for example, appoint people with close ties to the labor movement, business interests, or some of the regional strongholds of the party. Only in rare exceptions were cabinet officials not active members of the PRI. When the PAN assumed the presidency, the selection of a cabinet and close advisers was more difficult. Until then, the party had elected officials only to state and local governments and to congress. As a consequence, the range of people with executive experience to whom Fox could turn was limited. He

appointed U.S.-trained economists for his economic team and business executives for many other important posts. Few of these appointees had close ties to the PAN, and few had prior experience in government. Over the years, few women have been selected for ministry-level posts—there are a handful of examples in recent administrations—and thus far they have only presided over agencies with limited influence over decision making, like the ministries of tourism, ecology, and foreign relations.

The president has the authority to fill numerous other high-level positions, which allows him to provide policy direction and keep tabs on what is occurring throughout the government. The range of appointments that a chief executive can make means that the beginning of each administration is characterized by extensive turnover of positions, and as a result progress on the president's policy agenda can be slow during his first year in office as newly appointed officials learn the ropes and assemble their staffs. The president's power to make appointments provides him with the capacity to build a team of like-minded officials in government and ensure their loyalty to him. This system traditionally served the interests of presidents and the PRI well; under the PAN, given the limited number of its partisans who have experience at national levels, the system has not guaranteed the president as much power over the workings of the executive branch. In addition, with pressure mounting for a less politicized civil service in a more democratic Mexico, Fox committed himself to retaining qualified people in their positions and making many fewer changes than was customary.

Mexican presidents, though powerful, are not omnipotent. They must, for example, abide by a deeply held constitutional norm, fully adhered to since 1940, by stepping down at the end of their term, and they must adhere to tradition by removing themselves from the political limelight to allow their successors to assume full presidential leadership. All presidents, regardless of party, must demonstrate their loyalty to the myths and symbols of Mexican nationalism, such as the indigenous roots of much of its culture and the agrarian origins of the revolution, and they must make a rhetorical commitment to social justice and sovereignty in international affairs. Moreover, in the 1990s, President Zedillo relinquished a number of the traditional powers of the presidency. He announced, for example, that he would not select his PRI successor but would leave it up to the party to determine its candidate. In doing so, however, he created considerable conflict and tension as the PRI had to take on unaccustomed roles and as politicians sought to fill the void left by the "abandonment" of presidential power. Fox inherited a system in which he was expected to set the policies and determine the priorities for a very wide range of government activity. Without a strong party in congress to back him or many experienced people in his government, he was often unable to deliver. In the absence of strong presidential leadership, Mexico's government often seemed to flounder.

The Bureaucracy

Mexico's executive branch is large and powerful. Almost 1.5 million people work in the federal bureaucracy, most of them in Mexico City. An additional 1 million work for the large number of state-owned industries and semiautonomous agencies of the government. State and local governments employ over 1.5 million people.

Officials at lower levels in the bureaucracy are unionized and protected by legislation that gives them job security and a range of benefits. At middle and upper levels, most officials are called "confidence employees"; they serve as long as their bosses have confidence in them. These officials have been personally appointed by their superiors at the outset of an administration. Their modest salaries are compensated for by the significant power that they can have over public affairs. For aspiring young professionals, a career in government is often attractive because of the challenge of dealing with important problems on a daily basis. Some employees also benefit from opportunities to take bribes or use other means to promote their personal interests.

The Para-Statal Sector

The **para-statal** sector—composed of semiautonomous or autonomous government agencies, many of which produce goods and services—was extremely large and powerful in Mexico. Because the government provided significant support for the development of the economy as part of its post-1940 development strategy, it engaged in numerous activities that in other

countries are carried out by the private sector. Thus, until the Salinas administration, the country's largest steel mill was state-owned, as were the largest fertilizer producer, sugar mills, and airlines. In addition, the national electricity board still produces energy and supplies it at subsidized prices to industries. The state-owned petroleum company, PEMEX, grew to enormous proportions in the 1970s and 1980s under the impact of the oil boom. NAFIN, a state investment corporation, provides a considerable amount of investment capital for the country. At one point, a state marketing board called CONASUPO was responsible for the importation and purchase of the country's basic food supplies, and in the 1970s, it played a major role in distributing food, credit, and farm implements in rural areas.

This large para-statal sector was significantly trimmed by the economic policy reforms that began in the 1980s. In 1970, there were 391 para-statal organizations in Mexico. By 1982, their number had grown to 1,155, in part because of the expansion of government activities under presidents Echeverría and López Portillo and in part because of the nationalization of private banks in 1982. Shortly afterward, concerted efforts were made to privatize many of these industries, including the telephone company, the national airlines, and the nationalized banks. By 1994, only 215 state-owned industries remained, and efforts continued to sell or liquidate many of them. However, some core components of the para-statal sector will likely remain in government hands for the foreseeable future because an influential bloc of nationalist political actors insist on the symbolic importance of public ownership of key industries. The Fox government, a partisan of the private sector, raised the possibility of privatizing PEMEX and the electricity board, but quickly retreated to very partial measures in the face of extensive opposition to private ownership of the "national patrimony."

Other State Institutions

The Military

Mexico is one of only a few countries in the developing world, particularly in Latin America, to have successfully marginalized the military from centers of political power. Although former military leaders dominated Mexican politics during the decades immediately after the Revolution of 1910, Calles, Cárdenas, and subsequent presidents laid the groundwork for civilian rule by introducing the practice of rotating regional military commands so that generals could not build up geographic bases of power. In addition, postrevolutionary leaders made an implicit bargain with the military leaders by providing them with opportunities to engage in business so that they did not look to political power as a way of gaining economic power. After 1946, the military no longer had institutional representation within the PRI and became clearly subordinate to civilian control. No military officer has held the presidency since that time.

This does not mean that the military has existed outside politics. It has been called in from time to time to deal with domestic unrest: in rural areas in the 1960s, in Mexico City and other cities to repress student protest movements in 1968, in 1988 in the arrest of a powerful labor leader, in 1989 to break a labor strike, in 1990 to deal with protest over electoral fraud, in Chiapas beginning in late 1994, and to manage the Mexico City police in 1997. The military was also called in to deal with the aftermath of the earthquake in Mexico City in 1985, but its inadequate response to the emergency did little to enhance its reputation in the eyes of the public. In recent years, the military has been heavily involved in efforts to combat drug trafficking, and rumors abound about deals struck between military officials and drug barons. Such fears were confirmed when General Jesús Gutierrez Rebollo, the head of the antidrug task force, was arrested in 1997 on accusations of protecting a drug lord. When the PAN government made it possible for citizens to gain greater access to government information, it was discovered that the military had been involved in political repression, torture, and killing in the 1970s and 1980s. The scandal created by such revelations further lowered its reputation.

Whenever the military is called in to resolve domestic conflicts, some Mexicans become concerned that the institution is becoming politicized and may come to play a larger role in political decision making. Thus far, such fears have not been realized, and many believe that as long as civilian administrations are able to maintain the country's tradition of stability, the military will not intervene directly in politics. The fact that the country successfully observed the transfer of power from the PRI to the PAN also has increased a sense that the military will remain subordinate to civilian control.

The Judiciary

Unlike Anglo-American legal systems, Mexico's law derives from the Roman and Napoleonic tradition and is highly formalized and explicit. The Constitution of 1917 is a lengthy document that has been amended many times and contains references to a wide range of civil rights, including items as broad as the right to a healthy environment. Because Mexican law tends to be very explicit and because there are no punitive damages allowed in court cases, there are fewer lawsuits than in the United States. One important exception to this is the *amparo,* whereby individual citizens may ask for a writ of protection claiming that their constitutional rights have been violated by specific government actions or laws.

There are federal and state courts in Mexico. The federal system is composed of the Supreme Court, which decides the most important cases in the country; circuit courts, which take cases on appeal; and district courts, where all cases enter the system. As in the United States, Supreme Court justices are nominated by the president and approved by the Senate. Since most of the important laws in Mexico are federal, state courts have played a subordinate role. However, this is changing. As Mexican states become more independent from the federal government, state law has been experiencing tremendous growth. In addition, there are many important specialized federal courts, such as labor courts, military courts, and electoral courts.

Like other political institutions in Mexico, the judiciary was for many decades politically, though not constitutionally, subordinate to the executive. The courts occasionally slowed the actions of government by issuing *amparos*; however, in almost every case in which the power of government or the president was at stake, the courts ruled on the side of the government. The Zedillo administration tried to change this by emphasizing the rule of law over that of powerful individuals. Increasing interest in human rights issues by citizens' groups and the media has added pressure to the courts to play a stronger role in protecting basic freedoms. Zedillo's refusal to interfere with the courts' judgments also strengthened the judiciary. This trajectory continued under Fox. Nevertheless, the judicial system remains the weakest branch of government.

Subnational Government

As with many other aspects of the Mexican political system, regional and local government in Mexico is quite different from what is described in the constitution. Mexico has a federal system, and each state has its own constitution, executive, unicameral legislature, and judiciary. Municipalities (equivalent to U.S. counties) are governed by popularly elected mayors and councils. But most state and municipal governments are poor. Most of the funds they command are transferred to them from the central government, and they have little legal or administrative capacity to raise their own revenue. States and localities also suffer greatly from the lack of well-trained and well-paid public officials. As at the national level, many jobs are distributed as political patronage, but even officials who are motivated to be responsive to local needs are generally ill equipped to do so. Since the early 1990s, the government has made several serious efforts to decentralize and devolve more power to state and local governments. At times, governors and mayors have resisted such initiatives because they meant that regional and local governments would have to manage much more complex activities and be the focus of demands from public sector workers and their unions. Local governments were also worried that they would be unable to acquire the budgetary resources necessary to carry out their new responsibilities.

There are exceptions to this picture of regional and local government impoverishment and lack of capacity. The governments of some northern states, such as Nuevo León, have been more responsive to local needs and better able to administer public services. In such states, local municipalities have become famous for the extent to which they differ from the norm in most of Mexico. The city of Monterrey, for example, has a reputation for efficient and forward-looking municipal government. Much of this local capacity can be credited to a regional political tradition that has stressed independence from—and

even hostility to—Mexico City and the PRI. In addition, states and localities that have stronger governments and a tradition of better service tend to be areas of greater wealth, largely in the north of the country. In these cases, entrepreneurial groups and private citizens have often invested time and resources in state and local government.

Until 1988, all governors were from the PRI, although many believe that only electoral fraud kept two governorships out of the hands of an opposition party in 1986. Finally, in 1989, a non-PRI governor assumed power in Baja California, an important first. By late 2005, 13 states and the Federal District were governed by parties other than the PRI. Also, municipalities have increasingly been the focus of authentic party competition. As opposition parties came to control these levels of government, they were challenged to improve services such as police protection, garbage collection, sanitation, and education. PRI-dominated governments have also tried to improve their performance because they are now more threatened by the possibility of losing elections.

The Policy-Making Process

The Mexican system is very dependent on the quality of its leadership and on presidential understanding of how economic and social policies can affect the development of the country. As indicated throughout this chapter, the six-year term of office, the *sexenio,* is an extremely important fact of political life in Mexico. New presidents can introduce extensive change in positions within the government. They are able to bring in "their" people, who build teams of "their" people within ministries, agencies, and party networks. This generally provides the president with a group of high- and middle-level officials who share a general orientation toward public policy and are motivated to carry out his goals. When the PRI was the dominant party, these officials believed that in following presidential leadership, they enhanced their chances for upward political mobility. In such a context, even under a single party, it was likely that changes in public policies could be introduced every six years, creating innovation or discontinuity, or both. As indicated, the limited experience of the PAN in executive office and the increasing role of congress in policymaking meant that the influence of the president on government became less strong after 2000. Nevertheless, Mexicans continue to look to the president and the executive branch for policy leadership.

Together with the bureaucracy, the president is the focal point of policy formulation and political management. Until 1997, the legislature always had a PRI majority and acted as a rubber stamp for presidentially sponsored legislation. Since then, the congress has proven to be a more active policymaker, blocking and forcing the negotiation of legislation, and even introducing its own bills. The president's skills in negotiating, managing the opposition, using the media to acquire public support, and maneuvering within the bureaucracy can be important for ensuring that his program is fully endorsed.

Significant limits on presidential power occur when policy is being implemented. In fact, in areas as diverse as the regulation of working conditions, antipollution laws, tax collection, election monitoring, and health care in remote rural areas, Mexico has extremely advanced legislation on the books. Yet the persistence of unsafe factory conditions, pollution in Mexico City, tax evasion, electoral fraud, and poor health care suggests that legislation is not always translated into practice. At times, policies are not implemented because public officials at the lower levels disagree with them or make deals with affected interests in order to benefit personally. This is the case, for example, with taxes that remain uncollected because individuals or corporations bribe officials to overlook them. In other cases, lower-level officials may lack the capacity or skills to implement some policies, such as those directed toward improving education or rural development services. For various reasons, Mexican presidents cannot always deliver on their intentions. Traditionally, Mexican citizens have blamed lower-level officials for such slippage, but exempting the president from responsibility for what does or does not occur during his watch has become much less common since the 1970s.

Section **4** Representation and Participation

How do citizen interests get represented in Mexican politics, given the high degree of centralization, presidentialism, and, until recently, PRI domination? Is it possible for ordinary citizens to make demands on government and influence public policy? In fact, Mexico has had a relatively peaceful history since the revolution in part because the political system offers some channels for representation and participation. Throughout this long history, the political system has emphasized compromise among contending elites, behind-the-scenes conflict resolution, and distribution of political rewards to those willing to play by the formal and informal rules of the game. It has also responded, if reluctantly and defensively, to demands for change.

Often, citizens are best able to interact with the government through a variety of informal means rather than through the formal processes of elections, campaigns, and interest group lobbying. Interacting with government through the personal and informal mechanisms of clientelism usually means that the government retains the upper hand in deciding which interests to respond to and which to ignore. For many interests, this has meant "incorporation without power."[17] Increasingly, however, Mexican citizens are organizing to alter this situation, and the advent of truly competitive elections has increased the possibility that citizens who organize can gain some response from government.

The Legislature

Students in the United States are frequently asked to study complex charts explaining how a bill becomes a law because the formal process of lawmaking affects the content of legislation. Under the old reign of the PRI in Mexico, while there were formal rules that prescribed such a process, studying them would not have been useful for understanding how the legislature worked. Because of the overwhelming presence of this political party, opposition to presidential initiatives by Mexico's two-chamber legislature, the Senate and the Chamber of Deputies, was rarely heard. If representatives did not agree with policies they were asked to approve, they counted on the fact that policy implementation was flexible and allowed for after-the-fact bending of the rules or disregard of measures that were harmful to important interests.

Members of the Mexican congress are elected through a dual system of "first past the post" (that is, the candidate with the most votes wins) and proportional representation. Each state elects three senators. Two of them are determined by majority vote, and the third is determined by whichever party receives the second highest number of votes. In addition, thirty-two senators are determined nationally through a system of proportional representation that awards seats based on the number of votes cast for each party. Senators serve six-year terms. The same type of electoral system works in the Chamber of Deputies, with 300 selected on the basis of majority vote and 200 additional representatives chosen by proportional representation. Deputies are elected for three-year terms. Representation in congress has become somewhat more diverse since the end of the 1980s. In 2004, women held 15.6 percent of seats in the Senate and 22.6 percent in the Chamber of Deputies. Some representatives also emerged from the ranks of community activists who had participated in activities such as urban popular movements.

The PRI's grip on the legislature was broken in 1988. The growing strength of opposition parties, combined with legislation that provided for greater representation of minority parties in the congress, led to the election of 240 opposition deputies (out of 500) that year, depriving the PRI of the two-thirds majority it needed for major pieces of legislation or constitutional amendments. After that, when presidential legislation was sent to the chamber, the opposition challenged the tradition of legislative passivity and insisted on real debate about issues. The two-thirds PRI majority was returned in 1991—amid allegations of voter fraud—and presidentialism was reasserted. Nevertheless, the strong presence of opposition parties continued to encourage debate as PRI delegates were challenged to defend proposed legislation. The 1994 elections returned a clear PRI majority of 300 deputies, but in 1997, the PRI lost this majority when 261 deputies were elected from opposition parties. For

the first time in its history, the PRI did not have an absolute majority in the Chamber of Deputies. The party composition of the Chamber of Deputies and the Senate after the elections of 2003 is shown in Figure 1.

Since the late 1990s, the role of congress in the policy process has been strengthened considerably.[10] The cost of greater power sharing between the executive and the legislature, however, has been to stall the policy process. Several important pieces of legislation were stalled under President Zedillo. Even PRI legislators became more willing to slow or alter presidential initiatives. Under the Fox administration, relations with congress have been even more confrontational. The president lacks a party majority in congress and had a difficult time promoting his investment plan, labor code reform, and the liberalization of the energy sector. In a first-ever use of congressional power, in 2002, the Senate, angry over differences with the president about U.S.-Mexico relations, greatly embarrassed Fox by denying him the required permission to travel outside of Mexico for a visit to the United States and Canada. As a consequence of this kind of muscle flexing, congressional committees that once were important only for their control over patronage have acquired new relevance, and committee members and chairs are becoming somewhat more like their U.S. counterparts in terms of the power they can wield. Party caucuses have also emerged as centers of power in the legislature. In addition, interest groups, which before 1997 had scant interest in lobbying for legislative action because the legislature did not make important decisions, have increased their activities in congress. Thus, as a genuine multiparty system has emerged, the Mexican congress has become a more important forum for a variety of political voices and points of view.

Political Parties and the Party System

Even under the long reign of the PRI, a number of political parties existed in Mexico. By the mid-1980s, some of them were attracting more political support, a trend that continued into the 1990s and 2000s. Electoral reforms introduced by the López Portillo, de la Madrid, Salinas, and Zedillo administrations made it easier for opposition parties to contest elections and win seats in the legislature. In 1990, an electoral

Figure 1

Congressional Representation by Party, 2003

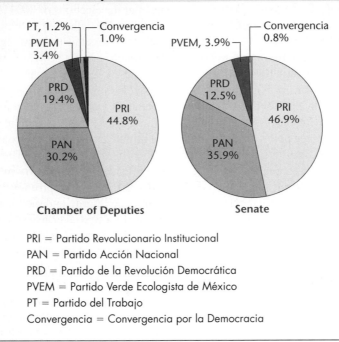

PT, 1.2% — — Convergencia 1.0%

PVEM 3.4%

PRD 19.4%

PAN 30.2%

PRI 44.8%

Chamber of Deputies

— Convergencia 0.8%

PVEM, 3.9% —

PRD 12.5%

PAN 35.9%

PRI 46.9%

Senate

PRI = Partido Revolucionario Institucional
PAN = Partido Acción Nacional
PRD = Partido de la Revolución Democrática
PVEM = Partido Verde Ecologista de México
PT = Partido del Trabajo
Convergencia = Convergencia por la Democracia

Source: CIA World Factbook, http://www.cia.gov/cia/publications/factbook/geos/mx.html; see also http://www.senado.gob.mx and http://www.camaradediputados.gob.mx.

commission was created to regulate campaigns and elections, and in 1996 it became fully independent of the government. Now all parties receive funding from the government and have access to the media. In addition to the PRI, two other political parties have demonstrated the capacity to win substantial support in elections.

The PRI

Mexico's Institutional Revolutionary Party (PRI) was founded by a coalition of political elites who agreed that it was preferable to work out their conflicts within an overarching structure of compromise than to continue to resort to violence. In the 1930s, the forerunner of the PRI (the party operated under different names until 1946) incorporated a wide array of interests, becoming a mass-based party that drew support from all classes in the population. Over seven decades, its

principal activities were to generate support for the government, organize the electorate to vote for its candidates, and distribute jobs and resources in return for loyalty to the system.

Until the 1990s, party organization was based largely on the corporate representation of class interests. Labor was represented within party councils by the Confederation of Mexican Workers (CTM), which includes industry-based unions at local, regional, and national levels. Peasants were represented by the National Peasant Confederation (CNC), an organization of *ejido* and peasant unions and regional associations. The so-called popular sector, comprising small businesses, community-based groups, and public employees, had less internal cohesion but was represented by the National Confederation of Popular Organizations (CNOP). Of the three, the CTM was consistently the best organized and most powerful. Traditionally, the PRI's strongest support came from the countryside, where *ejidatarios* and independent small farmers were grateful for and dependent on rewards of land or jobs. As the country became more urbanized, the support base provided by rural communities remained important to the PRI but produced many fewer votes than were necessary to keep the party in power.

Within its corporate structures, the PRI functioned through extended networks that distributed public resources—particularly jobs, land, development projects, and access to public services—to lower-level activists who controlled votes at the local level. In this system, those with ambitions to public office or to positions within the PRI put together networks of supporters from above (patrons), to whom they delivered votes, and supporters from below (clients), who traded allegiance for access to public resources. For well over half a century, this system worked

extremely well. PRI candidates won by overwhelming majorities until the 1980s (see Figure 2). Of course, electoral fraud and the ability to distribute government largesse are central explanations for these numbers, but they also attest to an extremely well-organized party. Although the PRI became much weaker in the 1980s and 1990s, it was still the only political party that could boast a network of constituency organizations in virtually every village and urban community in the country. Its vast political machinery also allowed it to monitor events, even in remote areas.

Within the PRI, power was centralized, and the sector organizations (the CTM, the CNC, and the CNOP) responded primarily to elites at the top of the political pyramid rather than to member interests. Over time, the corporate interest group organizations, particularly the

Figure 2

PRI Support in Congressional Elections, 1946–2003

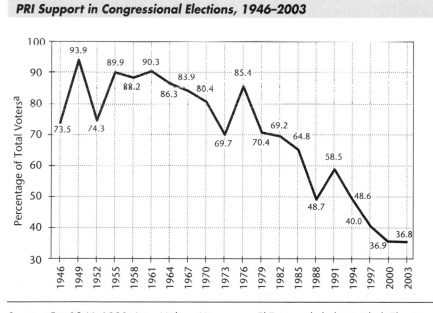

Sources: For 1946–1988: Juan Molinar Horcasitas, *El Tiempo de la legtimidad: Elecciones, autoritarismo y democracia en México* (México, D.F.: Cal y Arena, 1991). For 1991: Secretaría Nacional de Estudios, Partido Acción Nacional, *Análisis del Proceso Federal Electoral 1994, 1995.* For 1994: Instituto Federal Electoral, *Estadística de las Elecciones Federales de 1994, Compendio de Resultados* (Mexico, D.F., 1995). For 1997: http://www.ife.org.mx/ ww-worge/tablas/mrent.htm. For 2000 and 2003: Instituto Federal Electoral, http://www. ife.org.mx. Figures for 2003 include votes received by the Alianza para Todos (Alliance for Everyone), which brought the PRI and the much smaller PVEM together on a single ticket in some states.

CTM and the CNC, became widely identified with corruption, bossism, centralized control, and lack of effective participation. By the 1980s, new generations of voters were less beholden to patronage-style politics and much more willing to question the party's dominance. When the administrations of de la Madrid, Salinas, and Zedillo imposed harsh austerity measures, the PRI was held responsible for the resulting losses in incomes and benefits. Simultaneously, as the government cut back sharply on public sector jobs and services, the PRI had far fewer resources to distribute to maintain its traditional bases of support. Moreover, it began to suffer from increasing internal dissension between the old guard—the so-called dinosaurs—and the "modernizers" who wanted to reform the party.

Until 1988, PRI candidates easily won election to the presidency (see Table 2). After that year, however, the PRI was challenged by parties to the right and left, and outcomes were hotly contested by the opposition, which claimed fraudulent electoral practices. In 1994, Zedillo won primarily because the opposition was not well organized and failed to present a program other than its opposition to the PRI. Presidents Salinas and Zedillo also distanced themselves from the party during their administrations, giving the first clear signals in PRI history that there was a distinction between the party and the government.

As the PRI faced greater competition from other parties and continued to suffer from declining popularity, efforts were made to restructure and reform it. The CNOP was replaced by an organization that sought to incorporate a wide array of non-class-based citizen and neighborhood movements. In 1990, membership rules were altered to allow individuals and groups not identified with its corporate sector organizations to join. In addition, regional party organizations gained representation at the national level. Party conventions were introduced in an effort to democratize the internal workings of the party, and some states and localities began to hold primaries to select PRI candidates, a significant departure from the old system of selection by party bosses.

The PRI continues to face a difficult future. Voters are younger, better educated, more middle class, and more likely to live in urban areas than they were in the days of the PRI's greatest success—the 1940s, 1950s, and 1960s. The 1988 presidential elections demonstrated the relevance of changing demographic conditions when only 27.3 percent of the population of Mexico City voted for the PRI candidate and only 34.3 percent of the population in other urban areas supported him. By 2003, support for the party had fallen so far in the nation's capital that only 11.8 percent of voters in the Federal District cast their ballots for PRI congressional candidates. With the vast majority of the country's population now living in cities, the PRI will have to win the support of more urban voters in order to remain a relevant political force. That task looks all the more difficult after the historic election of 2000. Not only did opposition campaigns tap into a deep well of resentment against evidence of corruption and mismanagement in the PRI, but Fox's victory stripped the party of the aura of invincibility that had helped to cement its dominance of Mexican politics for decades.

In the immediate aftermath of the PRI's defeat, many analysts wondered how the party would be able to survive as an effective organization. Some predicted that the party would fall apart without one of its own in the presidency. However, public disappointment over Fox's inability to deliver on his promises of far-reaching change has allowed the PRI to remain a significant part of the Mexican political landscape. In recent years, despite initial uncertainty about the long-term direction of the party and a few defections, the PRI has for the most part remained disciplined and unified under the leadership of Roberto Madrazo, a former governor who is seen as representing the organization's old guard. The party has fared well in state and local elections, even winning back the governorship in the state of Chihuahua (in 1998 and 2004) and the mayor's office in Tijuana (2004), both places that were considered to be strongholds of the PAN. The PRI also continues to be the largest party in both chambers of the Mexican congress. Whether or not the PRI can return to the pinnacle of political power in Mexico by reoccupying the presidency remains to be seen.

The PAN

The National Action Party (PAN) was founded in 1939 to represent interests opposed to the centralization and anticlericalism of the PRI. It was founded by those who believed that the country needed more than

Table 2

Voting in Presidential Elections, 1934–2000

Year	Votes for PRI Candidate[a]	Votes for PAN Candidate	Votes for All Others[b]	Turnout (% Voters Among Eligible Adults)[c]
1934	98.2%	—	1.8%	33.8%
1940	93.9	—	6.1	57.5
1946	77.9	—	22.1	42.6
1952	74.3	7.8%	17.9	57.9
1958	90.4	9.4	0.2	49.4
1964	88.8	11.1	0.1	54.1
1970	83.3	13.9	1.4	63.9
1976[d]	93.6	—	1.2	29.6
1982	71.0	15.7	9.4	66.1
1988	50.7	16.8	32.5[e]	49.4[f]
1994	50.1	26.7	23.2	77.16
2000	36.1	42.5[g]	19.2[h]	64.0

[a]From 1958 through 1982, includes votes cast for the Partido Popular Socialista (PPS) and the Partido Auténtico de la Revolución Mexicana (PARM), both of which regularly endorsed the PRI's presidential candidate. In 1988, they supported opposition candidate Cuauhtémoc Cárdenas.

[b]Excludes annulled votes; includes votes for candidates of nonregistered parties.

[c]Eligible population base for 1934 through 1952 includes all males ages 20 and over (legal voting age: 21 years). Both men and women ages 20 and over are included in the base for 1958 and 1964 (women received the franchise in 1958). The base for 1970–1988 includes all males and females ages 18 and over (the legal voting age was lowered to 18, effective 1970).

[d]The PRI candidate, José Lopez Portillo, ran virtually unopposed because the PAN failed to nominate a candidate. The only other significant candidate was Valentín Campa, representing the Communist Party, which was not legally registered to participate in the 1976 election. More than 5 percent of the votes were annulled.

[e]Includes 31.1 percent officially tabulated for Cuauhtémoc Cárdenas.

[f]Estimated using data from the Federal Electoral Commission. However, the commission itself has released two different figures for the number of eligible voters in 1988. Using the commission's larger estimate of eligible population, the turnout would be 44.9 percent.

[g]Votes cast for Alianza por el Cambio, formed by the Partido Acción Nacional (PAN) and the Partido Verde Ecologista de Mexico (PVEM).

[h]Includes votes cast for Alianza por México, formed by the Partido de la Revolución Democrática (PRD), the Partido del Trabajo (PT), Convergencia por la Democracia, the Partido Alianza Social (PAS), and the Partido de la Sociedad Nacionalista (PSN).

Sources: From *Comparative Politics Today: A World View,* 4th ed. by Gabriel Almond and G. Bingham Powell, Jr. Copyright ©1988. Reprinted by permission of Addison-Wesley Educational Publishers, Inc. For 1994: Instituto Federal Electoral, *Estadística de las Elecciones Federales de 1994, Compendio de Resultados* (Mexico, D.F., 1995). For 2000: Instituto Federal Electoral, www.ife.org.mx.

one strong political party and that opposition parties should oppose the PRI through legal and constitutional actions. Historically, this party has been strongest in northern states, where the tradition of resistance to Mexico City is also strongest. It has also been primarily an urban party of the middle class and is closely identified with the private sector. The PAN has traditionally campaigned on a platform endorsing greater regional autonomy, less government intervention in the economy, reduced regulation of business, clean and fair elections, rapprochement with the Catholic Church, and support for private and religious education. When PRI governments of the 1980s and 1990s moved toward market-friendly and export-oriented policies, the policy differences between the two parties were significantly reduced. Nevertheless, a major difference of perspectives about religion continued to characterize the two parties. The PAN has always favored a closer relationship with the Catholic Church, and President Fox's public protestations of faith, including kissing Pope John Paul II's ring when the pontiff visited Mexico in 2002, raised many an eyebrow in a system long noted for its commitment to secularism.

For many years, the PAN was able to elect only 9 to 10 percent of all deputies to the national congress and capture control of a few municipal governments. Then, in the early 1980s, and especially after President López Portillo nationalized the banks, opposition to centralism and state control of the economy grew more popular. The PAN began to develop greater capacity to contest elections at higher levels of government. In particular, the party gained popularity among urban middle-class voters, won elections in several provincial cities, and came close to winning governorships in two states. In 1989, it won its first governorship, in the state of Baja California. In the 1994 elections, the PAN's candidate garnered 26 percent of the presidential vote, more than it had won in any previous election, and the party won 25 seats in the Senate and 119 in the Chamber of Deputies. In 1997, the party's legislative delegation grew to 33 senators and 121 deputies, and those numbers rose again in 2000, to 53 and 224, respectively. By late 2005, the PAN controlled the governorships in nine states, and in one more the governor had been elected as the candidate of an alliance between the PAN and another political party (see below). And, of course, the PAN won the presidency in 2000 with 42.7 percent of the total vote.

The PAN has traditionally set relatively high standards for activism among its party members; as a consequence, the membership of the party has remained small, even as its capacity to attract votes has grown. In their efforts to control the development of the party, its leaders have had a difficult relationship with the PAN standard bearer, Vicente Fox. As Fox's national political profile expanded while serving as the governor of the state of Guanajuato, leaders of the party became concerned that he would emerge as a favorite for the presidency. They considered him to be an opportunistic newcomer to the party, and they worked to limit his ability to run for office, forcing him to look for other sources of financing his campaign. In 1997, the "Friends of Fox" organization began to raise funds and promote his candidacy for president, and at the same time, the traditional leaders of the party were weakened significantly when the PAN made a poor showing in electoral contests. Fox gained in popularity throughout the country, and in 1999, the party had little option but to nominate him as its candidate. The Friends of Fox continued to provide the most important source of campaign support, however, and when Fox won the presidential election, the PAN organization was weak and not at all united in backing him. Furthermore, although the party made a very good showing in elections for the Chamber of Deputies and the Senate, it did not have a majority in either chamber.

President Fox hoped that mid-term congressional elections in 2003 would return a PAN majority, making it possible for him to push ahead with various initiatives that had been stalled by the legislative branch. Instead, many voters expressed their frustration with the administration's lack of effectiveness by casting their ballots for non-PAN candidates. The party's representation in the Chamber of Deputies dropped substantially, from 224 seats to 151. With Fox constitutionally barred from seeking a second term, the PAN will have to find a new presidential candidate in the 2006 elections.

The PRD

Another significant challenge to the PRI has come from the Democratic Revolutionary Party (PRD), a populist and nationalist alternative to the PRI whose policies are left of center. Its candidate in the 1988 and 1994 elections was Cuauhtémoc Cárdenas, the son of Mexico's most famous and revered president. He was a PRI insider until party leaders virtually ejected him for demanding internal reform of the party and a platform emphasizing social justice. In the 1988 elections, Cárdenas was officially credited with winning 31.1 percent of the vote, and his party captured 139 seats in the Chamber of Deputies. He benefited from massive political defection from the PRI and garnered support from workers disaffected with the boss-dominated unions as well as from peasants who remembered his father's concern for agrarian reform and the welfare of the poor.

Even while the votes were being counted, the party began to denounce widespread electoral fraud and claim that Cárdenas would have won if the election had been honest. The PRD challenged a number of vote counts in the courts and walked out on the inaugural speech given by the PRI's Salinas. Considerable public opinion supported the party's challenge. In the aftermath of the 1988 elections, then, it seemed that the PRD was a strong contender to become Mexico's second most powerful party. It was expected to have a real chance in future years to challenge the PRI's "right" to the presidency.

However, in the aftermath of these elections, the party was plagued by internal divisions over its platform, leadership, organizational structure, and election strategy. By 1994, it still lagged far behind the PRI and the PAN in establishing and maintaining the local constituency organizations needed to mobilize votes and monitor the election process. In addition, the PRD found it difficult to define an appropriate left-of-center alternative to the market-oriented policies carried out by the government. While the claims that such policies ignored the need for social justice were popular, policies to respond to poverty that did not imply a return to unpopular government intervention were difficult to devise. In the aftermath of the Colosio assassination, citizens also became more alarmed about violence, and some were concerned that the level of political rivalry represented by the PRD threatened the country's long-term political stability. In the 1994 elections, Cárdenas won only 17 percent of the votes, although the PRD elected seventy-one deputies and eight senators.

Thanks to the government's continued unpopular economic policies and the leadership of a successful grass-roots mobilizer named Andrés Manuel López Obrador, who was elected to head the party in 1996, the PRD began to stage a remarkable turnaround. Factional bickering was controlled, and organizational discipline increased. In addition, the PRD proved successful in moving beyond its regional strongholds and established itself as a truly national party. In 1997, the party increased its share of seats to 125 in the Chamber of Deputies and 16 in the Senate. Most important, Cárdenas became the first popularly elected mayor of Mexico City, providing him and the party with an opportunity to demonstrate their ability to govern. By this time, the PRD had managed to shed some of its reputation as a "one-horse show" and had won two governorships. In 2000, López Obrador was elected mayor of Mexico City with 39.5 percent of the vote, signaling again the political importance of the capital city. In the presidential race, Cárdenas ran again, but he was able to garner only 16.5 percent of the vote. The party's performance in the legislative race was equally disappointing. The PRD retained 16 seats in the Senate, but lost 58 in the Chamber of Deputies, holding only 67 seats.

The party's fortunes improved somewhat in 2003, when the size of its delegation in the Chamber of Deputies rose to 97. Although the problem of factional infighting had still not been completely resolved by 2005, by then four states and the Federal District were governed by the PRD. Another governor had been elected as the representative of a coalition between the PRD and the PAN, which put aside their divergent ideologies and worked together on the local level to unseat the PRI in the rural, traditional state of Chiapas.

Thanks largely to its control over the capital city and the existence of PRD administrations on the municipal level in parts of the country, the party was able to boast that about a quarter of the country's population lived under a PRD government. Although it continues to occupy fewer offices than the other two major parties, the party is still considered a significant contender for political power in Mexico, with Mexico City Mayor Andrés Manuel López Obrador seen by many as a front-runner in the 2006 presidential elections.

Other Parties

There are a number of smaller parties that contest elections in Mexico. In 2003, the Green Ecologist

Party of Mexico (PVEM), the Labor Party (PT), and Convergence for Democracy (Convergencia) each won between 2.3 and 4.0 percent of the vote for congressional seats. A handful of even smaller parties garnered less than 1 percent of the vote apiece. Since Mexican law requires parties to receive at least 2.5 percent of the vote to be able to compete in future elections, the long-term viability of some of these organizations is very doubtful. Small parties usually do win a few of the seats in the Chamber of Deputies and the Senate that are filled by proportional representation. Also, these groups sometimes wield influence on national politics by forming alliances with the larger parties, either endorsing their candidates for president or governor in national and state elections or backing a single slate of candidates for congress. For example, the PVEM joined with the PAN in the Alliance for Change to back Fox's bid for the presidency in 2000, while the PT, Convergencia, and two even smaller parties formed the Alliance for Mexico to support the PRD's candidate, Cuauhtémoc Cárdenas. In the congressional elections of 2003, the PVEM entered into another alliance, this time with the PRI, and in many states, candidates from the two parties ran for office as members of the Alliance for Everyone. Because these small parties often appear to be opportunistic in the shifting alliances that they make, and because a few of the most insignificant parties apparently exist only to tap into the public funding that finances election campaigns in Mexico, many Mexicans have a low regard for some of these organizations.

Elections

Each of the three main political parties draws voters from a wide and overlapping spectrum of the electorate. Nevertheless, a typical voter for the PRI is likely to be from a rural area or small town, to have less education, and to be older and poorer than voters for the other parties. A typical voter for the PAN is likely to be from a northern state, to live in an urban area, to be a middle-class professional, to have a comfortable lifestyle, and to have a high school or even a university education. A typical voter for the PRD is likely to be young, to be a political activist, to have an elementary or high school education, to live in one of the central states, and to live in a small town or an urban area. As we have seen, the support base for the PRI is the most vulnerable to economic and demographic changes in the country. Voting for opposition parties is an urban phenomenon, and Mexico continues to urbanize at the rate of 3 percent per year. This means that in order to stay competitive, the PRI will have to garner more support from urban areas. It must also be able to appeal to younger voters, especially the large numbers who are attracted to the PRD and the PAN.

Elections are becoming more competitive and fairer in Mexico. Electoral reforms introduced by the López Portillo, de la Madrid, Salinas, and Zedillo administrations made it easier for opposition parties to contest elections and win seats in the legislature. In 1990, an electoral commission was created to regulate campaigns and elections, and in 1996 it became fully independent from the government. Now all parties receive government funding and have guaranteed access to the media. These and other laws that limit campaign spending and campaign contributions were a response to demands that the government level the playing field between the PRI and the other parties. Voter registration was reformed to ensure that fraud would be more detectable. Election monitoring was also strengthened, and another reform increased the chances for opposition parties to win representation in the Senate. Beginning in 1994, elections have been much fairer, and subsequent congressional, state, and municipal elections reinforced the impression that electoral fraud is on the wane in many areas. The PAN's victory in 2000 substantially increased this impression. Some state and local elections continue to be questioned, however, especially in rural areas in the south, where local PRI bosses remain powerful.

Political Culture, Citizenship, and Identity

Most citizens in Mexico demonstrate overall commitment to the political system while expressing considerable criticism—and often cynicism—about how it works and how equitable it is. Many criticize corruption in government and the PRI, but remain proud that their country has become more democratic.

Institutional Intricacies: *Campaigning with Comic Books*

In the more democratic Mexico that has emerged since the 1990s, political leaders have found that they must find new and imaginative ways to communicate with voters and to seek their backing. As the effectiveness of the clientelist networks that guaranteed PRI hegemony for so many years declines, candidates for public office and government officials are increasingly turning to strategies used in other democratic systems to win support for themselves and their programs. For example, public opinion polling and elaborate marketing plans are now becoming important tools for Mexican politicians who previously relied on patronage and strategies of co-optation and accommodation to achieve their goals.

Even as they adopt some of the methods used by their counterparts in other countries, however, some politicians are also reaching out to their constituents in a distinctly Mexican way: through comic books. Though the comic books published by officials and aspirants to higher office tend to be less lurid and suggestive than the enormously popular pocket-sized publications sold at newsstands throughout the country, they reach a wide audience since they are generally distributed free of charge.

Mexico City Mayor Andrés Manuel López Obrador of the left-of-center Democratic Revolutionary Party (PRD) was among the first to use a comic book to trumpet his accomplishments. In a series entitled *Stories of the City*, the popular head of the government of the Federal District is depicted as a defender of the poor and downtrodden residents of the capital. Later, when allegations of corruption in his administration threatened to derail the mayor's bid for the presidency in 2006, the municipal government issued another edition of *Stories of the City* to expose what it called "the dark forces against López Obrador." The comic book reiterated the populist mayor's claim that elites and hidden special interests were attempting to manufacture scandals that would prevent him from reaching Los Pinos.

President Vicente Fox also recognized the potential usefulness of comic books as a means of disseminating his political message. In 2002, faced with the widespread perception that the Fox administration had failed to bring about substantial change, the president's office commissioned a comic book called *July 2nd: Now Nobody Will Stop Change in Mexico!* in which a group of university students convince skeptical classmates that the date of Fox's election—July 2, 2000—was a historic milestone for Mexico. After discussing the various achievements of the Fox administration, the students conclude that the president "always speaks openly, is honest, and works every day for the good of all Mexicans." At a time when Fox was seen by many as weak and ineffectual, *July 2nd* represented an unconventional effort to convince Mexicans that the president was getting results.

Mexican political comic books have even had an impact in the realm of international affairs. When the Mexican foreign ministry issued a comic book–style *Guide for the Mexican Migrant* late in 2004, a number of U.S. legislators complained that the Mexican government appeared to be offering its citizens tips on how to flout American immigration laws. Although the publication noted that the safest way to travel abroad was with a passport and a visa, it also explained how to avoid dehydration when passing through remote desert regions and how to reduce the danger of drowning when crossing rivers. The guide also advised migrants not to call attention to themselves and to avoid loud parties once they were across the border. Despite the outcry that arose over the publication in certain circles in Washington, D.C., the Mexican Foreign Ministry insisted that the guide had been prepared for humanitarian reasons, inasmuch as many migrants had lost their lives trying to reach the United States in recent years.

Politicians and government agencies alike have recognized that comic books can be an effective way to reach a large number of Mexican citizens. The speed with which publications of this sort have proliferated shows the resourcefulness of Mexican political actors as they seek to adapt to a new political landscape that is more competitive and open and that places more of a premium on successful communication with the citizenry.

Most Mexicans have a deep familiarity with how their political system works and the ways in which they might be able to extract benefits from it. They understand the informal rules of the game in Mexican politics that have helped maintain political stability despite extensive inequalities in economic and political power. Clientelism has long been a form of participation in the sense that through their connections, many people, even the poorest, are able to interact with public officials and get something out of the political system. This kind of participation emphasizes how limited resources, such as access to health care, can be distributed in a way that provides maximum political payoff. This informal system is a fundamental reason that many Mexicans continued to vote for the PRI for so long.

However, new ways of interacting with government are emerging, and they coexist along with the clientelistic style of the past. An increasing number of citizens are seeking to negotiate with the government on the basis of citizenship rights, not personal patron-client relationships. The movements that emerged in the 1980s sought to form broad but loose coalitions with other organizations and attempted to identify and work with reform-oriented public officials. Their suspicion of traditional political organizations such as the PRI and its affiliates also led them to avoid close alliances with other parties, such as the PAN and the PRD.

As politics and elections became more open and competitive, the roles of public opinion and the mass media have become more important. In the past, public opinion polling was often contaminated by the dominance of the PRI, and some polling organizations were even subsidized by the party or the government. Increasingly, however, even the PRI and the government are interested in objective information and analysis of public opinion. These data have influenced the content and timing of government decisions and the development of strategies in election campaigns. In 1994 and 2000, politicians, citizens, and political activists closely followed the popularity polls of the three major candidates for president, and party officials monitored how the image of their contender could be molded to capture higher voter approval ratings. Because extensive public opinion polling is comparatively new in Mexico, it is difficult to assess how attitudes toward government have changed over time. Surveys indicate that public confidence in government fell sharply during the 1980s but rebounded somewhat in the 1990s. Fewer Mexicans claim a party preference today than in the past, and the percentage of citizens who identify with the PRI has dropped dramatically in recent years.

Today, the media play an important role in public opinion formation in Mexico. In the past, it was not easy for newspapers, magazines, or radio and television stations to be openly opposed to the government. For many years, the government used access to newsprint, which it controlled, to reward sympathetic news coverage and penalize coverage it considered hostile. In addition, the government and ambitious officials paid stipends to reporters who covered their activities favorably. A considerable amount of the revenue of newspapers and other media organizations came from advertising placed by the government. Each of these mechanisms was used to encourage positive reporting of government activities and the quashing of stories that reflected ill on the party or the administration, without resorting to outright government control of the media.

As with other aspects of Mexican politics, the media began to become more independent in the 1980s, enjoying a "spring" of greater independence and diversity of opinion.[19] There are currently several major television networks in the country, and many citizens have access to CNN and other global networks. The number of newspapers is expanding, as is their circulation, and several news magazines play the same role in Mexico that *Time* and *Newsweek* do in the United States. Citizens in Mexico today clearly hear a much wider range of opinion and much greater reporting of debates about public policy and criticism of government than at any time previously.

Interests, Social Movements, and Protest

The Mexican system has long responded to groups of citizens through pragmatic **accommodation** to their interests. This is one important reason that political tensions among major interests have rarely escalated into the kind of serious conflict that can threaten stability. Where open conflict has occurred, it has generally been met with efforts to find some kind of compromise solution. Accommodation has been particularly apparent in response to the interests of business. Mexico's development strategy encouraged the growth of wealthy elites in commerce, finance, industry, and agriculture (see Section 2). Although these elites were the primary beneficiaries of the country's development, they were never directly incorporated into the PRI. Instead, they represent themselves through a set of business-focused interest groups and personal relationships with influential officials. Through these networks, business organizations and individuals seek policies favorable to their interests.

Labor has been similarly accommodated within the system. Wage levels for unionized workers grew fairly consistently between 1940 and 1982, when the economic crisis caused a significant drop in wages. At the same time, labor interests were attended to in terms of concrete benefits and limitations on the rights of employers to discipline or dismiss workers. Union leaders controlled their rank and file in the interest of their own power to negotiate with government, but at the same time, they sought benefits for workers who continued to provide support for the PRI. The power of the union bosses has declined, in part because the unions are weaker than in the past, in part because union members are demanding greater democratization, and in part because the PRI no longer monopolizes political power.

Under the PRI, accommodation was often coupled with **co-optation** as a means of incorporating dissidents into the system so that they did not threaten its continuity. In 1968, for example, students protesting against authoritarianism, poverty, and inequity challenged the government just prior to the opening of the Olympic Games. The government responded with force—in one instance killing several hundred students in Mexico City—sparking even greater animosity. When Luis Echeverría became president in 1970, he recruited large numbers of the student activists into his administration. He also dramatically increased spending on social services, putting many of the young people to work in expanding antipoverty programs in the countryside

and in urban slums. Through these actions, a generation of political and social activists was incorporated into the system, and there was some accommodation to their concerns. We also know now that his government allowed the military to kidnap, arrest, torture, and kill some political dissidents.

Despite the strong and controlling role of the PRI in Mexico's political history, the country also has a tradition of civic organizations that operate at community and local levels with considerable independence from politics. Local village improvement societies, religious organizations, and sports clubs are widespread. Many of their activities are not explicitly political, although they may have political implications in that they encourage individuals to work together to find solutions to problems or to organize around common interests. Other organizational experiences are more clearly political. The student movement of 1968 provided evidence that civil society in Mexico had the potential to contest the power of the state. The emergence of independent unionism in the 1970s was another indication of renewed willingness to question the right of the state to stifle the dissenting voices.

The economic crisis of 1982 combined with this civic tradition to heighten demands for assistance from the government. In October 1983, as many as 2 million people participated in a civic strike to call attention to the economic crisis and demand a forceful government response. In urban areas, citizen groups demanded land rights in squatter settlements, as well as housing, infrastructure, and urban services, as rights of citizenship rather than as a reward for loyalty to the PRI.[20] In the aftermath of the 1985 earthquake, citizen groups became especially dynamic in demanding that government respond to the needs of citizens without reference to their history of party loyalty.[21] Many also became active in groups that share concerns about quality-of-life issues such as clean air and safe neighborhoods (see "Citizen Action: Urban Popular Movements").

In subsequent years, a variety of groups in Mexico have continued to organize around middle-class and urban issues. Women, with a strong cultural role as caretakers of the home, have begun to mobilize in many cities to demand community services, equal

Citizen Action: *Urban Popular Movements*

In October 1968, hundreds of students and working-class people took to the streets of Mexico City to protest high unemployment and the authoritarianism of the government. What began as a peaceful rally in Tlaltelolco Plaza ended in a tragedy when government troops opened fire on the crowd and killed more than two hundred people. The political activism of the students heralded the birth of urban popular movements in Mexico. The massacre in Tlaltelolco became a symbol of a government that was unwilling or unable to respond to citizen demands for economic and political equity. The protest movements sparked by the events of 1968 sought to transcend class boundaries and unite voices around a range of urban issues, from housing shortages to inadequate urban services, to lack of land, to centralized decision making. Such social movements forged new channels for poor and middle-class urban residents to express their needs. They also generated forums for demanding democratic government that the traditional political system was not providing. In May 1980, the first national congress of urban movements was held in Monterrey in northern Mexico.

Urban popular movements, referring to activities of low- and modest-income (popular) groups, gained renewed vitality in the 1980s. When the economic crisis resulted in drastic reductions of social welfare spending and city services, working- and middle-class neighborhoods forged new coalitions and greatly expanded the national discussion of urban problems. The Mexico City earthquake of 1985 encouraged the formation of unprecedented numbers of grass-roots movements in response to the slow and poorly managed relief efforts of the government. Turning to each other, earthquake victims organized to provide shelter, food, and relocation. The elections of 1988 and 1994 provided these groups with significant opportunities to press parties and candidates to respond to their needs. They insisted on their rights to organize and protest without fear of repression or co-optation by the government or the PRI. As the opposition parties expanded rapidly, some leaders of urban movements enrolled as candidates for public office.

Urban popular movements bring citizens together around needs and ideals that cut across class boundaries. Neighborhood improvement, the environment, local self-government, economic development, feminism, and professional identity have been among the factors that have forged links among these groups. As such identities have been strengthened, the need of the political system to negotiate and bargain with a more independent citizenry has increased. Urban popular movements have helped to transform political culture on the most local level, one reason the PAN was able to garner so many votes in the 2000 election.

---

pay, legal equality, and opportunities in business traditionally denied them.[22] Religious groups, both Catholic and Protestant, have begun to demand greater government attention to problems of poverty and inequity, as well as more government tolerance of religious education and religious practices. In the early 1990s, the government's social development program, which many critics claim was a ploy by President Salinas to win back respect for his government after the flawed elections of 1988, helped organize thousands of grass-roots organizations and possibly contributed to a trend towards broader mobilization independent of PRI clientelist networks.[23] In 1997 and 2000, unprecedented numbers of citizens volunteered their time to civic associations that observed the vote to ensure, ballot box by ballot box, that the votes were counted accurately. Where this occurred, mostly in urban areas, there were few accusations of fraud.

In the countryside, too, rural organizations demanded greater independence from government and the leaders of the PRI and the CNC (the national peasant association) in the 1980s.[24] In addition to

Mexicans demonstrate for better housing in Mexico City's central plaza. *Source:* Robert Freck/Odyssey/Chicago.

greater access to land, they demanded better prices for the crops they produced, access to markets and credit, development of better infrastructure, and the provision of better education and health services. They began to form alliances with other groups. Since 1994, the rebels in Chiapas have become a focal point for broad alliances of those concerned about the rights of indigenous groups (ethnic minorities) and rural poverty. Indigenous groups have also emerged to demand that government be responsive to their needs and respectful of their traditions. Overall, then, civil society in Mexico is becoming more pluralist and less easily controlled, and there is broader scope for legitimate protest, opposition, and dissent.

Section ❺ Mexican Politics in Transition

Political Challenges and Changing Agendas

Mexico confronts a world of increasing interdependence among countries. For all countries, economic integration raises issues of national sovereignty and identity. Mexicans define themselves in part through a set of historical events, symbols, and myths that focus on the country's troubled relationship with the United States. Among numerous national heroes and martyrs are those who distinguished themselves in confrontations with the United States. The myths of the Revolution of 1910 emphasize the uniqueness of the country in terms of its opposition to the capitalists and militarists of the northern country. In the 1970s, Mexicans were encouraged to see themselves as leading Third World countries in arguing for enhanced bargaining positions in relation to the industrialized countries of the north. This view stands in strong contrast to more recent perspectives touting the benefits of an internationally oriented economy and the undeniable post-NAFTA reality of information, culture, money, and people flowing back and forth across borders.

The country's sense of national identity is affected by international migration. Of particular importance in the Mexican case is labor migration. Every year, large numbers of Mexicans enter the

United States as workers. Many return to their towns and villages with new values and new views of the world. Many stay in the United States, where Hispanics have become the largest ethnic population in the country. Most continue to believe that Mexican culture is preferable to American culture, which they see as excessively materialistic and violent. Although they believe that Mexico is a better place to nurture strong family life and values, they are nevertheless strongly influenced by U.S. mass culture, including popular music, movies, television programs, fast food, and consumer goods (see "Global Connection: Mexican Migration to the United States").

The inability of the Mexican economy to create enough jobs pushes additional Mexicans to seek work in the United States, and the cash remittances that migrants abroad send home to their families and communities are now almost as important a source of income for Mexico as PEMEX's oil sales. However, the issues surrounding migration have become even more complex since the attacks of September 11, 2001. Hopes for a bilateral accord that would permit more Mexicans to enter and work in the United States legally evaporated after U.S. officials suddenly found themselves under greatly increased pressure to control the country's borders. Illegal immigration has not abated, however, and Mexican

Global Connection: *Mexican Migration to the United States*

The contrast between the poverty of much of the developing world and the prosperity of industrialized nations is nowhere on more vivid display than it is along the 2,000-mile-long border between Mexico and the United States. Because of the economic disparities that exist between the two neighboring countries, Mexicans with limited opportunities at home have long been venturing north of the border in search of jobs and a higher standard of living. The money that these migrants send back to Mexico helps to sustain not just their own families but entire regions that have been left behind by the country's uneven pattern of growth and development. As the number of the Mexican migrants seeking opportunities abroad has grown in recent years, their presence in the United States has come to have profound ramifications for the politics of both nations.

Mexicans began moving to the United States in substantial numbers late in the nineteenth century, and their ranks grew as many fled the chaotic conditions that had been created by the Revolution of 1910. Although some of these early migrants found work in northern industrial centers such as Chicago, most settled in the border states of California and Texas, where they joined pre-existing Mexican communities that had been there since the days when the American southwest had been part of Mexico. Even greater numbers of migrants began to arrive during World War II, when the U.S. government allowed Mexican workers, known as *braceros,* to enter the country to help provide much-needed manpower for strategic production efforts. The *bracero* program remained in place after the war, and under it, a predominantly male Mexican workforce provided seasonal labor to U.S. employers, mostly in the agricultural sector.

After the *bracero* program came to an end in 1964, Mexicans continued to seek work in the United States, despite the fact that most then had to enter the country illegally. To a large extent, the U.S. government informally tolerated the employment of undocumented migrants until the 1980s, when policymakers came under pressure to assert control over the border. The 1986 Immigration Reform and Control Act (IRCA) allowed migrants who had been in the United States for a long period of time to gain legal residency rights, but it called for tighter controls on immigration in the future.

However, rather than cutting off the movement of Mexicans into the United States, IRCA and subsequent efforts to deter illegal immigration simply turned a pattern of seasonal migration into a flow of migrants that settled permanently north of the border. Before 1986, most Mexican migrant workers left their families at home and worked in the United States for only a few months at a time before returning to their country with the money they had earned. But many of the seasonal migrants who gained amnesty under IRCA then sent for their families to join them, creating a more permanent immigrant community. Also, with increased vigilance and new barriers making the crossing of the border more difficult, more of the migrants who arrived in the United States decided to remain there rather than risk apprehension by traveling back and forth between the two countries. High-profile efforts to patrol the border around urban areas such as San Diego and El Paso led migrants to use more remote crossing points, and although the number of Mexicans who died trying to reach the United States rose as many attempted to travel through the desolate deserts of Arizona, the overall rate of illegal immigration was not affected by the government's crackdown.

In the 1990s, growing Mexican communities in the United States spread into areas such as North Carolina, Georgia, Arkansas, and Iowa, where few Mexicans had lived before. They also became increasingly mobilized politically as they organized to resist anti-immigrant voter initiatives such as Proposition 187 in California in 1994 and Proposition 200 in Arizona in 2004, both of which threatened to cut off social services for undocumented migrants. At the same time, their political importance in Mexico has reached unprecedented heights as officials at all levels of government there

(continued)

Global Connection: *Mexican Migration to the United States (cont.)*

recognize the critical importance to the Mexican economy of the $16.6 billion that the country receives each year in remittances from migrants working in other countries. Mexican governors, mayors, and federal officials now regularly visit representatives of migrant groups in the United States, often seeking their support and funding for projects at home. Moreover, a 1996 law allowing Mexicans to hold dual citizenship could allow

many Mexican migrants to have a voice in the governance of both the country of their birth as well as the country where they now reside. In 2005, Mexican legislators finally approved a system under which registered Mexican voters living abroad could participate in federal elections using mail-in ballots, and it is easy to imagine that this huge group could play a decisive role in future electoral contests.

---

officials continue to try to convince their counterparts in Washington that allowing more migrants to cross the border legally would actually enhance U.S. security by reducing the number of unauthorized crossings. Whether or not the U.S. government approves, the difference in wages between the United States and Mexico will persist for a long time, which implies that migration will also persist.

There is disagreement about how to respond to the economic challenges that Mexico faces. Much of the debate surrounds the question of what integration into a competitive international economy really means. For some, it represents the final abandonment of Mexico's sovereignty. For others, it is the basis on which future prosperity must be built. Those who are critical of the market-based, outward-oriented development strategy are concerned about its impact on workers, peasants, and national identities. They argue that the state has abandoned its responsibilities to protect the poor from shortcomings of the market and to provide for their basic needs. They believe that U.S. and Canadian investors have come to Mexico only to find low-wage labor for industrial empires located elsewhere, and they argue that those investors will not hesitate to abandon Mexico for even lower-wage countries such as China when the opportunity arises. They see little benefit in further industrial development based on importation of foreign-made parts, their assembly in Mexico, and their

export to other markets. This kind of development, they argue, has been prevalent in the *maquiladoras*, or assembly industries, many of which are located along the U.S.-Mexico border. Those who favor closer integration with Canada and the United States acknowledge that some foreign investment does not promote technological advances or move the work force into higher-paying and more skilled jobs. They emphasize, however, that most investment will occur because Mexico has a relatively well-educated population, the capacity to absorb modern technology, and a large internal market for industrial goods.

In addition to the economic challenges it faces, Mexico provides a testing ground for the democratic idea in a state with a long history of authoritarian institutions. The democratic ideas of citizen rights to free speech and assembly, free and fair elections, and responsive government are major reasons that the power of the PRI came under so much attack beginning in the 1980s. Currently, Mexico is struggling with opening up its political institutions to become more democratic. Vicente Fox, for example, promised to make information about government activities much more widely available to the population, and extensive files about violent military and police repression of political dissent in the past have been made available to citizens. The government also created the independent National Human Rights Commission, which has been active in protecting citizens' rights (see "Current Challenges: Human Rights in Mexico"). However, efforts to bring about greater transparency in the Mexican political system have sometimes run up against obstacles as government ministries have resisted pressures to release sensitive documents and as investigations into the -repressive activities of the PRI regime in decades past have been stymied. These setbacks leave some Mexicans skeptical of claims that a truly open, democratic political culture is being forged. Mean-

while, when Fox demonstrated little capacity to set priorities and communicate a vision for his government, many government agencies found it difficult to act, given a long history of dependence on presidential leadership. This has left many citizens with questions about the effectiveness of democratic institutions.

Centralization of power and decision making is another legacy that Mexico is trying to revise. Countries around the globe increasingly recognize that the

Current Challenges: *Human Rights in Mexico*

The government of Vicente Fox (2000–2006) committed itself to opening up government and improving the state of human rights in Mexico. In the past, the government had been able to limit knowledge of its repressive actions, use the court system to maintain the political peace, and intimidate those who objected to its actions. The president appointed human rights activists to his cabinet and ordered that secret police and military files be opened to public scrutiny. He instructed government ministries to supply more information about their activities and the rights that citizens have to various kinds of services. He also invited the United Nations to open a human rights office in Mexico. He encouraged the ratification of the Inter-American Convention on Enforced Disappearance of Persons. The government also sought to protect the rights of Mexicans abroad, and the United States and Mexico have established a working group to improve human rights conditions for migrants.

The results of these actions have been dramatic. For the first time, Mexicans learned of cases of hundreds of people who had "disappeared" as a result of police and military actions. In addition, citizens have come forward to announce other disappearances, ones they were unwilling to report earlier because they feared reprisals. In 2002, former president Luis Echvererría was brought before prosecutors and questioned about government actions against political dissent in 1968 and 1971, a kind of accountability unheard of in the past. The National Human Rights Commission has been active in efforts to hold

government officials accountable and to protect citizens nationally and abroad from repetitions of the abuses of the past.

Yet challenges to human rights accountability remain. Opening up files and setting up systems for prosecuting abusers need to be followed by actions to impose penalties on abusers. The judicial system is weak and has little experience in human rights cases. In addition, action on reports of disappearances, torture, and imprisonment has been slowed by contention about civil and military jurisdictions. In an embarrassing revelation to the government, Amnesty International reported several cases of disappearances that occurred after Fox assumed leadership of the country. There were also reports of arbitrary detentions and extrajudicial executions. In October 2001, Digna Ochoa, a prominent human rights lawyer, was shot. In the aftermath of this assassination, the government was accused of not doing enough to protect her, even when it was widely known that she had been targeted by those opposed to her work. Human rights activists claimed that police and military personnel, in particular, still had impunity to the laws. The strength of the Fox administration was tested in these events, and although human rights were much more likely to be protected than in the past, the government continued to have a long way to go in safeguarding the rights of indigenous people, political dissidents, migrants, gays and lesbians, and poor people whose ability to use the judicial system is limited by poverty and lack of information.

solutions to many policy problems lie at regional and local levels. While the government has introduced the decentralization of a number of activities and services, state and municipal governments are struggling to meet the demands of citizens who want competence, responsiveness, and accountability from their local and regional public officials

Improving social conditions is an important challenge for Mexico. While elites enjoy the benefits of sumptuous lifestyles, education at the best U.S. universities for their children, and luxury travel throughout the world, large numbers of Mexicans remain ill educated, poorly served with health care, and distant from the security of knowing that their basic needs for food, shelter, and employment can be met. The Chiapas rebellion of 1994 made the social agenda a topic of everyday conversation by reminding Mexicans that some people lived in appalling conditions with little hope for the future.

As in the United States, some argue that the best solutions to these problems are economic growth and expanded employment. They believe that the achievement of prosperity through integration into the global economy will benefit everyone in the long run. For this to occur, however, they insist that education will have to be improved and made more appropriate for developing a well prepared work force. They also believe that improved education will come about when local communities have more control over schools and curricula and when parents have more choice between public and private education for their children. From their perspective, the solution to poverty and injustice is fairly clear: more and better jobs and improved education.

For those critical of the development path on which Mexico embarked in the 1980s and 1990s, the problems of poverty and inequity are more complex. Solutions involve understanding the diverse causes of poverty, including not only lack of jobs and poor education but also exploitation, geographic isolation, discriminatory laws and practices, as well as the disruptive impact of migration, urbanization, and the tensions of modern life. In the past, Mexicans looked to government for social welfare benefits, but their provision was deeply flawed by inefficiency and political manipulation. The government consistently used access to social services as a means to increase its political control and limit the capacity of citizens to demand equitable treatment. Thus, although many continue to believe that it is the responsibility of government to ensure that citizens are well educated, healthy, and able to make the most of their potential, the populace is deeply suspicious of the government's capacity to provide such conditions fairly and efficiently.

Finally, Mexico is confronting major challenges of adapting newly democratic institutions to reflect ethnic and religious diversity and provide equity for women in economic and political affairs. The past decade has witnessed the emergence of more organized and politically independent ethnic groups demanding justice and equality from government. These groups claim that they have suffered for nearly 500 years and that they are no longer willing to accept poverty and marginality as their lot. The Roman Catholic Church, still the largest organized religion in the country, is losing members to Protestant sects that appeal particularly to the everyday concerns of poor Mexicans. Women, who make up 32 percent of the formal labor force but 40 percent of professional and technical workers, are becoming more organized, but they still have a long way to go before their wages equal those of men or they have equal voice in political and economic decisions.

Mexican Politics in Comparative Perspective

Mexico faces many of the same challenges that beset other countries: creating equitable and effective democratic government, becoming integrated into a global economy, responding to complex social problems, and supporting increasing diversity without losing national identity. Indeed, these were precisely the challenges that the United States faced at the millennium, as did India, Nigeria, Brazil, Germany, and others. Mexico confronts these challenges within the context of a unique historical and institutional evolution. The legacies of its past, the tensions of the present, and the innovations of the future will no doubt evolve in ways that continue to be uniquely Mexican.

What will the future bring? How much will the pressures for change and the potential loss of national identity affect the nature of the political system? In 1980, few people could have foreseen the extensive economic policy reforms and pressures for democracy that Mexico would experience in the next two decades. Few would have predicted the defeat of the PRI in the elections of 2000. In considering the future of the country, it is important to remember that Mexico has a long tradition of relatively strong institutions. It is not a country that will easily slip into sustained political instability. A tradition of constitutional government, a strong presidency, a political system that has incorporated a wide range of interests, little military involvement in politics, and a deep sense of national identity: these are among the factors that need to be considered in predicting the political consequences of democratization, economic integration, and greater social equality in Mexico.

Mexico represents a pivotal case of political and economic transition for the developing world. If it can successfully bridge the gap between its past and its future and move from centralization to effective local governance, from regional vulnerability to global interdependence, and from the control of the few to the participation of the many, it will set a model for other countries that face the same kind of challenges.

Key Terms

mestizo	corporatist state
Amerindian	civil society
indigenous groups	state capitalism
maquiladoras	import substituting
coup d'état	industrialization (ISI)
anticlericalism	informal sector
ejidos	proportional
ejidatarios	representation
sexenio	technocrats
clientelism	para-statal
North American Free	accommodation
Trade Agreement	co-optation
(NAFTA)	

Suggested Readings

Babb, Sarah L. *Managing Mexico: Economists from Nationalism to Neoliberalism.* Princeton, N.J.: Princeton University Press, 2001.

Bethell, Leslie, ed. *Mexico Since Independence.* Cambridge: Cambridge University Press, 1991.

Castañeda, Jorge G. *Perpetuating Power: How Mexican Presidents Were Chosen.* New York: New Press, 2000.

Chand, Vickram K. *Mexico's Political Awakening.* Notre Dame, Ind.: University of Notre Dame Press, 2001.

Collier, Ruth Berins. *The Contradictory Alliance: State-Labor Relations and Regime Change in Mexico.* Berkeley: University of California Press, 1992.

Cook, Maria Lorena, Middlebrook, Kevin J., and Molinar, Juan (eds.). *The Politics of Economic Restructuring in Mexico.* San Diego: Center for U.S.-Mexican Studies, University of California, 1994.

Cornelius, Wayne A. "Nation-Building, Participation, and Distribution: The Politics of Social Reform Under Cárdenas." In Gabriel A. Almond, Scott Flanagan, and Robert J. Mundt (eds.), *Crisis, Choice, and Change: Historical Studies of Political Development.* Boston: Little, Brown, 1973.

Cornelius, Wayne A., Eisenstadt, Todd A., and Hindley, Jane (eds.). *Subnational Politics and Democratization in Mexico.* San Diego: Center for U.S.-Mexican Studies, University of California, 1999.

Davidow, Jeffrey. *The U.S. and Mexico: The Bear and the Porcupine.* Princeton, N.J.: Markus Wiener Publishers, 2004.

Dominguez, Jorge I., and Lawson, Chappell H. (eds.). *Mexico's Pivotal Democratic Election: Candidates, Voters, and the Presidential Campaign of 2000.* Stanford, Calif.: Stanford University Press, 2004.

Durand, Jorge, Douglas S. Massey, and Emilio A. Parrado. "The New Era of Mexican Migration to the United States," *The Journal of American History* 86: 2 (September 1999)

Foweraker, Joe, and Craig, Ann L. (eds.), *Popular Movements and Political Change in Mexico.* Boulder, Colo.: Lynne Rienner, 1990.

Grindle, Merilee S. *Challenging the State: Crisis and Innovation in Latin America and Africa.* Cambridge: Cambridge University Press, 1995.

Harvey, Neil. *The Chiapas Rebellion: The Struggle for Land and Democracy.* Durham, N.C.: Duke University Press, 1998.

Krauze, Enrique. *Mexico, Biography of Power: A History of Modern Mexico, 1810-1996.* Trans. by Hank Heifetz. New York: HarperCollins, 1997.

Lawson, Chappell H. *Building the Fourth Estate: Democratization and the Rise of a Free Press in Mexico.* Berkeley: University of California, 2002.

Levy, Daniel C., and Bruhn, Kathleen. *Mexico: The Struggle for Democratic Development.* Berkeley: University of California Press, 2001.

Lustig, Nora. *Mexico: The Remaking of an Economy.* 2nd ed. Washington, D.C.: Brookings Institution, 1998.

Meyer, Michael C., Sherman, William L., and Deeds, Susan M. *The Course of Mexican History.* 7th ed. New York: Oxford University Press, 2002.

Paz, Octavio. *The Labyrinth of Solitude: Life and Thought in Mexico.* New York: Grove Press, 1961.

Preston, Julia, and Dillon, Samuel. *Opening Mexico: The Making of a Democracy.* New York: Farrar, Straus and Giroux, 2004.

Salinas de Gortari, Carlos. *México: The Policy and Politics of Modernization.* Trans. by Peter Hearn and Patricia Rosas. Barcelona: Plaza & Janés Editores, 2002.

Suárez-Orozco, Marcelo, ed. *Crossings: Mexican Immigration in Interdisciplinary Perspective.* Cambridge: Harvard University Press, 1998.

Ugalde, Luis Carlos. *The Mexican Congress: Old Player, New Power.* Washington, D.C.: Center for Strategic and International Studies, 2000.

Womack, John, Jr. *Zapata and the Mexican Revolution.* New York: Vintage Books, 1968.

Suggested Websites

Office of the President (in Spanish and English)
www.presidencia.gob.mx
Secretariat of Foreign Relations (in Spanish and English)
www.src.gob.mx
El Universal newspaper (in Spanish and English)
estadis.eluniversal.com.mx/noticiash.html
The Mexico Project, National Security Archive
www2.gwu.edu/~nsarchiv/mexico
Washington Post (registration required, free)
**www.washingtonpost.com/wp-dyn/world/americas/
northamerica/mexico**
Federal Electoral Institute (in Spanish only)
www.ife.org.mx/InternetCDA/HOME/home.jsp

Endnotes

[1] This figure represents an estimate of the metropolitan area of Mexico City, which extends beyond the official boundaries of the city.

[2] An excellent history of this event is presented in Wayne A. Cornelius, "Nation-Building, Participation, and Distribution: The Politics of Social Reform Under Cárdenas," in Gabriel A. Almond, Scott Flanagan, and Robert J. Mundt (eds.), *Crisis, Choice and Change: Historical Studies of Political Development* (Boston: Little, Brown, 1973).

[3] Michael C. Meyer and William K. Sherman, *The Course of Mexican History,* 5th ed. (New York: Oxford UP, 1995), 598–599.

[4] Although the self-confessed "lone gunman" was jailed, the ensuing investigation raised concerns about a possible conspiracy involving party and law enforcement officials as well as drug cartels. Rumors circulated about a cover-up scandal. Eventually, skepticism about the integrity of the inquiry was so great that President Salinas called for a new investigation. At this point, little remains known about what exactly happened in Tijuana and why.

[5] United Nations Development Programme, *Human Development Report* (2004), http://hdr.undp.org/reports/global/2004/pdf/hdr04_HDI.pdf.

[6] World Bank, *World Development Indicators* database, August 2004, http://www.worldbank.org/data/countrydata/ countrydata.html.

[7] World Bank, *World Development Report, 2001* (New York: Oxford University Press, 2001).

[8] Merilee S. Grindle, *State and Countryside: Development Policy and Agrarian Politics in Latin America* (Baltimore: Johns Hopkins University Press, 1986), 63, quoting President Avila Camacho (1940–1946).

[9] Kevin J. Middlebrook (ed.), *Unions, Workers, and the State in Mexico* (San Diego: Center for U.S.-Mexican Studies, University of California Press, 1991).

[10] Grindle, *State and Countryside,* 79–111.

[11] For a description of this process, see Carlos Bazdresch and Santiago Levy, "Populism and Economic Policy in Mexico," in Rudiger Dornbusch and Sebastian Edwards (eds.), *The Macroeconomics of Populism in Latin America* (Chicago: University of Chicago Press, 1991), 72.

[12] For an assessment of the mounting problems of Mexico City and efforts to deal with them, see Diane E. Davis, *Urban Leviathan: Mexico City in the Twentieth Century* (Philadelphia: Temple University Press, 1994).

[13] Joe Foweraker and Ann L. Craig (eds.), *Popular Movements and Political Change in Mexico* (Boulder, Colo.: Lynne Rienner, 1989).

[14] Roger Hansen, *The Politics of Mexican Development* (Baltimore: Johns Hopkins University Press, 1971), 75.

[15] World Bank, *World Development Indicators, 2004,* 61.

[16] Economist Intelligence Unit, *Country Commerce, Mexico* (London: EIU, September 2001), 43.

[17] Daniel Levy and Gabriel Székely, *Mexico: Paradoxes of Stability and Change* (Boulder, Colo.: Westview Press, 1983), 100.

[18] See Luis Carlos Ugalde, *The Mexican Congress: Old Player, New Power* (Washington, D.C.: Center for International and Strategic Studies, 2000).

[19] See Chapell H. Lawson, *Building the Fourth Estate: Democratization and the Rise of a Free Press in Mexico* (Berkeley: University of California Press, 2002).

[20]Susan Eckstein (ed.), *Power and Popular Protest: Latin American Social Movements* (Berkeley: University of California Press, 1989).

[21]Wayne A. Cornelius and Ann L. Craig, "Politics in Mexico," in Gabriel Almond and G. Bingham Powell (eds.), *Comparative Politics Today,* 5th ed. (Boston: Scott Foresman, 1992), 502.

[22]Foweraker and Craig, *Popular Movements and Political Change in Mexico.*

[23]Jonathan Fox and Gustavo Gordillo, "Between State and Market: The Campesinos' Quest for Autonomy," in Wayne A. Cornelius, Judith Gentleman, and Peter H. Smith (eds.), *Mexico's Alternative Political Futures* (San Diego: Center for U.S.-Mexican Studies, University of California Press, 1989).

[24]Wayne A. Cornelius, Ann L. Craig, and Jonathan Fox (eds.), *Transforming State-Society Relations in Mexico: The National Solidarity Strategy* (San Diego: Center for U.S.-Mexican Studies, University of California Press, 1994).

CHAPTER 6

Nigeria

Darren Kew and Peter Lewis

Federal Republic of Nigeria

Land and People

Capital	Abuja
Total area (square miles)	356,669 (more than twice the size of California)
Population	135.7 million

Annual population growth rate (%)	1975–2002	2.9
	2002–2015 (projected)	2.2

Urban population (%)	47

Ethnolinguistic composition (% of population)	Hausa-Fulani	26
	Yoruba	21
	Igbo (Ibo)	18
	Ijaw	7
	Other	28

Note: There are more than 250 ethnic groups in Nigeria.

Official Language	English

Religious affiliation (%)	Muslim	48
	Christian	45
	Indigenous	7

Economy

Domestic currency	Naira (NGN) US$1 = 132.89 NGN (2004 av.)	
Total GNI (US$)	47.5 billion (2002)	
GNI per capita (US$)	350 (2002)	
Total GNI at purchasing power parity (US$)	122.6 billion	
GNI per capita at purchasing power parity (US$)	950	

GDP annual growth rate (%)	1983–1993	4.9
	1993–2003	2.9
	2002	1.5
	2003	10.7
	2004	6.2

GDP per capita average annual growth rate (%)	1983–1993	1.9
	1993–2003	0.3

Inequality in income or consumption (1996–1997) (%)	Share of poorest 10%	1.6
	Share of poorest 20%	4.4
	Share of richest 20%	55.7
	Share of richest 10%	40.8
	Gini Index (1996–1997)	50.6

Structure of production (% of GDP)	Agriculture	36.3
	Industry	30.5
	Services	33.3

Labor force distribution (% of total)	Agriculture	70
	Industry	10
	Services	20

Exports as % of GDP	50.0
Imports as % of GDP	40.9

Society

Life expectancy at birth	42.0	
Infant mortality per 1,000 live births	87	

Adult literacy (% of population age 15+) (%)	Male	75.7
	Female	60.6

Access to information and communications (per 1,000 population)	Telephone lines	5
	Mobile phones	4
	Radios	200
	Televisions	68
	Personal computers	6.8

Women in Government and Economy

Women in the national legislature (2003)		
Lower house or single house (%)		6.4
Upper house (%)		3.7
Women at ministerial level (2001) (%)		22.6
Female economic activity rate (age 15 and above) (%)		47.8
Female labor force (% of total)		38
Estimated earned income (PPP US$)	Female	562
	Male	1,322

Composite Ratings and Rankings

Human Development Index ranking (value) out of 177 countries	151 (.466)
Gender-related Development Index (GDI) ranking (value) out of 144 countries	122 (.458)
Gender Empowerment Measure (GEM) ranking (value) out of 78 countries	N/A
Corruption Perception Index (CPI) ranking (value) out of 146 countries	144 (1.6)
Environmental Sustainability Index (ESI) ranking (value) out of 146 countries	98 (45.4)
Freedom in World Rating	Partly Free (4.0)

Political Organization

Political System   Democracy.

Regime History   Democratic government took office in May 1999, after sixteen years of military rule. The most recent national elections were held in 2003.

Administrative Structure   Nigeria is a federation of thirty-six states, plus the Federal Capital Territory (FCT) in Abuja. The three tiers of government are federal, state, and local. Actual power is centralized under the presidency and the governors.

Executive   U.S.-style presidential system, under Olusegun Obasanjo.

Legislature   A bicameral civilian legislature was elected in April 2003. The 109 senators are elected on the basis of equal representation: three from each state, and one from the FCT. The 360 members of the House of Representatives are elected from single-member districts.

Judiciary   The Nigerian judicial system resembles that of the United States with a network of local and district courts as well as state-level courts. The state-level judiciaries are subordinate to the Federal Court of Appeal and the Supreme Court of Nigeria, which consists of fifteen appointed associate justices and the chief justice. Every state of the federation can also opt to establish a system of Islamic law (*shari'a*)

courts for cases involving only Muslims in customary disputes (divorce, property, etc.); the secular courts, however, retain supreme jurisdiction at the federal level if any conflict arises over which system to use. Most Nigerian states feature such courts, which share a Federal *Shari'a* Court of Appeal in Abuja. Twelve northern states since 1999 have also instituted the *shari'a* criminal code, which allows for amputation for stealing, stoning to death for adultery, and other extreme sentences. Non-Muslim states may also set up customary courts, based on local traditional jurisprudence.

Party System   Thirty parties have been registered by the Nigerian electoral commission since 2002. The largest are the People's Democratic Party (PDP), the All Nigerian People's Party (ANPP), the Alliance for Democracy (AD), and the All Progressive Grand Alliance (APGA). PDP won the presidency, majorities in both houses of the National Assembly, as well as a majority of governorships, state assemblies, and local governments.

Section ❶ The Making of the Modern Nigerian State

Politics in Action

Olusegun Obasanjo took office as president in May 1999 amid tremendous domestic and international goodwill as Nigeria's first elected civilian leader in nearly twenty years. Flanked by Nelson Mandela and other global dignitaries, Obasanjo boldly stated his intentions to reform the corrupt Nigerian state, reverse its economic decline, and restore the nation's international stature. A succession of oppressive, thieving military leaders in the 1980s and 1990s had stolen billions from the national coffers, leaving this oil-rich nation in tremendous debt and making it an international pariah; 130 million Nigerians looked to Obasanjo to rectify the political sins of the past and pull them out of impoverishment. The president promised to do both, and in 1999 he set out with an ambitious political agenda.

Three years later, the National Assembly set out to impeach him. Members of Obasanjo's own party, including the Speaker of the House, sponsored the resolution to instigate impeachment proceedings. The legislators spoke publicly of the president's

unconstitutional behavior, but in private they were more outraged by his heavy-handed methods (including attempts to make ad hoc changes to election laws, and efforts to unseat contentious legislative leaders), aggravated by the fact that he refused to disburse their personal allowances for the year.

President Obasanjo's struggles with the National Assembly are symptomatic of the larger obstacles his government faces in trying to revive the dysfunctional Nigerian state. His ambitious agenda has run aground on the many contradictions in governance left by years of military rule, including a disproportionately powerful presidency married to an inexperienced legislature, all enmeshed in a web of rivalries among various powerbrokers and their supporters. In addition, the young democracy faces the challenge of managing the country's contentious ethnic and religious diversity in conditions of scarcity and weak institutions. Furthermore, years of economic decline and political corruption have left most Nigerians with little patience for Obasanjo's fragile, internally divided government to deliver significant progress. The military left power in 1999 a discredited institution, but it is slowly rebuilding, and the clock is ticking against the civilians: Will public frustrations with the slow pace of reform hold off long enough for democracy to consolidate sufficiently to meet even minimal public expectations?

Nigeria encapsulates many characteristics that more broadly identify Africa. These opposing forces are rooted in the constant struggle in Nigeria between **authoritarian** and democratic governance, the push for development amidst persistent underdevelopment, the burden of public corruption, and the pressure for accountability. Nigeria, like all other African countries, has sought to create a viable nation-state out of the social incoherence created by its colonial borders. Over 250 competing ethnic groups, crosscut by two major religious traditions, have repeatedly clashed over economic and political resources, as well as issues of administrative and legal identity. All of these factors combine to produce the political entity known as Nigeria with low levels of popular **legitimacy** and **accountability,** and a persistent inability to meet the most basic needs of its citizens. The country therefore provides a crucible in which to examine questions of democracy and authoritarianism, the pressures and management of ethnic conflict, and economic underdevelopment brought about by both colonial oppression and independent Nigeria's mismanagement of its vast resources.

Much about Nigeria is contentious. Since gaining independence from British colonial rule in 1960, Nigeria has undergone several political transitions, from democratic governments to autocratic regimes, both military and civilian, and from one military regime to another. It has experienced six successful coups and many unsuccessful attempted coups (most recently in 2004), and it was torn by three years of civil war that claimed over 100,000 military and over 1 million civilian casualties. Against this background, Nigeria today remains essentially an **unfinished state** characterized by instabilities and uncertainties.

Nigeria reached another critical turning point in 1999 when a military government transferred power to civilians for the second time since the British left in 1960. The civilians held their own elections in 2003 for the first time since 1983, when the elections were so flawed that the public welcomed a military coup. The 2003 elections were also deeply flawed. Will Nigeria return to the discredited path of authoritarianism and greater underdevelopment, or will the civilian leadership rise to achieve a consolidated democracy and sustainable growth?

Geographic Setting

Nigeria, with 130 million people inhabiting 356,669 square miles, ranks as the most populous nation in Africa and among the ten largest in the world. A center of West African regional trade, culture, and military strength, Nigeria is bordered by four countries—Benin, Niger, Chad, and Cameroon, all of them Francophone—and by the Gulf of Guinea in the Atlantic Ocean to the south. The modern country of Nigeria, however, like nearly all the other contemporary states in Africa, is not even a century old.

Nigeria was a British colony from 1914 until its independence on October 1, 1960, although foreign domination of much of the territory had begun in the mid-nineteenth century. Nigeria's boundaries had little to do with the borders of the precolonial African societies in the territory that the British conquered. Instead, these boundaries merely marked the point where British influence ended and French began. Britain ruled northern and southern Nigeria as two separate colonies until 1914, when it amalgamated its Northern and Southern Protectorates. In short, Nigeria was an arbitrary creation reflecting British colonial interests. The consequences of this forced union of myriad African cultures and ruling entities under one political roof remain a central feature of Nigerian political life today.

Nigeria's location in West Africa, its size, and its oil-producing status have made it a hub of regional activity. Demographically, it overwhelms the other fifteen countries in West Africa, with a population that is nearly 60 percent of the region's total. Moreover, Nigeria's gross domestic product (GDP) typically represents more than half of the total GDP for the entire subregion.

Nigeria's ethnic map can be divided into six inexact areas or "zones." The northwest (or "core North") is dominated by Nigeria's single largest ethnic group, the Hausa-Fulani, two formerly separate groups that over the past century have largely merged. The northeast is a minority region, the largest of whom are the Kanuri. Both regions in the north are predominantly Muslim.

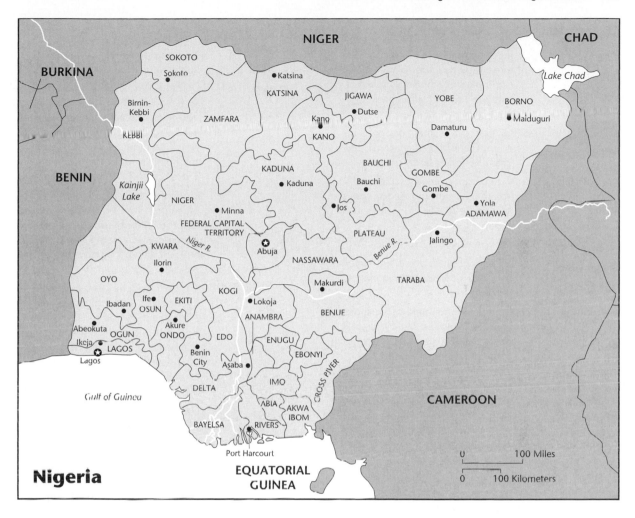

Nigeria

A large swath of territory stretching across the center of the country, called the Middle Belt, is also home to a wide range of minority groups of both Muslim and Christian faiths. The southwest (referred to as the Western Region in the First Republic) is dominated by the country's second largest ethnic group, the Yoruba, who are approximately 40 percent Muslim, 50 percent Christian (primarily Protestant), and 10 percent practitioners of Yoruba traditional beliefs. The southeast (which formed the hub of the First Republic's Eastern Region) is the Igbo homeland, Nigeria's third largest group, who are primarily Christian, and where Protestant evangelical movements have become popular. Between the Yoruba and Igbo regions of the south is the southern minority zone, which stretches across the Niger Delta areas and east along the coast as far as Cameroon.

Critical Junctures

A number of critical junctures have shaped the character of the Nigerian state and illustrate the difficult path that the country has taken during the past half-century. Nigeria's recent history reflects influences from the precolonial period, the crucial changes wrought by British colonialism, the post-colonial alternation of military and civilian rule, and the economic collapse since 1980, precipitated by Nigeria's political corruption and its overreliance on the petroleum industry.

Critical Junctures in Modern Nigerian Political Development

1960 Independence. Nigeria consists of three regions under a Westminster parliamentary model. Abubakar Tafawa Balewa, a northerner, is the first prime minister.

January 1966 Civilian government deposed in coup. General Aguiyi Ironsi, an Igbo, becomes head of state.

July 1966 Countercoup is led by General Yakubu Gowon (an Anga, from the Middle Belt) with aid from northern groups.

1967–1970 Biafran civil war

July 1975 Military coup deposes Gowon; led by General Murtala Muhammed, a northerner.

February 1976 Murtala Muhammed assassinated in failed coup led by Middle Belt minorities. Muhammed's second-in-command, General Olusegun Obasanjo, a Yoruba, assumes power.

September 1978 New constitution completed, marking the adoption of the U.S. presidential model in a federation with 19 states.

October 1979 Elections held. A majority in both houses is won by NPN, led by northern/Hausa-Fulani groups. Alhaji Shehu Shagari is elected Nigeria's first executive president.

December 1983 Military coup led by General Muhammadu Buhari, a northerner.

August 1985 Buhari is overthrown by General Ibrahim B. Babangida, a Middle Belt Muslim, in a palace coup. Babangida promises a return to democracy by 1990, a date he delays five times before being forced from office.

June 12, 1993 Moshood Abiola wins presidential elections, but Babangida annuls the election eleven days later.

August 1993 Babangida installs Ernest Shonekan as "interim civilian president" until new presidential elections could be held later that autumn.

November 1993 Defense Minister General Sani Abacha seizes power in a coup. Two years later he announces a three-year transition to civilian rule, which he manipulates to have himself nominated for president in 1998.

July–Sept. 1994 Prodemocracy strike by the major oil union, NUPENG, cuts Nigeria's oil production by an estimated 25 percent. Sympathy strikes ensue, followed by arrests of political and civic leaders.

June 1998 General Abacha dies; succeeded by General Abdulsalami Abubakar, a Middle Belt Muslim from Babangida's hometown. Abubakar releases nearly all political prisoners and installs a new transition program. Parties are allowed to form unhindered.

1999 Former head of state Olusegun Obasanjo and his party, the PDP, sweep the presidential and National Assembly elections, adding to their majority control of state and local government seats. The federation now contains thirty-six states.

November 1999 Zamfara state in the North is the first of twelve to institute the *shari'a* criminal code. That same month, President Obasanjo sends the army to the Niger Delta town of Odi to root out local militias, leveling the town in the process.

2000 Communal conflicts erupt in Lagos, Benue, Kaduna, and Kana states at different times over localized issues.

Spring 2002 The Supreme Court passes several landmark judgments, overturning a PDP-biased 2001 electoral law, and ruling on the control of offshore oil and gas resources. In November the Court opens the legal door for more parties to be registered.

August 2002	The National Assembly begins impeachment proceedings against President Obasanjo over budgetary issues. The matter ends by November, with the president apologizing.
July 2003	Rogue police units stage a coup in Anambra State, temporarily arresting the governor. The putsch soon collapses, but Anambra becomes a war zone between the governor and the state's political kingpin, who has family ties to the president.
May 2004	Politically motivated ethnic violence in Plateau State spreads to Benue and Kano states. The government imposes emergency rule in Plateau State, which ends in November.
March 2005	The presidency convenes a national political reform conference to debate the structure of the federation and to refine the constitution.

The Precolonial Period (800–1900)

Much of Nigeria's precolonial history before 1000 A.D. has been reconstructed from oral histories, since literate cultures evolved much later. In contrast to the peoples of the forest belt to the south, the more open terrain in the north, with its need for irrigation, encouraged the early growth of centralized states. Such states from the eighth century included Kanem-Bornu in the northeast and the Hausa states in the northwest. Another attempt at state formation led to the emergence of a Jukun kingdom, which by the end of the seventeenth century was a tributary state of the Bornu Empire.

A major element that shaped the course of events in the savanna areas of the north was trade across the Sahara Desert with northern Africa. Trade brought material benefits as well as Arabic education and Islam, which gradually replaced traditional spiritual, political, and social practices. In 1808, the Fulani, who came from lands west of modern Nigeria through a holy war (*jihad*) led by Uthman dan Fodio, established an Islamic empire, the Sokoto Caliphate. Portions of the region to the south, the present day Middle Belt,

were able to repel the *jihad* and preserve their independence and religious diversity. The Sokoto Caliphate used Islam and a common language, Hausa, to forge unity out of the disparate groups in the north. The Fulani Empire held sway until British colonial authority was imposed on northern Nigeria by 1900.

Toward the southern edge of the savanna lived such groups as the Tiv, whose political organization seldom extended beyond the village level. Within such societies, politics was generally conducted along kinship lines, and the fundamental political unit was the extended family. Political authority was diffuse rather than centralized, such that later Western contacts described them as "stateless," or **acephalous societies.** Because they lacked complex political hierarchies, these societies escaped much of the upheaval experienced under colonialism by the centralized states, and they retained much of their autonomy.

The development of collective identities in southern Nigeria was equally complex. Groups included the highly centralized Yoruba empires and kingdoms of Oyo and Ife; the Edo kingdom of Benin in the Midwest; the acephalous societies of the Igbo to the east; and the trading city-states of the Niger Delta and its hinterland, peopled by a wide range of ethnicities.

Several precolonial societies had democratic elements that scholars speculate might have led to more open and participatory polities had they not been interrupted by colonialism. Governance in the Yoruba and Igbo communities involved principles of accountability: rulers could not disregard the views and interests of the governed or they would risk revocation of consent and loss of their positions. Another element was representation, defined less in terms of formal procedures for selecting leaders, and more in terms of assurances that rulers adhered to culturally mandated principles and obligations that forced them to seek out and protect the interests of their subjects.

Among the Islamic communities of the north, political society was highly structured, reflecting local interpretations of Qur'anic principles. Leadership structures were considerably more hierarchical than those of the south, dominated by a few educated elites in positions of authority. In addition (although some of the pre-Islamic indigenous beliefs showed deference to important women spirit leaders), women were consigned to a subordinate position in systems

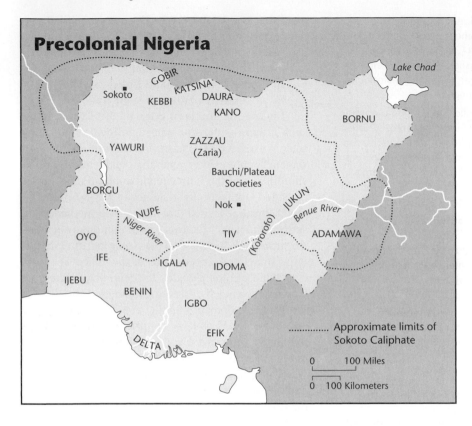

Precolonial Polities and Societies. *Source:* K. Michael Barbour, Julius Oguntoyinbo, J.O.C. Onyemelukwe, and James C. Nwafor, *Nigeria in Maps* (New York: Africana Publishing Company, 1982), 37.

of governance. The Islamic Fulani Empire was a confederation in which the rulers, **emirs,** owed allegiance to the sultan, who was the temporal and spiritual head of the empire. The sultan's powers, in turn, were circumscribed by the obligation to observe the principles of Islam in fulfilling his duties.

Colonial Rule and Its Impact (1860–1945)

Competition for trade and empire drove the European imperial powers further into Africa after 1860. Colonial rule deepened the extraction of Nigeria's natural resources and the exploitation of Nigerian labor, according to the economic and political requisites of Britain, the governing power. Colonialism left its imprint on all aspects of Nigeria's existence, bequeathing political and economic systems that have left enduring imprints on development and governance.

Where centralized monarchies existed in the north, the British ruled through a policy known as **indirect rule,** which allowed traditional structures to persist as subordinates to the British governor and a small administrative apparatus. Where more dispersed kingships ruled, as among the Yoruba, or where acephalous societies existed, particularly among the Igbo and other groups in the southeast, the colonizers either strengthened the authority of traditional chiefs and kings or appointed **warrant chiefs** (who ruled by warrant of the British Crown), weakening the previous practices of accountability and participation.

The British played off ethnic and social divisions to keep Nigerians from developing organized political resistance to colonial rule, and where resistance did develop, the colonizers were not afraid to employ repressive tactics, even as late as the 1940s. Yet the British also promoted the foundations of a democratic political system before they left in 1960. This dual standard left a conflicted democratic idea: formal democratic institutions yet an authoritarian political culture. Colonialism also strengthened the collective identities of Nigeria's multiple ethnic groups by fostering political competition among them, primarily among the three largest: the Hausa-Fulani, Yoruba, and Igbo.

Divisive Identities: Ethnic Politics Under Colonialism (1945–1960)

Based on their experience under British rule, leaders of the anticolonial movement came to regard the state as an exploitative instrument, and its control as an opportunity to pursue personal and group interests rather than broad national interests. Thus, when the British began to negotiate a gradual exit from Nigeria, the semblance of unity that had existed among the anticolonial leaders prior to the 1950s soon evaporated, and intergroup political competition became increasingly fierce.

Nigerian leaders quickly turned to ethnicity as the preferred vehicle to pursue competition and mobilize public support. The three largest ethnic groups, the Hausa-Fulani, Igbo, and Yoruba, though each a minority, together comprise approximately two-thirds of Nigeria's population, and they have long dominated the political process. By pitting ethnic groups against each other for purposes of divide and rule and by structuring the administrative units of Nigeria based on ethnic groups, the British ensured that ethnicity would be the primary element in political identification and mobilization.

Nigerian ethnic groups, championed by educated local elites, rallied followers based on common ethnic identity and challenged the colonial administration, while also competing with rivals from other ethnic groups. Initially, ethnically based associations were concerned with nonpolitical issues: promoting mutual aid for housing and education, as well as sponsoring cultural events. With the encouragement of ambitious leaders, however, these groups took on a more political character. Nigeria's first political party, the National Council of Nigeria and the Cameroons (later the National Convention of Nigerian Citizens, NCNC), initially drew supporters from across Nigeria. As the prospects for independence increased, however, indigenous elites began to divide along ethnic lines to mobilize support for their differing political agendas.

Recognizing the multiethnic character of their colony, the British divided Nigeria into a federation of three regions with elected governments in 1954. Each of the regions soon fell under the domination of one of the major ethnic groups and their respective parties. The Northern Region came under the control of the Northern Peoples Congress (NPC), dominated by Hausa-Fulani elites. In the southern half of the country, the Western Region was controlled by the Action Group (AG), which was controlled by Yoruba elites. The Igbo, the numerically dominant group in the Eastern Region, were closely associated with the NCNC, which became the ruling party there. Thus, ethnic and regional distinctions of modern Nigeria were reinforced in divisive ways during the transition to independence.[1]

Chief Obafemi Awolowo, leader of the AG, captured the sentiment of the times when he wrote in 1947 that "Nigeria is not a nation. It is a mere geographical expression. There are no 'Nigerians' in the same sense as there are 'English,' 'Welsh,' or 'French.' The word 'Nigerian' is merely a distinctive appellation to distinguish those who live within the boundaries of Nigeria from those who do not."[2]

The First Republic (1960–1966)

The British granted Nigeria independence in 1960 to an elected parliamentary government. Nigerians adopted the British Westminster model at the federal and regional levels, in which the chief executive, the prime minister, was chosen by the majority party. Northerners came to dominate the federal government by virtue of their greater population, based on the 1952–1953 census. The ruling coalition for the first two years quickly turned into a northern-only grouping when the NPC achieved an outright majority in the legislature. Having benefited less from the economic, educational, and infrastructural benefits of colonialism, the northerners who dominated the First Republic set out to redistribute resources to their benefit. This NPC policy of "northernization" brought them into direct conflict with their southern counterparts, particularly the Yoruba-based AG and later the Igbo-dominated NCNC.

When an AG internal conflict led to a political crisis in the Western regional assembly in 1962, the NPC-led national government seized the opportunity

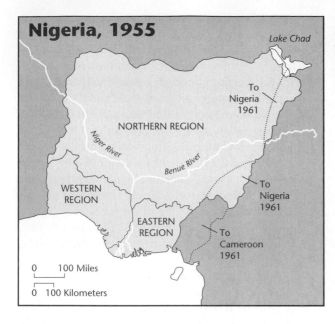

Nigeria, 1955

Lake Chad

To Nigeria 1961

NORTHERN REGION

Niger River

Benue River

WESTERN REGION

EASTERN REGION

To Nigeria 1961

To Cameroon 1961

0   100 Miles

0   100 Kilometers

Nigeria in 1955: Divided into Three Federated Regions. The administrative division of Nigeria into three regions later became the basis for ethnoregional conflicts. (Note: At the time of independence, the southeastern part of the country, which had been governed as a trust territory, opted to become part of independent Cameroon; two northern trust territories opted to become part of independent Nigeria.)
Source: K. Michael Barbour, Julius Oguntoyinbo, J.O.C. Onyemelukwe, and James C. Nwafor, *Nigeria in Maps* (New York: Africana Publishing Company, 1982), 39.

to subdivide the Western (largely Yoruba) Region in two—diluting Yoruba political power. Violence escalated among the Yoruba factions in the West as the NPC-dominated government engaged in extensive political corruption. A fraudulent census, falsified ballots in the general elections, widespread violence, and intimidation of supporters and candidates alike ensured the NPC a tarnished victory in 1965.

Rivalries intensified as the NPC sat atop an absolute majority in the federal parliament with no need for its former coalition partner, the NCNC. Nnamdi Azikiwe, the NCNC leader who was also president in the First Republic (then a largely symbolic position), and Tafawa Balewa, the NPC prime minister, separately approached the military to ensure that if it came to conflict, they could count on its loyalty. Thus, "in the struggle for personal survival both men, perhaps inadvertently, made the armed forces aware that they had a political role to play."[3]

Civil War and Military Rule (1966–1979)

With significant encouragement from contending civilian leaders, a group of largely Igbo officers seized power in January 1966. Aguiyi Ironsi, also an Igbo, became head of state by dint of being the highest-ranking

officer rather than a coup plotter. His announced aim was to end violence in the Western Region and to stop political corruption and abuses by the northern-dominated government by centralizing the state apparatus, thereby replacing the federation with a unitary state. Although Ironsi claimed to be ethnically plural in his outlook, other Nigerians, particularly northerners, were deeply suspicious of his revocation of federalism. A second coup in July 1966 killed General Ironsi and brought Yakubu Gowon, a Middle Belt Christian, to power as a consensus head of state among the non-Igbo coup plotters.[4]

Because many northern officials had been killed in the initial coup, a tremendous backlash against Igbos flared in several parts of the country during 1966, especially after the second coup. Igbo migrant laborers were persecuted in the north, and ethnic violence sent many Igbos fleeing to their home region in the east. By 1967, the predominantly Igbo population of eastern Nigeria attempted to secede and form its own independent nation, named Biafra. The secessionists wanted to break free from Nigeria, believing that the north, by virtue of its greater numbers, would permanently lock the other regions out of power. General Gowon built a military-led government of national unity in what remained of Nigeria (the North and West) and, after a bloody three-year war of attrition and starvation tactics, defeated Biafra by January 1970. The conflict exacted a heavy toll on Nigeria's populace, including at least a million deaths.

After the war, Gowon presided over a policy of national reconciliation, which proceeded fairly smoothly with the aid of growing oil revenues. In order to dilute the power of the "big three" ethnic groups, he broke the four-region federation into twelve states, later increased to nineteen by his successor. He also oversaw an increase in the armed forces from about 10,000 men in 1966 to nearly 250,000 by 1970. Senior officers reaped the benefits of the global oil boom in 1973–1974, and corruption was widespread. Influenced by the unwillingness of the military elite to relinquish power and the spoils of office, Gowon opted to postpone a return to civilian rule, which he had pledged originally to complete by 1976. He was overthrown in 1975 by Murtala Muhammad, who promptly reactivated the transition program.

Muhammed was committed to the restoration of democracy, but he was assassinated in 1976. General Olusegun Obasanjo, Muhammad's second-in-command who took power after the assassination, peacefully ceded power to an elected civilian government in 1979, which became known as the Second Republic. Obasanjo retired but would later reemerge as a civilian president in 1999.

The Second and Third Republics, and Predatory Military Rule (1979–1999)

The president of the 1979–1983 Second Republic, Shehu Shagari, and his ruling National Party of Nigeria (NPN, drawn largely from the First Republic's northern-dominated NPC), did little to assuage the mistrust between the various parts of the federation, or to stem rampant corruption. Regional and ethnic polarization persisted, the economy deteriorated rapidly, and the conspicuous misconduct of politicians and political parties eroded the legitimacy of civilian rule. Four years of factional infighting, weak leadership, declining public services, chronic economic mismanagement, a steady parade of corruption scandals, and growing political violence increased public restiveness toward the civilian regime. The NPN captured outright majorities in the 1983 state

General Olusegun Obasanjo was the Nigerian head of state who supervised the transition to civilian rule from 1976 to 1979. In 1995 he was arrested and convicted in a secret trial in connection with an alleged attempt to overthrow the regime of General Abacha. After his release, he won the presidency in 1999 as a candidate for the PDP. *Source:* Bettmann/Corbis.

and national elections through massive fraud and violence. The last vestiges of popular tolerance dissipated, and a few months later the military, led by Major General Muhammadu Buhari, seized power.

When General Buhari refused to pledge a rapid return to democratic rule and failed to revive a plummeting economy, his popular support wavered, and in August 1985 General Ibrahim Babangida seized power. Although Babangida quickly announced a program of transition to democratic rule, he and his cohort engaged in an elaborate series of stalling tactics in order to extend their tenure in office. What promised to be the dawn of a Third Republic ended in betrayal when Babangida annulled the presidential election of June 12, 1993, which should have preceded a full withdrawal of the military from the political scene. In stark contrast to all prior elections since independence, the 1993 election was widely acclaimed as fair (despite military restrictions on the scope of competition), and was evidently won by Yoruba businessman Chief Moshood Abiola. The annulment provoked angry reactions from a population weary of postponed transitions, lingering military rule, and the deception of rulers. Babangida could not resist pressures to resign, but he did manage to handpick his successor, Ernest Shonekan, to head a civilian caretaker government with no mandate or public foundation.

General Sani Abacha, who had been installed by Babangida as defense minister in the caretaker regime, seized power from Shonekan in November 1993. Shonekan's government, never regarded by the public as legitimate, was vulnerable to increasing agitation from both civilian and military ranks, providing an opportunity for Abacha to remove the caretaker council. As head of state, General Abacha prolonged the now established tradition of military dominance, combining repression with frequent public promises to restore constitutional democracy. Like Babangida, Abacha announced a new program of transition to civilian rule and regularly delayed the steps in its implementation. He cracked down on political opposition, severely constricted civil liberties and political rights, and fomented corruption on a stupendous scale. Only Abacha's sudden death in June 1998 saved the country from certain crisis, as his scheme to orchestrate the outcome of the transition to produce his own "election" as president became clearer. General Abdulsalami Abubakar, Abacha's successor, quickly established a new transition program and promptly handed it over to an elected civilian government led

General Sani Abacha, a prominent member of Nigerian military regimes since December 1983, took over the government in November 1993, disbanded all elective institutions, and suppressed opposition forces. His death in June 1998 was celebrated in the streets; he and his close supporters looted billions of U.S. dollars from the nation's coffers. *Source:* AP/Wide World Photos.

by President Olusegun Obasanjo and the People's Democratic Party (PDP) in May 1999.

The Fourth Republic (1999 to the Present)

Obasanjo was called out of retirement by the leaders of the PDP to run for president for several reasons. Many Yorubas felt that their group had long been cheated of the presidency by northern elites, especially when Moshood Abiola's 1993 election victory was annulled. Yet most northern leaders did not trust the prominent Yoruba politicians. Obasanjo, although a Yoruba, handed power as military head of state in 1979 to the northerner Shehu Shagari at the dawn of the Second Republic. The northern political establishment then concluded that Obasanjo was a Yoruba candidate they could trust. In addition, many perceived that an ex-military leader could better manage the thorny task of keeping the armed forces in the barracks once they left power.

Yet Obasanjo was initially unpopular among his own people, and he assumed the presidency in 1999 with few Yoruba votes in an election marred by irregularities at the polls. Nonetheless, he claimed a broad mandate to arrest the nation's decline by reforming the state and economy. Within weeks, he electrified the nation by retiring all the military officers who had held positions of political power under previous military governments, seeing them as the most likely plotters of future coups.

Obasanjo began to address the manifold issues surrounding the stagnant economy. The critical oil sector was targeted for new management, while the president lobbied foreign governments to forgive Nigeria's massive debts. The minimum wage was raised significantly, a "truth and reconciliation" commission was set up to address past abuses, an anticorruption commission addressed previous misconduct as well as current offenses, and a special commission was created to channel a greater portion of oil revenues back to the impoverished and environmentally ravaged Niger Delta region, where oil is extracted. Civil society groups thrived on renewed political freedom, and the media grew bold in exposing corrupt practices in government, forcing a Speaker of the House of Representatives and two Senate presidents to resign.

Despite his ambitions for reform, Obasanjo had political debts to his party, and his first cabinet included many of the corrupt politicians who had brought down the nation's previous republics and had colluded with Generals Babangida and Abacha in the 1980s and 1990s. Veteran politicians along with newcomers at all levels of government grew increasingly bold in lining their own pockets with public funds. Obasanjo's political survival, notably his bid for re-election in 2003, required many of these same politicians to deliver the support of their constituencies, rendering the president's anticorruption machinery largely dormant in his first term, and bringing his reform agenda to a halt.

Having surrounded himself with politicians for whom he held little trust, Obasanjo largely kept his own counsel on matters of state. The president was openly disdainful of the National Assembly, and he eventually faced two motions to impeach him. After weeks of tense negotiations, the impeachment drive relented.

Having avoided impeachment, President Obasanjo secured renomination from his party in the 2003 elections through a series of political accommodations with key party barons. The PDP political machinery charged with organizing the election effort engaged in widespread electoral malpractices. In the states of the Niger Delta and the southeast, the ruling party brazenly rigged the elections, while in other regions, the veracity of election outcomes were highly questionable. There were also questions about a number of opposition victories in the northern and northeastern states that they controlled.

Political deals and sharp election practices saved the president's second term and secured the PDP's dominance, but public confidence in the president and the new democratic system plummeted in the wake of the second election. Political feuds led to political upheavals in the states, and the declaration of a state of emergency in violence-wracked Plateau state. Faced with increasing political turmoil and social conflict, the president called a National Political Reform Conference in early 2005, ostensibly to review the constitution and the structure of the federation, with the unstated goal of shoring up his government's sagging legitimacy.

Themes and Implications

Historical Junctures and Political Themes

Federalism and democracy have been important strategies in Nigeria for realizing "unity in diversity" (the national motto), with the goals of building a coherent nation-state out of over 250 different ethnic groups and blending democratic values with accountable government. In reality, the legacy of colonial rule and many years of military domination have yielded a unitary system in federal guise: a system with an all-powerful central government surrounded by weak and economically insolvent states.

When the military returned to the barracks in 1999, it left an overdeveloped executive arm at all levels of government—federal, state, and local—at the expense of weak legislative and judicial institutions. Unchecked executive power under the military, and a dominant executive under the civilians, has encouraged the arbitrary exercise of authority, accompanied by patronage politics, which sap the economy of its vitality, prevent accountability, and undermine the rule of law.

Since the return of democratic rule, the state governments, the National Assembly, and the judiciary have been whittling away at the powers of the national executive. The president, however, remains the dominant figure in Nigerian politics.

Nigeria in the World of States: Oil Dependence and Decline. Although Nigeria enjoys economic and military power within the West African region, on a global level, it is marginalized and vulnerable. Nigeria, with its natural riches, has long been regarded as a potential political and economic giant of Africa. Yet the World Bank lists it among the poorest 20 percent of the countries of the world, with a GDP per capita of just over $300. Instead of independent growth, today Nigeria depends on unpredictable oil revenues, sparse external loans, and aid—a victim of its leaders' bad policies and poor management. Owing to neglect of agriculture, Nigeria moved from self-sufficiency in the production of basic foodstuffs in the mid-1960s to heavy dependence on imports less than twenty years later. Manufacturing activities, after a surge of investment by government and foreign firms in the 1970s,

suffered from inefficiency and disinvestment in subsequent decades, sagging to levels not seen since independence.

Nigeria's economy remains dependent on oil, and its heavy indebtedness gives foreign creditors and the International Monetary Fund (IMF) considerable leverage over its macroeconomic policies. Years of predatory military rule made Nigeria a political and economic pariah in the 1990s, and deteriorating political institutions made the country a way station for international drug trafficking to the United States and for international commercial fraud. Although the most recent accession of democratic government ended the nation's political isolation, its economy remains subject to the vicissitudes of the international oil market. The government has been favored in the short term by high oil prices and increasing U.S. consumption of Nigerian oil and gas, but there has been no effective restructuring or diversification of the petroleum monoculture.

Governing Nigeria's Economy.   Nigeria's oil dependence is a symptom of deeper structural problems. The very concept of the state was introduced into the colony in large part to restructure and subordinate the local economy to European capitalism. The Nigerian colonial state was conceived and fashioned as **interventionist,** with broad license to intrude into major sectors of the economy and society. The principal goals of the British colonial enterprise were to control the Nigerian economy and to marshal the flow of resources from the colonies to the metropole. A secondary concern was the creation of an economy hospitable to free markets and private enterprise. Nigeria's interventionist state extended its management of the economy, including broad administrative controls and significant ownership positions in areas as diverse as agriculture, banking, commerce, manufacturing, transportation, mining, education, health, employment, and, eventually, oil and natural gas.

After independence in 1960, Nigeria's civilian and military rulers alike expanded the interventionist state, which came to dominate all facets of the nation's economic life. Successive governments began in the late 1980s to reverse this trend, but privatization and economic reform have been piecemeal at best. President Obasanjo promised to sell off government interests in the telephone, power, and oil sectors, although the state remains by far the largest source of economic activity. The new regime's efforts to promote better macroeconomic management and to root out endemic corruption have not borne results in the form of economic growth, employment, or the reduction of poverty.

Democratic Ideas Amid Colonialism and Military Rule. Colonialism introduced a cultural dualism—a clash of customs, values, and political systems—between the traditions of social accountability in precolonial society, and emerging Western ideas of individualism. These pressures weakened indigenous democratic bases for the accountability of rulers and responsibility to the governed, along with age-old checks on abuses of office. Although the colonial rulers left Nigeria with the machinery of parliamentary democracy, they largely socialized the local population to be passive subjects rather than responsive participants. Even as colonial rule sought to implant democracy in principle, in practice it bequeathed an authoritarian legacy to independent Nigeria. Military rule continued this pattern from 1966 to 1979 and again from 1983 to 1999, as juntas promised democratization yet governed with increasing severity.

This dualism promoted two public realms to which individuals belonged: the communal realm, in which people identified by ethnic or subethnic groups (Igbo, Tiv, Yoruba, and others), and the civic realm under the colonial administration and its successors in which citizenship was universal.[5] The realms influenced each other, but the communal realm was usually stronger in certain respects than the civic realm, posing Nigerians a loyalty dilemma: Does one serve the interests of one's ethnic group or those of a greater Nigeria? Because the colonial state and its "civic" realm began as an alien, exploitative force, Nigerians came to view the state as the realm from which rights must be extracted, duties and taxes withheld, and resources plundered (see Section 4), whereas morality was reserved for the ethnic or communal realm. Military regimes in the postcolonial era continued this pattern, and when they left in 1999, the democratic government faced the task of governing amid strong communal loyalties and an amoral civic realm.

In addition to suffering the burden of two public realms, the democratic idea in Nigeria has also been filtered through deep regional divisions. The British policy of indirect rule had profoundly different effects on the northern and southern regions. The south experienced both the benefits and burdens of colonial occupation. The coastal location of Lagos, Calabar, and their regions made them important hubs for trade and shipping activity, around which the British built the necessary infrastructure—schools (promoting Christianity and Western education), roads, ports, and the like—and a large African civil service to facilitate colonialism. In northern Nigeria, where indigenous hierarchical political structures were better established, the British used local structures and left intact the emirate authorities and Islamic institutions of the region. The north consequently received few infrastructural benefits, little Christian missionary activity, and its traditional administration was largely preserved.

A pattern of uneven development resulted, with the south enjoying the basis for a modern economy and exposure to democratic institutions and the north remaining largely agricultural and monarchical. These disparities between northern and southern Nigeria propelled northern leaders in the First and Second Republics to secure control of the federal government in order to redistribute resources to the north, while military rulers selectively colluded with northern elites and manipulated their fears and weathered southern resentments.

Despite these setbacks, the democratic idea remained vibrant across Nigeria throughout even the darkest days of military rule, and it remains strong even as frustrations rise over the imperfections of the current democratic government. Nigeria's incredible diversity continually demands constant processes of negotiation and protections of interests that democracy promises, albeit after a difficult period of transition.

Nigeria's Fragile Collective Identity. This division between north and south is overlaid with hundreds of ethnic divisions across the nation, which military governments and civilians alike have been prone to manipulate for selfish ends. Over three decades after the Biafran civil war, Nigeria often seems as divided as it was in the prelude to that conflict. Fears of another civil war rose during the mid-1990s.

These many cultural divisions have been continually exacerbated by the triple threats of **clientelism,** corruption, and unstable authoritarian governing structures, which together foster ethnic group competition and hinder economic potential.[6] Clientelism is the practice by which particular individuals or segments receive disproportionate policy benefits or political favors from a political patron, usually at the expense of the larger society. In Nigeria, patrons are often linked to clients by ethnic, religious, or other cultural ties, and these ties have generally benefited only a small elite. By fostering political competition along cultural lines, clientelism tends to undermine social trust and political stability, which are necessary conditions for economic growth. Clientelism thus reduces the state to an arena of struggle over distribution of the "national cake" among primarily ethnic clients rather than serving as a framework of governance.

Despite the prevalence of ethnicity as the primary form of political identity and the accompanying scourge of ethnic-based clientelism, the idea of Nigeria has taken root among the country's ethnic groups over forty years of independence. Most public discourse does not question the idea of a single cohesive country, but instead revolves around finding an equitable balance among different ethnic groups within the context of a united Nigeria. This can be seen in recent calls from some organizations for a "national conference" to restructure the federation. Most Nigerians enjoy many personal connections across ethnic and religious lines, and elites in both the north and the south have significant business activities throughout the country. Nevertheless, ethnicity remains a critical flashpoint that has led to localized ethnic violence on many occasions, and politicians continue to use ethnic identification to forward their political objectives, often divisively.

Implications for Comparative Politics

The saying that "as Nigeria goes, so goes the rest of sub-Saharan Africa" may again be relevant. With a population of over 130 million growing at nearly 3 percent annually, Nigeria is by far the largest country in Africa and among the ten most populous countries in the world. One out of every five black Africans is Nigerian. Unlike most other countries on the continent, Nigeria has the human and material resources to overcome the vicious cycle of poverty and **autocracy.** Hopes for this breakthrough, however, have been regularly frustrated over four decades of independent rule. If Nigeria, with its vast resources, cannot succeed in breaking this cycle, what does that mean for the rest of sub-Saharan Africa?

Nigeria remains the oldest surviving federation in Africa, and it has managed through much travail to maintain its fragile unity. That cohesion has come under increasing stress, and a major challenge is to ensure that Nigeria does not ultimately collapse. One fact is certain: Nigeria's multiethnic, multireligious, multiclass, and multiregional nature makes it an especially valuable case for the study of social cleavages in conflict and cooperation. Even the United States, which is nearing a demographic transition from a white majority, can learn from Nigeria's efforts to find unity amid cultural diversity.

Nigeria's past failures to sustain democracy and economic development also render it an important case for the study of resource competition and the perils of corruption, and its experience demonstrates the interrelationship between democracy and development. Democracy and development depend on leadership, political culture, institutional autonomy, and the external economic climate; Nigeria has much to teach us on all these topics.

At this stage, it is uncertain whether Nigeria will return to the path of autocracy, underdevelopment, and fragmentation or continue on a course toward democratic consolidation and national construction. In the following sections, we will explore these issues and evaluate how they may shape Nigerian politics in the years ahead.

Section ❷ Political Economy and Development

We have seen how colonialism bequeathed Nigeria an interventionist state and how governments in the postindependence period continued this pattern.

The state became the central fixture in the Nigerian economy, stunting the private sector and encumbering industry and commerce. As the state began to unravel in the late 1980s and 1990s, leaders grew more predatory, plundering the petroleum sector, the nation's remaining source of revenues, and preventing the nation's vast economic potential from being realized.

State and Economy

Through direct ownership of industry and services or through regulation and administrative control, the Nigerian state plays the central role in making decisions about the extraction, deployment, and allocation of scarce economic resources. Any major economic activity involves the state in some way, whether through licenses, taxes, contracts, legal provisions, trade and investment policy, or direct involvement of government agencies. The state's premier role in the economy arises from control of the most productive sectors, particularly the oil industry. Most of the nation's revenues, and nearly all of its hard currency, are channeled through the government. The discretion of leaders in spending those earnings, known as **rents,** forms the main path for channeling money through the economy. Consequently, winning government contracts—for supplies, construction, services, and myriad functions connected to the state—becomes a central economic activity, and those who control the state become the gatekeepers of contracting, licenses, and other areas of economic gain. [7]

As individuals, groups, and communities jostled for state control or access, economic and social life became thoroughly politicized and consumed by **rent-seeking** behavior, best understood as competition over politically regulated economic gains (rents), which are furnished to those with political connections. In most societies, access to the state and its leadership confers some economic advantages, but it can literally be a matter of life and death in impoverished countries like Nigeria.

Perhaps 70 percent of Nigerians struggle along without such access, surviving on petty trade and subsistence agriculture—the so-called informal sector of the economy—where taxes and regulation rarely reach. A number of analysts estimate that the Nigerian informal sector can be valued at approximately 20 percent of the entire Nigerian GDP, much of it earned through cross-border trade.

Origins of Economic Decline

In the colonial and immediate postcolonial periods, Nigeria's economy was centered on agricultural production for domestic consumption as well as for export. Peasant producers were induced by the colonial state to produce primary export commodities—cocoa in the west, palm oil in the east, and groundnuts and cotton in the north—through direct taxation, forced cultivation, and the presence of European agricultural firms. Despite the emphasis on exports, Nigeria was self-sufficient in food production at the time of independence. Vital to this effort was small-scale local production of sorghum and maize in the north and cassava and yams in the south. Some rice and wheat were also produced. It was not until later in the 1960s that emphasis shifted to the development of nonfood export crops through large-scale enterprises.

Nearly exclusive state attention to large-scale, nonfood production meant that small farmers were left out and received scant government support. Predictably, food production suffered, and food imports were stepped up to meet the needs of a burgeoning population. Despite such government neglect, agriculture was the central component of the national economy in the First Republic. A combination of three factors effectively undermined the Nigerian agricultural sector. [8] The first was the Biafran War (1967–1970), which drastically reduced palm oil production in the east, where the war was concentrated. Second, severe drought in 1969 produced a famine from 1972 through 1974. Finally, the development of the petroleum industry caused a total shift in economic focus from agriculture (in terms of both labor and capital investment) to petroleum production. Agricultural export production plummeted from 80 percent of exports in 1960 to just 2 percent by 1980. To compensate for widening food shortfalls, food imports surged by 700 percent between 1970 and 1978.

With the 1970s boom in revenues from oil, Nigeria greatly increased its expenditures on education, defense, and infrastructure. The university system was expanded, roads and ports were built, and industrial and office buildings were constructed. Imports of capital goods and raw materials required to support this expansion rose more than seven-fold between 1971 and 1979. Similarly, imports of consumer goods rose dramatically (600 percent) in the same period as an increasingly wealthy Nigerian elite developed a taste for expensive imported goods.[9] By 1978, the Nigerian government had outspent its revenues and could no longer finance many of its ambitious projects; consequently, the government was forced to borrow money to make up the deficit, causing external debt to skyrocket.

The acceleration in oil wealth was mirrored by a corresponding increase in corruption. Many public officials became very wealthy by setting up joint ventures with foreign oil companies. Other officials simply stole public funds for their own benefit. The economic downturn of the 1980s created even greater incentives for government corruption, and the Babangida and Abacha administrations became infamous for avarice. A Nigerian government commission reported that some $12.2 billion had been diverted to special off-budget accounts between 1988 and 1993. These funds were supposedly earmarked for national security and infrastructure, but they were never audited, and their expenditure remains entirely unaccounted.[10] Within three years of seizing power in 1993, General Abacha allowed all of Nigeria's oil refineries to collapse, forcing this giant oil-exporting country into the absurd situation of having to import refined petroleum. Abacha's family members and friends, who served as fronts, shamelessly monopolized the contracts to import this fuel in 1997. Elsewhere outside the oil sector, small-time scam artists proliferated such that by 2002, Internet scams had become one of Nigeria's top five industries, earning over $100 million annually.

In sum, the oil boom was a double-edged sword for Nigeria. On the one hand, it has generated tremendous income; on the other, it has become a source of external dependence and has badly skewed the Nigerian economy. Since the early 1970s, Nigeria has relied on oil for over 90 percent of its export earnings and about three-quarters of government revenues, as shown in Table 1. Hasty, ill-managed industrial and infrastructural expansion under both military and civilian regimes, combined with the neglect of the agricultural

sector, further weakened the Nigerian economy. As a result, the economy was unable to compensate for the sharp fall in world oil prices after 1981 and descended into crisis.

From 1985 to the Present: Deepening Economic Crisis and the Search for Solutions

Structural Adjustment.   The year 1985 marked a turning point for the Nigerian state and economy. It ushered in Ibrahim Babangida's eight-year rule and revealed the economy's precarious condition. Within a year of wresting power from General Buhari in August 1985, the Babangida regime developed an economic **structural adjustment program (SAP)** with the active support of the World Bank and the IMF (also referred to as the **international financial institutions,** or **IFIs**). The decision to embark on the SAP was made against a background of increasing economic constraints arising from the continued dependence of the economy on waning oil revenues, a growing debt burden, **balance of payments** difficulties, and lack of fiscal discipline.[11] (See "Global Connection: Structural Adjustment Programs.")

The large revenues arising from the oil windfall enabled the state to increase its involvement in direct production. Beginning in the 1970s, the government created a number of para-statals (state-owned enterprises; see Section 3) including large shares in major banks and other financial institutions, manufacturing, construction, agriculture, public utilities, and various services. Although the government has since sold many of its para-statals, the state remains the biggest employer as well as the most important source of revenue, even for the private sector. By the 1980s, the public bureaucracy in Nigeria had swollen to over 3 million employees (most employed by the federal and state governments), representing more than 60 percent of employment in the modern, formal sector of the economy.

Privatization, which is central to Nigeria's adjustment program, means that state-owned businesses would be sold to private (nonstate) investors, domestic or foreign. Privatization is intended to generate revenue, reduce state expenditures for loss-making operations, and improve efficiency. Expectations that privatization would encourage Nigerian and foreign

Table 1

Oil Sector Statistics, 1970–2003

	Annual Output (million barrels)	Average Price Index	Oil Exports as Percent of Total Exports	Government Oil Revenue (Naira millions)	Percent of Total Revenue
1970	396	37	58	100	26
1971	559	43	74	510	44
1972	643	40	82	767	54
1973	750	39	83	1,016	60
1974	823	162	93	3,726	82
1975	651	109	93	4,271	77
1976	756	115	94	5,365	79
1977	761	115	93	6,081	76
1978	692	100	89	4,556	62
1979	840	237	93	8,881	81
1980	753	220	96	12,353	81
1981	525	225	97	8,563	70
1982	470	212	99	7,814	66
1983	451	200	96	7,253	69
1984	508	190	97	8,268	74
1985	544	180	97	10,915	75
1986	534	75	94	8,107	66
1987	464	90	93	19,027	76
1988	507	60	91	20,934	77
1989	614	87	95	41,334	82
1990	–	125	–	–	–
1991	–	80	–	–	–
1992	714	79	98	164,078	86
1993	720	62	91	162,102	84
1994	733	70	85	160,192	79
1995	705	65	95	244,902	53
1996	783	95	95	266,000	51
1997	803	85	95	250,000	80
1998	700	62	90	248,500	70
1999	1,950	–	–	–	76
2000	2,040	–	–	–	65
2001	2,083	–	98	1,668,000	79
2002	2,068	–	94	1,884,000	80
2003*	2,291	–	91	2,194,000	78

*Projected.

Sources: Output is from *Petroleum Economist* (1970–1989); price index and exports are from IMF, *International Financial Statistics* (1970–1984) and from Central Bank of Nigeria, *Annual Reports* (1985–1989); revenues are from Central Bank of Nigeria, *Annual Reports* (various years). From Tom Forrest, *Politics and Economic Development in Nigeria* (Boulder: Westview Press, 1993), 134. 1990s statistics are from the Nigerian Federal Office of Statistics, *Annual Abstract of Statistics: 1997 Edition*, from the 1998 IMF *Annual Report*, and from Vision 2010, *Report of the Vision 2010 Committee: Main Report* (Abuja: Federal Government of Nigeria, September 1997). Nigerian Economic Summit Group, *Economic Indicators* (Vol. 8, no. 2, April–June 2002). Compilation and some calculations by Darren Kew.

Global Connection: *Structural Adjustment Programs*

The solutions to Nigeria's economic woes depend, in the first instance, on its own people and government, but assistance must also come from outside its borders. In addition to bilateral (country-to-country) assistance, multilateral economic institutions are a key source of loans, grants, and other forms of development aid. Two multilateral institutions that have become familiar players on the African economic scene are the International Monetary Fund (IMF) and the World Bank. These international financial institutions (IFIs) were established after World War II to provide short-term credit facilities to encourage growth and expansion of trade and longer-term financing packages to rebuild the countries of war-torn Europe. Today, the functions of the IFIs have adapted and expanded to meet contemporary needs, including efforts to stabilize and restructure faltering economies. One area of emphasis by the IFIs, particularly among African countries, is the structural adjustment program (SAP).

Assistance from the World Bank and the IMF comes with many strings attached, which typically include SAPs. These rigorous programs, which are intended to reduce government intervention and develop free markets, call for immediate austerity measures by recipient governments. SAPs generally begin with currency devaluation and tariff reductions. These actions are followed by measures aimed at reducing budget deficits, restructuring the public sector (particularly employment practices), privatizing state-owned enterprises, agricultural reform (especially raising producer prices), and the reduction of consumer subsidies on staple foods. The social and economic hardships of these programs, particularly in the short term, can be severe. SAPs result in considerable economic, and frequently social, dislocation; dramatic price increases in foodstuffs and fuel, rising unemployment, and new fees for

public services are seldom popular with the general population.

At Babangida's insistence, Nigeria's SAP was developed and deployed in 1986 independently of the IMF. The program was, however, endorsed by the IFIs, making Nigeria eligible to receive disbursements of funds from the IMF and the World Bank and to reschedule $33 billion of external debt with the Paris and London clubs of lenders. Ironically, Nigeria's SAP was in many regards more rigorous than an initial program designed by the IMF. Like SAPs elsewhere, the Nigerian program was designed to encourage economic liberalization and promote private enterprise in place of a reliance on state-owned enterprises and public intervention. The logic was that competition leads to more efficient products and markets. Recovery among Africa's struggling economies has, however, been limited. Africa's economic problems are deeply entrenched; although an economy may be stabilized relatively quickly, comprehensive structural adjustment takes considerably longer. Nigeria's SAP—in part because of the popular reaction to austerity measures, corruption in its implementation, and the complicating factor of unstable military rule—generally failed to revitalize the economy and achieve its stated goals. The final years of the Babangida administration (1985–1993) saw a marked slippage in the reform program, and the Abacha regime continued that trend. Abacha did enact a number of economic policies in 1995 and 1996 that lowered inflation, stabilized the exchange rate, and fostered mild GDP growth, but by 1997, these achievements had been squandered. President Obasanjo has sought to uphold the overall policies of SAP without calling it such, including attempts to end subsidies on fuel and to complete the privatization of the major government para-statals.

---

investments in manufacturing have been largely disappointed. On a domestic level, Nigerian entrepreneurs have found that trading, government contracting, and currency speculation offer more reliable yields than manufacturing. Potential foreign investors remain hesitant to risk significant capital in an environment characterized by political and social instability, unpredictable economic policies, and endemic corruption.

Only a few attractive areas such as telecommunications, utilities, and oil and gas are likely to draw significant foreign capital.

Economic Planning.   Beginning in 1946, when the colonial administration announced the ten-year Plan for Development and Welfare, national plans have been prepared by ministries of finance, economic development, and planning. Five-year plans were the norm from 1962 through 1985, when their scope was extended to fifteen years. The national plan, however, has not been an effective management tool. The reasons are the absence of an effective database for planning and a great lack of discipline in plan implementation. The state strives to dictate the pace and direction of economic development, but lacks the tools and political will to deliver on its obligations.

Nigerian and foreign business leaders revived dialogue with government on economic direction with the 1994 establishment of the annual Nigerian Economic Summit Group (NESG). This differed from previous planning efforts in that it was based on the coequal participation of government and private sector representatives. Two years later, General Abacha initiated the Vision 2010 process (see "Current Challenges: From Vision 2010 to NEEDS"). Participants in Vision 2010 advocated reductions in government's excessive role in the economy with the goals of increasing market efficiency and reducing competition for control of the state. The Obasanjo administration accepted much of the Vision 2010 agenda at the outset of its first term, although it did not say so publicly because of the plan's association with General Abacha's predatory regime. Many of the private sector participants in Vision 2010 continue to meet regularly through the Economic Summit. Advice from the NESG continues to influence the economic policies of both the Obasanjo administration and the National Assembly.

President Obasanjo opened his second term in office in 2003 with a renewed focus on economic reform and development. His appointment of a bold, reformist economic team won the praise of international financial institutions, and the president unveiled an ambitious package of economic reforms combined with social development initiatives, called the National Economic Empowerment and Development Strategy (NEEDS). In addition to stable macroeconomic policy,

especially promising developments have included a restructuring of the banking sector by the new governor of the Central Bank of Nigeria, and the activities of a second anticorruption agency established by the president, the Economic and Financial Crimes Commission (EFCC). Since its foundation in 2003, the EFCC has already indicted a cabinet minister, the inspector general of the police (the head of the nation's police force), and the governor of Plateau State—a far more successful record than Obasanjo's first anticorruption commission, the ICPC, which since its establishment in 2000 has yet to prosecute a single prominent figure.

Ambitious goals followed by lackluster implementation plagued the reform agenda in the president's first term, and many problems must still be overcome in the economy: low investment, low capacity utilization, unreliable distribution, stifling corruption, and overregulation. Average annual GDP growth rates were negative from 1981 through 1987 and have risen only moderately above the rate of population growth since Obasanjo took office in 1999. Consumption and investment have also recorded negative growth (see Table 2). Buoyant oil revenues have helped to float the economy, though poverty has not significantly diminished, and there remain basic questions about the sustainability of growth without a more diversified productive foundation.

Nigeria's heavy foreign debt exacerbates the nation's economic stagnation (see Table 3). President Obasanjo made debt relief one of his highest priorities on taking office in 1999 and promptly undertook numerous visits to the capitals of Europe, Asia, and the United States to urge the governments of those countries to forgive most of Nigeria's obligations. For a long time, his pleas fell largely on deaf ears as Nigeria's National Assembly showed little inclination to spend within the nation's means and the president himself showered funds on wasteful projects such as a half-billion-dollar soccer stadium. Nigeria, once considered a country likely to achieve self-sustaining growth, now ranks among the more debt-distressed countries in the developing world. It cannot earn enough from the export of goods to service its foreign debt—which eats over a quarter of the national budget—and also meet the basic needs of the population. After persistent international lobbying, along with progress on economic reforms during Obasanjo's second term, Nigeria eventually secured an agreement

Current Challenges: *From Vision 2010 to NEEDS*

In the early 1990s, concerned with the nation's economic decline, a number of the larger Nigerian businesses and key multinational corporations decided to pursue new initiatives. With the involvement of then head of state Ernest Shonekan, they arranged the first Economic Summit, a high-profile conference that advocated numerous policies to move Nigeria toward becoming an "emerging market" that could attract foreign investment along the lines of the high-performing states in Asia.

Shortly after the first Economic Summit, however, General Abacha took control and continued the ruinous economic approach of Babangida's later years. The Economic Summit meanwhile continued to meet annually. After his flawed 1994 budget sent the Nigerian economy into a tailspin, Abacha was ready to listen to the summit participants. He accepted several of their recommendations, and by 1996 the economy began to make modest gains. Therefore, when key members of the summit proposed Vision 2010, General Abacha seized the opportunity presented and endorsed it in September 1996. Chief Shonekan was named the chair.

Through Vision 2010, the government pledged to adopt a package of business-promoting economic reforms, while business pledged to work toward certain growth targets consistent with governmental priorities in employment, taxation, community investment, and the like. Along with government and business leaders, key figures were invited to participate from nearly all sectors of society, including the press, nongovernmental organizations, youth groups, marketwomen's associations, and others. Government-owned media followed Vision 2010's pronouncements with great fanfare, while the private media reviewed them with a healthy dose of skepticism regarding Abacha's intentions and the elitist nature of the exercise. Vision 2010's final report called for

- restoring democratic rule
- restructuring and professionalizing the military
- lowering the population growth rate

- rebuilding education
- meaningful privatization
- diversifying the export base beyond oil
- supporting intellectual property rights
- central bank autonomy

Whatever its merits, Vision 2010 was imperiled because of its association with Abacha. When the new Obasanjo administration took office in 1999 lacking a comprehensive economic plan of its own, however, it quietly approached Shonekan for the detailed recommendations and data produced by Vision 2010. Consequently, the general economic strategy and objectives of Vision 2010 are largely echoed in those of the current government. The Economic Summit, meanwhile, continues to provide annual assessments of the Nigerian economy and critical economic advice to policy makers.

President Obasanjo repackaged and developed many of these goals into a new economic initiative for his second term, the National Economic Empowerment and Development Strategy (NEEDS). NEEDS lists several ambitious objectives for restructuring the Nigerian economy. First is government reform, particularly in terms of anticorruption, greater transparency, rule of law, and contract enforcement, which are all important political institutional supports for a properly functioning economy. Second, NEEDS seeks to spur private sector development through a renewed privatization effort, infrastructure development, agricultural support, and industrial expansion. In addition, NEEDS targets the development concerns of the nation's poor majority, through government assistance for Nigeria's ailing health, education, unemployment, and anti-poverty programs. Since announcing these efforts in 2003, however, the Obasanjo administration has been slow to implement them, although it has promised a number of redoubled initiatives toward these goals for 2005.

Source: Vision 2010 Final Report, September 1997; Federal Government of Nigeria, the *National Economic Empowerment and Development Strategy,* March 2004.

Table 2

Selected Economic Indicators, 1980–2003

	Real GDP (Naira billions) (1993 = 100)	GDP (% Growth)	Manufacturing Capacity Utilization (%)*	Inflation Rate (%)
1980	96.2	5.5	70.1	9.9
1985	68.9	9.4	37.1	5.5
1990	90.3	8.1	40.3	7.4
1991	94.6	4.8	42.0	13.0
1992	97.4	3.0	41.8	44.6
1993	100.0	2.7	37.2	57.2
1994	101.0	1.3	30.4	57.0
1995	103.5	2.2	29.3	72.8
1996	106.9	3.3	32.5	29.3
1997	111.1	3.9	–	8.5
1998	113.3	2.0	–	9.0
1999	114.4	1.0	–	6.7
2000	118.8	3.8	–	6.9
2001	123.5	4.0	–	18.9
2002	127.7	3.4	–	16.9
2003	133.1	4.2	–	13.5

GDP % Growth

1976–1986	–1.3
1987–1997	1.6

*Manufacturing capacity utilization is the average (across the economy) percentage of full production capabilities at which manufacturers are producing.

Sources: Vision 2010. *Report of the Vision 2010 Committee: Main Report.* Abuja: Federal Government of Nigeria, September 1997; World Bank, "Nigeria at a Glance," 1998 (www.worldbank.org) the 1998 IMF *Annual Report.* Nigerian Economic Summit Group, *Economic Indicators* (Vol. 8, no. 2, April–June 2002).

Table 3

Nigeria's Total External Debt (millions of US$; current prices and exchange rates)

1975–1979	1980	1981	1982	1983
3,304	8,934	12,136	12,954	18,340
1984	**1985**	**1986**	**1987**	**1988**
18,537	19,551	24,043	31,193	31,947
1989	**1994**	**1995**	**1996**	**1997**
32,832	34,000	35,010	33,442	32,906
1999	**2000**	**2001**	**2002**	**2003**
29,358	34,134	33,766	33,723	33,740

Nigeria's Debt Compared to its Earnings:

	1976	1986	1996	1997	1999
Total Debt/GDP	3.7	109.9	72.0	63.1	83.8
Total Debt Service/ Exports	3.7	28.4	15.2	15.9	204

	2000	2001	2002	2003
Total Debt/GDP	97.3	86.9	76.5	72.6
Total Debt Service/ Exports	147.6	147	177.5	159.5

Sources: UNDP, World Bank, *African Development Indicators* (Washington, D.C.: World Bank, 1992), 159; UNDP *1998 Human Development Report;* World Bank, "Nigeria at a Glance," 1998 (www.worldbank.org). Nigerian Economic Summit Group, *Economic Indicators* (Vol. 8, no. 2, April–June 2002).

for a substantial reduction of the country's debt. In June 2005, the Paris Club of official creditors approved a package of debt repayments, repurchases and write-offs that would effectively reduce Nigeria's external debt by 90 percent within two years. Obasanjo's efforts in the international arena appeared to be paying dividends,

Social Welfare.   Given the continued decline in its economic performance since the early 1980s, it is not surprising that Nigeria's social welfare has suffered greatly as well. Since 1986, there has been a marked deterioration in the quantity and quality of social services, complicated by a marked decline in household incomes (see Table 4). The SAP program and subsequent austerity measures emphasizing the reduction of state expenditures have forced cutbacks in spending on social welfare.

Budgetary austerity and economic stagnation have hurt vulnerable groups such as the urban and rural poor, women, the young, and the elderly. Indeed, Nigeria performs poorly in meeting basic needs: life expectancy is barely above forty years, and infant mortality is estimated at more than 80 deaths per

Table 4

Index of Real Household Incomes of Key Groups 1980/81–1986/87, 1996, 2001 (Rural self-employed in 1980/81 = 100)

	1980/81	1981/82	1982/83	1983/84	1984/85	1985/86	1986/87	1996*	2001*
Rural self-employed	100	103	95	86	73	74	65	27	32
Rural wage earners	178	160	147	135	92	95	84	48	57
All rural households	105	107	99	89	74	84	74	28	33
Urban self-employed	150	124	106	94	69	69	61	41	48
Urban wage earners	203	177	164	140	101	101	90	55	65
All urban households	166	142	129	109	80	80	71	45	53

*Estimated, based on 1980/81 figures adjusted for a 73 percent drop in per capita GDP from 1980 to 1996, and an 18 percent increase in per capita GDP from 1996 to 2001. The FOS lists annual household incomes for 1996 as $75 (N 6,349) for urban households and $57 (N 4,820) for rural households, suggesting that the gap between urban and rural households is actually 19 percent closer than our estimate.

Sources: National Integrated Survey of Households (NISH), Federal Office of Statistics (FOS) consumer price data, and World Bank estimates. As found in Paul Collier, *An Analysis of the Nigerian Labour Market,* Development Economics Department Discussion Paper (Washington, D.C.: World Bank, 1986). From Tom Forrest, *Politics and Economic Development in Nigeria* (Boulder: Westview Press, 1993), 214. 1996 data from FOS *Annual Abstract of Statistics: 1997 Edition*, p. 80.

1,000 live births. Nigeria's provision of basic education is also inadequate. Moreover, Nigeria has failed to develop a national social security system, with much of the gap filled by family-based networks of mutual aid. President Obasanjo took an important step in meeting basic needs when he raised the minimum wage nearly tenfold in 1999. Since wage levels had hardly been raised in years despite the inflation of the previous decade, the gains for workers with formal sector jobs were more meager than the increase suggests. Moreover, most Nigerians do not have access to formal sector jobs, and roughly 70 percent of the population must live on less than a dollar per day.

The provision of health care and other social services—water, education, food, and shelter—remains woefully inadequate in both urban and rural areas. Beyond the needless loss of countless lives to preventable and curable maladies, Nigeria's neglect of the health and social net will likely bear more bitter fruit. The nation stands on the verge of an AIDS epidemic of catastrophic proportions. The United Nations estimates—conservatively—that HIV infection rates are at approximately 6 percent of the population and are likely to spread to 10 percent by the end of the decade, dooming perhaps 15 million Nigerians. The government has made AIDS a secondary priority, leaving much of the initiative to a small group of courageous but underfunded nongovernmental organizations. The Obasanjo administration began providing subsidized antiretroviral medications through a small number of clinics in 2002, and in early 2005 announced that it planned to raise the numbers of patients with access to these medications from 14,000 to 100,000, but several million Nigerians are estimated to be HIV positive.

Society and Economy

Because the central government in Nigeria controls access to most resources and economic opportunities, the state has become the major focus for competition among ethnic, regional, religious, and class groups.[12] A partial explanation for the failure of economic strategies can be found within Nigerian society itself—a complex mix of contending ethnic, religious, and regional constituencies.

Ethnic and Religious Cleavages

Nigeria's ethnic relations have generated tensions that sap the country's economy of much needed vitality.[13]

Competition among the largest groups is centered on access to national economic and political resources. The dominance of the Hausa-Fulani, Igbo, and Yoruba in the country's national life, and the conflicts among political elites from these groups, distort economic affairs. Religious cleavages have also affected economic and social stability. Some of the federation's states in the far north are populated mainly by Muslims, whereas others, particularly in the middle and eastern parts of the south, are predominantly Christian.

Government ineptitude (or outright manipulation), and growing Islamic and Christian assertion, have heightened conflicts between adherents.[14] Christians have perceived past northern-dominated governments as being pro-Muslim in their management and distribution of scarce resources as well as in their policy decisions, some of which jeopardized the secular nature of the state. These fears have increased since 1999, when several northern states instituted expanded versions of the Islamic legal code, the *shari'a*. For their part, Muslims now fear that President Obasanjo, a born-again Christian, is tilting the balance of power and thus the distribution of economic benefits against the north. The decline in the Nigerian economy also contributed to the rise of Christian and Muslim fundamentalisms, which have spread among unemployed youths and others in a society suffering under economic collapse. Disputes over economic and political issues have sometimes escalated into physical attacks on Christians, Muslims, and members of ethnic groups resident outside their ethnoreligious homelands

Northern-led governments after independence, fearing a "southern tyranny of skills,"[15] sought to use the political clout of their numerical majority to keep the south in check and to redistribute resources to the north. Early military governments (1966–1979) tried to maintain some measure of ethnic and religious balance, but the Babangida regime in the 1980s became increasingly northern-dominated and more willing than any of its predecessors to manipulate Nigeria's ethnic divisions. General Abacha's regime tilted overwhelmingly in favor of northerners, specifically Hausa-Fulani, in its membership. Numerous attacks were perpetrated against prominent southern civilians, particularly Yoruba, often using Abacha's secret hit squads. His regime also closed universities and detained a number of activists, particularly in the south.

Other groups were adversely affected by Abacha's rule. The Ogoni, Ijaw, and other southern minorities of the oil-producing regions were brutalized by military and police forces when they protested the scant oil revenues remitted to the region, as well as the environmental degradation from the irresponsible oil industry. The Ogoni in particular were organized through the Movement for the Survival of the Ogoni People (MOSOP), under the leadership of internationally renowned writer and environmentalist Ken Saro-Wiwa. The military's abrupt hanging of Saro-Wiwa and eight Ogoni compatriots in 1995 following a kangaroo trial was widely criticized as "judicial murder" by human rights groups, and led to Nigeria's suspension from the Commonwealth (an international organization composed of Britain and its former colonies). A subsequent UN mission of inquiry declared the executions illegal under both Nigerian and international law.

MOSOP under Saro-Wiwa effectively blended claims for **self-determination,** which in this case meant increased local political autonomy and national political representation, with concerns over oil industry pollution in the Niger Delta, primarily on the part of global oil giant Royal Dutch/Shell, as a platform to forge alliances with international environmental and human rights organizations. Many other Niger Delta minority groups have subsequently followed MOSOP's lead in pushing for a combination of self-determination, political rights, environmental concerns, and demands for greater control over the oil pumped from their lands.

Since the return of democracy in 1999, many ethnic-based and religious movements have taken advantage of renewed political freedoms to organize around their interests and to press the government to address their grievances. Some mobilization has been peaceful, but many armed groups have also formed, at times with the encouragement or complicity of the mainstream political movements. In the oil-producing regions, these militias live off oil "bunkering": tapping into pipelines, siphoning oil, and reselling it on the black market. While armed gangs are primarily responsible, there have been allegations of complicity by members of the armed forces and senior officials.

Youths from the Niger Delta minorities, primarily the Ijaw, have occupied Shell and Chevron facilities on several occasions to protest their economic marginalization. One spectacular incident on an offshore oil platform in 2002 saw a group of local women stage a peaceful takeover using a traditional form of protest: disrobing in order to shame the oil companies and local authorities. Some of these protests have ended peacefully, although a large-scale upheaval in the Warri region in 2003 caused the deaths of several policemen, soldiers, and oil workers. The Obasanjo government has periodically responded to these incidents and other disturbances with excessive force. After Ijaw militias killed several policemen in the village of Odi in late 1999, the military subsequently flattened the village, raping and killing many innocent people. Army units committed similar retaliatory atrocities in 2001 among villages in the Middle Belt state of Benue, when ethnic militias apparently killed several soldiers engaged in a peacekeeping mission during an interethnic dispute.

In the Niger Delta, the struggle of the minority communities with the federal government and multinational oil corporations has been complicated by clashes among the minority groups themselves over control of land and access to government rents. Fighting among the Ijaws and the Itsekiris near Warri in 2003 claimed more than 100 lives. Ethnic-based mobilization, including the activities of militias and vigilante groups, has increased across the country since the transition to civilian rule. Political leaders have sometimes built alliances with such groups and are increasingly using them to harass and even kill political opponents. These practices have reached a dangerous threshold in the Niger Delta, where an ethnic militia attacked a state capital in late 2004 and forced the flight of the governor, who was originally instrumental in organizing the militia and used them to rig his re-election in 2003. The president ultimately mediated among these warlords and offered them an amnesty package for disarming.

These divisive practices overshadow certain positive aspects of sectional identities. For example, associations based on ethnic and religious affinities often serve as vehicles for mobilizing savings, investment, and production, such as informal credit associations. Sectional groups such as the Igbo *Ohaneze* or the Yoruba *Afenifere* have also advocated more equitable federalism and continued democratic development.

These groups, which form an important foundation of civil society, have continued to provide a vehicle for political expression while also reflecting the divisive pressures of Nigeria's cultural pluralism.

Gender Differences

Although the Land Use Act of 1978 stated that all land in Nigeria is ultimately owned by the government, land tenure in Nigeria is still governed by traditional practice, which is largely patriarchal. Despite the fact that women, especially from the south and Middle Belt areas, have traditionally dominated agricultural production and form the bulk of agricultural producers, they are generally prevented from owning land, which remains the major means of production. Trading, in which women feature prominently, is also controlled in many areas by traditional chiefs and local government councilors, who are overwhelmingly male.

Women have not succeeded in transforming their economic importance into political clout, but important strides are being made in this direction. Their struggle to achieve access to state power is a reflection of several factors. Women's associations in the past tended to be elitist, urban based, and mainly concerned with issues of trade, children, household welfare, and religion. The few that did have a more political orientation have been largely token appendages of the male-dominated political parties or instruments of the government. An example of the latter was the Better Life Program, directed by the wife of Babangida, and its successor, the Family Support Program, directed by Abacha's wife. Women are grossly underrepresented at all levels of the governmental system; only eight (of 469) national legislators are women.[16]

Reflecting the historical economic and educational advantages of the south, women's interest organizations sprouted in southern Nigeria earlier than in the north. Although these groups initially focused generally on nonpolitical issues surrounding women's health and children's welfare, organizations like Women in Nigeria began to form in the 1980s with explicit political goals, such as getting more women into government and increasing funds available for education.

As in the south, northern women's NGOs at first focused on less politicized issues, but by the end of the 1990s, explicitly political organizations emerged such as the 100 Women Groups, which sought to elect 100 women to every level of government. Northern groups also showed tremendous creativity in using Islam to support their activities, which was important considering that tenets of the religion have been regularly used by Nigerian men to justify women's subordinate status. Women's groups in general have been more dynamic in developing income-generating projects to make their organizations and constituents increasingly self-reliant, compared with male-dominated NGOs that depend heavily on foreign or government funding.

Nigeria in the Global Economy

At the international level, the Nigerian state has remained comparatively weak and dependent on Western industrial and financial interests. The country's acute debt burden, now set to be reduced, is roughly three-quarters the value of its annual GDP, while Nigeria is reliant on the developed industrial economies for finance capital, production and information technologies, basic consumer items, and raw materials. Mismanagement, endemic corruption, and the vagaries of international commodity markets have largely squandered the country's economic potential. Apart from its standing in global energy markets, Nigeria has receded to the margins of the global economy.

Nigeria and the Regional Political Economy

Nigeria's aspirations to be a regional leader in Africa have not been dampened by its declining position in the global political economy. Nigeria was a major actor in the formation of the **Economic Community of West African States (ECOWAS)** in 1975 and has carried a disproportionately high financial and administrative burden for keeping the organization afloat. Under President Obasanjo's initiative, ECOWAS voted in 2000 to create a parliament and a single currency for the region as the next step toward a European Union–style integration. These lofty goals will take years of concerted efforts from the region's troubled governments to become a reality, and the lackluster results of past integration efforts do not bode well for success.

Nigeria was also the largest contributor of troops to the West African peacekeeping force, the ECOWAS Monitoring Group (known as ECOMOG). Under Nigerian direction, the ECOWAS countries dispatched ECOMOG troops to Liberia from 1990 to 1997 to restore order and prevent the Liberian civil war from destabilizing the subregion. Ironically, despite military dictatorship at home, Nigerian ECOMOG forces invaded Sierra Leone in May 1997 to restore its democratically elected government, a move generally endorsed by the international community. The United Nations assumed leadership of the operation in 1999, but Nigeria continues to contribute troops. Nigeria under President Obasanjo has also sought to mediate crises in Guinea-Bissau, Togo, and Ivory Coast, and in Congo and Zimbabwe outside the ECOWAS region.

Because it is the largest economy in the West African subregion, Nigeria has at times been a magnet for immigration. At the height of the 1970s oil boom, many West African laborers, most of them Ghanaians, migrated to Nigeria in search of employment. When the oil-based expansion ceased and jobs became scarce, Nigeria sought to protect its own workers by expelling hundreds of thousands of West Africans in 1983 and 1985. Many Nigerians now flock to the hot Ghanaian economy for work and to countries across the continent, including far-off South Africa.

Nigeria and the Political Economy of the West

Nigeria's global influence peaked in the 1970s at the height of the oil boom. Shortly after the 1973–1974 global oil crisis, Nigeria's oil wealth was perceived by the Nigerian elite as a source of strength. In 1975, for example, Nigeria was selling about 30 percent of its oil to the United States and was able to apply pressure to the administration of President Gerald Ford in a dispute over Angola.[17] By the 1980s, however, the global oil market had become a buyers' market. Thereafter, it became clear that Nigeria's dependence on oil was a source of weakness, not strength. The depth of Nigeria's international weakness became more evident with the adoption of structural adjustment in the mid-1980s. Given the enormity of the economic crisis, Nigeria was compelled to seek IMF/World Bank support to improve its balance of payments and facilitate economic restructuring and debt rescheduling, and it has had to accept direction from foreign agencies ever since.

In addition to its dependence on oil revenues, Nigeria remains dependent on Western technology and expertise for exploration and extraction of its oil reserves. Nevertheless, oil can be an important political resource. For example, after General Babangida cancelled presidential elections in 1993, pressure by U.S. and European oil companies on their home governments ensured that severe economic sanctions on Nigeria were not imposed. The United States is now turning toward Nigerian oil to diversify its supply base beyond the Middle East, which should improve Nigerian government revenues but may not significantly alter the overall dependency of the economy.

Nigeria remains a highly visible and influential member of the Organization of Petroleum Exporting Countries (OPEC), selling on the average 2 million barrels of petroleum daily and contributing approximately

8 percent of U.S. oil imports. Britain, France, and Germany each have over $1 billion in investments. Nigeria's oil wealth and its great economic potential have tempered the resolve of Western nations in combating human rights and other abuses, notably during the Abacha period from 1993 to 1998.

Although President Obasanjo enjoyed much goodwill among Western governments when he assumed office, they were hesitant to discuss cancellation of Nigeria's enormous debt without some evidence of fiscal responsibility. Given the government's inconsistency in this regard, international donors remained largely unmoved, until economic reforms gained momentum midway through the administration's second term.

The West has nevertheless been supportive of the return of Nigerian leadership across Africa. Together with President Thabo Mbeki of South Africa, Obasanjo

Despite being sub-Saharan Africa's largest crude oil exporter, Nigeria faces chronic fuel shortages. General Abacha allowed the nation's four refineries to collapse, forcing the country into the absurd situation of importing fuel—through middlemen who gave enormous kickbacks to Abacha and his family. Shortages have resurfaced periodically since 1999. *Source:* Jay Oguntuwase-Asope, *The Guardian* (Lagos), August 12, 1998.

was instrumental in convincing the continent's leaders to transform the OAU into the African Union (AU) in 2002, modeled on European-style processes to promote greater political integration across the continent. The AU's first item of business, largely promoted by Mbeki and Obasanjo, was to endorse the New Partnership for Africa's Development (NEPAD), through which African governments committed good governance and economic reforms in return for access to Western markets and financial assistance. NEPAD remains a central element in Nigerian and South African foreign policy, but their hesitancy to apply pressure for reforms in important countries, such as Zimbabwe, has led to significant ambivalence toward NEPAD among Western governments.

Despite its considerable geopolitical resources, Nigeria's economic development profile is bleak. Nigeria is listed very close to the bottom of the UNDP's Human Development Index (HDI), 142 out of 174, behind India and Haiti. Gross national product (GNP) per capita in 2001 was $300, less than 2 percent of which was recorded as public expenditures on education and health, respectively. These figures compare unfavorably with the $860 per capita GNP for China and $390 per capita for India. On the basis of its per capita GDP, the Nigerian economy is the nineteenth poorest in the world in a 1997 World Bank ranking. For comparative purposes, the same study ranks Ghana as thirty-first poorest and India twenty-seventh.

Section ❸ Governance and Policy-Making

The rough edges of what has been called the "unfinished Nigerian state" can be seen in its institutions of governance and policy-making. What seemed like an endless political transition under the Babangida and Abacha regimes was rushed through in less than a year by their successor, Abdulsalami Abubakar. President Obasanjo thus inherited a government that was close to collapse, riddled with corruption, unable to perform basic tasks of governance, yet facing high public expectations to deliver rapid progress.

Organization of the State

The National Question and Constitutional Governance

After four decades as an independent nation, Nigerians are still debating the basic political structures of the country, who will rule and how, and indeed, even if the country should remain united. They call this fundamental governance issue the "national question." How is the country to be governed given its great diversity? What should be the institutional form of the government? How can all sections of the country work in harmony and none feel excluded or dominated by the others? Nigerian leaders have attempted to answer these questions in various ways. Since independence,

one path has been reliance on Anglo-American models of democracy and constitutionalism. Another path has been military domination. Nigeria has stumbled along under hybrids of these two tendencies. As a consequence, the country has produced many constitutions but has yet to entrench constitutionalism.

Since the amalgamation of northern and southern Nigeria in 1914, the country has drafted nine constitutions—five under colonial rule (in 1922, 1946, 1951, 1954, and 1960) and four after colonial rule: the 1963 Republican Constitution, the 1979 Constitution of the Second Republic, the 1989 Constitution intended for the Third Republic, and the current 1999 Constitution, which essentially amended the 1979 version. Although huge sums were spent on constitution making by the Babangida and Abacha regimes, Nigeria actually conducted national elections in 1998–1999 without a settled constitutional document. Public pressure to revise the 1999 constitution has remained strong, and the president inaugurated a National Political Reform Conference in early 2005 to recommend changes in the constitution and the structure of the federation. The conference lacked broad legitimacy, however, since the president appointed delegates and the ruling party and presidential allies have significant influence over the deliberations. Consequently, a number of political parties and civil society groups condemned the conference, and threatened to hold their own national "confab" later in the year.

In contrast, Nigerian constitutions have earned little respect from military or civilian leaders, who have often been unwilling to observe legal and constitutional constraints. Governance and policymaking in this context are conducted within fragile institutions that are swamped by personal and partisan considerations. Military rule bolstered these tendencies and personalized governance and policymaking. With this in mind, we will discuss key elements of recent periods of military rule, their continued influence in the present, and the young institutions of the Fourth Republic.

Federalism and State Structure

Nigeria's First Republic experimented with the parliamentary model, in which the executive is chosen directly from the legislative ranks. The First Republic was relatively decentralized, with the locus of political power in the three federal units: the Northern, Eastern, and Western Regions. The Second Republic constitution, which went into effect in 1979, adopted a U.S.-style presidential model. The Fourth Republic continues with the presidential model: a system with a strong executive who is constrained by a system of checks and balances on authority, a bicameral legislature, and an independent judicial branch charged with matters of law and constitutional interpretation.[18]

Like the United States, Nigeria also features a federal structure comprising 36 states and 774 local government units empowered to enact their own laws within their individual jurisdictions, but limited in scope by the constitution and federal laws. Together, these units constitute a single national entity with three levels of government. The judicial system also resembles that of the United States with a network of local and district courts, as well as state-level courts.

Under a true federal system, the formal powers of the different levels of government would be derived from the constituent members of the federation, such as the states. In Nigeria, by contrast, these institutions have been created top-down, by military fiat. The military left a 1999 constitution that retains enormous powers in the federal government, and the executive in particular. In addition, so many years of military rule

left a pattern of governance—a political culture—that retains many authoritarian strains despite the formal democratization of state structures.

The control of oil wealth by this centralized command structure has further cemented economic and political control in the center, resulting in a skewed federalism in which states enjoy nominal powers, but in reality are totally dependent on the central government. The powers of the state and local governments are delineated by the federal constitution, and they receive virtually their entire budget from the federally determined share of the oil revenues.

Another aspect of federalism in Nigeria has been the effort to arrive at some form of elite accommodation to moderate some of the more divisive aspects of cultural pluralism. A similar practice, known as "federal character," was introduced into the public service and formally codified by the 1979 constitution, while ethnic quotas have long been observed by the armed forces. (See "Current Challenges: Nigeria's Federal Character.")

Because federal character is also perceived as a tool of ethnic management, disputes about its application have tended to focus on ethnic representation rather than on representation of state interests. Although this principle was originally regarded as a positive Nigerian contribution to governance in a plural society, its application has tended to intensify rather than to reduce intergroup rivalries and conflicts. In recent years, there have been calls for the use of merit over federal character in awarding public sector jobs. (See "Current Challenges: Federalism in Nigeria.")

The Executive

Evolution of the Executive Function

In the Second Republic, the earlier parliamentary system was replaced by a presidential system based on the American model. The president was chosen directly by the electorate rather than indirectly by the legislature, based on a widespread belief that a popularly elected president could serve as a symbol of national unity. The framers of the Second Republic's constitution believed that placing the election of the president in the hands of the electorate, rather than parliament, would mitigate a lack of party discipline in the selection of the executive.

Current Challenges: *Nigeria's Federal Character*

Federal character, in principle, is an affirmative action program to ensure representation of all ethnic and regional groups, particularly in the civil service. Although *federal character* is regarded as a euphemism for *ethnic balancing,* in practice it has provoked ethnic instability, rivalry, and conflict. Federal character goes beyond federalism in the traditional Western and territorial sense. Federalism as a principle of government has a positive connotation (especially with regard to mitigating ethnic conflict); however, federal character elicits the unevenness and inequality in Nigerian politics, especially when it comes to the controversial use of ethnic-based quotas in hiring, the awarding of government contracts, and the disbursement of political offices.

The pursuit of ethnic balancing has had numerous ill effects, several of which are identified by Nigerian scholar Peter Ekeh.[*] Federal character has created benefit-seeking and autonomy-seeking groups in areas where they did not previously exist. Second, federal character and federalism have overloaded the political system in terms of personnel and other costs. Federal character has also "invaded the integrity of the public bureaucracy" by ignoring merit. Finally, the thirty-six states that currently exist in Nigeria are vying for control of the center in order to extract the greatest benefits, using ethnic quotas as a lever. None of these conditions is likely to change in the near future. Federal character, and everything that goes with it, appears to be a permanent part of Nigeria's political and social landscape.

_____

[*]See Peter Ekeh, "The Structure and Meaning of Federal Character in the Nigerian Political System," in Peter Ekeh and Eghosa E. Osaghae (eds.), *Federalism and the Federal Character in Nigeria* (Ibadan: Heinemann, 1989).

Current Challenges: *Federalism in Nigeria*

The federal system has historically enjoyed wide support within Nigeria. With the "national question" unanswered, however, the federal structure endures increasing strain. At the conclusion of the civil war in 1970, many assumed that the question of national unity had been finally settled. Attempts to include clauses on the right to secede in the constitutions of 1979 and 1989 were roundly rejected by the drafting committees. Yet the most recent transition period featured a number of public debates about partition, particularly among the Yoruba, while other groups have continually lamented their political marginalization. Questions have also been raised as to whether Nigeria will continue to be a secular state and persist as a federation if it is to accommodate the country's ethnic, cultural, and religious heterogeneity.

To resolve these issues, some Nigerians have called for a national conference to review the basis of national unity and even to consider the restructuring of Nigeria into a loose confederation of autonomous states, perhaps along the lines of the First Republic. Such calls were ignored by the military, which foreclosed any debate on the viability of a united Nigeria, thus maintaining the geographic status quo. After resisting pressures for a national conference, President Obasanjo surprised the public by convening the National Political Reform Conference in early 2005. He insists that national unity is nonnegotiable, but several proposals to restructure the federation and to alter Nigeria's presidential system have been advanced. A number of political leaders and civil society groups have criticized the conference as being overly beholden to the president, and some groups are threatening to hold their own national conference as well.

The Second Republic's experiment with presidentialism lasted for only four years before it was ended by the 1983 coup. Although some Nigerian intellectuals call for a return to parliamentarism, the presidential model has become entrenched in the nation's political arena. The return of military rule in 1983 further concentrated power in the hands of the chief executive. Thus, when Obasanjo took office, the first elected Nigerian president since Shehu Shagari in 1983, he inherited an executive structure that towered above all other arms of the federal government, far beyond the careful balance envisioned when the model was adopted in 1979.

The Executive Under Military Rule

The leadership styles among Nigeria's seven military heads of state varied widely. The military regime of General Gowon (1966–1975) was initially consensual, with major national decisions made by a council of officers from across the federation, but the head of state clung to power for several years after the war; his authority declined while he increasingly relied on a small group of advisers. Generals Muhammad and Obasanjo ruled through expanded collegial institutions, though their executive control was strengthened in practice. General Buhari, after ousting the civilian Second Republic, made no pretense of political transition, and instituted stern authoritarian control.

After a few years of relatively consensual governance, the Babangida regime (1985–1993) drifted into a more personalized and repressive mode of governance. Abacha (1993–1998) exceeded his predecessors in his harsh autocratic rule. General Abubakar, in contrast, moved quickly to relax political controls, institute a rapid democratization program, and curb the abuses of the security services. Nearly all military leaders have talked of "transitions to democracy," though only Generals Obasanjo and Abubakar fulfilled the pledge of yielding power to an elected government.

Under military administrations, the president, or head of state, made appointments to most senior government positions.[19] Since the legislature was disbanded, major executive decisions (typically passed by decrees) were subject to the approval of a ruling council of high-level military officers. By the time of Abacha's Provisional Ruling Council (PRC), however, this council had become virtually a rubber stamp for the ruler. Given the highly personalistic character of military politics, patron-client relationships flourished during this period. Not surprisingly, ethnic, religious, and regional constituencies have paid close attention to the pattern of appointments to the executive branch.

The military was structurally weakened during its long years in power, having been politicized and divided by these patron-client relationships. Under Babangida and Abacha, the military was transformed from an instrument that guarantees national defense and security into another predatory apparatus, one more powerful than political parties. Four decades after the first military coup of January 1966, most Nigerians now believe that the country's political and economic development has been profoundly hampered by military domination and misrule. Within days of his taking office in 1999, President Obasanjo retired over ninety military officers who had held political offices (such as military governorships) under the previous military juntas, seeing them as the most likely plotters of future coups. While there have been media reports of several coup plots, the military establishment has apparently remained loyal and outside of politics.

In addition, President Obasanjo has paid close attention to keeping the military professionally oriented—and in the barracks. Because he is an ex-military head of state himself, this should not be surprising. U.S. military advisers and technical assistance have been invited to redirect the Nigerian military toward regional peacekeeping expertise—and to keep them busy outside of politics. So far, this strategy seems effective, but the military remains a threat should the civilians fail to gain popular approval.

The Obasanjo Administration

As noted earlier, President Obasanjo's first six months in office were marked by a number of initiatives to reform the armed forces, revitalize the economy, address public welfare, and improve standards of governance.

Prominent among these priorities, the president sought to root out misconduct and inefficiency in the public sector. His initial appointments to manage the oil industry drew early praise for their clean management and contracting policies, and the persistent fuel scarcities of the Abacha years abated. Soon, however, familiar patterns of clientelism and financial kick-backs for oil licenses resurfaced. Obasanjo proposed an anticorruption commission with sweeping statutory powers to investigate and prosecute public officials. Delayed in its establishment, the commission had little impact, and was accused by detractors of being a political tool of the presidency. A second anticorruption commission founded in 2003, the Economic and Financial Crimes Commission (EFCC), has had an impressive record of indictments, as discussed in Section 2.

In response to calls by civil society groups for some accounting for the injustices committed during years of military rule, Obasanjo set up the Peace and Reconciliation Commission in 1999. Unlike the famous Truth and Reconciliation Commission set up by South Africa at the end of the apartheid years, the Nigerian Commission did not have the power to grant amnesty in exchange for admissions of guilt, which would better ensure that testimony would be accurate. The stories and mutual recriminations of former Abacha henchmen riveted the nation in nightly television broadcasts and created high political drama. The commission conducted some of its most sensitive inquiries in secret, and submitted its report confidentially to the president, who refused to make its findings public. The report, however, was leaked to several civil society organizations who promptly published it.

A major impediment to reform came from the ruling party itself. The PDP is a collection of powerful politicians from Nigeria's First and Second Republics, many of whom had grown rich from their complicity with the Babangida and Abacha juntas. These "big men" approached Obasanjo and engineered political machines that delivered him the 1999 election victory, through a poll marked by numerous procedural violations. As apparent reward for this support, Obasanjo filled his cabinet with many of these dubious political kingpins and did not scrutinize their handling of ministry budgets. With a difficult re-election bid in 2003, these fixers again delivered a victory for the president and the PDP, accomplished through massive fraud in a third of Nigeria's states, and questionable practices in at least another third of the country. Not surprisingly, allegations of corruption at the highest levels of the Obasanjo administration have increased, and several high officials at the cabinet and gubernatorial levels

have been investigated. Personal differences between President Obasanjo and PDP leaders in the National Assembly, particularly the Speaker of the House, meanwhile, led them to instigate impeachment proceedings against the president in mid-2002, as will be discussed in Section 4.

An important area of attention has been the conflict-ridden Niger Delta. The president's initial goodwill from visiting the region and meeting local leaders, including youths, soon turned to hostility when he refused to negotiate claims by delta communities for greater control of the revenues from oil drilled on their lands. Instead, he proposed a Niger Delta Development Commission (NDDC) to disburse the 13 percent of oil revenues constitutionally mandated to return to the delta states. Community groups rejected the plan, governors of the Niger Delta states took Obasanjo to court, and youth militias returned to harassing the police, stealing oil, and kidnapping oil workers for ransom. One such attack killed several policemen in November 1999, whereupon military units destroyed the village of Odi and massacred many of its inhabitants.[20] The NDDC was slow to take shape and had little impact on the region's development. Meanwhile, ethnic militias, living off stolen oil, continue to grow bolder and more restive. Violence in Delta State in 2003 shut down nearly 40 percent of the country's oil exports for several days.

The fraud in the 2003 elections undermined the PDP government's legitimacy and signaled to "big men" across Nigeria that any method to achieve power was acceptable in Nigerian politics. Shortly after the governor of Anambra state was "elected" in a race that was by all accounts rigged—President Obasanjo himself later publicly admitted as much—the governor sought to distance himself from the "godfather" who had rigged the election for him. After the governor was abducted and released by rogue police officers, Anambra was reduced to a war zone between supporters of the governor and those of his patron. Obasanjo and other PDP leaders sought to mediate, but tellingly, the president refused to give the governor police protection or to arrest his political adversary.

A similar struggle between the governor of Plateau State (whose most recent election was also tainted) and other big men turned violent, as both sides used ethnic and religious grievances to incite communities across these divides. Christian attacks on Muslim communities in the town of Yelwa in May 2004 prompted revenge attacks by Muslims against Christians in several Middle Belt states and in Kano, forcing the president to declare a state of emergency in Plateau and to impose a military administrator for six months. Surprisingly, President Obasanjo restored the governor to office once the emergency was lifted, despite the fact that the British government had subsequently brought charges of money laundering against the governor.

The events in Anambra and Plateau states, as well as the chaos in the Niger Delta region, demonstrated deficits of legitimacy for the government as well as the democratic system. As Nigeria's political elites continue to flout the rules of the system, it is inevitable that patronage, coercion, and personal interest will drive policy more than the interests of the public. The president sought to renew his reform agenda in 2005 with high-profile anticorruption and economic reform policies, but the titanic struggles of the big men at all levels of Nigerian politics continue to dilute and undermine the impact of these reforms. The president's occasional ambivalence about legal restraints on his own powers, as in the case of Plateau State, also offsets his own reform agenda.

The Bureaucracy

The bureaucracy touches upon all aspects of Nigerian government. The colonial system relied on an expanding bureaucracy to govern Nigeria. As government was increasingly "Africanized," the bureaucracy became a way to reward individuals in the patrimonial system (see "Current Challenges: Prebendalism").

Current Challenges: **Prebendalism**

Prebendalism, the peculiarly Nigerian version of corruption, is the disbursing of public offices and state rents to one's ethnic-based clients.* It is an extreme form of clientelism that refers to the practice of mobilizing cultural and other sectional identities by political aspirants and officeholders for the purpose of corruptly appropriating state resources. Prebendalism is an established pattern of political behavior that justifies the pursuit of and the use of public office for the personal benefit of the officeholder and his clients. The official public purpose of the office becomes a secondary concern. As with clientelism, the officeholder's clients comprise a specific set of elites to which he is linked, typically by ethnic or religious ties, and this linkage is key to understanding the concept. There are thus two sides involved in prebendalism, the officeholder and the client, and expectations of benefits by the clients (or supporters) perpetuate the prebendal system.

As practiced in the Babangida and Abacha eras, when official corruption occurred on an unprecedented scale, prebendalism deepened sectional cleavages and eroded the resources of the state. It also discouraged genuinely productive activity in the economy and expanded the class of individuals who live off state patronage.

As long as prebendalism remains the norm of Nigerian politics, a stable democracy will be elusive. These practices are now deeply embedded in Nigerian society and are therefore more difficult to uproot. The corruption resulting from prebendal practices is blamed in popular discourse for the enormous overseas flight of capital into private accounts. The lion's share of the $12.2 billion windfall of the early 1990s is believed to have been pocketed by Babangida and senior members of his regime, an example of the magnitude of the systematic pilfering of public resources. General Abacha continued this pattern and diverted $5 billion from the Nigerian central bank. There are so many current officeholders in Nigeria who indulge in corrupt practices that Transparency International regularly lists Nigeria among the most corrupt countries.

*Richard Joseph, *Democracy and Prebendal Politics in Nigeria: The Rise and Fall of the Second Republic* (Cambridge: Cambridge University Press, 1987) 55–68.

Bureaucratic growth was no longer determined by function and need; increasingly, individuals were appointed on the basis of patronage, ethnic group, and regional origin rather than merit.

It is conservatively estimated that federal and state government personnel increased from a modest 72,000 at independence to well over 1 million by the mid 1980s. The salaries of these bureaucrats presently consume roughly half of government expenditures, which after another 30 percent or more for debt servicing leaves a paltry 10 percent or so for the other responsibilities of government, from education and health care to building the roads.

Para-statals

Among the largest components of the national administration in Nigeria are numerous state-owned enterprises, or **para-statals.** Para-statals in Nigeria are corporate enterprises, owned by the state, created for specific commercial and social welfare services. They are a hybrid, somewhere between institutions that engage in traditional government operations, such as customs or the postal service, and those in the private sector that operate primarily for profit. Para-statals are similar to private enterprises in having their own boards of directors. In principle, they are autonomous of the government that established them. In reality, however, such autonomy is limited since their boards are politically appointed and ultimately answerable to the government. In general, para-statals are established for several reasons. First, they furnish public facilities, including water, power, telecommunications, ports, and other transportation. A second rationale for the establishment of para-statals is the need to accelerate economic development by controlling the commanding heights of the economy, including steel production, petroleum and natural gas production, refining, petrochemicals, fertilizer, and certain areas of agriculture. Third, para-statals are intended to provide basic utilities and services to citizens at low costs, held below the levels that would be needed by private firms to generate profit. Finally, there is a nationalist dimension that relates to issues of sovereignty over sectors perceived sensitive for national security.

Para-statals such as agricultural commodity boards and the Nigerian National Petroleum Corporation (NNPC) have served as major instruments of the interventionist state. They have been used to co-opt and organize business and societal interests for the purpose of politically controlling the economy and dispensing state largesse. These enterprises are major instruments of patronage and rent seeking. In Nigeria, as in the rest of Africa, most para-statal enterprises are a tremendous drain on the economy. It is not surprising, therefore, that one of the major requirements of the economic structural adjustment program discussed in Section 2 is the privatization of most of these enterprises. Privatizing the para-statals remains a central part of reform strategy under the Obasanjo administration. The telecommunications and power industries are already up for sale, and the administration has promised to sell parts of the oil industry.

Other State Institutions

Other institutions of governance and policymaking, including the federal judiciary and subnational governments (incorporating state and local courts), operate within the context of a strong central government dominated by a powerful chief executive.

The Judiciary

At one time, the Nigerian judiciary enjoyed relative autonomy from the executive arm of government. Aggrieved individuals and organizations could take the government to court and expect a judgment based on the merits of their case. This situation changed as each successive military government demonstrated a profound disdain for judicial practices, and eventually it undermined not only the autonomy but also the very integrity of the judiciary as a third branch of government.

The Babangida and Abacha regimes, in particular, issued a spate of repressive decrees disallowing judicial review. Clauses were regularly inserted in government decrees barring any consideration of their legality by the courts, as well as any actions taken by government officials under them. Other methods included intimidation by the security services, the creation of parallel special military tribunals that could dispense with various legal procedures and due process, and disrespect for courts of record.

Through the executive's power of appointment of judicial officers to the high bench, as well as the executive's control of funds required for the running of the judiciary, the government can dominate the courts at all levels. In addition, what was once regarded as a highly competent judiciary has been undermined severely by declining standards of legal training as well as by bribery.

The decline of court independence reached a new low in 1993 when the Supreme Court, in what some analysts labeled "judicial terrorism," endorsed a government position that literally placed all actions of the military executive beyond the pale of judicial review. The detention and hanging of Ken Saro-Wiwa and eight other Ogoni activists in 1995 (see Section 2) underscored the politicization and compromised state of the judicial system. With the return of civilian rule, however, the courts have slowly begun to restore some independence and credibility. The Supreme Court in particular has returned as a critical player in national political development after years of docility and self-imposed irrelevance. In early 2002, it passed two landmark judgments. The first struck down a 2001 election law that would have prevented new parties from contesting the national elections in 2003—a decision that contravened the wishes of the president and the ruling party. The Court also decided against the governors of Nigeria's coastal states over control of the vast offshore gas reserves, declaring these to be under the jurisdiction of the federal government.

State and Local Judiciaries.   The judiciaries at the state level are subordinate to the Federal Court of Appeal and the Supreme Court. Some of the states in the northern part of the country with large Muslim populations maintain a parallel court system based on the Islamic *shari'a* (religious law). Similarly, some states in the Middle Belt and southern part of the country have subsidiary courts based on customary law. Each of these maintains an appellate division. Otherwise, all courts of record in the country are based on the English common law tradition, and all courts are ultimately bound by decisions handed down by the Supreme Court.

How to apply the *shari'a* has been a source of continuing debate in Nigerian politics. For several years, some northern groups have participated in a movement to expand the application of *shari'a* law in predominantly Muslim areas of Nigeria, and some even have advocated that it be made the supreme law of the land. Prior to the establishment of the Fourth Republic, *shari'a* courts had jurisdiction only among Muslims in civil proceedings and in questions of Islamic personal law. In November 1999, however, the northern state of Zamfara instituted a version of the *shari'a* criminal code, which included cutting off hands for stealing, and stoning to death for those (especially women) who committed adultery. Eleven other northern states adopted the criminal code by 2001, prompting fears among Christian minorities in these states that the code might be applied to them and creating a divisive national issue. Although the *shari'a* criminal code appears to contradict Nigeria's officially secular constitution, the administration has so far been unwilling to take these states to court and appears to be pushing for a political solution.

State and Local Government

Because the creation of new states and local governments opens new channels to the oil wealth accumulated at the federal level, localities and groups are constantly clamoring for further subdivision. Periodic changes in these federal arrangements, including the creation of new states and the addition of a third level of local government, has generally occurred under nondemocratic auspices of colonial and military rule. Sensing opportunities to buy support for their regimes, Babangida and Abacha nearly doubled the number of states and tripled that of local governments (see Table 5). Although they touted these moves as answering the "national question" by increasing opportunities for local self-determination, the limited fiscal and political autonomy of these units has in fact bolstered central government control. Several states have added local governments since 2000, but the federal government has argued that they do not have the constitutional authority to do so.

The Nigerian experience has promoted a distributive approach to federalism. The lofty claims for federalism as a way of promoting unity through diversity are lost amid the intense competition among local communities and elites for access to national patronage, which

Table 5

Political Divisions, 1963–1996					
1963	*1967*	*1976*	*1987*	*1991*	*1996*
					(Northwest zone)
Northern Region	North Central	Kaduna	Kaduna	Kaduna	Kaduna
			Katsina	Katsina	Katsina
	Kano	Kano	Kano	Kano	Kano
				Jigawa	Jigawa
	North Western	Sokoto	Sokoto	Sokoto	Sokoto
					Zamfara
				Kebbi	Kebbi
					(North-Central zone)
		Niger	Niger	Niger	Niger
	Benue-Plateau	Benue-Plateau	Benue-Plateau	Benue	Benue
				Plateau	Plateau
					Nassarawa
		Abuja	Abuja	FCT (Abuja)[c]	FCT (Abuja)
	West Central	Kwara	Kwara	Kwara	Kwara
				Kogi[a]	Kogi
					(Northeast zone)
	North Eastern	Bauchi	Bauchi	Bauchi	Bauchi
					Gombe
		Borno	Borno	Borno	Borno
				Yobe	Yobe
		Gongola	Gongola	Adamawa	Adamawa
				Taraba	Taraba
					(Southeast zone)
Eastern Region	East Central	Anambra	Anambra	Anambra	Anambra
				Enugu	Enugu
					Ebonyi
		Imo	Imo	Imo	Imo
				Abia	Abia
					(South-south zone)
	South Eastern	Cross River	Cross River	Cross River	Cross River
			Akwa Ibom	Akwa Ibom	Akwa Ibom
	Rivers	Rivers	Rivers	Rivers	Rivers
					Bayelsa
Mid-West Region	Mid-Western	Bendel	Bendel	Edo	Edo
				Delta	Delta
					(Southwest zone)
Western Region	Western	Ogun	Ogun	Ogun	Ogun
		Ondo	Ondo	Ondo	Ondo
					Ekiti
		Oyo	Oyo	Oyo	Oyo
				Osun	Osun
Lagos[b]	Lagos	Lagos	Lagos	Lagos	Lagos

[a]Kogi state was created by combining parts of Benue and Kwara states.

[b]Lagos was excised from the Western Region in 1954 and became the federal capital. In 1967, it also became capital of the new Lagos State, which included Badagry, Ikeja, and Epe districts from the Western Region.

[c]Abuja replaced Lagos as the federal capital in December 1991, although its boundaries were first delineated in the 1970s.

Source: Tom Forrest, *Politics and Economic Development in Nigeria* (Boulder, Colo.: Westview Press, 1993), 214; Darren Kew.

comes in the form of oil revenues that are collected, and then appropriated or redistributed, by the federal administration through the states. (See Table 6.)

State governments are generally weak and dependent on federally controlled revenues. Most of them would be insolvent and unable to sustain themselves without substantial support from the central government because of the states' weak resource and tax base. About 90 percent of state incomes are received directly from the federal government, which includes a lump sum based on oil revenues, plus a percentage of oil income based on population. The states and local governments, however, must generate more resources of their own to increase the efficiency of both their administrations and private economic sectors. In

all likelihood, only Lagos and Kano states could survive without federal subsidies.

In response to the proliferation of states, the political parties have turned to the notion of six zones in Nigeria, correlated roughly with the major ethnic regions in the country: Hausa-Fulani, Igbo, Yoruba, and three minority-dominated areas. Political appointments are roughly balanced among the six zones and rotate over time.[21] For instance, the presidency is currently held by the southwest (Yoruba) zone; the next president, by informal agreement, will likely be from one of the Middle Belt minorities, the Northeast, or from the South-South zone—the Niger Delta.

In the same way that states depend on federal handouts, local governments have remained dependent

Table 6

Percentage Contribution of Different Sources of Government Revenue to Allocated Revenue, 1980–2003

	Oil Revenue Petroleum Profits Tax	Mining Rents and Royalties	Nonoil Revenue Customs and Excise Duties	Others	Total
1980	58.1	25.7	12.3	3.9	100.0
1981	55.5	19.6	20.4	4.5	100.0
1982	44.5	27.3	21.5	6.7	100.0
1983	35.7	33.4	18.9	12.0	100.0
1984	44.8	32.4	15.2	7.6	100.0
1985	47.8	30.0	14.7	7.5	100.0
1986	40.5	25.3	14.6	19.6	100.0
1987	50.6	25.4	14.3	9.7	100.0
1988	46.7	31.5	15.9	5.9	100.0
	Oil Revenues (Combined)		Nonoil Revenue	Other	Total
1992	86.2		8.4	5.4	100.0
1993	84.0		8.0	8.0	100.0
1994	79.3		9.1	11.6	100.0
1995	53.2		8.1	38.7*	100.0
1996	51.1		10.6	38.3*	100.0
2001	79.7		17.6	2.7	100.0
2002	78.6		19.4	2.0	100.0
2003	78.1		19.9	2.0	100.0

*Beginning in 1995, the Nigerian government began including surplus foreign exchange as federally collected revenue in its accounting.

Sources: Federal Ministry of Finance and Economic Development, Lagos. From Adedotun Phillips, "Managing Fiscal Federalism: Revenue Allocation Issues," *Publius: The Journal of Federalism*, 21, no. 4 (Fall 1991), p. 109. Nigerian Federal Office of Statistics, *Annual Abstract of Statistics: 1997 Edition*. Nigerian Economic Summit Group, *Economic Indicators* (Vol. 8, no. 2, April–June 2002).

on both state and federal governments. This practice has continued despite the 1988 reforms of the local government system initiated by the Babangida regime, supposedly to strengthen that level of government. Dissatisfaction with local government performance persists, and President Obasanjo appointed a high-level committee to recommend reforms, which has yielded little concrete action. The current National Political Reform Conference may issue new proposals.

The state and local governments have the constitutional and legal powers to raise funds through taxes. However, Nigerians share a pronounced unwillingness, especially those in self-employment, trade, and other informal sector activities, to pay taxes and fees to a government with such a poor record of delivering basic services. The result is a vicious cycle: government is sapped of resources and legitimacy and cannot adequately serve the people. Communities, in turn, are compelled to resort to self-help measures to protect these operations and thus withdraw further from the reach of the state. Because very few individuals and organizations pay taxes, even the most basic government functions are starved of resources (see Table 7).

The return of democratic rule has meant the return of conflict between the state and national governments, much like during the Second Republic (1979–1983). The primary vehicle for conflict since 1999 has been a series of "governors' forums," one for the seventeen southern governors, one for the nineteen northern governors, and one for all thirty-six governors. Ad hoc committees on specific issues have also arisen. Southern governors have been particularly active in asserting greater legal control over the resources in their states (such as oil) and over the offshore oil and gas reserves. Much as at the national level, the state-level executives have far more power than their legislatures. These state assemblies, however, have not been docile, and on several occasions they have moved to impeach their state governors.

A number of governors, particularly in the Igbo-dominated southeast, have turned to armed militias and vigilante groups to provide security in their states and to intimidate political opponents. Many of these groups were initially local responses to the corrupt and ineffective police force, but several of the governors have sensed the larger political usefulness of these groups. Consequently, and disturbingly, political assassinations and violence increased as the 2003 elections approached. Some of these militias in the Niger Delta have turned on their former masters, on

Table 7

Share of Total Government Expenditure (%)

	1961	1965	1970	1975	1980	1987	1992	1996	2001	2002
Federal Government	49	53	73	72	66	75	72	74	57	52.3
State Government	51	47	27	28	34	25	28*	26*	24	26
Local Government**	–	–	–	–	–	–	–	–	20	21.7
Total Expenditure (millions Naira)	336	445	1,149	10,916	21,349	29,365	128,476	327,707	1,008,780	1,111,950

* Note that 67% of state spending in 1992 and 49% of it in 1996 came from federal government oil earnings, part of which are allocated annually to all the states roughly in proportion to their population size.

**Local government expenditures are included in state government figures in 1961 and 1965, and federal figures from 1970 through 1996.

Sources: Central Bank of Nigeria, *Annual Report and Statement of Accounts;* Federal Office of Statistics, *Abstract of Annual Statistics* (Lagos: Federal Government Printer, 1961, 1965, 1970, 1975, 1980, 1987, and 1997). From Izeubuwa Osayimwese and Sunday Iyare, "The Economics of Nigerian Federalism: Selected Issues in Economic Management," *Publius: The Journal of Federalism,* 21, no. 4 (Fall 1991), p. 91. Nigerian Economic Summit Group, Economic Indicators (Vol. 8, no. 2, April–June 2002). 1990s percentage calculations by Darren Kew.

one occasion forcing the Rivers State governor to flee to Abuja for protection.

The Policy-Making Process

Nigeria's prolonged experience with military rule has resulted in a policy process based more on top-down directives than on consultation, political debate, and legislation. Several years of democratic government have seen important changes, as the legislatures, courts, and state governments have begun to force the presidency to negotiate its policies and work within a constitutional framework.

First, we must explore how military rule shaped policymaking in Nigeria. Because of their influence in recruitment and promotions, as well as through their own charisma or political connections, senior officers often developed networks of supporters of the same or lower rank, creating what is referred to as a "loyalty pyramid."[22] Once in power, the men at the top of these pyramids in Nigeria gained access to tremendous oil wealth, passed on through the lower echelons of the pyramid to reward support. Often these pyramids reflect ethnic or religious affiliations (see the discussions of corruption in Section 2 and **prebendalism** in Section 3) such as the "Kaduna Mafia" of northern elites, but pyramids like the "Babangida" or "Abacha Boys" included a patchwork of officers beyond their ethnic circle. In addition, the well-developed pyramids had allies or personal connections in the bureaucracy and business. The personal ambitions of leaders commonly eclipsed the corporate mission of the military. Personal goals and interests became the defining characteristic of the regime and its policies, with the only check on personal power being another coup.

General Babangida signified a turning point within the military as national concerns were increasingly subsumed by personal ambitions.[23] He was a master at playing the different loyalty pyramids against each other, lavishing the nation's oil wealth on friends and buying the support of opponents he could not crush. Once in power, General Abacha made little pretense of accommodating other factions, instead ruthlessly centralizing nearly all government decision making and spreading little patronage.

Abacha's personal plunder of the nation's revenues dispelled the notion that the military was a cohesive, nationalist institution capable of governing Nigeria any more efficiently than the civilians. A parallel structure of junior officers loyal to Abacha acted as his gatekeepers, circumventing and humiliating the military's normal chain of command. General Abubakar thus took the reins of a military that was divided and demoralized. Abubakar was more of a professional than his predecessors, purging the government of "Abacha boys" and swiftly returning the country to civilian rule. Despite having returned to the barracks, others in the military may well yearn for their turn at the top.

Because the military dominated Nigeria for three-quarters of its independent existence, civilian politics bears a strong resemblance to the politics of loyalty pyramids among the military.[24] Many of the current civilian politicians belonged to the loyalty pyramids of different military men—as bureaucrats, members of military cabinets, business partners to exploit Nigeria's oil wealth, and so on. Now that the politicians are in power, some of them former military officers, they are taking up the reins of the civilian portions of these pyramids, while they undoubtedly retain some influence with military figures.

Nigerians often refer to the politicians who sit atop these civilian loyalty pyramids as "big men." Unlike the military leaders, however, the civilian big men do not typically have access to formal coercive instruments, so to maintain their pyramids they must rely on financial kickbacks and promises of rents from the state: government jobs, contracts, and so on. (Section 4 discusses these clientelistic and prebendal patterns of the loyalty pyramids in greater detail.)

Thus, in patterns reminiscent of the struggles among military loyalty pyramids, the policymaking process today in Nigeria under democratic rule is a function of the clash of interests among the big men and their clients. The vice president, party leaders of the PDP, many of the ministers, and leaders in the National Assembly are all big men vying for larger rents from the state and increased influence and status. Ironically, Obasanjo was not a "big man" when he was elected; he rode to power on the backs of these big men and their supporters who are now in intense competition with each other.

Civilian policymaking in present-day Nigeria centers largely on presidential initiative in proposing reform policies, which are then filtered through the interests of the "big men." Invariably, their agendas conflict with those of the president and with each other, and policies are consequently blocked or significantly altered. Frequently, the reformist agenda is stalled or ineffectual. The president became increasingly adept at navigating these interests in his first term, but soon enough the reformist agenda took a

back seat to his own concern for reelection. On this point his ministers were agreed, and policymaking by the administration was harnessed to the goal of getting the president reelected by any possible means. After the elections, the president turned back to a reform agenda, though these policies remain mired in the competition of interests among the big men of the political class.

Section **4** Representation and Participation

Representation and participation are two vital components in modern democracies. Nigerian legislatures have commonly been sidelined or reduced to subservience by the powerful executive, while fraud, elite manipulation, and military interference have marred the party and electoral systems. Consequently, Nigerian society has found modes of participation outside the official structures. An important focus of this section will therefore be unofficial (that is, nongovernmental) methods of representation and participation through the institutions of civil society. The institutions of political society include such entities as parties, constitutions, and legislatures, while those of **civil society** include professional associations, trade unions, religious organizations, and various interest groups.

The patterns outlined in this section reflect the complexities of the relationship between representation and participation. Formal representation does not necessarily enhance participation. In fact, there are situations in which the most important modes of political participation are found outside institutional channels such as elections and legislatures—or even in opposition to them.

The Legislature

Not surprisingly, Nigeria's legislature has been a victim of the country's political instability. Legislative structures and processes historically suffered abuse, neglect, or peremptory suspension by the executive arm. As a consequence, the politicians who took office at the state and federal levels in 1999 had little understanding, and less experience, of legislative functions

and responsibilities. In addition, they stood in the shadow of the overly powerful executive that had dominated Nigerian politics under the military.

Until the first coup in 1966, Nigeria operated its legislature along the lines of the British Westminster model, with an elected lower house and a smaller upper house composed of individuals selected by the executive. For the next thirteen years of military rule, a Supreme Military Council performed legislative functions by initiating and passing decrees at will. During the second period of civilian rule, 1979–1983, the bicameral legislature was structured similar to the U.S. system, with a Senate and House of Representatives (together known as the National Assembly) consisting of elected members.

Election to the Senate is on the basis of equal state representation, with three senators from each of the thirty-six states, plus one senator from the federal capital territory, Abuja. The practice of equal representation in the Senate is identical to that of the United States, except that each Nigerian state elects three senators instead of two. Election to the Nigerian House of Representatives was also based on state representation but weighted to reflect the relative size of each state's population, again after the U.S. example. Only eight women were elected in 1999 to sit in the Fourth Republic's National Assembly. This reflects the limited political participation of Nigerian women in formal institutions, as discussed in Section 2.

An innovation added during the failed transition to the Third Republic is that local government structures now enjoy greater autonomy from control by the state governments. The federal executive has, however, dominated other branches of government, partly as a consequence of military rule, and also by virtue of the strong fiscal centralization of the oil-based state.

Thus, Nigerian legislatures under military government were either powerless (as during the brief sitting of the Assembly in 1992–1993) or nonexistent. Even under previous elected civil administrations, however, Nigerian legislatures were subjected to great pressure by the executive and never assumed their full constitutional role. Because the executive and majority interests in the National Assembly belonged to the same party, influence has been easily exercised through party machines and outright bribery. This situation has been exacerbated by legislative dependence on the executive for their allowances and the resources to meet the relentless demands from their constituents for jobs, contracts, and other favors. This is the critical difference between the Nigerian and U.S. systems: in Nigeria, the president controls and disburses public revenues, which the Assembly only influences by its right to pass the budget. The U.S. Congress, by contrast, controls the public purse.

The National Assembly that took office in 1999 therefore began its work with great uncertainty over its role in Nigerian politics. Both the House and the Senate were controlled by the People's Democratic Party (PDP), as was the presidency. Thus, many observers expected the familiar pattern of executive dominance of the legislature through the party structures to continue as it had under the Second and Third Republics.

Initially, these expectations were fulfilled. Legislators spent most of their time clamoring for their personal spending funds to be disbursed by the executive. Some of their first acts were to vote themselves pay raises and exorbitant furniture expenditures (thus provoking a protest strike by trade unions). Other legislators tested the waters for the first time with a variety of radical bills that never emerged from committee, including one that would have asked the United States to invade Nigeria if the military staged another coup. The first Speaker of the House was forced to resign when a newspaper discovered that he had lied about his age and was too young to run for office. Three Senate presidents were also forced to resign when the media unearthed evidence of irregularities and corruption. The president, meanwhile, referred to legislators as "small boys" and rarely accorded them the respect of an equal branch of government.

Gradually, however, the National Assembly began to fight back and gain some relevance. The one constitutional power of the Assembly that President Obasanjo could not circumvent was the authority to approve the national budget. In 2001, negotiations between the president and Assembly leaders over the budget became deadlocked, and it was eventually passed several months after it was due. The 2002 budget negotiations were even more bruising, and the president was ultimately forced to sign a budget higher than the revenues expected for that year. When oil revenues dipped even lower than expected, Obasanjo unilaterally chose to disburse only a portion of the budgeted funds to programs of his choosing. Among the funds withheld were those for the National Assembly. In August 2002, the House and the Senate, including members of Obasanjo's own party, began impeachment proceedings against the president. A face-saving compromise, and an apology from the president, was reached through a combination of negotiation and reported side payments to key legislators.

The impeachment move was not so much a serious attempt to remove the president as it was a statement to Obasanjo that he had to deal with the legislature with respect and as an equal partner in governance. The motives of legislators were hardly pure, since most were primarily concerned with getting their personal slices of the budget, but the president had clearly overstepped his constitutional role by arbitrarily choosing which portions of the budget he would respect. Some of the big men in the Assembly, particularly the Speaker of the House, had personal grudges against Obasanjo that were also at play in the impeachment move. Overall, however, the legislature emerged strengthened from the encounter.

The president, however, ensured that this victory for the institution came at a heavy price for its members: Nearly 80 percent of legislators elected in 1999 were not returned in 2003—not because their constituents voted them out, but because they were removed in the PDP primaries, a process that President Obasanjo and the governors largely controlled. Not taking any chances, the PDP leadership even went so far as to have a court reverse the 2003 election results against one of their defeated candidates and then to have the man elected Senate president. Despite these efforts to ensure a more compliant leadership in the

National Assembly, the president has been more respectful of the prerogatives of the legislature in his second term, and legislators continue to demonstrate that they have their own minds on budget matters and significant legislation.

Legislatures at the state level face a similar imbalance of power with the governors, who control large local bureaucracies and disburse the funds received from the federally shared revenues. The politics of these state assemblies have been chaotic and often vicious, with behavior ranging from throwing chairs to storming the assembly hall with supporters, and increasingly, the use of political violence.

The Party System and Elections

An unfortunate legacy of the party and electoral systems after independence was that political parties were associated with particular regions and ethnic groups.[25] The tendency to perceive politics as a zero-sum (or winner-take-all) struggle for access to scarce state resources encouraged political and social fragmentation. Unlike Ghana, Mexico and, to some extent, India, Nigeria did not develop an authoritarian dominant-party system after independence, which might have transcended some of these social cleavages. Instead, the multiparty system deepened existing social divisions.

Nigeria's use of a first-past-the-post plurality electoral system produced legislative majorities for parties with strong ethnic and regional identities. Nigerian parties during the First Republic were dominated by the largest ethnic group in each of the three regions. During subsequent democratic experiments, many of the newer parties could trace their roots to their predecessors in the first civilian regime. In consequence, parties were more attentive to the welfare of the regions from which they drew their support than to the development of Nigeria as a whole. Control of the center, or special political access, assured claims to substantial financial resources. In a polity as potentially volatile as Nigeria, these tendencies intensified political polarization and resentment among the losers.

In the Second Republic, the leading parties shared the same ethnic and sectional support, and often the same leadership, as the parties prominent in the first civilian regime. The Unity Party of Nigeria, UPN (mainly Yoruba), was headed by former Action Group leader Chief Obafemi Awolowo; the Nigerian Peoples Party, NPP (mainly Igbo), was led by Nnamdi Azikiwe (formerly of the NCNC); the Peoples Redemption Party, PRP (centered in Kano city in northern Nigeria), was led by Mallam Aminu Kano, while the Great Nigeria Peoples Party, GNPP (organized around the Kanuri northeast), was a newer tendency under Waziri Ibrahim. The dominant party in the Second Republic, the National Party of Nigeria (NPN), brought together a diverse cross-ethnic coalition under a predominantly northern leadership that had been previously associated with the Northern People's Congress (NPC). In its wavering steps toward the civilian Third Republic, General Babangida announced a landmark decision in 1989 to establish only two political parties by decree.[26] The state provided initial start-up funds, wrote the constitutions and manifestos of these parties, and designed them to be "a little to the right and a little to the left," respectively, on the political-ideological spectrum. Interestingly, the elections that took place under these rules from 1990–1993 indicated that, despite their inauspicious beginnings, the two parties cut across the cleavages of ethnicity, regionalism, and religion, demonstrating the potential to move beyond ethnicity.[27] The Social Democratic Party (SDP), which emerged victorious in the 1993 national elections, was an impressive coalition of Second Republic party structures, including elements of the former UPN, NPP, PRP, and GNPP. The opposing National Republican Convention (NRC) was seen as having its roots in northern groups that were the core of the National Party of Nigeria (NPN)

Table 8 shows historical trends in electoral patterns and communal affiliations. As clearly outlined, northern-based parties dominated the first and second experiments with civilian rule. Given this background, it is significant that Moshood Abiola was able to win the presidency in 1993, the first time in Nigeria's history that a southerner electorally defeated a northerner. Abiola, a Yoruba Muslim, won a number of key states in the north, including the hometown of his opponent. Southerners therefore perceived the decision by the northern-dominated Babangida regime to annul the June 12 elections as a deliberate attempt by the military and northern interests to maintain their decades-long domination of the highest levels of government.

Table 8

Federal Election Results in Nigeria, 1959–2003

Presidential Election Results, 1979–2003

	Victor (% of the vote)	Leading Contender (% of the vote)
1979	Shehu Shagari, NPN (33.8)	Obafemi Awolowo, UPN (29.2)
1983	Shehu Shagari, NPN (47.3)	Obafemi Awolowo, UPN (31.1)
1993	M.K.O. Abiola, SDP (58.0)	Bashir Tofa, NRC (42.0)
1999	Olusegun Obasanjo, PDP (62.8)	Olu Falae, AD/APP alliance (37.2)
2003	Olusegun Obasanjo, PDP (61.9)	Mohammadu Buhari, ANPP (31.2)

Parties Controlling the Parliament/National Assembly (Both Houses) by Ethno-Regional Zone, First to Fourth Republics

		Northwest	North-Central	Northeast	Southwest	South-South	Southeast
First	1959	**NPC**	**NPC** (NEPU)	**NPC**	AG	AG	NCNC*
	1964–65	**NPC**	**NPC**	**NPC**	NNDP* (AG)**	NNDP* (AG)**	NCNC
Second	1979	**NPN**	PRP **(NPN, UPN)**	GNPP **(NPN)**	UPN **(NPN)**	**NPN** (UPN)	NPP*
	1983	**NPN**	**NPN** (PRP)	**NPN**	UPN **(NPN)**	**NPN**	NPP**
Third	1992	**NRC**	SDP **(NRC)**	SDP **(NRC)**	SDP	**NRC** (SDP)	**NRC**
Fourth	1999	**PDP** (APP)	**PDP**	**PDP** (APP)	AD **(PDP)**	**PDP** (APP)	**PDP**
	2003	ANPP **(PDP)**	ANPP **(PDP)**	**PDP** (ANPP)	**PDP** AD	**PDP** (ANPP)	**PDP** (APGA)

Boldfaced: Ruling party

Italicized: Leading opposition

*: Coalition with ruling party

**: Coalition with opposition

National Assembly and State Level Elections

Senate	1999	2003
PDP	63	73
APP/ANPP	26	28
AD	20	6

House	1999	2003
PDP	214	213
APP/ANPP	77	95
AD	69	31
Other		7

Table 8 *(continued)*

Federal Election Results in Nigeria, 1959–2003

Governorships	1999	2003
PDP	21	28
APP/ANPP	9	7
AD	6	1
State Houses of Assembly	1999	2003
PDP	23	28
APP/ANPP	8	7
AD	5	1

List of Acronyms Used in Table 8

AG	Action Group
AD	Alliance for Democracy
ANPP	All Nigerian Peoples Party (formerly APP)
APGA	Alll People's Grand Alliance
APP	All People's Party
GNPP	Great Nigerian Peoples' Party
NAP	Nigerian Advance Party
NCNC	National Convention of Nigerian Citizens (formerly National Council of Nigeria and the Cameroons)
NEPU	Northern Elements Progressive Union
NNDP	Nigerian National Democratic Party
NPC	Northern People's Congress
NPF	Northern Progressive Front
NPN	National Party of Nigeria
NPP	Nigerian People's Party
NRC	National Republican Convention
PRP	People's Redemption Party
PDP	People's Democratic Party
SDP	Social Democratic Party
UPN	Unity Party of Nigeria

Old Roots and New Alignments: The PDP and the Other Parties of the Fourth Republic

Nigerians generally reacted with anger to General Abacha's 1993 coup and his subsequent banning of the SDP and NRC, although party members themselves, with few exceptions, offered a muted response. Southern-based human rights and prodemocracy groups, in alliance with student unions and other organizations, launched street demonstrations, and trade union strikes brought the economy to a halt by mid-

1994. With the unions crushed and Abiola in jail by the end of 1994, Abacha started his own transition program in October 1995. It featured a series of elections from the local to the federal levels over the following three years in a manner reminiscent of the Babangida program. In late 1996, the Abacha government registered only five parties, most of whose members had no public constituency and little political experience. By the time local government elections were held in January 1997, the few people who did vote had little idea for whom they were voting; some of the candidates confessed publicly that they had never seen their party's manifesto.

During 1997, the five parties, branded by the opposition as "five fingers of a leprous hand," began to clamor for General Abacha to run for president. Public participation in state assembly elections in December 1997 was abysmal, as each of the parties proclaimed, one after another, that Abacha was their candidate. The presidential election scheduled for August 1998 was reduced to a mere referendum, endorsed by the chief justice of the Supreme Court as legally permissible. The "transition" process had become a travesty.[28] Once Abacha's plan to be certified as president became a certainty, domestic opposition increased. A group of former governors and political leaders from the north (many former NPN and PRP members) publicly petitioned Abacha not to run for president. They were later joined by colleagues from the south, forming what they called the Group of 34 (G-34). Human rights and prodemocracy organizations began again to form alliances to organize protests, and critical press coverage recovered some of its former boldness. Even General Babangida voiced his opposition to Abacha's continuing as president. The only real obstacle to Abacha's plan for "self-succession" was whether the military would allow it.

Although there had been frequent rumors of Abacha's ill health, his death on June 8, 1998, was still a great surprise. The following day, General Abubakar, chief of Defense Staff, was sworn in as head of state. Shortly afterward, he promised a speedy transition to democracy and began releasing political prisoners. There were immediate calls for Chief Abiola's release and his appointment to head an interim government of national unity. Abiola's fatal heart attack a month after Abacha's death raised considerable suspicion, since Abiola had remained the sole obstacle to a fresh political process and new elections, which the military establishment clearly preferred. The political process, however, proceeded apace. New parties quickly formed, and even Yoruba political leaders agreed to participate, although they insisted that the next president should be a Yoruba to compensate their people for having been robbed of their first elected presidency.

Once again, political associations centered on well-known personalities, and intense bargaining and mergers took place. The G-34, the prominent group of civilian leaders who had condemned Abacha's plans to perpetuate his power, created the People's Democratic Party (PDP) in late August, minus most of their Yoruba members, who joined the Alliance for Democracy (AD). At least twenty more parties applied for certification to the electoral commission (INEC); many of them were truly grass-roots movements, including a human rights organization and a trade union party.

To escape the ethnic-based parties of the First and Second Republics, INEC required that parties earn at least 5 percent of the votes in twenty-four of the thirty-six states in local government elections in order to advance to the later state and federal levels. This turned out to be an ingenious way of reducing the number of parties, while obliging viable parties to broaden their appeal. The only parties to meet INEC's requirements were the PDP, AD, and the All Peoples Party (APP); the APP included a mixture of groups from the Middle Belt, the southeast, and the far north. With the big men of the PDP backing him, General Obasanjo went on to defeat an AD/APP alliance candidate, Chief Olu Falae, also Yoruba, in the presidential contest in February 1999.

These parties rely on elite-centered structures established during previous civilian governments and transition programs, and demonstrate the cross-ethnic alliances that have animated politics over the last quarter-century. The PDP includes core members of the northern established NPN, the northern progressive PRP, and the Igbo-dominated NPP of the Second Republic, as well as prominent politicians from the Niger Delta. The APP (now ANPP) drew from the Second Republic's GNPP, a party dominated by the Kanuri and groups from the Middle Belt, and also features southern politicians who had prominent roles in the Abacha-sponsored parties. The ANPP is also a multiethnic collection, drawing northern politicians of royal lineage, northeastern and Middle Belt minorities, Igbo business moguls, and southern minority leaders. The AD, however, is as Yoruba-centered as its predecessors, the UPN in the Second Republic and the AG in the First Republic. Yet like these earlier parties, it has attracted dynamic politicians from other areas. The rise of multiethnic political parties, however, is one of the most significant democratic developments of the Fourth Republic.

The haste of the Abubakar-supervised electoral process benefited civilian politicians and recently retired military officers with access to substantial financial resources. The civil society groups that led much of the struggle against the Abacha dictatorship found themselves at a disadvantage in trying to influence the processes of party formation and development. Thus, the leaders of the political parties in the Fourth Republic essentially represent alliances of convenience among powerful individuals, the big men who retain their own resource and client bases, while lacking a common ideology or clear policy agenda. The parties stand for little beyond the interests of their leading patrons, and loyalties among their members are weak, as are their connections to the wider populace. The Fourth Republic has enjoyed no real opposition movement at the national level. The PDP came together sufficiently to dominate the 2003 elections, but thereafter its internal divisions resurfaced, and the many competing interests of its leaders have continued to threaten party unity.

The Independent National Electoral Commission (INEC) complicated matters in 2002 when it registered three new political parties, each of them pragmatic alliances among disgruntled politicians from the existing parties, primarily the PDP. Late in 2002, the Supreme Court overruled the INEC's restrictive policies on registering parties, and dozens of new parties were permitted to contest the 2003 elections. In all, some thirty associations participated at the polls. Revealing its pro-Abacha roots, the ANPP nominated as its 2003 presidential candidate former head of state, General (retired) Muhammadu Buhari, a well-known supporter of the *shari'a* movement. The AD declined to nominate a 2003 presidential candidate in exchange for a PDP promise not to mount serious challenges against other AD candidates in the Yoruba region. The PDP, however, reneged on the backroom deal and defeated the AD at all levels in five of the six southwestern states in 2003.

Faced with the absolute dominance of the PDP in the 2003 elections, the other parties apart from the ANPP formed the Conference of Nigerian Political Parties (CNPP). The CNPP has subsequently been more vocal than the ANPP in its opposition to PDP policies. For their part, the ANPP, which holds seven of the northern governorships, has generally shown more interest in working with the PDP and the president than in playing the role of loyal opposition. Unless the PDP implodes, there appears to be no clear challenger to its dominance for the 2007 elections.

Political Culture, Citizenship, and Identity

Society is mobilized and represented politically by legislatures, political parties, trade unions, and elements of civil society. In the process, these institutions help to shape, organize, and express political culture and identities, thus nurturing qualities of citizenship. During long periods of military rule, these institutions were proscribed and disbanded (in the case of legislatures and political parties) or muzzled (in the case of labor unions). Their roles were filled at times by other groups and institutions, including ethnic and religious organizations, the mass media, and professional and trade groups. In many of these circles, the state is regarded as a distant entity of questionable legitimacy. The state's unwillingness or inability to deliver appropriate services, the rampant corruption among officials, and the prevalence of authoritarian rule have fostered a political culture of apathy and alienation among many Nigerians, accompanied by militant opposition among particular communities and groups.

Military rule left Nigeria with strong authoritarian influences in its political culture. Most of the younger politicians of the Fourth Republic came of age during military rule and naturally learned the business of politics from Abacha, Babangida, and their military governors. Nigeria's deep democratic traditions discussed in Section 1 remain vibrant among the larger polity, but they are in constant tension with the values imbibed during years of governance when political problems were often solved by military dictate, power, and violence rather than by negotiation and respect for law. This tension was manifest in the irony that the leading presidential contenders in 2003 were all former military men, one of whom—Buhari—was the ringleader of the 1983 coup that overthrew the Second Republic.

Modernity Versus Traditionalism

The terrain of political culture, citizenship, and identity is a contested arena within Nigeria. The interaction of modern (colonial, Western) elements with traditional (precolonial, African) practices has created the tensions of a modern sociopolitical system that rests uneasily on traditional foundations. Nigerians straddle two worlds, each undergoing constant evolution. On one hand, the strong elements in communal societies that promoted accountability have been weakened by the intrusion of Western culture oriented toward individuality. On the other hand, the modern state has been unable to free itself fully from rival ethnic claims organized around narrow, exclusivist constituencies.

As a result, exclusivist identities continue to dominate Nigerian political culture and to define the nature of citizenship.[29] Individuals tend to identify with their immediate ethnic, regional, and religious (or subethnic, subregional, and subreligious) groups rather than with state institutions, especially during moments of crisis. Nigerians usually seek to extract as many benefits as possible from the state but hesitate when it comes to performing basic civic duties such as paying taxes or taking care of public property. Entirely missing from the relationship between state and citizen in Nigeria is a fundamental reciprocity—a working social contract—based on the belief that there is a common interest that binds them.

Religion

Religion has been a persistent basis of conflict in Nigerian history. Islam began to filter into northeast Nigeria in the eleventh and twelfth centuries, spread to Hausaland by the fifteenth century, and greatly expanded in the early nineteenth century. In the north, Islam first coexisted with, then gradually supplanted, indigenous religions. Christianity arrived in the early nineteenth century, but expanded rapidly through missionary activity in the south. The amalgamation of northern and southern Nigeria in 1914 brought together the two regions and their belief systems.

These religious cultures have consistently clashed over political issues such as the secular character of the state. The application of the *shari'a* criminal code in the northern states has been a focal point for these tensions. For many Muslims, the *shari'a* represents a way of life and supreme (personal) law that transcends secular and state law; for many Christians, the expansion of *shari'a* law threatens the secular nature of the Nigerian state and their position within it. The pull of religious versus national identity becomes even stronger in times of economic hardship. The Babangida period corresponded to a rise in both Islamic fundamentalist movements and evangelical Christian fundamentalism that has continued through the present. Where significant numbers of southern Christians are living in predominantly Muslim states (for example, Kaduna State), many clashes have erupted, with great loss of life and the extensive destruction of churches, mosques, and small businesses.

The Press

The plural nature of Nigerian society, with the potential to engender a shared political culture, can be seen in virtually all aspects of public life. The Nigerian press, for instance, has long been one of the liveliest and most irreverent in Africa. The Abacha regime moved to stifle its independence, banning several publications and threatening the suspension of others. In this regard, Abacha was following the example of his predecessor, Babangida, especially during the final years of his rule. A northern paper, the *New Nigerian,* published in Kaduna, succumbed at times to overt sectionalism. The fact that the media are sometimes regarded as captives of ethnic and regional constituencies has weakened their capacity to resist attacks on their rights and privileges. Significantly, most of the Nigerian press has been based in a Lagos-Ibadan axis in the southwestern part of Nigeria and has frequently been labeled "southern." Recently, however, independent television and radio stations have proliferated around the country, and forests of satellite towers now span Nigerian cities to support the boom in Internet cafés and telecommunications. The freer environment of democracy has also allowed investigative journalism to flourish. Several legislative leaders have been brought down by timely media exposés of their misconduct, and other public figures, including prominent governors, cabinet officers, and the inspector-general of police, are being scrutinized in the press.

Interests, Social Movements, and Protest

Political attitudes, political culture, and sectional identities are still dominated and defined largely by elite, urban-based interests. These interests include ethnic as well as professional and associational groups. The few nonelite groups, such as urban-based marketwomen's associations, often serve as channels for disseminating the decisions and agendas of elite groups. In essence, nonelite and rural elements continue to be marginalized and manipulated by elites and urban groups. Lacking competence in the language of public discourse, namely, English, and access to financial networks, nonelites have difficulty confronting, on their own, the decision-making centers of the state and society.

Elite and nonelite Nigerians alike come together in civic organizations and interest groups such as labor unions and student and business associations. Because the political machinery was in the hands of the military, Nigerian citizens sought alternative means of representation and protest in an effort to affect political life. Historically, labor has played a significant role in Nigerian politics, as have student groups, some women's organizations, and various radical and populist organizations. Business groups have frequently supported and colluded with corrupt civilian and military regimes. In the last year of the Abacha regime, however, even the business class, through mechanisms like Vision 2010, began to suggest an end to such arbitrary rule. The termination of military rule has seen civil society groups flourish across Nigeria.

Labor

Organized labor has played an important role in challenging governments during both the colonial and postcolonial eras in several African countries, Nigeria among them. Continuous military pressure throughout the 1980s and 1990s forced a decline in the independence and strength of organized labor in Nigerian politics. The Babangida regime implemented strategies of **state corporatism** designed to control and co-opt various social forces such as labor. When the leadership of the Nigerian Labour Congress (NLC), the umbrella confederation, took a vigorous stand against the government, the regime sacked the leaders and appointed conservative replacements. Prodemocracy strikes in mid-1994 by the National Petroleum Employees Union (NUPENG) and other sympathetic labor groups significantly reduced oil production and nearly brought the country to a halt, whereupon the Abacha regime arrested and disbanded its leadership.

The Nigerian labor movement has been vulnerable to reprisals by the state and private employers. The government has always been the biggest single employer of labor in Nigeria, as well as the recognized arbiter of industrial relations between employers and employees. Efforts by military regimes to centralize and co-opt the unions caused their militancy and impact to wane. Moreover, ethnic, regional, and religious divisions have often hampered labor solidarity, and these differences have been periodically manipulated by the state.

General Abubakar removed government-appointed union administrators in 1998 and allowed the unions once again to elect their own leaders. Within a year, labor had regained its footing. Several waves of national strikes forced the Obasanjo government to forgo plans to raise the price of fuel, and additional strikes prompted significant wage increases. At moments during these campaigns, the Nigerian Labour Congress appeared to play a more commanding role as the political opposition to government than did any of the parties nominally in opposition.

Labor still claims an estimated 2 million members across Nigeria and remains one of the most potent forces in civil society. The unions have a great stake in the consolidation of constitutional rule in the Fourth Republic and the protections that allow them to organize and act freely on behalf of their members. Given the strength of the NLC, the PDP has sought to break it into its constituent unions to dilute its impact, but has so far been unsuccessful.

The Business Community

Nigeria has a long history of entrepreneurialism and business development. This spirit is compromised by tendencies toward rent-seeking and the appropriation of state resources. Members of the Nigerian business class have been characterized as "pirate capitalists" because of the high level of corrupt practices and collusion with state officials.[30] Many wealthy individuals have served in the military or civilian governments, while others protect their access to state resources by sponsoring politicians or entering into business arrangements with bureaucrats. Nevertheless, as economic and political conditions in Nigeria have deteriorated, the state has afforded fewer avenues for businesspeople, as well as a declining capacity to provide the necessary infrastructure for business development.

Nonetheless, private interests have proven surprisingly resilient, as organized groups have emerged to represent the interests of the business class and to promote general economic development. There are numerous associations throughout Nigeria representing a broad variety of business activities and sectoral interests. Many local or regional groups are also members of national organizations. National business associations, such as the Nigerian Association of Chambers of Commerce, Industry, Mines, and Agriculture (NACCIMA), the largest in the country, have taken an increasingly political stance. Business groups pressed the military leadership to resolve the June 12 crisis in 1993, and they have had a strong voice in advocating better governance. In their bid to reduce uncertainty, halt economic decline, and protect their economic interests, business associations increasingly perform what are clearly political roles. The continuing influence of the Economic Summit and other business associations in shaping government policies underscores this trend.

Other Social Groups

Student activism continues to be an important feature of Nigerian political life. University and other student groups play an important political role. Along with their teachers, students have suffered countless closings of the universities during the Babangida and Abacha regimes in addition to direct government harassment, banning, and attempts to engineer divisions in their unions and associations. Many professional associations of doctors and lawyers have also become champions of democracy and human rights, often supporting campaigns conducted by human rights organizations.

The activities of these organizations increased significantly with the introduction of the structural adjustment program (SAP) in the 1980s. Politically marginal groups, including women, youth, the urban poor, and people in rural areas, perceived an imbalance in the distribution of the benefits and burdens generated by the economic reform program. Not surprisingly, flagrant displays of wealth by senior members of the military alienated these groups and encouraged a "culture of rage" among many disenfranchised segments of urban society. Growing restiveness over economic hardship and military oppression led to a sharp increase in the number of human rights groups and other nongovernmental organizations (NGOs) in the 1990s.[31] Greater funding for NGOs from foreign governments and private foundations assisted the growth of this sector, most notably in the south but gradually in the north as well. They have generally focused on such issues as civil protection, gender law, health care, media access, and public housing. Most are urban based, although efforts to develop rural networks are underway.

Personality conflicts, ethnic divisions, and scarce resources hampered the efforts of civil society to resist military dictatorship.[32] Prodemocracy efforts by NGOs peaked in the 1993–1994 struggle over June 12, when they managed to stage numerous successful stay-home strikes in Lagos and other southern cities. The Campaign for Democracy in 1993 and then the National Democratic Coalition (NADECO) in 1994 built an antimilitary front that also included students, academics, some labor unions, and women's and professional groups. As Abacha moved forward with his self-succession campaign in 1997–1998, this sector attempted to counter the regime's machinations, although it faced very restrictive political conditions.

The return of political freedoms under the Fourth Republic has allowed organizations in civil society to proliferate and become influential. The end of military government has also left many of the prodemocracy and human rights groups without the strong central focus they had in the 1990s, and specialized groups are gradually supplanting the older, broader organizations that were active in preceding decades.

Civil society groups are making a substantial contribution to consolidating democracy in Nigeria. Their relationships with the political parties, however, remain distant, although many are engaged in advocacy, and some leaders of the prodemocracy struggles of the 1990s ran for office in the 2003 elections. Nigeria's prospects for building a sustainable democracy during the Fourth Republic will depend, in part, on the willingness of many of these advocacy groups to increase their collaboration with the political parties, while maintaining a high level of vigilance and activism.

Section ⑤ Nigerian Politics in Transition

Despite the slow progress of the Fourth Republic, Nigerians overwhelmingly favor democratic government over military rule. About 70 percent of respondents in a recent survey said that they still prefer democracy to any other alternative, although popular frustration is growing with the slow pace of reform and continued corruption in politics.[33] Will democracy in Nigeria be consolidated sufficiently to meet minimal levels of public satisfaction, or will the nation again succumb to destructive authoritarian rule?

Nigerian politics must change in fundamental ways for democracy to become more stable and legitimate. First and foremost, the nation must turn from a system of politics dominated by "big men"—for all intents and purposes, a semi-competitive oligarchy—to a more representative mode of politics that addresses the fundamental interests of the public. Second, Nigerians must conclusively settle the national question and commit to political arrangements that accommodate the nation's diversity. In short, Nigeria's Fourth Republic must find ways of moving beyond prebendal politics and develop a truly national political process in which mobilization and conflicts along ethnic, regional, and religious lines gradually diminish.

Political Challenges and Changing Agendas

Nigeria's fitful transition to democratic rule between 1985 and 1999 was inconclusive, largely because it was planned and directed from above. This approach contrasts sharply with the popular-based movements that unseated autocracies in Central and Eastern Europe. The military periodically made promises for democratic transition as a ploy to stabilize and legitimate their governments. General Abubakar dutifully handed power to the civilians in 1999, but only after ensuring that the military's interests would be protected under civilian rule and creating an overly powerful executive that reinforces **patrimonialism,** a system of power in which authority is maintained through patronage. The military's rapid transition program produced a tenuous, conflicted democratic government that faces daunting tasks of restoring key institutions, securing social stability, and reforming the economy. The continuing strength and influence of collective identities, defined on the basis of religion or ethnicity, are often more binding than national allegiances. The parasitic nature of the Nigerian economy is a further source of instability. Rent-seeking and other unproductive, often corrupt, business activities remain accepted norms of wealth accumulation.

Nonetheless, Nigerians are sowing seeds of change in all of these areas. Attitudes toward the military in government have shifted dramatically. The decline in the appeal of military rule can be attributed to the abysmal performances of the Babangida and Abacha regimes in economic oversight and governance. Many now recognize that the military, apart from its contributions to national security, is incapable of promoting economic and social progress in Nigeria. With the armed forces discredited for the moment, the nature of the struggles among civilian political elites will decide the direction of political and economic change. Thus, democratic development may be advanced in the long run if stable coalitions appear over time in a manner that balances the power among contending groups, and if these key elites adapt to essential norms and "rules of the game.

Initially, members of the new political class confined their struggles within the constraints of the democratic system: using the courts, media, legislatives struggles, and even legal expediencies such as impeachment. Political actors largely worked through formal institutions, contending openly and offsetting the power of a single group or faction. Disturbingly, the 2003 elections reflected a growing willingness of the political elite to use extra-systemic measures to forward their interests through election rigging, corruption, and militia-led violence. Many of these tendencies have persisted.

The next critical step down the long road of democratic development for Nigeria is the creation of a viable, multiethnic opposition party that is also loyal, meaning that it plays by the rules of the system. Opposition parties help to reduce corruption in the system because they have an interest in exposing the misconduct of the ruling party, which in turn pressures them to restrain their own behavior. Furthermore, in order to unseat the ruling party and win elections, opposition parties need to engage the public to win their votes. In this manner, issues of interest to the public are engaged by the parties.

The introduction of so many new parties in 2002 has yet to facilitate the development of a viable, loyal opposition, but it could provide some of the groundwork if the PDP continues to exhibit strong internal divisions. It is also possible that the new parties may further dilute the opposition and allow the PDP to govern largely unchecked. If some minor parties manage to win only narrow ethnic constituencies, and the electoral commission does not rigorously apply the multiethnic rules of contestation, Nigeria may return to the ruinous ethnic politics of the past.

The project of building a coherent nation-state out of competing nationalities remains unfinished. Ironically, because the parties of the Fourth Republic generally do not represent any particular ethnic interest—indeed, they do not represent anyone's interests except those of the leaders and their clients—ethnic associations and militias have risen to articulate ethnic-based grievances. Ethnic consciousness cannot be eliminated from society, but ethnicity cannot be the main basis for political competition. If the current ethnic mobilization can be contained within ethnic associations arguing over the agenda of the parties, then it can be managed. If any of the ethnic associations captures one of the political parties or joins with the militias to foment separatism, instability will result.

Democratic development also requires further decentralization of power structures in Nigeria. The struggle on the part of the National Assembly and the state governors to wrest power from the presidency has advanced this process. The administration's efforts to privatize government para-statals could also reduce the power of the presidency over time, since it will no longer control all the productive sectors of the economy. A more decentralized system allows local problems to be solved within communities rather than involving national institutions and the accompanying interethnic competition. Decentralization also lowers the stakes for holding national offices, thereby reducing the destructive pressures on political competition and political office. The devolution of power and resources to smaller units, closer to their constituents, can substantially enhance the accountability of leaders and the transparency of government operations.

Civil society groups are the final link in democratic consolidation in Nigeria. These groups are critical players in connecting the Nigerian state to the Nigerian people. They aggregate and articulate popular interests into the policy realm, and they provide advocacy on behalf of their members. If the political parties are to reflect anything more than elite interests and clientelist rule, the parties must reach out and build alliances with the institutions of civil society. For opposition parties to become a viable opposition movement capable of checking the power of the PDP, they will have to build alliances with civil society groups in order to mobilize large portions of the population. Foreign pressure also plays an important role in maintaining the quest for democracy and sustainable development. In recent years, major external forces have been more forthright in supporting civil society and democratization in Nigeria. The United States, Britain, and some member states of the European Union quite visibly exerted pressure on Babangida to leave and applied modest sanctions in support of democracy. This has been made possible, in part, by a changing international environment, especially the willingness of the major industrial countries and the international financial institutions to support democracy around the world. Nigeria's weak economy and heavy debt, now estimated at $33 billion, have made it susceptible to this kind of pressure.

Western commitment to development and democracy in Africa is not guaranteed. Much of the initiative for Africa's growth therefore needs to emerge from within. In Nigeria, such initiatives will depend on substantial changes in the way Nigerians do business. It will be necessary to develop a more sophisticated and far less corrupt form of capitalist enterprise and the development of entrepreneurial interests within Nigeria who will see their interests tied to the principles of democratic politics and economic initiative. The middle class is beginning to grow under democratic rule, but it remains small and vulnerable to economic and political instability.

Nigerian politics has been characterized by turmoil and periodic crises ever since the British relinquished colonial power. Over forty years later, the country is still trying to piece together a fragile democracy, while per capita incomes are scarcely higher than at independence. Despite a number of positive trends, the nation continues to wrestle with slow growth in major productive sectors, enfeebled infrastructure and institutions, heightened sociopolitical tensions, an irresponsible elite, and an expanding mass culture of despondency and rage. Only responsible government combined with sustained civil society action can reverse this decline and restore the nation to what President Obasanjo has called "the path to greatness."

Nigerian Politics in Comparative Perspective

The study of Nigeria has important implications for the study of African politics and, more broadly, of comparative politics. The Nigerian case embodies a number of key themes and issues that can be generalized. We can learn much about how democratic regimes are established and consolidated by understanding Nigeria's pitfalls and travails. Analysis of the historical dynamics of Nigeria's ethnic conflict helps to identify institutional mechanisms that may be effective in reducing ethnic conflict in other states. We can also learn much about the necessary and sufficient conditions for economic development, and the particular liabilities of oil-dependent states. Each of these issues offers comparative lessons for the major themes explored in this book: the world of states, governing the economy, the democratic idea, and the politics of collective identities.

A World of States

Nigeria exists in two "worlds" of states: one in the global political economy and the other within Africa. We have addressed at length Nigeria's position in the world. Economically, Nigeria was thrust into the world economy in a position of weakness, first as a British colony and later as an independent nation. Despite its resources and the potential of oil to provide the investment capital needed to build a modern economy, Nigeria has grown weaker. It has lost much of its international clout, and in place of the international respect it once enjoyed as a developing giant within Africa, the country became notorious throughout the 1990s for corruption, human rights abuses, and failed governance. The return of democracy has restored some of Nigeria's former stature, but its economic vulnerability and persistent corruption keep it a secondary player in the world of states.

This chapter has remarked, "As Nigeria goes, so goes the rest of sub-Saharan Africa." The future of democracy, political stability, and economic renewal in other parts of Africa, and certainly in West Africa, will be greatly influenced for good or ill by unfolding events in Nigeria. Beyond the obvious demonstration effects, the economy of the West African subregion could be revitalized by substantial growth of the Nigerian economy. In addition, President Obasanjo has conducted very active public diplomacy across Africa, seeking to resolve major conflicts, promote democracy, and improve trade. Thus far, international political and business attention has shifted elsewhere on the continent, focusing on such countries as South Africa, Botswana, and Ghana. This portends a danger of greater marginalization, reflecting the expanding patchwork of Africa among areas of stability and growth, contrasted with areas of turmoil and decay.

Governing the Economy

Nigeria provides important insights into the political economy of underdevelopment. At independence in 1960, Nigeria was stronger economically than its Southeast Asian counterparts Indonesia and Malaysia. Independent Nigeria appeared poised for growth, with a wealth of natural resources, a large population, and the presence of highly entrepreneurial groups in many regions of the country. Today, Nigeria is among the poorest countries in the world in terms of per capita income, while many of its Asian counterparts have joined the ranks of the newly industrializing countries. One critical lesson Nigeria teaches is that a rich endowment of resources is not enough to ensure economic development. In fact, it may encourage rent-seeking behavior that undermines more productive activities.[34] Sound political and institutional development must come first.

Other variables are critically important, notably democratic stability and a capable developmental state. A developmentalist ethic, and an institutional structure to enforce it, can set limits to corrupt behavior and constrain the pursuit of short-term personal gain at the expense of national economic growth. Institutions vital to the pursuit of these objectives include a professional civil service, an independent judiciary, and a free press. Nigeria has had each of these, but they were gradually undermined and corrupted under military rule. The public "ethic" that has come to dominate Nigerian political economy has been prebendalism. Where corruption is unchecked, as in Nigeria, the Philippines under

Ferdinand Marcos, or Latin American countries such as Ecuador and Venezuela, economic development suffers accordingly.

Nigeria also demonstrates that sustainable economic development requires sound economic policy. Without export diversification, commodity-exporting countries are buffeted by the price fluctuations of one or two main products. This situation can be traced back to overreliance on primary commodity export-oriented policies bequeathed by the British colonial regime. Yet other former colonies, such as Malaysia and Indonesia, have managed to diversify their initial export base. Nigeria, by contrast, has substituted one form of commodity dependence for another, and it has allowed its petroleum industry to overwhelm all other sectors of the economy. Nigeria even became a net importer of products (for example, of palm oil and palm nuts) for which it was once a leading world producer. In comparative perspective, we can see that natural resource endowments can be tremendously beneficial. The United States, for example, has parlayed its endowments of agricultural, mineral, and energy resources into one of the world's most diversified modern economies. Meanwhile Japan, which is by comparison poorly endowed with natural resources, has one of the strongest economies in the world, achieved in large part through its unique developmental strategies. Each of these examples illustrates the primacy of sound economic policies implemented through consolidated political systems.

The Democratic Idea

Many African countries have experienced transitions from authoritarian rule.[35] With the end of superpower competition in Africa and the withdrawal of external support for Africa's despots, many African societies experienced a resurgence of popular pressures for greater participation in political life and more open forms of governance. Decades of authoritarian, single-party, and military rule in Africa have left a dismal record of political repression, human rights abuses, inequality, deteriorating governance, and failed economies. A handful of elites have acquired large fortunes through wanton corruption. Consider Nigeria's "missing" $12.2 billion windfall in oil revenues after the Gulf War in 1991 or the fact that former Zairian president Mobutu Sese Seko's personal wealth was estimated to be several billion dollars—perhaps as much as the country's entire external debt. Kenya's former president Daniel arap Moi is considered among the richest men in Africa, a group to which Ibrahim Babangida and the late Sani Abacha of Nigeria have belonged. The exercise of postcolonial authoritarian rule in Africa has contributed to economic stagnation and decline. The difficulties of such countries as Cameroon, Togo, and Zimbabwe in achieving political transitions reflects, in large part, the ruling elites' unwillingness to cede control of the political instruments that made possible their self-enrichment.

Nigeria exemplifies the harsh reality of authoritarian and unaccountable governance. Nigerians have endured six military regimes, countless attempted coups, and a bloody civil war that claimed over 1 million lives. They have also seen a once-prospering economy reduced to a near shambles. Today, democracy has become a greater imperative be cause only such a system provides the mechanisms to limit abuses of power and render governments accountable.

Collective Identities

Nigeria presents an important case in which to study the dangers of communal competition in a society with deep cultural divisions. How can multiethnic countries manage diversity? What institutional mechanisms can be employed to avert tragedies such as the 1967–1970 civil war or the continuing conflicts that have brought great suffering to Rwanda and the former Yugoslavia? This chapter has suggested institutional reforms such as multiethnic political parties, decentralization, and a strengthened federal system that can contribute to reducing tensions and minimizing conflict.

Insights from the Nigerian experience may explain why some federations persist, while identifying factors that can undermine them. Nigeria's complex social map, and its varied attempts to create a nation out of its highly diverse population, enhances our understanding of the politics of cultural pluralism and the difficulties of accommodating sectional interests under conditions of political and economic insecurity. Federal character in Nigeria has become a form of ethnic and regional favoritism and a tool for dispensing patronage. Yet the country has benefited in some ways from the attention devoted to creating state and local governments, and from giving people in different regions a sense of being stakeholders in the entity called Nigeria.

Nigeria's challenges reflect the frustrated hopes of its people for a better life, stable government, and a democratic political order, while suggesting the potential contributions that this country could make to the African continent and the wider international arena. The quest for responsive and capable democratic governance leads in one direction, while another direction presents the specter of military entrepreneurs, or ethnic and religious extremists, plunging Nigeria into another cycle of coups, decline, and possibly collapse.

Key Terms

authoritarian
legitimacy
accountability
unfinished state
jihad
acephalous societies
emirs
indirect rule
warrant chiefs
interventionist
clientelism
autocracy
rents
rent-seeking
structural adjustment
 program (SAP)

international financial
 institutions (IFIs)
balance of payments
privatization
self-determination
Economic Community
 of West African
 States (ECOWAS)
para-statals
shari'a
prebendalism
civil society
state corporatism
patrimonialism

Suggested Readings

Aborisade, Oladimeji, and Mundt, Robert J. *Politics in Nigeria,* 2nd ed. New York: Longman, 2002.

Achike, Okay. *Public Administration: A Nigerian and Comparative Perspective.* London: Longman, 1978.

Adamolekun, L. *Politics and Administration in Nigeria.* London: Hutchinson, 1986.

Agbaje, Adigun. *The Nigerian Press: Hegemony and the Social Construction of Legitimacy, 1960–1983.* Lewiston, N.Y.: Edwin Mellen Press, 1992.

———. "Twilight of Democracy in Nigeria." *Africa Demos* 3, no. 3:5. Atlanta: The Carter Center of Emory University, 1994.

Beckett, Paul A., and Young, Crawford, eds. *Dilemmas of Democracy in Nigeria.* Rochester, N.Y.: University of Rochester Press, 1997.

Bienen, Henry. *Political Conflict and Economic Change in Nigeria.* London: Frank Cass, 1988.

Diamond, Larry. *Class, Ethnicity and Democracy in Nigeria: The Failure of the First Republic.* London: Macmillan, 1988.

———. "Nigeria: The Uncivic Society and the Descent into Praetorianism." In Larry Diamond, J. Linz, and S. M. Lipset, eds. *Politics in Developing Countries: Comparing Experiences With Democracy,* 2nd ed. Boulder, Colo.: Lynne Rienner Publishers, 1995, 417–491.

Decalo, Samuel. *Coups and Army Rule in Africa,* 2nd ed. New Haven, Conn.: Yale University Press, 1990.

Dudley, Billy. *An Introduction to Nigerian Government and Politics.* Bloomington: Indiana University Press, 1982.

Ekeh, Peter P., and Osaghae, Eghosa E., eds. *Federal Character and Federalism in Nigeria.* Ibadan: Heinemann, 1989.

Falola, Toyin. *Violence in Nigeria: The Crisis of Religious Politics and Secular Ideologies.* Rochester, N.Y.: University of Rochester Press, 1999.

Forrest, Tom. *Politics and Economic Development in Nigeria.* Boulder, Colo.: Westview Press, 1993.

Horowitz, Donald L. *Ethnic Groups in Conflict.* Berkeley: University of California Press, 1985.

Joseph, Richard A. *Democracy and Prebendal Politics in Nigeria: The Rise and Fall of the Second Republic.* Cambridge: Cambridge University Press, 1987.

Kew, Darren. "Political Islam in Nigeria's Transition Crisis," *Muslim Politics Report* (Council on Foreign Relations: New York), May–June, 1996.

Kirk-Greene, Anthony, and Rimmer, Douglas. *Nigeria Since 1970: A Political and Economic Outline.* London: Hodder and Stoughton, 1981.

Lewis, Peter M. "Endgame in Nigeria? The Politics of a Failed Democratic Transition." *African Affairs* 93 (1994): 323–340.

Lewis, Peter M., Rubin, Barnett R., and Robinson, Pearl T. *Stabilizing Nigeria: Pressures, Incentives, and Support for Civil Society.* New York: Century Foundation, for the Council on Foreign Relations, 1998.

Lubeck, Paul. *Islam and Urban Labor in Northern Nigeria.* Cambridge: Cambridge University Press, 1987.

Luckham, Robin. *The Nigerian Military: A Sociological Analysis of Authority and Revolt, 1960–67.* Cambridge: Cambridge University Press, 1971.

Melson, Robert, and Wolpe, Howard, eds. *Nigeria: Modernization and the Politics of Communalism,* East Lansing: Michigan State University Press, 1971.

Nyang'oro, Julius, and Shaw, Tim, eds. *Corporatism in Africa: Comparative Analysis and Practice.* Boulder, Colo.: Westview Press, 1989.

Olukoshi, Adebayo, ed. *The Politics of Structural Adjustment in Nigeria.* London: James Currey Publishers, 1993.

Osaghae, Eghosa. *Crippled Giant: Nigeria Since Independence.* Bloomington: Indiana University Press, 1998.

Oyediran, Oyeleye, ed. *Nigerian Government and Politics Under Military Rule.* London: Macmillan, 1979.

Reno, William. *Warlord Politics and African States.* Boulder, Colo.: Lynne Rienner Publishers, 1998.

Sklar, Richard L. *Nigerian Political Parties: Power in an Emergent African Nation.* New York: NOK Publishers, 1983.

Soyinka, Wole. *Open Sore of a Continent.* Oxford: Oxford University Press, 1996.

Suberu, Rotimi. *Federalism and Ethnic Conflict in Nigeria.* Washington, D.C.: U.S. Institute of Peace, 2001.

Watts, Michael, ed. *State, Oil, and Agriculture in Nigeria.* Berkeley: University of California Press, 1987.

Wunsch, James S., and Olowu, Dele, eds. *The Failure of the Centralized State: Institutions and Self-Governance in Africa.* Boulder, Colo.: Westview Press, 1990.

Young, Crawford. *The Rising Tide of Cultural Pluralism: The Nation-State at Bay?* Madison: University of Wisconsin Press, 1993.

Suggested Websites

British Broadcasting Corporation: A 2002 interview with President Obasanjo
news.bbc.co.uk/2/hi/talking_point/1800826.stm
Gamji: A collection of news stories from Nigerian newspapers, as well as opinion pieces and other news links
www.gamji.com
The Guardian, Nigeria's leading daily newspaper
www.ngrguardiannews.com
Human Rights Watch reports
hrw.org/doc/?t=africa&c=nigeri
International Institute for Democracy and Electoral Assistance
archive.idea.int/frontpage_nigeria.htm
Stanford University's Center for African Studies
www.stanford.edu/dept/AFR/

Endnotes

[1]Much of this context is recounted in James S. Coleman, *Nigeria: Background to Nationalism* (Berkeley: University of California Press, 1958).

[2]Obafemi Awolowo, *Path to Nigerian Freedom* (London: Faber and Faber, 1947), 47–48.

[3]Billy Dudley, *An Introduction to Nigerian Government and Politics* (Bloomington: Indiana University Press, 1982), 71.

[4]Robin Luckham, The Nigerian Military: A Sociological Analysis of Authority and Revolt 1960–67 (Cambridge: Cambridge University Press, 1971).

[5]Peter Ekeh, "Colonialism and the Two Publics in Africa: A Theoretical Statement," *Comparative Studies in Society and History* 17, no. 1 (January 1975).

[6]Richard A. Joseph, *Democracy and Prebendal Politics in Nigeria: The Rise and Fall of the Second Republic* (Cambridge: Cambridge University Press), 55–58.

[7]Gavin Williams and Terisa Turner, "Nigeria," in John Dunn, ed., *West African States: Failure and Promise* (Cambridge: Cambridge University Press, 1978), 156–157.

[8]Michael J. Watts, *State, Oil and Agriculture in Nigeria* (Berkeley: University of California Press, 1987), 71.

[9]Watts, *State Oil and Agriculture in Nigeria,* 67.

[10]See Peter M. Lewis, "From Prebendalism to Predation: The Political Economy of Decline in Nigeria," *Journal of Modern African Studies* 34, no. 1 (1996), 79–103.

[11]Tom Forrest, *Politics and Economic Development in Nigeria,* 2nd ed. (Boulder, Colo.: Westview Press, 1995), 207–212.

[12]Dele Olowu, "Centralization, Self-Governance, and Development in Nigeria," in James S. Wunsch and Dele Olowu, eds., *The Failure of the Centralized State: Institutions and Self-Governance in Africa,* (Boulder, Colo.: Westview Press, 1991), 211.

[13]Robert Melson and Howard Wolpe, *Nigeria: Modernization and the Politics of Communalism* (East Lansing: Michigan State University Press, 1971).

[14]Toyin Falola, Violence in Nigeria: The Crisis of Religious Politics and Secular Ideologies (Rochester, N.Y.: University of Rochester Press, 1998).

[15]Billy J. Dudley, *Instability and Political Order: Politics and Crisis in Nigeria* (Ibadan: Ibadan University Press, 1973), 35.

[16]Pat A. Williams, "Women and the Dilemma of Politics in Nigeria," in Crawford Young and Paul Beckett, eds., *Dilemmas of Democracy in Nigeria* (Rochester, N.Y.: University of Rochester Press, 1997), 219–241.

[17]Anthony Kirk-Greene and Douglas Rimmer, *Nigeria Since 1970: A Political and Economic Outline* (London: Hodder and Stoughton 1981), 49.

[18]Rotimi Suberu, *Federalism and Ethnic Conflict in Nigeria* (Washington, D.C.: U.S. Institute of Peace, 2001).

[19]Henry Bienen, *Armies and Parties in Africa* (New York: Africana Publishing, 1978), 193–211.

[20]Human Rights Watch, *The Destruction of Odi and Rape in Choba* (New York: Human Rights Watch, December 22, 1999).

[21]Suberu, *Federalism and Ethnic Conflict in Nigeria,* 119–120.

[22]Samuel DeCalo, *Coups and Army Rule in Africa* (New Haven, Conn.: Yale University Press, 1976), 18.

[23]Larry Diamond, "Nigeria: The Uncivic Society and the Descent into Praetorianism," in Larry Diamond, J. Linz, and S.M. Lipset, eds., *Politics in Developing Countries: Comparing Experiences With Democracy,* 2nd ed. (Boulder, Colo.: Lynne Rienner Publishers, 1995).

[24]Joseph, *Democracy and Prebendal Politics in Nigeria,* 52–53.

[25]Richard Sklar, *Nigerian Political Parties* (Princeton: Princeton University Press, 1963).

[26]Babafemi Badejo, "Party Formation and Party Competition" in Larry Diamond, Anthony Kirk-Greene, and Oyeleye Oyediran, eds., *Transition Without End: Nigerian Politics and Civil Society Under Babangida* (Boulder, Colo.: Lynne Rienner Publishers, 1997), 179.

[27]Eghosa Osaghae, *Crippled Giant: Nigeria Since Independence* (Bloomington: Indiana University Press 1999), 233–239.

[28]Peter M. Lewis, Barnett Rubin, and Pearl Robinson, *Stabilizing Nigeria: Pressures, Incentives and Support for Civil Society* (New York: Council on Foreign Relations, 1998), 87.

[29]Rotimi Suberu, *Public Policies and National Unity in Nigeria,* Research Report No. 19 (Ibadan: Development Policy Centre, 199), 9–10.

[30]Sayre Schatz, "'Pirate Capitalism' and the Inert Economy of Nigeria," *Journal of Modern African Studies* 22, no. 1 (March 1984), 45–57.

[31]Adebayo Olukoshi, "Associational Life" in Diamond, Kirk-Greene, and Oyediran, *Transition Without End,* 385–86.

[32]Osaghae, *Crippled Giant,* 301.

[33]Peter Lewis, Etannibi Alemika, and Michael Bratton, *Down to Earth: Changes in Attitudes to Democracy and Markets in Nigeria,* Afrobarometer Working Paper No. 20, Michigan State University, August 2002.

[34]See Terry Lynn Karl, *The Paradox of Plenty* (Berkeley: University of California Press, 1997); and Michael Ross, "The Political Economy of the Resource Curse," *World Politics* 51 (January 1999), 297–322.

[35]Michael Bratton and Nicolas van de Walle, *Democratic Experiments in Africa* (Cambridge: Cambridge University Press, 1997).

PART 4
Authoritarian Regimes

CHAPTER 7

Iran

Ervand Abrahamian

Islamic Republic of Iran

Land and People

Capital	Tehran	
Total area (square miles)	634,562 (slightly larger than Alaska)	
Population	68,017,860	
Annual population growth rate (%)	1975–2000	3.0
	2005–2015 (projected)	0.7
Urban population (%)	67.0	
Ethnic composition (% of total population)	Persian	51
	Azeri	24
	Gilaki and Mazandarani	8
	Kurd	7
	Arab	3
	Turkman	2
	Baluchi	2
	Other	3
Major language(s) (%)	Persian (Farsi)	58
	Turkic	26
	Kurdish	9
	Other	7
Religious affiliation (%)	Shi'a Muslim	89
	Sunni Muslim	9
	Zoroastrian, Jewish, Christian, and Baha'I	2

Economy

Domestic currency	Rial (IRR)	
	US$1: 8,614 IRR (2004 av.)	
Total GNI (US$)	133.2 billion	
GNI per capita (US$)	2010	
Total GNI at purchasing power parity (US$)	465.00 billion	
GNI per capita at purchasing power parity (US$)	$7,000	
GDP annual growth rate (%)	1983–1993	2.2
	1993–2003	3.7
	2003	6.6
	2004	6.3
GDP per capita average annual growth rate (%)	1983–1993	–0.5
	1993–2003	2.2
	2003	5.2
Inequality in income or consumption (1996–1997)	Data Not Available for Iran	

Structure of production (% of GDP)	Agriculture	11.2
	Industry	40.9
	Services	48.7
Labor force distribution (% of total)	Agriculture	30
	Industry	25
	Services	45
Exports as % of GDP	25.3	
Imports as % of GDP	22.9	

Society

Life expectancy at birth	71	
Infant mortality per 1,000 live births	30	
Adult literacy (% over age 15)	Male	83.2
	Female	70
Access to information and communications (per 1,000 population)	Telephone lines	169
	Mobile phones	32
	Radios	281
	Televisions	163
	Personal computers	69.7

Women in Government and the Economy

Women in the national legislature		
Lower house or single house (%)		4.1
Women at ministerial level (%)		9.4
Female economic activity rate (age 15 and above) (%)		30
Female labor force (% of total)		27
Female legislators, senior officials, and managers (% of total)		13
Female professional and technical workers (% of total)		33
Estimated earned income (PPP US$)	Female	2,835
	Male	9,946

Composite Ratings and Rankings

Human Development Index (HDI) ranking (value) out of 177 countries	101 (.732)
Gender-Related Development Index (GDI) ranking (value) out of 144 countries	82 (.713)
Gender Empowerment Measure (GEM) ranking (value) out of 78 countries	72 (.313)
Corruption Perception Index (CPI) ranking (value) out of 145 countries	87 (2.9)
Environmental Sustainability (ESI) Index ranking (value) out of 146 countries	132 (39.8)
Freedom in World Rating	6.0 (Not Free)

Political Organization

Political System   A mixture of democracy and theocracy (rule of the clergy) headed by a cleric with the title of the Leader.

Regime History   Islamic Republic since the 1979 Islamic Revolution.

Administrative Structure   Centralized administration with 30 provinces. The interior minister appoints the provincial governor-generals.

Executive   President and his cabinet. The president is elected by the general electorate every four years. The president chooses his cabinet ministers, but they need to obtain the approval of the *Majles* (parliament).

Legislature   Unicameral. The *Majles*, formed of 270 seats, is elected every four years. It has multiple member districts with the top runners in the elections taking the seats. Bills passed by the *Majles* do not become law unless they have the approval of the clerically dominated Council of Guardians.

Judiciary   A Chief Judge and a Supreme Court independent of the executive and legislature but appointed by the Leader.

Party System   The ruling clergy restricts most party and organizational activities.

Section ❶   The Making of the Modern Iranian State

Politics in Action

Iran shook the world, not to mention its own establishment, first in 1997 by electing Muhammad Khatami, a relatively unknown moderate cleric, as president of the Islamic Republic in a landslide victory, and then again in 2001 by reelecting him with even a larger majority. Khatami, a former director of the National Library, was a mild-mannered middle-ranking cleric, a hojjat al-Islam ("Proof of Islam"), not a high-ranking **ayatollah** or grand ayatollah ("Sign of God"). In the elections, he vigorously campaigned on the theme of creating "civil society" and improving the "sick economy." He stressed the importance of an open society that would protect individual liberties, freedom of expression, women's rights, political pluralism, and, most essential, the rule of law. He had even authored books applauding Western thinkers such as Locke, Voltaire, and Rousseau. His electoral campaigns also stressed the need for a "dialogue between civilizations." This was a far cry from the early days of the 1979 Iranian Revolution, when its leader, Grand Ayatollah Ruhollah Khomeini, had denounced the United States as the "Great Satan" and incited students to seize the U.S. embassy. This takeover and the resulting hostage crisis lasted 444 days and prompted a break in U.S.-Iranian diplomatic relations that lasts to this day.

Khatami's initial electoral success was especially surprising since much of the religious establishment had openly endorsed his rival. Most commentators, both inside and outside the country, had considered the election a shoo-in for this conservative candidate. After all, he had been endorsed by an impressive array of newspapers, radio stations, television programs, state institutions, quasi-state foundations, clerical organizations, and local **mosques** (Muslim houses of worship). They had warned that any opening up of the system could endanger the whole regime and that Khatami could become another Mikhail Gorbachev, the reformist leader who had inadvertently presided over the demise of the Soviet Union. Even Ayatollah Ali Khamenei, the Leader who is often mistitled in the West as Iran's Supreme Leader, had implicitly endorsed the conservative candidate. In the upset election, Khatami took 70 percent of the vote in a campaign that attracted 80 percent of the electorate. Much of Khatami's vote came from women, university students, and young adults throughout the country—even from those serving in the armed forces. He followed up his victory by trying to liberalize the press, establishing political parties, and initiating a dialogue with the United States. He even bolstered the case for liberalization by citing *Democracy in America,* the classic book by nineteenth-century French writer Alexis de Tocqueville. Khatami also assured the West that Iran had no intention of implementing the *fatwa* (religious decree) that the late Ayatollah Khomeini had placed on the Muslim-born British writer Salman Rushdie in 1989. Khomeini had condemned Rushdie to death on the grounds that his book, *Satanic Verses,* blasphemed Islam and thus proved that its author was an apostate from Islam, which is a capital offense according to a narrow interpretation of Islamic law. The 2001 presidential elections, as well as the 2000 parliamentary elections, further strengthened Khatami's mandate. In 2005, former president Clinton observed that Iran was the only country in the world where "liberals" and "progressives" had, in recent years, won a series of resounding electoral victories.

These elections vividly illustrated the main dilemmas confronting the Islamic Republic that had been established by Ayatollah Khomeini in the aftermath of the 1979 revolution. The Islamic Republic of Iran today is a mixture of **theocracy** and democracy: it is a political system based on clerical authority as well as popular sovereignty, based on the divine right of the clergy as well as the rights of the people, based on concepts derived from early Islam as well as from modern democratic principles such as the separation of powers. The country has regular elections for the presidency and the *Majles* (Parliament), but a clerically dominated **Guardian Council** determines who can and cannot run in these elections. The president is the formal head of the executive branch of government, but he can be overruled, even dismissed, by the chief cleric known as the **Leader.** The president appoints the minister of justice, but the whole judiciary is under the supervision of the chief judge, who is appointed directly by the Leader. The *Majles* is the legislative branch of government, but its bills do not become law unless the Guardian Council deems them compatible with Islam and the Islamic constitution. In short, contemporary Iranian politics resonates with both *vox dei* (the voice of God) and *vox populi* (the voice of the people).

Geographic Setting

Iran—three times the size of France, slightly larger than Alaska, and much larger than its immediate neighbors—is notable for two geographic features. The first is that most of its territory is inhospitable to agriculture. A vast arid zone known as the Great Salt Desert covers much of the central plateau from the capital city, Tehran, to the borders with Afghanistan and Pakistan. The Zagros mountain range takes up the western third of the country. Another range, the Elborz, stretches across the north. Rain-fed agriculture is confined mostly to the northwest and the provinces along the Caspian Sea. In the rest of the country, population settlements are located mostly on oases, on the few rare rivers, and on constructed irrigation networks. Only pastoral nomads can survive in the semiarid zones and in the high mountain valleys. Thus, 67 percent of the total population of 68 million is concentrated on 27 percent of the land—mostly in the Caspian region, in the northwest provinces, and in the cities of Tehran, Qom, Isfahan, Shiraz, and Ahwaz.

In the past, Iran's inhospitable environment was a major obstacle to economic development. In recent decades, this obstacle has been partly overcome by oil revenues that totaled $28 billion in 2004. Iran is the second largest oil producer in the Middle East and the fourth largest in the world, and oil revenues account for the fact that Iran is now an urbanized and partly industrialized country. Nearly 67 percent of the population lives in urban centers; 70 percent of the labor force is employed in industry and services; 77 percent of adults are literate; life expectancy has reached seventy years; and the majority of Iranians enjoy a standard of living well above that found in most of Asia and Africa.

Iran's second notable geographic feature is that it lies on the strategic crossroads between Central Asia and Turkey, between the Indian subcontinent and the Middle East, and between the Arabian Peninsula and the Caucasus Mountains, which is often considered a boundary between Europe and Asia. This has made the region vulnerable to invaders: Indo-Europeans in the distant past (they gave the country the name of Iran, Land of the Aryans), Islamic Arab tribes in the seventh century, and a series of Turkic incursions in the Middle Ages.

The population today reflects these historic invasions. Some 51 percent of the country speaks Persian **(Farsi),** an Indo-European language, as their first language; 26 percent speak various dialects of Turkic, mainly Azeri and Turkman; 8 percent speak Gilaki or Mazandarani, distant Persian dialects; 7 percent speak Kurdish, another Indo-European language; and

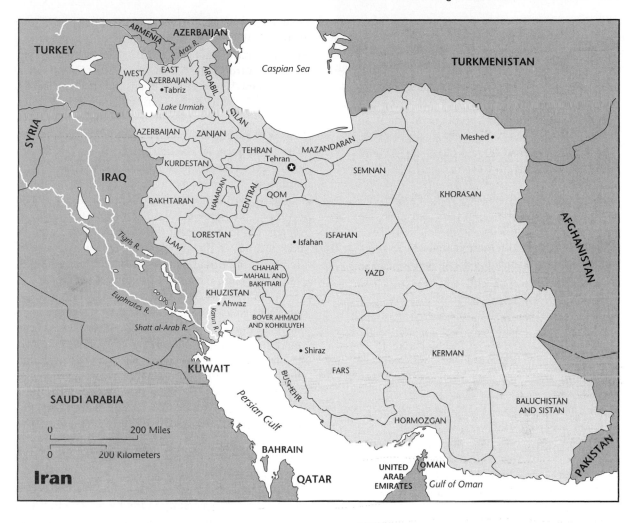

Iran

3 percent speak Arabic. Europeans long referred to the country as Persia, but since the third century Iranians have called their country Iran and their main language Farsi, after the central province (Fars), the original home of the languages. In 1935, Iran formally asked the international community to cease calling the country Persia.

Critical Junctures

Although modern Iran traces its roots to an ancient empire of the sixth century B.C. and its Islamic religion to the Arab invasions of the seventh century, its current national identity, geographic boundaries, particular interpretation of Islam—**Shi'ism**—and political system were formed by four more recent critical junctures: the Safavid (1501–1722), Qajar (1794–1925), and Pahlavi (1925–1979) dynasties, and the Revolution of 1979, which led to establishment of the current Islamic Republic.

The Safavids (1501–1722)

Modern Iran, with its Shi'i Islamic identity and its present-day boundaries, can be traced to the sixteenth century, when the Safavid family conquered the territory with the help of fellow Turkic-speaking tribes. They revived the ancient Iranian titles of shah-in-shah

Critical Junctures in Modern Iran's Political Development

1921	Colonel Reza Khan's military coup
1925	Establishment of the Pahlavi dynasty
1941–1945	Allied occupation of Iran
1951	Nationalization of the oil industry
1953	Coup against Mosaddeq
1963	White Revolution
1975	Establishment of the Resurgence Party
1979	Islamic Revolution
1979–1981	U.S. hostage crisis
December 1979	Referendum on the constitution
January 1980	Bani-Sadr elected president
March 1980	Elections for the First Islamic *Majles*
1980–1988	War with Iraq
June 1981	President Bani-Sadr ousted
October 1981	Khamenei elected president
1984	Elections for the Second Islamic *Majles*
1988	Elections for the Third Islamic *Majles*
1989	Khomeini dies; Khamenei appointed Leader; Rafsanjani elected president
1992	Elections for the Fourth Islamic *Majles*
1996	Elections for the Fifth Islamic *Majles*
1997	Khatami elected president on reform platform
2000	Reformers win elections for the Sixth Islamic *Majles*
2000	Khatami reelected president for the Sixth Islamic *Majles*
2004	Elections for the Seventh Islamic *Majles*

(King of Kings) and Shadow of God on Earth, and proceeded to forcibly convert their subjects to Shi'ism. Although small Shi'i communities had existed in this area since the beginning of Islam, the vast majority had adhered to the majority Sunni branch (see "Background: Islam and Shi'ism"). The Safavid motivation for this drastic conversion was to give their kingdom and population a distinct identity separate from the surrounding Sunni powers: the Ottomans in the west, the Uzbeks in the north, and the Afghans in the east.

By the mid-seventeenth century, the Safavid dynasty had succeeded in converting nearly 90 percent of their subjects to Shi'ism. Sunnism survived only among the tribal groups at the periphery: Kurds in the northwest, Turkmans in the northeast, Baluchis in the southeast, and Arabs in the southwest. It should be noted that the Safavids failed to capture from the Ottomans Shi'i's two most holy sites (both located in modern Iraq): Karbala, where Imam Husayn, one of their most important martyrs, had been killed in 680 A.D.; and Najaf, the nearby theological center.

In addition to the Sunni minority, Safavid Iran contained small communities of Jews, Zoroastrians, and Christians (Armenians and Assyrians). These small minorities lived mostly in Isfahan, Shiraz, Kerman, Yazd, and Azerbaijan. Jews had lived in Iran since ancient times, predating the great diaspora prompted by the Roman destruction of Jerusalem. Zoroastrians were descendants of Iranians who retained their old religion after the Arab invasions. The Christians had lived in the northwest long before the advent of Islam. To strengthen their foothold in central Iran, the Safavids transported there some 100,000 Armenians, encouraging them to become craftsmen and merchants, especially in the lucrative silk trade. The Safavids, like most other Muslim rulers, but unlike medieval Christian kings, tolerated religious minorities as long as they paid special taxes and accepted royal authority. According to Islam, Christians, Jews, and Zoroastrians were to be tolerated as legitimate **People of the Book.** They were respected both because they were mentioned in the Holy **Qur'an** and because they had their own sacred texts: the Bible, the Torah, and the Avesta.

The Safavids established their capital in Isfahan, a Persian-speaking city, and recruited Persian scribes into their court administration. Such families had helped administer the ancient Iranian empires. They proceeded to govern not only through these Persian scribes and Shi'i clerics but also through tribal chiefs, large landowners, religious notables, city merchants, guild elders, and urban ward leaders.

Background: Islam and Shi'ism

Islam, with some 1 billion adherents, is the second largest religion in the world. Islam means literally "submission to God," and a Muslim is someone who has submitted to God—the same God that Jews and Christians worship. Islam has one central tenet: "There is only one God, and Muhammad is His Prophet." Muslims, in order to consider themselves faithful, need to perform the following four duties to the best of their ability: give to charity; pray every day facing Mecca, where Abraham is believed to have built the first place of worship; make a pilgrimage at least once in a lifetime to Mecca, which is located in modern Saudi Arabia; and fast during the daytime hours in the month of Ramadan to commemorate God's revelation of the Qur'an (Koran, or Holy Book) to the Prophet Muhammad. These four duties, together with the central tenet, are known as the Five Pillars of Islam.

From its earliest days, Islam has been divided into two major branches: Sunni, meaning literally "followers of tradition," and Shi'i, literally "partisans of Ali." Sunnis are by far in the majority worldwide. Shi'is constitute less than 10 percent of Muslims worldwide and are concentrated in Iran, southern Iraq, Bahrain, eastern Turkey, Azerbaijan, and southern Lebanon.

Although both branches accept the Five Pillars, they differ mostly over who should have succeeded the Prophet Muhammad (d. 632). The Sunnis recognized the early dynasties that ruled the Islamic empire with the exalted title of caliph ("Prophet's Deputy"). The Shi'is, however, argued that as soon as the Prophet died, his authority should have been passed on to Imam Ali, the Prophet's close companion, disciple, and son-in-law. They further argue that Imam Ali passed his authority to his direct male heirs, the third of whom, Imam Husayn, had been martyred fighting the Sunnis in 680, and the twelfth of whom had supposedly gone into hiding in 941.

The Shi'is are also known as Twelvers, since they follow the Twelve Imams. They refer to the Twelfth Imam as the *Mahdi,* the Hidden Imam, and believe him to be the Messiah who will herald the end of the world. Furthermore, they argue that in his absence, the authority to interpret the *shari'a* (religious law) should be in the hands of the senior clerical scholars—the ayatollahs. Thus, from the beginning, the Shi'is harbored ambivalent attitudes toward the state, especially if the rulers were Sunnis or lacked genealogical links to the Twelve Imams. For Sunnis, the *shari'a* is based mostly on the Qur'an and the teachings of the Prophet. For Shi'is, it is based also on the teachings of the Twelve Imams.

The Safavid army was formed mostly of tribal cavalry led by tribal chieftains. Financial constraints prevented the Safavids from creating a large bureaucracy or an extensive standing army. Their revenues came mostly from land taxes levied on the peasantry. In theory, the Safavids claimed absolute power; in reality, their power was limited since they lacked a central state and had no choice but to work along with many semi-independent local leaders. The central government was linked to the general population not so much through coercive institutions as through provincial and hereditary notables. It survived for the most part because the society below was sharply fragmented by geographic barriers (especially mountains) as well as by tribal, communal, and ethnic differences. Moreover, many senior clerics who might have opposed the dynasty resided in Najaf, Iraq, at a safe distance from the seat of power of Iran. The Safavid shah did not control Iranian society. Rather, he hovered over it, systematically orchestrating its many existing rivalries.

The Qajars (1794–1925)

The Safavid dynasty collapsed in 1722 when Afghan tribesmen invaded the capital. The invasion was followed by a half-century of civil war until the Qajars, another Turkic tribe, reconquered much of Iran. The Qajars moved the capital to Tehran and recreated the

Safavid system of central manipulation and court administration, including the Persian scribes. They also declared Shi'ism to be the state religion even though they, unlike the Safavids, did not boast of genealogical links to the Twelve Imams. This was to have far-reaching repercussions. Since these new shahs did not pretend to wear the imam's mantle, the Shi'i clerical leaders could claim to be the main interpreters of Islam. In addition, many of them safeguarded their independence from the state by continuing to reside in Iraq and collecting religious contributions directly from the faithful in Iran. These contributions came mainly from wealthy merchants.

Qajar rule coincided with the peak of European imperialism in the nineteenth century. The Russians seized parts of Central Asia and the Caucasus region from Iran and extracted a series of major economic concessions, including a monopoly to fish for sturgeon (the source of the delicacy, caviar) in the Caspian Sea and exemption from import duties, internal tariffs, and the jurisdiction of local courts. The British Imperial Bank won the monopoly to issue paper money. The Indo-European Telegraph Company got a contract to extend communication lines through the country. Exclusive rights to drill for oil in the southwest were sold to a British citizen. The later Qajars also borrowed heavily from European banks to meet lavish court expenses. By the end of the century, these loans had become so heavy that the Qajars were obliged to guarantee repayments by placing the country's entire customs service under European supervision. Iranians felt that their whole country had been auctioned off and that the shah had given away far too many concessions, or capitulations, as they called them.

These resentments culminated in the constitutional revolution of 1905–1909. The revolution began with shopkeepers and moneylenders demonstrating against the handing over of customs collections to Europeans. They suspected that the shah would renege on local debts in favor of repaying his foreign loans. They also protested that the government was not doing enough to protect native merchants and industries. The protests intensified when the government, faced with soaring sugar prices due to political turmoil in Russia (Iran's major source of the commodity) publicly whipped two major sugar merchants.

The revolutionary movement peaked in 1906, when some 14,000 protesters took sanctuary inside the gardens of the British legation in Tehran and demanded a written constitution. After weeks of haggling, the shah conceded because the British diplomats advised compromise and because his army, led by Russians and called the Cossack Brigade, threatened to join the protesters. A British diplomat commented, "The shah with his unarmed, unpaid, ragged, starving soldiers, what can he do in face of the menace of a general strike and riots?"[1]

The 1906 constitution introduced essential features of modern government into Iran: elections, separation of powers, laws made by a legislative assembly, and the concepts of popular sovereignty and the nation (*mellat*). It also generated a heated debate, with some arguing that democracy was inherently incompatible with Islam and others countering that true Islam could not be practiced unless the government was based on popular support. Some even argued in favor of secularism—complete separation of religion from politics, church from state, and clergy from government authority. The new constitution retained the monarchy, but centered political power in a national assembly called the *Majles*. It hailed this assembly as "the representative of the whole people" and guaranteed seats to the recognized religious minorities: Jews, Zoroastrians, and Christians. Significantly, no seats were given to the Baha'is, a nineteenth-century offshoot of Shi'ism. The clerical leaders deemed the Baha'is to be apostates from Islam and "sinister heretics linked to the imperial powers."

The constitution endowed the *Majles* with extensive authority over all laws, budgets, treaties, loans, concessions, and the composition of the cabinet. The ministers were accountable to the *Majles,* not to the shah. "Sovereignty," declared the constitution, "is a trust confided (as a divine gift) by the people to the person of the shah." The constitution also included a bill of rights guaranteeing equality before the law, protection of life and property, safeguards from arbitrary arrest, and freedom of expression and association.

Although the constitution was modeled on the European liberal secular system of government, it made some concessions to Shi'ism. Shi'ism was declared Iran's official religion. Only Shi'is could hold cabinet posts. Clerical courts retained the right to implement the *shari'a* (religious law), especially in family matters. A Guardian Council formed of senior clerics elected by the *Majles* was given veto power over parliamentary bills deemed un-Islamic. In short, popular sovereignty was to be restricted by clerical veto power. In actual fact, this Guardian Council was not convened until the 1979 Islamic Revolution because of divisions within the clerical establishment and opposition from parliament.

The initial euphoria that greeted the 1905 constitutional revolution gave way to deep disillusionment in the subsequent decade. Pressures from the European powers continued, and a devastating famine after World War I took some 1 million lives, almost 10 percent of the total population. Internal conflicts polarized the *Majles* into warring liberal and conservative factions. The former, mostly members of the intelligentsia, championed social reforms, especially the replacement of the *shari'a* with a modern legal code. The latter, led by landlords, tribal chiefs, and senior clerics, vehemently opposed such reforms, particularly land reform, women's rights, and the granting of full equality to religious minorities.

Meanwhile, the central government, lacking any real army, bureaucracy, or tax-collecting machinery, was unable to administer the provinces, especially the regions inhabited by the Kurds, Turkmans, and Baluchis. Some tribes, equipped with modern European rifles, had more firepower than the central government. Moreover, during World War I, Russia and Britain formally carved up Iran into three zones. Russia occupied the north and Britain the south. Iran was left with a small "neutral zone" in the middle.

By 1921, Iran was in complete disarray. The shah was gathering his crown jewels to flee south. The British, in their own words, were hoping to "salvage" some "healthy limbs" of the fractured country in their southern zone. Left-wing rebels, helped by the new communist regime in Russia, had taken over Gilan province and were threatening nearby Azerbaijan, Mazandaran, and Khorasan. According to a British diplomat, the propertied classes, fearful of communism, were anxiously seeking "a savior on horseback."[2]

The Pahlavis (1925–1979)

That savior appeared in February 1921 in the person of Colonel Reza Khan, the recently appointed commander of the elite 3,000-strong Cossack Brigade. Carrying out a typical military **coup d'état**, he replaced the cabinet and, while paying lip service to the monarch, consolidated power in his own hands, especially the post of commander in chief of the armed forces. Four years later, he emerged from behind the throne; deposed the Qajars; crowned himself shah-in-shah in the style of his hero, the French emperor Napoleon; and established the Pahlavi dynasty, adopting a name associated with the glories of ancient Iran. This was the first nontribal dynasty to rule the whole of Iran. To forestall opposition from Britain and the Soviet Union, he assured both countries that Iran would remain strictly nonaligned. A compliant *Majles* endorsed this transfer of power from the Qajars to the Pahlavis.

Reza Shah ruled with an iron fist until 1941, when the British and the Soviets invaded Iran to stop Nazi Germany from establishing a foothold there. Reza Shah promptly abdicated in favor of his son, Muhammad Reza Shah, and went into exile, where he soon died. In the first twelve years of his reign, the young shah retained control over the armed forces but had to live with a free press, an independent judiciary, competitive elections, assertive cabinet ministers, and boisterous parliaments. He also had to confront two vigorous political movements: the communist Tudeh (Masses) Party and the National Front, led by the charismatic Dr. Muhammad Mosaddeq (1882–1967).

The Tudeh drew its support mostly from working-class trade unions. The National Front drew its support mainly from the salaried middle classes and campaigned to nationalize the British company that controlled the whole of the petroleum industry in Iran. Mosaddeq also wanted to sever the shah's links with the armed forces. He argued that according to the constitution, the monarch should reign, not rule, and that the armed forces should be supervised by cabinet ministers responsible to parliament. In 1951, Mosaddeq was elected prime minister and promptly nationalized the oil industry. The period of relative freedom, however, ended abruptly in 1953, when royalist army officers overthrew Mosaddeq and installed the shah with absolute power. The coup was financed by the U.S. Central Intelligence Agency (CIA) and the British, which intensified anti-British sentiment and created a deep distrust of the United States. It also made the shah appear to be a puppet of foreign powers. Muhammad Reza Shah ruled much in the style of his autocratic father until he was overthrown by the 1979 Islamic Revolution.

During its fifty-four-year rule, the Pahlavi dynasty built the first highly centralized state in Iran's history. This state rested on three pillars: the armed forces, the bureaucracy, and the royal patronage system. The armed forces grew from fewer than 40,000 in 1925 to 124,000 in 1941, and to over 410,000 in 1979, by which time Iran had the fifth largest army in the world, the largest navy in the Persian Gulf, the largest air force in western Asia, and one of the best-equipped tank brigades in the Third World. The armed forces were supplemented by a pervasive secret police known as SAVAK—the Persian acronym for the Organization to Protect and Gather Information for the State.

Iran's bureaucracy expanded from a haphazard collection of hereditary scribes, some without fixed offices, to twenty-one ministries employing over 300,000 civil servants in 1979. The Education Ministry grew twentyfold, administering 26,000 primary schools with some 4 million children and 1,850 secondary schools with 740,000 pupils. Meanwhile, the Ministry of Higher Education supervised 750 vocational schools with 227,000 students and thirteen universities with 154,000 students. The powerful Interior Ministry appointed provincial governors, town mayors, district superintendents, and village headmen. Since it also appointed electoral supervisors, it could rig *Majles* elections and provide the shah with rubber-stamp parliaments.

The Justice Ministry supplanted the *shari'a* with a European-style civil code and the clerical courts with a modern judicial system culminating in a Supreme Court. Lawyers and judges had to pass government-administered exams based on European jurisprudence. The legal system was further secularized in the 1960s, when the shah decreed a controversial Family Protection Law that contradicted the traditional interpretation of the *shar'ia* on a number of points, including raising the marriage age to twenty for men and eighteen for women. It also allowed women to override spousal objections and work outside the home if they got court permission and restricted polygamy by stipulating that husbands could marry more than one wife only if they first obtained permission from previous wives and the courts.

Other ministries experienced similar expansion. For example, the Transport Ministry built an impressive array of bridges, ports, highways, and railroads known as the Trans-Iranian Railway. The Ministry of Industries financed the construction of numerous factories specializing in consumer goods. The Agricultural Ministry attained prominence in 1962 when the shah made land reform the centerpiece of his much-heralded "White Revolution," which was designed partly to forestall the possibility of a communist-led "red revolution." The government bought land from large absentee owners and sold it to small farmers through low-interest, long-term mortgages. It also undertook the task of transforming small farmers into modern commercial entrepreneurs by providing them with fertilizers, cooperatives, distribution centers, irrigation canals, dams, and tractor repair shops. The White Revolution included the extension of the vote to women and a Literacy Corps to eradicate illiteracy in the countryside. Thus, by the late 1970s, the state had set up a modern system of communications, initiated a minor industrial revolution, and extended its reach into even the most outlying villages.

The state also controlled a number of major institutions: the National and the Central Banks; the Industrial and Mining Development Bank, which channeled money to private entrepreneurs; the Plan Organization in charge of economic policy; the national radio-television network, which monopolized the airwaves; and most important, the National Iranian Oil Company, which grew from a leasing firm in the 1950s to become a large exploring, drilling, refining, and exporting corporation.

The Pahlavi state was further bolstered by court patronage. The dynasty's founder, Reza Shah, the son of a small landowner, used coercion, confiscations, and diversion of irrigation water to make himself one of the largest landowners in the Middle East. As a British diplomat put it, Reza Shah had an "unholy interest in property," especially other people's property.[3] This wealth transformed the shah's court into a large military-landed complex, providing work for thousands in its numerous palaces, hotels, casinos, charities, companies, and beach resorts. This patronage system grew under his son, Muhammad Reza Shah, particularly after he established his tax-exempt Pahlavi Foundation, which by the 1970s, controlled 207 large companies active in tourism, insurance, banking, agribusiness, mining, construction, and manufacturing.

The Pahlavi drive for secularization, centralization, industrialization, and social development won some favor from the urban propertied classes. But arbitrary rule, the 1953 coup that overthrew a popular prime minister, the disregard for constitutional liberties, and the stifling of independent newspapers, political parties, and professional associations produced widespread resentment, particularly among the clergy, the intelligentsia, and the urban masses. In short, this state was strong in the sense that it controlled the modern instruments of coercion and administration. But its roots were very shallow because of its failure to link the new state institutions to the country's social structure. The Pahlavi state, like the Safavids and the Qajars, hovered over, rather than embedding itself into, Iranian society. Furthermore, much of the civil society that had existed in traditional Iran had now been suffocated by the modern state.

In 1975, the shah announced the formation of the Resurgence Party. He declared Iran to be a one-party state and threatened imprisonment and exile to those refusing to join the party. In heralding the new order, the shah replaced the traditional Islamic calendar with a new royalist one, jumping from the Muslim year 1355 to the royalist year 2535; 2,500 years were allocated to the monarchy in general and 35 years for the shah's own reign. The King of Kings and the Shadow of God also accrued two new titles: Leader to the New Great Civilization and Light of the Aryans (Aryamehr).

The Resurgence Party was designed to create yet another organizational link with the population, especially with the **bazaars** (traditional marketplaces), which, unlike the rest of society, had managed to retain their guilds and thus escape direct government control. The Resurgence Party promptly established its own bazaar guilds as well as newspapers, women's organizations, professional associations, and labor unions. It also prepared to create a Religious Corps, modeled on the Literacy Corps, to go into the countryside to teach the peasants "true Islam." The Resurgence Party promised to establish an "organic relationship between rulers and ruled," "synthesize the best of capitalism and socialism," and chart the way toward the New Great Civilization. It also praised the shah for curbing the "medieval clergy," eradicating "class warfare," and

becoming a "spiritual guide" as well as a world-renowned statesman. For his part, the shah told an English-language newspaper that the party's philosophy was "based on the dialectical principles of the White Revolution" and that nowhere else in the world was there such a close relationship between a ruler and his people. "No other nation has given its commander such a *carte-blanche* [blank check]."[4] The Western terminology, as well as the boast, revealed much about the shah at the height of his power—or, as some suspected, his megalomania.

The Islamic Revolution (1979–2001)

On the eve of the 1979 Islamic Revolution, a newspaper published by Iranian exiles denounced the Pahlavis in an issue entitled "Fifty Indictments of Treason During Fifty Years of Treason."[5] It charged the shah and his family with establishing a military dictatorship, collaborating with the CIA, trampling on the constitution, creating SAVAK, rigging parliamentary elections, organizing a fascistic one-party state, taking over the religious establishment, and undermining national identity by disseminating Western culture. It also accused the regime of inducing millions of landless peasants to migrate into urban shantytowns, widening the gap between rich and poor, funneling money away from the small bourgeoisie into the pockets of the wealthy comprador bourgeoisie (the entrepreneurs linked to foreign companies and multinational corporations), wasting resources on bloated military budgets, and granting new capitulations to the West—the most controversial being the extension of diplomatic immunity to U.S. military advisers in Iran.

These grievances were given greater articulation when a leading anti-shah cleric, Ayatollah Ruhollah Khomeini—from his exile in Iraq—began to formulate a new version of Shi'ism (see "Leaders: Ayatollah Ruhollah Khomeini"). His version has often been labeled Islamic **fundamentalism;** it would better be described as Shi'i populism or political Islam. The term *fundamentalism,* derived from American Protestantism, implies religious dogmatism, intellectual inflexibility and purity, political traditionalism, social conservatism, rejection of the modern world, and the literal interpretation of scriptural texts. Khomeini, however, was less concerned about literal interpretations of the Qur'an

Leaders: Ayatollah Ruhollah Khomeini

Ruhollah Khomeini was born in 1902 into a landed clerical family well known in central Iran. During the 1920s, he studied in the famous Fayzieh Seminary in Qom with the leading theologians of the day, most of whom were scrupulously apolitical. He taught at the seminary from the 1930s through the 1950s, avoiding politics even during the mass campaign to nationalize the British-owned oil company. His entry into politics did not come until 1962, when he, along with most other clerical leaders, denounced Muhammad Reza Shah's White Revolution. Forced into exile, Khomeini taught at the Shi'i center of Najaf in Iraq from 1964 until 1978.

During these years, Khomeini developed his own version of Shi'i populism by incorporating socioeconomic grievances into his sermons and denouncing not just the shah but the whole ruling class. Returning home triumphant in the midst of the Iranian Revolution after the Shah was forced from power in 1979, he was declared the Imam and Leader of the new Islamic Republic. In the past, Iranian Shi'is, unlike the Arab Sunnis, had reserved the special term *imam* only for Imam Ali and his twelve direct heirs, whom they deemed to be semidivine and thereby infallible. For many Iranians in 1979, Khomeini was charismatic in the true sense of the word: a man with a special gift from God. Khomeini ruled as Imam and Leader of the Islamic Republic until his death in 1989.

---

than about articulating resentments against the elite and the United States. He was more of a political revolutionary than a social conservative.

Khomeini denounced monarchies in general and the Pahlavis in particular as part and parcel of the corrupt elite exploiting the oppressed masses. For him, the oppressors consisted of courtiers, large landowners, high-ranking military officers, wealthy foreign-connected capitalists, and millionaire palace dwellers. The oppressed consisted of the masses, especially landless peasants, wage earners, bazaar shopkeepers, and shantytown dwellers. His proclamations often cited the Qur'anic term *mostazafin* (dispossessed) and the biblical promise that "the poor (meek) shall inherit the earth."

In calling for the overthrow of the Pahlavi monarchy, Khomeini injected a radically new meaning into the old Shi'i term *velayat-e faqih* (**jurist's guardianship**). He argued that jurist's guardianship gave the senior clergy—namely, the grand ayatollahs such as himself—all-encompassing authority over the whole community, not just over widows, minors, and the mentally disabled, as had been the interpretation previously. He insisted that only the senior clerics had the sole competence to understand the *shari'a*, that the divine authority given to the Prophet and the imams had been passed on to their spiritual heirs, the clergy; and that throughout history, the clergy had championed the rights of the people against bad government and foreign powers. He further insisted that the clergy were the people's true representatives since they lived among them, listened to their problems, and shared their everyday joys and pains. He claimed that the shah secretly planned to confiscate all religious endowment funds and replace Islamic values with "cultural imperialism." These pronouncements added fuel to an already explosive situation.

By 1977, Iran needed a few sparks to ignite the revolution. These sparks came in the form of minor economic difficulties and international pressures to curb human rights violations. In 1977–1978, the shah tried to deal with a 20 percent rise in consumer prices and a 10 percent decline in oil revenues by cutting construction projects and declaring war against "profiteers," "hoarders," and "price gougers." Not surprisingly, shopkeepers felt that the shah was diverting attention from court corruption and planning to replace them with government-run department stores and that he was intending to destroy the bazaar, which some felt was the real pillar of Iranian society.

The pressure for human rights came from Amnesty International, the United Nations, and the Western press, as well as from the recently elected Carter administration in the United States. In 1977, after meeting with the International Commission of Jurists, the shah permitted Red Cross officials to visit prisons and allowed defense attorneys to attend political trials. This international pressure had allowed the opposition to breathe again after decades of suffocation.[6]

This slight loosening of the reins, coming in the midst of the economic recession, sealed the fate of the shah. Political parties, labor organizations, and professional associations—especially lawyers, writers, and university professors—regrouped after years of being banned. Bazaar guilds regained their independence from the government party. College, high school, and seminary students, especially in the religious center of Qom, took to the streets to protest the quarter-century of repression. On September 8, 1978, known as Bloody Friday, troops in Tehran fired into a crowded square, killing hundreds of unarmed demonstrators. By late 1978, a general strike had brought the whole economy to a halt, paralyzing not only the oil industry, the factories, the banks, and the transport system but also the civil service, the media, the bazaars, and the whole educational establishment. Oil workers vowed that they would not produce any petroleum for export until they had exported the "shah and his forty thieves."[7]

Meanwhile, in the urban centers, local committees attached to the mosques and financed by the bazaars were distributing food to the needy, supplanting the police with militias known as *pasdaran* (Revolutionary Guards), and replacing the judicial system with ad hoc courts applying the *shari'a*. Equally significant, antiregime rallies were now attracting as many as 2 million protesters. The largest rally was held in Tehran in December 1978 on the day commemorating the martyrdom of Imam Husayn in the seventh century. Protesters demanded the abolition of the monarchy, the return from exile of Khomeini, and the establishment of a republic to preserve national independence and provide the masses with social justice in the form of decent wages, land, and a proper standard of living.

Although these rallies were led by pro-Khomeini clerics, they drew support from a broad variety of organizations: the National Front; the Lawyer's, Doctor's, and Women's associations; the communist Tudeh Party; the Fedayin, a Marxist guerrilla group; and the Mojahedin, a Muslim guerrilla group formed of nonclerical intellectuals. The rallies also attracted students, from high schools and colleges, as well as shopkeepers and craftsmen from the bazaars. A secret Revolutionary Committee in Tehran coordinated protests throughout the country, kept in telephone contact with Khomeini in Paris, and circulated recordings of his messages within Iran. This was a revolution made in the streets and propelled forward by audiotapes. It was also one of the first revolutions to be televised worldwide. Later on, many felt that these demonstrations inspired the revolutions that swept through Eastern Europe in the 1980s.

After a series of such mass rallies in late 1978, the *Washington Post* concluded that "disciplined and well-organized marches lent considerable weight to the opposition's claim of being an alternative government."[8] Similarly, the *Christian Science Monitor* stated that the "giant wave of humanity sweeping through the capital declared louder than any bullet or bomb could the clear message, 'The shah must go.'"[9] Confronted by this opposition and aware that increasing numbers of soldiers were deserting to the opposition, the shah decided to leave Iran. A year later, when he was in exile and dying of cancer, there was much speculation, especially in the United States, that he might have mastered the upheavals if he had been healthier, possessed a stronger personality, and received full support from the United States. But even a man with an iron will and full foreign backing would not have been able to deal with millions of demonstrators, massive general strikes, and debilitating desertions from his own pampered military.

On February 11, 1979—three weeks after the shah's departure from Iran and ten days after Khomeini's return—armed groups, especially Fedayin and Mojahedin guerrillas, supported by air force cadets, broke into the main army barracks in Tehran, distributed arms, and then assaulted the main police stations, the jails, and eventually the national radio-television station. That same evening, the radio station made the historic announcement: "This is the voice of Iran, the voice of true Iran, the voice of the Islamic Revolution." A few hours of street fighting had completed the destruction of the fifty-four-year-old dynasty that claimed a 2,500-year-old heritage.

The Islamic Republic (1979–2001)

Seven weeks after the February revolution, a nationwide referendum replaced the monarchy with an Islamic Republic. Of the 21 million eligible voters, over 20 million—97 percent—endorsed the change. Liberal and lay supporters of Khomeini, including Mehdi Bazargan, his first prime minister, had hoped to offer the electorate a third choice: that of a democratic Islamic Republic. But Khomeini overruled them on the grounds that the term *democratic* was redundant because Islam itself was democratic. The structure of this new republic was to be determined later. Khomeini was now hailed as the Leader of the Revolution, Founder of the Islamic Republic, Guide of the Oppressed Masses, Commander of the Armed Forces, and most potent of all, Imam of the Muslim World.

A new constitution was drawn up in late 1979 by a body named the Assembly of Religious Experts (*Majles-e Khebregan*). Although this 73-man assembly—later increased to 85—was elected by the general public, almost all secular organizations as well as clerics opposed to Khomeini boycotted the elections on the grounds that the state media were controlled, independent papers had been banned, and voters were being intimidated by club-wielding vigilantes known as the **Hezbollahis** ("Partisans of God"). The vast majority of those elected, including forty **hojjat al-Islams** and fifteen ayatollahs, were pro-Khomeini clerics. They proceeded to draft a highly theocratic constitution vesting much authority in the hands of Khomeini in particular and the clergy in general—all this over the strong objections of Prime Minister Bazargan, who wanted a French-style presidential republic that would be Islamic in name but democratic in structure.

When Bazargan threatened to submit his own secular constitution to the public, the state television network, controlled by the clerics, showed him shaking hands with U.S. policymakers. Meanwhile, Khomeini declared that the U.S embassy had been a "den of spies" plotting a repeat performance of the 1953 coup. This led to mass demonstrations, a break-in at

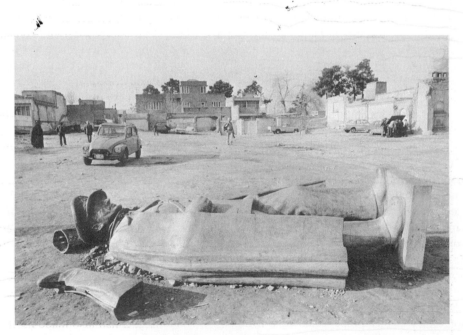

The Shah's statue on the ground, February 1979.
Source: © Abbas/ Magnum Photos.

the embassy, and the seizure of dozens of American hostages, and the resignation of Bazargan. Some suspect that the hostage crisis was engineered to undercut Bazargan.

A month after the embassy break-in, Khomeini submitted the theocratic constitution to the public and declared that all citizens had a divine duty to vote. Although 99 percent of the electorate endorsed it, voter participation was down to 75 percent despite full mobilizations by the mass media, the mosques, and the Revolutionary Guards. Some 5 million voters abstained. The clerics had won their constitution but at the cost of eroding some of their broad support.

In the first decade after the revolution, a number of factors helped the clerics consolidate power. First, few people could challenge Khomeini's overwhelming charisma and popularity. Second, the Iraqi invasion of Iran in 1980—prompted by Saddam Hussein's ambition to gain control over vital borders—rallied the Iranian population behind their endangered homeland. Third, international petroleum prices shot up, sustaining Iran's oil revenues. The price of a barrel of oil, which had hovered around $30 in 1979, jumped to over $50 by 1981, which enabled the new regime, despite war and revolution, to continue to finance existing development programs. In fact, in the 1980s, modern amenities, especially electricity, indoor plumbing, televisions, telephones, refrigerators, motorcycles, and medical clinics, made their first significant appearance in the countryside.

The second decade after the revolution brought the clerics serious problems. Khomeini's death in June 1989 removed his decisive presence. His successor, Ali Khamenei, lacked not only his charisma but also his scholastic credentials and seminary disciples. Khamenei had been considered a mere hojjat al-Islam until the government-controlled press elevated him to the rank of ayatollah and Leader. Few grand ayatollahs deemed him their equal. The 1988 UN-brokered cease-fire in the Iran-Iraq War ended the foreign danger. A drastic fall in world oil prices, which plunged to less than $10 a barrel by 1998, placed a sharp brake on economic development. Even more serious, by the late 1990s, the regime was facing a major ideological crisis, with many of Khomeini's followers, including some of his closest disciples, now stressing the importance of public participation over clerical hegemony,

of political pluralism over theological conformity, of populism over fundamentalism, and of civil society over state authority—in other words, of democracy over theocracy. The regime was grappling with the difficult problem of how to permit mass participation without undermining the entrenched conservative clergy.

Iran after September 11th (2001 to the Present)

The terrorist attacks of September 11, 2001, and the subsequent American invasions of Afghanistan in October 2001 and Iraq in March 2002, had profound consequences on Iran—probably more profound than on any other country with the exception of these three directly involved in the so-called War on Terror. The effect became even more pronounced in January 2002, when President Bush, in his famous "Axis of Evil" speech, specifically mentioned Iran, accusing it of secretly building nuclear weapons and aiding "international terrorists." He also urged the "people" of Iran to "liberate themselves" from their "unelected leaders."

The United States and Iran have entered a new cold war with one another in which both enjoy some advantages. On one hand, Iran is no match to the U.S. military—especially since it is now surrounded by American bases in Iraq, Afghanistan, Turkey, the Persian Gulf, and Central Asia. What is more, the United States could always further tighten the economic sanctions it has imposed on Iran ever since the 1979 hostage crisis. On the other hand, Iran, unlike Iraq and Afghanistan, is far too big a country to occupy—especially since the U.S. military is already overextended. Ironically, the United States, by invading these two countries, had eliminated Iran's two main regional enemies—Saddam Hussein in Iraq and the Taliban in Afghanistan. In addition, the Shi'i in Iraq and the anti-Taliban forces in Afghanistan are long-standing allies of Iran who could make the difficult American task in those occupied countries even more difficult if they chose to do so. Ironically, the United States, by invading these two countries, had eliminated Iran's two main local enemies—Saddam Hussein and the Taliban. And by occupying these two countries, it had also made itself more vulnerable to Iranian pressures since the Shi'i in Iraq and the anti-Taliban forces in Afghanistan had long-standing ties with Iran. The United States and Iran have entered a new cold war—one that is likely to last a long time.

Themes and Implications

Historical Junctures and Political Themes

The critical historical junctures discussed above have shaped contemporary Iran, especially the way it deals with the democratic idea, its role in the world of states, its attempts to govern the economy and meet the rising expectations of its citizens, and its need to overcome internal ethnic divisions.

In internal affairs, by far the most important challenge facing the republic is the task of reconciling Islam with democracy. Iran has been a Muslim country since the seventh century and Shi'i Muslim since the sixteenth century. It has also aspired to attain democracy, mass participation, and popular sovereignty since the 1905 constitutional revolution. The dual aspirations for Islam and for democracy culminated in the 1979 Islamic Revolution. Khomeini argued that Islam and democracy were compatible since the vast majority supported the clerics, had faith in them, respected them as the true interpreters of the *shari'a,* and wanted them to oversee the activities of state officials. Islam and democracy, however, appear less reconcilable now that the public has lost its enthusiasm for clerical rule. Some Khomeini followers have continued to give priority to his concept of theocracy, but others have begun to emphasize the need for democracy. In other words, Khomeinism has divided into two divergent branches in Iran: political liberalism and clerical conservatism.

The fate of democracy in Iran is bounded by the very nature of the *shari'a.* Democracy is based partly on the two principles that all individuals are equal, especially before the law, and that all people have inalienable natural rights, including the right to choose their own religion. The *shari'a,* at least in its traditional and conventional interpretations, rejects both of these democratic principles. Formulated in the seventh century, the *shari'a* is based on the principle of inequality, especially between men and women, between Muslims and non-Muslims, between legitimate minorities, known as the People of the Book, and illegitimate ones, known as unbelievers. In addition, the

shari'a, like all other religious law, not only considers rights to emanate from God rather than nature, but also deems the individual to be subordinate to the larger religious community. This is of special concern for Muslims who lose their faith or join another religion since the *shari'a* can condemn them to death as apostates. This is no mere technicality; over 250 Baha'is and over 400 leftist prisoners who professed atheism have been executed in Iran on just such grounds. But there are many moderate clerics in Iran who want to reform the *shari'a* to make it compatible with the modern concepts of individual freedom and human rights. They also favor treating those who do not believe in religion in the traditional manner of "don't ask, don't tell."

In international affairs, the Islamic Republic is determined to remain the dominant power in the Persian Gulf, even though it attained this position under the shah thanks mainly to the support of the United States. In his last years, the shah had become known as the American policeman in the Gulf region. By denouncing the United States as an "arrogant imperialist," canceling military agreements with the West, and condoning the taking of U.S. diplomats as hostages, Khomeini asserted Iranian autonomy in the region, but he also inadvertently prompted Saddam Hussein to launch the Iraq-Iran War. When Khomeini's government ministers suggested that the Persian Gulf be renamed the Muslim Gulf to improve relations with Arab countries, he responded that it should remain what it had always been: the Persian Gulf. Khomeini was as much an Iranian nationalist as a Muslim revolutionary.

Before he died, Khomeini initiated policies that have made it difficult for his successors to improve relations with the West, especially the United States. He called for revolutions throughout the Muslim world, denouncing Arab rulers in the region, particularly in Saudi Arabia, as the "corrupt puppets of American imperialism." He strengthened Iran's navy, and bought nuclear submarines from Russia. He launched a research program to build medium-range missiles and nuclear installations—possibly even nuclear weapons. He denounced the proposals for Arab-Israeli negotiations over Palestine. He sent money as well as arms to Muslim dissidents abroad, particularly Shi'i groups in Lebanon, Iraq, and Afghanistan. He permitted the intelligence services to assassinate some one hundred exiled opposition leaders living in Western Europe, and he issued the *fatwa* death decree against the British writer Salman Rushdie. These policies helped isolate Iran not only from the United States but also from the European Community, human rights organizations, and the United Nations. Khomeini's successors have had to grapple with this heritage, especially since these acts have direct bearing on economic development and prospects for obtaining foreign investment.

The Islamic Republic began with the conviction that it could rapidly develop the economy if it relied less on oil exports and more on agriculture and manufacturing. It blamed the shah for the single-export economy, the migration of peasants into the towns, the increasing gap in incomes, the continued high illiteracy rate, the lack of medical and educational facilities, and, in general, the low standard of living.

The new regime soon discovered that the country's underlying economic problems were formidable. Peasants continue to migrate to the cities because of the lack of both agricultural land and irrigation. Industry in Iran remains limited because of the lack of investment capital. Inflation and unemployment are high. Meanwhile, the population has steadily increased, and real per capita income has fallen due to forces outside the control of the state, particularly the price fluctuations of the international petroleum market. To deal with this economic crisis, some leaders have favored conventional state-interventionist strategies: price controls, five-year plans, and further redistribution of wealth through high taxation and social investment. Others have advocated equally conventional **laissez-faire** strategies: open markets, removal of state controls, more business incentives, and the wooing of foreign capital. Some clerics now openly admit that religion does not have answers to such problems as inflation, unemployment, and the volatility of world oil prices. This is a sharp contrast to the early days of the revolution, when Khomeini had confidently declared that Islam had all the solutions and that economics was a subject best left to "donkeys."

Finally, the Islamic Republic began with a strong and widely shared collective identity since 99 percent of Iran's population is Muslim. But this major asset was squandered in the two decades after the revolution. The stress on Shi'ism naturally alienated the 10 percent of Iranians who are Sunnis. In addition, the regime's insistence on a theocratic constitution on Khomeini's antagonized other top clerics as well as lay secular Muslims, who lead most of the political parties. Similarly, the inadvertent association of Shi'ism with the central Persian-speaking regions of Iran carries with it the potential danger of eventually alienating the important Turkic minority in Azerbaijan province. Thus, the Iranian regime, like most other developing states, has to solve the problem of how to allocate scarce resources without exacerbating ethnic, regional, and sectarian differences.

Implications for Comparative Politics

The Iranian Revolution, the emergence of religion as a force in Middle Eastern politics, and the collapse of the Soviet Union convinced many Americans that a new specter was haunting the West: that of Islamic fundamentalism. Some scholars predicted that a "clash of civilizations" would replace the cold war, arguing that the fault lines in world politics would no longer be over political ideology but over religion and culture. One of the main clashes would be between the West and the Muslim world, headed by the Islamic Republic of Iran.[10] Islam was seen as a major threat not only because of its size but also because it was deemed "inherently bellicose," "militant," and antagonistic to the West.

Such dire predictions have turned out to be gross exaggerations. It is true that the early Islamic Republic began denouncing the United States, arming militants in other parts of the Middle East, and calling for a struggle, sometimes termed a *jihad* (crusade), against the West. But these rhetorical denunciations have become muted, as reflected in the election of the reformist Muhammad Khatami as president. The call for Muslim unity has fallen on deaf ears, especially in Sunni countries, such as Saudi Arabia, which remains a very close ally of the United States. Iranian assistance to Shi'i Muslims is limited to Iraq, Lebanon, and Afghanistan. In Afghanistan, Iran even pressured its Shi'i allies to help the United States overthrow the Taliban after 9/11. In Iraq, it urged the Shi'i population not to resist the American invasion and to channel their activities into the electoral arena. What is more, Iranians themselves, including the clerics, have divided sharply into ultraconservative, conservative, liberal, and radical political camps. They even use the Western terms *left, right,* and *center* to describe themselves. Contemporary Iran shows that Muslim politics comes in many forms and, that as a blanket category, it has as little meaning as that of Christian politics. In the same way that one does not study the Bible to understand modern Europe, one does not need the Qur'an to analyze Middle Eastern politics.

Iran is a major power in the Middle East. It has one of the region's biggest armies and the largest navy in the Persian Gulf, a large land mass, considerable human resources, a respectable gross domestic product (GDP), and vast oil production. Iran also has plans, predating the Islamic Revolution, to become a nuclear power, which remains a major issue of tension in U.S.-Iranian relations.

But Iran is also, in many ways, a much weakened power. Its GDP is only about that of New Jersey, and its armed forces are a mere shadow of their former selves. The brutal eight-year conflict with Iraq (1980–1988) made the military war-weary. The officer ranks have been decimated by constant purges. The country's military hardware has been depleted by war, age, and lack of spare parts. In the last years of the shah, military purchases accounted for 17 percent of the GDP; they now account for 2 percent. Plans to build nuclear plants have been delayed, largely because the U.S. has successfully persuaded Europe not to transfer potentially dangerous technology to Iran.

Iran is unlikely to obtain nuclear weapons in the immediate future. Moreover, the United States, after 9/11 and the occupation of Iraq in March 2003, surrounded Iran with a string of military bases in the Gulf, Turkey, Azerbaijan, Georgia, Afghanistan, and Central Asia.

It is true that Iran has viewed itself as the vanguard of the Islamic world. But that world turns out to be as illusory for its champions as for its detractors. Just as there never was a communist monolith seeking global domination, the Muslim world is formed not of one unitary bloc but of many rival states, each with its own national self-interest. In theory, their rulers stress the importance of Islamic solidarity. In reality, they pursue conventional national interests, even allying with non-Muslims against Muslims, if necessary. For example, at the height of the American hostage crisis, Iran obtained military equipment from Israel and the United States to pursue the war against Iraq. Similarly, in recent years, Iran has sided with Hindu India against Muslim Pakistan, with Christian Armenia against Muslim Azerbaijan, and with Russia against Muslim Chechnya. Those who see the future as a clash of civilizations and a replay of the medieval Crusades forget that during those wars, both Muslims and Christians were often divided and sometimes sided against their own coreligionists. The Muslim world is no more united now than it was then. Iran, like its neighbors, formulates policies based on state and national interests, not on cultural, religious, and so-called civilizational sentiments.

Section ❷ Political Economy and Development

State and Economy

In 2002, Iran drafted a dramatically new investment law permitting foreigners to own as much as 100 percent of any firm in the country, to repatriate profits, to be free of state meddling, and to have assurances against both arbitrary confiscations and high taxation. Its intention was to attract foreign investments, especially from the European Union, and pave the way for joining the World Trade Organization (WTO). In the past, Iran's application to join the WTO had failed in

part because of its legal impediments against foreign investments and in part because of U.S. opposition. The new investment law was a far cry from the early days of the revolution when Khomeinists had vociferously denounced foreign investors as imperialist exploiters, waxed eloquent about economic self-sufficiency, and criticized the 1965 investment law, which limited foreign capital to less than 49 percent of any firm, as another example of the shah selling the country to Western corporations. Although some leaders continued to warn against Western consumerism and cultural imperialism, the regime as a whole was now eager to attract foreign investment and to rejoin the world economy.

The Economy in the Nineteenth Century

The integration of Iran into the world system began in a modest way in the latter half of the nineteenth century. Before then, commercial contact with the outside world had been limited to a few luxury goods and the famous medieval silk route to China. A number of factors account for this nineteenth-century integration: the economic concessions granted to the European powers; the opening up of the Suez Canal and the building of the Trans-Caspian and the Batum-Baku railways; the laying of telegraph lines across Iran to link India with Britain; the outflow of capital from Europe after 1870; and, most important, the Industrial Revolution in Europe and the subsequent export of European manufactured goods to the rest of the world.

In the course of the nineteenth century, Iran's foreign trade increased tenfold. Over 83 percent of this trade was with Russia and Britain; 10 percent with Germany, France, Italy, and Belgium; and less than 7 percent with countries in the Middle East. Exports were confined to carpets and agricultural products, including silk, raw cotton, opium, dried fruits, rice, and tobacco. Imports were mostly tea, sugar, kerosene, and such industrial products as textiles, glassware, and guns. Modest foreign investment also flowed into banking, fishing, carpet weaving, transport, and telegraph communications within Iran.

Contact with the West had far-reaching repercussions. It produced economic dependency, a situation common to much of the Third World, in which less developed countries become too reliant on developed countries; poorer nations are vulnerable to sudden fluctuations in richer economies and dependent on the export of raw materials, the prices of which often stagnate or decline, while the prices of the manufactured products they import invariably increase. Some scholars argue that this type of dependency lies at the root of the present-day economic problems in much of Africa, Latin America, and Asia, including the Middle East.

The nineteenth-century influx of mass-manufactured goods into Iran devastated some traditional handicrafts, especially cotton textiles. The import of cheap, colorful cotton goods undercut not only the local weavers, dyers, and carders but also the thousands of women who in the past had supplemented their family incomes with cottage industries and home spindles.[11] They naturally blamed foreign imports for their plight. Carpet manufacturers, however, benefited, since they found a ready market in Europe and North America.

The introduction of cash crops to be sold on the market, especially cotton, tobacco, and opium, reduced the acreage available for wheat and other edible grains. Many landowners ceased growing food and turned to commercial export crops. This paved the way for a series of disastrous famines in 1860, 1869–1872, 1880, and 1918–1920. Opium cultivation in Iran was particularly encouraged by British merchants eager to meet the rising demands of the Chinese market brought about by the notorious Opium Wars between China and Britain in the mid-nineteenth century.

Furthermore, the foreign competition, together with the introduction of the telegraph and the postal systems, brought many local merchants, shopkeepers, and workshop owners in the bazaars together into a national propertied middle class aware for the first time of their common interests against both the central government and the foreign powers. This new class awareness played an important role in Iran's constitutional revolution of 1905.

The Oil Economy

Deeper integration of Iran into the world system came in the twentieth century. Its main engine was oil. British prospectors struck oil in Khuzistan province in 1908, and the British government in 1912 decided to fuel its navy with petroleum rather than coal. It also decided to buy most of its fuel from the Anglo-Iranian Oil Company, in which it was a major shareholder. Iran's oil revenues increased modestly in the next four decades, reaching $16 million in 1951. After the nationalization of the oil industry in 1951 and the agreement with a consortium of U.S. and British companies in 1955, oil revenues rose steadily, from $34 million in 1955 to $5 billion in 1973 and, after the quadrupling of oil prices in 1974, to over $23 billion in 1976.

Between 1953 and 1978, Iran's cumulative oil income came to over $100 billion.

Oil became known as Iran's black gold. It financed over 90 percent of imports and 80 percent of the annual budget and far surpassed total tax revenues. Oil also enabled Iran not to worry about feeding its population, a problem that confronts many developing countries. Instead, it could undertake ambitious development programs that other states implemented only if they could squeeze scarce resources from their populations. In fact, oil revenues created in Iran what is known as a **rentier state,** a country that obtains a lucrative income by exporting raw materials or leasing out natural resources to foreign companies. Iran as well as Iraq, Algeria, and the Gulf states received enough money from their oil wells to be able to disregard their internal tax bases. The Iranian state thus became relatively independent of society. Society, in turn, had few inputs into the state. Little taxation meant little representation. It also meant that the state was totally reliant on one commodity, oil, whose worth was dependent on the vagaries of the world market.

Muhammad Reza Shah tried to reduce Iran's dependency on oil by encouraging other exports and attracting foreign investment into non-oil ventures. Neither policy succeeded. Despite some increase in carpet and pistachio exports, oil continued to dominate: on the eve of the 1979 Islamic revolution, it still provided 97 percent of the country's foreign exchange. Even after the oil boom, foreign firms, mostly U.S., European, and Japanese, invested no more than $1 billion in Iran, and much of this was not in industry but in banking, trade, and insurance. In Iran, as in the rest of the Middle East, foreign investors were put off by government corruption, labor costs, small internal markets, potential instability, and fear of confiscations. Apparently Western companies did not share their own government's confidence that Iran was an "island of stability" under the shah.

Society and Economy

Some oil revenue was squandered by Muhammad Reza Shah's regime on palaces, bureaucratic waste, outright corruption, ambitious nuclear projects, and ultrasophisticated weapons too expensive even for many NATO countries. But significant sums were also channeled into socioeconomic development. GNP grew at the average rate of 9.6 percent every year from 1960 to 1977, making Iran one of the fastest developing countries in the Third World at that time. The land reform project, the linchpin of the White Revolution, created over 644,000 moderately prosperous farms (see Table 1). The number of modern factories tripled from fewer than 320 to over 980 (see Table 2). Enrollment in primary schools grew from fewer than 750,000 to over 4 million; in secondary schools, from 121,000 to nearly 740,000; in vocational schools, from 2,500 to nearly 230,000; and in universities, from under 14,000 to more than 154,000. The Trans-Iranian Railway was completed, linking Tehran with Tabriz, Meshed, Isfahan, and the Gulf. Roads were built connecting most villages with the provincial cities.

Table 1

Land Ownership in 1977

Size (hectares)	Number of Owners
200+	1,300
51–200	44,000
11–50	600,000
3–10	1,200,000
Landless	700,000

Note: One hectare is equal to approximately 2.47 acres.
Source: E. Abrahamian, "Structural Causes of the Iranian Revolution," *Middle East Research and Information Project,* no. 87 (May 1980).

Table 2

Number of Factories

Size	1953	1977
Small (10–49 workers)	Fewer than 1,000	More than 7,000
Medium (50–500 workers)	300	830
Large (over 500 workers)	19	159

Source: E. Abrahamian, "Structural Causes of the Iranian Revolution," *Middle East Research and Information Project,* no. 87 (May 1980).

The expansion in health services was equally impressive. Between 1963 and 1977, the number of hospital beds increased from 24,126 to 48,000; medical clinics, from 700 to 2,800; nurses, from 1,969 to 4,105; and doctors, from 4,500 to 12,750. These improvements, together with the elimination of epidemics and famines, mainly due to food imports, lowered infant mortality and led to a population explosion. In the two decades prior to the 1979 revolution, the overall population doubled from 18 million to nearly 36 million. This explosion gave the country a predominantly youthful age structure. By the mid-1970s, half the population was under sixteen years of age. This was to have far-reaching repercussions in the street politics of 1977–1979 when young people were one of the driving forces leading up to the Islamic Revolution.

Socioeconomic development did not necessarily make the shah popular. On the contrary, his approach to development tended to increase his unpopularity with many sectors of Iranian society. The Industrial and Mining Development Bank channeled over $50 billion of low-interest loans to court-connected entrepreneurs, industrialists, and agribusinessmen. The shah believed that if economic growth benefited those who were already better off, some of the wealth that was produced would gradually trickle down to the lower levels of society. But in Iran, as elsewhere, the benefits of this development strategy got stuck at the top of society and never trickled down. By the mid-1970s, Iran was one of most unequal countries in the world in terms of income distribution.[12] Similarly, land reform, despite high expectations, created a small stratum of prosperous farmers but left the vast majority of peasants landless or nearly landless; over 1.2 million received less than 10 hectares (approximately 24.7 acres), not enough to survive as independent farmers given the productivity of agricultural land in Iran (see Table 1). Not surprisingly, many of the rural poor flocked to the urban shantytowns in search of work.

The factories spawned by the shah's modernization program drew criticism on the grounds that they were mere assembly plants and poor substitutes for real industrial development (see Table 3). His medical programs still left Iran with one of the worst doctor-patient ratios and child mortality rates in the Middle East. Educational expansion created only one place for

Table 3

Industrial Production

Product	1953	1977
Coal (tons)	200,000	900,000
Iron ore (tons)	5,000	930,000
Steel (tons)	—	275,000
Cement (tons)	53,000	4,300,000
Sugar (tons)	70,000	527,000
Tractors (no.)	—	7,700
Motor vehicles (no.)	—	109,000

Source: E. Abrahamian, "Structural Causes of the Iranian Revolution," *Middle East Research and Information Project,* no. 87 (May 1980), 22.

every five university applicants, failed to provide primary schools for 60 percent of children, and had no impact on the rate of illiteracy, which was 68 percent. In fact, the population explosion increased the absolute number of illiterates in Iran. The priority given to the development of Tehran increased disparities between the capital and the provinces. By the mid-1970s, Tehran contained half the country's doctors and manufacturing plants. According to one study, the per capita income in the richest provinces was ten times more than in the poorest ones. By the end of the shah's rule, Iran had the second highest (after Brazil) regional income disparity in the developing world.[13] According to another study, the ratio of urban to rural incomes was 5 to 1, making it one of the worst in the world.[14]

These inequalities created a **dual society** in Iran. On one side was the modern sector, headed by the elites with close ties to the oil state. On the other side was the traditional sector comprising the clergy, the bazaar middle class, and the rural masses. Each sector, in turn, was sharply stratified into unequal classes. Thus, Iranian society was divided vertically into the modern and the traditional, and horizontally into a number of urban as well as rural classes (see Figure 1).

The upper class—the Pahlavi family, the court-connected entrepreneurs, the military officers, and the senior civil servants—constituted less than 0.01 percent of the population. In the modern sector, the middle class—professionals, civil servants, salaried personnel, and college students—formed about 10

Iranian society was divided sharply not only into horizontal classes, but also into vertical sectors—the modern and the transitional, the urban and the rural. This is known as a dual society.

Figure 1

Iran's Class Structure in the Mid-1970s

Upper Class

Pahlavi Family; Court-Connected Entrepreneurs; Senior Civil Servants and Military Officers	0.1%

Middle Class

Traditional (Propertied) 13%	Modern (Salaried) 10%
Clerics Bazaaris Small Factory Owners Commercial Farmers	Professionals Civil Servants Office Employees College Students

Lower Classes

Rural 45%	Urban 32%
Landed Peasants Near Landless Peasants Landless Peasants Unemployed	Industrial Workers Wage-Earners in Small Factories Domestic Servants Construction Workers Peddlers Unemployed

percent of the population. The bottom of the modern sector—the urban working class, which included factory workers, construction laborers, peddlers, and unemployed—constituted over 32 percent. In the traditional sector, the middle class—bazaar merchants, small retailers, shopkeepers, workshop owners, and well-to-do family farmers—made up 13 percent. The rural masses—landless and near-landless peasants, nomads, and village construction workers—made up about 45 percent of the population.

The government's own statistics reveal the widening inequality. In 1972, the richest 20 percent of urban households accounted for 47.1 percent of total urban family expenditures; by 1977, it accounted for 55.5 percent. In 1972, the poorest 40 percent accounted for 16.7 percent of urban family expenditures; by 1977, it accounted for 11.7 percent (see Table 4).

These inequalities fueled resentments against the ruling elite, which were expressed more in cultural and

Table 4

Measures of Inequality of Urban Household Consumption Expenditures

Year	Percentage Share in Total Expenditures		
	Poorest 40%	Middle 40%	Richest 20%
1972	16.7	36.2	47.1
1977	11.7	32.8	55.5

Source: V. Nowshirvani and P. Clawson, "The State and Social Equity in Postrevolutionary Iran," in M. Weiner and A. Banuazizi (eds.), *The Politics of Social Transformation in Afghanistan, Iran, and Pakistan* (Syracuse, N.Y.: Syracuse University Press, 1994), 248.

religious terms than in economic and class terms. Among those who articulated these resentments was a gadfly writer named Jalal Al-e-Ahmad (1923–1969). A former communist who had rediscovered his Shi'i roots in the 1960s, Al-e-Ahmad shook his contemporaries by publishing a polemical pamphlet entitled *Gharbzadegi* (*The Plague from the West*). He argued that the ruling class was destroying Iran by mindlessly imitating the West; neglecting the peasantry; showing contempt for popular religion; worshipping mechanization, regimentation, and industrialization; and flooding the country with foreign ideas, tastes, luxury items, and mass-consumption goods. He stressed that developing countries such as Iran could survive this "plague" of Western imperialism only by returning to their cultural roots and developing a self-reliant society, especially a fully independent economy. Al-e-Ahmad inspired the long search for cultural authenticity and economic self-sufficiency that would culminate in the Islamic Revolution of 1979.

These themes were developed further by another young intellectual, Ali Shariati (1933–1977). Studying in Paris during the turbulent 1960s, Shariati was influenced by Marxist sociology, Catholic liberation theology, the Algerian revolution, and, most important, Frantz Fanon's theory of violent Third World revolutions against colonial oppression as laid out in his book, *Wretched of the Earth*. Shariati returned home with what can be called a fresh and revolutionary interpretation of Shi'ism, echoes of which would later appear in Khomeini's writings.

Shariati argued that history was a continuous struggle between oppressors and oppressed. Each class had its own interests, its own interpretations of religion, and its own sense of right and wrong, justice and injustice, morality and immorality. To help the oppressed, Shariati believed, God periodically sent down prophets, such as Abraham, Moses, Jesus, and Muhammad. Muhammad had been sent to launch a dynamic community in "permanent revolution" toward the ultimate utopia: a perfectly classless society.

Although Muhammad's goal had been betrayed by his illegitimate successors, the caliphs, his radical message had been preserved for posterity by the Shi'i imams, especially by Imam Husayn, who had been martyred to show future generations that human beings had the moral duty to fight oppression in all places at all times. Shariati equated Imam Husayn with

Che Guevara, the Latin American guerrilla fighter who helped lead the Cuban Revolution and was killed in Bolivia in 1967. According to Shariati, the contemporary oppressors were the imperialists, the modern-day feudalists, the corrupt capitalists, and their hangers-on, especially the "tie-wearers" and "the palace dwellers," the carriers of the "Western plague." He criticized the conservative clerics who had tried to transform revolutionary religion into an apolitical public opiate. Shariati died on the eve of the 1979 revolution, but his prolific works were so widely read and so influential that many felt that he, rather than Khomeini, was the true theorist of the Islamic Revolution.

Iran in the Global Economy

Under the Shah

The oil boom in the 1970s gave the shah the opportunity to play a significant role in international politics. As the second most important member (after Saudi Arabia) of the **Organization of Petroleum Exporting Countries (OPEC),** Iran could cast decisive votes for raising or moderating oil prices. At times, the shah curried Western favor by moderating prices. At other times, he pushed for higher prices to finance his ambitious projects and military purchases. These purchases rapidly escalated once President Richard Nixon began to encourage U.S. allies, such as the shah, to take a greater role in policing their regions. Moreover, Nixon's secretary of state, Henry Kissinger, openly argued that the United States should finance its ever-increasing oil imports, most of them from the Persian Gulf, by exporting more military hardware to the region. The shah was now able to buy from the United States almost any weapon he desired. Arms dealers began to jest that the shah read their technical manuals in the same way that some men read *Playboy*. The shah's arms buying from the United States jumped from $135 million in 1970 to a peak of $5.7 billion in 1977. Between 1955 and 1978, Iran spent more than $20.7 billion on U.S. arms alone.

This military might gave the shah a reach well beyond his immediate boundaries. He occupied three small but strategically located Arab islands in the Strait of Hormuz, thus controlling the oil lifeline through the Persian Gulf but also creating distrust among his Arab neighbors. He talked of establishing a presence well beyond the Gulf on the grounds that Iran's national interests reached into the Indian Ocean. "Iran's military expenditures," according to a 1979 U.S. congressional report, "surpassed those of the most powerful Indian Ocean states, including Australia, Indonesia, Pakistan, South Africa, and India."[15]

In the mid-1970s, the shah dispatched troops to Oman to help the local sultan fight rebels. He offered Afghanistan $2 billion to break its ties with the Soviet Union, a move that probably prompted the Soviets to intervene militarily in that country. The shah, after supporting Kurdish rebels in Iraq, forced Baghdad to concede to Iran vital territory on the Shatt al Arab estuary. This had been a bone of contention between the two countries ever since Iraq had come into existence after World War I. A U.S. congressional report summed up Iran's overall strategic position: "Iran in the 1970s was widely regarded as a significant regional, if not global, power. The United States relied on it, implicitly if not explicitly, to ensure the security and stability of the Persian Gulf sector and the flow of oil from the region to the industrialized Western world of Japan, Europe, and the United States, as well as to lesser powers elsewhere."[16]

These vast military expenditures, as well as the oil exports, tied Iran closely to the industrial countries of the West and to Japan. Iran was now importing millions of dollars' worth of rice, wheat, industrial tools, construction equipment, pharmaceuticals, tractors, pumps, and spare parts, the bulk of which came from the United States. Trade with neighboring and other developing countries was insignificant. In the words of the U.S. Department of Commerce, "Iran's rapid economic growth [provided America with] excellent business opportunities."[17]

The oil revenues thus had major consequences for Iran's political economy, all of which paved the way for the Islamic Revolution. They allowed the shah to pursue ambitious programs that inadvertently widened class and regional divisions within the dual society. They drastically raised public expectations without necessarily meeting them. They made the rentier state independent of society. They also made Iran an oil-addicted rentier state highly dependent on oil prices and imported products and vulnerable to the world market. Economic slowdowns in the industrial countries could lead to a decline in their oil demands, which could diminish Iran's ability to buy such essential goods as food, medicine, and industrial spare parts. One of the major promises made by the Islamic Revolution was to end this economic dependency on oil and the West.

Iran's Economy Under The Islamic Republic

The Islamic Republic began with high hopes of rapidly developing the economy and becoming fully independent of oil and the West. The results have been mixed.

The main economic problem plaguing the Islamic Republic has been instability in the world oil market despite OPEC's attempts to preserve prices by limiting production and setting quotas for its members. The price of a barrel of oil, which had quadrupled from $5 to $20 in 1974, peaked at $52 in late 1980 but plunged sharply thereafter, reaching $18 in 1985, hovering around $12 to $14 in the late 1980s and 1990s, and descending to a new low of $10 in 1999. This meant that Iran's oil revenues, which continued to provide the state with 80 percent of its hard currency and 75 percent of its total revenues, fell from $20 billion in 1978 to less than $10 billion in 1998. They did not improve until the early 2000s when oil prices began to edge upwards again. Still a rentier state, Iran remains vulnerable to the vagaries of the international petroleum market.

The decline in oil prices during the 1980–1990s was due to a number of factors outside Iran's control: the slackening of the demand in the industrialized countries (especially with the recession in the late 1990s); the glutting of the international market by the entry of non-OPEC producers, such as Britain and Mexico; and the tendency of some OPEC members to preserve their revenues by cheating on their production quotas. Iran's oil revenues were also affected by the war with Iraq and its own failure to raise production. In some years, Iran was not able to meet even its OPEC quotas. To raise oil production, Iran needs an influx of capital and new deep-drilling technology, both of which can be found only in the West. This explains why the Islamic Republic has so dramatically changed its policy towards foreign investment.

Iran's economic problems have been compounded by the population explosion, the Iran-Iraqi war, and the emigration of some 3 million Iranians. The annual population growth rate, which had hit 2.5 percent in the late 1970s, jumped to nearly 4 percent by the late 1980s, mainly because the new regime encouraged large families. This was the highest rate in the world, causing a major strain on government resources, especially social services and food imports. The Iraqi war not only hurt the oil industry but also wrought as much as $600 billion in property damage whole border cities were flattened. It also led to half a million Iranian casualties. The Islamic Revolution itself frightened many professionals and highly skilled technicians, as well as wealthy entrepreneurs, and industrialists into fleeing to the West. Of course, they carried their portable assets with them.

The overall result was a twenty-year economic crisis that lasted into the late 1990s. GNP fell 50 percent, per capita income declined 45 percent, and inflation hovered around 20 to 30 percent every year. The value of real incomes, including salaries and pensions, dropped by as much as 60 percent. Unemployment hit 20 percent; over two-thirds of entrants into the labor force could not find jobs. The absolute number of illiterates increased. Peasants continued to flock to urban shantytowns. Tehran grew from 4.5 million to 12 million people. The total number of families living below the poverty level increased. By the late 1990s, over 9 million urban dwellers lived below the official poverty line.[18] Shortages in foreign exchange curtailed vital imports, even of essential manufactured goods. The value of the currency plummeted. Before the revolution, the U.S. dollar had been worth 70 Iranian rials; by 1998, it was worth as much as 1,750 rials on the official exchange rate, and more than 9,000 rials on the black market. What is more, the regime that came to power advocating self-sufficiency now owed foreign banks and governments over $30 billion, forcing it to renegotiate foreign loans constantly.

Despite this ongoing economic crisis, the Islamic Republic has scored some notable successes. The Reconstruction Ministry, established mainly for the rural population, built 30,000 miles of paved roads, 40,000 schools, and 7,000 libraries. It brought electricity and running water to more than half of the country's 50,000 villages. The number of registered vehicles on the roads increased from 27,000 in 1990 to over 2.9 million in 1996. More dams and irrigation canals were built, and the Agricultural Ministry distributed some 630,000 hectares of confiscated arable land to peasants and gave farmers more favorable prices, especially for wheat. By the late 1990s, most independent farmers had such consumer goods as radios, televisions, refrigerators, and pickup trucks. The extension of social services narrowed the gap between town and country and between the urban poor and the middle classes. The adult literacy rate grew from 50 percent to 76 percent, and by 2000 the literacy rate among those in the six to twenty-nine age range hit 97 percent. The infant mortality rate fell from 104 per 1,000 in the mid-1970s to 30 per 1,000 in 2003. Life expectancy climbed from fifty-five years in 1979 to sixty-eight in 1993 and further to seventy in 2004—one of the best in the Middle East. The UN estimates that by 2000, 94 percent of the population had access to health services and 95 percent to safe water. On the whole, the poor in Iran are better off now than their parents had been before the Islamic Revolution. Moreover, the country, despite initial setbacks, was able to become more self-sufficient in food production. By the mid-1990s, it was importing no more than 5 percent of its wheat, rice, sugar, and meat requirements. The regime has also been able to diversify foreign trade and become less dependent on the West. By 2000, Iran's main trade partners were Japan, South Korea, and Russia.

The Islamic Republic also made major strides toward population control. At first, it closed down birth control clinics, claiming that Islam approved of large families and that Iran needed workers. But it reversed direction once the ministries responsible for social services felt the full impact of this growth. The regime also realized that only food imports could meet the rising demands. In 1989, the government declared that Islam favored healthy rather than large families and that one literate citizen was better than ten illiterate ones. It reopened birth control clinics, cut subsidies to large families, and announced that the ideal family should consist of no more than two children. It even took away social benefits from those having more than two children. By 2003, the regime could boast that it had reduced the annual population growth to 1.2 percent. This is an impressive accomplishment. It is also a sign that the regime is highly pragmatic when it comes to economic issues.

The 2000–2005 rise in petroleum prices—from $19 per barrel in 1999 to $53 per barrel in 2005—further helped the situation. Oil revenues jumped from less than $10 billion in 1998 to over $28 billion in 2001 and $30 billion in 2004. Foreign reserves increased to $4.8 billion, wiping out the external debt, stabilizing the currency, and improving the country's creditworthiness. Iran became one of the few developing countries to be free of foreign debt and was even able set aside some oil revenues as a hedge against leaner times. The GDP grew 7.4 percent in 2002 and 6.6 percent in 2003. Both the official unemployment and inflation rates, while still high, have fallen, and the currency has stabilized. The

government has floated its first international bond and, despite U.S. opposition, foreign investments—to the tune of $12 billion—have been contracted to flow into oil and gas ventures, petrochemicals, minerals, and car factories. The World Bank lent Iran $232 million for medical services and sewage lines, again despite American opposition. Oil revenues have allowed the government to channel additional funds into the infrastructure, especially power stations, hydroelectric dams, and education. The earlier oil bust had brought Iran economic stagnation; the new boom has brought it some hope.

Section ❸ Governance and Policy-Making

Iran's political system is unique in the contemporary world. It is a theocracy with important democratic features. It is a theocracy (which means, from the Greek, "God's power") for the simple reason that the clergy—in other words, the theologians—control the most powerful political positions. The system nevertheless contains elements of democracy with some high officials, including the president, elected directly by the general public.

Organization of the State

The Iranian state rests on the Islamic constitution designed by the Assembly of Religious Experts immediately after the 1979 revolution. It was amended between April and June 1989 during the last months of Khomeini's life by the Council for the Revision of the Constitution, which was handpicked by Khomeini himself. The final document, with 175 clauses and some 40 amendments (ratified by a nationwide referendum in July 1989) is a highly complex mixture of theocracy and democracy.

The constitution's preamble affirms faith in God, Divine Justice, the Qur'an, the Day of Judgment, the Prophet Muhammad, the Twelve Imams, the eventual return of the Hidden Imam (the Mahdi), and, of course, Khomeini's doctrine of jurist's guardianship that give supreme power to senior clergy. All laws, institutions, and state organizations have to conform to these "divine principles."

The Leader

The constitution named Khomeini to be the Leader for life on the grounds that the public overwhelmingly recognized him as the "most just, pious, informed, brave, and enterprising" of the senior clerics—the grand ayatollahs. It further described him as the Leader of the Revolution, the Founder of the Islamic Republic, and, most important, the imam of the whole community. It stipulated that if no single Leader emerged after his death, then all his authority would be passed on to a leadership council of senior clerics. After Khomeini's death, however, his followers so distrusted the other senior clerics that they did not set up such a council. Instead, they elected one of their own, Ali Khamenei, a middle-ranking cleric, to be the new Leader. Most of Khomeini's titles, with the exception of imam, were bestowed on Khamenei. The Islamic Republic has often been described as a regime of the ayatollahs (high-ranking clerics). It could be more aptly called a regime of the hojjat al-Islams (middle-ranking clerics), since few senior clerics want to be associated with it. None of the grand ayatollahs and few of the ordinary ayatollahs subscribed to Khomeini's notion of jurist's guardianship. On the contrary, most disliked his radical populism and political activism.

The constitution gives wide-ranging powers to the Leader. Enshrined as the vital link between the three branches of government, he can mediate between the legislature, the executive, and the judiciary. He can

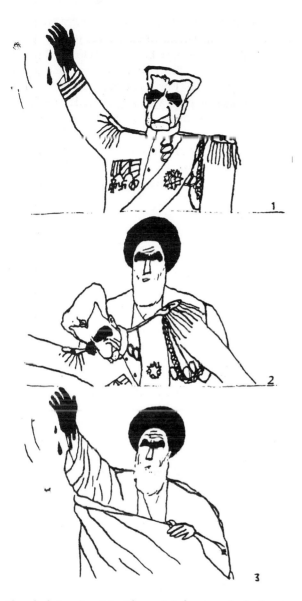

The shah turning into Khomeini, from an émigré newspaper. *Source:* Courtesy Nashriyeh.

"determine the interests of Islam," "supervise the implementation of general policy," and "set political guidelines for the Islamic Republic." He can eliminate presidential candidates as well as dismiss the duly elected president. He can grant amnesty. As commander in chief, he can mobilize the armed forces, declare war and peace, and convene the Supreme Military Council. He can appoint and dismiss the commanders of Revolutionary Guards as well as those of the regular army, navy, and air force.

The Leader has extensive power over the judicial system. He can nominate and remove the chief judge, the chief prosecutor, and the revolutionary tribunals. He can dismiss lower court judges. He also nominates six clerics to the powerful twelve-man Guardian Council, which can veto parliamentary bills. It has also obtained (through separate legislation) the right to review all candidates for elected office, including the presidency and the national legislature, the *Majles.* The other six members of the Guardian Council are jurists nominated by the chief judge and approved by the *Majles.* Furthermore, the Leader appoints the powerful **Expediency Council,** which has the authority to resolve differences between the Guardian Council and the *Majles* (the legislature) and to initiate laws on its own.

The Leader is also authorized to fill a number of important nongovernment posts: the preachers (**Imam Jum'ehs**) at the main city mosques, the director of the national radio-television network, and the heads of the main religious endowments, especially the **Foundation of the Oppressed** (see below). By 2001, the Office of the Leader employed over six hundred in Tehran and had representatives placed in the most sensitive institutions throughout the country. The Leader has obtained more constitutional powers than dreamed of by the shah.

The later constitutional amendments expanded and transformed the Assembly of Religious Experts into an eighty-six-man house elected every four years. Packed with clerics, the assembly not only elected Khamenei as Khomeini's successor but also reserved the right to dismiss him if it found him "mentally incapable of fulfilling his arduous duties." In effect, the Assembly of Religious Experts has become an upper chamber to the *Majles.* Its members are required to have a seminary degree equivalent to a master's degree. Figure 2 illustrates the hierarchy established by the constitution of the Islamic Republic of Iran.

The general public elects the *Majles,* the president, and the Assembly of Religious Experts. But the Leader and the Guardian Council decide who can compete in these elections.

The general public elects the *Majles,* the president, and the Assembly of Religious Experts. But the Supreme Leader and the cleric-dominated Guardian Council decide who can compete in these elections.

Figure 2

The Islamic Constitution

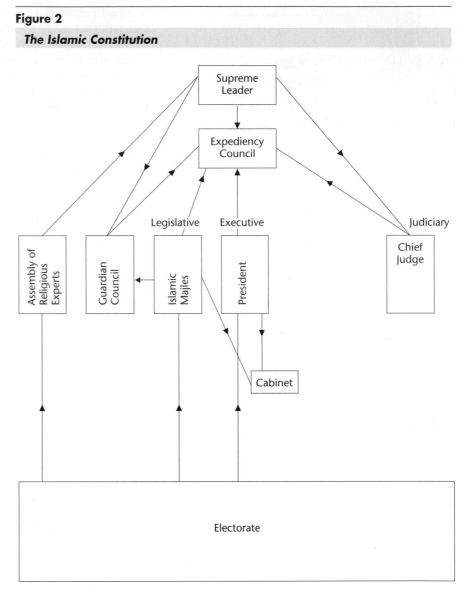

Because the constitution is based on Khomeini's theory of jurist's guardianship, it gives wide-ranging judicial powers to the Leader in particular and to the clerical strata in general. Laws are supposed to conform to the religious law, and the clergy are regarded as the ultimate interpreters of the *shari'a.* In fact, the constitution makes the judicial system the central pillar of the state, overshadowing the executive and the legislature. Bills passed by the Islamic *Majles* are reviewed by the Guardian Council to ensure that they conform to the *shari'a.* All twelve members of this Guardian Council are either clerics or lay jurists knowledgeable in the *shari'a.* The minister of justice is chosen by the president but needs the approval of both the *Majles* and the chief judge. The judicial system itself has been Islamized all the way down to the district courts, with seminary-trained jurists replacing university-educated judges. The Pahlavis purged the clergy from the judicial system; the Islamic Republic purged the university-educated.

The Executive

The President and the Cabinet

The constitution, particularly after the amendments, reserves some power for the president. He is described as the chief executive and the highest state official after the Leader. He is chosen every four years through a national election. He must be a pious Shi'i faithful to the principles of the Islamic Republic. He cannot be elected to more than two terms. He draws up the annual budget, supervises economic matters, and chairs the plan and budget organization. He can propose legislation to the *Majles*. He conducts the country's internal and external policies. He signs all international treaties, laws, and agreements. He chairs the National Security Council responsible for defense matters. The president has the power to select the vice presidents and cabinet ministers. A separate parliamentary law, however, stipulates that he has to choose his minister of intelligence from the ranks of the clergy.

The president appoints most senior officials, including provincial governors, town mayors, and ambassadors. Furthermore, he names the directors of some of the large public organizations, such as the National Iranian Oil Company, the National Electricity Board, and the National Bank.

Khomeini often promised that trained officials would run the executive branch in the Islamic Republic, but clerics—also called mullahs have, in fact, dominated the presidency. Of the five presidents since the revolution, three have been mullahs: Khamenei, Rafsanjani, and Khatami. The main exception, Abol-Hasan Bani-Sadr, was ousted in 1981 precisely because he denounced the regime as "a dictatorship of the mullahtariat," comparing it to a communist-led "dictatorship of the proletariat." The fifth was assassinated.

The Bureaucracy

The president, as the chief of the executive branch, heads a huge bureaucracy. In fact, this bureaucracy continued to proliferate after the revolution, even though Khomeini had often taken the shah to task for having a bloated government. It expanded, for the most part, to provide jobs for the many college and high school graduates. On the eve of the revolution, the ministries had 300,000 civil servants and 1 million employees. By the early 1990s, they had over 600,000 civil servants and 1.5 million employees. The Iranian Revolution, like many others, ended up creating a bigger bureaucracy.

Leaders: Ayatollah Ali Khamenei

Ali Khamenei succeeded Khomeini as Leader in 1989. He was born in 1939 in Meshed into a minor clerical family originally from Azerbaijan. He studied theology under Khomeini in Qom and was briefly imprisoned in 1962. Active in the anti-shah opposition movement in 1978, he was given a series of influential positions immediately after the revolution, even though he held only the middle-level clerical rank of hojjat al-Islam. He became Friday prayer leader of Tehran, head of the Revolutionary Guards, and, in the last years of Khomeini's life, president of the republic. After Khomeini's death, he was elevated to the rank of Leader even though he was neither a grand ayatollah nor a recognized senior expert on Islamic law. He had not even published a theological treatise. The government-controlled media, however, began to refer to him as an ayatollah. Some ardent followers even referred to him as a grand ayatollah qualified to guide the world's whole Shi'i community. After his elevation, he built a constituency among the regime's more diehard elements: traditionalist judges, conservative war veterans, and antiliberal ideologues. Before 1989, he often sported in public a pipe, a mark of an intellectual, but gave up the habit upon becoming Leader.

Among the most important ministries of the Islamic Republic are Culture and Islamic Guidance, which has responsibility for controlling the media and enforcing "proper conduct" in public life; Intelligence, which has replaced the shah's dreaded SAVAK as the main security organization; Heavy Industries, which manages the nationalized factories; and Reconstruction, which has the dual task of expanding social services and taking "true Islam" into the countryside. Its mission is to build bridges, roads, schools, libraries, and mosques in the villages so that the peasantry will learn the basic principles of Islam. "The peasants," declared one cleric, "are so ignorant of true Islam that they even sleep next to their unclean sheep."[19]

The clergy dominate the bureaucracy as they do the presidency. They have monopolized the most sensitive ministries—Intelligence, Interior, Justice, and Culture and Islamic Guidance—and have given posts in other ministries to their relatives and protégés. These ministers appear to be highly trained technocrats, sometimes with advanced degrees from the West, but in fact are powerless individuals chosen by, trusted by, and related to the ruling clergy.

Semipublic Institutions

The Islamic Republic has set up a number of semipublic institutions. They include the Foundation of the Oppressed, the Alavi Foundation (named after Imam Ali), the Martyrs Foundation, the Pilgrimage Foundation, the Housing Foundation, the Foundation for the Publication of Imam Khomeini's Works, and the Fifteenth of Khordad Foundation, which commemorates the date (according to the Islamic calendar) of Khomeini's 1963 denunciation of the shah's White Revolution. Although supposedly autonomous, these foundations are directed by clerics appointed personally by the Leader. According to some estimates, their annual income may be as much as half that of the government.[20] They are exempt from paying state taxes and are allocated foreign currencies, especially U.S. dollars, at highly favorable exchange rates subsidized by the oil revenues. Most of their assets are property confiscated from the old elite.

The largest of these institutions, the Foundation for the Oppressed, administers over 140 factories, 120 mines, 470 agribusinesses, and 100 construction companies. It also owns the country's two leading newspapers, *Ettela'at* and *Kayhan.* The Martyrs Foundation, in charge of helping war veterans, controls confiscated property that was not handed over to the Foundation for the Oppressed. It also receives an annual subsidy from the government. These foundations together control $12 billion in assets and employ over 400,000 people. They can be described as states within a state—or rather, as clerical fiefdoms favored by the Leader.

Leaders: Sayyid Muhammad Khatami

Muhammad Khatami was elected president of the Islamic Republic in 1997 and reelected in 2000. He was born in 1944 into a prominent clerical family in central Iran. His father, an ayatollah, was a close friend of Khomeini. His mother came from a prosperous landed family. He studied theology in Qom and philosophy at Isfahan University. At the outbreak of the revolution, he was in charge of a Shi'i mosque in Germany. After the revolution, he first headed a state publishing house, was a member of the *Majles,* and then served as minister of culture and Islamic guidance. Arousing the wrath of the conservatives, he resigned from the last post in 1992 and took up the teaching of philosophy at Tehran University. He uses the title *sayyid* and wears a black turban to indicate that he is a male descendant of the Prophet. Although a cleric by appearance and training, he seems to many more like a university professor interested in liberal political philosophy.

Other State Institutions

The Military

The clergy have taken special measures to control Iran's armed forces—both the regular military of 370,000, including 220,000 conscripts, and the irregular forces formed of 120,000 Revolutionary Guards established immediately after 1979, and 200,000 volunteers of the Mobilization of the Oppressed (*Basej-e Mostazafin*) created during the war against Iraq. The Leader, as commander in chief, appoints the chiefs of staff as well as the top commanders. He also fills the post of defense minister with his own confidant, who reports directly to him, bypassing the president and the cabinet. Moreover, he places chaplains in military units to watch over regular officers.

After the revolution, the new regime purged the top ranks of the military, placed officers promoted from the ranks of the Revolutionary Guards in command positions over the regular divisions, and built up the Revolutionary Guards as a parallel force with its own uniforms, budgets, munitions factories, recruitment centers, and even small air force and navy. According to the constitution, the regular army defends the borders, while the Revolutionary Guards protect the republic from internal enemies. Despite these measures, political sentiments within the regular military about the Islamic Republic remain unknown, if not ambivalent, especially among the 18,000 professionals in the navy, 45,000 in the air force, and 150,000 in the regular army.

The Judiciary

The Islamic Republic regime Islamized the judiciary by enacting a penal code, the Retribution Law, based on a reading of the *shari'a* that was so narrow that it prompted many modern-educated lawyers to resign in disgust, charging that it contradicted the United Nations Charter on Human Rights. It permitted injured families to demand blood money on the biblical and Qur'anic principle of "an eye for an eye, a tooth for a tooth, a life for a life." It mandated the death penalty for a long list of "moral transgressions," including adultery, homosexuality, apostasy, drug trafficking, and habitual drinking. It sanctioned stoning, live burials, and finger amputations. It divided the population

into male and female and Muslims and non-Muslims, and treated them unequally. For example, in court, the evidence of one male Muslim is equal to that of two female Muslims. The regime also passed a "law on banking without usury" to implement the *shari'a* ban on all forms of interest taking and interest giving.

Although the law was Islamized, the modern centralized judicial system was not dismantled. For years, Khomeini argued that in a truly Islamic society, the local *shari'a* judges would pronounce final verdicts without the intervention of the central authorities. Their verdicts would be swift and decisive. This, he insisted, was the true spirit of the *shari'a*. After the revolution, however, he discovered that the central state needed to retain ultimate control over the justice system, especially over life and death issues. Thus, the revolutionary regime retained the appeals system, the hierarchy of state courts, and the power to appoint and dismiss all judges. State interests took priority over the spirit of the *shari'a*.

Practical experience led the regime to gradually broaden the narrow interpretation of the *shari'a*. To permit the giving and taking of interest, without which modern economies would not function, the regime allowed banks to offer attractive rates as long as they avoided the taboo term *usury*. To meet public sensitivities as well as international objections, the courts rarely implemented the harsh penalties stipulated by the *shari'a*. They adopted the modern method of punishment, imprisonment, rather than the traditional one of corporal public punishment. By the early 1990s, those found guilty of breaking the law were treated much as they would be in the West: fined or imprisoned rather than flogged in the public square.

Subnational Government

Although Iran is a highly centralized state, it is divided administratively into provinces, districts, subdistricts, townships, and villages. Provinces are headed by governors-general, districts by governors, subdistricts by lieutenant governors, towns by mayors, and villages by headmen.

The constitution declares that the management of local affairs in every village, town, subdistrict, district, and province will be under the supervision of councils whose members would be elected directly by

Leaders: *Hojjat al-Islam Ali-Akbar Hashemi Rafsanjani Ali-Akbar*

Rafsanjani was born in 1934 into a fairly prosperous business and farming family in the heartland of the Shi'i and Persian-speaking provinces. He studied in Qom under Khomeini; found himself in prison four times during the 1960s; set up a number of commercial companies, including one that exported pistachios; and wrote a book praising a nineteenth-century prime minister who had made an abortive attempt to industrialize the country. Nevertheless, Rafsanjani remained active enough in clerical circles to be considered a hojjat al-Islam. After the revolution, he became a close confidant of Khomeini and attained a number of cabinet posts, culminating with the presidency in 1989. After serving two four-year terms, the maximum allowed by the constitution, he was given the chairmanship of the powerful Expediency Council. In some ways, his institutional power rivals that of President Khatami, but not, of course, that of Leader Khamenei.

the local population. It also declares that governors-general, governors, mayors, and other regional officials appointed by the Interior Ministry have to consult local councils. These clauses creating local councils had been incorporated into the constitution mainly because of mass demonstrations organized in 1980 by the left—notably the Mojahedin and the Fedayin. The **Assembly of Experts** would have preferred to have remained silent on the issue.

Because of conservative opposition, no steps were actually taken to hold council elections until 1999 when Khatami, the new president, insisted on holding the country's very first nationwide local elections. Over 300,000 candidates, including 5,000 women, competed for 11,000 council seats—3,900 in towns and 34,000 in villages. Khatami's supporters won a landslide victory, taking 75 percent of the seats, including twelve of the fifteen in Tehran. The top vote getter in Tehran was Khatami's former interior minister, who had been impeached by the conservative *Majles* for issuing too many publishing licenses to reform-minded journals and newspapers. These elections showed that the vitality of participatory democracy on the grassroots. But in February 2003, in a second round of local elections, conservatives won fourteen of the fifteen council seats in Tehran. This political swing was due largely to widespread voter abstention. Following appeals by reformers for their supporters to boycott the elections, only about 10 percent of the electorate in Tehran cast ballots.

The Policy-Making Process

Policy-making in Iran is highly complex in part because of the cumbersome constitution and in part because factionalism within the ruling clergy has resulted in more amendments, which have made the original constitution even more complicated. Laws can originate in diverse places, and they can be modified by pressures coming from numerous directions. They can also be blocked by a wide variety of state institutions. In short, the policy-making process is highly fluid and diffuse, often reflecting the regime's factional divisions.

The clerics who destroyed Iran's old order remained united while building the new one. They formed a distinct social stratum as well as a cohesive political group. They were convinced that they alone had the divine mandate to govern. They followed the same leader, admired the same texts, cited the same potent symbols, remembered the same real and imaginary indignations under the shah, and, most important, shared the same vested interest in preserving the Islamic Republic. Moreover, most had studied at the same seminaries and came from the same lower-middle-class backgrounds. Some were even related to each other through marriage and blood ties.

But once the constitution was in place, the same clerics drifted into two loose but identifiable blocs: the Society (*Majmu'eh*) of the Militant Clergy, and the Association (*Jam'eh*) of the Militant Clergy. The former can be described as statist reformers or populists, and the latter as laissez-faire (free-market) conservatives. The radicals hoped to consolidate lower-class support by using state power for redistributing wealth, eradicating unemployment, nationalizing enterprises, confiscating large estates, financing social programs, rationing and subsidizing essential goods, and placing price ceilings on essential consumer goods. In short, they espoused the creation of a comprehensive welfare state. The conservatives hoped to retain middle-class support, especially in the bazaars, by removing price controls, lowering business taxes, cutting red tape, encouraging private entrepreneurs, and balancing the budget, even at the cost of sacrificing subsidies and social programs. In recent years, the statist reformers have begun to emphasize the democratic over the theocratic features of the constitution, stressing the importance of individual rights, the rule of law, and government accountability to the electorate. In many ways, they have become like social democrats the world over.

The conservatives were originally labeled middle-of-the-roaders and traditionalists. The statists were labeled progressives, seekers of new ideas, and followers of the imam's line. The former liked to denounce the latter as extremists, leftists, and pro-Soviet Muslims. The latter returned the insult by denouncing the free-marketers as medievalists, rightists, capitalists, mafia bazaaris, and pro-American Muslims. Both could bolster their arguments with apt quotes from Khomeini.

This polarization created a major constitutional gridlock since the early Islamic *Majles* was dominated by the reformers, whereas the Guardian Council was controlled by the conservatives who had been appointed by Khomeini. Between 1981 and 1987, over one hundred bills passed by the reformer-dominated *Majles* were vetoed by the Guardian Council on the grounds that they violated the *shari'a,* especially the sanctity of private property. The vetoed legislation included a labor law, land reform, nationalization of foreign trade, a progressive income tax, control over urban real estate transactions, and confiscation of the property of émigrés whom the courts had not yet found guilty of counterrevolutionary activities. Introduced by individual deputies or cabinet ministers, these bills had received quick passage because the

The clerical regime and its two stilts: the sword and the oil wells. *Source:* Courtesy *Mojahed* (in exile).

radical statists controlled the crucial *Majles* committees and held a comfortable majority on the *Majles* floor. Some ultraconservatives had countered by encouraging the faithful not to pay taxes and instead to contribute to the grand ayatollahs of their choice. After all, they argued, one could find no mention of income tax anywhere in the *shari'a.*

Both sides cited the Islamic constitution to support their positions. The conservative free-marketers referred to the long list of clauses protecting private property, promising balanced budgets, and placing agriculture, small industry, and retail trade in the private sector. The reformers referred to an even longer list promising education, medicine, jobs, low-income housing, unemployment benefits, disability pay, interest-free loans, and the predominance of the public sector in the economy.

To break the constitutional gridlock, Khomeini boldly introduced into Shi'ism the Sunni Islamic concept of **maslahat**—that is, "public interest" and "reasons of state." Over the centuries, Shi'i clerics had denounced this as a Sunni notion designed to bolster illegitimate rulers. Khomeini now claimed that a truly Islamic state could safeguard the public interest by suspending important religious rulings, even over prayer, fasting, and the pilgrimage to Mecca. He declared public interest to be a primary ruling and the others mere secondary rulings. In other words, the state could overrule the views of the highest-ranking clerics. In the name of public interest, it could destroy mosques, confiscate private property, and cancel religious obligations. Khomeini added that the Islamic state had absolute authority, since the Prophet Muhammad had exercised absolute (*motalaq*) power, which he had passed on to the imams and thus eventually to the Islamic Republic. Never before had a Shi'i religious leader claimed such powers for the state, especially at the expense of fellow clerics.

As a follow-up, Khomeini set up a new institution named the Expediency Council for Determining the Public Interest of the Islamic Order—known for short as the Expediency Council. He entrusted it with the task of resolving conflicts between the Islamic *Majles* and the Guardian Council. He packed it with thirteen clerics, including the president, the chief judge, the Speaker of the *Majles,* and six jurists from the Guardian Council. The Expediency Council eventually passed some of the more moderate bills favored by the reformers. These included a new income tax, banking legislation, and a much-disputed labor law providing workers in large factories with a minimum wage and some semblance of job security.

The constitutional amendments introduced after Khomeini's death institutionalized the Expediency Council. The new Leader could now not only name its members but also determine its tenure and jurisdiction. Not surprisingly, Khamenei packed it with his supporters—none of them prominent grand ayatollahs. He also made its meetings secret and allowed it to promulgate new laws rather than restrict itself to resolving legislative differences between the Guardian Council and the *Majles.* In effect, the Expediency Council is now a secretive supraconstitutional body accountable only to the Leader. In this sense, it has become a powerful body rivaling the Islamic *Majles* even though it did not exist in the original constitution. By 2002, the Expediency Council contained thirty-two members. These included the president; chief judge; speaker of the *Majles;* ministers of intelligence, oil, culture, and foreign affairs; chief of the General Staff; commander of the Revolutionary Guards; jurists from the Guardian Council; directors of radio and television as well as of the Central Bank, Atomic Energy Organization, and National Oil Company; heads of the main religious foundations; chairman of the Chamber of Commerce; and editors of the main conservative newspapers. Seventeen were clerics. These thirty-two can be considered the inner circle of the ruling elite.

Section ❹ Representation and Participation

Although the Islamic Republic is predominantly a theocracy, some claim that it is also a democracy. According to the constitution, the general electorate chooses the president as well as the Assembly of Experts, which in turn chooses the Leader. What is more, the elected legislature, the *Majles,* exercises considerable power, and according to one of the founders of the regime, it is the centerpiece of the Islamic constitution.[21] Another architect of the constitution has argued that the people, by carrying out the Islamic Revolution, implicitly favored a type of democracy confined within the boundaries of Islam and the guardianship of the jurist.[22] But another declared that if he had to choose between the democracy and power of the clergy as specified in the concept of jurist's guardianship, he would not hesitate to choose the latter since it came directly from God.[23] On the eve of the initial referendum, Khomeini himself declared: "This constitution, which the people will ratify, in no way contradicts democracy. Since the people love the clergy, have faith in the clergy, want to be guided by the clergy, it is only right that the supreme religious authority oversee the work of the [government] ministers to ensure that they don't make mistakes or go against the Qur'an."[24]

The Legislature

According to Iran's constitution, the *Majles* "represents the nation" and is granted many powers, including enacting or changing ordinary laws (with the approval of the Guardian Council), investigating and supervising all affairs of state, and approving or ousting the cabinet ministers. In describing this branch of government, the constitution uses the term *qanun* (statutes) rather than *shari'a* (divine law) so as to gloss over the fundamental question of whether legislation passed by the *Majles* is derived from God or the people. It accepts the rationale that God formulates divine law (*shari'a*) but elected representatives can draw up worldly statutes (*qanuns*).

The *Majles* has 290 members and is elected by citizens over the age of sixteen. It can pass *qanun* as long as the Guardian Council deems them compatible with the *shari'a* and the constitution. It can choose, from a list drawn up by the chief judge, six of the twelve-man Guardian Council. It can investigate at will cabinet ministers, affairs of state, and public complaints against the executive and the judiciary. It can remove cabinet members—with the exception of the president—through a parliamentary vote of no confidence. It can withhold approval for government budgets, foreign loans, international treaties, and cabinet appointments. It can hold closed debates, provide members with immunity from arrest, and regulate its own internal workings, especially the committee system.

The *Majles* plays an important role in everyday politics in Iran. On occasion, it has changed government budgets, criticized cabinet policies, modified development plans, and forced the president to replace some of his ministers. In 1992, 217 deputies circulated an open letter that explicitly emphasized the prerogatives of the *Majles* and thereby implicitly downplayed those of the Leader. Likewise, the speaker of the House in 2002 threatened to close down the whole *Majles* if the judiciary violated parliamentary immunity and arrest one of the liberal deputies.

Political Parties and the Party System

Iran's constitution guarantees citizens the right to organize, and a law passed in 1980 permits the Interior Ministry to issue licenses to political parties. But political parties were not encouraged until Khatami's 1997 election as president. Since then, three parties have been active: the Islamic Iran Participation Front and the Islamic Labor Party, both formed by Khatami reformist supporters, and the conservative Servants of Reconstruction created by Hojjat al-Islam Ali-Akbar Hashemi Rafsanjani, the former president and now chairman of the Expediency Council. According to the Interior Ministry, licenses have been granted to some seven hundred political, social, and cultural organizations, but all are led by people deemed politically acceptable by the regime. Real political opposition has been forced into exile, mostly in Europe. The most important opposition groups are

- **The Liberation Movement.** Established in 1961 by Mehdi Bazargan, the Islamic Republic's first prime minister. Bazargan had been appointed premier in February 1979 by Khomeini himself, but had resigned in disgust ten months later when the Revolutionary Guards had permitted students to take over the U.S. embassy. The Liberation Movement is a moderate Islamic party, which despite its religious orientation is secular and favors the strict separation of mosque from state.
- **The National Front.** Originating in the campaign to nationalize the country's oil resources in the early 1950s, the National Front remains committed to Mossadeq's twin political ideals of nationalism and secularism. Because the conservative clergy feel threatened by the National Front's potential appeal, they have banned the organization.
- **The Mojahedin.** Formed in 1971 as a guerrilla organization to fight the shah's regime, the Mojahedin tried to synthesize Marxism and Islam. It interpreted Shi'i Islam to be a radical religion favoring equality, social justice, martyrdom, and redistribution of wealth. Immediately after the

revolution, the Mojahedin opposed the clerical regime and attracted a large following among students. The regime retaliated with mass executions, forcing the Mojahedin to move their base of operations to Iraq. Not unexpectedly, the Mojahedin became associated with a national enemy and thereby lost much of its appeal.

- **The Fedayin.** Also formed in 1971, the Fedayin modeled itself after the Marxist guerrilla movements of the 1960s in Latin America, especially those inspired by Che Guevara and the Cuban revolution. Losing more fighters than any other organization in the struggle against the shah, the Fedayin came out of the revolution with great mystique and popular urban support. But it soon lost much of its strength because of massive government repression and a series of internal splits.

- **The Tudeh (Party of the Masses).** Established in 1941, the Tudeh is a mainstream, formerly pro-Soviet communist party. Although the Tudeh initially supported the Islamic Republic as a "popular anti-imperialist state," it was banned, and most of its organizers were executed during the 1980s.

Elections

Iran's constitution promises free elections. In practice, however, *Majles* elections have varied from relatively free but disorderly in the early days of the republic, to controlled and highly unfair in the middle years, and back again to relatively free—and now orderly—in the last decade. The main obstacle to fair elections has been the Guardian Council with its powers to approve all candidates. For example, in 1996, this Council excluded over 44 percent of some 5,000 parliamentary candidates by questioning their loyalty to the concept of jurist's guardianship. Electoral freedom is also restricted by the government-controlled radio-television network, the main source of information for the vast majority. The Interior Ministry can ban dissident organizations, especially their newspapers on the grounds that they are anti-Islamic. In some years, especially in the 1980s, ballot boxes were placed in mosques with Revolutionary Guards supervising the voting. Neighborhood clerics were on hand to help illiterates complete their ballots. Club-wielding gangs, the pro-regime Hezbollahis, assaulted their opponents.

Moreover, the electoral law, based on a winner-take-all majority system rather than on proportional representation, was designed to minimize the voice of the opposition. There have been seven elections since the founding of the Islamic Republic in 1979. The course and the outcomes of those elections reveal a lot about the evolution of representation and participation in Iran.

The First Majles (1980)

In the election in 1980 for the First *Majles* after the revolution, there were over 4,400 candidates, over 40 parties, over 200 dailies and weeklies, and thousands of political organizations in the bazaars, campuses, high schools, factories, and offices. The parties represented the whole range of the ideological spectrum from the far right to the extreme left. By shattering the old state structures, the revolution had unleashed a wide variety of political, social, and ethnic groups. It was as if, after years of silence, every professional and occupational association, every political party and ideological viewpoint, and every interest and pressure group rushed into the open to air its views, print its newspapers and broadsheets, and field its parliamentary candidates.

On the political right was the Islamic Republican Party (IRP), established immediately after the revolution by Khomeini's closest disciples. It had the support of the Islamic Chamber of Commerce, Islamic Association of Bazaar Guilds, Islamic Association of Teachers, Islamic Association of University Students, Association of Qom Seminary Teachers, and, most important of all, Association of Militant Clergy. Not surprisingly, it championed Khomeini's notion of jurist's guardianship.

At the center was Bazargan's Liberation Movement, which favored free markets, limited government, cordial relations with the United States, and a pluralistic political system. It also advocated a liberal interpretation of Islam, arguing that the clergy should advise rather than rule. Bazargan was a veteran of the nationalist movement against the British, but also liked to couch his politics with quotations from Islamic scriptures.

Closely allied with the Liberation Movement was the National Front, which was led by Western-educated, middle-aged professionals and technocrats. Unlike the Liberation Movement, they avoided making political use of Islam and separated politics from religion and treated the latter as a private matter.

The political left in the 1980 elections was fragmented into religious and nonreligious groups. The religious left included Islamic yet anticlerical groups such as the Mojahedin, Movement of Militant Muslims, and Movement for the Liberation of the Iranian People. The nonreligious groups included Marxist and ethnic parties: the Tudeh, the Fedayin, the Kurdish Democratic Party, and at least a dozen smaller Marxist-Leninist organizations. To complicate matters further, Abul-Hassan Bani-Sadr, a left-leaning French-educated intellectual supporter of Khomeini who had been elected president of Iran in January 1980, fielded his own candidates. Many of these parties had their own student, labor, professional, and women's organizations. Tehran alone had over a dozen women's organizations.

Not surprisingly, the elections for this First *Majles* were extremely lively, even though the IRP manipulated the state machinery to favor its candidates. On the eve of the voting, the minister of the interior declared that all were free to run, but only "true Muslims" would be permitted to sit in parliament.[25] Some 80 percent of the electorate participated in the first round.

The competition in the 1980 election was so intense in some constituencies that the Interior Ministry stepped in, impounded the ballot boxes, harassed candidates, and indefinitely postponed the second round of run-off elections. By the time the second round was held, the regime had cracked down on the opposition, forcing Bani-Sadr into exile, banning many leftist parties, and executing hundreds of Mojahedin.

Of the 216 deputies elected in 1980, 120 were supporters of the IRP, 33 of Bani-Sadr (who were later purged), and 20 of the Liberation Movement. Thirty-three described themselves as independents. Some of these had their parliamentary credentials promptly rejected on the grounds that documents found in the recently occupied U.S. embassy "proved" them to be U.S. spies. The IRP had won only 35 percent of the popular vote but had collected over 60 percent of the seats in the *Majles*. The Mojahedin, on the other hand, got 25 percent of the popular vote but did not obtain a single seat. In the end, the conservative IRP wound up

with a solid majority in the Islamic Republic's first "elected" legislature.

The Second Majles (1984)

The elections for the Second *Majles* were carried out under very different circumstances. The spring of the Iranian Revolution was over. The opposition was now either banned outright or else highly restricted in its activities. The IRP monopolized the political scene, manipulating state institutions and controlling a vast array of organizations, including large foundations, local mosques, Revolutionary Guards, and thousands of town preachers. Not surprisingly, it won a landslide victory, leaving a few seats to independent-minded clerics with their own local followings. Also not surprisingly, voter participation fell sharply, to less than 60 percent, even though Khomeini declared that abstaining was tantamount to betraying Islam. Over 54 percent of the 270 deputies were clerics, almost all middle ranking.

The Third (1988), Fourth (1992), and Fifth (1996) Majleses

In 1987, Khomeini abruptly dissolved the IRP. No official reason was given, but the decision was prompted by the intense conflict within the party between statists demanding economic reforms and conservative free marketers favoring the bazaars. One radical deputy claimed that "the party had been infiltrated by opportunistic time-servers pretending to be devout followers of the Imam's Line."[26]

In dissolving the IRP, Khomeini declared that the clergy were free to establish two competing organizations as long as both opposed imperialism, communism, and capitalism, but supported Islam, the Islamic Republic, and the jurist's guardianship. "Political differences," he commented, "are natural. Throughout history our religious authorities have differed among themselves. . . . Besides Iranians should be free to express themselves."[27] He could have added, "within reason and within the context of Islam as defined by myself."

In preparation for the 1988 elections, the reformers left the Association of Militant Clergy and formed their own Society of Militant Clergy. From then on, there were two rival clerical organizations: on one side, the statist reformers with their Society and at least five major newspapers; on the other side, the conservative free marketers with their Association and a major newspaper called *Resalat (Message)*. The conservatives became known as the Resalat group. Both groups had adherents in the seminaries and among the local preachers (Imam Jum'ehs).

The reformers won the lackluster elections for the Third *Majles*. The new parliament had eighty-six clerics, a 23 percent decline from the previous assembly. This, however, did not signify the demise of clerical power. Some clerics had gone on to higher positions, especially to the Assembly of Religious Experts. Moreover, many of the new lay deputies were young protégés of the clerics recruited into their fold from the students who had taken over the U.S. embassy.

Although the reformist clerics began the Third *Majles* with a clear majority, their influence soon ebbed because of Khomeini's death in June 1989, and because the new Leader Khamenei and President Rafsanjani began to adopt free-market policies once the war with Iraq ended. During the war, both men had been vocal advocates of price controls, rationing, high taxes, nationalization, and large government budgets. Now, with peace, they argued that the best way to jump-start the economy was to encourage private enterprise and cut state expenditures. In his eulogy for the late founder of the Islamic Republic, Rafsanjani downplayed Khomeini as the revolutionary leader of the downtrodden and instead praised him as a world-famous statesman who had restored Iran's national sovereignty.

In the following months, Rafsanjani, and to a lesser extent Khamenei, asked their followers to put away "childish slogans" and acknowledge the fact that the revolution had been "guilty of excesses." They talked increasingly of realism, stability, efficiency, managerial skills, work discipline, expertise, individual self-reliance, modern technology, entrepreneurship, and business incentives. They warned that the worst mistake a state could make was to spend more than its revenue. Rafsanjani declared, "Some people claim that God will provide. They forget that God provides only for those willing to work." Khamenei sermonized on how Imam Ali, the founder of Shi'i Islam, had taken great pride nourishing his plantations. Khomeini had often depicted Imam Ali as a humble water carrier; Khamenei now depicted him as an entrepreneurial plantation owner.

To ensure a smooth change of course, Khamenei handed over control of the two main newspapers, *Kayhan* and *Ettela'at,* to the conservatives and authorized the Guardian Council to monitor the 1992 *Majles* elections. The Guardian Council announced that all candidates had to prove their "practical commitment to the Leader and the Islamic Republic." The Council further restricted the campaign to one week, permitting candidates to speak in mosques and run newspaper advertisements but not to debate each other in open forums. The head of the Guardian Council announced that he would use pesticides to cleanse parliament of anyone with "difficult attitudes." Seventy-five radical candidates withdrew. Forty were disqualified by the Guardian Council. Only a handful of reformers were allowed to be elected. Voter participation dropped to a new low. In Tehran, less than 55 percent of the eligible voters bothered to cast ballots despite Khamenei's proclamation that every true Muslim had the "religious obligation to vote."

Ayatollah Khalkhali, a prominent judge, was barred from running on the grounds that he did not have appropriate theological training. He retorted that conservatives who had sat out the revolution were now weaseling their way into the Guardian Council. Another disqualified candidate, who had earlier dismissed human rights as a "foreign conspiracy," now complained that the Guardian Council had violated his rights by failing to inform him of why he had been barred. The Guardian Council replied that its reasons had been kept out of the mass media in order to protect both state secrets and the public reputations of those deemed unqualified. Those who had been purged were expected to be grateful for this sensitivity. It also argued that it had followed precedent, reminding reformers that they themselves had used similar procedures to keep out "undesirables" from the previous three parliaments.

The conservative purge of the *Majles* was relatively easy to carry out. For one thing, the extensive constitutional powers entrusted to the Leader left the reformers vulnerable. As Hojjat al-Islam Mohtashami, a leading reformer, complained, the institution of jurist's guardianship was now being used to clobber revolutionary heads. When reformers complained that they were being slandered as traitors for merely questioning the turn to free-market economic policies, their opponents countered that disobedience to the Leader was tantamount to disobedience to God. They argued that only proponents of "American Islam" would dare question the decisions of the Leader. They also reminded them that the new oath of office required parliamentary deputies to obey the Leader as the Vice Regent of the Hidden Twelfth Imam." Khamenei may not have inherited Khomeini's title of imam, but he had obtained the new exalted position of the Hidden Imam's Vice Regent.

The conservatives also threw populist rhetoric at the reformers. They described them as the "newly moneyed class" and as "Mercedes-Benz clerics." They accused them of misusing official positions to line their own pockets, give lucrative contracts to their friends, and deceive the masses with unrealistic promises. "They," exclaimed one conservative, "act like a giant octopus, giving with one tentacle but taking away with the others." They also placed the responsibility for the country's economic malaise squarely on the shoulders of the radicals. They argued that a decade of the kind of statist policies favored by the reformers had increased poverty, illiteracy, inflation, unemployment, and slum housing. Before the revolution, these problems were blamed on the shah and his family. Now they were blamed on the "pseudo-clerical radicals."

The purge was so decisive that immediately after the Fourth *Majles* elections the reformers temporarily suspended the activities of their Society of Militant Clergy. Some reformers went to head foundations, seminaries, and libraries. Others began to write for newspapers, arguing that the public should choose the Leader and that the Guardian Council should stay out of the electoral process. Yet others remained in the political arena, mildly criticizing the regime and quietly awaiting a better day.

This expectation was not far-fetched. The conservative majority began to splinter once President Rafsanjani implemented probusiness policies. He relaxed price controls, liberalized imports, ended rationing, disbanded courts that penalized price gougers, returned some confiscated property, and ended all talk of land reform, nationalization, and income distribution. He also set up a stock exchange in Tehran and free-trade zones in the Persian Gulf. Some 170 deputies associated with Khamenei supported these measures but continued to favor highly conservative policies in the cultural realm. They demanded strict control over the media, silencing of liberal intellectuals, and rigid implementation of the dress code for women. They were also reluctant to challenge the financial privileges of the large foundations or open up the economy to international and émigré capital; they saw foreign competition as a threat to the bazaar. Meanwhile, some forty deputies, associated more with President Rafsanjani, favored cultural liberalization and the attraction of foreign capital as well as the probusiness policies. They also favored balancing the budget by downsizing the clerical foundations and cutting state subsidies. The remaining sixty deputies were independent, voting sometimes with the cultural conservatives, sometimes with the cultural liberals.

To get a working majority, President Rafsanjani had to water down his programs. He took only limited measures to privatize large enterprises, trim the foreign exchange privileges of the huge clerical foundations, and cut subsidies that absorbed much of the oil revenue. Moreover, he was unable to increase business taxes; all the taxes raised by the bazaar guilds together still constituted less than 9 percent of the government's annual tax income. Moreover, he had to shelve his daring bill designed to attract foreign investment. This bill would have raised the share that foreign interests could own in Iranian enterprises from 49 percent to 100 percent. It would have been a total policy reversal since the Islamic revolutionaries had relished accusing the shah of selling the country to foreign capitalists. Rafsanjani now argued that he could not revive the ailing economy without an injection of massive foreign capital.

Frustrated by these setbacks, Rafsanjani created a new political organization, Servants of Reconstruction, to run candidates for the Fifth *Majles*. Although supported by many cabinet ministers and the popular mayor of Tehran, who had made the city livable by building highways, libraries, and parks, Rafsanjani's party won only eighty seats. Over 140 seats went to the conservatives, who were able to prevent the implementation of economic and cultural changes favored by Rafsanjani. The conservative judiciary also imprisoned the mayor of Tehran on trumped-up embezzlement charges and closed down the newspaper, *Zanan* (*Women*), edited by Rafsanjani's daughter, on the grounds that it had offended religious sensibilities. Furthermore, term limits inevitably turned Rafsanjani into a lame duck president.

The Sixth Majles (2000)

The upset victory of the reform-minded Khatami in Iran's 1997 presidential election paved the way for the Sixth *Majles* elections in 2000, the first to be both orderly and competitive since the founding of the Islamic Republic. The reformers—labeling themselves the Khordad Front after the month (in the Iranian calendar) when Khatami had won the presidency—ran a highly successful campaign in 2000. The Khordad Front brought together the Islamic Iran Participation Front (headed by Khatami's brother); the Society of Militant Clergy; the Islamic Labor Party and the Workers House, a quasi-union; the Mojahedin Organization of the Islamic Revolution (a twenty-year-old group of reformist technocrats not to be confused with the guerrilla Mojahedin); a new campus organization called the Office for Strengthening Solidarity; a number of recently established and highly popular newspapers; and a host of liberal Muslim organizations, including the Islamic Association of Women. The Front was even supported, at least initially, by former president Rafsanjai's Servants of Reconstruction.

The associations that backed the Kordad Front had previously been proregime but had started to speak out in favor of a free press, government accountability, and fewer privileges for the clergy. Their views were articulated by a number of prominent intellectuals and journalists who had started their careers as staunch regime supporters—some had even participated in the takeover of the U.S. embassy in 1979–1980—but who had come to the conclusion that the democratic features of the constitution should take priority over the theocratic ones.

The best known of these intellectuals was Abdol-Karim Soroush who had been a follower of the Islamist ideologue Shariati. But Soroush now argued that Islam had become an "overbloated ideology" transgressing its true role in the realm of personal ethics and individual morality. He and his fellow reformers often denounced intolerant conservatives as "religious fascists." If the works of Shariati and Khomeini had been replete with concepts like revolution, imperialism, cultural roots, martyrdom, the dispossessed, and the Western plague, those of Soroush and the new reformers were full of concepts such as pluralism, democracy, freedom, equality, modernity, citizenship, dialogue, civil society, human rights, rule of law, and political participation. These reformers not only championed democratic concepts but also tried to make them compatible with Islam.

The reformers won the Sixth *Majles* elections in 2000 in a landslide, winning 80 percent of the vote in a campaign that drew over 70 percent of the electorate. In elections held for the Assembly of Experts a few months earlier, the reformers had abstained, and consequently voter participation had dropped to 46 percent. Over 6,800 candidates competed for the 290 seats in the Sixth *Majles*. Although the Guardian Council barred some prominent reformers from the election, it permitted most to participate, probably because of pressure from the Leader. Many supporters of secular parties—all banned from the campaign—voted for the reformers, who won over 195 seats. Candidates endorsed by the most prominent conservative organizations won fewer than forty seats, while the total number of "turbaned deputies" (clerics) fell to a new low of thirty-seven. President Khatami's brother, who had created the reformist Islamic Iran Participation Party, topped the winners in Tehran. Many prominent conservatives with long experience in high positions failed to get elected. Even the country's religious capital, Qom, voted overwhelmingly for the reformers. Former president Rafsanjani, who in the last days had openly courted the conservatives, was humiliated. He came in thirtieth in the first round of the Tehran election and quietly withdrew instead of continuing in the runoffs. After the elections, the London *Economist* magazine commented: "Iran, although an Islamic state, imbued with religion and religious symbolism, is an increasingly anti-clerical country. In a sense, Iran resembles some Roman Catholic countries where religion is taken for granted, without public display, and with ambiguous feeling towards the clergy. Iranians tend to mock their mullahs, making mild little jokes about them; they certainly want them out of their bedrooms. In particular, they dislike their political clergy."[28]

In the next two years, the reformist majority in the *Majles* drew up over one hundred bills, some of which implicitly challenged the conventional interpretations of the *shari'a*. The measures supported by the reformers eliminated the distinction between men and women, Muslims and non-Muslims, in weighing court evidence and awarding compensation. They raised the marriageable age for girls from nine to fifteen; gave scholarships to women to study abroad; ruled that divorce courts should divide property on an equal basis between husbands and wives; allowed women deputies to wear the *hejab* (headscarf) rather than the *chadour* (full covering); permitted school girls to wear colorful clothing; and ratified the UN Declaration on the Elimination of Discrimination against Women—a declaration too egalitarian even for the U.S. Congress. They permitted private banking, denationalized some enterprises, unified the exchange rate, diminished the privileges enjoyed by the clerical foundations, and liberalized the foreign investment law, thereby attracting some capital from Europe and Japan. The reformers purged the Intelligence Ministry of "rogue elements" who had carried out a series of political assassinations. They set up committees to investigate prison conditions and hosted a visit from the European Union's Commission on Human Rights. They proposed a special press court—outside the authority of the conservative judiciary—to handle libel and censorship cases. They nourished a "thousand flowers to bloom" by channeling subsidies into cultural activities and encouraging the publication as well as translation of thousands of works. They stipulated that trials were to be held before juries; that the function of the prosecutor was separate from that of the judge; that judges in serious cases had to have at least ten years' experience; that defendants had the right to counsel and access to their families; and that prisoners under no circumstances were to be blindfolded, deprived of sleep, or placed in solitary confinement. Equally contentious, they passed a bill (which was later vetoed) transferring the authority to approve parliamentary candidates and supervise elections from the Guardian Council to the Interior Ministry.

The conservative Guardian Council as well as the judiciary—often supported by the Leader—retaliated against the reformers. They vetoed much of their legislation on the grounds that they violated the *shari'a* and the constitution. They closed down over fifty papers in what became known as the "great newspaper massacre," and hauled reformist journalists before the courts, accusing them of libel, slander, and blasphemy. They even tried unsuccessfully to strip deputies of parliamentary immunity.

Far more serious, the Guardian Council—this time even against the advice of the Leader—barred some 3,533 candidates including 87 reform deputies—among them Khatami's brother—from running in the Seventh *Majles* elections in 2004. Another 40 deputies resigned in protest. Ironically this drastic purge was greatly facilitated by the United States—both by President Bush's Axis of Evil speech and by the military occupation of Afghanistan and Iraq. Reluctant to rock the boat at a time of apparent and imminent national danger, most reformers restrained themselves and withdrew from active politics. Not surprisingly, the conservatives won a hollow victory in the 2004 elections. They received a clear majority, but the voter turnout was less than 51 percent, and in Tehran only 28 percent. This was the worst showing since 1979. For a regime that liked to boast about mass participation, this was seen as a major setback—even as a crisis of legitimacy.

The 2005 Presidential Elections

These elections were a mirror image of the 1997 presidential elections—except in reverse. Mahmoud Ahmadinezhad, a little known forty-nine-year-old university lecturer who had been appointed mayor of Tehran by the conservatives, won not only a surprise but a landslide surprise victory over Rafsanjani, the well-known seventy-year old ex-president now running on a broad reform platform that included the hope to improve relations with the United States. Ahmadinezhad received 17.2 million votes (62 percent); Rafsanjani, 10 million (36 percent). The turnout, however, was considerably less than in 1997. The following four reasons explain the reversal of fortunes.

First, the reformers were sharply divided. Some encouraged their followers to boycott the election as a protest against the Leader and the Guardian Council. Others had to split their votes among two reform candidates in addition to Rafsanjani.

Second, Ahmadinezhad skillfully tapped into class resentments. He campaigned on the theme that he was a hard-working "man of the people" who could speak on their behalf against "nepotism," "cronyism," "elitism," "corruption," "profiteering," and "luxury living." While keeping the language of reform and development, he revived Khomeini's populist rhetoric about the "mostazafin," "social justice," and "palace dwellers." He argued that the "real problem" confronting the nation had little to do with "what people wore," but much to do with jobs, decent wages, work conditions, housing, pensions, health coverage, and unemployment insurance. He opposed privatization, favored interest-free loans for small farmers, and advocated more state expenditures for welfare programs and the underdeveloped provinces. He implied that his main rival had siphoned off oil revenues to his family. These themes resonated well among the poor; for, although their actual standard of living had improved since the revolution, their relative standard of living compared to the upper middle class had not. What is more, the regime has so far failed to meet their rising expectations. These themes also resonated since he himself came from a poor family and had achieved success by doing well in university examinations and by volunteering to fight in the Iraqi war. His own father had been a blacksmith—an occupation potent with symbolic meaning since the Robin Hood of Iranian mythology had been a blacksmith. On the eve of the elections, Ahmadinez had invited television crews into his home where the public could see that he lived in a modest working class apartment—in sharp contrast to his competitor.

Third, Ahmadinez had received military support. On the eve of the elections, the heads of the revolutionary guards, the basij militia, and veteran organizations encouraged their members to rally votes for him. It is estimated these forces, together with their families, could muster some six million votes. This helped expand the conservative "base," which in the previous elections had been no more than 20 percent of the electorate.

Finally, the Bush administration inadvertently helped the conservatives. The administration's vocal calls for "regime change," together with the invasions of Afghanistan and Iraq, the courting of such unpopular exiles as the Mojahedin, the establishment of military bases around the country, and the insistence that the nuclear program should be dismantled, created within Iran the fear that the country was in "mortal danger." Such a mood inevitably undermined the reformers whom the public associated with the West. Some reformers blamed the Bush administration for undermining their position. Conversely, some conservatives thanked the administration.

Political Culture, Citizenship, and Identity

In theory, the Islamic Republic of Iran should be a highly viable state. After all, Shi'ism is the religion of both the state and the vast majority of the population. Shi'ism can also be described as the central component of Iranian popular culture. Moreover, the constitution guarantees basic rights to religious minorities as well as to individual citizens. All citizens, regardless of race, color, language, or religion, are promised the rights of free expression, worship, and organization. They are guaranteed freedom from arbitrary arrest, torture, and police surveillance.

The constitution extends additional rights to the recognized religious minorities: Christians, Jews, and Zoroastrians. Although Christians (Armenians and Assyrians), Jews, and Zoroastrians form just 1 percent of the total population, they are allocated five *Majles* seats. They are permitted their own community organizations, including schools, their own places of worship, and their own family laws. The constitution, however, is ominously silent about Baha'is and Sunnis. The former are deemed heretics from Islam; the latter are treated in theory as full citizens but their actual status is not spelled out.

The constitution also gives guarantees to non-Persian speakers. Although 83 percent of the population understands Persian, thanks to the educational system, over 50 percent continue to speak non-Persian languages at home—languages such as Azeri, Kurdish, Turkic, Gilaki, Mazandarani, Arabic, and Baluchi. The constitution promises them rights unprecedented in Iranian history. It states that "local and native languages can be used in the press, media, and schools." It also states that local populations have the right to elect provincial, town, and village councils. These councils can watch over the governors-general and the town mayors, as well as their educational, cultural, and social programs.

These generous promises have often been honored more in theory than in reality. The local councils—the chief institutional safeguard for the provincial minorities—were not convened until twenty years after the revolution. Subsidies to non-Persian publications and radio stations remain meager. Jews have been so harassed as "pro-Israeli Zionists" that more than half—40,000 out of 80,000—have left the country since the revolution. Armenian Christians have had to end co-educational classes, adopt the government curriculum, and abide by Muslim dress codes, including the veil. The Christian population has declined from over 300,000 to fewer than 200,000.

The Baha'is, however, have borne the brunt of religious persecution. Their leaders have been executed as "apostates" and "imperialist spies." Adherents have been fired from their jobs, had their property confiscated, and been imprisoned and tortured to pressure them to convert to Islam. Their schools have been closed, their community property expropriated, and their shrines and cemeteries bulldozed. It is estimated that since the revolution, one-third of the 300,000 Baha'is have left Iran. The Baha'is, like the Jews and Armenians, have migrated mostly to Canada and the United States. This persecution did not ease until the election of President Khatami in 1997.

The Sunni population, which forms as much as 10 percent of the total, has its own reasons for being alienated. The state religion is Shi'ism, and high officials have to be Shi'i. Citizens must abide by Khomeini's concept of jurists' guardianship, a notion derived from Shi'ism. Few institutions cater to Sunni needs. There is not a single Sunni mosque in the whole of Tehran. Iran's Kurds, Turkmans, Arabs, and Baluchis are also Sunnis, and it is no accident that in the immediate aftermath of the 1979 revolution, the newborn regime faced its most serious challenges in precisely the areas of the country where these linguistic minorities lived. It crushed these revolts by rushing in Revolutionary Guards from the Persian Shi'i heartland of Isfahan, Shiraz, and Qom.

The regime's base among the Azeris, who are Shi'i but not Persian speakers, remains to be tested. In the past, the Azeris, who form 24 percent of the population and dwarf the other minorities, have not posed a serious problem to the state. They are part of the Shi'i community and have prominent figures in the Shi'i hierarchy—most notably the current Leader, Khamenei. What is more, many Azeri merchants, professionals, and workers live and work throughout Iran. In short, Azeris can be considered well integrated into Iran.

But the 1991 creation of the Republic of Azerbaijan on Iran's northeastern border following the disintegration of the Soviet Union has raised new concern since some Azeris on both sides of the border have begun to talk of establishing a larger unified Azerbaijan. It is no accident that in the war between Azerbaijan and Armenia in the early 1990s, Iran favored the latter. So far, the concept of a unified Azerbaijan has little appeal among Iranian Azeris.

Interests, Social Movements, and Protest

In the first two decades after its founding, the government of the Islamic Republic often violated its own constitution. It closed down newspapers, professional associations, labor unions, and political parties. It banned demonstrations and public meetings. It incarcerated tens of thousands without due process. It systematically tortured prisoners to extract false confessions and public recantations. And it executed some 25,000 political prisoners, most of them without due process of law. The United Nations, Amnesty International, and Human Rights Watch all took Iran to task for violating the UN Human Rights Charter as well its own Islamic constitution. Most victims were Kurds, military officers from the old regime, and leftists, especially members of the Mojahedin and Fedayin.

Although the violation of individual liberties affected the whole population, it aroused special resentment among three social groups: the modern middle class, educated women, and organized labor. The modern middle class, especially the intelligentsia, has been secular and even anticlerical ever since the 1905 revolution. Little love is lost between it and the Islamic Republic. Not surprisingly, the vast majority of those executed in the 1980s were teachers, engineers, professionals, and college students. Youth, especially college students, are a force to be reckoned with: over half the current population was born after 1979 and as many as 1.15 million are enrolled in higher education. In 1999, eighteen different campuses, including Tehran University, erupted into mass demonstrations against the chief judge, who had closed down a reformist newspaper. Revolutionary Guards promptly occupied the campuses, killing and seriously injuring an unknown number of students. Again in late 2002, thousands of students protested the death sentence handed down to a reformist academic accused of insulting Islam. But in 2004, when the Guardian Council barred thousands of reformers from the elections, the campuses remained quiet—partly out of fear, partly out of disenchantment with the reformers for failing to deliver on their promises, and partly because of the concern about the looming danger from the United States military presence in Iraq.

Educated women in Iran also harbor numerous grievances against the conservative clerics in the regime, especially in the judiciary. Although the Western press often dwells on the veil, Iranian women consider the veil one of their less important problems. Given a choice, most would probably continue to wear it out of personal habit and national tradition. More important are work-related grievances: job security, pay scales, promotions, maternity leave, and access to prestigious professions. Despite patriarchal attitudes held by the conservative clergy, educated women have become a major factor in Iranian society. They now form 54 percent of college students, 45 percent of doctors, 25 percent of government employees, and 13 percent of the general labor force, up from 8 percent in the 1980s. They have established their own organizations and journals, reinterpreting Islam to conform with modern notions of gender equality. Women do serve in the Majles and on local councils, but one grand ayatollah has even argued that they should be able to hold any job, including president, Leader, and court judge, positions from which women have been barred since 1979.

Factory workers in Iran are another significant social group with serious grievances. Their concerns deal mostly with high unemployment, low wages, declining incomes, lack of decent housing, and an unsatisfactory labor law, which, while giving them mandatory holidays and some semblance of job security, denies them the right to call strikes and organize independent unions. Since 1979, wage earners have had a Workers' House—a government-influenced organization—and its affiliated newspaper, *Kar va Kargar* (*Work and Worker*), and, since 1999, the Islamic Labor Party to represent their interests. In most years, the Workers' House flexes its political muscle by holding a May Day rally. In 1999, the rally began peacefully with a greeting from a woman reform deputy who had received the second-most votes in the 1996 Tehran municipal elections. But the rally turned into a protest when workers began to march to parliament denouncing conservatives who had spoken in favor of further watering down of the Labor Law. Bus drivers spontaneously joined the protest, shutting down most of central Tehran.

President Khatami's reform movement drew much of its core support precisely from these three social groups: college youth, women, and workers. In the 1997 and 2001 presidential campaigns, as well as in the elections for municipal councils and the Sixth *Majles,* crucial roles were played by the Islamic Student Associations, the Office of Student Solidarity, the Islamic Women's Association, and the Workers' House. The reformers were also supported by a number of newspapers, which have quickly gained a mass circulation, even though they initially catered mainly to the intelligentsia. For example, the reformist *Hayat-e No,* launched in late 2000, had a circulation of over 235,000 by April 2001, almost double that of the long-established conservative newspaper *Ettela'at.*

Section ⑤ Iranian Politics in Transition

Political Challenges and Changing Agendas

Contemporary Iran faces two major challenges—one internal, the other external. Internally, the Islamic Republic continues to grapple with the vexing question of how to synthesize theocracy with democracy, and clerical authority with mass participation. The conservative clerics, who already controlled the judiciary, took over the *Majles* in 2004 and the presidency in June 2005. Even though the conservatives appear to control the political heights, they have lost much of their support in the general public. The conservatives thus, face the challenge of how to maintain some semblance of mass participation while not actually sharing power with the reformers.

This challenge is particularly vexing since the country has in recent decades gone through a profound cultural revolution embracing such key concepts as political pluralism, mass participation, civil society, human rights, and individual liberties. Even the conservatives have begun to incorporate such terms into their language and openly describe themselves as "neoconservatives" and "pragmatic" in order to broaden their appeal.

Meanwhile, those in the general public who feel excluded from national politics remain active in vibrant nongovernmental organizations. The most visible of these is a human rights group headed by Shirin Ebadi, the winner of the Nobel Peace in 2003. If completely excluded from the political arena, activists such as Ebadi may well conclude that reform is not possible within the system and that the whole regime has to be changed either through constitutional or other, perhaps less peaceful, means.

The external challenge to the Islamic Republic comes from the United States. The Bush administration, by naming Iran as a member of the Axis of Evil and openly calling for "regime change," dramatically increased pressures on Iran—pressures that already existed because of economic sanctions, lack of diplomatic relations, and successful barring of Iran from the World Trade Organization. In the past, the United States has accused Iran of sabotaging the Arab-Israeli peace process; helping terrorist organizations, especially Hamas in Palestine and Hezbollah in Lebanon; and "grossly violating" democratic and human rights of its own citizens. More recently, it has highlighted the danger of weapons of mass destruction in Iran and accused the country of intending to transform its nuclear energy program into a nuclear weapons program. Of course, the external challenge to Iran drastically increased once the United States occupied Iran's neighbors, Afghanistan and Iraq.

The conservative clerics, however, have been able to inadvertently transform this external threat into an asset. They intimidated many reformers into toning down their demands, even silencing them, by declaring that the country was in danger, that the enemy was at the gates, and that any opposition to the government in such times would play into the hands of foreigners. Few were willing to appear unpatriotic at a time when the nation was perceived as facing imminent invasion.

Iranian Politics in Comparative Perspective

Iran is unlike most developing countries in that it is an old state with institutions that go back to ancient times. It is also not a country that only relatively recently achieved independence since it was never formally

Electoral campaigners
Source: Lynsey
Adderio/New York Times

colonized by the European imperial powers. Unlike many other Third World states that have a weak connection with their societies, Iran has a religion that links the elite with the masses, the cities with the villages, the government with the citizenry. Shi'ism, as well as Iranian national identity, serves as a social and cultural cement, giving the population a strong collective identity. Iran also has the advantage of rich oil resources that give it the potential for rapid economic growth that would be the envy of most developing countries. Finally, Iran produced two popular upheavals in the twentieth century: the constitutional (1905) and the Islamic (1979) revolutions in which the citizenry actively intervened in politics, overthrew the old regime, and shaped the new. Both of these revolutions were the result of authentic homegrown political movements, not foreign imports.

Yet Iran shares some problems with other Third World countries. It has failed to establish a full-fledged democracy. Its economy remains underdeveloped, highly dependent on one commodity, and unable to meet the rising expectations of its population. Iran's collective identity, although strong in religious terms, is strained by other internal fault lines, especially those of class, ethnicity, gender, and interclerical political conflicts. And its ambition to enter the world of states as an important player has been thwarted by international as well as domestic and regional realities, which have combined to keep the country pretty much on the global sidelines. Democracy in Iran has been constricted by theocracy. Some argue that Islam has made this inevitable. But Islam, like Christianity and the other major religions, can be interpreted in ways that either support or oppose the democratic idea. Some interpretations of Islam stress the importance of justice, equality, and consultation as political principles. Islam also has a tradition of tolerating other religions, and the *shari'a* explicitly protects life, property, and honor. In practice, Islam has often separated politics from religion, government legal statutes from holy laws, spiritual affairs from worldly matters, and the state from the clerical establishment.

Moreover, theocracy in Iran originates not in Islam itself but in the concept of the jurist's guardianship as developed by Khomeini. On the whole, Sunni Islam considers clerics to be theological scholars, not a special political stratum, which helps explain why the Iranian regime has found it difficult to export the revolution to other parts of the Muslim world. The failure of democracy in Iran should be attributed less to anything intrinsic in Islam than to the confluence of crises between 1979 and 1981 that allowed a particular group of clerics to seize power. Whether they remain in power depends not so much on Islam but on how they handle economic problems and the demands for public participation—in other words, how they deal with the challenges of governing the economy and synthesizing theocracy with the democratic idea.

Politics in the Islamic Republic of Iran remains sharply divided over the question of how to manage an economy beset by rising demands, wildly fluctuating petroleum revenues, and the nightmarish prospect that in the next two generations, the oil wells will run dry. Most clerics favor a rather conventional capitalist road to development, hoping to liberalize the market, privatize industry, attract foreign capital, and encourage the propertied classes to invest. Others envisage an equally conventional statist road to development, favoring central planning, government industries, price controls, high taxes, state subsidies, national self-reliance, and ambitious programs to eliminate poverty, illiteracy, slums, and unemployment. President Khatami charted a third way, combining elements of state intervention with free enterprise that is strikingly similar to the social democracy favored in some other parts of the world such as the Labour Party in Britain

As the clock of history ticks, Iran's population grows, oil revenues fluctuate, and the per capita national income could fall again. Economic problems like those that undermined the monarchy could well undermine the Islamic Republic. The country's collective identity has also come under great strain in recent years. The emphasis on Shi'ism has antagonized Iran's Sunnis as well as its non-Muslim citizens. The emphasis on clerical Shi'ism has further alienated all secularists, including lay liberals, radical leftists, and moderate nationalists. Furthermore, the official emphasis on Khomeini's brand of Shi'ism has alienated those Shi'is who reject the whole notion of jurist's guardianship. The elevation of Khamenei as the Leader has also antagonized many early proponents of jurist's guardianship on the grounds that he lacks the scholarly qualifications to hold the position that embodies the sacred and secular power of the Islamic Republic.

In sum, Iran's ruling regime has gradually reduced the social base that brought it to power. Only time will tell whether growing discontent will be expressed through apolitical channels, such as drug addiction, emigration, and quietist religion, or whether those seeking change will look to reformist movements or turn to more radical insurrectionary organizations or ethnic-based movements.

Finally, the Islamic Republic's initial attempt to enter the international arena as a militant force for the spread of its theocratic version of Islam proved counterproductive. This effort diverted scarce resources to the military. It frightened Saudi Arabia and the Gulf sheikdoms into the arms of the United States. It prompted the United States to isolate Iran, discouraging investment and preventing international organizations from extending economic assistance. Iran's militancy also alarmed nearby secular Islamic states such as Turkey, Tadzhikistan, and Azerbaijan. In recent years, the regime has managed to overcome many of these problems. It has won over the Arab states and has established cordial relations with its neighbors. Most important, it has managed to repair bridges to the European Community. Only time will show how its tortuous relations with the United States will work out and how this will affect the future of politics in Iran.

Key Terms

ayatollah

mosques

fatwa

theocracy

Majles

Guardian Council

Leader

Farsi

Shi'ism

People of the Book

Qur'an

shari'a

coup d'état

bazaars

fundamentalism

jurist's guardianship

pasdaran

Hezbollahis

hojjat al-Islam

laissez-faire

jihad

rentier state

dual society

Organization of
    Petroleum Exporting
    Countries (OPEC)

Expediency Council

Imam Jum'ehs

Foundation of the
    Oppressed

Assembly of Experts

Maslahat

Suggested Readings

Abrahamian, E. *Iran Between Two Revolutions.* Princeton, N.J.: Princeton University Press, 1982.

———. *Khomeinism.* Berkeley: University of California Press, 1993.

Akhavi, S. *Religion and Politics in Contemporary Iran.* Albany: State University of New York Press, 1980.

Bakhash, S. *Reign of the Ayatollahs.* New York: Basic Books, 1984.

Baktiari, B. *Parliamentary Politics in Revolutionary Iran.* Gainesville: University Press of Florida, 1966.

Bill, J. *The Eagle and the Lion.* New Haven, Conn.: Yale University Press, 1988.

Brumberg, D. *Reinventing Khomeini: The Struggle for Reform in Iran.* Chicago: University of Chicago Press, 2001.

Buchta, W. *Who Rules Iran?* Washington, D.C.: Washington Institute for Near East Policy, 2000.

Chehabi, H. *Iranian Politics and Religious Modernism.* Ithaca, N.Y.: Cornell University Press, 1990.

Dabashi, H. *Theology of Discontent: The Ideological Foundation of the Islamic Revolution in Iran.* New York: New York University Press, 1993.

Fischer, M. *Iran: From Religious Dispute to Revolution.* Cambridge: Harvard University Press, 1980.

Garthwaite, F. *The Persians.* Oxford: Blackwell, 2005.

Hooglund, E. *Twenty Years of Islamic Revolution.* Syracuse, N.Y.: Syracuse University Press, 2002.

Kazemi, F. "Civil Society and Iranian Politics." In A. Norton (ed.), *Civil Society in the Middle East.* Leiden: Brill, 1996.

Keddie, N. *Modern Iran: Roots and Results of Revolution.* New Haven, Conn.: Yale University Press, 2004.

Kurzman, C. *The Unthinkable Revolution in Iran.* Cambridge: Harvard University Press, 2004.

Milani, M. *The Making of Iran's Islamic Revolution.* Boulder, Colo.: Westview Press, 1994.

Mir-Hosseini, Z. *Islam and Gender.* Princeton, N.J.: Princeton University Press, 1999.

Moin, B. *Khomeini: Life of the Ayatollah.* London: Tauris, 1999.

Mottahedeh, R. *The Mantle of the Prophet.* New York: Simon & Schuster, 1985.

Schirazi, A. *The Constitution of Iran.* London: Tauris, 1997.

Suggested Websites

The Story of the Revolution, British Broadcasting Corporation
www.bbc.co.uk/persian/revolution
Iranian Mission to the United Nations
www.un.int/iran

Islamic Republic News Agency
www.irna.ir/en
Iran Report, Radio Free Europe
www.rferl.org/reports/iran-report
News Related to Iran
www.farsinews.net

Endnotes

[1]Quoted in E. Browne, *The Persian Revolution* (New York: Barnes and Noble, 1966), 137.

[2]British Financial Adviser to the Foreign Office in Tehran, *Documents on British Foreign Policy, 1919–39* (London: Her Majesty's Stationery Office, 1963), First Series, XIII, 720, 735.

[3]British Minister to the Foreign Office, *Report on the Seizure of Lands,* Foreign Office 371/Persia 1932/File 34–16007.

[4]*Kayhan International,* November 10, 1976.

[5]"Fifty Indictments of Treason During Fifty Years of Treason," *Khabarnameh,* no. 46 (April 1976).

[6]M. Bazargan, "Letter to the Editor," *Ettela'at,* February 7, 1980.

[7]*Iran Times,* January 12, 1979.

[8]*Washington Post,* December 12, 1978.

[9]*Christian Science Monitor,* December 12, 1978.

[10]Samuel P. Huntington, *The Clash of Civilizations and the Remaking of World Order* (New York: Simon & Schuster, 1996).

[11]Mirza Hosayn Khan Tahvildar-e Isfahan, *Jukhrafiha-ye Isfahan* [The Geography of Isfahan] (Tehran: Tehran University Press, 1963), 100–101.

[12]International Labor Organization, "Employment and Income Policies for Iran" (Unpublished report, Geneva, 1972), Appendix C, 6.

[13]A. Sharbatoghilie, *Urbanization and Regional Disparity in Post-Revolutionary Iran* (Boulder, Colo.: Westview Press, 1991), 4.

[14]*Wall Street Journal,* November 4, 1977.

[15]U.S. Congress, *Economic Consequences of the Revolution in Iran* (Washington, D.C.: U.S. Government Printing Office, 1979), 184.

[16]U.S. Congress, *Economic Consequences of the Revolution in Iran,* 5.

[17]U.S. Department of Commerce, *Iran: A Survey of U.S. Business Opportunities* (Washington, D.C.: U.S. Government Printing Office, 1977), 1–2.

[18]Cited in H. Amirahmadi, *Revolution and Economic Transition* (Albany: State University of New York Press, 1960), p. 201.

[19]Cited in *Iran Times,* July 9, 1993.

[20]J. Amuzegar, *Iran's Economy Under the Islamic Republic* (London: Taurus Press, 1994), 100.

[21]A. Rafsanjani, "The Islamic Consultative Assembly," *Kayhan,* May 23, 1987.

[22]S. Saffari, "The Legitimation of the Clergy's Right to Rule in the Iranian Constitution of 1979," *British Journal of Middle Eastern Studies* 20, no. 1 (1993): 64–81.

[23]Ayatollah Montazeri, *Ettela'at,* October 8, 1979.

[24]O. Fallaci, "Interview with Khomeini," *New York Times Magazine,* October 7, 1979.

[25]*Kayhan,* March 6, 1980.

[26]*Kayhan,* April 21, 1987.

[27]*Kayhan-e Hava'i,* November 16, 1988.

[28]*Economist,* February 9, 2000.

CHAPTER 8

China

William A. Joseph

People's Republic of China

Land and People

Capital	Beijing
Total area	3,705,286 sq mi/ 9,596,960 sq km (slightly smaller than the United States)
Population	1.306 billion
Annual population growth rate (%)	1975–2000 1.2 2002–2015 (projected) 0.6
Urban population (%)	39
Ethnic composition (%)	Chinese (Han) 91.9 Others (Hui, Uygur, Tibetan, Zhuang) 8.1
Major language(s)	Standard Chinese or Mandarin (based on the Beijing district); plus many other dialects such as Cantonese and Shanghaiese, and minority languages
Religious affiliation (%)	Officially atheist. Daoist (Taoist), Buddhist, Muslim 1–2 Christian 3–4

Economy

Domestic currency	Yuan (CNY) (Note: also referred to as the *renminbi* (RMB) *US$1: 83 CNY* (2004)
Total GNI (US$)	1.4 trillion
GNI per capita (US$)	1,100
GNI at purchasing power parity (US$)	6.4 trillion
GNI per capita at purchasing power parity (US$)	4,980
GDP annual growth rate (%)	1983–1993 9.5 1993–2003 8.6 2002 8.3 2003 9.1
GDP per capita average annual growth rate (%)	1983–1993 7.9 1993–2003 7.6
Inequality in income or consumption (2001) (%)	Share of poorest 10% 2 Share of poorest 20% 5

	Share of richest 20%	50
	Share of richest 10%	33
	Gini Index (2001)	44.7
Structure of production (% of GDP)	Agriculture	13.8
	Industry	52.9
	Services	33.3
Labor force distribution (% of total)	Agriculture	49
	Industry	22
	Services	29
Exports as % of GDP		34.3
Imports as % of GDP		31.8

Society

Life expectancy at birth	72.27	
Infant mortality per 1,000 live births	24.18	
Adult illiteracy (% of population of age 15+)	9	
Access to information and communications (per 1,000 population)	Telephone lines	137
	Mobile phones	110
	Radios	339
	Televisions	312
	Personal computers	19

Women in Government and the Economy

Women in the national legislature		
Lower house or single house (%)		20.2
Women at ministerial level (%)		5.1
Female economic activity rate (age 15 and above) (%)		72.5
Estimated earned income (PPP US$)	Female	3,571
	Male	5,435

Composite Ratings and Rankings

Human Development Index (HDI) ranking (value) out of 177 countries	94 (.745)
Gender-related Development Index (GDI) ranking (value) out of 78 countries	71 (.741)
Gender Empowerment Measure (GEM) ranking (value) (out of 78 countries)	N/A
Corruption Perception Index (CPI) ranking (value) out of 146 countries	71 (3.4)
Environmental Sustainability Index (ESI) ranking (value) out of 146 countries	133 (38.6)
Freedom in World Rating	Not Free (6.5)

Section ❶   The Making of the Modern Chinese State

Politics in Action

When the International Olympics Committee announced in July 2001 that Beijing had been chosen as the site of the 2008 summer games, an estimated 200,000 Chinese citizens poured into Tiananmen ("Gate of Heavenly Peace") Square in the heart of China's capital to celebrate the honor that had been bestowed on their country. They saw the awarding of the games to Beijing as overdue recognition of the remarkable modernization of the Chinese economy, the stunning successes of Chinese athletes in international sports competitions, and the emergence of the People's Republic of China (PRC) as a major global power.

But there were also many voices that were extremely critical of the IOC's decision. Human rights organizations such as Amnesty International argued that the decision rewarded one of the world's most oppressive governments. Some compared the Beijing Games to those held in Berlin, Germany, in 1936, shortly after Hitler had come to power, games that the Nazis used to gain international legitimacy. The Dalai Lama, the exiled spiritual leader of Tibet, which has been occupied by China since 1950, strongly objected to awarding the games to Beijing. As his spokesman noted, "This will put the stamp of international approval on Beijing's human rights abuses and will encourage China to escalate its repression."[1] Critics of the Beijing games also pointed out the irony that the Olympics celebrations in Tiananmen Square were held very near the place where, in 1989, China's Communist leaders ordered troops to crush a prodemocracy movement and killed hundreds of civilians, many of them college students.

Others argued that hosting the Olympics could be a force for positive change in China. PRC leaders would not want to risk an international boycott of the Beijing Games by engaging in highly visible repression. This, in turn, could embolden China's democracy activists, who have been largely silent since the Tiananmen massacre. In this way, the 2008 Beijing Olympics might spur much-needed political reform, as did the 1988 Olympics in Seoul, an important impetus to South Korea's transition from a military dictatorship to a democracy.

The controversy over the Beijing Olympics reflects the fundamental contradiction that defines contemporary Chinese politics. The People's Republic of China is one of only a few countries in the world that is still a **communist-party state** in which the ruling party claims an exclusive monopoly on political power and proclaims allegiance (at least officially) to the ideology of **Marxism-Leninism.** At the same

361

time, the country has experienced dramatic economic and social liberalization—and even considerable political relaxation since the bloodshed in Tiananmen—and is more fully integrated into the world than at any other time in its history. But the Chinese Communist Party (CCP) rejects any meaningful movement toward democracy, and the rift between a tyrannical political system and an increasingly modern and globalized society remains deep and ominous.

Geographic Setting

The PRC is located in the eastern part of mainland Asia at the heart of one of the world's most strategically

important and regions. It shares land borders with more than a dozen countries, including Russia, India, Pakistan, Vietnam, and the Democratic People's Republic of Korea (North Korea) and is a relatively short distance by sea from Japan, the Philippines, and Indonesia. China, which had largely assumed its present geographic identity by the eighteenth century, is slightly smaller than the United States in land area, and is the fourth largest country in the world, after Russia, Canada, and the United States.

The PRC is bounded on all sides by imposing physical barriers: the sea to the east; mountains to the north, south, and west (including the world's highest, Mount Everest); deserts, vast grasslands, and dense

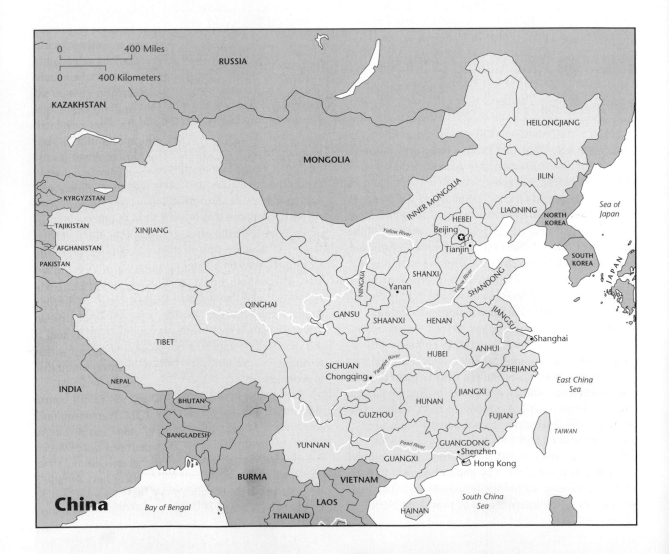

forests in various parts of the north; and tropical rain forests to the south. In traditional times, these barriers isolated China from extensive contact with other peoples and contributed to the country's sense of itself as the "Middle Kingdom" (which is the literal translation of the Chinese term for China, *zhongguo*) that lay not only at the physical, but also at the political and cultural center of the world.

Administratively, the **PRC** is made up of twenty-two provinces, five **autonomous regions,** four centrally administered cities (including the capital, Beijing), and two Special Administrative Regions (Hong Kong and Macao). The sparsely populated but territorially vast western part of the country is mostly mountains, deserts, and high plateaus. The northeast, which is much like the U.S. plains states in terms of weather and topography, is both a wheat-growing area and China's industrial heartland. Southern China has a much warmer, and in places even semitropical, climate, which allows year-round agriculture and intensive rice cultivation. The country is very rich in natural resources, particularly coal and petroleum (including significant, but untapped onshore and offshore reserves), and is considered to have the world's greatest potential for hydroelectric power. Still, China's astounding economic growth in recent decades has created an almost insatiable demand for energy resources, which has, in turn, led the PRC to look abroad for critical raw materials.

Although China and the United States are roughly equal in geographic size, China's population of about 1.3 billion—the world's largest—is five times greater. But only a relatively small part of China's land is usable for agriculture. China has a little over 20 percent of the world's population but only 10 percent of the world's arable land. The precarious balance between people and the land needed to feed them has been a dilemma for China for centuries and remains one of the government's major concerns.

China has more than 140 cities with a population of a million or more, the three largest being Shanghai (17.1 million), Beijing (14.5 million), and Tianjin (10.1 million). In 1997, the former British colony of Hong Kong, one of the world's great commercial centers (population 6.9 million), became part of the PRC. Nevertheless, about 60 percent of China's people still live and work in rural areas. The countryside has played—and continues to play—a very important role in China's political development.

China's population is highly concentrated along the eastern seaboard and in the most agriculturally fertile areas around three great rivers: the Yellow River in north China, the Yangtze (Yangzi) in the central part of the country, and the Pearl River in the south. The vast majority (92 percent) of China's citizens are ethnically Chinese (referred to as the Han, after one of China's earliest dynasties). The remaining 8 percent is made up of more than fifty ethnic minorities, who differ from the Han in at least one of several major ways, including race, language, culture, and religion. Most of these minority peoples live in the country's geopolitically sensitive border regions, including Tibet. This makes the often uneasy and sometimes hostile relationship between China's minority peoples and the central government in Beijing a crucial and volatile issue in Chinese politics today.

Critical Junctures

The People's Republic of China was founded in 1949. But understanding the critical junctures in the making of the modern Chinese state requires that we go back much further into China's political history. Broadly considered, that history can be divided into three periods: the imperial period (221 B.C.–1911 A.D.), during which China was ruled by a series of dynasties and emperors; the relatively brief republican period (1912–1949), when the country was plagued by civil war and foreign invasion; and the communist period, from the founding of the PRC in 1949 to the present.

From Empire to Republic (221 B.C. –1911 A.D.)

Modern China is heir to one of the world's oldest cultural and political traditions. The roots of Chinese culture date back more than 4,000 years, and the Chinese empire first took political shape in 221 B.C., when a number of small kingdoms were unified under China's first emperor, who laid the foundation of an imperial system that lasted for more than twenty centuries until its overthrow in 1911. During those many centuries, China was ruled by more than a dozen different family-based dynasties and experienced extensive geographic expansion and far-reaching political, economic, social, and cultural changes. Nevertheless, many of the core features of the imperial system remained remarkably consistent over time.

There are several reasons that the Chinese empire survived for such a long time. First, imperial China developed an effective national government with a merit-based bureaucracy chosen through competitive examinations long before the strong monarchical states of Europe took form in the seventeenth century. Second, the traditional Chinese economy was a source of great strength to the empire. Urbanization expanded in China much sooner than it did in Europe, and Westerners, like Marco Polo, who journeyed to China as early as the thirteenth century, were amazed by the grandeur of the Middle Kingdom's cities.

Third, the structure of traditional Chinese society, especially in the million or more small villages that were its foundation, gave imperial China great staying power. The vast majority of the village population was made up of poor and relatively poor peasants. But life was dominated by landlords and other local elites who worked with the national government to maintain and sustain the system.

Fourth, the traditional order was supported by the enduring influence in Chinese society of Confucianism. This philosophy, based on the teachings of Confucius (c. 551–479 B.C.), stresses the importance of the group over the individual, deference to one's elders and superiors, and the need to maintain social harmony. Confucianism did contain a teaching, the "Mandate of Heaven," that said the people had the right to overthrow an unjust ruler. Nevertheless, Confucianism was, in essence, a conservative philosophy that justified an autocratic state, a patriarchal culture, and a highly stratified society. Finally, the Chinese imperial system endured because, throughout most of its history, China was by far the dominant political, military, and cultural force in its known world. Even when it was conquered from the outside, as it was in 1214 A.D. by the Mongols and in 1644 A.D. by the Manchus, the invaders wound up establishing a new dynasty much on the pattern of the old and adapting many aspects of Chinese civilization.

Imperial China experienced many internal rebellions, often quite in large scale, during its lengthy history. Some even led to the overthrow of the ruling dynasty, but the result was always the establishment of a new dynasty built on traditional foundations. However, in the late eighteenth and nineteenth centuries, the Chinese empire was confronted with an unprecedented combination of internal crises and external challenges. A population explosion (the result of a long spell of peace and prosperity under the Qing dynasty) contributed to the onset of economic stagnation, which along with a significant rise in official corruption and exploitation of the peasants by both landlords and the government fomented widespread social unrest. The internal disorder culminated in the Taiping Rebellion (1850–1864), a massive revolt that took 20 million lives and nearly toppled the Qing.

In the meantime, the West, which had surged far ahead of China in industrial and military development, was pressing the country to open its markets to foreign trade. China showed little interest in such overtures and tried to limit the activities of Westerners in China. But Europe, most notably Britain, in the midst of its era of mercantile and colonial expansion, used its military supremacy to compel China to engage in "free" trade with the West. China's efforts to stop Britain from selling opium in China led to military conflict between the two countries. After suffering a humiliating defeat in the Opium War (1839–1842), China was literally forced to sign a series of unequal treaties that opened its borders to foreign merchants, missionaries, and diplomats on terms dictated by Britain and other Western powers. China also lost control of significant pieces of its territory to foreigners (including Hong Kong), and important sectors of the Chinese economy fell into foreign hands.

There were many efforts to revive or reform the Qing dynasty in the late nineteenth and early twentieth centuries, but political power in China remained largely in the hands of staunch conservatives who resisted change. As a result, when change came, it was in the form of a revolution in 1911 that both toppled the ruling dynasty and brought an end to the 2,000-year-old imperial system.

Warlords, Nationalists, and Communists (1912–1949)

The Republic of China was established on January 1, 1912, with Dr. Sun Yat-sen,[*] then China's best-known revolutionary, as president. However, the

---

[*] In China, family names come first. For example, Sun Yat-sen's family name was "Sun," and his given name was Yat-sen, and he is referred to as Dr. Sun.

Critical Junctures in Modern China's Political Development

1911   Revolution led by Sun Yat-sen over-throws 2,000-year-old imperial system and establishes the Republic of China.

1912   Sun Yat-sen founds the Nationalist (*Guomindang*) Party to oppose warlords who have seized power in the new republic.

1921   Chinese Communist Party (CCP) is founded.

1927   Civil war between Nationalists (now led by Chiang Kai-shek) and Communists begins.

1934   Mao Zedong becomes leader of the CCP.

1937   Japan invades China, marking the start of World War II in Asia.

1949   Chinese Communists win the civil war and establish the People's Republic of China.

1958–1960   Great Leap Forward.

1966–1976   Great Proletarian Cultural Revolution.

1976   Mao Zedong dies.

1978   Deng Xiaoping becomes China's paramount leader.

1989   Tiananmen massacre.

1997   Deng Xiaoping dies; Jiang Zemin becomes China's most powerful leader.

2002–2003   Hu Jintao succeeds Jiang as head of the CCP and president of the People's Republic of China.

Western-educated Sun was not able to hold onto power, and China soon fell into a lengthy period of conflict and disintegration, with parts of the country run by rival military leaders known as warlords. Sun set about organizing another revolution to reunify the country under his Nationalist Party (the *Guomindang*).

In 1921, the Chinese Communist Party (CCP) was established by a few intellectuals who had been inspired by the Russian revolution in 1917 and by the anti-imperialism of the newly founded Soviet Union to look for more radical solutions to China's problems. In 1924, the small Communist Party, acting on Soviet advice, joined with Sun Yat-sen's Nationalists to fight the warlords. After some initial successes, this alliance came to a tragic end in 1927 when Chiang Kai-shek, a military leader who had become the head of the Nationalist Party after Sun's death in 1925, turned against his coalition partners and ordered a bloody suppression that nearly wiped out the communists. Chiang then proceeded to unify the Republic of China under his personal rule, largely by striking an accommodation with some of the country's most powerful remaining warlords who supported him in suppressing the communists.

In order to survive, the Communist Party had to relocate its headquarters deep into the Chinese countryside. Ironically, this retreat created the conditions for the eventual rise to power of the man who would lead the CCP to nationwide victory, Mao Zedong. Mao, who had been one of the junior founders of the Communist Party, strongly advocated paying more attention to China's suffering peasants as a potential source of support. "In a very short time," he wrote in 1927, "several hundred million peasants will rise like a mighty storm, like a hurricane, a force so swift and violent that no power, however great, will be able to hold it back."[2] It was while the CCP was based in the rural areas that Mao began his climb to the top of the party leadership.

In 1934–1935, the Chinese communists undertook their mythologized Long March, an epic journey of 6,000 miles through some of China's roughest terrain, to escape attack by Chiang's forces. At the end of the Long March, the CCP established a base in Yanan, which was located in a remote and impoverished area of northwestern China. In Yanan, Mao consolidated his political and ideological control of the CCP, sometimes through ruthless means, and was elected party chairman in 1943, a position he held until his death in 1976.

Japan's invasion of China in 1937 started World War II in Asia and pushed the Nationalist government to the far southwestern part of the country, effectively eliminating it as an active combatant against Japanese aggression. In contrast, the CCP base in Yanan was on the front line against Japan's troops in northern China, and Mao and the Communists successfully mobilized the peasants to use **guerrilla warfare** to fight the invaders. By the end of World War II in 1945, the CCP had vastly expanded its membership and controlled much of the countryside in north China. The Nationalists, on the other hand, were isolated and unpopular with many Chinese because of the corruption, political repression, and economic mismanagement of Chiang Kai-shek's regime.

After the Japanese surrender, the Chinese civil war quickly resumed. The Communists won a decisive victory over the U.S.-backed Nationalists, who were forced to retreat to the island of Taiwan, 90 miles off the Chinese coast. (See "Global Connection: The Republic of China on Taiwan.") On October 1, 1949, Mao Zedong stood on a rostrum in Tiananmen near the entrance to the former imperial palace in Beijing and declared the founding of the People's Republic of China.

Mao in Power (1949–1976)

The CCP came to power on the crest of an enormous wave of popular support because of its reputation as a party of social reformers and patriotic fighters. Chairman Mao and the CCP quickly turned their attention to some of the country's most glaring problems. For instance, a massive land reform campaign redistributed property from the rich to the poor and increased productivity in the countryside. Highly successful drives eliminated opium addiction and prostitution from the cities, and a national law greatly enhanced the legal status of women in the family and allowed many women to free themselves from unhappy arranged marriages. Although the CCP did not hesitate to use violence to achieve its objectives and silence opponents, the party gained considerable legitimacy because of its successful policies during these years.

Between 1953 and 1957, the PRC implemented a Soviet-style five-year economic plan. The complete nationalization of industry and **collectivization** of agriculture carried out as part of this plan were decisive steps away from the mixed state-private economy of the early 1950s and toward **socialism.** Although the plan achieved good economic results for the country, Mao was troubled by the growth of the government bureaucracy and the persistence of inequalities, especially those caused by the emphasis on industrial and urban development and the relative neglect of the countryside.

In 1956, Mao used the media to issue a call to the Chinese people to "let a hundred flowers bloom, let a hundred schools of thought contend"; that is, they should come forward to offer their frank opinions about how the Communist Party was governing China. His goals for this **Hundred Flowers Movement** were to shake up the bureaucrats and encourage broader participation in making public policy, especially among the country's intellectuals. But the outpouring of public criticism and a wave of large-scale industrial strikes revealed the fact that many people were harboring deep resentments about Communist policies and about the growing political dictatorship.

Mao's reaction to the unexpectedly severe Hundred Flowers criticism was to order a vicious crackdown—the **Anti-Rightist Campaign** of 1957—in which hundreds of thousands of people were accused of being enemies of the revolution ("Rightists") and punished by being demoted, fired, or sent to labor camps. This campaign completely stifled political debate in China and "destroyed the hope that China's 'transition to socialism' might proceed on the basis of some form of popular democracy and with some real measure of intellectual freedom. It reinforced . . . that the exercise of state power was a monopoly of the Communist Party."[3]

Mao's discontent with the direction in which he perceived the PRC was heading continued to build, even after his critics had been silenced. In response, he launched the **Great Leap Forward** (1958–1960), a utopian effort to accelerate the country's economic development by relying on the labor power and revolutionary enthusiasm of the masses while also propelling China into a radically egalitarian era of true **communism.**

The Great Leap was a great flop and turned into "one of the most extreme, bizarre, and eventually catastrophic episodes in twentieth-century political history."[4] In the rural areas, irrational policies, wasted resources, poor management, and the lack of labor incentives combined with bad weather to produce a famine that claimed between 20 and 30 million lives. An industrial depression soon followed the collapse of agriculture, causing a terrible setback to China's economic development.

In the early 1960s, Mao took a less active role in day-to-day decision making. Two of China's other top leaders at the time, Liu Shaoqi and Deng Xiaoping,

Global Connection: *The Republic of China on Taiwan*

Despite the victory of the Chinese Communist Party in the civil war and the founding of the People's Republic of China on the Chinese mainland in October 1949, the Republic of China (ROC) under Chiang Kai-shek and the Nationalist Party continued to function on the island of Taiwan, just 90 miles off the coast. The Chinese Communists would likely have taken over Taiwan at the end of the civil war if the United States had not intervened to protect the island. The U.S. government, alarmed by the outbreak of the Korean War in 1950, saw the defense of the Nationalist government on Taiwan as part of the effort to stop the further expansion of communism in Asia.

When Chiang Kai-shek and his supporters fled across the Taiwan Strait in 1949, the island was already firmly under the control of Nationalists, who had killed or arrested many of their opponents on Taiwan in the aftermath of a popular uprising in February 1947. The harsh dictatorship imposed by Chiang's Nationalists deepened the sharp divide between the mainlanders, who had come over to escape the communists, and the native Taiwanese majority, whose ancestors had settled on the island centuries before and who spoke a distinctive Chinese dialect.

Economically, Taiwan prospered under Chiang Kai-shek's rule. With large amounts of U.S. aid and advice, the Nationalist government sponsored a successful and peaceful program of land reform and rural development, attracted extensive foreign investment, and encouraged an export-led strategy of economic growth that made Taiwan a model newly industrializing country (NIC) by the 1970s. The government also invested heavily in the modernization of Taiwan's roads and ports, and it promoted policies that have given the island health and education levels that are among the best in the world and a standard of living that is one of the highest in Asia.

Political change, however, came more slowly to Taiwan. After his death in 1975, Chiang Kai-shek was succeeded as president by his son, Chiang Ching-kuo, whom most people expected to continue the authoritarian rule of his father. Instead, the younger Chiang permitted some opposition and dissent, and he gave important government and party positions, previously dominated by mainlanders, to Taiwanese. When he died in 1988, the presidency of the republic passed to the Taiwanese vice president, Lee Teng-hui, who also became head of the Nationalist Party.

Under President Lee, Taiwan made big strides toward democratization. Laws used to imprison dissidents were revoked, the media were freed of all censorship, and open multiparty elections were held for all local and island-wide positions. In presidential elections in 1996, Lee Teng-hui won 54 percent of the vote in a hotly contested four-way race, reflecting both the new openness of the political system and the credit that Taiwan's voters gave the Nationalist Party for the island's progress.

But in 2000, an opposition party candidate, Chen Shui-bian of the Democratic Progressive Party (DPP), won the presidency, which many observers saw as reflecting a further maturing of Taiwan's democracy. Chen's victory was due in part to a combination of the desire for change, especially in light of a serious downturn in the island's economic growth and a split within the Nationalist Party.

The most contentious political issue in Taiwan, which is still formally called the Republic of China, is whether the island should continue to work, however slowly, toward reunification with the mainland, as was the Nationalists' policy under Lee Teng-hui, or declare formal independence. A big factor in Chen's election was the growing popularity of the DPP's position that Taiwan should seriously consider the independence option. Public opinion is sharply divided, with most people seeming to prefer the status quo in which Taiwan is, for all intents and purposes (including its own strong military), a separate political entity from China, but not an internationally recognized independent country. Chen was re-elected in 2004 in a close and contentious election, but he and the DPP have toned down

(continued)

Global Connection: *The Republic of China on Taiwan (cont.)*

their independence rhetoric. The political status of Taiwan is also a very sensitive matter in relations between the United States and the People's Republic of China. The U.S. is committed to a "peaceful solution" of the situation in the Taiwan Strait and continues to sell military technology to Taiwan. Beijing regards Taiwan as an inalienable part of China and has refused to renounce the use of force if the island moves toward formal separation. The PRC government often criticizes American policy toward Taiwan as interference in China's internal affairs.

Taiwan and China have developed extensive economic relations with each other, and millions of people from Taiwan have gone to the mainland to do business, visit relatives, or just sightsee. The PRC and ROC have engaged in some negotiations about further reconciliation and possible reunification, and in 2005 the current head of the Nationalist Party went to the mainland and held talks with CCP leader (and PRC president) Hu Jintao, in the first direct contact between the two political parties since the end of the civil war. Nevertheless, the governments that rule mainland China and Taiwan remain far apart because of their vastly differing political, economic, and social systems.

Taiwan

Land area	13,895 sq mi/ 35,980 sq km (slightly smaller than Maryland and Delaware combined)
Population	22.9 million
Ethnic composition	Taiwanese 84%, mainland Chinese 14%, aborigine 2%
GDP at purchasing power parity (US$)	$576 billion
GDP per capita at purchasing power parity (US$)	$25,300
GDP growth rate (2004)	6.0%
Life expectancy	77.3
Infant mortality (per 1,000 live births)	6.4
Literacy	96%

were put in charge of efforts to revive the economy and used a combination of careful government planning and market-oriented policies to stimulate production, particularly in agriculture.

This strategy did help the Chinese economy, but once again Mao found himself profoundly unhappy with the consequences of China's development. By the mid-1960s, the chairman had concluded that the policies of Liu and Deng had led to a resurgence of elitism and inequality that were threatening his revolutionary goals for China by setting the country on the road to capitalism.

The result of Mao's disquiet was the **Great Proletarian Cultural Revolution** (1966–1976), an ideological crusade designed to jolt China back toward his

vision of socialism. Like the Great Leap Forward, the Cultural Revolution was a campaign of mass mobilization and utopian idealism, but its methods were much more violent, and its main objective was the political purification of the party and the nation through struggle against so-called class enemies, not accelerated economic development. Using his unmatched political clout and charisma, Mao put together a potent coalition of radical party leaders, loyal military officers, and student rebels (called Red Guards) to purge anyone thought to be guilty of **revisionism,** that is, betrayal of his version of communist ideology known as Mao Zedong Thought.

In the Cultural Revolution's first phase (1966–1969), 20 million or so Red Guards went on a rampage across the country, harassing, torturing, and killing people accused of being class enemies, particularly intellectuals and discredited party leaders. During the next phase (1969–1971), Mao used the People's Liberation Army (PLA) to restore political order, while the final phase (1972–1976) involved intense factional conflict over who would succeed the aging Mao as party chairman. Mao died in September 1976 at age eighty-two. A month later, the power struggle was settled when a coalition of relatively moderate leaders masterminded the arrest of their radical rivals, the so-called Gang of Four, who were led by Mao's wife, Jiang Qing. The arrest of the Gang (who were sentenced to long prison terms) marked the end of the Cultural Revolution, which had claimed at least a million lives and brought the nation to the brink of civil war.

Deng Xiaoping and the Transformation of Chinese Communism (1977–1997)

In order to help them repair the damage caused by the Cultural Revolution, China's new leaders restored to office many of the veteran officials who had been purged by Mao and the radicals, including Deng Xiaoping. By 1978, Deng had clearly become the most powerful member of the CCP leadership—although he preferred to install a loyal lieutenant in the formal position of party leader rather than take it for himself. He lost little time in putting China on a path of reform that dramatically transformed the nation.

Deng's policies were a profound break with the Maoist past. State control of the economy was significantly reduced, and market forces were allowed to play an increasingly important role in all aspects of production. Private enterprise was encouraged, and the economy was opened to unprecedented levels of foreign investment. On the cultural front, Chinese artists and writers saw the shackles of party dogma that had bound them for decades greatly loosened. Deng took major steps to revitalize China's government by bringing in younger, better-educated officials. The results of Deng's initiatives were, by any measure, extraordinary. After decades of stagnation, the Chinese economy experienced spectacular growth throughout the 1980s and beyond (see Section 2).

Then came June 1989 and the massacre near Tiananmen Square. Discontent over inflation and official corruption, as well as a desire, especially among students and intellectuals, for more political freedom, inspired large-scale demonstrations in Beijing and several other Chinese cities that spring. The demonstrations in Beijing grew through April and May, and at one point more than a million people from all walks of life gathered in and around Tiananmen. For several months, the CCP, constrained by internal divisions about how to handle the protests and intensive international media coverage, did little other than engage in some threatening rhetoric to dissuade the demonstrators. But China's leaders ran out of patience, and the army was ordered to clear the square during the very early morning hours of June 4. By the time dawn broke in Beijing, Tiananmen Square had indeed been cleared, but with a death toll that still has not been revealed.

Following the Tiananmen massacre, China went through a few years of intensified political repression and economic retrenchment. Then in early 1992, Deng Xiaoping took some bold steps to accelerate reform of the economy. He did so in large part because he hoped reform would help the PRC avoid a collapse of the Communist system such as had occurred just the year before in the Soviet Union.

From Revolutionary Leaders to Technocrats (1997 to the Present)

Another important consequence of the 1989 Tiananmen crisis was the replacement as formal head of the CCP of one Deng protégé, Zhao Ziyang, by another, Jiang Zemin. Zhao was ousted by Deng because he was considered too sympathetic to the student demonstrators, and Jiang was promoted from his previous posts as mayor and CCP chief of Shanghai because of his firm but relatively bloodless handling of similar protests in that city. Although Deng remained the power behind the throne for several years, he gradually turned over greater authority to Jiang, who, in addition to his positions as head (general secretary) of the CCP and chair of the powerful Central Military Commission, became president of the PRC in 1993. When Deng Xiaoping died in February 1997, Jiang was secure in his position as China's top leader.

Under Jiang's leadership, China continued the process of economic reform and its record of remarkable

This cartoon captures the contradiction between economic reform and political repression that characterized China under the leadership of Deng Xiaoping. *Source:* © 1992, *The Boston Globe*. Distributed by Los Angeles Times Syndicate. Reprinted with permission.

economic growth. The PRC became even more fully integrated into the global economy, as exemplified by its admission to the World Trade Organization (WTO) in 2001, and enhanced both its regional and international stature as a rising power. Overall, the country was politically stable during the Jiang era. But the CCP still repressed any individual or group perceived as challenging its authority, and the country faced serious problems, including mounting unemployment, pervasive corruption, and widening gaps between the rich and the poor.

Upon his retirement, Jiang was succeeded as CCP general secretary in November 2002 and PRC president in March 2003 by Hu Jintao, who had previously served as China's vice president. At age sixty when he took these offices, Hu Jintao was considerably younger than most of China's recent leaders. But both Jiang and Hu represented a new kind of leader for the PRC. Mao Zedong and Deng Xiaoping were career revolutionaries who had participated in the CCP's long struggle for power and were among the founders of the Communist regime when it was established in 1949. In contrast, Jiang and Hu were technocrats, officials with academic training (in their cases, as engineers) who worked their way up the party ladder by a combination of professional competence and political loyalty.

Another significant aspect of the transfer of power from Jiang to Hu was how predictable and orderly it

was. In fact, some observed that it was the first relatively tranquil top-level political succession in China in more than 200 years. Jiang had retired after two terms in office, as required by both party rules and the state constitution, and Hu had, for several years, been expected to succeed Jiang.

This smooth leadership transition, however, masked much that echoed the secretive and highly personalistic methods that have long characterized Chinese politics. First, Hu Jintao had been designated years before by Deng Xiaoping to be Jiang's successor. So Hu's "election" to the posts of CCP general secretary and PRC president was less the result of an institutionalized process than of personal and factional machinations.

Second, despite retiring from all party and government positions, Jiang Zemin retained considerable political power and influence. He was, in various ways, able to orchestrate his enshrinement as the successor to Mao and Deng as one of the great luminaries in party history. He also kept at least an ear in the inner sanctum of decision making through the placement of numerous close associates in the party's most powerful organizations Nevertheless, the coming to power of Jiang Zemin and then Hu Jintao did mark a critical juncture in China's political history, in that it reflected the passing of power from the revolutionary to the technocratic generation of Chinese Communist leaders.

In early 2005, Hu further consolidated his hold on power when he took over from Jiang as chair of the Central Military Commission (which controls the armed forces). He has also started to stake out a distinctive program and approach to leadership. On the one hand, he has tried to project himself as something of a populist by placing more emphasis on dealing with the country's most serious socioeconomic problems, such as enormous inequalities between regions, that have resulted from China's rapid economic growth over the last two decades. On the other hand, Hu appeared to be more hardline than Jiang in limiting dissent in society and even disagreement within the party leadership. In any case, there is little reason to expect that Chinese politics at the top will change much under Hu Jintao or that he will deviate significantly from the combination of economic reform and political repression that has been the CCP's formula for retaining power since the days of Deng Xiaoping.

Themes and Implications

Historical Junctures and Political Themes

The World of States.   When the People's Republic was founded in 1949, China was in a weak position in the international system. For more than a century, its destiny had been shaped by incursions and influences from abroad that it could do little to control. Mao made many tragic and terrible blunders, but one of his great achievements was to build a strong state able to affirm and defend its sovereignty. China's international stature has increased as its economic and military strength have grown in recent decades. Although still a relatively poor country by many per capita measures, the sheer size of its economy makes the PRC an economic powerhouse whose import and export policies have an important impact on many other countries. China is a nuclear power with the world's largest conventional military force, and it is an active and influential member of nearly all international organizations, including the United Nations, where it sits as one of the five permanent members of the Security Council. Clearly, China has become a major player in the world of states.

The making of the modern Chinese state has also been profoundly influenced at several critical points by

Student demonstrators erected a statue called the "Goddess of Democracy" in Beijing's Tiananmen Square in late May 1989 to symbolize their demands for greater political freedom in China. In the background is an official portrait of former Chinese Communist Party leader, Mao Zedong. Chinese troops toppled and destroyed the statue after they occupied the square on June 4, 1989, a process that also resulted in the death of many protestors.   *Source:* AP/ Wide World Photos.

China's encounters with other countries. The end of the Middle Kingdom's relative isolation from the non-Asian world and the conflict with the militarily superior West in the nineteenth century was a major factor in the collapse of the imperial system in 1911. Anger over European and U.S. treatment of China, admiration for the Russian Revolution, and the invasion of

China by Japan in the 1930s all played a role in propelling the CCP to power in 1949.

American hostility to the new Communist regime in Beijing helped push the PRC into an alliance with the Soviet Union and follow the Soviet model of development in the early 1950s. But Mao's disapproval of the direction in which Soviet Communist leaders were taking their country greatly influenced his decisions to launch both the Great Leap Forward in 1958 and the Cultural Revolution in 1966. The former communist allies became embroiled in an ideological dispute that eventually spilled over into global diplomatic rivalry, serious border tensions, and even small-scale military conflict that could have escalated into all out war. In the early 1970s, Mao supported the beginnings of détente with the United States in response to what he saw as a growing and more immediate threat to China from the Soviet Union. The relationship between China and the United States deepened throughout the 1970s and helped pave the way for the marketization and globalization of the Chinese economy under Deng Xiaoping.

Sino-American interaction (*sino* means "China," as derived from the Latin) is, arguably, the most important bilateral diplomatic relationship in the post–cold war world. There have been numerous ups and downs in that relationship ever since the two countries resumed ties in the 1970s. U.S. presidential administrations (and even presidential advisors within a single administration) have differed about whether China's rise as a great power should be seen as an opportunity for the United States, particularly in terms of trade and investment, or a threat to American interests. A particularly low point came after the 1989 Tiananmen massacre, when the United States cut back contacts with the Beijing regime. But shared economic and geopolitical interests have brought the United States and China closer since then., However, disagreements over issues like human rights and the political status of Taiwan and incidents such as the accidental bombing of the PRC embassy in Belgrade, Yugoslavia, by U.S. aircraft during the Kosovo war in July 1999 and the collision of an American spy plane with a Chinese jet fighter off the coast of China in April 2001 have, at times, caused serious friction.

The terrorist attacks of September 11, 2001, had a significant impact on Sino-American relations. The PRC became a key ally in the U.S.-led war on terrorism, which put almost all of the disputes between Beijing and Washington on the diplomatic back-burner. China's leaders were quite happy to have tensions with the United States off their already overly burdened agenda. Indeed, one observer concluded, "the country that has benefited most from 9/11 is China."[5] The United States also needs the PRC's help to resolve the conflict with North Korea (China's neighbor and one-time close communist ally) over that country's nuclear weapons program.

Nevertheless, U.S-China relations are, at best, in a rather uncertain stage. On the one hand, in late 2004, then secretary of state, Colin Powell, declared that Sino-American relations were "the best" they had been "in over 30 years," and, a few months later, his successor, Condoleezza Rice, affirmed "the constructive, growing, and deepening relationship with China."[6] But, in mid-2005, secretary of defense Donald Rumsfeld and an official Pentagon report injected a note of caution in the Bush administration's assessment of U.S. ties with the PRC when they emphasized the threat posed to Asian security and American interests by China's military buildup.[7]

Governing the Economy. Economic issues were central to the revolutionary process that resulted in the founding of the People's Republic. The Western powers were primarily motivated by the lure of the China market in their aggressive policies toward the Chinese empire in the nineteenth century. Chiang Kai-shek's Nationalist government lost popular support partly because of its mismanagement of the economy and its inability to control corruption. Mass poverty and extreme economic inequality fueled the Chinese revolution and led millions of peasants and workers to back the Communist Party in the civil war.

The history of the PRC is largely the story of experimentation with a series of very different economic systems: a Soviet-style planning system in the early 1950s, the radical egalitarianism of the Maoist model, and market-oriented policies implemented by Deng Xiaoping and his successors. Ideological disputes within the CCP over which of these development strategies China should follow were the main cause of the ferocious political struggles, such as the Cultural Revolution, that have so often wracked the country.

Deng's bold reforms were, in large measure, motivated by his hope that improved living standards would restore the legitimacy of the CCP, which had been badly tarnished by the economic failings of the Maoist era. The remarkable successes of those reforms have helped sustain the CCP in power at a time when most other Communist regimes have disappeared. Continuing China's economic progress will be one of the most important challenges facing Hu Jintao and China's other leaders.

The Democratic Idea.   The CCP also faces major political challenges, especially the challenge of the democratic idea, which has had a troubled history in modern China. The revolution of 1911 that overthrew the imperial system and established the Republic of China under Sun Yat-sen was the culmination of the first effort to establish a Chinese government in which citizens would have a voice. But the combination of warlordism, civil war, world war, and Chiang Kaishek's sharp turn toward dictatorship undermined any real progress toward democracy. Any hope that the democratic idea might take root in the early years of Communist rule in China was violently dispelled by the building of a one-party Communist state and Mao's unrelenting campaigns against alleged enemies of his revolution. The Deng Xiaoping era brought much greater economic, social, and cultural freedom for the Chinese people, but time and again the CCP acted to strangle the stirrings of the democratic idea, most brutally in Tiananmen Square in 1989. Jiang Zemin and Hu Jintao have been faithful disciples of Deng; they have not only vigorously championed economic reform in China, but also made sure that the CCP retains its firm grip on power.

The Politics of Collective Identity.   Because of its long history and high degree of cultural homogeneity, China has a very strong sense of national identity. Memories of past humiliations and suffering at the hands of foreigners still influence the international relations of the PRC. For example, Beijing's insistence that Britain return Hong Kong to Chinese control in 1997, largely on its terms, was shaped by the desire to redress what it saw as one of the most blatant injustices of China's defeat in the Opium War of the mid-nineteenth century. China also believes that Japan should apologize more fully for atrocities committed by the Japanese army during World War II before the two Asian powers can have completely cordial diplomatic relations. And as faith in communist ideology has weakened, party leaders have increasingly turned to nationalism as a means to rally the Chinese people behind their government, as reflected in the large-scale public celebrations that greeted Beijing's selection as the site for the 2008 Summer Olympics.

China's cultural homogeneity has also spared it the kind of widespread ethnic or religious violence that has plagued so many other countries in the modern world. The exception has been in the border regions of the country, where there is a large concentration of minority peoples, particularly in Tibet and the Muslim areas of China's northwest (see Section 4).

But China did experience a particularly vicious and destructive kind of identity politics during the Maoist era. Although landlords and capitalists had lost their private property and economic power by the mid-1950s, Mao continued to promote violent class struggle that pitted workers, peasants, and loyal party activists against "capitalist roaders" and other alleged counterrevolutionaries. When he took over in the late 1970s, Deng Xiaoping called for an end to such divisive class struggles and proclaimed an era of social harmony in which the whole nation could concentrate its energies on the overarching goal of economic development, a trend that was continued and deepened by his successors. But economic reform has led to new (or renewed) cleavages in Chinese society, including glaring inequalities between those who have profited handsomely from the marketization of the economy and those who have done less well or even been disadvantaged by the changes. These inequalities could become the basis of class, regional, or other kinds of identity-based conflicts that severely test the economic and political management skills of China's leaders.

Implications for Comparative Politics

China is a particularly important case for the study of comparative politics. First, the PRC can be compared with other communist party-states with which it shares or has shared many political and ideological features. From this perspective, China raises intriguing questions: Why has China's communist party-state so far proved more durable than that of the Soviet Union and nearly all other similar regimes? By what combination of reform and repression has the CCP held onto power? What signs are there that it is likely to continue to be able to do so for the foreseeable future? What signs suggest that Communist rule in China may be weakening? Studying Chinese politics is important for understanding the past, present, and future of a type of political system, the communist party-state, that has had a major impact on the modern world.

China can also be fruitfully compared with other developing nations that face similar economic and political challenges. Although the PRC is part of the Third World as measured by the average standard of living of its population, its record of growth in the past several decades has been far better than almost all other developing countries. Furthermore, the educational and health levels of the Chinese people are quite good when compared with many other countries at a similar level of development, for example, India and Nigeria. How has China achieved such relative success in its quest for economic and social development? On the other hand, while much of the Third World has gone through a wave of democratization in recent decades, China remains a one-party dictatorship. How and why has China resisted this wave of democracy? What does the experience of other developing countries say about how economic modernization might influence the prospects for democracy in China?

Napoleon Bonaparte, emperor of France in the early nineteenth century, is said to have remarked, "Let China sleep. For when China wakes, it will shake the world."[8] There is no doubt China has awakened. Given the country's geographic size, vast resources, huge population, surging economy, and formidable military might, the PRC is certain to be among the world's great powers in the near future and surely deserves the attention of all students of comparative politics.

Section ❷ Political Economy and Development

The growth of China's economy since the late 1970s has been called "one of the century's greatest economic miracles," which has led to "one of the biggest improvements in human welfare anywhere at any time."[9] Such superlatives seem justified in describing overall economic growth rates that have averaged around 9 percent per year for more than two decades, while most of the world's other economies have been growing much more slowly. Measured in terms of purchasing power parity (which adjusts for price differences between countries), China now has the second largest economy in the world after the United States, and per capita incomes in the rural areas (where most people still live) have increased twentyfold, while urban incomes are up about fifteen times. Although there are still many very poor people in China, more than 300 million have been lifted from absolute poverty to a level where they have a minimally adequate supply of food, clothing, and shelter. China's economic miracle has involved much more than growth in GDP and personal income. There has also been a profound transformation of the basic nature of economic life in the PRC from what it had been during the Maoist era.

State and Economy

The Maoist Economy

When the CCP came to power in 1949, the Chinese economy was suffering from the devastating effects of more than a hundred years of rebellion, invasion, civil war, and bad government. The first urgent task of China's new communist rulers was the stabilization and revival of the economy. Although a lot of property was seized from wealthy landowners, rich industrialists, and foreign companies, much private ownership and many aspects of capitalism were allowed to continue in order to gain support for the government and get the economy going again.

Once production had been restored, the party turned its attention to economic development by following the Soviet model of state socialism. The essence of this model was a **command economy,** in which the state owns or controls most economic resources, and economic activity is driven by government planning and commands rather than by market forces.

The command economy in China was at its height during the First Five-Year Plan of 1953–1957, when the government took control of the production and distribution of nearly all goods and services. The Plan yielded impressive economic results, but it also created huge bureaucracies and new inequalities, especially between the heavily favored industrial cities and the investment-starved rural areas. Both the Great Leap Forward (1958–1961) and the Cultural Revolution (1966–1976) embodied the Maoist approach to economic development that was intended to be less bureaucratic and more egalitarian than the Soviet model.

For example, in the Great Leap, more than a million backyard furnaces were set up throughout the country to prove that steel could be produced by peasants in every village, not just in a few huge modern factories in the cities. In the Cultural Revolution, revolutionary committees, controlled by workers and communist activists, replaced the Soviet-style system of letting managers run industrial enterprises. Both of these Maoist experiments were less than successful. The backyard furnaces yielded great quantities of useless steel and squandered precious resources, while the revolutionary committees led many factories to pay more attention to politics than production.

The economic legacy of Maoism was mixed. Under Mao, the PRC "did accomplish, in however flawed a fashion, the initial phase of industrialization of the Chinese economy, creating a substantial industrial and technological base that simply had not existed before."[10] In addition, by the end of the Maoist era, the people of China were much healthier and more literate than they had been in the early 1950s. But for all of its radical rhetoric, the Maoist strategy of development never broke decisively with the basic precepts of the command system. Political interference, poor management, and ill-conceived projects led to wasted resources of truly staggering proportions. Overall, China's economic growth rates, especially in agriculture, barely kept pace with population increases, and the average standard of living changed little between the 1950s and Mao's death in 1976.

China Goes to Market

After he consolidated power in 1978, Deng Xiaoping took China in an economic direction far different from Mao's, or from that which had ever been followed by a communist party-state anywhere. His pragmatic views on how to promote development were captured in his famous 1962 statement, "It doesn't matter whether a cat is white or black, as long as it catches mice."[11] Deng meant that China should not be overly concerned about whether a particular policy was socialist or capitalist if it in fact helped the economy. It was just such sentiment that got him in trouble with Mao and made Deng one of the principal victims of the Cultural Revolution.

Once he was in charge, Deng spearheaded a program of sweeping reforms that remade the Chinese economy, touched nearly every aspect of life in the PRC, and redefined the role of the communist party and the meaning of socialism in China. These reforms greatly reduced the role of government control while allowing market mechanisms, such as the profit motive, to operate in increasingly large areas of the economy. They also involved a significant degree of decentralization in the economy. Authority for making economic decisions passed from bureaucrats to individual families, factory managers, and private entrepreneurs, all of them presumably motivated by the desire to make more money.

Almost all prices are now set according to supply and demand, as in a capitalist economy, rather than by administrative decree, and in most sectors of the economy decisions about what to produce and how to produce it are no longer dictated by the state. Many government monopolies have given way to fierce competition between state-owned and non-state-owned firms. For example, the government-run national airline, which was the country's only airline until 1985, now competes with dozens of foreign and domestic carriers. Reflecting a new awareness of the importance of consumer appeal, the name of the state-owned airline was also changed from the bureaucratic-sounding "Civil Aviation Administration of China" (CAAC) to the more market-friendly "Air China."

A decade ago there were over 100,000 state-owned enterprises (SOEs) in China; now there are about a quarter of that number. In 1978, SOEs generated about 80 percent of China's gross domestic product; by 2003 that figure had dropped to 17 percent. These economic dinosaurs still employ nearly 70 millions workers. They also dominate critical parts of the economy such as the production of steel and petroleum.

But even SOEs must now be responsive to market forces. Those that are unable to turn a profit are forced to restructure or even threatened with bankruptcy. Some have been semiprivatized, but many of those that remain are vastly overstaffed and have outdated facilities and machinery that make them unattractive to potential foreign or domestic buyers. SOEs also hinder modernization of key sectors of the Chinese economy and remain a huge drain on the country's banks (mostly government-controlled), which are still required to bail out many failing state-owned enterprises with large loans that are rarely, if ever, paid back. More drastic SOE reform has been stymied because the country's leaders are understandably concerned about the political and social consequences that would result from an even more massive layoff of industrial workers.

Overall, the role of the state sector in China's economy continues to shrink as private and collective enterprises (which are usually run by combinations of local governments and private entrepreneurs) are expanding at a much faster rate. The Chinese government encourages private ownership, and the private sector now accounts for more than a third of China's total GDP. In Beijing, about 90 percent of retail and service businesses are privately owned, and these employ over 70 percent of the city's workers.

The economic results of China's move to the market have been phenomenal (see Figure 1). The PRC has been the fastest-growing major economy in the world for more than two decades and even weathered, relatively unscathed, the severe financial crisis that struck the rest of East Asia in the late 1990s. China's GDP per capita (that is, the total output of the economy divided by the total population) grew at an average rate of 7.6 percent per year from 1993–2003. By way of comparison, the per capita GDP of the United States grew at

Figure 1

The Economic Transformation of China

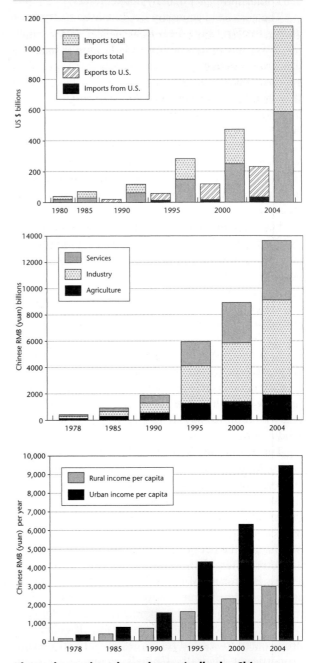

These charts show how dramatically the Chinese economy has been transformed since the market reforms introduced by Deng Xiaoping in 1978.

Sources: U.S.-China Business Council; United States Census Bureau; Xinhua; Chinability.com.

3.4 percent per year during the same period, Japan's at 1.2 percent, and India's at 4.1 percent.

A booming economy and rapidly rising incomes have unleashed a consumer revolution in the PRC. In the late 1970s, the only places people in the cities could shop for most consumer goods were at state-run stores that carried a very limited range of products, many of which were of shoddy quality. Today most of China's urban areas are becoming shopping paradises, with domestic and foreign stores of every kind, huge malls, fast food outlets, and a myriad of entertainment options. Whereas just a few decades ago, hardly anyone owned a television; now nearly every urban household has a color TV, and a large proportion of rural families have at least a black-and-white set. And cell phones are everywhere.

The PRC says that it currently has a **socialist market economy.** Although this terminology may seem to be mere ideological window dressing to allow the introduction of capitalism into a country still ruled by a communist party, the phrase conveys the fact that China's economy now combines elements of both socialism and capitalism. In theory, the market remains subordinate to government planning and CCP leadership, which is supposed to prevent too much capitalist-like exploitation and inequality.

Despite these comprehensive changes, the Chinese economy is not fully marketized. Central planning, although greatly refined and reduced, has not been eliminated altogether, and national and local bureaucrats still exercise a great deal of control over the production and distribution of goods, resources, and services. The extent of private property is still restricted, and unproductive state enterprises continue to exert a considerable drag on major economic sectors. Although the market reforms have gained substantial momentum that would be nearly impossible to reverse, the CCP still wields the power to decide the future direction of China's economy.

Remaking the Chinese Countryside

The economic transformation of China has been particularly striking in the countryside, where over 700 million people live and work.

One of the first revolutionary programs launched by the CCP after it came to power in 1949 was a land reform campaign that confiscated the property of landlords and redistributed it as private holdings to the poorer peasants. But in the mid-1950s, as part of the transition to socialism, China's peasants were reorganized into collective farms made up of about 250 families each. The land then belonged to the collective, and local officials working in coordination with the state plan directed production and labor. Individuals were paid according to how much they worked on the collective land, while most crops and other farm products had to be sold to the state at low fixed prices. During the Great Leap Forward, the collective farms were merged into gigantic **people's communes,** each made up of several thousand families. Although the size of the communes was scaled back following failure of the Leap, the commune system remained the foundation of the rural economy throughout the rest of the Maoist period. The system of collectivized agriculture proved to be one of the weakest links in China's command economy. Per capita agricultural production and rural living standards were essentially stagnant from 1957 to 1977.

The first changes in the organization of agriculture in post-Mao China came from the spontaneous actions of local leaders who were looking for ways to boost production. They moved to curtail the powers of the commune and allow peasants more leeway in planting and selling their crops. In the early 1980s, Deng Xiaoping used his newly won political power to support this trend and moved to "bury the Maoist model once and for all" in the countryside.[12] The communes were replaced by a **household responsibility system,** which remains in effect today. Under this system, farmland is contracted out to individual families, who take full charge of the production and marketing of crops. Families can sign contracts for thirty years or more, but there has been no move to privatize agriculture fully by selling the land to individuals. The freeing of the rural economy from the constraints of the communal system led to a sharp increase in agricultural productivity and income for most farm families.

But nothing contributed more to the remaking of the Chinese countryside than the spread of a rural industrial and commercial revolution that, in speed and scope, was unprecedented in the history of the modern world. Although the foundations of rural industrialization were laid during the Maoist period, **township and**

This picture, taken in Shanghai in the 1990s, graphically captures how the modern and the traditional exist side-by-side in China. It also shows how the market-style reforms introduced by Deng Xiaoping greatly increased disparities in wealth, a problem that could lead to growing social and political tensions in the future. *Source:* Dan Habib.

village enterprises (TVEs) expanded enormously under Deng Xiaoping's economic reforms. These rural factories and businesses, which vary greatly in size, from a handful of employees to thousands, are generally owned and run by local governments and private entrepreneurs, and are now attracting a considerable amount of foreign investment. Although they are called collective enterprises, TVEs operate outside the state plan, make their own decisions about all aspects of the business process, and are responsible for their profits and losses.

For much of the 1980s and 1990s, TVEs were the fastest-growing sector of the Chinese economy. But the economic Darwinism of the market caught up with the rapid expansion of TVEs by the turn of the century, and many were forced out of business. Nevertheless, there are over 20 million TVEs in China, employing nearly 130 million people and generating over 34 percent of GDP. They have become increasingly important in producing for the export market, particularly in areas such as textiles and toys.

The transformation of the Chinese countryside has not been without serious problems. Local officials who run TVEs "often behave more like business tycoons than public servants" and pay more attention to making money for themselves than to their civic duties.[13] Peasant protests, which sometimes turn violent, against high taxes, corrupt local officials, environmental desecration, illegal land seizures, and delays in payments for agricultural products purchased by the government have increased significantly in recent years.

The growth of agriculture has slowed considerably since the first burst of reform: from a high of 12.5 percent growth in 1985, it averaged a little over 4 percent per year in the 1990s and dropped to under 3 percent in the early 2000s. Agricultural output appeared to be bouncing back with an increase of 7 percent in 2004 in response to government efforts to stimulate the rural economy. Nevertheless, there is a huge gap between the average incomes of urban residents and those who live in the countryside (see Fig. 1) and farmers in

China's poorer areas have faced years of stagnating or even declining incomes. Furthermore, the social services safety net provided for China's rural dwellers by the communes has all but disappeared with the return to household-based farming and the market economy. Many rural clinics and schools closed once government financial support was eliminated. The availability of health care, educational opportunities, disability pay, and retirement funds now depends on the relative wealth of families and villages. China's controversial one-child population control policy (see "Current Challenges: China's One-Child Policy") has particularly disadvantaged poor rural families who need more household labor.

The Political Impact of Economic Reform

Efforts to transform the economy through market-style policies have had an important impact on China's domestic politics. First, both Deng Xiaoping and then Jiang Zemin faced opposition from other party leaders who believed that China was moving too fast and too far toward a market economy. The critics of reform worried about the spread of capitalist influences, including calls for more democracy, at home and from abroad. Deng was able to accommodate such challenges, and the emergence of Jiang and, more recently, Hu Jintao as Deng's successors has kept power in the hands of leaders strongly committed to continuing economic reform. But a major economic setback or widespread political turmoil could still lead to a resurgence of antireform elements in the party.

Second, the **decentralization** of economic decision making, which has been an important factor in the success of the market reforms, has also greatly increased the autonomy of subnational governments in China. Local governments often defy or ignore the central government by, for example, evading taxes or undertaking massive construction projects without consulting Beijing.

Finally, China's economic transformation has brought far-reaching social change to the country, creating new pressures on the political system and new challenges to the CCP. The party wants the Chinese people to believe that economic growth depends on the political stability that only its firm leadership can provide. CCP leaders hope that growing prosperity will leave most people satisfied with the communist party and reduce demands for political change. But economic reform has created many groups—entrepreneurs, professionals, middle-class consumers, the hundreds of thousands of Chinese students who have studied abroad—who cannot be repressed if the party wants to sustain the country's economic progress. In time, these and other emerging groups are likely to press their claims for a more independent political voice and to confront the regime with some fundamental questions about the nature of Communist power in China.

Society and Economy

Market reform and globalization of the Chinese economy have created a much more diverse and open society. People are vastly freer to choose careers, travel about the country and internationally, practice their religious beliefs, buy private homes, join nonpolitical associations, and engage in a wide range of other activities that were prohibited or severely restricted during the Maoist era. But economic change has also caused grave social problems. There has been a sharp increase in crime, prostitution, and drug use; although such problems are still far less prevalent in China than in many other countries, they are serious enough to be a growing concern for national and local authorities.

Economic reform has also brought significant changes in China's basic system of social welfare. The Maoist economy was characterized by what was called the **iron rice bowl.** As in other state socialist economies such as the Soviet Union, this meant that employment, a certain standard of living (albeit, a low one), and basic cradle-to-grave benefits were guaranteed to most of the urban and rural labor force. In the cities, the workplace was more than just a place to work and earn a salary; it also provided its employees with housing, health care, day care, and other services.

China's economic reformers believe that such guarantees led to poor work motivation and excessive costs for the government and enterprises, and they have implemented policies designed to break the iron rice bowl. Income and employment are no longer guaranteed but are more directly tied to individual effort.

Current Challenges: **China's One-Child Policy**

While he was in power, Mao Zedong did not see a reduction of China's population growth rate as an important national priority. On the contrary, he viewed vast amounts of human labor and the revolutionary enthusiasm of the masses as precious national assets. As a result, little was done to promote family planning in China during most of the Maoist era.

By the early 1970s, China's population had reached over 800 million, and because of greatly improved health conditions, it was growing at about 2.8 percent per year. This meant that the number of people in China would double in just twenty-five years, which threatened to put a great strain on the country's resources. Cutting the birthrate came to be seen as a major prerequisite to economic development. Since the 1980s, the Chinese government has enforced a stringent population control policy that has, over time, used various means to encourage or even force couples to have only a single child. Intensive media campaigns have lauded the patriotic virtues and material benefits of small families. Positive incentives such as more farmland or preferred housing have been offered to couples with only one child, and fines or demotions have been meted out to those who violate the policy. In some places, workplace medics or local doctors monitor contraceptive use and women's fertility cycles, and a couple must have official permission to have a child. Defiance has sometimes led to forced abortion or sterilization.

The one-child campaign, the modernizing economy, and a comparatively strong record in improving educational and employment opportunities for women have all played a role in bringing China's population growth rate to about 0.8 percent per year. This figure is *very* low for a country at China's level of economic development. India, for example, has also had some success in promoting family planning, but its annual population growth rate is 1.6 percent, while Nigeria's is 2.4 percent. These may not seem like big differences, but consider this: at these respective growth rates, it will take eighty-seven years for China's population to double, whereas India's

population will double in forty-three years and Nigeria's in just twenty-nine years!

There have been some very serious problems with China's population policy. The compulsory, intrusive nature of the family planning program and the extensive use of abortion as one of the major means of birth control have led to some international criticism, which Beijing has rejected as interference in its domestic affairs.

Many farmers have evaded the one-child policy—for example, by not registering births—because the return to household-based agriculture has made the quantity of labor an important ingredient in family income. The still widespread belief that male children will contribute more economically to the family and that a male heir is necessary to carry on the family line causes some rural families to take drastic steps to make sure that they have a son. Female infanticide and the abandonment of female babies have increased dramatically, and the spread of ultrasound technology has led to large number of sex-selective abortions of female fetuses. As a result, China has an unusual gender balance among its young population: normally, 103 to 107 boys are born for every 100 girls, but China's last census, completed in 2000, showed a gender ratio of nearly 120 boys for every 100 girls and as high as 135 to 100 in some regions. As a result, there are hundreds of thousands (perhaps millions) of "missing girls" in China's population under the age of thirty. One estimate suggests that there are 70 million more males in China than females, and some worry this has already led to "bride stealing" and other kinds of trafficking in women.

Partly in response to rural resistance and international pressure, the Chinese government has relaxed its population policies somewhat; forced abortion is now infrequent, although sex-selective abortion is not. Rural couples are now often allowed to have two children. In the cities, where there has been more voluntary compliance with the policy because of higher incomes and limited living space, the one-child policy is still basically in effect.

Workers in the remaining state-owned enterprises still have rather generous health and pension plans, but employees in the rapidly expanding semiprivate and private sectors usually have few benefits.

The breaking of the iron rice bowl has motivated people to work harder in order to earn more money. But it has also led to a sharp increase in urban unemployment. An estimated 45 to 60 million workers have been laid off in recent years. Many are too old or too unskilled to find good jobs in the modernized and marketized economy, and China has very little in the way of unemployment insurance or social security for its displaced workers. The official unemployment rate is about 4 percent of the urban labor force, but it is generally believed to be at least twice that and to be as high as 40 percent in some parts of the country. China's health care system—once touted as a model for the Third World—is in shambles. Less than a quarter of the urban population, and only 10 percent of those who live in the rural area, have health insurance. The World Health Organization ranks China among the worst countries in terms of the allocation of medical resources.

Work slowdowns, strikes, and demonstrations (in some cases with tens of thousands of participants) are becoming more frequent, particularly in China's northeastern rust belt, where state-owned industries have been particularly hard hit. In the past, the CCP has not dealt gently with protesting workers: the army was ordered to crush the 1989 Tiananmen demonstrations partly because party leaders were alarmed by the large number of workers who had joined the protests under the banner of an unauthorized union. If unemployment continues to surge, labor unrest could be a political time bomb for China's communist party-state.

Market reforms have also opened China's cities to a flood of rural migrants. After the agricultural communes were disbanded in the early 1980s, many of the peasants who were not needed in the fields found work in the rapidly expanding township and village enterprises. But many others, no longer constrained by the strict limits on internal population movement enforced in the Mao era, headed to the urban areas to look for jobs. The more than 100 million people who make up this so-called "floating population" are mostly employed in low-paying temporary jobs such as unskilled construction work. These migrants are filling an important niche in China's changing labor market, but they are also putting increased pressure on urban housing and social services. Their presence in Chinese cities could become politically destabilizing if they find their economic aspirations thwarted by a stalled economy or if they are treated too roughly or unfairly by local governments, which often see them as intruders. With another 150 million un- or underemployed rural dwellers, the floating population is expected to keep growing for years to come.

China's economic boom has also created enormous opportunities for corruption. In a country in transition from a command to a market economy, officials still control numerous resources and retain power over many economic transactions from which large profits can be made. Bribes are common in this heavily bureaucratized and highly personalized system. Because the rule of law is often weaker than personal connections (called **guanxi** in Chinese), nepotism and cronyism are rampant. Recognizing the threat that corruption poses to its legitimacy, the government has repeatedly launched well-publicized campaigns against official graft, with severe punishment, including execution, for some serious offenders, but with little effect in curbing such nefarious practices.

The benefits of economic growth have reached most of China to one degree or another. But there has also been a significant rise in inequality—a contradiction for a country led by a party that still claims to believe in communist ideals. China's market reforms and economic boom have created sharp class differences, generally benefiting people who live in the cities much more than those in the countryside. There is also widening gap between the more developed coastal regions and the inland areas, although recent poverty alleviation programs, including a "Develop the West" campaign, have brought a little economic progress to some of poorest parts of the country. The PRC government has been touting what it calls the *xiaokang* (or "well-off society") model of development, which emphasizes not only achieving a higher average standard of living, but a more equitable distribution of income and basic social welfare, including health and education.

Gender inequalities also appear to have increased in some ways since the introduction of the market reforms. There is no doubt that the overall situation of women in China has improved enormously since 1949 in terms of social status, legal rights, employment, and education. Women have also benefited from rising living standards and expanded economic opportunities that the reforms have brought. But the trend toward marketization has not benefited men and women equally. In the countryside, it is almost always the case that only male heads of households sign contracts for land and other production resources, and therefore men dominate rural economic life. This is true despite the fact that farm labor has become increasingly feminized as many men move to jobs in rural industry or migrate to the cities. Only 1 percent of the leaders in China's 700,000 villages are women. Economic and cultural pressures have also led to an alarming suicide rate (the world's highest) among rural women. Over 70 percent (about 120 million) of illiterate adults in China are female. Although China has one of the world's highest rates of female urban labor participation, the market reforms have "strengthened and in some cases reconstructed the sexual division of labor, keeping urban women in a transient, lower-paid, and subordinate position in the workforce."[14] Women workers are the first to be laid off or are forced to retire early when a collective or state-owned enterprise downsizes.

Finally, the momentous economic changes in China have had serious environmental consequences. As in the former Soviet Union and East-Central Europe, China's environment suffered greatly under the old state socialist system, but in some ways, ecological damage has become even worse in the profit-at-any-cost atmosphere of the market reforms. Industrial expansion is fueled primarily by the use of highly polluting coal, which has made the air in China's cities and even many rural areas among the dirtiest in the world. Soil erosion, the loss of arable land, and deforestation are serious problems for the countryside. The dumping of garbage and toxic wastes goes virtually unregulated, and it is estimated that 80 percent of China's rivers are badly polluted. One of the most serious problems is a critical water shortage in north China due to urbanization and industrialization. Private automobile use is just starting to take off and will greatly add to the country's pollution concerns (and demand for more oil) in the very near future.

There are signs of increasing environmental awareness among China's citizens. A large number of green groups are active on the national and local levels, and in April 2005, a protest over chemical plant pollution in rural central China turned into a violent clash between villagers and armed riot police. The government has begun to enact policies to address some of these problems, and environmental protection is another goal of the *xiaokang* model of development. However, as one journalist with long experience in China observed, "It still seems that every environmentally friendly measure is offset by a greater number of abuses" in the quest for rapid economic development.[15]

Dealing with some of the negative consequences of fast growth and market reforms is one of the main challenges facing China's government. The ability of citizen associations—including labor, women's, and environmental organizations—to place their concerns about these problems on the nation's political agenda remains limited by the party's tight control of political life and by restrictions on the formation of autonomous interest groups (see Section 4).

China in the Global Economy

Deng Xiaoping's program for transforming the Chinese economy rested on two pillars: the market-oriented reform of the domestic economy and the policy of opening China to the outside world. The extensive internationalization of the Chinese economy in recent decades contrasts sharply with the semi-isolationist policy of economic self-reliance pursued by Mao Zedong.

China was not a major trading nation when Deng took power in 1978. Total foreign trade was around $20 billion (approximately 10 percent of GDP), and foreign investment in China was minuscule, since the stagnant economy, political instability, and heavy-handed bureaucracy were not attractive to potential investors from abroad.

In the early 1980s, China embarked on a strategy of using trade as a central component of its drive for economic development, following in some ways the model of export-led growth pioneered by Japan and **newly industrializing countries** (NICs) such as the Republic of Korea (South Korea). The essence of this model is to take advantage of low-wage domestic labor to produce goods that are in demand internationally and then to use the earnings from the sale of those goods to finance the modernization of the economy.

By 2004, China was the world's third largest trading nation (after the United States and Germany), with imports and exports totaling more than $1.1 trillion, an increase of about 35 percent from just the year before. China's main exports are office machines, data-processing and telecommunications equipment, clothing and footwear, toys, and sporting goods. For many products, China dominates the world market. For example, 75 percent of DVD players and microwave ovens come from the PRC, as do over 60 percent of the world's bicycles: nine out of ten bikes sold in the United States are made in China. The PRC imports mostly industrial machinery, technology and scientific equipment, iron and steel, and raw materials needed to support economic development. Despite having large domestic sources of petroleum and significant untapped reserves, China became a net importer of oil for the first time in 1993 because of the huge energy demands of its economic boom. And in 2002, in order to meet the voracious appetite for steel generated by a construction boom and a surge in automobile production, China surpassed the United States as the world's largest importer of that commodity, even though it already produces more steel than the United States and Japan combined.

Much of China's trade is in East Asia, particularly with Japan, South Korea, Taiwan, and Hong Kong (which is now administratively part of the PRC, but is a highly developed, capitalist economy; see "Global Connection: Hong Kong: From China to Britain—and Back Again").

The United States has also become one of the PRC's major trading partners and is now the biggest market for Chinese exports (over 20 percent of the total in 2003). In 2000, China surpassed Japan as the country with which the United States had the largest trade deficit (that is, imports exceed exports) by a small margin, but as Japan continued to be mired in a deep recession, the U.S. deficit with China ($162 billion in 2004) is now larger than it is with Japan ($75 billion). This huge imbalance has become a source of tension in U.S.-China relations, particularly because quite a few Americans think that the PRC is engaging in trade practices (such as undervaluing its currency) that give

its products an unfair advantage in global commerce. Some politicians, business leaders, and labor union officials, who also believe that Americans are losing jobs because U.S. companies are "outsourcing" production to China because of its very low labor costs, are calling for the government to impose restrictions on Chinese imports. But others point out how trade with the PRC benefits the U.S. economy—for example, by bringing inexpensive goods into stores that have saved American consumers hundreds of billions of dollars over the last decade or so. They also note that China uses some of its export earnings to buy U.S. government bonds. These bonds provide the U.S. government with revenue to finance America's large budget deficit, the result of spending on the war in Iraq and tax cuts enacted by the Bush administration. If China (and other nations) did not purchase these government bonds, U.S. interest rates (including mortgages) would probably rise. Rising interest rates could result in a slowdown in the U.S. economy, which would have a ripple effect throughout the global economy.

Foreign investment in the PRC has also skyrocketed. There was literally no investment from abroad in China during the Maoist era, since letting foreigners own property, employ Chinese workers, or take profits out of the country was considered an infringement of national sovereignty and dignity. China is now the world's largest absorber of foreign direct investment ($150 billion in 2004), and more than 400 of the world's 500 top corporations have operations in the PRC. Although foreign firms generally pay Chinese workers considerably more than the average manufacturing wage of about 60 cents per hour, the low cost of labor in China is still a major attraction to investors from abroad.

Another lure to foreign investment is the huge Chinese domestic market, particularly as disposable incomes rise, and corporations, like Coca-Cola, General Motors, and Starbucks, have poured huge amounts of money into China in an effort to attract Chinese consumers. American tobacco companies are hoping that China's 350 million smokers can make up for sharply declining cigarette sales in the United States: in 2005, Philip Morris signed an agreement with a Chinese company to jointly produce Marlboros (2 billion in the first year!) to be sold in China. China is itself becoming a foreign investor, and in a sign of just

Hong Kong became a British colony in three stages during the nineteenth century as a result of what China calls the "unequal treaties" imposed under military and diplomatic pressure from the West. Two parts of Hong Kong were ceded permanently to Britain in 1842 and 1860, respectively, but the largest part of the tiny territory was given to Britain in 1898 with a ninety-nine-year lease. It was the anticipated expiration of that lease that set in motion negotiations between London and Beijing in the 1980s over the future status of Hong Kong. In December 1984, a joint declaration was signed by the two countries in which Britain agreed to return all of Hong Kong to Chinese sovereignty on July 1, 1997. On that date, Hong Kong became a Special Administrative Region (SAR) of the People's Republic of China.

Britain ruled Hong Kong in a traditional, if generally benevolent, colonial fashion. A governor sent from London presided over an administration in which foreigners rather than the local people exercised most of the power. There was a free press, a fair and effective legal system, and other important features of a democratic system. In the last years of British rule, there were efforts to appoint more Hong Kong Chinese to higher administrative positions and expand the scope of elections in choosing some members of the colony's executive and representative bodies. The British, who controlled Hong Kong for over a century, were criticized for taking steps toward democratization only on the eve of their departure from the colony. They allowed only a small number of Hong Kong residents to emigrate to the United Kingdom before the start of Chinese rule.

Hong Kong flourished economically under the free-market policies of the British and became one of the world's great centers of international trade and finance, and now has the highest standard of living in Asia outside of Japan and Singapore. Hong Kong is also characterized by extremes of wealth and poverty. When it took over Hong Kong in 1997, China, under the principle of "one country, two systems," pledged not to impose socialism and to preserve capitalism in the HKSAR for fifty years. Because of the extensive integration of the economies of Hong Kong and southern China, the PRC has a strong motivation not to do anything that might destroy the area's economic dynamism.

Although the PRC took over full control of Hong Kong's foreign policy and has stationed troops of the People's Liberation Army in Hong Kong, Beijing has generally fulfilled its promise that the SAR will have a high degree of political as well as economic autonomy. Civil liberties, the independence of the judiciary, and freedom of the press have largely been maintained.

China has, nevertheless, made sure that it keeps a grip on power in Hong Kong. The SAR is headed by a chief executive, who along with other top civil servants must be approved by the PRC. Politicians favoring democracy in Hong Kong have a strong presence in the SAR's elected legislature, but the legislature itself is relatively powerless when it comes to policymaking. In a telling example of the tug of war over the direction of Hong Kong's political future, the PRC's plan to implement a law prohibiting "any act of treason, secession, sedition, subversion against the Central People's Government, or theft of state secrets" was withdrawn in 2004 after large-scale protests by those who worry that British colonialism in Hong Kong might be replaced by Chinese authoritarianism.

Hong Kong

Land area	401.5 sq mi/ 1,092 sq km (about six times the size of Washington, D.C.)
Population	6.9 million
Ethnic composition	Chinese, 95%; other, 5%
GDP at purchasing power parity (US$)	$235 billion
GDP per capita at purchasing power parity (US$)	$34,200
GDP growth rate (2004)	7.9%
Life expectancy	81.39
Infant mortality (per 1,000 live births)	2.97
Literacy	94%
Human Development Index (HDI) ranking (value) out of 177 countries:	23 (.903)

how far the PRC has come as an economic actor in the world of states, the Chinese Lenovo Group bought the majority stake in IBM's personal computer business in late 2004. In a much more controversial move in mid-2005, the partly government-owned China National Offshore Oil Company (CNOOC) became embroiled in a multibillion-dollar bidding war with Chevron to purchase Unocal, a relatively small American company with valuable oil and gas holdings in Southeast Asia and elsewhere. Although the Chinese company eventually withdrew its offer, the episode sparked a debate in Congress and the media about whether CNOOC's efforts to acquire Unocal was another example of globalization at work and the rise of China as a major economic power or a serious threat to the energy and military security of the United States.

The admission of the PRC to the World Trade Organization (WTO) in December 2001 was another significant step in the country's integration into the global economy. The WTO is the major international organization that oversees and regulates commerce between nations, and membership in it is a great benefit to any country that engages in foreign trade. The United States and other highly developed countries agreed to admit China only after they felt that its economy was more "market" than "state" dominated and that China would play by the rules of free trade.

In agreeing to the terms of joining the WTO, China had to promise to make fundamental changes in its trade practices and domestic economic policies. Most important is the further opening of the Chinese economy to foreign investment and competition. Tariffs (that is, taxes) on imported goods must be drastically cut, and sectors of the economy that have been largely closed to foreign companies, such as banking, insurance, and agriculture, will have to be unbarred. China's state-owned enterprises, government monopolies, and rural economy will likely find this step toward deeper globalization particularly challenging, but the advantages to the PRC are an expected large increase in foreign trade and investment.

China occupies an important, but somewhat contradictory, position in the global economy. On the one hand, the PRC's relatively low level of economic and technological development, compared to the industrialized countries, makes it very much a part of the Third World. On the other hand, the total output and rapid growth of its economy, expanding trade, and vast resource base (including its population) make it a potential economic superpower among nations. Indeed, that day may have already come: In mid-2005, the highly respected British weekly magazine, *The Economist,* ran a cover story entitled "How China Runs the World Economy" arguing that "Beijing, not Washington, increasingly takes the decisions that affect workers, companies, financial markets and economies everywhere."[16] In the years ahead, China is certain to become an even more active participant in the global economy. At the same time, international influences are likely to play an increasingly important role in China's economic and political development.

Section ③   Governance and Policy-making

The People's Republic of China, Cuba, Vietnam, North Korea, and Laos are the only remaining communist party-states in the world. Like the Soviet Union before its collapse in 1991, the political systems of these countries are characterized by Communist Party domination of all government and social institutions, the existence of an official state ideology based on Marxism-Leninism, and, to varying and changing degrees, state control of key aspects of the economy. The CCP, which has about 70 million members, claims that only it can govern in the best interests of the entire nation and therefore has the right to exercise the "leading role" throughout Chinese society. Although China has moved sharply toward a market economy in recent decades, the CCP still asserts that it is building socialism with the ultimate objective of creating an egalitarian and classless communist society.

Organization of the State

"The force at the core leading our cause forward is the Chinese Communist Party," observed Mao Zedong in a speech given in 1954 at the opening session of China's legislature, the National People's Congress, which according to the constitution adopted at that meeting, was the "highest organ of state power" in the People's Republic.[17] Chairman Mao's statement was a blunt reminder that the party was in charge of the national legislature and all other government organizations. This same line was the very first entry in *The Little Red Book,* the bible of Mao quotes used by the Red Guards who ransacked the country in the name of ideological purity during the Cultural Revolution. Although many party members became targets of the Cultural Revolution, the prominence of this quotation reflected the fact that at the height of the movement's near anarchy, Mao and his supporters did not intend to call into question the primacy of Communist rule in China.

Even Deng Xiaoping, the architect of China's economic reforms, was unwavering in his view that the country should "never dispense with leadership by the party."[18] Despite the many fundamental changes that have taken place in recent decades, party leadership remains an unchallengeable principle of political life in China, and the nation's rulers still claim allegiance to communist ideology. Any analysis of governance and policymaking in China therefore must begin with a discussion of the ideology and power of the Communist Party.

Mao Zedong is said by the CCP to have made a fundamental contribution to communist ideology by adapting Marxism-Leninism to China's special circumstances, particularly its emphasis on the peasant-based revolution that brought the party to power. Mao's ideology ("Maoism") is officially referred to in China as "Mao Zedong Thought." The party continues to praise Mao, although they acknowledge that he made serious mistakes and that some of his ideas were wrong, such as his views about class struggle that led to the Cultural Revolution.

In 1997, the CCP added "Deng Xiaoping Theory" to its official ideology to reflect the late leader's role in justifying a self-proclaimed socialist country's use of market forces to promote the growth of the economy. And in 2002, when he retired as general secretary, even Jiang Zemin's ideas (the "Three Represents") about expanding the CCP to incorporate all sectors of

Chinese society, including private entrepreneurs, were enshrined in the party constitution (see Section 4).

Although the focus of Chinese communism has shifted from an emphasis on revolutionary change to economic development, most people in China have lost faith in the ideology because of the CCP's erratic and repressive leadership over the past several decades, or else they simply consider ideology largely irrelevant to their daily lives. Many of those who join the party now do so mainly for career advancement. There are numerous other sources of beliefs and values in society, such as family and religion, that are more important to most people than the official ideology. But the latest Chinese communist variant of Marxism-Leninism still provides the framework for governance and policymaking and sets the boundaries for what, in the party's view, is permissible in politics.

The underlying organizing principles of China's party-state are clearly laid out in the PRC constitution, which is a totally different document from the party (CCP) constitution.[19] The preamble makes repeated reference to the fact that the country is under "the leadership of the Communist Party of China." Article 1 defines the PRC as "a socialist state under the people's democratic dictatorship" and declares that "disruption of the socialist system by any organization or individual is prohibited." Such provisions imply that the Chinese "people"—implicitly defined as those who support socialism and the leadership of the party—enjoy democratic rights and privileges; but the Chinese constitution also gives the CCP the authority to exercise dictatorship over any person or organization that it believes is opposed to socialism and the party.

China's constitution is less a governing document than it is a political statement, and constitutional change (from amendments to total replacement) during the last 50 years has reflected the shifting political winds in China. The character and content of the constitution in force at any given time bear the ideological stamp of the prevailing party leadership. For example, the constitution adopted in 1975 toward the end of the Cultural Revolution noted prominently the yet unfinished "struggle between the socialist road and the capitalist road," whereas the current PRC constitution (adopted in 1982) was amended in 1993 to replace references to the superiority of central planning and state ownership with phrases more consistent with capitalist economic reforms, including the statement (Article 15) that China "practices a socialist market economy."

The constitution of the People's Republic specifies the structures and powers of subnational levels of government, including the country's provinces, autonomous regions, and centrally administered cities. But China is not a federal system (like Brazil, Germany, India, Nigeria, and the United States), in which subnational governments have considerable policymaking autonomy. Provincial and local authorities operate "under the unified leadership of the central authorities" (Article 3), which makes China a unitary state (like France and Japan), in which the national government exercises a high degree of control over other levels of government.

The Executive

The government of the People's Republic of China is organizationally and functionally distinct from the Chinese Communist Party. For example, the PRC executive consists of both a premier (prime minister) and a president, whereas the CCP is headed by a general secretary. But there is no alternation of parties in power in China, and the Communist Party exercises direct or indirect control over all government organizations and personnel. All high-ranking government officials with any substantive authority are also members of the CCP. Therefore, real executive power in the Chinese political system lies with the top leaders and organizations of the CCP (see Table 1). The government of the PRC essentially acts as the administrative agency for carrying out and enforcing policies made by the party. Nevertheless, to fully understand governance and policymaking in China, it is necessary to look at the structure of both the Chinese Communist Party and the government of the People's Republic of China (the "state") and the relationship between the two.

The Chinese Communist Party

The constitution of the CCP specifies national and local party structures and functions, the distribution of authority among party organizations, the requirements

for joining, the behavior expected of members, and procedures for dealing with infractions of party rules. Despite such organizational and procedural details, individual power, factional maneuvering, and personal connections (*guanxi*) are ultimately more important than formal constitutional arrangements for understanding how the party works.

For example, Deng Xiaoping, who was indisputably the most powerful individual in China from 1978 until he became physically incapacitated a year or so before his death in 1997, never occupied any of the top executive offices in the party or the government. Even when he no longer played an active role in day-to-day governance, no major decision was made without his approval, and he was regularly referred to as China's "paramount leader." The sources of Deng's immense power came from informal factors, such as his seniority as one of the founders of the regime, his *guanxi* with other key political and military leaders, and his long advocacy of now widely supported ideas about how China should develop into a strong and modern nation.

Despite the persisting strong influence of retired elders (such as Jiang Zemin) and personal connections in Chinese politics, the formal structures of power have assumed greater importance for understanding who has power and how decisions are made. According to the CCP constitution, the "highest leading bodies" of the party are the National Party Congress and the Central Committee (see Figure 2). But its infrequent, short meetings (for one week every five years) and large size (more than 2,100 delegates) mean that the role of the Congress in the party is more symbolic than substantive. The essential function of the National Party Congress is to approve decisions already made by the top leaders and to provide a showcase for the party's current policies. For instance, the party congress that convened in November 2002 was a highly orchestrated celebration of Jiang Zemin's leadership, as well as the occasion for installing Hu Jintao as the new general secretary. There was little debate about policy and no contested voting of any consequence.

The Central Committee, which currently has 198 full and 158 alternate members, is the next level up in the pyramid of party power and consists of CCP leaders from around the country who meet annually

Table 1

Who's Who in Beijing: China's Most Important Party and State Leaders Since 1949

Leader	Highest Positions Held	Comment
Mao Zedong (1893–1976)	CCP Chairman (1943–1976) PRC President (1949–1959) Military Commission Chair (1949–1976)	Became effective leader of the CCP in 1934–1935 during the Long March, although not elected chairman of the Politburo until 1943.
Liu Shaoqi (1898–1969)	PRC President (1959–1966) CCP Vice-Chairman (1949–1966)	Purged as a "capitalist roader" during the Cultural Revolution. Died in detention.
Zhou Enlai (1898–1976)	PRC Premier (1949–1976) PRC Foreign Minister (1949–1958) CCP Vice-Chairman (1949–1969; 1973–1976)	Longtime Mao ally, but a moderating influence during the Cultural Revolution. Architect of détente with U.S. in early 1970s.
Lin Biao (1907–1971)	CCP Vice-Chairman (1958–1971) PRC Vice-Premier (1954–1971) PRC Defense Minister (1959–1971)	One of Mao's strongest supporters in the Cultural Revolution. Allegedly killed in plane crash after failure of attempted coup against Mao.
Jiang Qing (1914–1991)	Deputy Director, Cultural Revolution Group (1966–1969) Member, CCP Politburo (1969–1976)	Former movie actress who married Mao in 1939. One of the leaders of the Cultural Revolution. Arrested after Mao's death in 1976 and sentenced to life in prison, where she died.
Hua Guofeng (1920–)	CCP Chairman (1976–1981) PRC Premier (1976–1980) Military Commission Chair (1976–1981)	Became CCP chairman after Mao's death and purge of Jiang Qing and her radical followers. Removed from power by Deng Xiaoping, who saw him as too weak and a neo-Maoist.
Deng Xiaoping (1904–1997)	PRC Vice-Premier (1952–1966; 1973–1976; 1977–1980) CCP Vice-Chairman (1975–1976; 1977–1987) Military Commission Chair (1981–1989)	Purged twice during Cultural Revolution. Became China's most powerful leader in 1978 and remained so until shortly before his death.
Jiang Zemin (1926–)	CCP General Secretary* (1989–2002) PRC President (1993–2003) Military Commission Chair (1989–2004)	Former Shanghai mayor promoted by Deng a safe choice to carry out his policies after Tiananmen crisis. Consolidated his own power after Deng's death in 1997.
Hu Jintao (1942–)	CCP General Secretary (2002–) PRC President (2003–) Military Commission Chair (2004–)	Chosen by Deng Xiaoping before his death to succeed Jiang Zemin as head of the CCP. A relatively young technocrat.

*The position of CCP chairman was abolished in 1982 and replaced by the general secretary as the party's top position.

for about a week. Members are elected for a five year term by the National Party Congress by secret ballot, and there is limited choice of candidates. Contending party factions may jockey to win seats, but the overall composition of the Central Committee is closely controlled by the top leaders to ensure compliance with their policies. The Central Committee elected in late 2002 continued the trend toward promoting younger and better-educated party members who are strong supporters of economic reform.

The Central Committee directs party affairs when the National Party Congress is not in session, but its

Figure 2

The Chinese Communist Party (CCP)

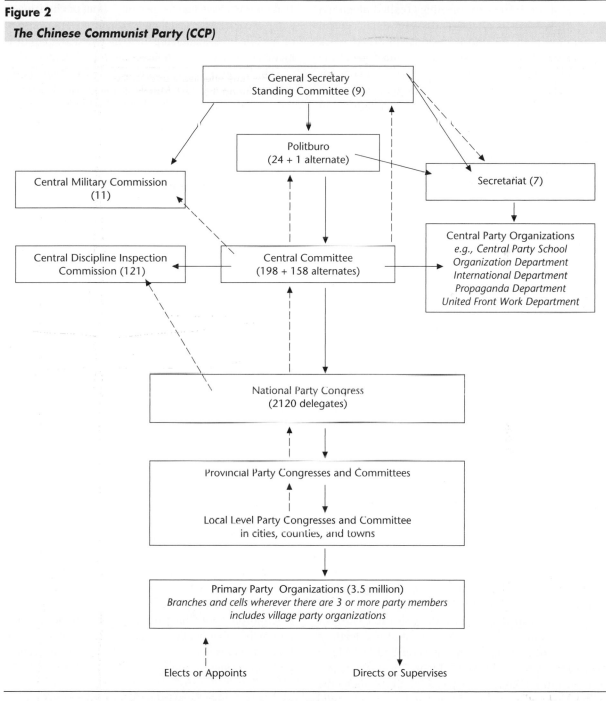

Numbers in parentheses refer to the number of members as of 2005.

size and short, infrequent meetings (called plenums) also greatly limit its effectiveness. However, Central Committee plenums and occasional informal work conferences do represent significant gatherings of the party elite, which can be a very important arena of political maneuvering and decision making.

The most powerful political organizations in China's communist party-state are the two small executive bodies at the very top of the CCP's structure: the Politburo (or Political Bureau) and its even more exclusive Standing Committee. These bodies are elected by the Central Committee from among its own members under carefully controlled conditions. The current Politburo has twenty-four members (plus one alternate), nine of whom also belong to the Standing Committee, the formal apex of power in the CCP. People who study Chinese politics scrutinize the membership of the Politburo and Standing Committee for clues about leadership priorities, the balance of power among party factions, and the relative influence of different groups in policymaking. The Politburo and Standing Committee are not responsible to the Central Committee or any other institution in any meaningful sense. The operations of these organizations are generally shrouded in secrecy. Most of their work goes on, and many of the top leaders live, in a high-security compound called Zhongnanhai ("Central and Southern Seas"), which is adjacent to the former imperial palace near Tiananmen Square. There is now a little more openness about the frequency (once a month) and subjects covered at Politburo meetings. Since becoming party leader, Hu Jintao has also regularized the practice of holding study sessions at which Politburo members are briefed on important policy issues by leading academic specialists.

Prior to 1982, the top position in the party was the chairman of the Politburo's Standing Committee, which was occupied by Mao Zedong (hence *Chairman* Mao) for more than three decades until his death in 1976. The title of chairman was abolished in 1982 to symbolize a break with Mao's highly personalistic and often arbitrary style of leadership. Since then, the party's leader has been the general secretary, who presides over the Politburo and the Standing Committee, a position most recently held by Jiang Zemin (1989–2002) and Hu Jintao (2002–present). Neither Jiang nor Hu have had the personal clout or charisma of either Deng or Mao and therefore have governed as part of a collective leadership that included their fellow members on the Standing Committee and Politburo.

Hu Jintao is said to be the core of the "fourth generation" of CCP leadership, while Jiang was the core of the "third generation." (Mao Zedong and Deng Xiaoping were, respectively, the core leaders of the first and second generations.) The transition of power from the Mao-Deng generations to the Jiang-Hu generations represents a shift from revolutionary to technocratic leadership. Indeed, both Jiang and Hu, as well as all the other currents members of the Politburo Standing Committee elected in 2002, were trained and worked as engineers before embarking on political careers.

Two other party organizations deserve brief mention. The Secretariat manages the day-to-day work of the Politburo and Standing Committee and coordinates the party's complex and far-flung structure with considerable authority in organizational and personnel matters. The Central Commission for Discipline Inspection is responsible for monitoring the compliance of party members with the CCP constitution and other rules. Recently, the commission has been used as a vehicle against corruption. In 2004, it disciplined 164,831 party members, including 15 at the ministerial level; most cases ended in some type of organizational punishment, such as demotion or expulsion from the party, but nearly 5,000 were turned over to judicial authorities for additional legal action.

Below the national level, the CCP has a hierarchy of local party organizations in provinces, cities, and counties, each headed by a party committee. There are also more than 3 million primary party organizations, called branches or cells, which are found in workplaces, government offices, schools, urban neighborhoods, rural towns, villages, and army units throughout the country. Local and primary organizations extend the CCP's reach throughout Chinese society and are designed to ensure the subordination of each level of party organization to the next higher level and ultimately to the central party authorities in Beijing.

The Government of the PRC

Government (or state) authority in China is formally vested in a system of people's congresses that begins

Former Chinese president and communist party leader Jiang Zemin confers with his successor, Hu Jintao, during a meeting of the National People's Congress in March 2003. *Source:* © Reuters NewMedia, Inc. / Corbis.

with the National People's Congress at the top and continues in hierarchically arranged levels down through provincial people's congresses, municipal people's congresses, rural township people's congresses, and so on (see Figure 3). In theory, these congresses (the legislative branch) are empowered to supervise the work of the "people's governments" (the executive branch) at the various levels of the system, but in reality, government executives (such as cabinet ministers, provincial governors, and mayors) are ultimately subject to party authority rather than to the people's congresses. For example, the city of Shanghai has both a mayor and a party secretary, each with distinct and important power. But the party secretary's power is more consequential, as was reflected in 2001 when the popular mayor of Shanghai (himself a party member) was forced to resign as the result of a political dispute with the local party head.

The National People's Congress elects the president and vice president of China. But there is only one candidate, chosen by the Communist Party, for each office. The president's term is concurrent with that of the congress (five years), and there is a two-term limit. The position is largely ceremonial, although a senior party leader has always held it. As China's head of state, the president meets and negotiates with other world leaders. Jiang Zemin revived the practice that the leader of the CCP serves concurrently as PRC president, as Mao had done from 1949 to 1959. Hu Jintao followed Jiang's example and was elected

president of China at the National People's Congress in March 2003.

The premier (prime minister) is the head of the government and has authority over the bureaucracy and policy implementation. The premier is formally appointed by the president with the approval of the National People's Congress. But in reality, the Communist Party decides who will serve as premier, and that post has always been held by a very high-ranking member of the CCP Standing Committee. Like the president, the premier may serve only two five-year terms. Wen Jiabao, a geological engineer and a former vice premier in charge of agriculture, the financial system, flood control, and poverty alleviation, was chosen as premier in March 2003.

The Bureaucracy

The premier directs the State Council, which is constitutionally "the highest organ of state administration" (Article 85) in the PRC. The State Council is formally appointed by the National People's Congress, although its membership is determined by the party leadership. It functions much like the cabinet in a parliamentary system and includes the premier, a few vice premiers, the heads of government ministries and commissions, and several other senior officials.

The size of the State Council varies as ministries and commissions are created, merged, or disbanded to meet changing policy needs. At the height of the state

Figure 3

Government of the People's Republic of China

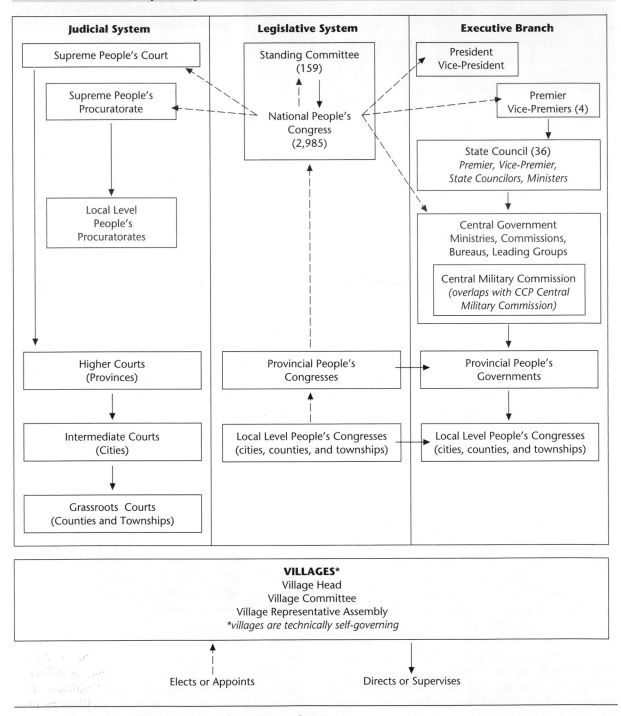

Numbers in parentheses refer to the number of members as of 2005.

socialist planned economy, there were more than one hundred ministerial-level officials. In the 1990s, there were forty ministries and commissions, and in 2003 the number was cut to twenty-eight, reflecting the decreased role of central planning and the administrative streamlining undertaken to make the government more efficient. The ministers run either functionally specific departments, such as the Ministry of Health, or organizations with more comprehensive responsibilities, such as the State Development and Reform Commission. Beneath the State Council is an array of support staffs, research offices, and other bureaucratic agencies charged with policy implementation. The work of the State Council (and the CCP Politburo) is supported by flexible issue-specific task forces called "leadership small groups." These informal groups bring together officials from various ministries and commissions in order to coordinate policymaking and implementation on matters that cross the jurisdiction of any single organization. Some groups, such the Central Leading Group on Foreign Affairs, are more or less permanent fixtures in the party-state structure, while others may be convened on an ad hoc basis, such the one that was formed to deal with the Severe Acute Respiratory Syndrome (SARS) public health crisis that China faced in 2003.

China's bureaucracy is immense in size and expansive in the scope of its reach throughout the country. The total number of **cadres** in the PRC—people in positions of authority who are paid by the government or party—is in the range of 40 million. A minority of these work directly for the government or the CCP. The remainder occupy key posts in economic enterprises (such as factory directors); schools (such as principals); and scientific, cultural, and other state-run institutions. Not all party members are cadres; in fact, most party members are ordinary workers, farmers, teachers, and so on. And most cadres are not party members, although party cadres ultimately have power over nonparty cadres. In 2001, the government announced a plan to reduce the size of the bureaucracy by 10 percent over the next five to ten years, particularly at the city, county, and township levels. There have also been substantive moves toward professionalizing the bureaucracy, particularly at the city level of government, by making more official positions subject to competition through civil service exams rather than the still-prevalent method of appointment from above.

One of the most significant administrative reforms of the post-Mao era—and one that is quite unprecedented in a communist party-state—has been the implementation of measures to limit how long officials can stay in their jobs. Depending on their position, both government and party cadres must now retire between the ages of sixty and seventy. A two-term limit has been set for all top cadres. In 1998, Premier Li Peng became the first central leader of the People's Republic to leave office at the end of a constitutionally specified term limit. But exceptions are still sometimes made for core leaders such as Jiang Zemin (born in 1926), who stayed on as CCP general secretary until he was seventy-six.

Other State Institutions

The Military and the Police

China's People's Liberation Army (PLA), which encompasses all of the country's ground, air, and naval armed services, is the world's largest military force, with about 2.3 million active personnel (down from nearly 4 million in 1989). In the early 2000s, the PRC had 2.18 active military personnel per 1,000 population, considerably smaller than the U.S. ratio of 4.70 per 1,000. The PLA also has a formal reserve of another 1 million or so and a backup people's militia of 12 to 15 million, which could be mobilized in the event of war, although the level of training and weaponry available to the militia are generally minimal. China has a Military Service Law that applies to all citizens between the ages of eighteen and twenty-two and gives the government the power to conscript both men and women as necessary to meet the country's security needs (although only males must register when they turn 18). But the military has not had to rely on conscription to fills its ranks since serving in the PLA is considered a prestigious option for many young people, particularly for rural youth who might not have many other opportunities for upward mobility.

The PRC has increased military spending by double-digit percentages nearly every year for more than a decade (12.6 percent in 2005) in order to modernize its armed forces and raise the pay of military personnel. China said that it spent $29.9 billion on defense in 2005, compared with $401.7 billion by the

United States. Many analysts think that the PRC vastly understates its defense budget and estimate that it is really closer to three times the official figures; still, China spends much less in total and vastly less per capita on military expenditures than does the United States.

The military has never held formal political power in the PRC, but it has been a very important influence on politics and policy. Ever since the days of the revolution and the civil war, there have been close ties between the political and military leaders of the CCP, with many top leaders (such as Mao and Deng) serving in both political and military capacities. One of the most famous quotes from Chairman Mao's writings, "Political power grows out of the barrel of a gun," conveyed his belief that the party needed strong military backing in order to win and keep power. However, the often overlooked second half of the quote, "Our principle is that the party commands the gun, and the gun must never be allowed to command the party," made the equally important point that the military had to be kept under civilian (that is, CCP) control.[20] Although there have been a few periods when the role of the military in Chinese politics appeared to be particularly strong (such as during the Cultural Revolution), the party has always been able to keep the "gun" under its firm command. The CCP extends its control of the PLA through a system of party committees and political officers who are attached to all military units.

There are no military officers on the party's most elite body, the Standing Committee, but two of the twenty-four full members of the Politburo are generals, and PLA representatives make up about 20 percent of the full members of the Central Committee. Nevertheless, the PLA continues to play a significant, if muted, role in Chinese politics. Military support remains a crucial factor in the factional struggles that still figure prominently in inner-party politics.

The key organizations in charge of the Chinese armed forces are the CCP and PRC Central Military Commissions (CMC). On paper, these are two distinct organizations, but, in fact, they overlap entirely in membership and function. The chair of the state Military Commission is "elected" by the National People's Congress, but is always the same person as the chair of the party CMC. The CMC chair is, in effect, the commander in chief of China's armed forces. This position has almost always been held by the most powerful party leader, for example, by Deng Xiaoping from 1981 to 1989, or his protégé, as was the case when Jiang Zemin took over the chairmanship in 1989 under Deng's auspices. Hu Jintao is the current chair of China's Central Military Commission.

China's internal security apparatus consists of several different organizations. The Ministry of State Security is responsible for combating espionage and gathering intelligence at home and abroad. A 1 million strong People's Armed Police (under the PLA) guards public officials and buildings, carries out some border patrol and protection, and is used to quell serious public disturbances, including worker or peasant unrest. The Ministry of Public Security is responsible for the maintenance of law and order, the investigation of crimes, and the surveillance of Chinese citizens and foreigners in China suspected of being a threat to the state. Local Public Security Bureaus are under the command of central ministry authorities in Beijing. In effect, then, China has a national police force stationed throughout the country. There are also local police forces, but they do little more than supervise traffic.

For people convicted of serious crimes, including political ones, the Ministry of Public Security maintains an extensive system of labor reform camps. These camps, noted for their harsh conditions and remote locations, are estimated to have millions of prisoners. They have, at times, become a contentious issue in U.S.-China relations because of claims that they use political prisoners as slave labor to produce millions of dollars worth of products (such as toys) that are then exported to U.S. and other foreign markets. China has agreed to curtail the export of prison-produced goods, but it maintains that productive work by prison inmates (common in many countries, including the United States) helps to rehabilitate prisoners and is a legitimate part of the penal system.

Public Security Bureaus have the authority to detain indefinitely people suspected of committing a crime without making a formal charge and can use administrative sanctions, that is, penalties imposed outside the court system, to levy fines or sentence detainees for up to four years of "re-education through labor." There is a special system of more than 300 labor camps for such detainees (estimated at 300,000), who include prostitutes, drug users, petty criminals, as well as some who might be considered political prisoners. But in a sign of the somewhat freer political environment, a few lawyers and scholars in China have begun openly claiming that administrative sanctions are contrary to the country's efforts to establish a fairer legal system.

The Judiciary

China has a four-tiered "people's court" system reaching from a Supreme People's Court down through higher (provincial-level), intermediate (city-level), and grassroots (county- and township-level) people's courts. The Supreme People's Court supervises the work of lower courts and the application of the country's laws, but it hears few cases and does not exercise judicial review over government policies. A nationwide organization called the "people's procuratorate" serves in the courts as public prosecutor and also has investigatory functions in criminal cases. Citizen mediation committees based in urban neighborhoods and rural villages play an important role in the judicial process by settling a large majority of civil cases out of court.

China's judicial system came under attack as a bastion of elitism and revisionism during the Cultural Revolution. The formal legal system pretty much ceased to operate during that period, and many of its functions were taken over by political or police organizations, which often acted arbitrarily in making arrests or administering punishments.

In recent decades, the legal system of the PRC has been revitalized. There are now more than 100,000 lawyers in China (by way of comparison, there are about a million in the United States), and legal advisory offices have been established throughout the country to provide citizens and organizations with legal assistance. Many laws and regulations have been enacted, including new criminal and civil codes, in the effort to regularize the legal system.

There has been an enormous surge in the number of lawsuits filed (and often won) by people against businesses, local officials, and government agencies. Chinese courts can provide a real avenue of redress to the public for a wide range of nonpolitical grievances, including loss of property, consumer fraud, and even unjust detention by the police.

China's criminal justice system works swiftly and harshly. Great faith is placed in the ability of an official investigation to find the facts of a case, and the outcome of cases that actually do come to trial is pretty much predetermined: there is a conviction rate of 98 to 99 percent for all criminal cases. Prison terms are long and subject to only cursory appeal. A variety of offenses in addition to murder—including, in some cases, rape and particularly serious cases of embezzlement and other "economic crimes"—are subject to capital punishment, which is carried out within days of sentencing by a single bullet in the back of the convicted person's head. Particularly large numbers of people are executed during the periodic government-sponsored anticrime "Strike Hard" campaigns. In 2004, China led the world in the application of the death penalty with about 3,500 executions, followed by Iran (159), Vietnam (64), and the United States (59).

Although the PRC constitution guarantees judicial independence, China's courts and other legal bodies remain under party control. The appointment of judicial personnel is subject to party approval, and the CCP can and does bend the law to serve its interests. Legal reform in China has been undertaken because China's leaders are well aware that economic development requires detailed laws, professional lawyers and judicial personnel, predictable legal processes, and binding documents such as contracts. China has, by and large, become a country where there is rule *by* law, which means that the party-state uses the law to carry out its policies and enforce its rule. But it is still far from having established the rule *of* law, in which everyone and every organization, including the Communist Party, is accountable and subject to the law.

Subnational Government

There are four main layers of state structure beneath the central government in China: provinces, cities, counties, and rural towns. There are also four very large centrally administered cities (Beijing, Shanghai, Tianjin, and Chongqing) and five autonomous regions, which are areas of the country with large minority populations (such as Tibet and Mongolia). Each of these levels has a representative people's congress that meets infrequently, and plays only a limited role in managing affairs in the area under its jurisdiction.

Subnational government organizations in China are under the supervision of both the next higher level of government and the Communist Party at their own level. For example, the organization in charge of education in one of China's provinces would be subject both to administrative supervision by the Ministry of Education in Beijing and to political control by the province's CCP committee. Such a system leads to complex and sometimes conflicting lines of authority within the Chinese bureaucracy. It also reinforces two key aspects of governance in the PRC: centralization and party domination. Nevertheless, since the 1980s, government administration in China has become increasingly decentralized as the role of central planning has been reduced and more power has been given to provincial and local authorities, particularly in economic matters. Efforts have also been made to reduce party interference in administrative work.

Despite decentralization, the central government still retains considerable power to intervene in local affairs when and where it wants. This power of the central authorities derives not only from their ability to set binding national priorities but also from their control over the military and the police, critical energy sources, resource allocation, and the construction of major infrastructure projects. A number of political scientists in China and abroad have suggested that the PRC, given its continental size and great regional diversity, would be better served by a federal system with a more balanced distribution of power between the national, provincial, and local levels of government, but such a move would be inconsistent with the highly centralized structure of a communist party-state.

Beneath the formal layers of state administration are China's 700,000 or so rural villages, which are home to the majority of the country's population. These villages, with an average population of 500–1,000 each, are technically self-governing and are not formally responsible to a higher level of state authority. In recent years, village leaders have been directly and competitively elected by local residents, and village representative assemblies have become more active in managing local affairs, trends that have brought an important degree of grass-roots democracy to village government (see Section 4). However, the single most powerful person in Chinese villages is still the local Communist Party leader (the party secretary) and the most powerful organization is the village party committee.

The Policy-making Process

At the height of Mao Zedong's power, many scholars described policy-making in China as a simple top-down "Mao-in-command" system. Then the Cultural Revolution led analysts to conclude that policy outcomes in the PRC were best understood as a result of factional and ideological struggles within the Chinese political elite. Now, a much more complex model, "fragmented authoritarianism," is often used to explain Chinese policy-making. This model recognizes that China is still fundamentally an authoritarian state and is far from being a democracy in which public opinion, party competition, media scrutiny, and independent interest groups have an impact on policy decisions. But it also takes into account that power in China has become much more dispersed, or fragmented, than it was during the Maoist era and sees policy as evolving from a complex process of cooperation, conflict, and bargaining among political actors at various levels of the system.[21] The decentralization of power that has accompanied economic reform has given provincial and local governments a lot more clout in the policy process, and the national focus on economic development has also led to the growing influence of nonparty experts and organizations in the policy loop.

The fragmented authoritarian model acknowledges that policymaking in China is still ultimately under the control of the Chinese Communist Party and that the top two dozen or so party leaders wield nearly unchecked power. The CCP uses a weblike system of organizational controls to make sure that the government bureaucracy complies with the party's will in policy implementation. In the first place, almost all key government officials are also party members. Furthermore, the CCP exercises control over the policy process through party organizations that parallel government agencies at all levels of the system. For example, each provincial government works under the watchful eye of a provincial party committee. In addition, the communist party maintains an effective presence inside every government organization through a "leading party group" that is made up key officials who are also CCP members.

The CCP also influences the policy process by means of the "cadre list," or as it was known in the Soviet Union where the practice was developed, the ***nomenklatura*** system. The cadre list covers millions of positions in the government and elsewhere (including institutions such as universities, banks, trade unions, and newspapers). Any personnel decision involving appointment, promotion, transfer, or dismissal that affects a position on this list must be approved by a party organization department, whether or not the person involved is a party member. In recent years, the growth of nonstate sectors of the economy and administrative streamlining have led to a reduction in the number of positions directly subject to party approval. Nevertheless, the *nomenklatura* system remains one of the major instruments by which the CCP tries to "ensure that leading institutions throughout the country will exercise only the autonomy granted to them by the party."[22]

No account of the policy process in China is complete without noting again the importance of *guanxi* ("connections"), the personal relationships and mutual obligations based on family, friendship, school, military, professional, or other ties. The notion of *guanxi* has its roots in Confucian culture and has long been an important part of political, social, and economic life in China. These connections are still a basic fact of life within the Chinese bureaucracy, where personal ties are often the key to getting things done. Depending on how they are used, *guanxi* can either help cut red tape and increase efficiency or bolster organizational rigidity and feed corruption.

In sum, the power of the Communist Party is the most basic fact of political life in China. Party domination, however, does not mean that the system "operates in a monolithic way"; in fact, it "wriggles with politics" of many kinds, formal and informal.[23] In order to get a more complete picture of governance and policymaking in China, it is important to look at how various influences, including ideology, factional struggles, bureaucratic interests, citizen input, and *guanxi,* shape the decisions ultimately made by Communist Party leaders and organizations.

Section ❹ Representation and Participation

The Chinese Communist Party claims to represent the interests of all the people of China and describes the People's Republic as a **socialist democracy** that it says is superior to democracy in capitalist countries where wealthy individuals and corporations dominate politics and policy-making despite multi-party politics. China's *socialist* democracy is based on the unchallengeable role of the CCP as the country's only ruling party and should not be confused with the *social* democracy of Western European center-left political parties, which is rooted in a commitment to competitive politics.

Representation and participation play important roles as instruments of socialist democracy in the PRC political system. There are legislative bodies, elections, and organizations like labor unions, all of which are meant to provide citizens with ways of influencing public policymaking and the selection of some government leaders. But such democratic elements in Chinese politics are strictly controlled and bounded by the CCP.

The Legislature

China's constitution grants the National People's Congress (NPC) the power to enact and amend the country's laws, approve and monitor the state budget, and declare and end war. The NPC is also empowered to elect (and recall) the president and vice president, the chair of the state Central Military Commission, the head of China's Supreme Court, and the procurator-general (something like the U.S. attorney general). The NPC has final approval over the selection of the premier and members of the State Council. At least on paper, these powers make China's legislature the most powerful branch of the government. In fact, these powers are exercised only in the manner allowed by the Communist Party.

The National People's Congress is a unicameral legislature. It is elected for a five-year term and meets annually for only about two weeks in March. Deputies to the NPC are not full-time legislators but remain in their regular jobs and home areas except for the brief time when the congress is in session. The size of the NPC is set by law prior to each five-year electoral cycle. The NPC that was elected in 2003 consisted of nearly 3,000 deputies. All the delegates, except those who represent the People's Liberation Army, are chosen on a geographic basis from China's provinces, autonomous regions, and major municipalities. About 73 percent of the deputies elected in 2003 were members of the CCP, while the others either belonged to one of China's few non-Communist (and powerless) political parties or had no party affiliation.

Workers and farmers made up about 18 percent of the deputies elected in 2003, intellectuals and professionals made up another 21 percent, government and party cadres accounted for a little under a third, 9 percent were from the military, and the remainder consisted of representatives of other occupational categories, such as entrepreneurs. Women made up 20 percent and ethnic minorities 14 percent of the deputies.

The annual sessions of the NPC are hailed with great fanfare in the Chinese press as an example of socialist democracy at work, but generally legislation is passed and state leaders are elected by an overwhelming majority. For instance, Hu Jintao was elected president of China in March 2003 by a vote of 2,937 for, 4 against, and 3 abstentions. Nevertheless, some debate and dissent do occur. For example, in 1992, about a third of NPC deputies either voted against or abstained from voting on the construction of the hugely expensive ($70 billion) and ecologically controversial Three Gorges dam project now being built on the Yangtze River. On very rare occasions, government legislative initiatives have even been defeated. But all NPC proceedings are subject to party scrutiny, and the congress never debates politically sensitive issues. The CCP also monitors the election process to make sure that no outright dissidents are elected as deputies.

Still, as economics has replaced ideology as the main priority of China's leaders, the NPC has become a much more significant and lively part of the Chinese political system than it was during the Mao era. Many NPC deputies are now chosen because of their ability to contribute to China's modernization rather than simply on the basis of political loyalty, and some have become a bit more assertive in expressing their opinions on various issues like corruption and environmental problems.

Political Parties and the Party System

China is usually called a one-party system because the country's politics are so thoroughly dominated by the Chinese Communist Party. In fact, China has eight political parties in addition to the CCP, but these parties neither challenge the basic policies of the CCP nor play a significant part in running the government, although they do sometimes provide advice in the policymaking process.

The Chinese Communist Party

The Chinese Communist Party has about 70 million members. The party has grown steadily since it came to power in 1949, when it had just under 4.5 million members. Only during the Cultural Revolution was there a sharp drop in membership due to the purge of "capitalist roaders" from party ranks, and many of those purged were welcomed back into the CCP after the death of Mao.

The CCP is the largest political party in the world in terms of total formal membership. But as with all other former and current ruling communist parties, its members make up a small minority of the country's population. CCP members are now about 5 percent of China's population, or about 8 percent of those over eighteen, the minimum age for joining the party.

The social composition of the CCP's membership has changed considerably in recent decades. In the mid-1950s, peasants made up nearly 70 percent of party membership. In 2002, a generic category that included "industrial workers, laborers in township enterprises, farmers, herdsman, and fishermen" accounted for only 45 percent of the CCP even though the party constitution still claims that "Members of the Communist Party of China are vanguard fighters of the Chinese working class imbued with communist consciousness" (Article 2). The majority of CCP members are not manual laborers of any sort, but are government officials, office workers, enterprise managers, military personnel, and professionals, including scientists, technical experts, and academics. In the last few years, the CCP has made an effort to get private entrepreneurs (capitalists) to join the party. This is quite a change from the Maoist era when any hint of capitalism was crushed. It is also a recognition of the increasing importance of the private sector in China's economy and a strategy by which the party hopes to prolong its rule by adapting to a rapidly modernizing society. But it will also likely change the social composition of the CCP and perhaps even lead to a gradual redefinition of the party's political role in China.

Women make up less than 20 percent of the CCP as a whole and only 2.5 percent of full members of Central Committee (and 14 percent of alternates) elected in 2002. There is one female member of the Politburo, Wu Yi, who is also a vice premier and former minister of foreign trade (and, by training, a petroleum engineer). There are no women on the party's most powerful organization, the Politburo Standing Committee.

Nearly 70 million people between the ages of fourteen and twenty-eight belong to the Communist Youth League, which serves as a training ground for party membership. Despite the fact that many Chinese believe that communist ideology is irrelevant to their lives and the nation's future, the CCP enrolls about 2 million new members each year. Being a party member still provides unparalleled access to influence and resources and remains a prerequisite for advancement in many careers in China, particularly in government.

China's Noncommunist Parties

The eight noncommunist political parties in the PRC are officially referred to as the "democratic parties," a designation meant to signify the role they play in representing different interests in the political process. This is meant to lend credibility to the CCP's claim that China is a democracy. Each noncommunist party draws its membership from a particular group in Chinese society. For example, the China Democratic League consists mostly of intellectuals, whereas the Chinese Party for the Public Interest draws on returned overseas Chinese and experts with overseas connections.

The democratic parties, all of which were founded before the CCP came to power, have a total membership of fewer than 500,000. These parties do not contest for power or challenge CCP policy. Their function is to provide advice to the CCP and generate support within their particular constituencies for CCP policies. Individual members of the parties may assume important government positions. But organizationally these parties are relatively insignificant and function as little more than "a loyal non-opposition."[24]

The main forum through which the noncommunist parties express their views on national policy is the Chinese People's Political Consultative Conference (CPPCC). The CPPCC is an advisory, not a legislative body, which according to its charter operates under the guidance of the Communist Party. It meets in full session once a year for about two weeks at the same time as the National People's Congress (NPC), which CPPCC members attend as nonvoting deputies. The large majority of the more than 2,000 delegates to the CPPCC are noncommunists, representing the "democratic parties" or various constituencies such as education, the arts, and medicine, But all delegates are chosen through a process supervised by the CCP, and a high-ranking party leader heads the CPPCC itself. CPPCC delegates are increasingly speaking out about national problems, but they do not express serious dissent from the party line on any matter. The severe prison sentences given to the activists who tried to establish an independent China Democratic Party in 1998 showed just how determined China's leaders are to prevent the formation of any political organization not subservient to the CCP.

Elections

Elections in the PRC are basically mechanisms to give the communist party-state greater legitimacy by allowing large numbers of citizens to participate in the political process under very controlled circumstances.

Most elections in China are "indirect' elections in which members of a one government body elect those who will serve at the next highest level. For example, provincial representatives to the National People's Congress are elected, not by all voters in the province, but by the deputies who are already serving in the provincial-level people's congress, who were, themselves elected by the county-level people's congresses in the province. Direct elections are most common at the village level, although there have been a few experiments with letting all eligible citizens choose officials and representatives at the next rung up the administrative ladder (the township). The authorities have been very cautious in expanding the scope of direct elections in order to prevent them from becoming a forum for dissent or a vehicle for the formation of an opposition party.

For several decades after the founding of the PRC, only one candidate stood for each office, so the only choice facing voters was to approve or abstain. Since the early 1980s, many direct and indirect elections have had multiple candidates for each slot, with the winner chosen by secret ballot. The nomination process has also become more open. Any group of more than ten voters can nominate candidates for an election, and there have been a significant number of cases where independently nominated candidates have defeated official nominees, although even independent candidates are basically approved by the CCP.

The most significant progress toward real democratic representation and participation in China has occurred in the rural villages. Laws implemented since the late 1980s have provided for the direct election of village committees, which are made up of local leaders (including the village head) who were previously appointed by and responsible to higher levels of government. These elections are, for the most part, multi-candidate and secret ballot, although they are still closely monitored by the village CCP committee. Village representative assemblies, with members chosen from each household or group of households, have taken a more active role in supervising the work of local officials and decision making in matters affecting community finances and welfare. Outside observers have been split on whether such direct grass-roots elections and the representative assemblies are seeds of real democracy in China or merely a facade designed by the Communist Party to appease international critics and give the rural population a way to express discontent with some officials without challenging the country's fundamental political organization.

Recent electoral reform has certainly increased popular representation and participation in China's government. But elections in the PRC still do not give citizens a means by which they can exercise effective control over the party officials and organizations that have the real power in China's political system. Top Chinese communist leaders, from Mao to now, have repeatedly rejected multiparty democracy as unsuited to China's traditions and conditions. In a major speech in 2004 marking his consolidation of power in the transition from Jiang Zemin, CCP general secretary and PRC president Hu Jintao said that indiscriminately copying western political systems would be a "blind alley" for China and that the "Communist Party of China logically came into the position to shoulder the historic mission of leading the Chinese people . . ."[25] There is little reason to think that this bottom-line framework for political representation and participation in China will change much in the foreseeable future.

Political Culture, Citizenship, and Identity

From Communism to Consumerism

Since its founding in 1949, the PRC's official political culture has been based on communist ideology, and the party-state has made extensive efforts to get people's political attitudes and behavior to conform to whatever was the currently prevailing version of Marxism-Leninism in the CCP. But this ideology has gone through such severe crises and profound changes during the turbulent decades of Communist rule that its future in China is seriously in doubt.

At the height of the Maoist era, Mao Zedong Thought was hailed as "an inexhaustible source of strength and a spiritual atom bomb of infinite power" that held the answer to all of China's problems in domestic and foreign policy.[26] By the mid-1970s, however, the debacles of the Mao years had greatly tarnished the appeal, to most people in China, not only of Maoism, but of communist ideology in general.

After Deng Xiaoping came to power in 1978, he set about trying to restore the legitimacy of the Communist Party through economic reforms and to revive communist ideology by linking it directly to China's development aspirations. After Deng's death in 1997, the CCP amended the party constitution to add "Deng Xiaoping Theory" to its official ideology. One key part of Deng's theory, often referred to under the rubric of "Building Socialism with Chinese Characteristics," was a major departure from Maoism in its central claim that, given China's relative poverty, the main task of the CCP was to promote economic development by any means necessary, even capitalist ones.

The other central components of Deng's ideology, which are fully consistent with Maoist theory and practice, are his so-called **Four Cardinal Principles:** upholding the socialist road, the people's democratic dictatorship, the leadership of the Communist Party, and Marxism-Leninism. In essence, then, Deng Xiaoping Theory is an ideological rationale for the combination of economic liberalization and party dictatorship that characterizes contemporary China.

In an effort to have himself placed on a historical pedestal equal to that of Deng and Mao, as he neared retirement Jiang Zemin offered his own variation on Chinese communism, the "Three Represents," which was said to sum up his contribution to the party's ideology. According to the, yet again, amended party constitution, the Three Represents depict the CCP as the faithful representative of the "development trend of China's advanced productive forces, the orientation of China's advanced culture, and the fundamental interests of the overwhelming majority of the Chinese people." This is a reaffirmation of Deng's emphasis on economic development, but it is also an ideological rationale for recruiting private entrepreneurs into the Communist Party and accommodating the many existing party members who have gone into private business (and often made large fortunes) in recent years. These so-called red capitalists are seen as the driving force in China's modernization, and the Three Represents theory is the latest ideological adaptation in the CCP's persistent claim to be a vanguard party that is best able and uniquely suited to lead the country to achieve its national and international objectives.

The CCP tries to keep communist ideology—now officially called "Marxism-Leninism, Mao Zedong Thought, Deng Xiaoping Theory, and the Important Thought of the Three Represents"—viable and visible by continued efforts to influence public opinion and socialization—for instance, by controlling the media and overseeing the educational system. Although China's media are much livelier and more open than during the Maoist period, there is no true freedom of the press. Reduced political control of the media has, to a large extent, meant only the freedom to publish more

entertainment news, human interest stories, local coverage, and some nonpolitical investigative journalism. The arts, in general, are the area of life in which there has been the greatest political change in China in recent years, in the sense that there is much less direct (but not totally absent) censorship. The Chinese film industry, for example, has emerged as one of the best in the world, with many of its directors, stars, and productions winning international acclaim.

Internet access is exploding in the PRC, with nearly 100 million users as of mid-2005 and Web connections available even in some quite remote towns. The government, worried about the potential influence of email and electronic information it cannot control, has blocked access to certain foreign websites, shut down unlicensed cyber cafés, which it likened to the opium dens of the past, and arrested people it has accused of disseminating subversive material over the Internet, including, in January 2005, a political essayist who was sentenced to five years in prison for subversion of state power and the socialist system.

Web access in China is tightly controlled by the licensing of just a few Internet Service Providers, who are themselves responsible for who uses their systems and how. A special state organization, with an estimated 50,000 employees, has been established to police the Internet, and the government is investing huge sums in developing (with technical assistance from western companies) stronger firewalls and monitoring systems. Microsoft, Yahoo, and Google have all been criticized by human rights organizations for agreeing to political restrictions on websites, news sources, chat rooms, and blogs in exchange for the right to do business in China. The Chinese party-state knows that cutting-edge technology is critical to its modernization plans—even the CCP has its own Web sites—and wants citizens to become computer literate; but, as with so much else in China, the party-state wants to define the way and dictate the rules.

Schools are one of the main institutions through which all states instill political values in their citizens. Educational opportunities have expanded enormously in China since 1949. Although enrollment rates drop sharply at the secondary school level, primary school enrollment is close to 100 percent of the age-eligible population (ages six to eleven). In Maoist China, students at all levels spent a considerable amount of time studying politics and working in fields or factories, and teaching materials were often overlaid with a heavy dose of political propaganda. Today, political study (recently with an emphasis on learning the "Three Represents") is a required but relatively minor part of the curriculum at all levels of education. Much greater attention is paid to urging students to gain the skills and knowledge they need to further their own careers and help China modernize.

Yet schools in China are by no means centers of critical or independent thinking, and teachers and students are still monitored for political reliability. In March 2005, a journalism professor at Beijing University (China's most prestigious) was fired for his public criticism of party censors, whom he compared to those in Nazi Germany. More than 80 percent of China's students between the ages of seven and fourteen belong to the Young Pioneers, an organization designed to promote good social behavior, patriotism, and loyalty to the party.

But efforts to keep communist ideology alive in China do not appear to be having much success with the younger generation. Alternative sources of socialization are growing in importance, although these do not often take expressly political forms because of the threat of repression. In the countryside, peasants have replaced portraits of Mao and other Communist heroes with statues of folk gods and ancestor worship tablets, and the influence of extended kinship groups such as clans often outweighs the formal authority of the party in the villages. In the cities, popular culture, including gigantic rock concerts, shapes youth attitudes much more profoundly than do party messages about the "Three Represents." Throughout China, consumerism and the desire for economic gain rather than communist ideals of self-sacrifice and the common good provide the principal motivation for much personal and social behavior. Many observers, both inside China and outside, have spoken of a moral vacuum in the country, which is not uncommon for a society that is undergoing such rapid, multifaceted change.

Religion, which was ferociously repressed during the Mao era, is attracting an increasing number of Chinese adherents. Buddhist temples, Christian churches, and other places of worship operate more freely than they have in decades. However, despite the fact that freedom of religion is guaranteed by the PRC constitution (as is the freedom not to believe in any religion), religious life is strictly controlled and limited to officially approved organizations and venues. Clergy of any religion who defy the authority of the party-state are still imprisoned. Clandestine Christian communities, called house churches, have sprung up in many areas of China among people who reject the government's control of religious life and are unable to worship in public. Though local officials sometime tolerate the existence of these churches, there have been numerous cases in which house church leaders and lay people have been arrested and the private homes where services are held have been bulldozed. The Chinese Catholic Church is prohibited from recognizing the authority of the pope, although there have been recent signs of a thaw between Beijing and the Vatican.

Citizenship and National Identity

China's citizens certainly have a strong sense of national identity in cultural terms. But their national identity in terms of what ties them to the state is going through a profound and uncertain transformation. Party leaders realize that most citizens are skeptical or dismissive of communist ideology and that appeals to socialist goals and revolutionary virtues no longer work to inspire loyalty. Therefore, the CCP has turned increasingly to patriotic themes to rally the country behind its leadership and goes to great lengths to portray itself as the best guardian of China's national interests. The official media put considerable emphasis on the greatness and antiquity of Chinese culture, with the not-so-subtle message that it is time for the Chinese nation to reclaim its rightful place in the world order—under the leadership of the CCP.

The party-state also does all it can to get political capital by touting its role in managing China's impressive economic achievements, winning the 2008 Summer Olympics for Beijing, and securing the return to China of territories like Hong Kong and Macao (a former Portuguese colony) that were lost long ago to Western imperialist powers. In the view of some, such officially promoted nationalist sentiments could lead to a more aggressive foreign and military policy, particularly, given the country's growing need for energy resources, toward areas such as the potentially oil-rich South China Sea, where the PRC's historical territorial claims conflict with those of other countries including Vietnam and the Philippines.

China's Non-Chinese Citizens

The PRC calls itself a multinational state with fifty-six officially recognized ethnic groups, one of which is the majority Han people. The defining elements of a minority group in China involve some combination of language, culture (including religion), and race that distinguish them from the Han. The fifty-five minorities number a little more than 100 million, or about 8.5 percent of the total population of the PRC. These groups range in size from 16 million (the Zhuang of southwest China) to about 2,000 (the Lhoba in the far west of the country). Most of these minorities have come under Chinese rule over many centuries through territorial expansion rather than through migration into China.

China's minorities are highly concentrated in the five autonomous regions of Guangxi, Inner Mongolia, Ningxia, Tibet, and Xinjiang, although only in the last two do minority people outnumber Han Chinese, who have been encouraged to migrate to these regions. The five autonomous regions are sparsely populated, yet they occupy about 60 percent of the total land area of the PRC. Some of these areas are resource rich, and all are located on strategically important borders of the country, including those with Vietnam, India, and Russia. In addition to the autonomous regions, which are the equivalent of provinces in the state structure, there are also numerous autonomous counties and other administrative units in many parts of the country where the majority or a large percentage of the population consists of ethnic minorities.

The Chinese constitution grants these autonomous areas the right of self-government in certain matters, such as cultural affairs, but their autonomy is in fact very limited, and the minority regions are kept firmly under the control of the central authorities. Minority peoples are given some latitude to develop their local economies as they see fit, religious freedom is generally respected, and the use of minority languages in the media and literature is encouraged, as is bilingual education. In order to keep the already small minority

populations from dwindling further, China's stringent family planning policy is applied much more loosely among minorities, who are often allowed to have two or more children per couple rather than the one-child prescribed limit for most Chinese.

There has been a concerted effort to recruit and promote minority cadres to run local governments in autonomous areas. But the most powerful individual in these areas, the head of the Communist Party, is likely to be Han Chinese; for example, the party secretary in all five autonomous regions is Han. Also, despite significant progress in modernizing the economies of the minority regions, these areas remain among the poorest in China.

The most extensive ethnic conflict in China has occurred in Tibet, which has been under Chinese military occupation since the early 1950s. Hu Jintao, the current president of the PRC and general secretary of the CCP, served as the party chief in Tibet from 1988 to 1992. This gives him vastly more personal experience in this troubled part of the country than any previous national leader. Some see this experience as a cause for optimism, while others are critical of Hu's record of enforcing repressive Chinese control of the region (see "Current Challenges: Tibet and China").

According to official PRC statistics, there are about 20 million Muslims in China (although some outside observers put the number at several times that). China's Muslims live in many parts of the country and are spread among several different ethnic minorities, the largest of which are the Hui (9 million) and Uyghur (8 million). The highest concentration of Muslims is in the far west of China in the Ningxia Hui and Xinjiang Uyghur autonomous regions, the latter of which borders the Islamic nations of Afghanistan and Pakistan and the Central Asian states of the former Soviet Union.

There is growing unrest among Uyghurs in Xinjiang (the more secular Hui are better integrated into Han Chinese society). The government has clashed with Uyghur militants who want to create a separate Islamic state of "East Turkestan" and have sometimes used violence, including bombings and assassinations, to press their cause. One of the reasons that the PRC became an eager ally of the United States in the post–September 11 war on terrorism was that it

Current Challenges: *Tibet and China*

Tibet is located in the far west of China on the border with India, Burma, Nepal, and Bhutan. It is a large area (about 470,000 square miles, which is nearly 13 percent of China's total area) and is ringed by some of the world's highest mountains, including the Himalayas and Mt. Everest. Ninety-three percent of Tibet's 2.6 million people are Tibetans, who are ethnically, linguistically, and culturally distinct from the Chinese. Another 3 million ethnic Tibetans live elsewhere in China, mostly in provinces adjacent to Tibet.

In the thirteenth century, Tibet became a theocracy in which absolute power was held by a Buddhist priest, called the Dalai Lama, who ruled the country with the help of other clergy and the aristocracy. Traditional Tibetan society was sharply divided between the tiny ruling class and the common people, most of whom were serfs living and working under difficult and often brutal conditions.

Tibet became subordinate to China in the early eighteenth century, although the Dalai Lama and other Tibetan officials continued to govern the country. After the collapse of China's imperial system in 1911, Tibet achieved de facto independence. However, Britain, which saw Tibet in the context of its extensive colonial rule in South Asia, exercised considerable influence in Tibetan affairs.

Shortly after coming to power in 1949, the Chinese Communists made known their intention to end foreign intervention in Tibet, which they, like previous Chinese governments, considered to be part of China. In 1951, the Dalai Lama agreed to the peaceful incorporation of Tibet into the People's Republic of China rather than face a full-scale military assault. Although some Chinese troops and officials were sent to Tibet, the Dalai Lama remained in a position of symbolic authority for much of the 1950s. In 1959, a widespread revolt against Chinese rule led to the invasion of Tibet by the People's Liberation Army. The Dalai Lama and over 50,000 of his supporters fled to exile in India, and Chinese rule was even more

firmly established. In 1965, the Tibetan Autonomous Region was officially formed, but Chinese political and military officials have kept a firm grip on power in Tibet.

During the Maoist era, traditional Tibetan culture was suppressed by the Chinese authorities. Since the late 1970s, Buddhist temples and monasteries have been allowed to reopen, and Tibetans have gained a significant degree of cultural freedom; the Chinese government has also significantly increased investment in Tibet's economic development. However, China still considers talk of Tibetan political independence to be treason, and Chinese troops have violently crushed several anti-China demonstrations in Lhasa, the capital of Tibet.

The Dalai Lama is very active internationally in promoting the cause of independence for Tibet. In 1989, he was awarded the Nobel Peace Prize. He has met with several U.S. presidents (mostly recently with President Bush in September 2003), addressed Congress, and spoken widely at colleges and to other audiences in the United States. In 1999, the U.S. State Department appointed a special coordinator for Tibetan issues. The Chinese government considers these events as proof of tacit American support for Tibetan independence.

In recent years, high-level delegations from the Dalai Lama's government-in-exile have visited Beijing and Lhasa to further explore better relations. The Dalai Lama appears willing to return to Tibet and accept Chinese sovereignty in exchange for guarantees of real autonomy in managing local, particularly religious and cultural, affairs. But the PRC is fearful that his presence would incite greater opposition to Chinese rule and has rejected the Dalai Lama's offer of a compromise as a "disguised" plan to gain independence for Tibet. The two sides appear far from any agreement, and tensions between Tibetans and Chinese in Tibet remain high and potentially explosive.

allowed China to justify its crackdown on the Xin-jiang-based East Turkestan Islamic Movement (ETIM), which Washington has included on its list of organizations connected to Osama bin Laden and al Qaeda.

China's minority population is relatively small and geographically isolated, and where ethnic unrest has occurred, it has been limited, sporadic, and easily quelled. Therefore, the PRC has not had the kind of intense identity-based conflict experienced by countries with more pervasive religious and ethnic cleavages, such as India and Nigeria. But it is possible that in the future, both domestic and global forces will cause issues of ethnic identity to become more visible and volatile on China's national political agenda.

Interests, Social Movements, and Protest

The formal structures of the Chinese political system are designed more to extend party-state control of political life than to facilitate citizen participation in politics. Therefore, people make extensive use of their personal connections (*guanxi*) based on kinship, friendship, and other ties to help ease their contacts with the bureaucrats and party officials who wield such enormous power over so many aspects of their lives.

Patron-client politics is also pervasive at the local level in China, as it is in many other developing countries where ordinary people have little access to the official channels of power. For example, a village leader (the patron) may help farmers (the clients) avoid paying some taxes by reporting false production statistics in exchange for their support to keep him in office. Such clientelism can be an important way for local communities to resist state policies that they see as harmful to their interests.

Organized interest groups and social movements that are truly independent of party-state authority are not permitted to influence the political process in any significant way. The CCP uses official "mass organizations" as one means to preempt the formation of autonomous groups and movements. Still, these organizations provide a way for interest groups to express their views on policy matters within strict limits.

China has numerous mass organizations formed around social or occupational categories, with a total

membership in the hundreds of millions. Two of the most important mass organizations are the All-China Women's Federation, the only national organization representing the interests of women in general, and the All-China Federation of Trade Unions (ACFTU), to which about 90 million Chinese workers belong. Both federations are top-down, party-controlled organizations, and neither constitutes an independent political voice for the groups they are supposed to represent. But they do sometimes act as an effective lobby in promoting the nonpolitical interests of their constituencies. For example, the Women's Federation has become a strong advocate for women on issues ranging from domestic violence to economic rights, and the Trade Union Federation has pushed for legislation to reduce the standard workweek from six to five days. The ACFTU also represents individual workers with grievances against management, though it always does so within the context of its role as an organization whose first loyalty is to the Chinese communist party-state.

The AFCTU's relationship with Wal-Mart is a telling example of the kind of labor union it really is. The corporation (which imports more than $8 billion of Chinese goods for sale in the United States) does not allow unions to organize in its American stores, but it has agreed to let the AFCTU establish a branch in its several dozen stores in the PRC. As *The New York Times* put it, "Only in China, with its inimitable bend of Dickensian capitalism and authoritarian communism, has Wal-Mart found a union to its liking. And small wonder . . . the role of the state-sanctioned unions isn't to channel the discontent [of workers] into achievable gains; it's to contain it to the employer's benefit."[27]

Since the late 1990s, there has been a huge increase in the number of nongovernmental organizations (NGOs) less directly subordinate to the CCP than the traditional mass organizations. There is an enormous variety of national and local NGOs, including those that deal with the environment (such as the China Green Earth Volunteers), health (for instance, the China Foundation for the Prevention of STDs and AIDS), charitable work (such as the China Children and Teenagers Fund), and legal issues (for instance, the Beijing Center for Women's Law Services). These NGOs, which still must register with the government, have considerable latitude to operate within their functional areas without direct party interference *if* they steer clear of politics and do not challenge official policies.

Although the various representative bodies and other citizen organizations discussed in this section remain subordinate to the CCP, they should not be dismissed as inconsequential in China's political system. They do "provide important access points between the Party and the organized masses, which allow the voicing of special interests in ways that do not threaten Party hegemony and yet pressure the shaping of policy."[28]

Mechanisms of Social Control

While China has certainly loosened up politically since the days of Mao Zedong, the party-state's control mechanisms still penetrate to the basic levels of society and serve the CCP's aim of preventing the formation of groups or movements that might defy its authority. In the rural areas, the small-scale, closely knit nature of the village facilitates control by the local party and security organizations. The major means of control that has been used by the party-state in urban China, called the work unit (or *danwei*) system, is more complex. For most of the history of the People's Republic, almost all urban adults belonged to a work unit, and the *danwei* was the center of economic, social, and political life for most urban residents.

At the height of their influence, the work units were the source not only of a person's salary, but also of housing, health care, and other benefits. The *danwei* would hold mandatory meetings to discuss the official line on important policies or events, and its personnel department kept employment and political dossiers on every person who worked in that unit. If a person changed jobs, which often could be done only with the *danwei*'s approval, the dossier moved too. In these and other ways, the unit acted as a check on political dissent and social deviance. The *danwei* system is still in effect, particularly in economic, educational, and other organizations with official government ties, but its influence in people's daily lives is greatly diminished.

Residents' committees are another instrument of control in urban China. These neighborhood-based organizations, each of which cover 100–1,000 households depending on the size of the city, effectively extend the unofficial reach of the party-state down to the most basic level of urban society. They used to be staffed mostly by appointed retired persons (often elderly women), but now, as their functions shift from surveillance to service, many are led by younger and better educated residents, and in some places committee members are elected by their neighbors.

As Chinese society continues to change under the impact of economic reform and globalization, government control mechanisms are weakening. The growth of private enterprise, increasing labor and residential mobility, and new forms of association (such as discos and coffeehouses) and communication (for example, cell phones, email, fax machines) are just some of the factors that are making it much harder for the party-state to monitor citizens as closely as it has in the past.

Protest and the Party-State

The Tiananmen massacre of 1989 showed the limits of protest in China. The leadership was particularly alarmed at signs that a number of grass-roots organizations, such as the Beijing Federation of Autonomous Student Unions and the Beijing Workers' Autonomous Union, were emerging from the demonstrations. The success of Solidarity, the independent Polish workers' movement, in challenging the power of the Communist Party in Poland in the late 1980s was much in the minds of China's leaders as they watched the Tiananmen protests unfold. Severe repression was their way of letting it be known that what Deng Xiaoping referred to as the "Polish disease" would not be allowed to spread to China and that neither open political protest nor the formation of autonomous interest groups would be tolerated.

There have been no large-scale political demonstrations in China since 1989, and prodemocracy groups have been driven deep underground or abroad. Known dissidents are continuously watched, harassed, imprisoned, and, recently and more benevolently, expelled from the country, sometimes as a conciliatory diplomatic gesture. In late December 2002, one of China's leading democratic activists, Xu Wenli, was released and sent to the United States for medical care after spending sixteen of the previous twenty-one years in prison: he had been most recently sentenced to a thirteen-year jail term in 1998 for his efforts to organize an independent political party.

But repression has by no means put an end to all forms of citizen protest in the PRC. Ethnic protests occur sporadically on China's periphery. The biggest and most continuous demonstrations against the party-state in recent years have been carried out by the Falun Gong (literally, "Dharma Wheel Practice"). Falun Gong (FLG) is a spiritual movement that combines philosophical and religious elements drawn from Buddhism and Taoism with traditional Chinese physical exercises (similar to *tai chi*) and meditation. It was founded in the early 1990s by Li Hongzhi, a one-time low-level PRC government employee now living in the United States. The movement claims 70 million members in China and 30 million in more than seventy other countries: these numbers may be exaggerated, but there is no doubt that the FLG has an enormous following. Its promise of inner tranquility and good health has proven very appealing to a wide cross-section of people in China as a reaction to some of the side effects of rapid modernization, including crass commercialism, economic insecurity, and the rising crime rate.

The Chinese authorities, reacting to the movement's growing popularity, began a crackdown on Falun Gong in 1999. Ten thousand FLG followers responded that April by holding a peaceful protest outside the gates of Zhongnanhai, the walled compound in the center of Beijing where China's top leaders live and work. The government then outlawed Falun Gong and deemed it an "evil cult" that spread lies, fooled people to the point that they rejected urgently needed medical care, encouraged suicides, and generally threatened social stability. It is not only the movement's size that alarms the Chinese party-state but also its ability to communicate with and mobilize its members and spread its message through both electronic means and by word of mouth.

The intense suppression of Falun Gong has included destruction of related books and tapes, jamming of websites, and the arrest of thousands of practitioners, many of whom, the movement claims, have been not only jailed but also beaten (sometimes to death) and sent to psychiatric hospitals or labor camps. There have been a few small demonstrations by FLG followers in recent years, including one in Tiananmen Square in January 2001 that involved self-immolation by five believers. But, by and large, the crackdown seems to have been successful, or, at least, Falun Gong has decided not to overtly challenge the party-state for the time being.

Labor unrest is becoming more frequent in China, with reports of thousands of strikes and other actions in recent years. There have been big demonstrations at state-owned factories by workers angry about the ending of the iron rice bowl system, layoffs, the nonpayment of pensions or severance packages, and the arrest of grass-roots labor leaders. Workers at some foreign-owned enterprises have gone on strike to protest unsafe working conditions or low wages. Most of these actions have remained limited in scope and duration, so the government has usually not cracked down on the protesters and has, on occasion, actually pressured the employers to meet the workers' demands.

The countryside has also seen a rising tide of protest. In the poorer regions of the country—especially in central China—farmers have attacked local officials and rioted over corruption, exorbitant taxes and extralegal fees, and the government's failure to pay on time for agricultural products it has purchased. In areas that have tasted some of the fruits of China's economic growth, people have protested environmental damage done by factories whose owners care for little other than profit and illegal land seizures by greedy developers working in cahoots with local officials.

These protests have not spread beyond the locales where they started and have focused on farmers' immediate material concerns, not on grand-scale issues like democracy. They have usually been contained by the authorities through a combination of coercion and concessions to some of the farmers' demands. The government has lately become more open in acknowledging rural discontent, going so far as to issue a report saying that, in 2003, there were 58,000 protests in the countryside, involving more than three million people—an increase of 15 percent over the year before. However, in mid-2005, a front-page commentary published in the communist party's national newspaper, the *People's Daily,* and clearly aimed the wave of rural protest, reiterated the importance of maintaining stability above all else and warned that lawbreakers would face the full sanction of the law.

The overall political situation in China presents a rather contradictory picture. Although people are much freer in many ways than they have been in decades, repression can still be intense, and open political dissent is almost nonexistent. But there are many signs that the Chinese Communist Party is losing some of its ability to control the movements and associations of its citizens and can no longer easily limit access to information and ideas from abroad. Some forms of protest also appear to be increasing and may come to pose a serious challenge to the authority of the party-state.

Section ⑤ Chinese Politics in Transition

Political Challenges and Changing Agendas

Scenes from the Chinese Countryside

The economic and political circumstances of China's vast rural population differ dramatically depending on where in the countryside you look.[29]

Huaxi, Jiangsu Province. In many ways, this rural village looks like an American suburb: spacious roads lined with two-story townhouses, potted plants on doorsteps, green lawns, and luscious shade trees. Homes are air-conditioned and have leather living room furniture, studies with computers, and exercise rooms, and most families have at least one car. There's even a fifteen-story pagoda-style hotel to accommodate the visitors who come to see China's richest village.

Things were not always so prosperous in Huaxi. In the early 1980s, most villagers were farmers living in tiny houses and hoping to save enough money to buy a bicycle. Now the residents are entrepreneurs and investors, and have an annual per capita income of nearly $10,000 per year—more than thirty times the rural average—(plus dividends). This remarkable transformation began about two decades ago when the Maoist communes were dissolved and replaced with household-based farming. Under the leadership of a savvy leader (who was criticized as a "capitalist roader" during the Cultural Revolution), enough funds were accumulated to allow the establishments of a few village industries, and over the years these have expanded into an array of fifty-eight different enterprises, many of which are now staffed by migrants from poorer rural areas.

Nanliang, Shaanxi Province. This village is located in one of the areas known as China's Third World, where persistent poverty rather than growing prosperity is still the common lot in life. There are no townhouses here; per capita income is less than $50 a year, and most families live in one-room, mud-brick houses with no running water that they often share with pigs or other farm animals. One muddy waterhole is used for bathing—by both people and livestock. There are no paved roads. The children, dressed in grimy clothes and ragged cloth shoes, are not starving, but they do not seem to be flourishing either. Education, professional health care, and other social services are minimal or nonexistent. There is no industry, and the poor quality land barely supports those who work it. Tens of millions of Chinese peasants in villages like Nanliang remain mired in poverty and have benefited little from the country's economic boom.

Beihe, Shandong Province. This may be, in many ways, a rather typical Chinese village, nowhere near as wealthy as Huaxi nor as poor as Nanliang. Per capita income is about $600 per year, derived mostly from a number of small, privately-owned factories. Lots of residents have mobile phones and own consumer electronics. But they are worried. The local enterprises are struggling to survive fierce market competition, and the village-owned malt factory that once employed 200 workers has gone bankrupt. Many hope to revive village fortunes by leasing out land—its last remaining valuable commodity—to expanding businesses.

Daolin, Hunan Province. A few years ago, thousands of angry farmers marched on the township government headquarters to protest excessive taxes and the gross corruption of local officials. One farmer was killed and dozens injured when the police used clubs and tear gas to disperse the crowd. Shortly afterward, nine people suspected of being ringleaders of the protests were arrested. The demonstrations had been spurred by a grass-roots organization called Volunteers for Publicity of Policies and Regulations, formed to bring attention to local violations of a national law that limits taxes on farmers to 5 percent of their income. In many parts of rural China, villagers are subject to a wide range of arbitrary fees: charges for slaughtering pigs, for sending children to school, for permits to get married or to have a baby, for registering land, and for outhouse renovations—to name just a few. As a result of such local fees, Daolin's farmers were paying double the legal tax rate, which for people with an annual per capita income of only $170 was quite a burden. People were even more furious because the extra fees often went to support the wining and dining of township bureaucrats rather than for worthy local projects.

Beiwang, Hebei Province.   This was one of the first villages in China to establish a representative assembly and hold democratic elections for local officials. Among the first decisions made by the assembly was to reassign the contracts for tending the village's 3,000 pear trees. After the rural communes were disbanded in the 1980s, each of the five hundred or so families in the village was given six trees to look after under the new household responsibility system. The assembly, however, decided that it would be better to reassign the trees to a very small number of families who would care for them in a more efficient and productive manner.

The local Communist Party branch objected on the grounds that the village might lose much of the revenue that it earned from signing contracts with many households, which was used to pay for various public works projects such as road maintenance. The party was probably also concerned about the ideological implications of a less egalitarian distribution of the village's trees and the income derived from them. Nevertheless, assembly representatives were able to generate strong support in the village for their proposal, and the party branch agreed under pressure to recontract the trees to just eleven households. In a short time, pear production zoomed. The new system proved to be economically beneficial not only to the few families who looked after the trees but also to the village as a whole because of the local government's share of the increased profits.

The scenes just described make several important points about Chinese politics today. First, they remind us of the central role that China's rural areas will play in the nation's future. Most Chinese still live in the countryside, and China's political and economic fate will be greatly influenced by what goes on there. These scenes also reflect the enormous diversity of the Chinese countryside: prosperity and poverty, mass protests and peaceful politics. It is very hard to generalize about such a vast and varied nation by looking at what is going on in only one small part of the country.

The scene from Beiwang reminds us that in China, as in other countries, not all politics involves matters of national or international significance. For many, perhaps most, Chinese, the question of who looks after the village pear trees matters more than what goes on in the inner sanctums of the Communist Party or the outcomes of U.S.-China presidential summits. The victory of the Beiwang representative assembly on the pear tree issue shows that even in a one-party state, the people sometimes prevail against those with power, and democracy works on the local level—as long as the basic principle of party leadership is not challenged.

The Huaxi scene is just one example of the astonishing improvement in living standards in much of rural China brought about by decollectivization and industrialization. But huge pockets of severe poverty, like that in Nanliang, still persist, especially in inland regions that are far removed from the more prosperous coastal regions. Most of rural China falls somewhere between the affluence of Huaxi and the extreme poverty of Nanliang. And it is in these in-between areas, such as Beihe and Daolin, where the combination of new hopes brought about by economic progress and the anger caused by blatant corruption, growing inequalities, stagnating incomes, and other frustrations may prove to be politically explosive.

Economic reform has yielded a better life and higher hopes for most of China's farmers. The CCP must now deal with the challenge of having to satisfy those hopes or risk the wrath of a social group that for decades has been the bedrock of the party's support.

Economic Management, Social Tension, and Political Legitimacy

The problems of China's rural areas are part of a larger challenge facing the country's leadership: how to sustain and effectively manage the economic growth on which the CCP's legitimacy as China's ruling party is now largely based. The party is gambling that continued solid economic performance will literally buy it legitimacy in the eyes of the Chinese people and that most citizens will care little about democracy if their material lives continue to get better.

Despite the overall success of the reforms, the Chinese Communist Party faces a number of serious challenges in governing the economy that will affect the party's political fortunes. Failure to keep inequality under control, especially between city and countryside, or to continue providing opportunities for advancement for the less well off could become a source of social instability and a liability for a political party that still espouses a commitment to socialist goals. One of the government's most formidable tasks will be to create enough jobs not only for the millions of workers who are expected to be laid off by the closure or restructuring of state-owned enterprises, but also for the ten million or so new entrants to the labor force each year. This situation will very likely be compounded by those displaced from companies that are no longer competitive in China's increasingly globalized economy.

The considerable autonomy gained by provinces and localities as a result of the decentralization of economic decision making has had important benefits for China's development, but it has also fostered a kind of regionalism that is a potential threat to the political control of the central government and coordinated national economic policy. China's communist party leaders will also have to decide how to further nurture the private sector, which is an established and dynamic part of the socialist market economy, yet still faces significant restrictions and daunting obstacles to growth. Corruption affects the lives of most people more directly than does political repression and has become so blatant and widespread that it is probably the single most corrosive force eating away at the legitimacy of the Chinese Communist Party.

Two issues—age and AIDS—illustrate the kinds of serious challenges that confront China's leaders with crucial policy choices that will have to be made in the very near future. Simply put, the age issue is that China "is unique in growing old before it has grown rich."[30] The country has a large and growing percentage of people over sixty-five and, because of its stringent population control policy, a shrinking percentage of working age population (sixteen to sixty-four). Most countries don't experience this kind of demographic "graying"

until they are much more affluent than China is or will be for several decades. The bottom line is that there is an urgent need for the government to plan for much better pension and senior citizen health care programs than are currently in place.

The spread of AIDS in China has the potential to turn into a major crisis. Recent surveys estimate the number of infected citizens to be between 850,000 and 1 million. Unless the current infection rate is slowed, predictions are that there could be 10 million AIDS victims in China by 2010.

AIDS first spread in China in the early 1990s among needle-sharing heroin users, mostly in the border regions of the west and southwest. It has since spread to all areas of the country through injecting drugs with contaminated needles and sexual activity, particularly prostitution. There was also an extensive outbreak of AIDS in several provinces among blood donors and their families. In these cases, poor farmers had sold their blood for cash at unscrupulous and unsafe collection stations run by local "entrepreneurs," doctors, and officials. Some villages in Henan province have an HIV infection rate of over 60 percent of the population.

The government has recently taken active steps to deal with the situation, including new laws regulating the blood supply, increased funding for AIDS prevention, support for AIDS awareness campaigns, improved access to cheaper drugs, and cooperation with international organizations. The premier, Wen Jiabao, made a well-publicized visit to AIDS patients in a Beijing hospital in December 2003 that reflected an unprecedented level of official acknowledgement of the disease. But responding effectively to AIDS will require concerted action on the national and local levels and the involvement of nongovernmental organizations and experts best equipped to address the root causes of the looming epidemic. As one authoritative article observed, "There are few countries in the world with a comparable level of governmental infrastructure and control, or that have experienced such steady and dynamic economic growth. China must muster the political will and resources to prevent this progress from quickly unraveling as a result of AIDS."[31]

A comparative study by the World Bank that was published in May 2005 concluded that China's "governance"—a composite category measuring corruption, government accountability and effectiveness, political stability, rule of law, and market-friendly policies—had actually declined in recent years.[32] Clearly, the leaders of the PRC will have to make some difficult policy choices in deciding how to manage China's rapidly modernizing economy and respond to its radically changing society.

China and the Democratic Idea

China has evolved in recent decades toward a system of what has been called "Market-Leninism," a combination of increasing economic openness and continuing political rigidity under the leadership of a ruling party that adheres to a remodeled version of communist ideology.[33] The major political challenges now facing the CCP and the country emerge from the sharpening contradictions and tensions of this hybrid system.

In the short run, the CCP's gamble that the country's economic boom would divert the attention of most Chinese from politics to profits has paid off. However, as the people of China become more secure economically, better educated, and more aware of the outside world, they are likely to become politically less quiescent. The steadily expanding class of private entrepreneurs may want political clout to match their economic wealth. Scholars, scientists, and technology specialists may become more outspoken about the limits on intellectual freedom. And the many Chinese citizens who travel or study abroad may find the political gap between their party-state and the world's growing number of democracies to be increasingly intolerable.

There are reasons to be both optimistic and pessimistic about the future of the democratic idea in China.[34] On the negative side, China's long history of bureaucratic and authoritarian rule and the hierarchical values of still-influential Confucian culture seem to be mighty counterweights to democracy. And although its political legitimacy may be weak and some aspects of its social control have broken down, the coercive power of China's communist party-state remains formidable. The PRC's relatively low per capita standard of living, a largely rural population and vast areas of extreme poverty, and state-dominated media and means of communications also impose some impediments to democratization. Finally, many in China are apathetic about politics or fearful of the violence and chaos that radical political change might unleash.

On the positive side, the impressive success of democratization in Taiwan in the past decade, including free and fair multiparty elections from the local level up to the presidency, strongly suggests that the values, institutions, and process of democracy are not incompatible with Confucian culture. And though it is still a developing country, China has a higher literacy rate, more extensive industrialization and urbanization, a faster rate of economic growth, and a larger middle class than most countries at its level of economic development—conditions widely seen by social scientists as favorable to democracy.

Despite the CCP's continuing tight hold on power, there have been a number of significant political changes in China that could be planting the seeds of democracy: the decentralization of political and economic power to local governments; the setting of a mandatory retirement age and term limits for all officials; the coming to power of younger, better educated, and more worldly leaders; the increasingly important role of the National People's Congress in the policymaking process; the introduction of competitive elections in rural villages; the strengthening and partial depoliticization of the legal system; tolerance of a much wider range of artistic, cultural, and religious expression; and the important freedom (unheard of in the Mao era) for individuals to be apolitical.

Furthermore, the astounding spread of the democratic idea around the globe has created a trend that will be increasingly difficult for China's leaders to resist. The PRC has become a major player in the world of states, and its government must be more responsive to international opinion in order to continue the country's deepening integration with the international economy and growing stature as a responsible and mature global power.

One of the most important political trends in China has been the resurgence of **civil society,** a sphere of independent public life and citizen association, which, if allowed to thrive and expand, could provide fertile soil for future democratization. The development of civil society among workers in Poland and intellectuals in Czechoslovakia, for example, played an important role in the collapse of communism in East-Central Europe in the late 1980s by weakening the critical underpinnings of party-state control.

The Tiananmen demonstrations of 1989 reflected the stirrings of civil society in post-Mao China. But the brutal crushing of that movement showed the CCP's determination to thwart the growth of civil society before it could seriously challenge Communist authority. But as economic modernization and social liberalization have deepened in the PRC, civil society has begun to stir again. Some stirrings, like the Falun Gong movement, have met with vicious repression by the party-state. But others, such as the proliferation and growing influence of nongovernmental organizations, have been encouraged by the authorities. Academic journals and conferences have recently had surprisingly open, if tentative, discussions about future political options for China, including multiparty democracy.

At some point, the leaders of the CCP will face the fundamental dilemma of whether to accommodate or, as they have done so often in the past, suppress organizations, individuals, and ideas that question the principle of party leadership. Accommodation would require the party-state to cede some of its control over society and allow more meaningful citizen representation and participation. But repression would likely derail the country's economic dynamism and could have terrible costs for China.

Chinese Politics in Comparative Perspective

As mentioned at the end of Section 1, students of comparative politics should find it particularly interesting to compare China with other nations from two perspectives. First, the People's Republic of China can be compared with other communist party-states with which it shares or has shared many political characteristics. Second, China can be compared with other developing nations that face similar economic and political challenges.

China as a Communist Party-State

Why has the Chinese communist party-state been more durable than other regimes of its type? The PRC's successful economic restructuring and the rapidly rising living standard of most of the people have saved the CCP from the kinds of economic crises that greatly weakened other Communist systems, including the Soviet Union. China's leaders believe that one of the biggest mistakes made by the last Soviet party chief, Mikhail Gorbachev, was that he went too far with political reform and not far enough with economic change, and they are convinced that their reverse formula is a key reason that they have not suffered the same fate.

The fact that the Chinese Communists won power through an indigenous revolution with widespread popular backing and did not depend on foreign military support for their victory also sets China apart from the situation of most of the now-deposed East-Central European communist parties. Although repression and corruption may be harming the popularity of the CCP, the party still has a deep reservoir of historical legitimacy among large segments of the population.

But China also has many things in common with other past and present communist party-states, including the basic features of what has been often called its totalitarian political system. **Totalitarianism** (a term also applied to fascist regimes such as Nazi Germany) describes a system in which the ruling party prohibits all forms of meaningful political opposition and dissent, insists on obedience to a single state-determined ideology, and enforces its rule through coercion and terror. Such regimes also seek to bring all spheres of public activity (including the economy and culture) and even many parts of its citizens' private lives (including reproduction) under the total control of the party-state in the effort to modernize the country and, indeed, to transform human nature. Maoist China was, in many ways, a classic totalitarian political system.

China offers an interesting comparative perspective on the nature of change in totalitarian systems. Partly because of their inflexibility, totalitarian regimes in Russia and East-Central Europe collapsed quickly and thoroughly, to be replaced by democracies in the 1990s. The CCP appears to be trying to save communist rule in China by abandoning or at least moderating many, if not all, of its totalitarian features. In order to promote economic development, the CCP has relaxed its grip on many areas of life, and citizens are now free to pursue their interests without state interference as long as they steer clear of sensitive political issues.

In this sense, the PRC has evolved from totalitarianism toward a less intrusive, but still dictatorial, "consultative authoritarian regime" that "increasingly recognizes the need to obtain information, advice, and support from key sectors of the population, but insists on suppressing dissent . . . and maintaining ultimate political power in the hands of the Party."[35] Thus, China seems, at least for the moment to be going through a type of post-totalitarian transition characterized by bold economic and social reform that may, in time, nurture a transition to democracy, but that so far has helped sustain a still dictatorial political system.

China as a Third World State

The record of communist rule in China raises many issues about the role of the state in economic development. It also provides an interesting comparative perspective on the complex relationship between economic and political change in the Third World.

When the Chinese Communist Party came to power in 1949, China was a desperately poor country, with an economy devastated by a century of civil strife and world war. It was also in a weak and subordinate position in the post–World War II international order. Measured against this starting point, the PRC has made remarkable progress in improving the well-being of its citizens, building a strong state, and enhancing the country's global role.

Why has China been more successful than so many other nations in meeting some of major challenges of development? Third World governments have often served narrow class or foreign interests more than the national interest. Many political leaders in Africa, Asia, and Latin America have been a drain on development rather than a stimulus. The result is that Third World states have many times become defenders of a status quo built on extensive inequality and poverty rather than agents of needed change. In contrast, the PRC's recent rulers have been quite successful in creating what social scientists call a **developmental state,** in which government power and public policy are used effectively to promote national economic growth.

Whereas much of the Third World seems to be heading toward democracy without development—or at best very slow development—China seems to be following the reverse course of very fast development

without democracy. There is a sharp and disturbing contrast between the harsh political rule of the Chinese communist party-state and its remarkable accomplishments in improving the material lives of the Chinese people. This contrast is at the heart of what one journalist has called the "riddle of China" today, where the government "fights leprosy as aggressively as it attacks dissent. It inoculates infants with the same fervor with which it arrests its critics. Partly as a result, a baby born in Shanghai now has a longer life expectancy than a baby born in New York City."[36] This "riddle" makes it difficult to settle on a clear evaluation of the overall record of Communist rule in China, particularly in the post-Mao era. It also makes it hard to predict the future of the Chinese Communist Party, since the regime's economic achievements could provide it with the support, or at least compliance, it needs to stay in power despite its serious political shortcomings.

The CCP's tough stance on political reform is in large part based on its desire for self-preservation. But in keeping firm control on political life while allowing the country to open up in other important ways, Chinese Communist Party leaders also believe they are wisely following the model of development pioneered by the newly industrializing countries (NICs) of East Asia such as South Korea, Taiwan, and Singapore.

The lesson that the CCP draws from the NIC experience is that only a strong "neoauthoritarian" government can provide the political stability and social peace required for rapid economic growth. According to this view, democracy—with its open debates about national priorities, political parties contesting for power, and interest groups squabbling over how to divide the economic pie—is a recipe for chaos, particularly in a huge and still relatively poor country But another of the lessons from the East Asian NICs—one that most Chinese leaders have been reluctant to acknowledge so far—is that economic development, social modernization, and global integration also create powerful pressures for political change from below and abroad. In both Taiwan and South Korea, authoritarian governments that had presided over economic miracles in the 1960s and 1970s gave way in the 1980s and 1990s to the democracy, largely in response to domestic demands.

China's dynamic economic expansion and social transformation over the last twenty-five years suggest that the PRC is in the early stages of a period of growth and modernization that will lead it to NIC status. However, in terms of the extent of industrialization, per capita income, the strength of the private sector of the economy, and the size of the middle and professional classes, China's development is still far below the level at which democracy succeeded in Taiwan and South Korea. Before concluding that the China's communist rulers will soon yield to the forces of modernization, it is important to remember that "authoritarian governments in East Asia pursued market-driven economic growth for decades without relaxing their hold on political power."[37]

Nevertheless, economic reform in China has already created groups and processes, interests and ideas that are likely to evolve as sources of pressure for more and faster political change. And the experience of the NICs and other developing countries suggests that such pressures will intensify as the economy and society continue to modernize. Therefore, at some point in the not-too-distant future, the Chinese Communist Party may again face the challenge of the democratic idea. How China's new generation of leaders responds to this challenge is perhaps the most important and uncertain question about Chinese politics in the early twenty-first century.

Key Terms

communist party-state
Marxism-Leninism
autonomous regions
guerrilla warfare
collectivization
socialism
Hundred Flowers
    Movement
Anti-Rightist Campaign
Great Leap Forward
communism
Great Proletarian Cul-
    tural Revolution
revisionism
command economy
socialist market economy
people's communes

household responsibility
    system
township and village
    enterprises
decentralization
iron rice bowl
guanxi
newly industrializing
    countries
cadres
nomenklatura
socialist democracy
Four Cardinal Principles
danwei
civil society
totalitarianism
developmental state

Suggested Readings

Bernstein, Thomas P., and Xiaobo Lü. *Taxation Without Representation in Contemporary Rural China.* Cambridge: Cambridge University Press, 2003.

Blecher, Marc J. *China Against the Tides: Restructuring Through Revolution, Radicalism, and Reform.* 2nd ed. New York: Continuum, 2003.

Chang, Jung, and Jon Halliday, *Mao: The Unknown Story.* New York: Random House, 2005.

Chang, Jung. *Wild Swans: Three Daughters of China.* New York: Simon & Schuster, 1996.

Dickson, Bruce J. *Red Capitalists in China: The Party, Private Entrepreneurs, and Prospects for Political Change.* Cambridge, Mass.: Cambridge University Press, 2003.

Gao Yuan. *Born Red: A Chronicle of the Cultural Revolution.* Stanford, Calif.: Stanford University Press, 1987.

Goldman, Merle. *From Comrade to Citizen: The Struggle for Political Rights in China.* Cambridge: Harvard University Press, 2005.

Gries, Peter Hays. *China's New Nationalism: Pride, Politics, and Diplomacy.* Berkeley: University of California Press, 2004.

Hutchings, Graham. *Modern China: A Guide to a Century of Change.* Cambridge: Harvard University Press, 2001.

Judd, Ellen R. *The Chinese Women's Movement Between State and Market.* Stanford, Calif.: Stanford University Press, 2002.

Kraus, Richard Curt. *The Party and the Arty in China: The New Politics of Culture.* Lanham, Md.: Rowman & Littlefield Publishers, 2004.

Lampton, David M. *Same Bed, Different Dreams: Managing U.S.-China Relations, 1989–2000.* Berkeley: University of California Press, 2001.

Lardy, Nicholas R. *Integrating China into the Global Economy.* Washington, D.C.: Brookings Institution Press, 2002.

Lieberthal, Kenneth. *Governing China: From Revolution to Reform.* 2nd ed. New York: W.W. Norton, 2003.

MacFarquhar, Roderick, ed. *The Politics of China: The Eras of Mao and Deng.* 2nd ed. Cambridge: Cambridge University Press, 1998.

Perry, Elizabeth J. *Challenging the Mandate of Heaven: Social Protest and State Power in China.* Armonk, N.Y.: M. E. Sharpe, 2002.

Saich, Tony. *Governance and Politics of China.* 2nd ed. New York: Palgrave Macmillan, 2004.

Solinger, Dorothy J. *Contesting Citizenship in Urban China: Peasant Migrants, the State, and the Logic of the Market.* Berkeley: University of California Press, 1999.

Spence, Jonathan. *Mao Zedong.* New York: Viking, 1999.

Spence, Jonathan D., and Annping Chin. *The Chinese Century: A Photographic History of the Last Hundred Years.* New York: Random House, 1996.

Unger, Jonathan. *The Transformation of Rural China.* Armonk, N.Y.: M. E. Sharpe, 2002.

Suggested Websites

China Links, Professor William A. Joseph, Wellesley College
www.wellesley.edu/Polisci/wj/China/chinalinks.html
Embassy of the People's Republic of China in the United States
www.china-embassy.org
Finding News About China
www.chinanews.bfn.org
PRC China Internet Information Center
www.china.org.cn
China Leadership Monitor
www.chinaleadershipmonitor.org

Endnotes

[1]"Beijing Win Divides World Opinion," CNN.com, http://www.cnn.com/2001/WORLD/asiapcf/east/07/13/bcijing.win/.

[2]Mao Zedong, "Report on an Investigation of the Peasant Movement in Hunan," March 1927, in *Selected Readings from the Works of Mao Tsetung* (Beijing: Foreign Languages Press, 1971), 24.

[3]Maurice Meisner, *Mao's China and After: A History of the People's Republic,* 3rd ed. (New York: Free Press, 1999), 183.

[4]David Bachman, *Bureaucracy, Economy, and Leadership in China: The Institutional Origins of the Great Leap Forward* (Cambridge: Cambridge University Press, 1991), 2.

[5]Fareed Zakaria, "The Big Story Everyone Missed," *Newsweek,* December 30, 2002, 52.

[6]Interview on MSNBC "The Wall Street Journal Report with Maria Bartiromo," November 13, 2004, at http://www.state.gov/secretary/former/powell/remarks/38165.htm; U.S. Department of State, "Rice, Chinese Leaders Stress Constructive, Growing Relationship," March 20, 2005, at http://usinfo.state.gov/eap/Archive/2005/Mar/20-527426.html.

[7]"Rumsfeld issues a sharp rebuke to China on arms," *The New York Times,* June 4, 2005, p. A1; United States Department of Defense, Annual Report to Congress, *The Military Power of the People's Republic of China, 2005,* at http://www.defenselink.mil/news/Jul2005/d20050719china.pdf.

[8]See, for example, "When China Wakes," *Economist,* November 28, 1992; and Nicholas D. Kristof and Sheryl WuDunn, *China Wakes: The Struggle for the Soul of a Rising Power* (New York: Time Books, 1994).

[9]"When China Wakes," 3, 15.

[10]Barry Naughton, "The Pattern and Legacy of Economic Growth in the Mao Era," in Kenneth Lieberthal et al. (eds.), *Perspectives on Modern China: Four Anniversaries* (Armonk, N.Y.: M. E. Sharpe, 1991), 250.

[11]Deng Xiaoping first expressed his "cat theory" in 1962 in a speech, "Restore Agricultural Production," in the aftermath of the failure and famine of the Great Leap Forward. In the original speech, he actually quoted an old peasant proverb that refers to a "yellow cat or a black cat," but it is most often rendered "white cat or black cat." See *Selected Works of Deng Xiaoping (1938–1965)* (Beijing: Foreign Languages Press, 1992), 293.

[12]Kathleen Hartford, "Socialist Agriculture Is Dead; Long Live Socialist Agriculture! Organizational Transformation in Rural China," in Elizabeth J. Perry and Christine P. W. Wong (eds.), *The Political Economy of Reform in Post-Mao China* (Cambridge: Council on East Asian Studies, Harvard University, 1985), 55.

[13]Christine P. W. Wong, "China's Economy: The Limits of Gradualist Reform," in William A. Joseph (ed.), *China Briefing, 1994* (Boulder, Colo.: Westview Press, 1994), 50.

[14]Emily Honig and Gail Herschatter, *Personal Voices: Chinese Women in the 1980s* (Stanford, Calif.: Stanford University Press, 1988), 337.

[15]Jasper Becker, "China's Growing Pains," *National Geographic,* March 2004, p. 81.

[16]*The Economist,* July 28, 2005, p. 61.

[17]Mao Zedong, "Strive to Build a Great Socialist Country," September 15, 1954, in *Selected Works of Mao Tsetung,* vol. 5 (Beijing: Foreign Languages Press, 1977), 149.

[18]Deng Xiaoping, "Uphold the Four Cardinal Principles," March 30, 1979, in *Selected Works of Deng Xiaoping (1977–1982)* (Beijing: Foreign Languages Press, 1984), 178.

[19]The constitution of the People's Republic of China can be found on line at the website of the *People's Daily,* http://english.people.com.cn/constitution/constitution.html. The full text of the constitution of the Chinese Communist Party can be found at the website of the International Department of the CCP at: http://www.idcpc.org.cn/english/cpcbrief/constitution.htm.

[20]Mao Zedong, "Problems of War and Strategy," November 6, 1938, in *Selected Works of Mao Tsetung,* vol. 2 (Beijing: Foreign Languages Press, 1972), 224.

[21]Kenneth Lieberthal and David Michael Lampton (eds.), *Bureaucracy, Politics, and Decision-Making in Post-Mao China* (Berkeley: University of California Press, 1992).

[22]John P. Burns, *The Chinese Communist Party's Nomenklatura System: A Documentary Study of Party Control of Leadership Selection, 1979–1984* (Armonk, N.Y.: M. E. Sharpe, 1989), ix–x.

[23]Gordon White, *Riding the Tiger: The Politics of Economic Reform in Post-Mao China* (Palo Alto, Calif.: Stanford University Press, 1993), 20.

[24]James D. Seymour, *China's Satellite Parties* (Armonk, N.Y.: M. E. Sharpe, 1987), 87.

[25]"Copying Western Political Systems Would Lead to Blind Alley for China: Chinese President," *People's Daily,* September 15, 2004, http://english.people.com.cn/200409/15/eng20040915_157076.html.

[26]Lin Biao, "Foreword to the Second Edition," *Quotations from Chairman Mao Tse-tung* (Beijing: Foreign Languages Press, 1967), iii.

[27]Harold Meyerson, "Wal-Mart Loves Unions (In China)," *The New York Times*, December 1, 2004. I would like to thank my student, Michele Park, for drawing my attention to this example and article.

[28]James R. Townsend and Brantly Womack, *Politics in China,* 3rd ed. (Boston: Little, Brown, 1986), 271.

[29]The following scenes are extrapolated from Jonathan Watts, "In China's richest village," *The Guardian*, May 10, 2005; Wang Zhe, "Behind the Dream of a Village," *Beijing Review,* June 14, 2001, 13–16; Lu Xueyi, "The Peasants Are Suffering, the Villages Are Very Poor," *Dushu* (Readings), January 2001, in U.S. Embassy (Beijing, China), PRC Press Clippings, http:// www.usembassy-china.org.cn/sandt/peasantsuffering .html); Hannah Beech, "In Rural China, It's a Family Affair" Time/Asia, May 27, 2002; "The Silent Majority: A Rare Look inside a Chinese Village," *The Economist*, April 7, 2005; Erik Eckholm, "Heated Protests by Its Farmers Trouble Beijing," *New York Times,* February 1, 1999, A; Susan V. Lawrence, "Democracy, Chinese-Style: Village Representative Assemblies," *Australian Journal of Chinese Affairs,* no. 32 (July 1994): 61–68.

[30]*The Economist,* "A Survey of India and China," March 3, 2005.

[31]Joan Kaufman and Jun Jing, "China and AIDS—The Time to Act Is Now," *Science,* June 28, 2002, 2340.

[32]D. Kaufmann, A. Kraay, and M. Mastruzzi, *Governance Matters IV: Governance Indicators for 1996–2004.* (Washington, D.C.: The World Bank), 2004. Available at: http://www .worldbank.org/wbi/governance/pubs/govmatters4.html.

[33]Nicholas D. Kristof, "China Sees 'Market-Leninism' as Way to Future," *New York Times,* September 6, 1993, 1, 5.

[34]Many of the points in this section are based on Martin King Whyte, "Prospects for Democratization in China," *Problems of Communism* (May–June 1992): 58–69; Michel Oksenberg, "Will China Democratize? Confronting a Classic Dilemma," *Journal of Democracy* 9, no. 1 (January 1998): 27–34; and Minxin Pei, "Is China Democratizing?" *Foreign Affairs* 77, no. 1 (January– February 1998), 68–82.

[35]Harry Harding, *China's Second Revolution: Reform After Mao* (Washington, D.C.: Brookings Institution, 1987), 200.

[36]Nicholas D. Kristof, "Riddle of China: Repression as Standard of Living Soars," *New York Times,* September 7, 1993, A1, A10.

[37]Nicholas Lardy, "Is China Different? The Fate of Its Economic Reform," in Daniel Chirot (ed.), *The Crisis of Leninism and the Decline of the Left* (Seattle: University of Washington Press, 1991), 147.

Glossary

accommodation an informal agreement or settlement between the government and important interest groups in response to the interest groups' concerns for policy or program benefits.

accountability a government's responsibility to its population, usually by periodic popular elections and by parliament's having the power to dismiss the government by passing a motion of no confidence. In a political system characterized by accountability, the major actions taken by government must be known and understood by the citizenry.

acephalous societies literally "headless" societies. A number of traditional Nigerian societies, such as the Igbo in the precolonial period, lacked executive rulership as we have come to conceive of it. Instead, the villages and clans were governed by committee or consensus.

Amerindians original peoples of North and South America; indigenous people.

anticlericalism opposition to the power of churches or clergy in politics. In some countries, for example, France and Mexico, this opposition has focused on the role of the Catholic Church in politics.

Anti-Rightist Campaign was launched by Chinese Communist Party (CCP) Chairman Mao Zedong in 1957 in the aftermath of the **Hundred Flowers Movement**. The Campaign was aimed at critics of the CCP who were labeled as "rightists," that is, counterrevolutionaries. Millions of people were affected and hundreds of thousands sent to labor reform camps, many were not released until after Mao's death in 1976.

Articles of Confederation the first governing document of the United States, agreed to in 1777 and ratified in 1781. The Articles concentrated most powers in the states and made the national government largely dependent on voluntary contributions of the states.

Assembly of Experts (Iran) nominates the and can replace him. The assembly is elected by the general electorate but almost all its members are clerics.

---

*Note: Boldface terms *within* a definition can be found as separate entries in the Glossary.

asymmetrical federalism a system of governance in which political authority is shared between a central government and regional or state governments, but where some subnational units in the federal system have greater or lesser powers than others.

authoritarianism a system of rule in which power depends not on popular legitimacy but on the coercive force of the political authorities. Hence, there are few personal and group freedoms. It is also characterized by near absolute power in the executive branch and few, if any, legislative and judicial controls. See also **autocracy; partrimonialism.**

autocracy a government in which one or a few rulers has absolute power, thus, a **dictatorship.** Similar to **authoritarianism.**

autonomous region in the People's Republic of China, a territorial unit equivalent to a province that contains a large concentration of ethnic minorities. These regions have some autonomy in the cultural sphere but in most policy matters are strictly subordinate to the central government.

autonomous republic a territorial unit in the Soviet Union that was a constituent unit of the **union republic** within which it was located. Autonomous republics were populated by a large national (ethnic) group, after which the autonomous republic was generally named. They enjoyed little actual autonomy in the Soviet period. Once Russia adopted its new constitution in 1993, those autonomous republics within Russian territory became constituent units (now called republics) of the Russian Federation.

ayatollah literally, "sign of God." High-ranking clerics in Iran. The most senior ones—often no more than half a dozen—are known as grand ayatollahs.

balance of payments an indicator of international flow of funds that shows the excess or deficit in total payments of all kinds between or among countries. Included in the calculation are exports and imports, grants, and international debt payments.

bazaar an urban marketplace where shops, workshops, small businesses, and export-importers are located.

bicameral a legislative body with two houses, such as the U.S. Senate and the U.S. House of Representatives. Just as the U.S. Constitution divides responsibilities between the branches of the federal government and between the federal government and the states, it divides legislative responsibilities between the Senate and the House.

Bill of Rights   the first ten amendments to the U.S. Constitution (ratified in 1791), which established limits on the actions of government. Initially, the Bill of Rights limited only the federal government. The Fourteenth Amendment and subsequent judicial rulings extended the provisions of the Bill of Rights to the states.

cabinet government   a system of government, as in Britain, in which the cabinet (rather than the prime minister) exercises responsibility for formulating policy and directing both the government and the executive branch. In the UK, cabinet government has been undermined as a check on the power of the prime minister.

cadre   a person who occupies a position of authority in a **communist party-state;**   cadres may or may not be Communist Party members.

checks and balances   a governmental system of divided authority in which coequal branches can restrain each other's actions. For example, the U.S. president must sign legislation passed by Congress for it to become law. If the president vetoes a bill, Congress can override that veto by a two-thirds vote of the Senate and the House of Representatives.

civil society   refers to the space occupied by voluntary associations outside the state, for example, professional associations (lawyers, doctors, teachers), trade unions, student and women's groups, religious bodies, and other voluntary association groups. The term is similar to *society*, although *civil society* implies a degree of organization absent from the more inclusive term *society*.

clientelism (or **patron-client networks**)   an informal aspect of policymaking in which a powerful patron (for example, a traditional local boss, government agency, or dominant party) offers resources such as land, contracts, protection, or jobs in return for the support and services (such as labor or votes) of lower-status and less powerful clients; corruption, preferential treatment, and inequality are characteristic of clientelist politics. See also **patrimonialism; prebendalism.**

collectivization   a process undertaken in the Soviet Union under Stalin in the late 1920s and early 1930s and in China under Mao in the 1950s, by which agricultural land was removed from private ownership and organized into large state and collective farms.

command economy   a form of **socialist** economic organization in which government decisions ("commands") rather than market mechanisms (such as supply and demand) are the major influences in determining the nation's economic direction; also called central planning.

communism   a system of social organization based on the common ownership and coordination of production. According to Marxism (the theory of German philosopher Karl Marx, 1818–1883), communism is a culminating stage of history, following capitalism and **socialism.** In historical practice, leaders of China, the Soviet Union, and other states that have proclaimed themselves seeking to achieve communism have ruled through a single party, the Communist Party, which has controlled the state and society in an authoritarian manner, and have applied **Marxism-Leninism** to justify their rule.

communist party-state   a type of nation-state in which the Communist Party attempts to exercise a complete monopoly on political power and controls all important state institutions. See also **communism.**

conditionality   the requirement that certain commitments be made by receiving governments in exchange for credits or other types of assistance provided by international or foreign agencies, to ensure that the goals of the donor agency are respected.

constitutional monarchy   a system of government in which the head of state ascends by heredity, but is limited in powers and constrained by the provisions of a constitution.

co-optation   incorporating activists into the system while accommodating some of their concerns.

corporatist state   a state in which **interest groups** become an institutionalized part of the structure. See also **corporatism; democratic corporatism; state corporatism.**

coup d'état   a forceful, extra-constitutional action resulting in the removal of an existing government.

danwei   a Chinese term that means "unit" and is the basic level of social organization and a major means of political control in China's **communist party-state.** A person's *danwei* is most often his or her workplace, such as a factory or an office.

decentralization   policies that aim to transfer some decision-making power from higher to lower levels of government, typically from the central government to subnational governments.

Declaration of Independence   the document asserting the independence of the British colonies in what is now the United States from Great Britain. The Declaration of Independence was signed in Philadelphia on July 4, 1776.

democratic centralism   a system of political organization developed by V. I. Lenin and practiced, with modifications, by all communist party-states. Its principles include a hierarchal party structure in which (1) party leaders are elected on a delegate basis from lower to higher party bodies; (2) party leaders can be recalled by those who elected them; and (3) freedom of discussion is permitted until a decision is taken, but strict discipline and unity should prevail in implementing a decision once it is made. In practice, in all Communist parties in China, the Soviet Union, and elsewhere, centralizing elements tended to predominate over the democratic ones.

demokratizatsiia   the policy of democratization identified by former Soviet leader Mikhail Gorbachev in 1987 as an essential component of *perestroika*. The policy was part of a gradual shift away from a **vanguard party** approach toward an acceptance of **liberal** democratic norms. Initially, the policy embraced multicandidate elections and a broadening of political competition within the Communist Party itself; after 1989, it involved acceptance of a multiparty system.

developmental state   a **nation-state** in which the government carries out policies that effectively promote national economic growth.

distributive policies   policies that allocate state resources into an area that lawmakers perceive needs to be promoted. For example, leaders today believe that students should have access to the Internet. In order to accomplish this goal, telephone users are being taxed to provide money for schools to establish connections to the Internet (which, in large part, uses telephone lines to transfer data).

dual society   a society and economy that are sharply divided into a traditional, usually poorer, and a modern, usually richer, sector.

Economic Community of West African Studies (ECOWAS)   the organization established in 1975 among the sixteen governments in West Africa. Its goals are to strengthen and broaden the economies in the region through the removal of trade barriers among its members (such as import quotas and domestic content laws), freedom of movement for citizens, and monetary cooperation.

ejidatario   recipient of *ejido* land grant in Mexico.

ejido   land granted by Mexican government to an organized group of peasants.

emir   traditional Islamic ruler. The emir presides over an "emirate," or kingdom, in northern Nigeria.

Expediency Council   a committee set up in Iran to resolve differences between the *Majles* and the **Guardian Council.**

Farsi   Persian word for the Persian language. Fars is a province in Central Iran.

fatwa   a pronouncement issued by a high-ranking Islamic cleric.

Federal Reserve Board   the U.S. central bank established by Congress in 1913 to regulate the banking industry and the money supply. Although the president appoints the chair of the board of governors (with Senate approval), the board operates largely independently. Many criticize its policies as reflecting the needs of banks and international capital over the needs of citizens, particularly workers.

federalism   a system of governance in which political authority is shared between the national government and regional or state governments. The powers of each level of government are usually specified in a federal constitution.

foreign direct investment   ownership of or investment in cross-border enterprises in which the investor plays a direct managerial role.

Foundation of the Oppressed   a clerically controlled foundation in Iran set up after the revolution there.

Four Cardinal Principles   ideas first enunciated by Chinese leader Deng Xiaoping in 1979 asserting that all policies should be judged by whether they uphold the socialist road, the dictatorship of the proletariat, the leadership of the Communist Party, and Marxism-Leninism–Mao Zedong Thought. The main purpose of the Four Cardinal Principles was to proscribe any challenge to the ultimate authority of the Chinese Communist Party, even during a time of far reaching economic reform. The Principles have been reaffirmed by Deng's successors and continue to define the boundaries of what is politically permissible in China.

free market   a system in which government regulation of the economy is absent or limited. Relative to other advanced democracies, the United States has traditionally had a freer market economically. See **laissez-faire.**

free trade   international commerce that is relatively unregulated or constrained by tariffs (special payments imposed by governments on exports or imports).

fundamentalism   a term recently popularized to describe radical religious movements throughout the world.

fusion of powers   a constitutional principle that merges the authority of branches of government, in contrast to the principle of **separation of powers.** In Britain, for example, Parliament is the supreme legislative, executive, and judicial authority. The fusion of legislature and executive is also expressed in the function and personnel of the cabinet.

gender gap   politically significant differences in social attitudes and voting behavior between men and women.

glasnost   Gorbachev's policy of "openness" or "publicity," which involved an easing of controls on the media, arts, and public discussion, leading to an outburst of public debate and criticism covering most aspects of Soviet history, culture, and policy.

Great Leap Forward   a movement launched by Mao Zedong in 1958 to industrialize China very rapidly and thereby propel it toward **communism**. The Leap ended in economic disaster in 1960, causing one of the worst famines in human history.

Great Proletarian Cultural Revolution   the political campaign launched in 1966 by Chairman Mao Zedong to stop what he saw as China's drift away from socialism and toward capitalism. The campaign led to massive purges in the Chinese Communist Party, the widespread persecution of China's intellectuals, extensive political violence, and the destruction of invaluable cultural objects. The Cultural Revolution officially ended in 1976 after Mao's death and the arrest of some of his most radical followers.

guanxi   a Chinese term that means "connections" or "relationships," and describes personal ties between individuals based on such things as common birthplace or mutual acquaintances. *Guanxi* are an important factor in China's political and economic life.

Guardian Council   a committee created in the Iranian constitution to oversee the *Majles* (the parliament).

guerrilla warfare   a military strategy based on small, highly mobile bands of soldiers (the guerrillas, from the Spanish word for war, "guerra") who use hit-and-run tactics like ambushes to attack a better-armed enemy.

hegemonic power   a state that can control the pattern of alliances and terms of the international order, and often shapes domestic political developments in countries throughout the world.

hezbollahis   literally "partisans of God." In Iran, the term is used to describe religious vigilantes. In Lebanon, it is used to describe the Shi'i militia.

hojjat al-Islam   literally, "the proof of Islam." In Iran, it means a medium-ranking cleric.

household responsibility system   the system put into practice in China beginning in the early 1980s in which the major decisions about agricultural production are made by individual farm families based on the profit motive rather than by a **people's commune** or the government.

Hundred Flowers Movement   refers to a period in 1956–57 when Chinese Communist Party Chairman Mao Zedong encouraged citizens, particularly intellectuals, to speak out ("Let a hundred flowers bloom, let a hundred schools of thought contend!") and give their views on how to improve China's government. Mao was shocked by the depth of the criticism of communist rule and cracked down by silencing and punishing the critics by launching the **Anti-Rightist Campaign** of 1957.

Imam Jum'ehs   prayer leaders in Iran's main urban mosques. Appointed by the **Supreme Leader,** they have considerable authority in the provinces.

import substituting industrialization (ISI)   strategy for industrialization based on domestic manufacture of previously imported goods to satisfy domestic market demands. See also **developmentalism.**

indigenous groups   population of **Amerindian** heritage in Mexico.

indirect rule   a term used to describe the British style of colonialism in Nigeria and India in which local traditional rulers and political structures were used to help support the colonial governing structure.

informal sector (economy)   that portion of the economy largely outside government control in which employees work without contracts or benefits. Examples include casual employees in restaurants and hotels, street vendors, and day laborers in construction or agriculture.

insider privatization   a term used in relation to Russia to refer to the transformation of formerly state-owned enterprises into **joint-stock companies** or private enterprises in which majority control of the enterprise is in the hands of employees and/or managers of that enterprise.

interest groups   organizations that seek to represent the interests—usually economic—of their members in dealings with the government. Important examples are associations representing people with specific occupations, business interests, racial and ethnic groups, or age groups in society.

international financial institutions (IFIs)   generally refers to the International Bank for Reconstruction and Development (the World Bank) and the International Monetary Fund (IMF), but can also include other international lending institutions. See also **structural adjustment program (SAP).**

interventionist   an interventionist state acts vigorously to shape the performance of major sectors of the economy.

iron rice bowl   a feature of China's socialist economy during the Maoist era (1949–76) that provided guarantees of lifetime employment, income, and basic cradle-to-grave benefits to most urban and rural workers. Economic reforms beginning in the 1980s that aimed at improving efficiency and work motivation sought to smash the iron rice bowl and link employment and income more directly to individual effort.

iron triangle relationships   a term coined by students of American politics to refer to the relationships of mutual support formed by particular government agencies, members of congressional committees or subcommittees, and interest groups in various policy areas. Synonymous with "cozy triangles," the term has been borrowed by some students of Japanese politics to refer to similar relationships found among Japanese ministry or agency officials, *Diet* (parliament) members, and special interest groups.

jihad   literally "struggle." Although often used to mean armed struggle against unbelievers, it can also mean spiritual struggle for more self-improvement.

joint-stock company   a business firm whose capital is divided into shares that can be held by individuals, groups of individuals, or governmental units. In Russia, formation of joint-stock companies has been the primary method for privatizing large state enterprises.

jurist's guardianship   Khomeini's concept that the Iranian clergy should rule on the grounds that they are the divinely appointed guardians of both the law and the people. He developed this concept in the 1970s.

Keynesianism   named after the British economist John Maynard Keynes, an approach to economic policy in which state economic policies are used to regulate the economy in an attempt to achieve stable economic growth. During recession, state budget deficits are used to expand demand in an effort to boost both consumption and investment, and to create employment. During periods of high growth when inflation threatens, cuts in government spending and a tightening of credit are used to reduce demand.

krai   one of the six territorial units in the Russian Federation that are defined by the constitution of 1993 to be among the eighty-nine members of the federation, with a status equal to that of the republics and *oblast.* Like the *oblasts* during the Soviet period, the *krai* were defined purely as territorial-administrative units within a particular **union republic** of the Soviet Union. A *krai* differed from an *oblast* in that part of its border was on an external boundary of the USSR or it included a mixture of diverse ethnic territories (or both). Generally a *krai* is a geographically large unit, but relatively sparsely populated.

laissez-faire   the doctrine that government should not interfere with commerce. Relative to other advanced democracies, the United States has traditionally taken a more laissez-faire

attitude toward economic regulation, although regulation increased in the twentieth century. See also **free market.**

law-based state   a state where the rule of law prevails, so that actions of the government as well of nongovernmental actors are subject to the requirements of the law. The creation of a law-based state in the Soviet Union was one of the explicit goals of Gorbachev's reform process, thus limiting the ability of state agencies or the Communist Party of the Soviet Union arbitrarily to circumvent laws or legal provisions.

legitimacy   a belief by powerful groups and the broad citizenry that a state exercises rightful authority. In the contemporary world, a state is said to possess legitimacy when it enjoys consent of the governed, which usually involves democratic procedures and the attempt to achieve a satisfactory level of development and equitable distribution of resources.

macroeconomic policy   government policy intended to shape the overall economic system at the national level by concentrating on policy targets such as inflation or growth.

mafia   a term borrowed from Italy and widely used in Russia to describe networks of organized criminal activity that pervade both economic and governmental securities in that country as well as activities such as the demanding of protection money, bribe taking by government officials, contract killing, and extortion.

majles   Arabic term for "assembly"; used in Iran to describe the parliament.

manifest destiny   the public philosophy in the nineteenth century that the United States was not only entitled but also destined to occupy territory from the Atlantic to the Pacific.

maquiladoras   factories that produce goods for export, often located along the U.S.-Mexican border.

Marbury v. *Madison*   the 1803 U.S. Supreme Court ruling that the federal courts inherently had the authority to review the constitutionality of laws passed by Congress and signed by the president. The ruling, initially used sparingly, placed the courts centrally in the system of checks and balances.

market reform   a strategy of economic transformation embraced by the Yeltsin government in Russia and the Deng Xiaoping government in China that involves reducing the role of the state in managing the economy and increasing the role of market forces. In Russia, market reform is part of the transition to postcommunism and includes the extensive transfer of the ownership of economic assets from the state to private hands. In China, market reform has been carried out under the leadership of the Chinese Communist Party and involves less extensive privatization.

Marxism-Leninism the theoretical foundation of communism based on the ideas of the German philosopher, Karl Marx (1818–1883), and the leader of the Russian Revolution, V. I. Lenin (1870–1924). Marxism is, in essence, a theory of historical development that emphasizes the struggle between exploiting and exploited classes, particularly the struggle between the bourgeoisie (capitalists) and the proletariat (the industrial working class). Leninism emphasizes the strategy and organization to be used by the communist party to overthrow capitalism and seize power as a first step on the road to communism.

maslahat Arabic term for "expediency," "prudence," or "advisability." It is now used in Iran to refer to reasons of state or what is best for the Islamic Republic.

mestizo a person of mixed white, indigenous (Amerindian), and sometimes African descent.

mir the traditional form of communal peasant organization in Russia that survived until the collectivization campaign of the late 1920s and involved a periodic redistribution of strips of land among families of the commune.

monetarism an approach to economic policy that assumes a natural rate of unemployment determined by the labor market, emphasizes setting targets for the rate of growth of the monetary supply, gives highest priority to controlling inflation, and rejects the instrument of government spending to run budgetary deficits for stimulating the economy.

mosque **Muslim** place of worship, equivalent to a church, temple, or synagogue.

neoliberalism a term used to describe government policies aiming to promote free competition among business firms within the market. Neoliberal policies include **monetarism**, **privatization**, reducing trade barriers, balancing government budgets, and reducing social spending.

newly industrializing countries (NICs) a term used to describe a group of countries that achieved rapid **economic development** beginning in the 1960s, largely stimulated by robust international trade (particularly exports) and guided by government policies. The core NICs are usually considered to be Taiwan, South Korea, Hong Kong, and Singapore, but other countries, including Argentina, Brazil, Malaysia, Mexico, and Thailand, are often included in this category.

nomenklatura a system of personnel selection under which the Communist Party maintained control over the appointment of important officials in all spheres of social, economic, and political life. The term is also used to describe individuals chosen through this system and thus refers more broadly to the privileged circles in the Soviet Union and China.

North American Free Trade Agreement (NAFTA) a treaty among the United States, Mexico, and Canada implemented on January 1, 1994, that largely eliminates trade barriers among the three nations and establishes procedures to resolve trade disputes. NAFTA serves as a model for an eventual Free Trade Area of the Americas zone that could include most Western Hemisphere nations.

oblast one of forty-nine territorial units in the Russian Federation defined by the constitution of 1993 to be among the eighty-nine members of the federation, with a status equal to that of the republics and *krai.* An *oblast* generally lacks a non-Russian national/ethnic basis. During the Soviet period, the *oblasts* were defined purely as territorial-administrative units located within a particular **union republic** of the Soviet Union. See also *okrug;* **autonomous republic.**

okrug one of ten territorial units in the Russian Federation that are defined by the constitution of 1993 to be among the eighty-nine members of the federation with a status equal to that of the republics, *oblasts,* and *krai.* An *okrug* generally was originally formed due to the presence of a non-Russian national/ethnic group residing in the territory. Alongside their status as equal units of the Russian Federation, most of the *okrugs* are physically located within and constituent parts of an *oblast* or *krai.* This situation has created ambiguity regarding the relationship between the *okrug* and the *oblast* or *krai* they are located in.

oligarchs a small group of powerful and wealthy individuals who gained ownership and control of important sectors of Russia's economy in the context of the privatization of state assets in the 1990s.

OPEC Organization of Petroleum Exporting Countries. Founded in 1960 by Iran, Venezuela, and Saudi Arabia, it now includes most oil-exporting states with the notable exceptions of Mexico and former members of the Soviet Union. It tries to regulate prices by regulating production.

para-statals state-owned, or at least state-controlled, corporations, created to undertake a broad range of activities, from control and marketing of agricultural production to provision of banking services, operation of airlines, and other transportation facilities and public utilities. See also **interventionist.**

parliamentary democracy system of government in which the chief executive is answerable to the legislature and may be dismissed by it. Parliamentary democracy stands in contrast to a presidential system, in which the chief executive is elected in a national ballot and is independent of the legislative branch.

parliamentary sovereignty   a constitutional principle of government (principally in Britain) by which the legislature reserves the power to make or overturn any law without recourse by the executive, the judiciary, or the monarchy. Only Parliament can nullify or overturn legislation approved by Parliament; and Parliament can force the cabinet or the government to resign by voting a motion of no confidence.

pasdaran   Persian term for guards, used to refer to the army of Revolutionary Guards formed during Iran's Islamic Revolution.

patrimonial state   See **patrimonialism.**

patrimonialism (or **ncopatrimonialism**)   a system of governance in which a single ruler treats the state as personal property (patrimony). Appointments to public office are made on the basis of unswerving loyalty to the ruler. In turn, state officials exercise wide authority in other domains, such as the economy, often for their personal benefit and that of the ruler, to the detriment of the general population. See also **authoritarianism; autocracy; prebendalism.**

patron-client networks (or patron-client politics)   See **clientelism.**

People of the Book   the Muslim term for recognized religious minorities, such as Christians, Jews, and Zoroastrians.

people's communes   large-scale rural communities first implemented during the **Great Leap Forward** that were in charge of nearly all aspects of political, social, and economic life in the Chinese countryside from the late 1950s until the early 1980s, when they were disbanded and replaced by a system of household and village-based agricultural production.

perestroika   the policy of restructuring embarked on by Gorbachev when he became head of the Communist Party of the Soviet Union in 1985. Initially, the policy emphasized decentralization of economic decision making, increased enterprise autonomy, expanded public discussion of policy issues, and a reduction in the international isolation of the Soviet economy. Over time, restructuring took on a more political tone, including a commitment to *glasnost* and *demokratizatsiia*.

police powers   powers that are traditionally held by the states to regulate public safety and welfare. Police powers are the form of interaction with government that citizens most often experience. Even with the growth in federal government powers in the twentieth century, police powers remain the primary responsibility of the states and localities.

political action committee (PAC)   a narrow form of interest group that seeks to influence policy by making contributions to candidates and parties in U.S. politics.

power vertical   a term used by Vladimir Putin to describe a unified and hierarchical structure of executive power ranging from the federal level to the local level, which can be reinforced by various mechanisms such as appointment of lower officials by higher-level officials and oversight of activities of lower organs by higher ones.

prebendalism   patterns of political behavior that rest on the justification that official state offices should be utilized for the personal benefit of officeholders as well as of their support group or clients. Thus, prebendal politics is sustained by the existence of **patron-client networks.** See also **patrimonialism; clientelism.**

privatization voucher   a certificate worth 10,000 rubles issued by the government to each Russian citizen in 1992 to be used to purchase shares in state enterprises undergoing the process of privatization. Vouchers could also be sold for cash or disposed of through newly created investment funds.

privatization   the sale of state-owned enterprises to private companies or investors. Those who support the policy claim that private ownership is superior to government ownership because for-profit entities promote greater efficiency. Privatization is a common central component of **structural adjustment programs** to curtail the losses associated with these enterprises and generate state revenue when they are sold. For Russia, see **spontaneous privatization.**

property taxes   taxes levied by local governments on the assessed value of property. Property taxes are the primary way in which local jurisdictions in the United States pay for the costs of primary and secondary education. Because the value of property varies dramatically from neighborhood to neighborhood, the funding available for schools—and the quality of education—also varies from place to place.

proportional representation (PR)   a system of political representation in which seats are allocated to parties within multimember constituencies, roughly in proportion to the votes each party receives. PR usually encourages the election to parliament of more political parties than single-member-district winner-take-all systems.

pyramid debt   a situation when a government or organization takes on debt obligations at progressively higher rates of interest in order to pay off existing debt. In some cases, a structure of pyramid debt can result in a default on the entire debt obligation if interest owed becomes unmanageable.

quangos   acronym for quasi-nongovernmental organizations, the term used in Britain for nonelected bodies that are outside traditional governmental departments or local authorities. They have considerable influence over public policy in areas such s education, health care, and housing.

Qur'an   the Muslim Bible.

redistributive policies   policies that take resources from one person or group in society and allocate them to a different, usually more disadvantaged, group. The United States has traditionally opposed redistributive policies to the disadvantaged.

regulations   the rules that explain the implementation of laws. When the legislature passes a law, it sets broad principles for implementation, but how the law is actually implemented is determined by regulations written by executive branch agencies. The regulation-writing process allows interested parties to influence the eventual shape of the law in practice.

rentier state   a country that obtains much of its revenue from the export of oil or other natural resources.

rents   above-market returns to a factor of production. Pursuit of economic rents (or "rent-seeking") is profit seeking that takes the form of nonproductive economic activity.

revisionism   a label used by the Chinese Communist Party (CCP) during the late Maoist era (1965–1976) to refer to the ideology of those political parties (particularly the Communist Party of the Soviet Union) or individuals (including members of the CCP) judged to have betrayed what they believed to be the true meaning of the theory and practice of **Marxism-Leninism** as interpreted by Mao Zedong.

self-determination   the right of a sovereign state or an ethnic or other group that shares cultural and historical ties to live together in a given territory and in a manner they desire. It is often the basis of the claim by a state or group for political independence and cultural autonomy.

separation of powers   an organization of political institutions within the state in which the executive, legislature, and judiciary have autonomous powers and no one branch dominates the others. This is the common pattern in presidential systems, as opposed to parliamentary systems, in which there is a **fusion of powers.**

sexenio   the six-year administration of Mexican presidents.

shari'a   Islamic law derived mostly from the **Qur'an** and the examples set by the Prophet Muhammad.

Shi'ism   a branch of Islam. It literally means the followers or partisans of Ali. The other branch is known as Sunni, or the followers of tradition.

shock therapy   a variant of **market reform** that involves the state simultaneously imposing a wide range of radical economic changes, with the purpose of "shocking" the economy into a new mode of operation. Shock therapy can be contrasted with a more gradual approach to market reform.

siloviki   derived from the Russian word *sil,* meaning "force." Russian politicians and government officials drawn from security and intelligence agencies (such as the Soviet KGB or its contemporary counterpart, the FSB), special forces, or the military, many of whom were recruited to important political posts under Vladimir Putin.

single-member plurality (SMP) electoral system   an electoral system in which candidates run for a single seat from a specific geographic district. The winner is the person who receives the most votes, whether or not that is a majority. SMP systems, unlike systems of proportional representation, increase the likelihood that two national coalition parties will form.

social security   national systems of contributory and noncontributory benefits to provide assistance for the elderly, sick, disabled, unemployed, and others similarly in need of assistance. The specific coverage of social security, a key component of the welfare state, varies by country.

socialism   in a socialist regime, the state plays a leading role in organizing the economy, and most business firms are publicly owned. A socialist regime, unlike a **communist party-state,** may allow the private sector to play an important role in the economy and be committed to political pluralism. In **Marxism-Leninism,** socialism refers to an early stage in development of communism. Socialist regimes can be organized in a democratic manner, in that those who control the state may be chosen according to democratic procedures. They may also be governed in an undemocratic manner when a single party, not chosen in free competitive elections, controls the state and society.

socialist democracy   the term used by the Chinese Communist Party to describe the political system of the People's Republic of China. Also called the *people's democratic dictatorship.* The official view is that this type of system, under the leadership of the Communist Party, provides democracy for the overwhelming majority of people and suppresses (or exercises dictatorship over) only the enemies of the people. Socialist democracy is contrasted to bourgeois (or capitalist) democracy, which puts power in the hands of the rich and oppresses the poor.

socialist market economy   the term used by the government of China to refer to the country's current economic system. It is meant to convey the mix of state control (socialism) and market forces (capitalism) that China is now following in its quest for economic development. The implication is that socialism will promote equality, while the market (especially the profit motive) will encourage people to work hard and foreign companies to invest.

special relationship   a term used to describe the close affinity between the United States and the United Kingdom since World War II, based on common language and close geopolitical ties and dramatized by Blair's decision to "stand shoulder to shoulder" with the United States when a coalition led by the U.S. invaded Iraq in 2003 to topple the regime of Saddam Hussein.

state corporatism   a political system in which the state requires all members of a particular economic sector to join an officially designated **interest group.** Such interest groups thus attain public status, and they participate in national policymaking. The result is that the state has great control over the groups, and groups have great control over their members. See also **corporatism; corporatist state.**

structural adjustment program (SAP)   medium-term (generally three to five years) programs (which include both action plans and disbursement of funds) established by the World Bank intended to alter and reform the economic structures of highly indebted Third World countries as a condition for receiving international loans. SAPs often involve the necessity for **privatization,** trade liberalization, and fiscal restraint. See also **international financial institutions (IFIs).**

tacit social contract   an idea put forth by some Western analysts that an unwritten informal understanding existed between the population and the party/state in the post-Stalinist Soviet Union, which helped form the basis of social and political stability; the implicit agreement involved citizens granting political support for Soviet rule in exchange for benefits such as guaranteed employment, free social services, a lax work environment, and limited interference in personal life.

technocrats   career-minded bureaucrats who administer public policy according to a technical rather than a political rationale. In Mexico and Brazil, these are known as the *técnicos.* For contrasting concepts, see **clientelism; patrimonial state; prebendalism.**

theocracy   a state dominated by the clergy, who rule on the grounds that they are the only interpreters of God's will and law.

totalitarianism   a political system in which the state attempts to exercise total control over all aspects of public and private life, including the economy, culture, education, and social organizations, through an integrated system of ideological, economic, and political control. Totalitarian states are said to rely largely on terror as a means to exercise power. The term has been applied to both **communist party-states** including Stalinist Russia and Maoist China and fascist regimes such as Nazi Germany.

township and village enterprises (TVEs)   nonagricultural businesses and factories owned and run by local governments and private entrepreneurs in China's rural areas. TVEs operate largely according to market forces and outside the state plan.

unfinished state   a state characterized by instabilities and uncertainties that may render it susceptible to collapse as a coherent entity.

unitary state   by contrast to the federal systems of Germany, India, Canada, or the United States, where power is shared between the central government and state or regional governments, in a unitary state (such as Britain) no powers are reserved constitutionally for subnational units of government.

USA PATRIOT Act   Legislation passed by the United States Congress in the wake of the September 11, 2001 attacks on New York and Washington. The legislation dramatically expanded the federal government's ability to conduct surveillance, to enforce laws, to limit civil liberties, and to fight terrorism.

vanguard party   a political party that claims to operate in the "true" interests of the group or class it purports to represent, even if this understanding doesn't correspond to the expressed interests of the group itself. The Communist parties of the Soviet Union and China are good examples of vanguard parties.

warrant chiefs   employed by the British colonial regime in Nigeria. A system in which "chiefs" were selected by the British to oversee certain legal matters and assist the colonial enterprise in governance and law enforcement in local areas.

welfare state   not a form of **state,** but rather a set of public policies designed to provide for citizens' needs through direct or indirect provisions of pensions, health care, unemployment insurance, and assistance to the poor.

Westminster model   a form of democracy based on the supreme authority of Parliament and the **accountability** of its elected representatives; named after the site of Parliament building in Westminster, a borough of London.

About the Editors and Contributors

Ervand Abrahamian is Distinguished Professor of History at Baruch College and the Graduate Center of the City University of New York. His recent publications include *Khomeinism: Essays on the Islamic Republic* (University of California Press, 1993) and *Tortured Confessions: Prisons and Public Recantations in Modern Iran* (University of California Press, 1999).

Joan DeBardeleben is Professor of Political Science and of European and Russian Studies at Carleton University in Ottawa, Ontario. She has published widely on Russian politics, with a focus on Russian federalism, public opinion, and elections. Recent articles have been published in *Europe-Asia Studies, Sotsiologicheskie issledovaniia* (Sociological Research), and *Party Politics.* She is a contributing author to *Microeconomic Change in Central and East Europe* (Carol S. Leonard, ed., Palgrave Macmillan, 2002) and *The Struggle for Russian Environmental Policy* (Ilmo Masso and Veli-Pekka Tynkkynen, eds., Kikimora, 2001). Dr. DeBardeleben is also Director of Carleton University's Centre for European Studies.

Louis DeSipio is an Associate Professor in the Department of Political Science and the Chicano/Latino Studies Program at the University of California, Irvine. He is the author of *Counting on the Latino Vote: Latinos as a New Electorate* (University Press of Virginia, 1996) and the coauthor, with Rodolfo O. de la Garza, of *Making Americans/Remaking America: Immigration and Immigrant Policy* (Westview Press, 1998). He is also the author and editor of a seven-volume series on Latino political values, attitudes, and behaviors. The seventh volume in this series, *Muted Voices: Latinos and the 2000 Elections*, was published in 2004.

Merilee S. Grindle is Edward S. Mason Professor of International Development at the John F. Kennedy School of Government, Harvard University. She is a specialist on the comparative analysis of policy-making, implementation, and public management in developing countries and has written extensively on Mexico. Her most recent book is *Audacious Reforms: Institutional Innovation and Democracy in Latin America* (The Johns Hopkins University Press, 2000).

William A. Joseph is Professor of Political Science at Wellesley College and an Associate of the Fairbank Center for East Asian Research at Harvard University. His research focuses on contemporary Chinese politics and ideology. He is the editor of *China Briefing: The Contradictions of Change* (M.E. Sharpe, 1997), co-editor of *New Perspectives on the Cultural Revolution* (Harvard University Press, 1991), and contributing editor of *The Oxford Companion to Politics of the World* (Oxford University Press, 2nd ed., 2001).

Mark Kesselman is Professor of Political Science at Columbia University. A specialist on the French and European political economy, his recent publications include contributions to *The Mitterrand Era: Policy Alternatives and Political Mobilization in France* (Macmillan, 1995), *Mitterrand's Legacy, Chirac's Challenge* (St. Martin's Press, 1996), and *Diminishing Welfare: A Cross-National Study of Social Provision* (Greenwood, 2002). He is the coauthor of *A Century of Organized Labor in France* (St. Martin's Press, 1997) and *The Politics of Power: A Critical Introduction to American Politics* (Wadsworth, 2005), coeditor of *Readings in Comparative Politics* (Houghton Mifflin, 2006), and editor of *Politics of Globalization: A Reader* (Houghton Mifflin, 2007).

Darren Kew is Assistant Professor in the Graduate Program in Dispute Resolution at the University of Massachusetts, Boston. He studies the role of civil society in democratic development and conflict prevention in Africa. Professor Kew has written on elections, civil society, and conflict prevention in Nigeria. He has worked with the Council on Foreign Relations' Center for Preventive Action to provide analysis and blueprints for preventing conflicts in numerous areas around the world, including Nigeria, Central Africa, and Kosovo, and he has also observed elections in Nigeria.

Joel Krieger is Norma Wilentz Hess Professor of Political Science at Wellesley College. His publications include *Globalization and State Power* (Pearson Longman, 2005), *Blair's War*, coauthored with David Coates (Polity Press, 2004), *British Politics in the Global Age: Can Social Democracy Survive?* (Polity Press, 1999), and *Reagan, Thatcher, and the Politics of Decline* (Oxford University Press, 1986). He is also editor-in-chief of *The Oxford*

Companion to Politics of the World (Oxford University Press, 1993; 2nd ed., 2001).

Peter Lewis is Associate Professor at the School of International Service, American University. He has written extensively on Nigerian political economy, as well as on broader regional issues of participation, democratic transition, and economic adjustment in Africa. He is currently working on a study of the comparative political economies of Indonesia and Nigeria.

Index

---

*Numbers in boldface indicate the page where a key term is defined.